PLANT-BASED DIET COOKBOOK

1001 Effortless Recipes To Overcome Today's Overly Meat Consumption Culture And Reduce The Risk Of Hearth Disease Without Any Type Of Medicines

ANNIE HART

TABLE OF CONTENTS

- INTRODUCTION 1
- BREAKFAST & SMOOTHIES 2
  - 01. Oatmeal & Peanut Butter Breakfast Bar 2
  - 02. Chocolate Chip Banana Pancake 2
  - 03. Avocado and 'Sausage' Breakfast Sandwich 2
  - 04. Black Bean Breakfast Burritos 3
  - 05. Cinnamon Rolls with Cashew Frosting ... 3
  - 06. Sundried Tomato & Asparagus Quiche .. 4
  - 07. Gingerbread Waffles 5
  - 08. Blueberry French Toast Breakfast Muffins 5
  - 09. Greek Garbanzo Beans on Toast 6
  - 10. Smoky Sweet Potato Tempeh Scramble ... 7
  - 11. Fluffy Garbanzo Bean Omelet 7
  - 12. Easy Hummus Toast 8
  - 13. No-Bake Chewy Granola Bars 8
  - 14. Hot Sausage and Pepper Breakfast 8
  - 15. Cardamom & Blueberry Oatmeal 9
  - 16. Cashew Cheese Spread 9
  - 17. Chilled Cantaloupe Smoothie 10
  - 18. High Protein Peanut Butter Smoothie ... 10
  - 19. Pineapple and Kale Smoothie 10
  - 20. Vanilla and Almond Smoothie 11
  - 21. Berry Blast Smoothie 11
  - 22. Choc-Banana Smoothie 11
  - 23. Greens and Berry Smoothie 11
  - 24. Peanut Butter Banana Quinoa Bowl 12
  - 25. Orange Pumpkin Pancakes 12
  - 26. Sweet Potato Slices With Fruits 13
  - 27. Breakfast Oat Brownies 13
  - 28. Spinach Tofu Scramble With Sour Cream 14
  - 29. Overnight Chia Oats 14
  - 30. Mexican Breakfast 15
  - 31. Amaranth Quinoa Porridge 15
  - 32. Cacao Lentil Muffins 16
  - 33. Chickpea Crepes With Mushrooms 16
  - 34. Goji Breakfast Bowl 17
  - 35. The 'Green Machine' Smoothie 17
  - 36. Sweet Coffee and Cacao Smoothie 18
  - 37. Amazing Blueberry Smoothie 18
  - 38. Go-Green Smoothie 18
  - 39. Creamy Chocolate Shake 18
  - 40. Hidden Kale Smoothie 19
  - 41. Blueberry Protein Shake 19
  - 42. Raspberry Lime Smoothie 19
  - 43. Peppermint Monster Smoothie 19
  - 44. Banana Green Smoothie 20
  - 45. Cinnamon Coffee Shake 20
  - 46. Orange Smoothie 20
  - 47. Pumpkin Smoothie 20
  - 48. Turmeric Smoothie 21
  - 49. Veggie Smoothie 21
  - 50. Very Berry Smoothie 21
  - 51. Coco Loco Smoothie 21
  - 52. Creamy Carrot Smoothie 22
  - 53. Date Chocolate Smoothie 22
  - 54. Date Banana Pistachio Smoothie 22
  - 55. Fall Green Smoothie 22
  - 56. Fig Protein Smoothie 23
  - 57. Frozen Berries Smoothie 23
  - 58. Fruit Medley Smoothie 23
  - 59. Green Healthy Smoothie 23
  - 60. Green Pina Colada 23
  - 61. Guava Smoothie 24
  - 62. Halva Smoothie 24
  - 63. Kale Smoothie 24
  - 64. Kiwi And Almonds Smoothie 24
  - 65. Mango Almonds Smoothie 25
  - 66. Mango Banana Smoothie 25
  - 67. Orange Nuts Smoothie 25
  - 68. Peanut Butter Green Smoothie 25
  - 69. Persimmon Mango Smoothie 25
  - 70. Pineapple, Orange, And Strawberry 26
  - 71. Pistachios Spinach Smoothie 26
  - 72. Peaches And Cream Oats 26
  - 73. Instant Pot Strawberries Breakfast 26
  - 74. Instant Pot Breakfast Quinoa 27
  - 75. Carrot Breakfast 27
  - 76. Special Instant Pot Vegan Oatmeal 27
  - 77. Instant Pot Breakfast Risotto 28
  - 78. Instant Pot Breakfast Porridge 28
  - 79. Delicious Apple Butter 28
  - 80. Instant Pot Vegan Chestnut Butter 29
  - 81. Delicious Breakfast Tapioca Pudding ... 29
  - 82. Breakfast Quinoa Salad 29
  - 83. Cinnamon Oatmeal 30
  - 84. Breakfast Coconut Risotto 30
  - 85. Pumpkin Oats 30
  - 86. Simple Tofu Mix 30
  - 87. Rich Quinoa Curry 31
  - 88. Breakfast Burgers 31
  - 89. Veggie Dumplings 32
  - 90. Breakfast Rice Bowl 32
  - 91. Millet And Veggie Mix 32
  - 92. Tapioca Pudding 33
  - 93. Breakfast Arugula Salad 33
  - 94. Protein Blueberry Smoothie 33
  - 95. Pumpkin Pie Smoothie 34
  - 96. Smoothie Bowl 34
  - 97. Soothing After Workout Smoothie 34
  - 98. Strawberry Coconut Smoothie 34
  - 99. Strawberry, Fruity And Nutty Smoothie 34
  - 100. Sunflower Seed Butter Smoothie 35
  - 101. Tropical Paradise Smoothie 35
  - 102. Veggie Omelet 35

Table of Contents

103. Veggies Quiche 36
104. Simple Bread 37
105. Quinoa Bread 37
106. Fruity Oatmeal Muffins 38
107. Oat Muffins 38
108. Tofu & Mushroom Muffins 39
109. Coconut & Seeds Granola 40
110. Nuts & Sees Granola 40
111. Banana Bread 41
112. Mini Italian Toast Crackers 41
113. 2-Minute Microwave Burger Bun 42
114. Almond Pan Loaf 42
115. Italian Herb Rolls 42
116. Tortilla Wraps 43
117. Keto-Vegan Pizza Crust 43
118. Panini Flat Bread 44
119. Herb Cracker Crisps 45
120. Dried Fruits And Nuts Breakfast Bread 45
121. Seed And Nut Topped Loaf 46
122. Low Carb Corn Bread 46
123. Low Carb Sub Bread 47
124. Plain Loaf 47
125. Seed-Based Crackers 48
126. 2-Minute Microwave Fruit Bread In A Mug! 48
127. Seed-Based Herb Crackers 49
128. Coconut Granola 49
129. Hot Pink Smoothie 50
130. Maca Caramel Frap 50
131. Peanut Butter Vanilla Green Shake 50
132. Green Colada 51
133. Chocolate Oat Smoothie 51
134. Peach Crumble Shake 51
135. Wild Ginger Green Smoothie 51
136. Berry Beet Velvet Smoothie 52
137. Spiced Strawberry Smoothie 52
138. Banana Bread Shake With Walnut Milk 52
139. Double Chocolate Hazelnut 53
140. Strawberry, Banana And Coconut Shake 53
141. Tropical Vibes Green Smoothie 53
142. Peanut Butter And Mocha Smoothie 54
143. Tahini Shake With Cinnamon And Lime 54
144. Ginger And Greens Smoothie 54
145. Two-Ingredient Banana Pancakes 55
146. Vegan Smoothie Bowl With Carrot 55
147. Vanilla Chia Pudding 55
148. Orange Pancakes 56
149. Oatmeal Energy Bars 56
150. Orange Chia Smoothie 57
151. Green Smoothie Bowl 57
152. Mango Craze Juice Blend 57
153. Pumpkin Apple Pie Smoothie 58
154. Pina Colada Smoothie (Vegan 58
155. Raw Mango Monster Smoothie 58
156. Acai Smoothie Bowl 59
157. Medium-Term Slow Cooker 59
158. Simple Vegan French Toast 59
159. Blueberry Chia Pudding 60
160. Zucchini Smoothie 60
161. Cushioned Vegan Pumpkin Pancakes. 60
162. Oatmeal-Banana Pancakes 61
163. Apple-Rosemary Steel-Cut Oats.............. 61
164. Mango Coconut Chia Pudding 62
165. Healthy Pumpkin Spice Oatmeal 62
166. Healthy Multigrain Seeded Bread 62
167. Warm Cinnamon Raisin Quinoa 63
168. Oatmeal Chia Hemp Chocolate 63
169. Duke Gray Chia Pudding 64
170. Peanut Butter-Banana Green Smoothie 64
171. Raspberry Mango Green Smoothie 64
172. Pineapple Orange Green Smoothie 64
173. Blueberry Green Smoothie 65
174. Strawberry Green Smoothie 65
175. Grape-Melon Green Smoothie 65
176. Raspberry Kale Smoothie 65
177. Banana Almond Green Smoothie 65
178. Kiwi Coconut Green Smoothie 65
179. Strawberry-Nectarine Green Smoothie 65
180. Triple Berry Green Smoothie 66
181. Orange Ginger Green Smoothie 66
182. Kale-Banana Power Smoothie 66
183. Cucumber-Apple Green Smoothie........... 66
184. Blackcurrant-Peach Green Smoothie.... 66
185. Papaya-Banana Green Smoothie 66
186. Grape Mint Green Smoothie 66
187. Tangerine Kale Smoothie 66
188. Pear Cucumber Smoothie 67
189. Cherry-Kiwi Green Smoothie 67
190. Avocado-Kale Smoothie 67
191. Coconut-Green Tea Smoothie 67
192. Orange-Carrot Green Smoothie 67
193. Pineapple-Coconut Green Smoothie 67
194. Vanilla-Almond Green Smoothie 67
195. Apple-Cucumber Smoothie 67
196. Strawberry-Lemon Green Smoothie 68
197. Energy Smoothie 68
198. Pink Grapefruit Green Smoothie 68
199. Mint- Cocoa Smoothie 68
200. Cranberry-Raspberry Smoothie 68
201. Plum Green Smoothie 68
202. Pineapple Lemon Green Smoothie 68
203. Blueberry Peach Green Smoothie 69
204. Tropical Papaya Smoothie 69
205. Pumpkin Banana Smoothie 69
206. Almond Chia Green Smoothie................ 69

207. Basic Green Smoothie 69
208. Apple Cinnamon Green Smoothie........ 69
209. Key Lime Green Smoothie 69
210. Avocado-Banana Green Smoothie........ 70
211. Spirulina Green Smoothie............... 70
212. Raspberry Green Smoothie 70
213. Mango-Orange Green Smoothie 70

MAINS 71
214. Grilled tempeh with green beans 71
215. Tofu Fajita Bowl............... 71
216. Indian Style Tempeh Bake 71
217. Tofu- Seitan Casserole 72
218. Ginger Lime Tempeh 72
219. Tofu Mozzarella 73
220. Seitan Meatza With Kale............... 73
221. Taco Tempeh Casserole 74
222. Broccoli Tempeh Alfredo 74
223. Avocado Seitan............... 75
224. Seitan Mushroom Burgers 75
225. Taco Tempeh Stuffed Peppers 75
226. Tangy Tofu Meatloaf............... 76
227. Vegan Bacon Wrapped Tofu 76
228. Veggie & Tofu Kebabs 77
229. Carrot And Radish Slaw............... 77
230. Spicy Snow Pea And Tofu Stir Fry........ 78
231. Roasted Veggies In Lemon Sauce 78
232. Lunch Recipes 79
233. Lemon Pepper Pasta 79
234. Lentils Salad With Lemon Tahini 80
235. Spanish Chickpea Spinach Stew 81
236. Lentils Bolognese With Soba Noodles.. 81
237. Red Burgers 82
238. Hemp Falafel With Tahini Sauce 82
239. Tempeh Skewers With Dressing 83
240. White Bean Salad With Spicy Sauce..... 84
241. Stuffed Sweet Hummus Potatoes 84
242. Crusted Tofu Steaks............... 85
243. Spicy Beans And Rice............... 85
244. Chili Quinoa Stuffed Peppers 86
245. Spinach With Walnuts & Avocado 87
246. Vegan Tacos 87
247. Grilled Broccoli with Chili Garlic Oil.. 87
248. Tomato Basil Pasta 88
249. Risotto With Tomato & Herbs 88
250. Tofu Shawarma Rice............... 89
251. Pesto Pasta 89
252. "Cheesy" Spinach Rolls............... 90
253. Grilled Summer Veggies............... 90
254. Superfood Buddha Bowl 91
255. Burrito & Cauliflower Rice Bowl 91
256. Seitan Zoodle Bowl 91
257. Tofu Parsnip Bake 92
258. Squash Tempeh Lasagna 93
259. Bok Choy Tofu Skillet 93
260. Quorn Sausage Frittata 94
261. Jamaican Jerk Tempeh 94
262. Zucchini Seitan Stacks 95
263. Curried Tofu Meatballs 95
264. Spicy Mushroom Collard Wraps 96
265. Pesto Tofu Zoodles............... 96
266. Cheesy Mushroom Pie 96
267. Tofu Scallopini With Lemon 97
268. Tofu Chops With Green Beans And Avocado Sauté 98
269. Mexican Quinoa And Lima Bean 98
270. Creole Tempeh Rice Bowls 99
271. Seitan Pesto Panini 99
272. Creamy Fettucine With Peas 100
273. Buckwheat Cabbage Rolls 100
274. Bbq Black Bean Burgers 101
275. Nutty Tofu Loaf............... 101
276. Taco Rice Bowls 102
277. Red Sauce Mushroom Pizza............... 102
278. Sweet Quinoa Veggie Burger 103
279. Green Bean And Mushroom Biryani. 104
280. Cabbage & Bell Pepper Skillet 104
281. Mixed Bean Burgers With Cashew 105
282. Beans, Tomato & Corn Quesadillas . 105
283. Bean & Rice Burritos 106
284. Baked Sweet Potatoes With Corn Salad 106
285. Cheesy Broccoli Casserole 107
286. Hummus & Vegetable Pizza 107
287. Chickpea Burgers With Guacamole... 108
288. Dark Bean And Quinoa Salad With Quick Cumin Dressing............... 108
289. Parmesan 109
290. Hemp Parmesan 109
291. Gluten Free White Bean And Summer Vegetable Pasta 109
292. Butternut Squash Curry............... 110
293. Crude Zucchini Alfredo With Basil And Cherry Tomatoes............... 110
294. Dark Bean And Corn Burgers 110
295. Eggplant Rollatini With Cashew 111
296. Ginger Lime Chickpea Sweet Potato.. 112
297. Sweet Potato And Black Bean Chili .. 112
298. Crude Cauliflower Rice With............... 113
299. Darker Rice And Lentil Salad............... 113
300. Crude "Nut" Noodles............... 113
301. Simple Fried Rice And Vegetables...... 114
302. Arugula Salad With Roasted Butternut Squash, Goji Berries, And Cauliflower...... 114
303. Simmered Vegetable Pesto Pasta Salad 114
304. Portobello "Steak" 115
305. Quinoa Enchiladas 115
306. Easy Flavored Potatoes Mix............... 116
307. Eggplant Sandwich............... 116
308. Veggie Salad 116

Table of Contents

309. Chickpeas Burgers 117
310. Potato Stew 117
311. Greek Veggie Mix 117
312. Herbed Mushrooms 118
313. Corn With Tofu 118
314. Garlicky Potatoes 118
315. Tasty Veggie Mix 119
316. French Mushroom Mix 119
317. Easy Broccoli Mix 119
318. Zucchini And Squash Salad 119
319. Indian Cauliflower Mix 120
320. "Baked" Potatoes 120
321. Squash Stew 120
322. Chinese Green Beans Mix 121
323. Chinese Tofu Mix 121
324. Tomato Stew 121
325. Ratatouille 122
326. Exotic Black Beans Mix 122
327. Creamy Beans Mix 122
328. Dark Bean And Quinoa Salad With Quick Cumin Dressing 123
329. Parmesan 123
330. Hemp Parmesan 123
331. Gluten Free White Bean 124
332. Butternut Squash Curry 124
333. Crude Zucchini Alfredo 125
334. Dark Bean And Corn Burgers .. 125
335. Eggplant Rollatini With 125
336. Ginger Lime Chickpea Sweet .. 126
337. Sweet Potato And Black Bean Chili .. 127
338. Crude Cauliflower Rice Pistachios 127
339. Darker Rice And Lentil Salad .. 127
340. Crude "Nut" Noodles 128
341. Simple Fried Rice And Vegetables 128
342. Arugula Salad With Roasted Butternut Squash, Goji Berries, And Cauliflower 128
343. Simmered Vegetable Pesto Pasta Salad 129
344. Portobello "Steak" And 129
345. Quinoa Enchiladas 130
346. Greek Okra And Eggplant Stew 130
347. Indian Chickpeas 131
348. White Beans Stew 131
349. Squash Bowls 131
350. Cauliflower Stew 132
351. Simple Quinoa Stew 132
352. Green Beans Mix 132
353. Chickpeas And Lentils Mix 133
354. Creamy Corn 133
355. Spinach And Lentils Mix 133
356. Cajun Mushrooms And Beans . 134
357. Eggplant Stew 134
358. Corn And Cabbage Salad 134
359. Okra And Corn Mix 135
360. Potato And Carrot Mix 135
361. Winter Green Beans 135
362. Green Beans Casserole 135
363. Chipotle Green Beans 136
364. Cranberry Beans Pasta 136
365. Mexican Casserole 136
366. Endives And Rice Casserole ... 137
367. Cabbage And Tomatoes 137
368. Simple Endive Mix 137
369. Eggplant And Tomato Sauce .. 138
370. Brown Rice And Mung Beans Mix .. 138
371. Lentils And Spinach Casserole 138
372. Red Potatoes And Tasty Chutney 139
373. Simple Veggie Salad 139
374. Chickpea And Black Olive Stew 139
375. Chili Seitan Stew With Brown Rice ... 140
376. Potato And Pea Stir-Fry 141
377. Mongolian Seitan 141
378. Alfredo Pasta With Cherry Tomatoes 141
379. Tempeh Tetrazzini With Garden Peas 142
380. Portobello Kale Florentine 143
381. Tempeh Oat Balls With Maple 143
382. Chili Mushroom Spaghetti 144
383. Zucchini Rolls In Tomato Sauce 144
384. Paprika & Tomato Pasta Primavera 145
385. Green Lentil Stew With Brown Rice ... 145
386. Cannellini Beans Bow Ties 146
387. Fresh Puttanesca With Quinoa 146
388. Quinoa Cherry Tortilla Wraps . 147
389. Quinoa With Mixed Herbs 147
390. Chickpea Avocado Pizza 147
391. White Bean Stuffed Squash ... 148
392. Grilled Zucchini And Spinach Pizza . 148
393. Crispy Tofu Burgers 149
394. Bean Lentil Salad With Lime Dressing 149
395. Lentil Arugula Salad 150
396. Red Cabbage And Cucumber Salad With Seitan 150
397. Protein Packed Chickpeas And Kidney Beans Salad 150
398. Quick Chickpeas And Spinach Salad 151
399. Carrot Slaw And Tempeh Triangles .. 151
400. Chili tofu 151
401. Lentil Soup (Vegan 152
402. Hot Black Beans And Potato .. 152
403. Low-Fat Bean Soup 152
404. Protein Rich Vegetable Minestrone ... 153
405. Quinoa Pumpkin Soup 153
406. Red Lentil Soup With Farro ... 153
407. Broccoli & Black Beans Stir Fry 154
408. Stuffed peppers 154
409. Sweet 'N Spicy Tofu 154
410. Eggplant & Mushrooms In Peanut Sauce 155
411. Green Beans Stir Fry 155

Table of Contents

412. Collard Greens 'N Tofu 155
413. Cassoulet 156
414. Double-Garlic Bean And Vegetable Soup 156
415. Mean Bean Minestrone 157
416. Sushi Rice And Bean Stew 158
417. Giardiniera Chili 159
418. Shorba (Lentil Soup 159
419. The Whole Enchilada 160
420. Black Bean And Avocado Salad 161
421. Mediterranean Quinoa And Bean Salad 161
422. Tabbouleh verde 162
423. Curried Bean And Corn Salad 162
424. Eggplant balela 163
425. Carrot and radish slaw with sesame dressing 164
426. Roasted veggies in lemon sauce 164
427. Spinach with walnuts & avocado 164
428. Vegan tacos 165
429. Grilled broccoli with chili garlic oil 165
430. Tomato basil pasta 165
431. Risotto with tomato & herbs 166
432. Tofu shawarma rice 166
433. Garlic pea shoots 166
434. Pesto pasta 167
435. Tomato Mint Salad with Rice Wine Vinaigrette 167
436. Greek Style Salad Wraps 167
437. Roasted Asparagus With Penne Salad 168
438. Grilled Eggplant Sandwiches 169
139. Vegan Paella 169
440. Tofu Vietnamese Style Sandwich 170
441. Artichoke And Nutritional Yeast Strata 170
442. Tofu Crisps With Greens 171
443. Polenta And Mushrooms 171
444. Roasted Cauliflower Penne With Olives 172
445. Grilled Vegetable Ratatouille With Tofu 172
446. Pasta With Lemon Cream Sauce, Asparagus, And Peas 173
447. Leek Chickpea And Quinoa 173
448. Spaghetti With Roasted Cherry Tomato 174
449. Vegetable Curry Samosas With Chutney 174
450. Lentil Burgers With Salsa 175
Baked Tofu Zucchini And Oregano Lasagna 176
452. Potato And Turnip French-Style Casserole 176
453. Chipotle Bean Burritos 177
454. Corn Quesadillas With Chile 177
455. Sautéed Tofu 178
456. Lentil-Rice Cakes With Salsa 178
457. Nutritional Yeast Tamales 179
458. Arugula Pizza 180
459. Rice Noodle Salad 180
460. Gemelli Salad With Almonds And Lime Vinaigrette 180
461. Grilled Portobello Tacos 181
462. Potato Hash With Beets And Vegan Eggs 181
463. Bean Chili 182
464. Sweet Potato Tamales 182
465. Beet Penne 183
466. Spinach-Feta Casserole 184
467. Curried Vegetables 185
468. Nutritional Yeast Stuffed Shells With Marinara Sauce 185

SIDES AND SALADS 186
469. Squash & Pomegranate Salad 186
470. French Style Potato Salad 186
471. Mango Salad With Peanut Dressing .. 187
472. Loaded Kale Salad 187
473. Cauliflower & Lentil Salad 188
474. Sweet Potato & Avocado Salad 188
475. Broccoli Sweet Potato Chickpea Salad 189
476. Penne Pasta Salad 189
477. Roasted Fennel Salad 190
478. Kale Salad With Tahini Dressing 190
479. Roasted Squash Salad 191
480. Vegetable Salad With Chimichurri 191
481. Thai Salad With Tempeh 192
482. Niçoise Salad 193
483. Avocado Kale Salad 193
484. Sesame Seed Simple Mix 194
485. Cherry Tomato Salad With Soy Chorizo 194
486. Roasted Bell Pepper Salad With Olives 194
487. Tofu-Dulse-Walnut Salad 194
488. Almond-Goji Berry Cauliflower Salad 195
489. Warm Mushroom And Orange Pepper Salad 195
490. Broccoli, Kelp, And Feta Salad 196
491. Roasted Asparagus With Feta Cheese Salad 196
492. Spicy Avocado Bites 196
493. Spicy Broccoli Salad 197
494. Spinach Hummus 197
495. Stir Fry Turmeric Butternut Squash .. 197
496. Rainbow Vegetable Bowl 198
497. Red Bell Pepper Hummus 198
498. Simple Peas Mix 198
499. Spinach Green Hummus 198
500. Stir-Fry Greens 199
501. Preparation Time: 20 minutes plus overnight soaking 199
502. Roasted Chili Potatoes 199
503. Roasted Parsnips With Zhoug 199
504. Roasted Broccoli With Peanuts And Kecap Manis 200
505. Roasted Red Cabbage Pesto 200
506. Roasted Garlic Toasts 201

507. Roasted Olive Oil Tomatoes 201
508. Rocket Chickpeas Salad 201
509. Savory Broccoli Mash 202
510. Savory Mango Chat 202
511. Som Tam Salad 202
512. Steamed Brinjal With Peanut Dressing 202
513. Sticky Seeds And Nuts 203
514. Sweet Potato Salad With Salad And Green Dip 203
515. Sweet Potato Spicy Bites 204
516. Tarragon Cauli Salad 204
517. Tarragon Spinach Cauliflower Salad . 205
518. Temaki 205
519. Tomato Chickpeas Salad 205
520. Tomato Salsa 206
521. Tex-Mex Salad 206
522. Treviso Walnut Salad 206
523. Turmeric Butternut Squash With Peas 207
524. Vegan Orzo Salad 207
525. White Bean Tamari Salad 207
526. White Protein Pesto 208
527. Black Bean Taco Salad Bowl 208
528. Romaine And Grape Tomato Salad With Avocado And Baby Peas 209
529. Warm Vegetable "Salad" 209
530. Puttanesca Seitan And Spinach Salad 209
531. Rice Salad With Cashews And Dried Papaya 210
532. Spinach Salad With Orange-Dijon Dressing 210
533. Caramelized Onion And Beet Salad . 211
534. Treasure Barley Salad 211
535. Golden Couscous Salad 212
536. Chopped Salad 212
537. Warm Lentil Salad With Red Wine Vinaigrette 212
538. Carrot And Orange Salad With Cashews And Cilantro 213
539. Not-Tuna Salad 213
540. Dazzling Vegetable Salad 214
541. Red Bean And Corn Salad 214
542. Mango And Snow Pea Salad 215
543. Cucumber-Radish Salad With Tarragon Vinaigrette 215
544. Italian-Style Pasta Salad 215
545. Tabbouleh Salad 216
546. Tuscan White Bean Salad 216
547. Indonesian Green Beansalad With Cabbage And Carrots 217
548. Cucumber And Onion Quinoa Salad . 217
549. Moroccan Aubergine Salad 217
550. Potato Salad With Artichoke Hearts . 218
551. Giardiniera 218
552. Creamy Avocado-Dressed Kale Salad. 219
553. Indonesian-Style Potato Salad 219
554. Roasted Beet And Avocado Salad 220
555. Creamy Coleslaw 220
SOUPS AND STEWS 222
556. Herby Cheddar Soup 222
557. Creamy Onion Soup 222
558. Creamy Tofu Mushroom Soup 223
559. Kale-Ginger Soup With Poached Eggs 223
560. Broccoli And Collard Soup 224
561. Chilled Lemongrass And Avocado Soup 224
562. Turnip–Tomato Soup 224
563. Spring Vegetable Soup 225
564. Zucchini-Dill Bowls With Ricotta Cheese 225
565. Cauliflower Soup 226
566. Greek Lentil Soup 226
567. Broccoli White Bean Soup 227
568. African Lentil Soup 227
569. Artichoke Bean Soup 228
570. Chinese Rice Soup 228
571. Black-Eyed Pea Soup With Greens ... 228
572. Beanless Garden Soup 229
573. Black-Eyed Pea Soup With Olive Pesto 229
574. Spinach Soup With Basil 230
575. Red Lentil Salsa Soup 230
576. Caldo Verde A La Mushrooms 231
577. Shiitake Mushroom Split Pea Soup.... 231
578. Velvety Vegetable Soup..................... 232
579. Sweet Potato And Peanut Soup 232
580. 3-Ingredient Carrot And Red Lentil Soup 233
581. 3-Ingredient Enchilada Soup 233
582. 3- Ingredient Lentil Soup 233
583. All Spices Lentils Bean Soup 234
584. Asparagus Cashew Cream Soup 234
585. Artichoke Spinach Soup 235
586. Beans With Garam Masala Broth 235
587. Black Beans And Potato Soup 236
588. Black Bean Cashew Soup 236
589. Black Beans Veggie Soup 236
590. Broccoli Corn Soup 237
591. Brown Lentils Tomato Soup 237
592. Brown Lentils Green Veggies Combo Soup 238
593. Cannellini Beans Tomato Soup 238
594. Cashew Chickpeas Soup 239
595. Charred Mexican Sweetcorn Soup 239
596. Chickpeas And Root Vegetable Soup. 240
597. Chickpeas Mushroom Broth 240
598. Chickpeas Puree Pumpkin Soup 241
599. Chickpeas Stew 241
600. Corns And Kale Potato Soup 242
601. Creamy Broccoli Soup 242
602. Easy Black Bean Stew 243

Table of Contents

603. Easy Split Pea Soup 243
604. Every Day One-Pot Lentil Soup 243
605. Garam Masala Lentil Stew 244
606. Green Chickpeas Soup 244
607. Green Lentils Tomato Soup 245
608. Green Peas Tomato Soup 245
609. Groundnut Sweet Potato Soup 246
610. Harissa Lentil Soup 246
611. Healthy Split Peas Spinach Soup 247
612. Kale And Kidney Beans Soup 247
613. Kidney Beans Soup 247
614. Serve with bread or rice 248
615. 3 Bean Chili 248
616. Root Vegetable Chili 249
617. Brown Rice Soup 249
618. Butternut Squash Soup 250
619. Green Beans Soup 250
620. Rich Chickpeas And Lentils Soup 250
621. Chard And Sweet Potato Soup 250
622. Chinese Soup And Ginger Sauce 251
623. Corn Cream Soup 251
624. Veggie Medley 252
625. Lentils Curry 252
626. Lentils Dal 252
627. Rich Jackfruit Dish 253
628. Vegan Gumbo 253
629. Eggplant Salad 253
630. Corn And Cabbage Soup 254
631. Okra Soup 254
632. Carrot Soup 254
633. Baby Carrots And Coconut Soup 255
634. Chinese Carrot Cream 255

SOUPS, STEWS & CHILIES 256
635. Cheesy Broccoli And Potato Soup 256
636. Split Peas & Carrot Soup 256
637. Black Beans Soup 256
638. Lentil And Mixed Vegetable Soup 257
639. Pumpkin Stew 257
640. Bean Onion Stew 258
641. Curried Carrot Kale Soup 258
642. Italian Plum Tomato Soup 258
643. Balsamic Hatchet Soup 259
644. Pearl Barley Tomato Mushroom Soup 259
645. Sweet Potato Soup 259
646. Corn Chowder 260
647. Onion Soup 260
648. Baby Spinach Coconut Soup 260
649. Cabbage Carrot Beet Soup 261
650. Tomato Tortilla Soup 261
651. Basil Marjoram Tomato Soup 261
652. Porcini Mushroom And Barley Soup . 261
653. Tofu Mushroom Kombu Soup 262
654. Basmati Rice Coconut Milk Soup 262
655. Rice Noodle Soup 263
656. Indian Red Split Lentil Soup 263
657. Light Vegetable Broth 263
658. Roasted Vegetable Broth 264
659. Root Vegetable Broth 264
660. Mushroom Vegetable Broth 265
661. Jamaican Red Bean Stew 265
662. Greens And Beans Soup 266
663. Hearty Chili 266
664. Golden Beet Soup With A Twist 267
665. Asian-Inspired Chili 267
666. African-Inspired Red Bean Stew 268
667. Chile-Lime Tortilla Soup 268
668. Weeknight Chickpea Tomato Soup ... 269
669. Shiitake Mushroom Soup With Sake . 269
670. Potato And Kale Soup 269
671. Coconut Watercress Soup 270
672. Roasted Red Pepper And Butternut Squash Soup 270
673. Mushroom Medley Soup 271
674. Tofu Coconut Indonesian Soup 271
675. Cabbage Scallion And Potato Soup 272
676. Lentil Soup 272
677. Black Bean Soup 272
678. Pepper Stew With Fire Roasted Tomatoes 273
679. Lentil Curry 273
680. Vegetarian Broth 273
681. Spicy Black Bean Soup 274
682. Kale And Cannellini Bean Soup 274
683. Tomato Lentil Soup 274
684. Spicy Chickpea Soup 274
685. Vegan Sausage Bean Soup 275
686. Instant Pot Corn Chowder 275
687. Carrot Split Pea Soup 276
688. Bread Cabbage Soup 276
689. Cannellini Potato Bean Soup 276
690. Vegan Gazpacho 277
691. Chickpeas Zucchini Pasta Soup 277
692. Brown Rice Herbes De Provence Soup 277
693. Milky Potato Soup 278
694. Hard Cider Harvest Soup 278
695. Homestyle Beet & Cabbage Borscht .. 278
696. Pureed Turnip & Carrot Soup 279

PASTA 280
697. 5-Ingredients Pasta 280
698. Brussels Sprout Penne 280
699. Bang Bang Sauce With Pasta 280
700. Beans And Pasta 281
701. Broccoli Elbow Macaroni 281
702. Broccoli Pasta 282
703. Caponata Pasta 282
704. Carbonara With Pine Nuts 283
705. Casarecce With Raw Tomato Sauce 283
706. Cauli Cabbage Pasta 283

- 707. Chickpeas Pasta 284
- 708. Chili Pasta With Chickpeas Gravy 284
- 709. Chickpeas Tomato Garlic Sauce Macaronis 285
- 710. Chinese Style Pasta 285
- 711. Cold Szechuan Noodles 286
- 712. Creamy Garlic Pasta 286
- 713. Fried Green Pasta 286
- 714. Gazpacho Spaghetti 287
- 715. Garlic Vegetable Pasta 287
- 716. Gochujang Cauliflower Spaghetti 288
- 717. Kale Chickpeas Pasta 288
- 718. Lemon Fusilli With Cauli 288
- 719. Lemony Pasta With Kidney Beans 289
- 720. Lentils Soup Savory Spaghetti 289
- 721. Long-Stemmed Broccoli With Spaghetti 290
- 722. Pasta With Beans 290
- 723. Peas Tomatoes Macaroni 290
- 724. Penne Bean Pasta With Roasted Tomato Sauce 291
- 725. Protein-Rich Chickpeas Pasta 291
- 726. Protein-Rich Zucchini Pasta 292
- 727. Raw Garlic Tomato Sauce Spaghetti .. 292
- 728. Red Pesto Pasta 292
- 729. Roasted Broccoli With Pasta 293
- 730. Roasted Veggie Lemon Salad 293
- 731. Savory Chickpeas Pasta 294
- 732. Saucy Brussels Macaroni 294
- 733. Simple Pasta With Chili Garlic Tarka 294
- 734. Spaghetti With Roasted Cauliflower .. 295
- 735. Spicy Bean Pasta 295
- 736. Split Peas Pasta 295
- 737. Stir-Fry Veggies With Pasta 296
- 738. Stuffed Veggie Balls With Pasta 296
- 739. Tomato Sauce Pasta 297
- 740. Two Beans Spaghetti 297
- 741. Vegetable Pasta With Tahini Dressing 298
- 742. Veggies Spaghetti 298
- 743. White Bean Pasta 299
- 744. Instant Pot Spaghetti 299
- 745. Mushrooms Creamed Noodles 300
- 746. Pasta With Peppers 300
- 747. Tofu & Dumplings 301
- 748. Fresh Tomato Mint Pasta 302
- 749. Lemon Garlic Broccoli Macaroni 302
- 750. Spinach Pesto Pasta 302
- 751. Paprika Pumpkin Pasta 303
- 752. Creamy Mushroom Herb Pasta 303
- 753. Cabbage And Noodles 303
- 754. Basil Spaghetti Pasta 304
- 755. Parsley Hummus Pasta 304
- 756. Creamy Spinach Artichoke Pasta 305
- 757. Easy Spinach Ricotta Pasta 305
- 758. Roasted Red Pepper Pasta 306
- 759. Cheese Beetroot Greens Maccheroni ... 306
- 760. Pastalaya 306
- 761. Corn And Chiles Fusilli 307
- Creamy Penne With Vegetables 307
- 763. Pasta With Eggplant Sauce 308
- 764. Creamy Pesto Pasta With Tofu & Broccoli 308
- 765. Chili Cheese Cottage Cheese Mac 309
- 76. Spicy Cauliflower Pasta 309
- 767. Tasty Mac And Cheese 310
- 768. Jackfruit And Red Pepper Pasta 310
- 769. Creamy Mushroom Pasta With Broccoli 310

SAUCES, AND CONDIMENTS 311

- 770. Green Goddess Hummus 311
- 771. Garlic, Parmesan And White Bean Hummus 311
- 772. Tomato Jam 312
- 773. Kale And Walnut Pesto 312
- 774. Buffalo Chicken Dip 312
- 775. Barbecue Tahini Sauce 313
- 776. Vegan Ranch Dressing 313
- 777. Cashew Yogurt 313
- 778. Nacho Cheese Sauce 314
- 779. Thai Peanut Sauce 314
- 780. Garlic Alfredo Sauce 314
- 781. Spicy Red Wine Tomato Sauce 315
- 782. Vodka Cream Sauce 315
- 783. Hot Sauce 315
- 784. Hot Sauce 316
- 785. Barbecue Sauce 316
- 786. Bolognese Sauce 317
- 787. Alfredo Sauce 317
- 788. Garden Pesto 317
- 789. Cilantro And Parsley Hot Sauce 318
- 790. Potato Carrot Gravy 318
- 791. Instant Pot Sriracha Sauce 319
- 792. Healthy One-Pot Hummus 319
- 793. Mushroom Gravy 319
- 794. Creamy Cheesy Sauce 319
- 795. Homemade Cashew Cream Cheese 320
- 796. Sunflower Seed, Potato & Brown Lentil Pâté 320
- 797. Chickpea & Artichoke Mushroom Pâté 320
- 798. Vegan Sauce 321
- 799. Pumpkin Butter 321
- 800. Vegan Cheese Dip 321
- 801. Artichoke Spinach Dip 322
- 802. Chipotle Bean Cheesy Dip 322
- 803. Pasta Sauce From Bologna 322
- 804. Delicious Bbq Sauce 323
- 805. Thai Curry Sauce 323
- 806. Sweet Peanut Sauce 323
- 807. Fast Hollandaise Sauce 323
- 808. Red Pepper Sauce 324

809. Divine Green Sauce 324
810. Smokey Tomato Sauce 324
811. Perfect Tomato Sauce 325
812. Merlot Sauce 325
813. Italian Gourmet Sauce 325
814. Cashew Alfredo 326
815. Aromatic Wine Sauce 326
816. Sweet And Sour Meatball Sauce 326
817. Brandy Nutmeg Cranberry Sauce 326
818. Instant Roasted Garlic 327
819. Spiced Rum & Orange Barbecue Sauce 327
820. Balsamic Onion Marmalade 327
821. Chipotle Ketchup 327
822. Classic Spinach Party Dip 328
823. Cheesy Chili Sausage Dip 328
824. Salsa Bean Dip 329
825. Cinnamon Ginger Syrup 329
826. Chai Green Tea Flavoring 329
827. Spiced Apple Spread 329
828. Balsamic Reduction 10 330
829. Butternut Squash Spread 330
830. Quick Apple Butter 330
831. Spiced Applesauce 330
832. Cranberry Apple Chutney 331
833. Spicy Sweet Chutney 331
834. Apple & Tomato Chutney 331
835. Blueberry Peach Chutney 332
836. Mango Chutney 332
837. Pear Confit 332
838. Cranberry Sauce 332
839. Peach Jam 333
840. Strawberry Jam 333
841. Tomato Jam 333
842. Ginger Syrup 333
843. Citrus Marmalade 334
844. Ketchup 334
845. Bbq 334
846. Pumpkin Sauce 335

SNACKS 336
847. Butter Carrots 336
848. Leeks With Butter 336
849. Juicy Brussel Sprouts 336
850. Parsley Potatoes 337
851. Fried Asparagus 337
852. Balsamic Artichokes 337
853. Tomato Kebabs 338
854. Eggplant And Zucchini Snack 338
855. Artichokes With Mayo Sauce 339
856. Fried Mustard Greens 339
857. Cheese Brussels Sprouts 340
858. Mushroom Stuffed Poblano 340
859. Mushroom Stuffed Tomatoes 341
860. Spinach Stuffed Portobello 341
861. Seasoned Potatoes 341

862. Black Bean Lime Dip 342
863. Beetroot Hummus 342
864. Zucchini Hummus 343
865. Chipotle And Lime Tortilla Chips 343
866. Carrot And Sweet Potato Fritters 343
867. Tomato And Pesto Toast 344
868. Avocado And Sprout Toast 344
869. Apple And Honey Toast 344
870. Thai Snack Mix 344
871. Zucchini Fritters 345
872. Zucchini Chips 345
873. Rosemary Beet Chips 345
874. Quinoa Broccoli Tots 346
875. Spicy Roasted Chickpeas 346
876. Nacho Kale Chips 346
877. Red Salsa 347
878. Tomato Hummus 347
879. Marinated Mushrooms 347
880. Hummus Quesadillas 348
881. Nacho Cheese Sauce 348
882. Avocado Tomato Bruschetta 349
883. Butter Carrots 349
884. Leeks With Butter 349
885. Juicy Brussel Sprouts 350
886. Parsley Potatoes 350
887. Fried Asparagus 350
888. Balsamic Artichokes 351
889. Tomato Kebabs 351
890. Eggplant And Zucchini Snack 352
891. Artichokes With Mayo Sauce 352
892. Fried Mustard Greens 353
893. Cheese Brussels Sprouts 353
894. Mushroom Stuffed Poblano 353
895. Mushroom Stuffed Tomatoes 354
896. Spinach Stuffed Portobello 354
897. Seasoned Potatoes 355
898. White Chocolate Fudge 355
899. Cheesecake With Blueberries 356
900. Lime Ice Creaminutes 356
901. Berry Coconut Yogurt Ice Pops 356
902. Berry Hazelnut Trifle 357
903. Avocado Truffles 357
904. Mint Ice Creaminutes 357
905. Cardamom Coconut Fat Bombs 358
906. Berries, Nuts, And Cream Bowl 358
907. Chocolate Peppermint Mousse 359
908. Keto Brownies 359
909. Chia Bars 360
910. Fruits Stew 360
911. Avocado And Rhubarb Salad 360
912. Plums And Nuts Bowls 360
913. Avocado And Strawberries Salad 360
914. Chocolate Watermelon Cups 361
915. Vanilla Raspberries Mix 361

- 916. Ginger Creaminutes 361
- 917. Chocolate Ginger Cookies 361
- 918. Coconut Salad................................... 362
- 919. Mint Cookies 362
- 920. Mint Avocado Bars........................... 362
- 921. Coconut Chocolate Cake................... 362
- 922. Mint Chocolate Creaminutes 363
- 923. Cranberries Cake 363
- 924. Sweet Zucchini Buns......................... 363
- 925. Lime Custard..................................... 363
- 926. Brussels Sprouts Chips 364
- 927. Baked Onion Rings 364
- 928. Roasted Almonds 364
- 929. Cheese Fries 365
- 930. Crunchy Parmesan Crisps................. 365
- 931. Cinnamon Coconut Chips.................. 365
- 932. Roasted Cashews 365
- 933. Crunchy Cauliflower Bites 366
- 934. Crispy Zucchini Fries 366
- 935. Crispy Kale Chips.............................. 366

DESSERT RECIPES........................... 367
- 936. Chocolate Brownies 367
- 937. Almond Butter Fudge 367
- 938. White Chocolate Fat Bomb 367
- 939. Brownie Balls 367
- 940. Peanut Butter Fudge 368
- 941. Instant Blueberry Ice Cream............. 368
- 942. Chia Raspberry Pudding 368
- 943. Choco Mug Brownie 368
- 944. Pistachio Ice Cream.......................... 369
- 945. Strawberry Ricotta 369
- 946. No-Bake Raspberry Cheesecake Truffles... 369

DESSERTS AND DRINKS 370
- 947. Oatmeal Raisin Muffins 370
- 948. Applesauce Muffins 370
- 949. Banana Cinnamon Muffins................. 371
- 950. Cashew Oat Muffins........................... 371
- 951. Banana Walnut Muffins 371
- 952. Carrot Flaxseed Muffins 372
- 953. Chocolate Peanut Fat Bombs 372
- 954. Protein Fat Bombs 373
- 955. Mojito Fat Bombs 373
- 956. Apple Pie Bites 373
- 957. Coconut Fat Bombs 374
- 958. Peach Popsicles 374
- 959. Green Popsicle 374
- 960. Strawberry Coconut Popsicles 375
- 961. Fudge Popsicles................................ 375
- 962. Tangerine Cake................................. 375
- 963. Sweet Tomato Bread 376
- 964. Lemon Squares 376
- 965. Sweet Cashew Sticks 376
- 966. Grape Pudding 377
- 967. Coconut And Seeds Bars 377
- 968. Chocolate Cookies............................. 377
- 969. Simple And Sweet Bananas 378
- 970. Coffee Pudding................................. 378
- 971. Almond And Vanilla Cake 378
- 972. Blueberry Cake................................. 379
- 973. Peach Cobbler................................... 379
- 974. Easy Pears Dessert 379
- 975. Sweet Strawberry Mix....................... 380
- 976. Sweet Bananas And Sauce 380
- 977. Orange Cake 380
- 978. Stuffed Apples 381
- 979. Apples And Mandarin Sauce 381
- 980. Almond Cookies................................. 381
- 981. Easy Pumpkin Cake........................... 381
- 982. Sweet Potato Mix 382
- 983. Summer Day Brownies...................... 382
- 984. Cranberry Cheesecake...................... 382
- 985. Fig Spread Dessert 383
- 986. Crème Brulée 384
- 987. Chocolate Cake 384
- 988. Crème Caramel 385
- 989. Lemon Dessert 385
- 990. Simple Fig Dessert 386
- 991. Sweet Pumpkin Pudding 386
- 992. Chill overnight.................................. 386
- 993. Marble Bread.................................... 387
- 994. Blueberry Strudel............................. 387
- 995. Vanilla Pancakes 388
- 996. Apple Pie Cups With Cranberries 388
- 997. Blueberry Peach Pie 389
- 998. Almond Cake 389
- 999. Agave Brownies 390
- 1000. Mango Cake..................................... 390
- 1001. Caramel Sauce 390
- 1002. Chocolate Pudding 391
- 1003. Chocolate Tapioca Pudding............... 391
- 1004. Brownies 391
- 1005. Chocolate-Orange Espresso Pudding 392
- 1006. Pumpkin Cinnamon Mini Cakes 392
- 1007. Oatmeal Cookies............................... 392
- 1008. Cherry Spread.................................. 393
- 1009. Creamy Coconut Eggs 393
- 1010. Pumpkin Pancakes............................ 394
- 1011. Orange Dessert 394
- 1012. Chocolate Bundt Cake...................... 395
- 1013. Chocolate Berry Cake 395
- 1014. Mocha Brownies 395
- 1015. Caramel Shortbread 396
- 1016. Easy Hazelnut Cake.......................... 397
- 1017. Pumpkin Parfait 397
- 1018. Banana Cheesecake.......................... 397
- 1019. Strawberry Pudding.......................... 398
- 1020. Cookies 'N' Cream Cupcakes............ 398

Table of Contents

1021. Carrot Cupcakes 399
1022. Coffee Cupcakes 399
1023. Pumpkin Gobs 400
1024. Saffron Cupcakes 401
1025. Mocha Cupcakes 401
1026. Raspberry Chocolate Mousse Cupcakes 402
1027. Chocolate Cake 403
1028. Simple Vanilla Cake 403
1029. Almond Ice Cream 403
1030. Raspberry Ice Cream 404
1031. Gelato 404
1032. Coconut Sorbet 404
1033. Chocolate Mousse 405
1034. Crème Brûlée 405
1035. Toffee Pudding 406
1036. Rice Pudding With Raisins 406
1037. French Custard 407
1038. Panna Cotta 407
1039. Trifle 407
1040. Hot Cocoa 408
1041. Pina Colada 408
1042. Pumpkin Spice Latte 408
1043. Simple Vanilla Milkshake 408
1044. Vanilla Raspberry Milkshake 408
1045. Frozen Mocha Latte 408
1046. Blueberry Margarita 409
1047. Peanut Butter Chocolate Chip Milkshake 409
1048. Lemonade And Rum Cocktail 409
1049. Peach Bellini 409
1050. Vanilla Ice Cream 409

CONCLUSION 409

INTRODUCTION

A large number of individuals who have deliberately inspected creature agribusiness have made plans to go veggie lover. In any case, regardless of whether you choose a veggie lover diet isn't for you, you'll likely leave away from perusing this exposition sold on the advantages of eating what individuals currently call a "plant-based" diet. For what reason am I so sure? Since the motivations to pick an eating routine that is at any rate generally plant-based are overpowering to such an extent that there truly aren't any solid counterarguments. That may clarify why the most unmistakable nourishment governmental issues journalists—including Michael Pollan, Mark Bittman, and Eric Schlosser—advocate an eating routine dependent on plants.

Plant-based weight control plans convey a significant number of the advantages of being vegetarian while requiring just the scarcest exertion. Since you haven't dedicated yourself to being 100 percent anything, there's no motivation to stress that you'll cheat, slip, or mess up. You can follow a plant-based eating routine and still eat Thanksgiving turkey or a late spring grill. In the event that being 100 percent veggie lover is something individuals focus on, being plant-based is more something they incline toward.

Perhaps the best thing about the plant-based idea is that it frequently gets under way an "idealistic cycle," where one positive change prompts another and afterward to another. At the point when you normally attempt new veggie lover nourishments, your top picks will in general consequently become piece of your ordinary eating regimen. So as time passes by, your eating regimen will probably move in a veggie lover heading with no deliberate exertion on your part. A lot of current veggie lovers arrived by bit by bit sliding down the plant-based slant. After some time spent eating expanding measures of plant-based nourishments, they understood that they were only a couple of little and simple advances from turning out to be absolutely vegetarian.

There are various adorable and accommodating neologisms appended to the plant-based camp: reducetarian, flexitarian, chegan, plant-solid, and even veganish. On the off chance that any of these terms impacts you, simply snatch tightly to it and start thinking thusly as you start attempting more veggie lover and vegetarian suppers.

Also, there are a few other related ideas you may discover supportive, including: Meatless Mondays, Mark Bittman's Vegan Before 6:00 arrangement, or taking a completely vegetarian diet out for a 21-day test drive. These conceivable outcomes can move huge change without forcing prerequisites for long lasting flawlessness.

Of the numerous motivations to go plant-based, maybe the best of all is the absence of a reasonable counterargument. In the entirety of my years expounding on nourishment legislative issues, I've not even once observed anybody (other than a couple paleo diet fan) make a genuine endeavor to contend against eating for the most part plants, since the preferences are unquestionable. Handfuls and many examinations show that eating more products of the soil can drastically diminish paces of malignant growth, diabetes, and circulatory malady. Furthermore, obviously, plant-based weight control plans likewise keep livestock from butcher, while all the while securing nature.

BREAKFAST & SMOOTHIES

01. Oatmeal & Peanut Butter Breakfast Bar

Preparation time: 10 minutes
Cooking Time 0 minutes
Servings 8

Ingredients
- 1½ cups date, pit removed
- ½ cup peanut butter
- ½ cup old-fashioned rolled oats

Directions:
1. Grease and line an 8" x 8" baking tin with parchment and pop to one side.
2. Grab your food processor, add the dates and whizz until chopped.
3. Add the peanut butter and the oats and pulse.
4. Scoop into the baking tin then pop into the fridge or freezer until set.
5. Serve and enjoy.

Nutrition:
Calories 459, Total Fat 8.9g, Saturated Fat 1.8g, Cholesterol 0mg, Sodium 77mg, Total Carbohydrate 98.5g, Dietary Fiber 11.3g, Total Sugars 79.1g, Protein 7.7g, Calcium 51mg, Potassium 926mg

02. Chocolate Chip Banana Pancake

Preparation time: 15 minutes
Cooking Time 3 minutes
Servings 6

Ingredients
- 1 large ripe banana, mashed
- 2 tablespoons coconut sugar
- 3 tablespoons coconut oil, melted
- 1 cup coconut milk
- 1 ½ cups whole wheat flour
- 1 teaspoon baking soda
- ½ cup vegan chocolate chips
- Olive oil, for frying

Directions:
1. Grab a large bowl and add the banana, sugar, oil and milk. Stir well.
2. Add the flour and baking soda and stir again until combined.
3. Add the chocolate chips and fold through then pop to one side.
4. Place a skillet over a medium heat and add a drop of oil.
5. Pour ¼ of the batter into the pan and move the pan to cover.
6. Cooking Time: for 3 minutes then flip and Cooking Time: on the other side.
7. Repeat with the remaining pancakes then serve and enjoy.

Nutrition:
Calories 315, Total Fat 18.2g, Saturated Fat 15.1g, Cholesterol 0mg, Sodium 221mg, Total Carbohydrate 35.2g, Dietary Fiber 2.6g, Total Sugars 8.2g, Protein 4.7g, Potassium 209mg

03. Avocado and 'Sausage' Breakfast Sandwich

Preparation time: 15 minutes
Cooking Time 2 minutes
Servings 1

Ingredients
- 1 vegan sausage patty
- 1 cup kale, chopped
- 2 teaspoons extra virgin olive oil
- 1 tablespoon pepitas
- Salt and pepper, to taste
- 1 tablespoon vegan mayo
- 1/8 teaspoon chipotle powder
- 1 teaspoon jalapeno chopped
- 1 English muffin, toasted
- ¼ avocado, sliced

Directions:
1. Place a sauté pan over a high heat and add a drop of oil.
2. Add the vegan patty and Cooking Time: for 2 minutes.

3. Flip the patty then add the kale and pepitas.
4. Season well then Cooking Time: for another few minutes until the patty is cooked.
5. Find a small bowl and add the mayo, chipotle powder and the jalapeno. Stir well to combine.
6. Place the muffin onto a flat surface, spread with the spicy may then top with the patty.
7. Add the sliced avocado then serve and enjoy.

Nutrition:
Calories 571, Total Fat 42.3g, Saturated Fat 10.1g, Cholesterol 36mg, Sodium 1334mg, Total Carbohydrate 38.6g, Dietary Fiber 6.6g, Total Sugars 3.7g, Protein 14.4g, Calcium 193mg

04. Black Bean Breakfast Burritos

Preparation time: 30 minutes
Cooking Time 10 minutes
Servings 4

Ingredients
- ¾ cup white rice
- 1 ½ cups water
- ¼ teaspoon sea salt
- ½ lime, juiced
- ¼ cup fresh cilantro, chopped
- 4 small red potatoes, cut into bite-sized pieces
- ½ red onion, sliced into rings
- 1-2 tablespoons olive oil
- Salt & pepper, to taste
- 1 cup cooked black beans
- ¼ teaspoon each ground cumin garlic powder, and chili powder
- Salt & pepper, to taste
- ¼ ripe avocado
- 1 lime, juiced
- 1 cup purple cabbage, thinly sliced
- 1 jalapeno, seeds removed, thinly sliced
- Pinch salt and black pepper
- 2 large vegan flour tortillas white or wheat
- ½ ripe avocado sliced
- ¼ cup salsa
- Hot sauce

Directions:
1. Place the rice, water and salt in a pan and bring to the boil.
2. Cover and Cooking Time: on low until fluffy then remove from the heat and pop to one side.
3. Place a skillet over a medium heat, add 1-2 tablespoons olive oil and add the potatoes and onion.
4. Season well then leave to Cooking Time: for 10 minutes, stirring often.
5. Remove from the heat and pop to one side.
6. Take a small pan then add the beans, cumin, garlic and chili. Stir well.
7. Pop over a medium heat and bring to simmer. Reduce the heat to keep warm.
8. Take a small bowl and add the avocado and lime. Mash together.
9. Add the cabbage and jalapeno and stir well. Season then pop to one side.
10. Grab the cooked rice and add the lime juice and cilantro then toss with a fork.
11. Gently warm the tortillas in a microwave for 10-20 seconds then add the fillings.
12. Roll up, serve and enjoy.

Nutrition:
Calories 588, Total Fat 17.1g, Saturated Fat 3.4g, Sodium 272mg, Total Carbohydrate 94.8g, Dietary Fiber 16.2g, Total Sugars 5g, Protein 18.1g, Calcium 115mg, Iron 6mg, Potassium 1964mg

05. Cinnamon Rolls with Cashew Frosting

Preparation time: 30 minutes
Cooking Time 25 minutes
Servings 12

Ingredients

- *3 tablespoons vegan butter*
- *¾ cup unsweetened almond milk*
- *½ teaspoon salt*
- *3 tablespoons caster sugar*
- *1 teaspoon vanilla extract*
- *½ cup pumpkin puree*
- *3 cups all-purpose flour*
- *2 ¼ teaspoons dried active yeast*
- *3 tablespoons softened vegan butter*
- *3 tablespoons brown sugar*
- *½ teaspoon cinnamon*
- *½ cup cashews, soaked 1 hour in boiling water*
- *½ cup icing sugar*
- *1 teaspoon vanilla extract*
- *2/3 cup almond milk*

Directions:

1. *Grease a baking sheet and pop to one side.*
2. *Find a small bowl, add the butter and pop into the microwave to melt.*
3. *Add the sugar and stir well then set aside to cool.*
4. *Grab a large bowl and add the flour, salt and yeast. Stir well to mix together.*
5. *Place the cooled butter into a jug, add the pumpkin puree, vanilla and almond milk. Stir well together.*
6. *Pour the wet ingredients into the dry and stir well to combine.*
7. *Tip onto a flat surface and knead for 5 minutes, adding extra flour as needed to avoid sticking.*
8. *Pop back into the bowl, cover with plastic wrap and pop into the fridge overnight.*
9. *Next morning, remove the dough from the fridge and punch down with your fingers.*
10. *Using a rolling pin, roll to form an 18" rectangle then spread with butter.*
11. *Find a small bowl and add the sugar and cinnamon. Mix well then sprinkle with the butter.*
12. *Roll the dough into a large sausage then slice into sections.*
13. *Place onto the greased baking sheet and leave in a dark place to rise for one hour.*
14. *Preheat the oven to 350°F.*
15. *Meanwhile, drain the cashews and add them to your blender. Whizz until smooth.*
16. *Add the sugar and the vanilla then whizz again.*
17. *Add the almond milk until it reaches your desired consistency.*
18. *Pop into the oven and bake for 20 minutes until golden.*
19. *Pour the glaze over the top then serve and enjoy.*

Nutrition:

Calories 226, Total Fat 6.5g, Saturated Fat 3.4g, Cholesterol 0mg, Sodium 113mg, Total Carbohydrate 38g, Dietary Fiber 1.9g, Total Sugars 11.3g, Protein 4.9g, Calcium 34mg, Iron 2mg, Potassium 153mg

06. Sundried Tomato & Asparagus Quiche

Preparation time: 1 hour 20 minutes
Cooking Time 40 minutes
Servings 8

Ingredients

- *1 ½ cup all-purpose flour*
- *½ teaspoon salt*
- *½ cup vegan butter*
- *2-3 tablespoons ice cold water*
- *1 tablespoon coconut or vegetable oil*
- *¼ cup white onion, minced*
- *1 cup fresh asparagus, chopped*
- *3 tablespoons dried tomatoes, chopped*
- *1 x 14 oz. block medium/firm tofu, drained*
- *3 tablespoons nutritional yeast*
- *1 tablespoon non-dairy milk*
- *1 tablespoon all-purpose flour*
- *1 teaspoon dehydrated minced onion*

- 2 teaspoons fresh lemon juice
- 1 teaspoon spicy mustard
- ½ teaspoon sea salt
- ½ teaspoon turmeric
- ½ teaspoon liquid smoke
- 3 tablespoons fresh basil, chopped
- 1/3 cup vegan mozzarella cheese
- Salt and pepper, to taste

Directions:
1. Preheat your oven to 350°F and grease 4 x 5" quiche pans and pop to one side.
2. Grab a medium bowl and add the flour and salt. Stir well.
3. Then cut the butter into chunks and add to the flour, rubbing into the flour with your fingers until it resembles breadcrumbs.
4. Add the water and roll together.
5. Roll out and place into the quiche pans.
6. Bake for 10 minutes then remove from the oven and pop to one side.
7. Place a skillet over a medium heat, add the oil and then add the onions.
8. Cooking Time: for five minutes until soft.
9. Throw in the asparagus and tomatoes and Cooking Time: for 5 more minutes. Remove from the heat and pop to one side.
10. Grab your food processor and add the tofu, nutritional yeast, milk, flour, onions, turmeric, liquid smoke, lemon juice and salt.
11. Whizz until smooth and pour into a bowl.
12. Add the asparagus mixture, the basil and the cheese and stir well.
13. Season with salt and pepper.
14. Spoon into the pie crusts and pop back into the oven for 15-20 minutes until set and cooked through.
15. Remove from the oven, leave to cool for 20 minutes then serve and enjoy.

Nutrition:
Calories 175, Total Fat 5.1g, Saturated Fat 2.3g, Cholesterol 1mg, Sodium 286mg, Total Carbohydrate 24.2g, Dietary Fiber 2.7g, Total Sugars 1.2g, Protein 9.4g, Calcium 118mg, Iron 3mg, Potassium 252mg

07. Gingerbread Waffles

Preparation time: 30minutes
Cooking Time 20 minutes
Servings 6

Ingredients
- 1 slightly heaping cup spelt flour
- 1 tablespoon ground flax seeds
- 2 teaspoons baking powder
- ¼ teaspoon baking soda
- ¼ teaspoon salt
- 1 ½ teaspoons ground cinnamon
- 2 teaspoons ground ginger
- 4 tablespoons coconut sugar
- 1 cup non-dairy milk
- 1 tablespoon apple cider vinegar
- 2 tablespoons black strap molasses
- 1½ tablespoons olive oil

Directions:
1. Find your waffle iron, oil generously and preheat.
2. Find a large bowl and add the dry ingredients. Stir well together.
3. Put the wet ingredients into another bowl and stir until combined.
4. Add the wet to dry then stir until combined.
5. Pour the mixture into the waffle iron and Cooking Time: on a medium temperature for 20 minutes
6. Open carefully and remove.
7. Serve and enjoy.

Nutrition:
Calories 256, Total Fat 14.2g, Saturated Fat 2g, Cholesterol 0mg, Sodium 175mg, Total Carbohydrate 31.2g, Dietary Fiber 3.4g, Total Sugars 13.2g, Protein 4.2g, Calcium 150mg, Iron 2mg, Potassium 369mg

08. Blueberry French Toast Breakfast Muffins

Preparation time: 55 minutes

Cooking Time 25 minutes
Servings 12

Ingredients

- 1 cup unsweetened plant milk
- 1 tablespoon ground flaxseed
- 1 tablespoon almond meal
- 1 tablespoon maple syrup
- 1 teaspoon vanilla extract
- 1 teaspoon cinnamon
- 2 teaspoons nutritional yeast
- ¾ cup frozen blueberries
- 9 slices soft bread
- ¼ cup oats
- 1/3 cup raw pecans
- ¼ cup coconut sugar
- 3 tablespoons coconut butter, at room temperature
- 1/8 teaspoon sea salt
- 9 slices bread, each cut into 4

Directions:

1. Preheat your oven to 375°F and grease a muffin tin. Pop to one side.
2. Find a medium bowl and add the flax, almond meal, nutritional yeast, maple syrup, milk, vanilla and cinnamon.
3. Mix well using a fork then pop into the fridge.
4. Grab your food processor and add the topping ingredients (except the coconut butter. Whizz to combine.
5. Add the butter then whizz again.
6. Grab your muffin tin and add a teaspoon of the flax and cinnamon batter to the bottom of each space.
7. Add a square of the bread then top with 5-6 blueberries.
8. Sprinkle with 2 teaspoons of the crumble then top with another piece of bread.
9. Place 5-6 more blueberries over the bread, sprinkle with more of the topping then add the other piece of bread.
10. Add a tablespoon of the flax and cinnamon mixture over the top and add a couple of blueberries on the top.
11. Pop into the oven and Cooking Time: for 25-25 minutes until the top begins to brown.
12. Serve and enjoy.

Nutrition:
Calories 228, Total Fat 14.4g, Saturated Fat 5.1g, Cholesterol 0mg, Sodium 186mg, Total Carbohydrate 22.9g, Dietary Fiber 4g, Total Sugars 7.8g, Protein 4.3g, Calcium 87mg, Iron 2mg, Potassiuminutes

09. Greek Garbanzo Beans on Toast

Preparation time: 30 minutes
Cooking Time 5 minutes
Servings 2

Ingredients

- 2 tablespoons olive oil
- 3 small shallots, finely diced
- 2 large garlic cloves, finely diced
- ¼ teaspoon smoked paprika
- ½ teaspoon sweet paprika
- ½ teaspoon cinnamon
- ½ teaspoon salt
- ½-1 teaspoon sugar, to taste
- Black pepper, to taste
- 1 x 6 oz. can peel plum tomatoes
- 2 cups cooked garbanzo beans
- 4 slices of crusty bread, toasted
- Fresh parsley and dill
- Pitted Kalamata olives

Directions:

1. Pop a skillet over a medium heat and add the oil.
2. Add the shallots to the pan and Cooking Time: for five minutes until soft.
3. Add the garlic and Cooking Time: for another minute then add the other spices to the pan.
4. Stir well then add the tomatoes.
5. Turn down the heat and simmer on low until the sauce thickens.
6. Add the garbanzo beans and warm

through.

7. *Season with the sugar, salt and pepper then serve and enjoy.*

Nutrition:
Calories 1296, Total Fat 47.4g, Saturated Fat 8.7g, Cholesterol 11mg, Sodium 1335mg, Total Carbohydrate 175.7g, Dietary Fiber 36.3g, Total Sugars 25.4g, Protein 49.8g, Calcium 313mg, Iron 17mg, Potassium 1972mg

10. Smoky Sweet Potato Tempeh Scramble

Preparation time: 17 minutes
Cooking Time 13 minutes
Servings 8

Ingredients

- *2 tablespoons olive oil*
- *1 small sweet potato, finely diced*
- *1 small onion, diced*
- *2 garlic cloves, minced*
- *8 oz. package tempeh, crumbled*
- *1 small red bell pepper, diced*
- *1 tablespoon soy sauce*
- *1 tablespoon ground cumin*
- *1 tablespoon smoked paprika*
- *1 tablespoon maple syrup*
- *Juice of ½ lemon*
- *1 avocado, sliced*
- *2 scallions, chopped*
- *4 tortillas*
- *2 tbsp. Hot sauce*

Directions:

1. *Place a skillet over a medium heat and add the oil.*
2. *Add the sweet potato and Cooking Time: for five minutes until getting soft.*
3. *Add the onion and Cooking Time: for another five minutes until soft.*
4. *Stir through the garlic and Cooking Time: for a minute.*
5. *Add the tempeh, pepper, soy, cumin, paprika, maple and lemon juice and Cooking Time: for two more minutes.*

6. *Serve with the optional extras then enjoy.*

Nutrition:
Calories 200, Total Fat 12.3g, Saturated Fat 2.2g, Cholesterol 0mg, Sodium 224mg, Total Carbohydrate 19g, Dietary Fiber 3.7g, Total Sugars 6.5g, Protein 7.5g, Calcium 64mg, Iron 2mg, Potassium 430mg

11. Fluffy Garbanzo Bean Omelet

Preparation time: 20 minutes
Cooking Time 7 minutes
Servings 2

Ingredients

- *¼ cup besan flour*
- *1 tablespoon nutritional yeast*
- *½ teaspoon baking powder*
- *¼ teaspoon turmeric*
- *½ teaspoon chopped chives*
- *¼ teaspoon garlic powder*
- *1/8 teaspoon black pepper*
- *½ teaspoon Ener-G egg replacer*
- *¼ cup water*
- *½ cup Romaine Leafy Green Fresh Express*
- *½ cup Veggies*
- *1 tablespoon Salsa*
- *1 tablespoon Ketchup*
- *1 tablespoon Hot sauce*
- *1 tablespoon Parsley*

Directions:

1. *Grab a medium bowl and combine all the ingredients except the greens and veggies. Leave to stand for five minutes.*
2. *Place a skillet over a medium heat and add the oil.*
3. *Pour the batter into the pan, spread and Cooking Time: for 3-5 minutes until the edges pull away from the pan.*
4. *Add the greens and the veggies of your choice then fold the omelet over.*
5. *Cooking Time: for 2 more minutes*

then pop onto a plate.
6. Serve with the topping of your choice.
7. Serve and enjoy.

Nutrition:

Calories 104, Total Fat 1.3g, Saturated Fat 0.2g, Cholesterol 0mg, Sodium 419mg, Total Carbohydrate 17.9g, Dietary Fiber 4.6g, Total Sugars 4.7g, Protein 6.6g, Calcium 69mg, Iron 3mg, Potassium 423mg

12. Easy Hummus Toast

Preparation time: 10 minutes
Cooking Time 0 minutes
Servings 1

Ingredients

- 2 slices sprouted wheat bread
- ¼ cup hummus
- 1 tablespoon hemp seeds
- 1 tablespoon roasted unsalted sunflower seeds

Directions:
1. Start by toasting your bread.
2. Top with the hummus and seeds then eat!

Nutrition:

Calories 445, Total Fat 16.3g, Saturated Fat 2.2g, Cholesterol 0mg, Sodium 597mg, Total Carbohydrate 54.5g, Dietary Fiber 10.5g, Total Sugars 6.1g, Protein 22.6g, Calcium 116mg, Iron 6mg, Potassium 471mg

13. No-Bake Chewy Granola Bars

Preparation time: 10 minutes
Cooking Time 10 minutes
Servings 8

Ingredients

- ¼ cup coconut oil
- ¼ cup honey or maple syrup
- ¼ teaspoon salt
- 1 teaspoon vanilla extract
- ½ teaspoon cardamominutes
- ¼ teaspoon cinnamon
- Pinch of nutmeg
- 1 cup old-fashioned oats
- ½ cup sliced raw almonds
- ¼ cup sunflower seeds
- ¼ cup pumpkin seeds
- 1 tablespoon chia seeds
- 1 cup chopped dried figs

Directions:
1. Line a 6" x 8" baking dish with parchment paper and pop to one side.
2. Grab a saucepan and add the oil, honey, salt and spices.
3. Pop over a medium heat and stir until it melts together.
4. Reduce the heat, add the oats and stir to coat.
5. Add the seeds, nuts and dried fruit and stir through again.
6. Cooking Time: for 10 minutes.
7. Remove from the heat and transfer the oat mixture to the pan.
8. Press down until it's packed firm.
9. Leave to cool completely then cut into 8 bars.
10. Serve and enjoy.

Nutrition:

Calories 243, Total Fat 13.3g, Saturated Fat 6.7g, Cholesterol 0mg, Sodium 78mg, Total Carbohydrate 30.8g, Dietary Fiber 4.3g, Total Sugars 21.1g, Protein 4.2g, Calcium 67mg, Iron 2mg, Potassium 285mg

14. Hot Sausage and Pepper Breakfast Casserole

Preparation time: 57 minutes
Cooking Time 50 minutes
Servings 8

Ingredients

- 10 cup white bread, cubed
- 2¾ cups ice water
- 1 ¼ cup plant-based unsweetened creamer
- 2 tablespoons extra-virgin olive oil
- 3 vegan sausage, sliced
- 1 bell pepper, seeded and chopped
- 1 medium onion, chopped
- 2 garlic cloves, minced
- 5 cups spinach leaves

- 1 cup vegan parmesan, grated
- 1 teaspoon ground sea salt, or to taste
- ½ teaspoon ground nutmeg
- ½ teaspoon ground black pepper
- 1 tablespoon fresh parsley, chopped
- 1 teaspoon fresh rosemary, chopped
- 1 teaspoon fresh thyme, chopped
- 1 teaspoon fresh oregano, chopped
- 1 tablespoon vegan butter

Directions:
1. Preheat your oven to 375°F and grease a 13" x 8" baking dish.
2. Grab a medium bowl and add the water, milk and nutmeg. Whisk well until combined.
3. Pop a skillet over a medium heat and add the oil.
4. Add the sausage to the pan and Cooking Time: for 8-10 minutes until browned. Remove from the pan and pop to one side.
5. Add the onions and Cooking Time: for 3 minutes.
6. Add the peppers and Cooking Time: for 5 minutes.
7. Add the garlic, salt and pepper and Cooking Time: for 2 minutes then remove from the pan and pop to one side.
8. Add the spinach to the pan and Cooking Time: until wilted.
9. Remove the spinach from the pan then chop. Squeeze out the water.
10. Grab the greased baking dish and add half the cubed bread to the bottom.
11. Add half the spinach to the top followed by half the spinach and half of the onion and pepper mixture.
12. Sprinkle with half the parmesan then repeat.
13. Whisk the egg mixture again then pour over the casserole.
14. Pop into the oven and bake for 30 minutes until browned.
15. Serve and enjoy.

Nutrition:
Calories 263, Total Fat 8.2g, Saturated Fat 1g, Cholesterol 0mg, Sodium 673mg, Total Carbohydrate 31.8g, Dietary Fiber 3.4g, Total Sugars 3.6g, Protein 12.9g, Calcium 239mg, Iron 3mg, Potassium 377mg

15. Cardamom & Blueberry Oatmeal

Preparation time: 10 minutes
Cooking Time 3 minutes
Servings 1

Ingredients
- ¾ cup quick oats
- 1¼ cup water
- ½ cup unsweetened almond milk, divided
- 2 tablespoons pure maple syrup
- ¼ heaping teaspoon cinnamon
- 1/8 teaspoon cardamominutes
- Handful walnuts
- Handful dried currants

Directions:
1. Place the water into a small saucepan and bring to the boil.
2. Add the oats, stir through, reduce the heat to medium and Cooking Time: for 3 minutes.
3. Add half of the milk, stir again and Cooking Time: for another few seconds.
4. Remove from the heat and leave to stand for 3 minutes.
5. Transfer to a bowl and to with the remaining ingredients.
6. Drizzle with the milk then serve and enjoy.

Nutrition:
Calories 568, Total Fat 24.4g, Saturated Fat 1.9g, Cholesterol 0mg, Sodium 118mg, Total Carbohydrate 77g, Dietary Fiber 10.4g, Total Sugars 26.8g, Protein 16.5g, Vitamin D 1mcg, Calcium 263mg, Iron 5mg, Potassium 651mg

16. Cashew Cheese Spread

Preparation Time: 5 minutes

Cooking Time: 0 minutes
Servings: 5
Ingredients:
- 1 cup water
- 1 cup raw cashews
- 1 tsp. nutritional yeast
- ½ tsp. salt

Optional: 1 tsp. garlic powder

Directions:
1. Soak the cashews for 6 hours in water.
2. Drain and transfer the soaked cashews to a food processor.
3. Add 1 cup of water and all the other ingredients and blend.
4. For the best flavor, serve chilled.
5. Enjoy immediately, or store for later.

Nutrition:
Calories 162, Total Fat 12.7g, Saturated Fat 2.5g, Cholesterol 0mg, Sodium 239mg, Total Carbohydrate 9.7g, Dietary Fiber 1.1g, Total Sugars 1.5g, Protein 4.6g, Calcium 15mg, Iron 2mg, Potassium 178mg

17. Chilled Cantaloupe Smoothie

Preparation time: 10 minutes
Servings 2
Ingredients:
- 1½ cups cantaloupe, diced
- 2 Tbsp frozen orange juice concentrate
- ¼ cup white wine
- 2 ice cubes
- 1 Tbsp lemon juice
- ½ cup Mint leaves, for garnish

Directions:
1. Blend all ingredients to create a smooth mixture.
2. Top with mint leaves, and serve.

Nutrition:
Calories 349, Total Fat 13.1g, Saturated Fat 11.3g, Cholesterol 0mg, Sodium 104mg, Total Carbohydrate 50.5g, Dietary Fiber 5.5g, Total Sugars 46.4g, Protein 6.5g, Vitamin D 0mcg, Calcium 117mg, Iron 5mg, Potassium 1320mg

18. High Protein Peanut Butter Smoothie

Preparation time: 3 minutes
Servings: 2

Ingredients
- 2 cups kale
- 1 banana
- 2 tbsp. hemp seeds
- 1 tbsp. peanut butter
- 2/3 cup water
- 2 cups ice
- 1 cup almond or cashew milk
- 2 tbsp. cacao powder
- 1 scoop Vega vanilla protein powder

Directions:
1. Pop the kale and banana in a blender, then add the hemp seeds and peanut butter.
2. Add the milk, water and ice and blend until ingredients are combined.
3. Add the protein powder.
4. Pour into glasses and serve.

Nutrition:
Calories 687, Total Fat 50.4g, Saturated Fat 38g, Cholesterol 0mg, Sodium 176mg, Total Carbohydrate 46.5g, Dietary Fiber 9.9g, Total Sugars 23.7g, Protein 20.4g, Vitamin D 0mcg, Calcium 150mg, Iron 8mg, Potassium 979mg

19. Pineapple and Kale Smoothie

Preparation time: 3 minutes
Servings 2

Ingredients
- 1 cup Greek yogurt
- 1½ cups cubed pineapple
- 3 cups baby kale
- 1 cucumber
- 2 tbsp, hemp seeds

Directions:
1. Pop everything in a blender and blitz
2. Pour into glasses and serve.

Nutrition:
Calories 509, Total Fat 8.9g, Saturated Fat 3.3g, Cholesterol 10mg, Sodium 127mg, Total Carbohydrate 87.1g, Dietary Fiber 10.3g, Total Sugars 55.3g, Protein 30.6g, Vitamin D 0mcg, Calcium 438mg, Iron 5mg, Potassium 1068mg

20. Vanilla and Almond Smoothie

Preparation time: 3 minutes
Servings 1

Ingredients

- 2 scoops vegan vanilla protein powder
- ½ cup almonds
- 1 cup water

Directions:

1. Pop everything in a blender and blitz
2. Pour into glasses and serve.

Nutrition:
Calories 415, Total Fat 33.8g, Saturated Fat 1.8g, Cholesterol 0mg, Sodium 108mg, Total Carbohydrate 18.2g, Dietary Fiber 7.9g, Total Sugars 2g, Protein 42.1g, Vitamin D 0mcg, Calcium 255mg, Iron 9mg, Potassium 351mg

21. Berry Blast Smoothie

Preparation time: 3 minutes
Servings: 2

Ingredients

- 1 cup raspberries
- 1 cup frozen blueberries
- 1 cup frozen blackberries
- 1 cup almond milk
- ¼ cup Soy Yogurt

Directions:

1. Pop everything in a blender and blitz
2. Pour into glasses and serve.

Nutrition:
Calories 404, Total Fat 30.4g, Saturated Fat 25.5g, Cholesterol 0mg, Sodium 22mg, Total Carbohydrate 34.5g, Dietary Fiber 12.5g, Total Sugars 19.6g, Protein 6.3g, Vitamin D 0mcg, Calcium 112mg, Iron 4mg, Potassium 581mg

22. Choc-Banana Smoothie

Preparation time: 3 minutes
Servings: 2

Ingredients

- 1 banana
- 2 tbsp. hemp seeds
- 2/3 cup water
- 2 cups ice
- 1 cup almond or cashew milk
- 2 scoop Vegan chocolate protein powder
- 2 tbsp. cacao powder

Directions:

1. Pop everything in a blender and blitz
2. Pour into glasses and serve.

Nutrition:
Calories 676, Total Fat 52.3g, Saturated Fat 38.1g, Cholesterol 0mg, Sodium 46mg, Total Carbohydrate 41.6g, Dietary Fiber 8.7g, Total Sugars 25.2g, Protein 22.4g, Vitamin D 0mcg, Calcium 80mg, Iron 6mg, Potassium 528mg

23. Greens and Berry Smoothie

Preparation time: 3 minutes
Servings 2

Ingredients

- 1 cup frozen berries
- 1 cup kale or spinach
- ¾ cup milk almond, oat or coconut milk
- ½ tbsp chia seeds

Directions:

1. Pop everything in a blender and blitz
2. Pour into glasses and serve.

Nutrition:
Calories 298, Saturated Fat 19.3g, Cholesterol 0mg, Sodium 29mg, Total Carbohydrate 20g, Dietary Fiber 7.4g, Total Sugars 8g, Protein 4.7g, Vitamin D 0mcg, Calcium 114mg, Iron 3mg, Potassium

520mg

24. Peanut Butter Banana Quinoa Bowl

Preparation time: 15 minutes
Cooking time: 15 minutes
Servings: 1
Ingredients:

- *175ml unsweetened soy milk*
- *85g uncooked quinoa*
- *½ teaspoon Ceylon cinnamon*
- *10g chia seeds*
- *30g organic peanut butter*
- *30ml unsweetened almond milk*
- *10g raw cocoa powder*
- *5 drops liquid stevia*
- *1 small banana, peeled, sliced*

Directions:
1. In a saucepan, bring soy milk, quinoa, and Ceylon cinnamon to a boil.
2. Reduce heat and simmer 15 minutes.
3. Remove from the heat and stir in Chia seeds. Cover the saucepan with lid and place aside for 15 minutes.
4. In the meantime, microwave peanut butter and almond milk for 30 seconds on high. Remove and stir until runny. Repeat the process if needed.
5. Stir in raw cocoa powder and Stevia.
6. To serve; fluff the quinoa with fork and transfer in a bowl.
7. Top with sliced banana.
8. Drizzle the quinoa with peanut butter.
9. Serve.

Nutrition:
Calories 718
Total Fat 29.6g
Total Carbohydrate 90.3g
Dietary Fiber 17.5g
Total Sugars 14.5g
Protein 30.4g

25. Orange Pumpkin Pancakes

Preparation time: 10 minutes
Cooking time: 15 minutes
Servings: 4
Ingredients:

- *10g ground flax meal*
- *45ml water*
- *235ml unsweetened soy milk*
- *15ml lemon juice*
- *60g buckwheat flour*
- *60g all-purpose flour*
- *8g baking powder, aluminum-free*
- *2 teaspoons finely grated orange zest*
- *25g white chia seeds*
- *120g organic pumpkin puree (or just bake the pumpkin and puree the flesh*
- *30ml melted and cooled coconut oil*
- *5ml vanilla paste*
- *30ml pure maple syrup*

Directions:
1. Combine ground flax meal with water in a small bowl. Place aside for 10 minutes.
2. Combine almond milk and cider vinegar in a medium bowl. Place aside for 5 minutes.
3. In a separate large bowl, combine buckwheat flour, all-purpose flour, baking powder, orange zest, and chia seeds.
4. Pour in almond milk, along with pumpkin puree, coconut oil, vanilla, and maple syrup.
5. Whisk together until you have a smooth batter.
6. Heat large non-stick skillet over medium-high heat. Brush the skillet gently with some coconut oil.
7. Pour 60ml of batter into skillet. Cooking Time: the pancake for 1 minute, or until bubbles appear on the surface.
8. Lift the pancake gently with a spatula and flip.
9. Cooking Time: 1 ½ minutes more. Slide the pancake onto a plate.

Repeat with the remaining batter.
10. *Serve warm.*

Nutrition:
Calories 301
Total Fat 12.6g
Total Carbohydrate 41.7g
Dietary Fiber 7.2g
Total Sugars 9.9g
Protein 8.1g

26. Sweet Potato Slices With Fruits

Preparation time: 10 minutes
Cooking time: 10 minutes
Servings: 2
Ingredients:

The base:
- *1 sweet potato*

Topping:
- *60g organic peanut butter*
- *30ml pure maple syrup*
- *4 dried apricots, sliced*
- *30g fresh raspberries*

Directions:
1. *Peel and cut sweet potato into ½ cm thick slices.*
2. *Place the potato slices in a toaster on high for 5 minutes. Toast your sweet potatoes TWICE.*
3. *Arrange sweet potato slices onto a plate.*
4. *Spread the peanut butter over sweet potato slices.*
5. *Drizzle the maple syrup over the butter.*
6. *Top each slice with an equal amount of sliced apricots and raspberries.*
7. *Serve.*

Nutrition:
Calories 300
Total Fat 16.9g
Total Carbohydrate 32.1g
Dietary Fiber 6.2g
Total Sugars 17.7g
Protein 10.3g

27. Breakfast Oat Brownies

Preparation time: 10 minutes
Cooking time: 40 minutes
Servings: 10 slices (2 per serving
Ingredients:
- *180g old-fashioned rolled oats*
- *80g peanut flour*
- *30g chickpea flour*
- *25g flax seeds meal*
- *5g baking powder, aluminum-free*
- *½ teaspoon baking soda*
- *5ml vanilla paste*
- *460ml unsweetened vanilla soy milk*
- *80g organic applesauce*
- *55g organic pumpkin puree*
- *45g organic peanut butter*
- *5ml liquid stevia extract*
- *25g slivered almonds*

Directions:
1. *Preheat oven to 180C/350F.*
2. *Line 18cm baking pan with parchment paper, leaving overhanging sides.*
3. *In a large bowl, combine oats, peanut flour, chickpea flour, flax seeds, baking powder, and baking soda.*
4. *In a separate bowl, whisk together vanilla paste, soy milk, applesauce. Pumpkin puree, peanut butter, and stevia.*
5. *Fold the liquid ingredients into dry ones and stir until incorporated.*
6. *Pour the batter into the prepared baking pan.*
7. *Sprinkle evenly with slivered almonds.*
8. *Bake the oat brownies for 40 minutes.*
9. *Remove from the oven and place aside to cool.*
10. *Slice and serve.*

Nutrition:
Calories 309
Total Fat 15.3g
Total Carbohydrate 32.2g
Dietary Fiber 9.2g

Total Sugars 9.1g
Protein 13.7g

28. Spinach Tofu Scramble With Sour Cream

Preparation time: 10 minutes
Cooking time: 15 minutes
Servings: 2
Ingredients:
Sour cream:
- 75g raw cashews, soaked overnight
- 30ml lemon juice
- 5g nutritional yeast
- 60ml water
- 1 good pinch salt

Tofu scramble:
- 15ml olive oil
- 1 small onion, diced
- 1 clove garlic, minced
- 400 firm tofu, pressed, crumbled
- ½ teaspoon ground cumin
- ½ teaspoon curry powder
- ½ teaspoon turmeric
- 2 tomatoes, diced
- 30g baby spinach
- Salt, to taste

Directions:
1. Make the cashew sour cream; rinse and drain soaked cashews.
2. Place the cashews, lemon juice, nutritional yeast, water, and salt in a food processor.
3. Blend on high until smooth, for 5-6 minutes.
4. Transfer to a bowl and place aside.
5. Make the tofu scramble; heat olive oil in a skillet.
6. Add onion and Cooking Time: 5 minutes over medium-high.
7. Add garlic, and Cooking Time: stirring, for 1 minute.
8. Add crumbled tofu, and stir to coat with oil.
9. Add the cumin, curry, and turmeric. Cooking Time: the tofu for 2 minutes.
10. Add the tomatoes and Cooking Time: for 2 minutes.
11. Add spinach and cook, tossing until completely wilted, about 1 minute.
12. Transfer tofu scramble on the plate.
13. Top with a sour cream and serve.

Nutrition:
Calories 411
Total Fat 26.5g
Total Carbohydrate 23.1g
Dietary Fiber 5.9g
Total Sugars 6.3g
Protein 25g

29. Overnight Chia Oats

Preparation time: 15 minutes + inactive time
Cooking time: 20 minutes
Servings: 4
Ingredients:
- 470ml full-fat soy milk
- 90g old-fashioned rolled oats
- 40g chia seeds
- 15ml pure maple syrup
- 25g crushed pistachios
- Blackberry Jam:
- 500g blackberries
- 45ml pure maple syrup
- 30ml water
- 45g chia seeds
- 15ml lemon juice

Directions:
1. Make the oats; in a large bowl, combine soy milk, oats, chia seeds, and maple syrup.
2. Cover and refrigerate overnight.
3. Make the jam; combine blackberries, maple syrup, and water in a saucepan.
4. Simmer over medium heat for 10 minutes.
5. Add the chia seeds and simmer the blackberries for 10 minutes.
6. Remove from heat and stir in lemon juice. Mash the blackberries with a fork and place aside to cool.
7. Assemble; divide the oatmeal among

four serving bowls.
8. Top with each bowl blackberry jam.
9. Sprinkle with pistachios before serving.

Nutrition:
Calories 362
Total Fat 13.4g
Total Carbohydrate 52.6g
Dietary Fiber 17.4g
Total Sugars 24.6g
Protein 12.4g

30. Mexican Breakfast

Preparation time: 10 minutes
Cooking time: 10 minutes
Servings: 4
Ingredients:

- 170g cherry tomatoes, halved
- 1 small red onion, chopped
- 25ml lime juice
- 50ml olive oil
- 1 clove garlic, minced
- 1 teaspoon red chili flakes
- 1 teaspoon ground cumin
- 700g can black beans* (or cooked beans), rinsed
- 4 slices whole-grain bread
- 1 avocado, peeled, pitted
- Salt, to taste

Directions:
1. Combine tomatoes, onion, lime juice, and 15ml olive oil in a bowl.
2. Season to taste and place aside.
3. Heat 2 tablespoons olive oil in a skillet.
4. Add onion and Cooking Time: 4 minutes over medium-high heat.
5. Add garlic and Cooking Time: stirring for 1 minute.
6. Add red chili flakes and cumin. Cooking Time: for 30 seconds.
7. Add beans and Cooking Time: tossing gently for 2 minutes.
8. Stir in ¾ of the tomato mixture and season to taste.
9. Remove from heat.
10. Slice the avocado very thinly.
11. Spread the beans mixture over bread slices. Top with remaining tomato and sliced avocado.
12. Serve.

Nutrition:
Calories 476
Total Fat 21.9g
Total Carbohydrate 52.4g
Dietary Fiber 19.5g
Total Sugars 5.3g
Protein 17.1g

31. Amaranth Quinoa Porridge

Preparation time: 5 minutes
Cooking time: 35 minutes
Servings: 2
Ingredients:

- 85g quinoa
- 70g amaranth
- 460ml water
- 115ml unsweetened soy milk
- ½ teaspoon vanilla paste
- 15g almond butter
- 30ml pure maple syrup
- 10g raw pumpkin seeds
- 10g pomegranate seeds

Directions:
1. Combine quinoa, amaranth, and water.
2. Bring to a boil over medium-high heat.
3. Reduce heat and simmer the grains, stirring occasionally, for 20 minutes.
4. Stir in milk and maple syrup.
5. Simmer for 6-7 minutes. Remove from the heat and stir in vanilla, and almond butter.
6. Allow the mixture to stand for 5 minutes.
7. Divide the porridge between two bowls.
8. Top with pumpkin seeds and pomegranate seeds.
9. Serve.

Nutrition:

Calories 474
Total Fat 13.3g
Total Carbohydrate 73.2g
Dietary Fiber 8.9g
Total Sugars 10g
Protein 17.8g

32. Cacao Lentil Muffins

Preparation time: 10 minutes
Cooking time: 15 minutes
Servings: 12 muffins (2 per serving

Ingredients:

- 195g cooked red lentils
- 50ml melted coconut oil
- 45ml pure maple syrup
- 60ml unsweetened almond milk
- 60ml water
- 60g raw cocoa powder
- 120g whole-wheat flour
- 20g peanut flour
- 10g baking powder, aluminum-free
- 70g Vegan chocolate chips

Directions:

1. Preheat oven to 200C/400F.
2. Line 12-hole muffin tin with paper cases.
3. Place the cooked red lentils in a food blender. Blend on high until smooth.
4. Transfer the lentils puree into a large bowl.
5. Stir in coconut oil, maple syrup, almond milk, and water.
6. In a separate bowl, whisk cocoa powder, whole-wheat flour, peanut flour, and baking powder.
7. Fold in liquid ingredients and stir until just combined.
8. Add chocolate chips and stir until incorporated.
9. Divide the batter among 12 paper cases.
10. Tap the muffin tin gently onto the kitchen counter to remove air.
11. Bake the muffins for 15 minutes.
12. Cool muffins on a wire rack.
13. Serve.

Nutrition:
Calories 372
Total Fat 13.5g
Total Carbohydrate 52.7g
Dietary Fiber 12.9g
Total Sugars 13g
Protein 13.7g

33. Chickpea Crepes With Mushrooms And Spinach

Preparation time: 20 minutes + inactive time
Cooking time: 15 minutes
Servings: 4

Ingredients:

Crepes:

- 140g chickpea flour
- 30g peanut flour
- 5g nutritional yeast
- 5g curry powder
- 350ml water
- Salt, to taste

Filling:

- 10ml olive oil
- 4 portabella mushroom caps, thinly sliced
- 1 onion, thinly sliced
- 30g baby spinach
- Salt, and pepper, to taste

Vegan mayo:

- 60ml aquafaba
- 1/8 teaspoon cream of tartar
- ¼ teaspoon dry mustard powder
- 15ml lemon juice
- 5ml raw cider vinegar
- 15ml maple syrup
- 170ml avocado oil
- Salt, to taste

Directions:

1. Make the mayo; combine aquafaba, cream of tartar, mustard powder. Lemon juice, cider vinegar, and maple syrup in a bowl.
2. Beat with a hand mixer for 30 seconds.

3. Set the mixer to the highest speed. Drizzle in avocado oil and beat for 10 minutes or until you have a mixture that resembles mayonnaise.
4. Of you want paler (in the color mayoadd more lemon juice.
5. Season with salt and refrigerate for 1 hour.
6. Make the crepes; combine chickpea flour, peanut flour, nutritional yeast, curry powder, water, and salt to taste in a food blender.
7. Blend until smooth.
8. Heat large non-stick skillet over medium-high heat. Spray the skillet with some cooking oil.
9. Pour ¼ cup of the batter into skillet and with a swirl motion distribute batter all over the skillet bottom.
10. Cooking Time: the crepe for 1 minute per side. Slide the crepe onto a plate and keep warm.
11. Make the filling; heat olive oil in a skillet over medium-high heat.
12. Add mushrooms and onion and Cooking Time: for 6-8 minutes.
13. Add spinach and toss until wilted, for 1 minute.
14. Season with salt and pepper and transfer into a large bowl.
15. Fold in prepared vegan mayo.
16. Spread the prepared mixture over chickpea crepes. Fold gently and serve.

Nutrition:
Calories 428
Total Fat 13.3g
Total Carbohydrate 60.3g
Dietary Fiber 18.5g
Total Sugars 13.2g
Protein 22.6g

34. Goji Breakfast Bowl

Preparation time: 10 minutes
Servings: 2
Ingredients:

- 15g chia seeds
- 10g buckwheat
- 15g hemp seeds
- 20g Goji berries
- 235mml vanilla soy milk

Directions:
1. Combine chia, buckwheat, hemp seeds, and Goji berries in a bowl.
2. Heat soy milk in a saucepan until start to simmer.
3. Pour the milk over "cereals".
4. Allow the cereals to stand for 5 minutes.
5. Serve.

Nutrition:
Calories 339
Total Fat 14.3g
Total Carbohydrate 41.8g
Dietary Fiber 10.5g
Total Sugars 20g
Protein 13.1g

35. The 'Green Machine' Smoothie

Preparation time: 3 minutes
Servings 2

Ingredients

- 1 cup spinach
- ½ cup broccoli
- 2 Sticks of Celery
- 4 tbsp desiccated coconut
- 1 banana
- 1 scoop vegan unflavored protein powder
- 1 cup almond milk
- 1 cupwater

Directions:
1. Pop everything in a blender and blitz
2. Pour into glasses and serve.

Nutrition:
Calories 780, Total Fat 66.5g, Saturated Fat 57.9g, Cholesterol 0mg, Sodium 224mg, Total Carbohydrate 38.8g, Dietary Fiber 15g, Total Sugars 18.4g, Protein 19.6g, Vitamin D 0mcg, Calcium 82mg, Iron 5mg, Potassium 1108mg

36. Sweet Coffee and Cacao Smoothie

Preparation time: 3 minutes
Servings 2

Ingredients
- 2 tsp Coffee
- ½ a Banana
- 1 cup Almond Milk
- 1 tsp Cashew Butter
- 2 tsp Cacao Powder
- 1 tsp maple Syrup
- 1 scoop vegan protein powder
- ½ cup Chocolate

Directions:
1. Pop everything in a blender and blitz
2. Pour into glasses and serve.

Nutrition:
Calories 614, Total Fat 43.2g, Saturated Fat 34.6g, Cholesterol 10mg, Sodium 146mg, Total Carbohydrate 44.7g, Dietary Fiber 5.4g, Total Sugars 31.2g, Protein 17.6g, Vitamin D 0mcg, Calcium 104mg, Iron 4mg, Potassium 614mg

37. Amazing Blueberry Smoothie

Preparation time: 5 minutes
Servings 2

Ingredients:
- ½ avocado
- 1 cup frozen blueberries
- 1 cup raw spinach
- ¼ tsp sea salt
- 1 cup soy
- 1 frozen banana

Directions:
1. Blend everything in a powerful blender until you have a smooth, creamy shake.
2. Enjoy your healthy shake and start your morning on a fresh note!

Nutrition:
Calories 269, Total Fat 12.3g, Saturated Fat 2.3g, Cholesterol 0mg, Sodium 312mg, Total Carbohydrate 37.6g, Dietary Fiber 8.2g, Total Sugars 22.9g, Protein 6.4g, Vitamin D 0mcg, Calcium 52mg, Iron 3mg, Potassium 528mg

38. Go-Green Smoothie

Preparation time: 5 minutes
Servings 1

Ingredients:
- 2 tablespoons, natural cashew butter
- 1 ripe banana
- 2/3 cup, unsweetened coconut
- ½ cup kale

Directions:
1. Put everything inside a powerful blender.
2. Blend until you have a smooth, creamy shake.
3. Enjoy your special green smoothie.

Nutrition:
Calories 500, Total Fat 33.2g, Saturated Fat 18.9g, Cholesterol 0mg, Sodium 161mg, Total Carbohydrate 48.6g, Dietary Fiber 10.4g, Total Sugars 19.8g, Protein 9.1g, Vitamin D 0mcg, Calcium 72mg, Iron 9mg, Potassium 777mg

39. Creamy Chocolate Shake

Preparation time: 10 minutes
Servings 2

Ingredients:
- 2 frozen ripe bananas, chopped
- 1/3 cup frozen strawberries
- 2 tbsp cocoa powder
- 2 tbsp salted almond butter
- 2 cups unsweetened vanilla almond milk
- 1 dash Stevia or agave nectar
- 1/3 cup ice

Directions:
1. Add all ingredients in a blender and blend until smooth.
2. Take out and serve.

Nutrition:
Calories 272, Total Fat 14.3g, Saturated Fat 1.5g, Cholesterol 0mg, Sodium 315mg, Total Carbohydrate 37g, Dietary Fiber 7.3g, Total

Sugars 16.8g, Protein 6.2g, Vitamin D 2mcg, Calcium 735mg, Iron 2mg, Potassium 732mg

40. Hidden Kale Smoothie

Preparation time: 5 minutes
Servings 2
Ingredients:
- 1 medium ripe banana, peeled and sliced
- ½ cup frozen mixed berries
- 1 tbsp hulled hemp seeds
- 2 cups frozen or fresh kale
- 2/3 cup 100% pomegranate juice
- 2¼ cups filtered water

Directions:
1. Add all ingredients in a blender and blend until smooth.
2. Take out and serve.

Nutrition:
Calories 164, Total Fat 2g, Saturated Fat 0.2g, Cholesterol 0mg, Sodium 51mg, Total Carbohydrate 34.2g, Dietary Fiber 3.9g, Total Sugars 17.7g, Protein 4.1g, Vitamin D 0mcg, Calcium 124mg, Iron 2mg, Potassium 776mg

41. Blueberry Protein Shake

Preparation time: 5 minutes
Servings 1
Ingredients:
- ½ cup cottage cheese
- 3 tbsp vanilla protein powder
- ½ cup frozen blueberries
- ½ tsp maple extract
- ¼ tsp vanilla extract
- 2 tsp flaxseed meal
- Sweetener, choice
- 10-15 ice cubes
- ¼ cup water

Directions:
1. Add all ingredients in a blender and blend until smooth.
2. Take out and serve.

Nutrition:
Calories 559, Total Fat 4.2g, Saturated Fat 1.9g, Cholesterol 14mg, Sodium 659mg, Total Carbohydrate 31.1g, Dietary Fiber 4.5g, Total Sugars 20.7g, Protein 98g, Vitamin D 0mcg, Calcium 518mg, Iron 3mg, Potassium 676mg

42. Raspberry Lime Smoothie

Preparation time: 5 minutes
Servings 2
Ingredients:
- 1 cup water
- 1 cup fresh or frozen raspberries
- 1 large frozen banana
- 2 tbsp fresh juice, lime
- 1 tsp oil, coconut
- 1 tsp agave

Directions:
1. In a blender put all ingredients and blend until smooth.
2. Take out and serve

Nutrition:
Calories 227, Total Fat 4g, Saturated Fat 1.3g, Cholesterol 0mg, Sodium 7mg, Total Carbohydrate 47.8g, Dietary Fiber 6g, Total Sugars 40.7g, Protein 0.9g, Vitamin D 0mcg, Calcium 22mg, Iron 1mg, Potassium 144mg

43. Peppermint Monster Smoothie

Preparation time: 5 minutes
Servings 1
Ingredients:
- 1 large frozen banana, peeled
- 1½ cups non-dairy milk
- A handful of fresh mint leaves, stems removed
- 1-2 handfuls spinach

Directions:
1. Add all ingredients in a blender and blend until smooth.
2. Take out and serve

Nutrition:
Calories 799, Total Fat 28.1g, Saturated Fat 16.7g, Cholesterol 110mg, Sodium 645mg, Total Carbohydrate 98.4g, Dietary Fiber 4.5g, Total Sugars 77.2g, Protein 46.2g, Vitamin D 7mcg, Calcium

1634mg, Iron 2mg, Potassium 1366mg

44. Banana Green Smoothie

Preparation time: 5 minutes
Servings 1
Ingredients:
- 1 cup coconut water
- ¼ cup plant-based milk
- ¼ tsp vanilla extract
- 1 heaping cup loosely packed spinach
- 2-3 cups frozen bananas, sliced

Directions:
Blend everything until smooth and serve.
Nutrition:
Calories 364, Total Fat 4.8g, Saturated Fat 2.6g, Cholesterol 15mg, Sodium 111mg, Total Carbohydrate 78g, Dietary Fiber 8g, Total Sugars 45.1g, Protein 9.6g, Vitamin D 1mcg, Calcium 257mg, Iron 1mg, Potassium 1241mg

45. Cinnamon Coffee Shake

Preparation time: 5 minutes
Servings 2
Ingredients:
- 1 cup cooled coffee, regular or decaf
- ¼ cup almond or non-dairy milk
- A few pinches cinnamon
- 2 tbsp hemp seeds
- Splash vanilla extract
- 2 frozen bananas, sliced into coins
- Handful of ice

Directions:
1. Chill some coffee in a sealed container for a couple of hours (or overnightbefore making this smoothie, or be ready to use more ice.
2. Add the non-dairy milk, cinnamon, vanilla, and hemp seeds to a blender and blend until smooth. Add the coffee and cut bananas and keep blending until smooth.
3. Add the ice and keep blending on high until there are no lumps remaining. Taste for sweetness and add your preferred plant-based sugar or sugar alternative.
4. Transfer to a glass and serve.

Nutrition:
Calories 197, Total Fat 6.4g, Saturated Fat 0.6g, Cholesterol 0mg, Sodium 5mg, Total Carbohydrate 31.3g, Dietary Fiber 5.2g, Total Sugars 15.8g, Protein 4g, Vitamin D 0mcg, Calcium 53mg, Iron 1mg, Potassium 582mg

46. Orange Smoothie

Preparation time: 5 minutes
Servings 2
Ingredients:
- 1 cup orange slices
- 1 cup mango chunks
- 1 cup strawberries, chopped
- 1 cup coconut water
- Pinch freshly grated ginger
- 1-2 cups crushed ice

Directions:
Place everything in a blender, blend, and serve.
Nutrition:
Calories 269, Total Fat 12.3g, Saturated Fat 2.3g, Cholesterol 0mg, Sodium 312mg, Total Carbohydrate 37.6g, Dietary Fiber 8.2g, Total Sugars 22.9g, Protein 6.4g, Vitamin D 0mcg, Calcium 52mg, Iron 3mg, Potassium 528mg

47. Pumpkin Smoothie

Preparation time: 5 minutes
Servings 2
Ingredients:
- 1 cup unsweetened non-dairy milk
- 2 medium bananas, peeled and cut into quarters and frozen
- 2 medjool dates, pitted
- 1 cup pumpkin puree, canned or fresh
- 2 cups ice cubes
- ¼ tsp cinnamon
- 2 tbsp ground flaxseeds
- 1 tsp pumpkin spice

Directions:
Blend all ingredients in a blender and serve.
Nutrition:
Calories 272, Total Fat 5.6g, Saturated Fat 2.2g, Cholesterol 10mg, Sodium 75mg, Total Carbohydrate 51.9g, Dietary Fiber 9.5g, Total Sugars 29.4g, Protein 8.2g, Vitamin D 1mcg, Calcium 204mg, Iron 4mg, Potassium 865mg

48. Turmeric Smoothie

Preparation time: 5 minutes
Servings 2
Ingredients:
- 2 cups non-dairy milk like coconut, almond
- 2 medium bananas, frozen
- 1 cup mango, frozen
- 1 tsp turmeric, ground grated, peeled
- 1 tsp fresh ginger, grated, peeled
- 1 tbsp chia seeds
- ¼ tsp vanilla extract
- ¼ tsp cinnamon, ground
- 1 pinch pepper, ground

Directions:
Blend all ingredients in a blender and serve
Nutrition:
Calories 785, Total Fat 62.4g, Saturated Fat 51.5g, Cholesterol 0mg, Sodium 41mg, Total Carbohydrate 60.2g, Dietary Fiber 15g, Total Sugars 33.9g, Protein 10g, Vitamin D 0mcg, Calcium 149mg, Iron 6mg, Potassium 1292mg

49. Veggie Smoothie

Preparation time: 10 minutes
Servings 1
Ingredients:
- 1 stalk celery
- 1 carrot peeled and roughly chopped
- ½ cup broccoli sprouts
- 1 cup kale, chopped
- ½ cup curly parsley
- ½ tomato roughly chopped
- ½ avocado
- 1 banana
- ½ green apple
- ½ cup non-dairy milk
- 1 tbsp chia seeds
- 1 tbsp flaxseeds

Directions:
1. Place all ingredients in a blender.
2. Blend until smooth. Serve immediately.

Nutrition:
Calories 696, Total Fat 34.1g, Saturated Fat 7g, Cholesterol 10mg, Sodium 190mg, Total Carbohydrate 90.5g, Dietary Fiber 29.5g, Total Sugars 37.2g, Protein 18.5g, Vitamin D 1mcg, Calcium 527mg, Iron 9mg, Potassium 2223mg

50. Very Berry Smoothie

Preparation time: 5 minutes
Servings 2
Ingredients:
- 2 cups, plant-based Milk
- 2 cups, Frozen or fresh berries
- ½ cup Frozen ripe bananas
- 2 teaspoons, Flax Seeds
- ¼ tsp, Vanilla
- ¼ tsp, Cinnamon

Directions:
1. Mix together milk, flax seeds, and fruit. Blend in a high-power blender.
2. Add cinnamon and vanilla. Blend until smooth.
3. Serve and enjoy!

Nutrition:
Calories 269, Total Fat 12.3g, Saturated Fat 2.3g, Cholesterol 0mg, Sodium 312mg, Total Carbohydrate 37.6g, Dietary Fiber 8.2g, Total Sugars 22.9g, Protein 6.4g, Vitamin D 0mcg, Calcium 52mg, Iron 3mg, Potassium 528mg

51. Coco Loco Smoothie

Preparation Time: 5 minutes
Servings: 2
Ingredients
- Coconut milk: 1 cup
- Frozen cauliflower florets: ½ cup

- Frozen mango cubes: 1 cup
- Almond butter: 1 tbsp

Directions:
1. Add all the ingredients to the blender
2. Blend on high speed to make it smooth

Nutrition:
Carbs: 18.2 g
Protein: 10.2 g
Fats: 27.0 g
Calories: 309 Kcal

52. Creamy Carrot Smoothie

Preparation Time: 5 minutes
Servings: 4

Ingredients
- Almond milk: 2 cups
- Prunes: 60 g
- Banana: 1
- Carrots: 150 g
- Walnuts: 30 g
- Ground cinnamon: ½ tsp
- Vanilla extract: 1 tsp
- Ground nutmeg: ¼ tsp

Directions:
1. Add all the ingredients to the blender
2. Blend on high speed to make it smooth

Nutrition:
Carbs: 14.9 g
Protein: 3 g
Fats: 4.5 g
Calories: 103 Kcal

53. Date Chocolate Smoothie

Preparation Time: 5 minutes
Servings: 2

Ingredients
- Unsweetened cocoa powder: 2 tbsp
- Unsweetened nut milk: 2 cups
- Almond butter: 2 tbsp
- Dried dates: 4 pitted
- Frozen bananas: 2 medium
- Ground cinnamon: ¼ tsp

Directions:
1. Add all the ingredients to the blender
2. Blend to form a smooth consistency

Nutrition:
Carbs: 72.1 g
Protein: 8 g
Fats: 12.7 g
Calories: 385 Kcal

54. Date Banana Pistachio Smoothie

Preparation Time: 5 minutes
Servings: 4

Ingredients
- Pistachios: 1 cup
- Raw pumpkin: 175 g
- Cloves: 1
- Nutmeg: 1/8 tsp
- Dates: 4
- Banana: 1
- Ground ginger: 1/8 tsp
- Ground cinnamon: 1 tsp
- Cashew milk: 500 ml
- Ice: as per your need

Directions:
1. Add all the ingredients to the blender
2. Blend on high speed to make it smooth

Nutrition:
Carbs: 32.9 g
Protein: 9.7 g
Fats: 15 g
Calories: 320 Kcal

55. Fall Green Smoothie

Preparation Time: 5 minutes
Servings: 1

Ingredients
- Persimmon: 1
- Spinach: 1 cup
- Orange: 1
- Water: 1 cup

- Chia seeds: 1 tbsp

Directions:
1. Add all the ingredients to the blender
2. Blend to form a smooth consistency
3. Add ice cubes from the top to chill it

Nutrition:
Carbs: 37.1 g
Protein: 6.5 g
Fats: 5.4 g
Calories: 183 Kcal

56. Fig Protein Smoothie

Preparation Time: 5 minutes
Servings: 1

Ingredients
- Fresh figs: 2
- Almond milk: 1 cup
- Dried date: 1 pitted
- Vanilla extract: ¼ tsp
- Sesame seeds: 2 tbsp

Directions:
1. Add all the ingredients to the blender
2. Blend to form a smooth consistency

Nutrition:
Carbs: 66.0 g
Protein: 16.1 g
Fats: 18 g
Calories: 435 Kcal

57. Frozen Berries Smoothie

Preparation Time: 5 minutes
Servings: 2

Ingredients
- Banana: 1 ripe
- Frozen berries: 200g
- Almond milk: 250ml

Directions:
1. Add all the ingredients in the blender
2. Blend to give a smooth consistency
3. Pour to the glasses and serve

Nutrition:
Carbs: 14.9 g
Protein: 2.2 g
Fats: 1.6 g
Calories: 92 Kcal

58. Fruit Medley Smoothie

Preparation Time: 5 minutes
Servings: 2

Ingredients
- Banana: 1 ripe sliced
- Almond milk: 1 cup
- Coconut oil: 1 tbsp
- Powdered ginger: 1 tsp
- Frozen fruit medley: 1 cup
- Chia seeds: 2 tbsp

Directions:
1. Add all the ingredients in the blender
2. Blend to give a smooth consistency
3. Pour to the glasses and serve

Nutrition:
Carbs: 52.8 g
Protein: 6.4 g
Fats: 22.5 g
Calories: 407 Kcal

59. Green Healthy Smoothie

Preparation Time: 5 minutes
Servings: 1

Ingredients
- Large banana: 1 frozen
- Fresh spinach: 1 cup
- Rolled oats: 2 tbsp
- Unsweetened almond milk: ¾ cup

Directions:
1. Add all the ingredients to the blender
2. Blend to form a smooth consistency

Nutrition:
Carbs: 41.2 g
Protein: 8.9 g
Fats: 3.9 g
Calories: 220 Kcal

60. Green Pina Colada

Preparation Time: 5 minutes
Servings: 2

Ingredients

- Full-fat coconut milk: 250 ml
- Fresh pineapple: 330 g chopped
- Banana: 1
- Fresh spinach: 30 g
- Water: 125 ml
- Sesame seeds: 2 tbsp

Directions:
1. Add all the ingredients to the blender
2. Blend to form a smooth consistency

Nutrition:
Carbs: 36.7 g
Protein: 6.4 g
Fats: 6.5 g
Calories: 198 Kcal

61. Guava Smoothie

Preparation Time: 5 minutes
Servings: 1

Ingredients
- Large banana: 1 frozen
- Guava: 2 cups deseeded and diced
- Unsweetened almond milk: ¾ cup

Directions:
1. Add all the ingredients to the blender
2. Blend to form a smooth consistency

Nutrition:
Carbs: 75g
Protein: 9.7 g
Fats: 3.6 g
Calories: 425 Kcal

62. Halva Smoothie

Preparation Time: 5 minutes
Servings: 1

Ingredients
- Dried date: 1 pitted
- Tahini: 1 tbsp
- Fresh figs: 2
- Almond milk: 1 cup
- Vanilla extract: ¼ tsp

Directions:
1. Add all the ingredients to the blender
2. Blend to form a smooth consistency

Nutrition:
Carbs: 66.0 g
Protein: 12.1 g
Fats: 16.5 g
Calories: 435 Kcal

63. Kale Smoothie

Preparation Time: 5 minutes
Servings: 1

Ingredients
- Almond butter: 1 tbsp
- Large banana: 1 frozen
- Fresh kale: 1 cup
- Unsweetened almond milk: ¾ cup

Directions:
1. Add all the ingredients to the blender
2. Blend to form a smooth consistency

Nutrition:
Carbs: 34.1
Protein: 12.8 g
Fats: 14 g
Calories: 244 Kcal

64. Kiwi And Almonds Smoothie

Preparation Time: 5 minutes
Servings: 2

Ingredients
- Almonds: ½ cup
- Coconut milk: 1 cup
- Kiwi: 1 medium peeled and sliced
- Banana: 1 sliced
- Ice cubes: 4
- Avocado: 1/2 small
- Baby spinach: 1 cup lightly packed

Directions:
1. Add all the ingredients to the blender
2. Blend to form a smooth consistency

Nutrition:
Carbs: 37.1 g
Protein: 15.2 g
Fats: 28.3 g

Calories: 427 Kcal

65. Mango Almonds Smoothie

Preparation Time: 5 minutes
Servings: 1

Ingredients
- *Frozen mango chunks: 1 cup*
- *Almonds: ¼ cup whole*
- *Oat milk: ½ cup*
- *Frozen banana: 1 large sliced*

Directions:
1. Add all the ingredients to the blender
2. Blend until smooth

Nutrition:
Carbs: 73.1 g
Protein: 10.5 g
Fats: 18.7 g
Calories: 486 Kcal

66. Mango Banana Smoothie

Preparation Time: 5 minutes
Servings: 1

Ingredients
- *Almond butter: 1tbsp*
- *Frozen mango chunks: ½ cup*
- *Banana: 1 small*
- *Flax seeds: 1 tsp*
- *Ground cinnamon: ¼ tsp*
- *Hemp seeds: 1 tsp*
- *Coconut milk: 1 cup beverage*

Directions:
1. Add all the ingredients to the blender
2. Blend to form a smooth consistency

Nutrition:
Carbs: 27.2 g
Protein: 10 g
Fats: 15.1 g
Calories: 270 Kcal

67. Orange Nuts Smoothie

Preparation Time: 5 minutes
Servings: 4 cups

Ingredients
- *Peanuts: 1 cup*
- *Almonds: 1 cup*
- *Strawberries: 6*
- *Orange: 1*
- *Pineapple: 1 cup chopped*
- *Water: 1 cup*

Directions:
1. Add all the ingredients to the blender
2. Blend to form a smooth consistency

Nutrition:
Carbs: 25.2 g
Protein: 15.5 g
Fats: 18.6 g
Calories: 462 Kcal

68. Peanut Butter Green Smoothie

Preparation Time: 5 minutes
Servings: 2

Ingredients
- *Coconut milk: 1 cup*
- *Peanut butter: 2 tbsp*
- *Frozen banana: 1 small sliced*
- *Frozen zucchini: 1/2 cup sliced*

Directions:
1. Add all the ingredients to the blender
2. Blend to form a smooth consistency

Nutrition:
Carbs: 33.1 g
Protein: 12.2 g
Fats: 18.0 g
Calories: 335 Kcal

69. Persimmon Mango Smoothie

Preparation Time: 5 minutes
Servings: 1

Ingredients
- *Frozen mango chunks: ½ cup*
- *Carrot: 1 small peeled and chopped*
- *Coconut milk: 1 cup beverage*
- *Ground cinnamon: ¼ tsp*
- *Ripe persimmon: ½ ripe*

- Flax seeds: 1 tsp
- Almond butter: 1 tbsp
- Hemp seeds: 1 tsp

Directions:
1. Add all the ingredients to the blender
2. Blend to form a smooth consistency

Nutrition:
Carbs: 27.2 g
Protein: 10 g
Fats: 15.1 g
Calories: 256 Kcal

70. Pineapple, Orange, And Strawberry Smoothie

Preparation Time: 5 minutes
Servings: 4 cups

Ingredients
- Strawberries: 6
- Orange: 1
- Pineapple: 1 cup chopped
- Water: 1 cup

Directions:
1. Add all the ingredients to the blender
2. Blend to form a smooth consistency

Nutrition:
Carbs: 12.2 g
Protein: 2 g
Fats: 0.2 g
Calories: 48 Kcal

71. Pistachios Spinach Smoothie

Preparation Time: 5 minutes
Servings: 1

Ingredients
- Large banana: 1
- Ice cubes: 4
- Pistachios: ¼ cup
- Fresh spinach: 1 cup
- Rolled oats: 2 tbsp
- Unsweetened almond milk: ¾ cup

Directions:
1. Add all the ingredients to the blender
2. Blend to form a smooth consistency

Nutrition:
Carbs: 49.2 g
Protein: 12.9 g
Fats: 21.9 g
Calories: 392 Kcal

72. Peaches And Cream Oats

Servings: 2
Preparation time: 10 minutes
Cooking time: 3 minutes

Ingredients:
- 2 peaches, chopped
- 1 cup coconut milk
- 1 cup steel cut oats
- ½ vanilla bean
- 2 cups water

Directions:
1. Put the peaches in your instant pot.
2. Add coconut milk, oats, vanilla bean and water and Cooking Time: for 3 minutes.
3. Leave aside for 10 minutes to release pressure and serve.
4. Enjoy!

Nutritional value: 130, fat 2, carbs 5, fiber 2, protein 3

73. Instant Pot Strawberries And Oats Breakfast

Servings: 2
Preparation time: 5 minutes
Cooking time: 10 minutes

Ingredients:
- 1/3 cup old-fashioned rolled oats
- 2 tablespoon dried strawberries
- A pinch of salt
- 2 cups water
- 2/3 cup almond milk
- ½ teaspoon coconut sugar

Directions:
1. Put the water in your instant pot.
2. Add strawberries, oats, almond milk and sugar.
3. Cooking Time: on High for 10

minutes, leave aside to release pressure, transfer the oats to breakfast bowls and serve.
4. Enjoy!

Nutritional value: *calories 200, fat 5, carbs 25, fiber 2.8, protein 8.6*

74. Instant Pot Breakfast Quinoa

Servings: 6
Preparation time: 10 minutes
Cooking time: 3 minutes
Ingredients:
- 1 and ½ cups quinoa
- 2 tablespoons maple syrup
- 2 and ¼ cups water
- ¼ teaspoon cinnamon, ground
- ½ teaspoon vanilla
- A pinch of salt
- Sliced almond for serving

Directions:
1. In your instant pot, mix water with maple syrup, quinoa, cinnamon, vanilla and salt.
2. Cooking Time: on high pressure for 1 minute, leave 10 minutes aside to release pressure, pour into breakfast bowls and serve with sliced almond on top.
3. Enjoy!

Nutritional value: *120, fat 10, carbs 12, fiber 4, protein 5*

75. Carrot Breakfast

Servings: 6
Preparation time: 20 minutes
Cooking time: 10 minutes
Ingredients:
- 1 cup steel cut oats
- 4 cups water
- 1 tablespoon coconut butter
- 2 teaspoons cinnamon, ground
- 1 cup carrots, finely grated
- 3 tablespoons maple syrup
- 1 teaspoon pumpkin pie spice
- A pinch of salt
- ¼ cup chia seeds
- ¾ cup raisins

Directions:
1. In your instant pot, mix coconut butter with water, cinnamon, carrots, maple syrup, salt and pumpkin pie spice and Cooking Time: on High for 10 minutes.
2. Leave pot aside to release pressure for 10 minutes, add oats, chia seeds and raisins, cover pot and leave it aside for another 10 minutes.
3. Transfer the carrot oatmeal to breakfast bowls and serve it right away!
4. Enjoy!

Nutritional value: *calories 150, fat 3, carbs 12, sugar 13, fiber 8, protein 8*

76. Special Instant Pot Vegan Pumpkin Oatmeal

Servings: 6
Preparation time: 10 minutes
Cooking time: 4 minutes
Ingredients:
- 1 and ½ cups steel cut oats
- 1 and ½ cups pumpkin puree
- 4 and ½ cups water
- 1 teaspoon allspice
- 1 teaspoon vanilla
- 2 teaspoons cinnamon powder
- ½ cup coconut sugar
- ¼ cup pecans, chopped
- 1 tablespoon cinnamon
- Almond milk for serving

Directions:
1. Put the water in your instant pot.
2. Add oats, pumpkin puree, 2 teaspoons cinnamon, vanilla and allspice.
3. Stir, cover, Cooking Time: on High for 3 minutes and then release pressure.
4. Meanwhile, in a bowl, mix pecans with sugar and 1 tablespoon cinnamon and stir well.

5. Sprinkle this over pumpkin oatmeal and serve with almond milk.
6. Enjoy!

Nutritional value: *calories 130, fat 3, carbs 12, fiber 3, protein 4, sugar 10*

77. Instant Pot Breakfast Risotto

Servings: 4
Preparation time: 10 minutes
Cooking time: 22 minutes
Ingredients:

- 1 and ½ cups arborio rice
- 2 apples, diced
- 2 tablespoons coconut butter
- A pinch of salt
- 1 and ½ teaspoons cinnamon
- 1/3 cup stevia
- 1 cup apple juice
- 3 cups almond milk
- ½ cup cherries, dried

Directions:

1. Put coconut butter and rice in your instant pot, cover and Cooking Time: on High for 6 minutes.
2. Uncover instant pot, stir the rice and mix it with apple juice, almond milk, apples, raw sugar, a pinch of salt and cinnamon, cover and Cooking Time: on High for 10 minutes.
3. Serve your breakfast rice in medium bowls with dried cherries on top.
4. Enjoy!

Nutritional value: *calories 178, fat 12, carbs 1, fiber 3, protein 12, sugar 11*

78. Instant Pot Breakfast Porridge

Servings: 6
Preparation time: 10 minutes
Cooking time: 35 minutes
Ingredients:

- ¼ cup split yellow gram, roasted
- 1 tablespoon split Bengal gram, roasted
- 1 and ½ cups banana, chopped
- 1 cup almond milk
- 1 cup rice, washed
- 3 cups water
- 2 cups jaggery, chopped
- 3 tablespoons cashews, chopped
- 1 teaspoon cardamom powder
- 2 tablespoons raisins
- ¼ teaspoon nutmeg powder
- Some saffron strands

Directions:

1. In your instant pot, mix yellow and Bengal gram with rice, almond milk and 2 and ½ cups water and Cooking Time: on High for 5-6 minutes.
2. Release pressure and leave aside for now.
3. In a bowl, mix jaggery with the rest of the water, stir and pour everything into a pan heated over medium high heat.
4. Cooking Time: for 7 minutes, stirring often and then add the rice and gram mix.
5. Stir again and Cooking Time: for 4 minutes.
6. Add raisins, cashews, stir and Cooking Time: for 2 minutes.
7. Add cardamom powder, nutmeg powder, saffron and bananas, stir and Cooking Time: for 1 minute.
8. Pour this into breakfast bowls and serve right away.
9. Enjoy!

Nutritional value: *calories 70, fat 1, carbs 5, fiber 1, protein 1*

79. Delicious Apple Butter

Servings: 80
Preparation time: 10 minutes
Cooking time: 1 hour
Ingredients:

- ½ cup cider vinegar
- 16 apples, cored and sliced
- 2 and ½ cups palm sugar

- ¼ teaspoon cloves, ground
- 3 teaspoons cinnamon

Directions:
1. Put the apples in your instant pot, cover and Cooking Time: on High for 1 hour.
2. Release pressure, transfer the apples to your food processor and blend them very well.
3. Return apples to your instant pot, add palm sugar, vinegar, cinnamon and cloves, stir well, cover the pot and Cooking Time: on Low for 15 minutes.
4. Transfer to jars and serve with some toasted bread in the morning.
5. Enjoy!

Nutritional value: calories 50, fat 0.1, carbs 11.2, fiber 0.9, sugar 10, protein 0.1

80. Instant Pot Vegan Chestnut Butter

Servings: 4
Preparation time: 10 minutes
Cooking time: 20 minutes
Ingredients:

- 1 and ½ pounds fresh chestnuts
- 11 ounces water
- 11 ounces coconut sugar

Directions:
1. Cut chestnuts in halves, peel them and put them in your instant pot.
2. Add water and sugar, cover lid and Cooking Time: on High for 20 minutes.
3. Release pressure for about 10 minutes, transfer the mix to your blender and pulse very well.
4. Pour into a bowl and serve in the morning on toasted and sliced bread.
5. Enjoy!

Nutritional value: calories 80, fat 0, carbs 20, sugar 17, protein 0

81. Delicious Breakfast Tapioca Pudding

Servings: 6
Preparation time: 10 minutes
Cooking time: 8 minutes
Ingredients:

- 1/3 cup tapioca pearls, washed and drained
- ½ cup water
- ½ cup coconut sugar
- 1 and ¼ cups almond milk
- Zest from ½ lemon

Directions:
1. Put the tapioca pearls in a bowl and mix with water, sugar, milk and lemon zest.
2. Stir well, transfer this to your instant pot and Cooking Time: on High for 8 minutes.
3. Release pressure, leave the pudding aside for 10 minutes, pour it into breakfast bowls and serve right away!
4. Enjoy!

Nutritional value: calories 180, fat 2.5, carbs 39, fiber 0.1, protein 2.5

82. Breakfast Quinoa Salad

Preparation time: 10 minutes
Cooking time: 20 minutes
Servings: 4
Ingredients:

- 1 yellow onion, chopped
- 3 tablespoons olive oil
- 1 carrot, chopped
- 2 cups mushrooms, sliced
- Zest from ½ lemon, grated
- 2 tablespoons lemon juice
- A pinch of salt and black pepper
- 4 garlic cloves, minced
- 1 cup quinoa
- 10 cherry tomatoes, halved
- 1 cup veggie stock
- 1 tablespoon spring onions, chopped

Directions:
1. Set your instant pot on sauté mode, add oil, heat it up, add onion and carrot, stir and sauté for 2 minutes.

2. Add mushrooms, stir and Cooking Time: for 3 minutes more.
3. Add salt, pepper, garlic, lemon juice and lemon zest, quinoa and stock, stir and Cooking Time: for 1 minute.
4. Add tomatoes, cover pot, Cooking Time: on High for 10 minutes, divide into bowls, sprinkle spring onion on top and serve cold for breakfast.
5. Enjoy!

Nutrition: calories 179, fat 2, fiber 3, carbs 18, protein 7

83. Cinnamon Oatmeal

Preparation time: 10 minutes
Cooking time: 4 minutes
Servings: 3
Ingredients:

- 3 cups water
- 1 cup steel cut oats
- 1 apple, cored and chopped
- 1 tablespoon cinnamon powder

Directions:
1. In your instant pot, mix water with oats, cinnamon and apple, stir, cover and Cooking Time: on High for 4 minutes.
2. Stir again, divide into bowls and serve for breakfast.
3. Enjoy!

Nutrition: calories 200, fat 1, fiber 7, carbs 12, protein 10

84. Breakfast Coconut Risotto

Preparation time: 10 minutes
Cooking time: 7 minutes
Servings: 4
Ingredients:

- 1 cup Arborio rice
- 2 cups almond milk
- 1 cup coconut milk
- 1/3 cup agave nectar
- 2 teaspoons vanilla extract
- ¼ cup coconut flakes, toasted

Directions:

1. Set your instant pot on simmer mode, add almond and coconut milk and bring to a boil.
2. Add agave nectar and rice, stir, cover and Cooking Time: on High for 5 minutes.
3. Add vanilla and coconut, stir, divide into bowls and serve warm.
4. Enjoy!

Nutrition: calories 192, fat 1, fiber 1, carbs 20, protein 4

85. Pumpkin Oats

Preparation time: 10 minutes
Cooking time: 3 minutes
Servings: 6
Ingredients:

- 4 and ½ cups water
- 1 and ½ cups steel cut oats
- 2 teaspoons cinnamon powder
- 1 teaspoon vanilla extract
- 1 teaspoon allspice
- 1 and ½ cup pumpkin puree
- ¼ cup pecans, chopped

Directions:
1. In your instant pot, mix water with oats, cinnamon, vanilla allspice and pumpkin puree, stir, cover and Cooking Time: on High for 3 minutes.
2. Divide into bowls, stir again, cool down and serve with pecans on top.
3. Enjoy!

Nutrition: calories 173, fat 1, fiber 5, carbs 20, protein 6

86. Simple Tofu Mix

Preparation time: 10 minutes
Cooking time: 10 minutes
Servings: 4
Ingredients:

- 1 pound extra firm tofu, cubed
- 1 cup sweet potato, chopped
- 3 garlic cloves, minced
- 2 tablespoons sesame seeds
- 1 yellow onion, chopped

- *2 teaspoons sesame seed oil*
- *1 carrot, chopped*
- *1 tablespoon tamari*
- *1 tablespoon rice vinegar*
- *2 cups snow peas, halved*
- *1/3 cup veggie stock*
- *2 tablespoons red pepper sauce*
- *2 tablespoons scallions, chopped*
- *2 tablespoons tahini paste*

Directions:
1. Set your instant pot on sauté mode, add oil, heat it up, add sweet potato, onion and carrots, stir and Cooking Time: for 2 minutes.
2. Add garlic, half of the sesame seeds, tofu, vinegar, tamari and stock, stir and Cooking Time: for 2 minutes more.
3. Cover pot and Cooking Time: on High for 3 minutes more.
4. Add peas, the rest of the sesame seeds, green onions, tahini paste and pepper sauce, stir, cover and Cooking Time: on Low for 1 minutes more.
5. Divide into bowls and serve for breakfast.
6. Enjoy!

Nutrition: *calories 172, fat 7, fiber 1, carbs 20, protein 6*

87. Rich Quinoa Curry

Preparation time: 10 minutes
Cooking time: 12 minutes
Servings: 6
Ingredients:

- *1 sweet potato, chopped*
- *1 broccoli head, florets separated*
- *1 small yellow onion, chopped*
- *15 ounces canned chickpeas, drained*
- *28 ounces canned tomatoes, chopped*
- *14 ounces coconut milk*
- *¼ cup quinoa*
- *1 tablespoon ginger, grated*
- *2 garlic cloves, minced*
- *1 tablespoon turmeric, ground*
- *2 teaspoons tamari sauce*
- *1 teaspoon chili flakes*
- *1 teaspoon miso*

Directions:
1. In your instant pot, mix potato with broccoli, onion, chickpeas, tomatoes, milk, quinoa, ginger, garlic, turmeric, tamari sauce, chili and miso, stir, cover and Cooking Time: on High for 12 minutes.
2. Stir one more time, divide into bowls and serve for breakfast.
3. Enjoy!

Nutrition: *calories 400, fat 20, fiber 11, carbs 50, protein 12*

88. Breakfast Burgers

Preparation time: 10 minutes
Cooking time: 30 minutes
Servings: 4
Ingredients:

- *1 cup mushrooms, chopped*
- *2 teaspoons ginger, grated*
- *1 cup yellow onion, chopped*
- *1 cup red lentils*
- *1 sweet potato, chopped*
- *2 and ½ cups veggie stock*
- *¼ cup hemp seeds*
- *¼ cup parsley, chopped*
- *1 tablespoon curry powder*
- *¼ cup cilantro, chopped*
- *1 cup quick oats*
- *4 tablespoons rice flour*

Directions:
1. Set your instant pot on sauté mode, add onion, mushrooms and ginger, stir and sauté for 2 minutes.
2. Add lentils, stock and sweet potatoes, stir, cover and Cooking Time: on High for 6 minutes.
3. Leave this mixture aside to cool down, mash using a potato masher, add parsley, hemp, curry powder, cilantro, oats and rice flour and stir well.

4. Shape 8 patties out of this mix, arrange them all on a lined baking sheet, introduce in the oven at 375 degrees F and bake for 10 minutes on each side.
5. Divide between plates and serve for breakfast.
6. Enjoy!

Nutrition: *calories 140, fat 3, fiber 4, carbs 14, protein 13*

89. Veggie Dumplings

Preparation time: 10 minutes
Cooking time: 15 minutes
Servings: 6
Ingredients:

- *1 tablespoon olive oil*
- *1 cup mushrooms, chopped*
- *1 and ½ cups cabbage, chopped*
- *½ cup carrots, grated*
- *1 and ½ cups water*
- *2 tablespoons soy sauce*
- *1 teaspoon ginger, grated*
- *1 tablespoon rice wine vinegar*
- *1 teaspoon sesame oil*
- *12 vegan dumpling wrappers*

Directions:
1. Set your instant pot on sauté mode, add olive oil, heat it up, add mushrooms, stir and Cooking Time: for 2 minutes.
2. Add carrot, cabbage, soy sauce and vinegar, stir and Cooking Time: for 3 minutes more.
3. Add sesame oil and ginger, stir and transfer everything to a bowl.
4. Arrange all wrappers on a working surface, divide veggie mix, wrap them and seal with some water.
5. Add the water to your instant pot, add steamer basket, add dumplings inside, cover pot and Cooking Time: on High for 7 minutes.
6. Divide between plates and serve for breakfast.
7. Enjoy!

Nutrition: *calories 100, fat 2, fiber 1, carbs 9, protein 3*

90. Breakfast Rice Bowl

Preparation time: 10 minutes
Cooking time: 30 minutes
Servings: 4
Ingredients:

- *1 tablespoon olive oil*
- *2 tablespoons chana masala*
- *1 red onion, chopped*
- *1 tablespoon ginger, grated*
- *1 tablespoon garlic, minced*
- *1 cup chickpeas*
- *3 cups water*
- *A pinch of salt and black pepper*
- *14 ounces tomatoes, chopped*
- *1 and ½ cups brown rice*

Directions:
1. Set your instant pot on sauté mode, add the oil, heat it up, add onion, stir and Cooking Time: for 7 minutes.
2. Add salt, pepper, chana masala, ginger and garlic, stir and Cooking Time: for 1 minute more.
3. Add tomatoes, chickpeas, rice and water, stir, cover and Cooking Time: on High for 20 minutes.
4. Stir one more time, divide into bowls and serve for breakfast.
5. Enjoy!

Nutrition: *calories 292, fat 4, fiber 3, carbs 9, protein 10*

91. Millet And Veggie Mix

Preparation time: 10 minutes
Cooking time: 16 minutes
Servings: 4
Ingredients:

- *1 cup millet*
- *½ cup oyster mushrooms, chopped*
- *2 garlic cloves, minced*
- *½ cup green lentils*
- *½ cup bok choy, chopped*
- *2 and ¼ cups veggie stock*

- 1 cup yellow onion, chopped
- 1 cup asparagus, chopped
- 1 tablespoon lemon juice
- ¼ cup parsley and chives, chopped

Directions:
1. Set your instant pot on sauté mode, heat it up, add garlic, onion and mushrooms, stir and Cooking Time: for 2 minutes.
2. Add lentils and millet, stir and Cooking Time: for a few seconds more.
3. Add stock, stir, cover and Cooking Time: on High for 10 minutes.
4. Add asparagus and bok choy, stir, cover and leave everything aside for 3 minutes.
5. Add parsley and chives and lemon juice, stir, divide into bowls and serve for breakfast.
6. Enjoy!

Nutrition: calories 172, fat 3, fiber 8, carbs 19, protein 5

92. Tapioca Pudding

Preparation time: 10 minutes
Cooking time: 8 minutes
Servings: 4
Ingredients:
- 1/3 cup tapioca pearls
- ½ cup water
- 1 and ¼ cups almond milk
- ½ cup stevia
- Zest from ½ lemon, grated

Directions:
1. In a heatproof bowl, mix tapioca with almond milk, stevia and lemon zest and stir well.
2. Add the water to your instant pot, add steamer basket, and heatproof bowl inside, cover and Cooking Time: on High for 8 minutes.
3. Stir your pudding and serve for breakfast.
4. Enjoy!

Nutrition: calories 187, fat 3, fiber 1, carbs 18, protein 3

93. Breakfast Arugula Salad

Preparation time: 10 minutes
Cooking time: 15 minutes
Servings: 6
Ingredients:
- 2 cups water
- 1 cup kamut grains, soaked for 12 hours, drained and mixed with some lemon juice
- 1 teaspoon sunflower oil
- A pinch of salt
- 4 ounces arugula
- 2 blood oranges, peeled and cut into medium segments
- 1 tablespoon olive oil
- 3 ounces walnuts, chopped

Directions:
1. In your instant pot, mix kamut grains with sunflower oil and the water, stir, cover and Cooking Time: on High for 15 minutes.
2. Drain kamut, transfer to a bowl, add a pinch of salt, arugula, orange segments, oil and walnuts, toss well and serve for breakfast.
3. Enjoy!

Nutrition: calories 125, fat 6, fiber 2, carbs 4, protein 3

94. Protein Blueberry Smoothie

Preparation Time: 5 minutes
Servings: 2
Ingredients
- Unsweetened coconut milk: 1 cup
- Blackberries: ½ cup
- Unsweetened coconut flakes: ¼ cup
- Banana: ½
- Chia Seeds Protein Powder: 2 scoops

Directions:
1. Add all the ingredients to the blender
2. Mix well and pour to the glass

Nutritional Facts
Carbs: 24.0 g

Protein: 23.1 g
Fats: 11.2 g
Calories: 376 Kcal

95. Pumpkin Pie Smoothie

Preparation Time: 5 minutes
Servings: 4

Ingredients

- Raw pumpkin:175 g
- Cloves:1
- Nutmeg:1/8 tsp
- Dates: 4
- Banana:1
- Ground ginger:1/8 tsp
- Ground cinnamon:1 tsp
- Cashew milk:500 ml
- Ice: as per your need

Directions:

1. Add all the ingredients to the blender
2. Blend on high speed to make it smooth

Nutrition:
Carbs: 24.9 g
Protein: 3.5 g
Fats: 1 g
Calories: 148 Kcal

96. Smoothie Bowl

Preparation Time: 5 minutes
Servings: 2

Ingredients

- Unsweetened almond milk: 250 ml
- Frozen Bananas: 2 large
- Peanut butter:2 tbsp
- Frozen blueberries:140 g
- Pistachios: 2 tbsp chopped

Directions:

1. Add all the ingredients to the blender except pistachios and blend well
2. Add fresh berries on top and pistachios and serve

Nutrition:
Carbs: 41.6 g

Protein: 7 g
Fats: 16.4 g
Calories: 261 Kcal

97. Soothing After Workout Smoothie

Preparation Time: 5 minutes
Servings: 2

Ingredients

- Strawberries: 1 cup chopped
- Oat milk: 1 cup
- Banana: 1
- Peanut butter: 1 tbsp

Directions:

1. Add all the ingredients to the blender
2. Blend on high speed to make it smooth

Nutrition:
Carbs: 26.7g
Protein: 7g
Fats: 8.5g
Calories: 198 Kcal

98. Strawberry Coconut Smoothie

Preparation Time: 5 minutes
Servings: 2

Ingredients

- Coconut milk: 1 cup
- Strawberry: 1 cup
- Almond butter: 1 tbsp
- Frozen mango cubes: ½ cup

Directions:

1. Add all the ingredients to the blender
2. Blend on high speed to make it smooth

Nutritional Facts
Carbs: 18.8 g
Protein: 8 g
Fats: 26 g
Calories: 329 Kcal

99. Strawberry, Fruity And Nutty Smoothie

Preparation Time: 5 minutes
Servings: 4 cups

Ingredients

- *Strawberries: 6*
- *Peanuts: 1 cup*
- *Orange: 1*
- *Pineapple: 1 cup chopped*
- *Water: 1 cup*

Directions:

1. *Add all the ingredients to the blender*
2. *Blend to form a smooth consistency*

Nutrition:
Carbs: 18.2 g
Protein: 8 g
Fats: 18.2 g
Calories: 258 Kcal

100. Sunflower Seed Butter Smoothie

Preparation Time: 5 minutes
Servings: 2

Ingredients

- *Coconut milk: 1 cup*
- *Frozen banana: 1 small sliced*
- *Sunflower Seed butter: 2 tbsp*
- *Spinach: 1/2 cup sliced*

Directions:

1. *Add all the ingredients to the blender*
2. *Blend to form a smooth consistency*

Nutritional Facts
Carbs: 33.1 g
Protein: 13.2 g
Fats: 18.0 g
Calories: 335 Kcal

101. Tropical Paradise Smoothie

Preparation Time: 5 minutes
Servings: 2

Ingredients

- *Frozen peeled banana: 1 thinly sliced*
- *Fresh mango: ½ cup diced*
- *Ice cubes: 4*
- *Full-fat coconut milk: 1 cup*
- *Pineapple chunks: ¾ cup*
- *Ground ginger: 1/8 tsp*
- *Chia seeds: 1 tbsp*
- *Toasted shredded coconut: 2 tbsp for topping*

Directions:

1. *Add all the ingredients to the blender except toasted coconuts*
2. *Blend to make smooth*
3. *Top with toasted coconuts and serve*

Nutritional Facts
Carbs: 33.3 g
Protein: 8 g
Fats: 26.4 g
Calories: 359 Kcal

102. Veggie Omelet

Preparation time: 15 minutes
Cooking time: 23 minutes
Servings: 2

Ingredients:

- *8 ounces fresh asparagus, trimmed and cut into 1-inch pieces*
- *¼ of red bell pepper, seeded*
- *¼ of green bell pepper, seeded*
- *1 tablespoon fresh chives, chopped*
- *¾ cup water*
- *½ cup superfine chickpea flour*
- *1 tablespoon chia seeds*
- *2 tablespoons nutritional yeast*
- *½ teaspoon baking powder*
- *1 teaspoon dried basil, crushed*
- *¼ teaspoon ground turmeric*
- *¼ teaspoon red pepper flakes, crushed*
- *Salt and ground black pepper, as required*
- *1 small tomato, chopped*

Directions:

1. *In a pan of the lightly salted boiling water, add the asparagus and Cooking Time: for about 5-7 minutes or until crisp tender.*

2. Drain the asparagus well and set aside.
3. Meanwhile, in a bowl, add the bell peppers, chives and water and mix.
4. In another bowl, add the remaining ingredients except tomato and mix well.
5. Add the water mixture into the bowl of flour mixture and mix until well combined.
6. Set aside for at least 10 minutes.
7. Lightly, grease a large nonstick skillet and heat over medium heat.
8. Add ½ of the mixture and with the back of a spoon, smooth it.
9. Sprinkle half of the tomato over mixture evenly.
10. Cover the skillet tightly and Cooking Time: for about 4 minutes.
11. Now, place half of cooked asparagus over one side of omelet.
12. Carefully, fold the other half over asparagus to cover it.
13. Cover the skillet and Cooking Time: for 3-4 minutes more.
14. Repeat with the remaining mixture.
15. Serve warm.

Tip:
1. In a resealable plastic bag, place the cooled omelet slices and seal the bag.
2. Refrigerate for about 2-3 days.
3. Reheat in the microwave on High for about 1 minute before serving.

Nutrition:
Calories: 271, Fats: 5.2g, Carbs: 44.7g, Fiber: 15.8g, Sugar: 9.5g, Proteins: 18.2g, Sodium: 104mg

103. Veggies Quiche

Preparation time: 15 minutes
Cooking time: 1 hour; Servings: 4
Ingredients:

- 1 cup water
- Pinch of salt
- 1/3 cup bulgur wheat
- ¾ tablespoon light sesame oil
- 1½ cups fresh cremini mushrooms, sliced
- 2 cups fresh broccoli, chopped
- 1 yellow onion, chopped
- 16 ounces firm tofu, pressed and cubed
- ¾ tablespoon white miso
- 1¼ tablespoons tahini
- 1 tablespoon soy sauce

Directions:
1. Preheat the oven to 350 degrees F. Grease a pie dish.
2. In a pan, add the water over medium heat and salt bring to a boil.
3. Stir in the bulgur and again bring to a boil.
4. Reduce the heat to low and simmer, covered for about 12-15 minutes or until all the liquid is absorbed.
5. Remove from the heat and let it cool slightly.
6. Now, place the cooked bulgur into the pie dish evenly and with your fingers, press into the bottom.
7. Bake for about 12 minutes.
8. Remove from the oven and let it cool slightly.
9. Meanwhile, in a skillet, heat oil over medium heat.
10. Add the mushrooms, broccoli and onion and Cooking Time: for about 10 minutes, stirring occasionally.
11. Remove from the heat and transfer into a large bowl to cool slightly.
12. Meanwhile, in a food processor, add the remaining ingredients and pulse until smooth.
13. Transfer the tofu mixture into the bowl with veggie mixture and mix until well combined.
14. Place the veggie mixture over the baked crust evenly.
15. Bake for about 30 minutes or until top becomes golden brown.
16. Remove from the oven and set aside for at least 10 minutes.
17. With a sharp knife, cut into 4 equal sized slices and serve.

Meal Preparation time: Tip:
1. In a resealable plastic bag, place the cooled quiche slices and seal the bag.
2. Refrigerate for about 2-4 days.
3. Reheat in the microwave on High for about 1 minute before serving.

Nutrition:
Calories: 212, Fats: 10.4g, Carbs: 19.6g, Fiber: 5.7g, Sugar: 3.4g, Proteins: 14.4g, Sodium: 425mg

104. Simple Bread

Preparation time: 15 minutes
Cooking time: 40 minutes
Servings: 16

Ingredients:
- 2 teaspoons maple syrup
- 2 cups warm water
- 4 cups whole-wheat flour
- 1 tablespoon instant yeast
- ½ teaspoon salt

Directions:
1. In a cup, dissolve the maple syrup in warm water.
2. In a large bowl, add the flour, yeast and salt and mix well.
3. Add the maple syrup mixture and mix until a sticky dough forms.
4. Transfer the dough into a greased 9×5-inch loaf pan.
5. Cover the loaf pan and set aside for about 20 minutes.
6. Preheat the oven to 390 degrees F.
7. Uncover the loaf pan and bake for about 40 minutes or until a toothpick inserted in the center comes out clean.
8. Remove the pan from oven and place onto a wire rack to cool for about 20 minutes.
9. Carefully, remove the bread from the loaf pan and place onto the wire rack to cool completely before slicing.
10. With a sharp knife, cut the bread loaf into desired sized slices and serve.
11. *Meal Preparation time: Tip:*
12. In a resealable plastic bag, place the bread and seal the bag after squeezing out the excess air.
13. Keep the bread away from direct sunlight and preserve in a cool and dry place for about 1-2 days.

Nutrition:
Calories: 118, Fats: 0.3g, Carbs: 24.7g, Fiber: 1g, Sugar: 0.6g, Proteins: 3.5g, Sodium: 76mg

105. Quinoa Bread

Preparation time: 15 minutes
Cooking time: 1½ hours
Servings: 12

Ingredients:
- 1¾ cups uncooked quinoa, soaked overnight and rinsed
- ¼ cup chia seeds, soaked in ½ cup of water overnight
- ½ teaspoon bicarbonate soda
- Salt, as required
- ¼ cup olive oil
- ½ cup water
- 1 tablespoon fresh lemon juice

Directions:
1. Preheat the oven to 320 degrees F. Line a loaf pan with parchment paper.
2. In a food processor, add all the ingredients and pulse for about 3 minutes.
3. Place the mixture into the prepared loaf pan evenly.
4. Bake for about 1½ hours or until a toothpick inserted in the center comes out clean.
5. Remove the pan from oven and place onto a wire rack to cool for about 20 minutes.
6. Carefully, remove the bread from the loaf pan and place onto the wire rack to cool completely before slicing.
7. With a sharp knife, cut the bread loaf into desired sized slices and serve.

Meal Preparation time: Tip:

8. In a resealable plastic bag, place the bread and seal the bag after squeezing out the excess air.
9. Keep the bread away from direct sunlight and preserve in a cool and dry place for about 1-2 days.

Nutrition:
Calories: 137, Fats: 6.5g, Carbs: 16.9g, Fiber: 2.6g, Sugar: 0g, Proteins: 4g, Sodium: 20mg

106. Fruity Oatmeal Muffins

Preparation time: 15 minutes
Cooking time: 20 minutes
Servings: 6
Ingredients:

- ½ cup hot water
- ¼ cup ground flaxseeds
- 1 banana, peeled and sliced
- 1 apple, peeled, cored and chopped roughly
- 2 cups rolled oats
- ½ cup walnuts, chopped
- ½ cup raisins
- ¼ teaspoon baking soda
- 2 tablespoons ground cinnamon
- ½ cup almond milk
- ¼ cup maple syrup

Directions:

1. Preheat the oven to 350 degrees F. Line a 12 cups muffin tin with paper liners.
2. In a bowl, add water and flaxseed and beat until well combined. Set aside for about 5 minutes.
3. In a blender, add the flaxseed mixture and remaining all ingredients except blueberries and pulse till smooth and creamy.
4. Transfer the mixture into prepared muffin cups evenly.
5. Bake for about 20 minutes or until a toothpick inserted in the center comes out clean.
6. Remove the muffin tin from oven and place onto a wire rack to cool for about 10 minutes.
7. Carefully invert the muffins onto the wire rack to cool completely before serving.

Meal Preparation time: Tip:

8. Carefully invert the muffins onto a wire rack to cool completely.
9. Line 1-2 airtight containers with paper towels.
10. Arrange muffins over paper towel in a single layer.
11. Cover the muffins with another paper towel.
12. Refrigerate for about 2-3 days.
13. Reheat in the microwave on High for about 2 minutes before serving.

Nutrition:
Calories: 351, Fats: 14.4g, Carbs: 51.8g, Fiber: 8.2g, Sugar: 22.4g, Proteins: 8.2g, Sodium: 61mg

107. Oat Muffins

Preparation time: 15 minutes
Cooking time: 20 minutes
Servings: 6
Ingredients:

- ½ cup unsweetened almond milk
- 1 tablespoon apple cider vinegar
- 1½ cups whole-wheat flour
- 1 teaspoon baking powder
- 1 teaspoon baking soda
- ½ teaspoon ground cinnamon
- ¼ teaspoon ground nutmeg
- ¼ teaspoon ground ginger
- ½ teaspoon sea salt
- ½ cup unsweetened applesauce
- ½ cup maple syrup
- 1 teaspoon vanilla extract
- 1 cup carrots, peeled and grated
- ¼ cup walnuts, chopped
- ¼ cup raisins

Directions:

1. Preheat the oven to 350 degrees F. Arrange a rack in the upper third of the oven. Grease a 12 cups muffin tin.
2. In a large bowl, add the almond

milk and vinegar and mix well. Set aside.

3. *In another large bowl, add the flour, baking powder, baking soda, spices and salt.*
4. *In the bowl of vinegar mixture, add the applesauce, maple syrup and vanilla extract and beat until well combined.*
5. *Add the flour mixture and mix until just combined.*
6. *Gently, fold in the carrots, walnuts and raisins.*
7. *Transfer the mixture into prepared muffin cups evenly and sprinkle with remaining oats.*
8. *Bake for about 17-20 minutes or until a toothpick inserted in the center comes out clean.*
9. *Remove from the oven and place the muffin tin onto a wire rack to cool for about 5 minutes.*
10. *Carefully invert the muffins onto the wire rack to cool completely before serving.*

Meal Preparation time: Tip:

11. *Carefully invert the muffins onto a wire rack to cool completely.*
12. *Line 1-2 airtight containers with paper towels.*
13. *Arrange muffins over paper towel in a single layer.*
14. *Cover the muffins with another paper towel.*
15. *Refrigerate for about 2-3 days.*
16. *Reheat in the microwave on High for about 2 minutes before serving.*

Nutrition:
Calories: 257, Fats: 3.8g, Carbs: 51.8g, Fiber: 2.3g, Sugar: 22.4g, Proteins: 5g, Sodium: 399mg

108. Tofu & Mushroom Muffins

Preparation time: 20 minutes
Cooking time: 20 minutes
Servings: 6

Ingredients:

- *1 teaspoon olive oil*
- *1½ cups fresh mushrooms, chopped*
- *1 scallion, chopped*
- *1 teaspoon garlic, minced*
- *1 teaspoon fresh rosemary, minced*
- *Ground black pepper, as required*
- *1 (12.3-ouncepackage lite firm silken tofu, drained*
- *¼ cup unsweetened almond milk*
- *2 tablespoons nutritional yeast*
- *1 tablespoon arrowroot starch*
- *1 teaspoon coconut oil, softened*
- *¼ teaspoon ground turmeric*

Directions:

1. *Preheat the oven to 375 degrees F. Grease a 12 cups of a muffin pan.*
2. *In a nonstick skillet, heat the oil over medium heat and sauté the scallion and garlic for about 1 minute.*
3. *Add the mushrooms and sauté for about 5-7 minutes.*
4. *Stir in the rosemary and black pepper and remove from the heat.*
5. *Set aside to cool slightly.*
6. *In a food processor, add the tofu and remaining ingredients and pulse until smooth.*
7. *Transfer the tofu mixture into a large bowl.*
8. *Fold in the mushroom mixture.*
9. *Place the mixture into prepared muffin cups evenly.*
10. *Bake for about 20-22 minutes or until a toothpick inserted in the center comes out clean.*
11. *Remove the muffin pan from the oven and place onto a wire rack to cool for about 10 minutes.*
12. *Carefully, invert the muffins onto wire rack and serve warm.*

Meal Preparation time: Tip:

1. *Carefully invert the muffins onto a wire rack to cool completely.*
2. *Line 1-2 airtight containers with paper towels.*
3. *Arrange muffins over paper towel in*

a single layer.

4. *Cover the muffins with another paper towel.*
5. *Refrigerate for about 2-3 days.*
6. *Reheat in the microwave on High for about 2 minutes before serving.*

Nutrition:
Calories: 74, Fats: 3.5g, Carbs: 5.3g, Fiber: 1.4g, Sugar: 1.1g, Proteins: 6.2g, Sodium: 32mg

109. Coconut & Seeds Granola

Preparation time: 10 minutes
Cooking time: 20 minutes
Servings: 15
Ingredients:

- *3 cups unsweetened coconut flakes*
- *1 cup walnuts, chopped*
- *½ cup flaxseeds*
- *2/3 cup pumpkin seeds*
- *2/3 cup sunflower seeds*
- *¼ cup coconut oil, melted*
- *1 teaspoon ground ginger*
- *1 teaspoon ground cinnamon*
- *1/8 teaspoon ground cloves*
- *1/8 teaspoon ground cardamom*
- *Pinch of salt*

Directions:

1. *Preheat the oven to 350 degrees F. Lightly, grease a large rimmed baking sheet.*
2. *In a bowl, add the coconut flakes, walnuts, flaxseeds, pumpkin seeds, sunflower seeds, coconut oil, spices and salt and toss to coat well.*
3. *Transfer the mixture onto the prepared baking sheet and spread in an even layer.*
4. *Bake for about 20 minutes, stirring after every 3-4 minutes.*
5. *Remove the baking sheet from the oven and let the granola cool completely before serving.*
6. *Break the granola into desired sized chunks and serve with your favorite non-dairy milk.*

Meal Preparation time: Tip:
Transfer granola in an airtight container and store in a cool, dry place for up to 2 weeks.
Nutrition:
Calories: 292, Fats: 26.4g, Carbs: 8.4g, Fiber: 5.3g, Sugar: 1.9g, Proteins: 6.2g, Sodium: 22mg

110. Nuts & Sees Granola

Preparation time: 15 minutes
Cooking time: 28 minutes
Servings: 12
Ingredients:

- *½ cup unsweetened coconut flakes*
- *1 cup raw almonds*
- *1 cup raw cashews*
- *¼ cup raw sunflower seeds, shelled*
- *¼ cup raw pumpkin seeds, shelled*
- *¼ cup coconut oil*
- *½ cup maple syrup*
- *1 teaspoon vanilla extract*
- *½ cup golden raisins*
- *½ cup black raisins*
- *Salt, as required*

Directions:

1. *Preheat the oven to 275 degrees F. Line a large baking sheet with parchment paper.*
2. *In a food processor, add the coconut flakes, almonds, cashews and seeds and pulse until chopped finely.*
3. *Meanwhile, in a medium nonstick pan, add the oil, maple syrup and vanilla extract over medium-high heat and Cooking Time: for about 3 minutes, stirring continuously.*
4. *Remove from the heat and immediately stir in the nuts mixture.*
5. *Transfer the mixture into the prepared baking sheet and spread evenly.*
6. *Bake for about 25 minutes, stirring twice.*
7. *Remove from the oven and immediately stir in the raisins.*
8. *Sprinkle with a little salt.*

9. With the back of a spatula, flatten the surface of mixture.
10. Set aside to cool completely.
11. Then break into desired size chunks and serve with your choice of non-dairy milk and fruit's topping.

Meal Preparation time: Tip:
Transfer granola in an airtight container and store in a cool, dry place for up to 2 weeks.
Nutrition:
Calories: 237, Fats: 18.4g, Carbs: 25.5g, Fiber: 2.6g, Sugar: 16.3g, Proteins: 5g, Sodium: 18mg

111. Banana Bread

Servings: 13
Preparation time: 5 minutes
Nutrition (per serving
Calories: 106 kcal
Carbs: 12.1g
Fat: 17.9g
Protein: 5.3g
Fiber: 2.3g
Sugar: 5.2g
Ingredients:

- 4 bananas
- 4 flax eggs
- 2 ½ cups almond flour
- ⅓ cup olive oil
- ½ tbsp. baking soda

Total number of ingredients: 5
Directions:
1. Preheat oven to 350 °F.
2. Slightly grease a loaf pan.
3. Chop bananas in quarter inch circular slices.
4. Place chopped bananas in a bowl.
5. Add flax eggs, almond flour, olive oil, and baking soda to bowl.
6. Mix with spoon until well blended.
7. Pour mixture into loaf pan.
8. Bake for one hour.
9. Remove from oven, and let cool at room temperature.

People on a ketogenic diet usually steer clear of eating bananas due to their high carb content (around 27g for an average sized banana). While this number seems scary, this recipe allows you to satisfy your banana sweet tooth while cutting the carb consumption per piece to about 12g.

112. Mini Italian Toast Crackers

Servings: 13
Preparation time: 5 minutes
Nutrition (about 4 crackers
Calories: 225 kcal
Carbs: 5.4g
Fat: 20.9g
Protein: 6.2g
Fiber: 0.5g
Sugar: 1g
Ingredients:

- 1 ¼ cups almond flour
- 1 flax egg
- 2 tbsp. olive oil
- ¾ tsp. salt
- 1 ½ tbsp. Italian seasoning (or ¼ tsp. each of: basil, garlic powder, thyme, oregano and onion powder).

Total number of ingredients: 5
Directions:
1. Preheat oven to 300 °F.
2. Place all ingredients into a bowl.
3. Mix ingredients into a dough-like consistency.
4. Once dough is formed, place on a cutting board.
5. Shape dough into a thin, long, rectangular prism.
6. Using a knife, cut dough into thin pieces of your liking.
7. Lightly grease a baking tray.
8. Place cut dough on baking tray.
9. Bake for 10 minutes or until crisp.

These Italian crackers are sure to hit that savory spot with the Italian herbs adding a twist to your everyday cracker! Use these as crackers when you're craving a quick, crispy snack, or munch on them in the morning, spreading avocado on them to make a quick breakfast.

113. 2-Minute Microwave Burger Bun

Servings: 1
Preparation time: 3 minutes

Nutrition (1 bun
Calories: 280 kcal
Carbs: 10g
Fat: 23.9g
Protein: 9.5g
Fiber: 4.4g
Sugar: 1.4g

Ingredients:

- ⅓ *cup almond flour (or any other nut flour of your choice*
- *1 flax egg*
- *½ tsp. baking powder*
- *½ tsp. cocoa powder*
- *¼ tsp. salt*
- *¾ tsp. sesame seeds*

Total number of ingredients: 6
Directions:

1. *In a bowl, add the almond flour, baking powder, cocoa powder, and salt. Mix thoroughly, or you will end up tasting weird bits of baking powder, salt, or cocoa in your burger bun!*
2. *Add the flax egg to mixture and stir until well blended.*
3. *Slightly grease a cup large enough to fit the batter.*
4. *Sprinkle some of the sesame seeds at the bottom of the cup.*
5. *Pour batter on top of the seeds.*
6. *Sprinkle the rest of the seeds on top of the batter.*
7. *Place cup in microwave.*
8. *Microwave for about 2 minutes or until firm.*

Sounds too easy to be true, right? Not to mention it makes the perfect complement to the perfect ketogenic vegan burger. This bun would be great with a seasoned tofu patty, grilled mushrooms, and crisp, fresh veggies like tomato and lettuce.

114. Almond Pan Loaf

Servings: 15
Preparation time: 10 minutes

Nutrition (per serving
Calories: 381 kcal
Carbs: 9.5g
Fat: 33g
Protein: 11.7g
Fiber: 5.2g
Sugar: 2.0g

Ingredients:

- *6 cups almond flour (or any other nut flour that you prefer*
- *3 flax eggs*
- *½ cup olive oil*
- *¼ cup almond milk (or water, if you want to reduce the caloric content*
- *2 tsp. baking powder*
- *1 tsp. baking soda*
- *¼ tsp. salt*

Total number of ingredients: 7
Directions:

1. *Preheat oven to 350 °F.*
2. *Lightly grease a large loaf pan with oil.*
3. *Combine all ingredients in a bowl, ensuring they are well mixed.*
4. *Pour mixture into loaf pan and bake for about 1 hour.*
5. *Remove pan from oven and let cool.*
6. *Once cooled, remove loaf by flipping pan upside down.*
7. *Slice evenly.*

Note: Though this bread does not rise as much as a "normal" loaf would, per se, its plain taste is the perfect complement to a sandwich on the go! Also, if you decide to use this to make a quick, easy lunch, two slices yield only 3 grams of carbs for your daily count compared to a whopping 22 grams of regular bread!

115. Italian Herb Rolls

Servings: 6
Preparation time: 10 minutes

Nutrition (per serving
Calories: 257 kcal
Carbs: 16.6g

Fat: 18.6g
Protein: 5.8g
Fiber: 11.7g
Sugar: 1.5g
Ingredients:

- 1 ¼ cups coconut flour
- ¾ tsp. baking soda
- 6 tbsp. melted coconut oil
- 3 tbsp. Italian seasoning (If you don't have this, you can just use 2/3 tsp. each of: basil, garlic powder, thyme, oregano and onion powder
- 2 flax eggs
- ¾ tsp. salt

Total number of ingredients: 6
Directions:

1. Preheat oven to 300 °F.
2. Add coconut flour, oil, baking soda, and flax eggs to a bowl.
3. Mix well.
4. Add Italian seasoning (or herbs if you don't have this seasoningand salt to the mix.
5. Using your hands, mold the dough, small handfuls at a time, to make mini rolls. You should have about 6 rolls when done.
6. Place on a greased baking sheet.
7. Bake at 300 °F for about 45 minutes.
8. Remove from oven and cool at room temperature.

TIP:

1. The bread is naturally a bit crumbly, but if you don't let it cool for an extended period of time, it will completely fall apart.
2. These lovely rolls are sure to satisfy cravings for carbs and make a delectable side roll to any balanced meal, whether it be a salad, soup, or even as a snack with a drizzle of olive oil.

116. Tortilla Wraps

Servings: 6
Preparation time: 10 minutes

Nutrition (per serving
Calories: 157 kcal
Carbs: 4.2g
Fat: 13.8g
Protein: 5.0g
Fiber: 1.9g
Sugar: 1.5g
Ingredients:

- ¼ cup ground flaxseed
- ¼ cup hot water
- 1 cup almond flour
- ¼ tsp. baking powder
- ½ tsp. salt

Total number of ingredients: 5
Directions:

1. Mix ground flaxseed with hot water until you get a gel-like substance.
2. In a separate bowl, mix almond flour, salt and baking powder.
3. Add ground flaxseed mixture to almond flour mixture.
4. Mix thoroughly.
5. Add hot water as needed in order to achieve a perfect dough-like consistency.
6. Knead dough, then separate dough into about 6 balls.
7. Flatten each ball as thinly as possible.
8. Grease a pan.
9. Place each tortilla on greased pan and bake each tortilla until brown on both sides.
10. Remove pan from oven.
11. Let cool completely before using as they are easier to mold and fold once cool.
12. This bread-based recipe comes in handy if you're craving a good old tofu wrap or even a vegan-styled quesadilla!

TIP: *Psyllium husk and flaxseed mixed with hot water allows for a gel-like substance to form, which is extremely convenient for achieving a dough-type consistency.*

117. Keto-Vegan Pizza Crust

Servings: 2
Preparation time: 10 minutes

Nutrition (1 Crust Slice
Calories: 134 kcal
Carbs: 3.4g
Fat: 11.8g
Protein: 4.9g
Fiber: 6.3g
Sugar: 1.6g

Ingredients:
- 1 tsp. salt
- 1 tbsp. olive oil
- 1 cup warm water
- 2 ½ tsp. active yeast
- 3 cups almond flour
- 1 pinch dried oregano, ground
- 1 pinch dried basil leaf

Total number of ingredients: 7

Directions:
1. Preheat oven to 300 °F.
2. Place warm water in a cup (Note: It must be the right temperature or it will not work).
3. Add yeast to cup.
4. Stir for one minute until you see a light brown mixture.
5. Let sit for 5 minutes until a thin layer of foam forms on top.
6. In a separate bowl, add almond flour and salt.
7. Mix almond flour and salt. Once done mixing, form a well in the middle of the almond flour-salt mixture.
8. Pour yeast mixture and olive oil into well center and begin mixing ingredients.
9. Mix until a dough is achieved. Add more or less flour depending on consistency of dough.
10. Separate into 2 balls.
11. Using a rolling pin, flatten balls into circles of dough.
12. Place dough in oven and allow to Cooking Time: halfway for about 6 minutes.
13. Take out dough.
14. Place pizza toppings on dough.
15. Place pizza dough back in oven to finish baking for 3-6 minutes.
16. Once baked, remove from oven.
17. Let cool for 2 minutes, then use a pizza slicer to slice into 8 pieces per pizza.

This adapted ketogenic vegan pizza crust is the perfect substitute if you're looking for a quick pizza without the excess carbs. This crust works best as thin to regular crust, but not deep dish. Pair with some fresh tomato sauce, vegan cashew-parmesan cheese, mushrooms, spinach, or even tofu if you like!

118. Panini Flat Bread

Servings: 10
Preparation time: 10 minutes

Nutrition (2 half slices/one sandwich
Calories: 280 kcal
Carbs: 8.1g
Fat: 24.4g
Protein: 8.5g
Fiber: 3.7g
Sugar: 3.1g

Ingredients:
- 3 cups almond flour
- 4 flax eggs
- ⅓ cup coconut flour
- 1 tsp. baking soda
- ½ tsp. garlic powder
- ¼ cup water
- ¼ cup olive oil

Total number of ingredients: 7

Directions:
1. Preheat oven to 350 °F.
2. Mix dry ingredients (coconut flour, almond flour, garlic powder and baking soda together in a bowl.
3. To this bowl, add in flax eggs, olive oil, and water, and mix completely until a dough forms (add extra flour or water accordingly; it should be a bit sticky!).
4. Place dough onto a parchment paper-covered tray and mold into a

rough rectangular loaf shape.
5. Place 1 piece of parchment paper on top of loaf.
6. Place loaf in oven and bake for 15-20 minutes until firm.
7. Remove loaf from oven.
8. Remove top piece of parchment paper and let loaf cool completely.
9. Once cool, cut into about 10 square pieces, then cut each piece in half.

119. Herb Cracker Crisps

Servings: 20
Preparation time: 5 minutes

Nutrition (about 4 crackers
Calories: 201 kcal
Carbs: 4.7g
Fat: 18.4g
Protein: 5.5g
Fiber: 0.4g
Sugar: 1.8g

Ingredients:
- 1 cup almond flour
- 2 flax eggs
- 2 tbsp. canola oil
- 2 tbsp. water
- 1 tbsp. rosemary (can be fresh or dried, but freshly chopped rosemary is preferable as it will give a beautiful, strong taste!
- ½ tsp. garlic powder
- ¼ tsp. dried oregano, ground
- ¼ tsp. dried basil leaf
- ¼ tsp. salt
- 1 pinch black pepper

Total number of ingredients: 10
Directions:
1. Preheat oven to 350 °F.
2. Place all ingredients in a bowl and mix well.
3. Line a pan with non-stick parchment paper.
4. Taking the dough formed in step 2, scoop ½ tbsp. of dough and place on pan. Flatten with your finger to make it as thin as a cracker.
5. Bake for about 5-10 minutes until the outsides are crisp and the insides are just the slightest bit soft (they'll harden even more when cooling).
6. Remove from oven, and let cool.
7. Eat these lovely crisps alone or with a spread to please any cracker-snack cravings you may be having. The infusion of herbs is sure to hit your taste buds and leave you satisfied, with only 4.7g of carbs and 1.8g of sugar per serving!

120. Dried Fruits And Nuts Breakfast Bread

Servings: 15
Preparation time: 15 minutes

Nutrition (per serving
Calories: 315 kcal
Carbs: 21.1g
Fat: 19.4g
Protein: 6.1g
Fiber: 3.6g
Sugar: 15.1g

Ingredients:
- 2 cups almond flour
- 1 medium banana
- 2 flax eggs
- ¼ cup coconut oil
- 2 tbsp. whole flax seeds
- ¼ tsp. salt
- ½ tsp. baking soda
- 1 ½ cups roughly chopped dried mixed fruit (e.g., cranberries, strawberries, pineapple, cherries)
- 1 ½ cups roughly chopped dried nuts (e.g., pecans, almonds, walnuts)

Total number of ingredients: 10
Directions:
1. Preheat oven to 300 °F.
2. Lightly grease a loaf pan with olive oil.
3. Place bananas in a bowl, and mash extremely well.
4. To the mashed bananas, add coconut oil and flax eggs.
5. Mix well.

6. Add in flour, baking powder, and salt to the mixture, and mix thoroughly.
7. Top with fruits, nuts, and seeds, and mix until everything is evenly mixed.
8. Pour batter in greased loaf pan, and let bake for about 45 minutes or until knife comes out of the center clean.
9. Remove pan from oven, and let cool completely before slicing.

Note:
1. This bread does not rise, so no worries if you don't see that happening!
2. You will realize how many nutrients you are getting when you eat a slice, as well as how satisfied and strengthened you feel! Due to the amount of dried fruits and nuts in the recipe, as well as the density of the loaf, one to two slices is more than enough to get you energized and full until lunch time. You can even grab a slice if you're looking for a boost in between your meals.
3. The great thing about this recipe is that it is very adaptable. You can choose whatever assortments of dried fruits or nuts you want to add to the recipe.

121. Seed And Nut Topped Loaf

Servings: 15
Preparation time: 15 minutes

Nutrition (per serving
Calories: 172 kcal
Carbs: 8.1g
Fat: 13.2g
Protein: 6.1g
Fiber: 3.5g
Sugar: 2.4
Ingredients:
- 2 cups almond flour
- 2 tbsp. coconut flour
- ⅓ cup coconut oil
- ½ cup whole almonds
- 3 tbsp. sesame seeds
- ½ cup pumpkin seeds
- ¼ cup whole flax seeds
- ½ tsp. salt
- 3 flax eggs
- 1 ½ tsp. baking soda
- ¾ cup almond milk
- 3 drops stevia sweetener
- 1 tbsp. apple cider vinegar

Total number of ingredients: 13
Directions:
1. Preheat oven to 350 °F.
2. Blend almonds in a blender until fine.
3. Add flax seeds, sesame seeds, and pumpkin seeds and blend.
4. Add almond flour, coconut flour, salt, and baking soda and blend.
5. In a separate bowl, add flax eggs, coconut oil, almond milk, vinegar, and sweetener. Stir well.
6. Add almond mixture to flax egg mixture and let sit for a few minutes.
7. Grease a loaf pan.
8. Pour batter in pan.
9. Sprinkle left over seeds atop batter (pumpkin, flax, and sesame seeds).
10. Bake for about 45 minutes, or until a knife comes clean out of the middle.
11. Remove from oven, and let cool completely before slicing.
12. This loaf recipe is a dry, nutty spin on a regular bread loaf. What makes it even better is its low-carb, high-fat content, allowing you to consume a few pieces guilt free.

122. Low Carb Corn Bread

Servings: 18
Preparation time: 10 minutes

Nutrition (per serving
Calories: 138 kcal
Carbs: 7.2g
Fat: 10.7g
Protein: 3.5g

Fiber: 1.2g
Sugar: 2.6g
Ingredients:
- 2 cups almond flour
- 6 drops stevia sweetener
- 1 tsp. salt
- 2 flax eggs
- 3 ½ tsp. baking powder
- ½ cup vanilla flavored almond milk
- ⅓ cup coconut oil
- 15 oz. can baby corn, finely chopped

Total number of ingredients: 8

Directions:
1. Preheat oven to 350 °F.
2. In a bowl, mix almond flour, salt, and baking powder.
3. Add stevia, chopped corn, flax eggs, almond milk, and coconut oil.
4. Mix well, ensuring no clumps.
5. Lightly grease a pan.
6. Pour batter in pan.
7. Place pan in oven and let bake 50-60 minutes or until knife comes cleanly out of the middle.

Note:
You would think that people on a ketogenic diet would need to steer clear of corn, but here's a recipe that has been tweaked to prove otherwise! The stevia acts as a natural sweetener with almond meal acting as a substitute for high carb flour options. You can eat a slice for breakfast or in between meals to satisfy cravings.

123. Low Carb Sub Bread

Servings: 4 mini subs
Preparation time: 5 minutes

Nutrition (per serving
Calories: 292 kcal
Carbs: 13.3g
Fat: 23.2g
Protein: 9.9g
Fiber 2,5g
Sugar: 3.2g
Ingredients:
- 1 ½ cups almond flour
- 5 tbsp. psyllium husk powder, finely ground
- 2 tsp. baking powder
- 1 tsp. salt
- 2 ½ tbsp. apple cider vinegar
- 2 flax eggs
- 1 cup boiling water

Total number of ingredients: 7

Directions:
1. Preheat oven to 350 °F.
2. In a bowl, mix together almond flour, psyllium husk powder, baking powder, and salt.
3. Add flax eggs and apple cider vinegar and mix well until a dough forms.
4. Add boiling water and continue mixing.
5. Mold dough into 4 mini subs or one large sub (remember the dough should and will rise).
6. Place dough on a slightly greased baking pan. Bake for 45 minutes or until firm.

Yes, while 13.3g carbs may seem like a lot, it must be taken in comparison to a traditional sub sandwich's carb levels: a whole 40g. Enjoy this recipe when you find yourself reminiscing on those tasty sub sandwiches, and simply indulge the guilt-free way!

124. Plain Loaf

Servings: 15
Preparation time: 5 minutes

Nutrition (per serving
Calories: 142 kcal
Carbs: 13.4g
Fat: 43.1g
Protein: 3.9g
Fiber: 3,5g
Sugar: 1.5g
Ingredients:
- 1 cup coconut flour
- 6 cups almond flour
- ¼ cup flax seed

- 5 flax eggs
- ½ cup water
- ½ cup MCT oil
- 3 tsp. baking powder
- 1 tsp. salt
- 1 tbsp. apple cider vinegar

Total number of ingredients: 8

Directions:

1. Preheat oven to 350 °F.
2. In a bowl, mix together dry ingredients: almond flour, coconut flour, baking powder, salt, and flax seeds.
3. In a separate bowl, mix together coconut oil, water and apple cider vinegar.
4. Combine dry and liquid ingredients from Steps 2 and Mix well.
5. Pour batter in a slightly greased large loaf pan.
6. Bake for 30-45 minutes or until firm.

Note: Make sure the loaf is completely cooled before slicing it.

Here is another spin on a plain bread type loaf that you could use a spread on, or for on-the-go sandwiches!

125. Seed-Based Crackers

Servings: 25 crackers
Preparation time: 5 minutes

Nutrition (per serving
Calories: 53 kcal
Carbs: 3.5g
Fat: 3.6g
Protein: 1.6g
Fiber: 1.6g
Sugar: 0.1g

Ingredients:

- 1 cup flaxseed, ground
- 1 cup pumpkin seeds
- ½ cup sesame seeds
- ½ tsp. salt
- 1 cup hot water

Total number of ingredients: 5

Directions:

1. Preheat oven to 300 °F.
2. Place all ingredients in a bowl and mix.
3. Let sit for five minutes (the flaxseed will form a gel with the water).
4. Spread mixture on a parchment paper-lined pan.
5. Using a knife, cut dough evenly into about 25 crackers.
6. Place in oven and bake until firm.
7. Turn oven off, leaving crackers in oven for about 1 hour so that crackers dry out.
8. Simple and quick homemade crackers are sure to satisfy your need of a quick snack, or even to use as a base for a low-carb spread.

126. 2-Minute Microwave Fruit Bread In A Mug!

Servings: 4 slices
Preparation time: 3 minutes

Nutrition (1 circled slice
Calories: 165 kcal
Carbs: 25.5g
Fat: 6.2g
Protein: 4.1g
Fiber: 0.8g
Sugar: 13.3g

Ingredients:

- ⅓ cup almond flour (or any other nut flour of your preference
- 1 flax egg
- ¼ tsp. baking soda
- ¼ tsp. salt
- 2 tbsp. of your desired dried fruit (For this recipe, raspberries and strawberries were chosen

Total number of ingredients: 5

Directions:

1. To a bowl, add almond flour, baking soda, dried fruits, and salt. Mix thoroughly.
2. Add flax egg and stir until evenly distributed. Also make sure dried fruits are evenly distributed in the batter.

3. Lightly grease a mug that is big enough to hold batter.
4. Pour batter into mug and microwave for about 2 minutes.
5. Remove mug from oven, and slice mini loaf into about 4 pieces.
6. This recipe is an adaptation of the new craze of "microwave bread" which allows you to exhaust minimal effort yet indulge to the maximum.

Raspberries and strawberries are great for those on a ketogenic diet as fresh raspberries contain 3.3g of carbs per ounce and strawberries 2.2g. Ultimately, this recipe is such an efficient, tasty, and filling way to put a spin on your normal loaf of bread.

127. Seed-Based Herb Crackers

Servings: 16
Preparation time: 50 minutes

Nutrition (per serving
Calories: 190 kcal
Carbs: 5.5g
Fat: 14.7g
Protein: 9.0g
Fiber: 5.3g
Sugar: 0.3g

Ingredients:
- 2 cups ground flaxseed
- 2 cups ground hemp seed
- 2 cups warm water
- 1 tsp. salt
- 1 tsp. black pepper
- Italian herbs or other herbs to taste

Total number of ingredients: 6

Directions:
1. Preheat oven to 350°F.
2. Line your baking plate with parchment paper.
3. Combine flax seeds, hemp seeds, salt, and herbs in mixing bowl and stir thoroughly.
4. Pour in water and stir.
5. Let mixture sit for 5 minutes until water is absorbed.
6. Spread out mixture evenly on the baking plate, about 1/8 inch thick.
7. Divide into 16 pieces without damaging parchment paper.
8. Bake for 50 minutes.
9. Remove from oven and cool down.
10. Break into 16 pieces for serving.
11. Can be stored up to a week or frozen.
12. Check out this delicious keto friendly cracker recipe that is suitable for ketogenic vegans and is extremely simple to make!

128. Coconut Granola

Preparation time: 10 minutes
Cooking time: 18 minutes
Servings: 4

Ingredients:
- 1 tablespoon coconut oil, melted
- 1 tablespoon coconut butter, melted
- 2-3 tablespoons maple syrup
- 1 teaspoon orange zest, grated freshly
- ½ teaspoon ground cinnamon
- Pinch of sea salt
- 2 cups coconut flakes

Directions:
1. Preheat the oven to 350 degrees F. Line a cookie sheet with parchment paper.
2. In a bowl, mix together all ingredients except coconut flakes.
3. Spread coconut flakes in prepared cookie sheet.
4. Pour coconut oil mixture over flakes and gently, stir to mix.
5. Bake for about 12-15 minutes.
6. Remove from the oven and set aside to cool completely.
7. Then break into desired size chunks and serve with your choice of non-dairy milk and fruit's topping.
8. Meal Preparation time: Tip:
9. Transfer granola in an airtight container and store in a cool, dry place for up to 2 weeks.

Nutrition:
Calories: 221, Fats: 19g, Carbs: 14g, Fiber: 4.4g, Sugar: 8.7g, Proteins: 1.6g, Sodium: 69mg

129. Hot Pink Smoothie

Preparation Time: 5 minutes
Cooking Time: 0 minute
Servings: 1
Ingredients:
- 1 clementine, peeled, segmented
- 1/2 frozen banana
- 1 small beet, peeled, chopped
- 1/8 teaspoon sea salt
- 1/2 cup raspberries
- 1 tablespoon chia seeds
- 1/4 teaspoon vanilla extract, unsweetened
- 2 tablespoons almond butter
- 1 cup almond milk, unsweetened

Directions:
1. Place all the ingredients in the order in a food processor or blender and then pulse for 2 to 3 minutes at high speed until smooth.
2. Pour the smoothie into a glass and then serve.

Nutrition:
Calories: 278 Cal
Fat: 5.6 g
Carbs: 37.2 g
Protein: 6.2 g
Fiber: 13.2 g

130. Maca Caramel Frap

Preparation Time: 5 minutes
Cooking Time: 0 minute
Servings: 4
Ingredients:
- 1/2 of frozen banana, sliced
- 1/4 cup cashews, soaked for 4 hours
- 2 Medjool dates, pitted
- 1 teaspoon maca powder
- 1/8 teaspoon sea salt
- 1/2 teaspoon vanilla extract, unsweetened
- 1/4 cup almond milk, unsweetened
- 1/4 cup cold coffee, brewed

Directions:
1. Place all the ingredients in the order in a food processor or blender and then pulse for 2 to 3 minutes at high speed until smooth.
2. Pour the smoothie into a glass and then serve.

Nutrition:
Calories: 450 Cal
Fat: 170 g
Carbs: 64 g
Protein: 7 g
Fiber: 0 g

131. Peanut Butter Vanilla Green Shake

Preparation Time: 5 minutes
Cooking Time: 0 minute
Servings: 1
Ingredients:
- 1 teaspoon flax seeds
- 1 frozen banana
- 1 cup baby spinach
- 1/8 teaspoon sea salt
- 1/2 teaspoon ground cinnamon
- 1/4 teaspoon vanilla extract, unsweetened
- 2 tablespoons peanut butter, unsweetened
- 1/4 cup ice
- 1 cup coconut milk, unsweetened

Directions:
1. Place all the ingredients in the order in a food processor or blender and then pulse for 2 to 3 minutes at high speed until smooth.
2. Pour the smoothie into a glass and then serve.

Nutrition:
Calories: 298 Cal
Fat: 11 g
Carbs: 32 g
Protein: 24 g
Fiber: 8 g

132. Green Colada

Preparation Time: 5 minutes
Cooking Time: 0 minute
Servings: 1
Ingredients:
- 1/2 cup frozen pineapple chunks
- 1/2 banana
- 1/2 teaspoon spirulina powder
- 1/4 teaspoon vanilla extract, unsweetened
- 1 cup of coconut milk

Directions:
1. Place all the ingredients in the order in a food processor or blender and then pulse for 2 to 3 minutes at high speed until smooth.
2. Pour the smoothie into a glass and then serve.

Nutrition:
Calories: 127 Cal
Fat: 3 g
Carbs: 25 g
Protein: 3 g
Fiber: 4 g

133. Chocolate Oat Smoothie

Preparation Time: 5 minutes
Cooking Time: 0 minute
Servings: 1
Ingredients:
- ¼ cup rolled oats
- 1 ½ tablespoon cocoa powder, unsweetened
- 1 teaspoon flax seeds
- 1 large frozen banana
- 1/8 teaspoon sea salt
- 1/8 teaspoon cinnamon
- ¼ teaspoon vanilla extract, unsweetened
- 2 tablespoons almond butter
- 1 cup coconut milk, unsweetened

Directions:
1. Place all the ingredients in the order in a food processor or blender and then pulse for 2 to 3 minutes at high speed until smooth.
2. Pour the smoothie into a glass and then serve.

Nutrition:
Calories: 262 Cal
Fat: 7.3 g
Carbs: 50.4 g
Protein: 8.1 g
Fiber: 9.6 g

134. Peach Crumble Shake

Preparation Time: 5 minutes
Cooking Time: 0 minute
Servings: 1
Ingredients:
- 1 tablespoon chia seeds
- ¼ cup rolled oats
- 2 peaches, pitted, sliced
- ¾ teaspoon ground cinnamon
- 1 Medjool date, pitted
- ½ teaspoon vanilla extract, unsweetened
- 2 tablespoons lemon juice
- ½ cup of water
- 1 tablespoon coconut butter
- 1 cup coconut milk, unsweetened

Directions:
1. Place all the ingredients in the order in a food processor or blender and then pulse for 2 to 3 minutes at high speed until smooth.
2. Pour the smoothie into a glass and then serve.

Nutrition:
Calories: 270 Cal
Fat: 4 g
Carbs: 28 g
Protein: 25 g
Fiber: 3 g

135. Wild Ginger Green Smoothie

Preparation Time: 5 minutes
Cooking Time: 0 minute
Servings: 1
Ingredients:

- 1/2 cup pineapple chunks, frozen
- 1/2 cup chopped kale
- 1/2 frozen banana
- 1 tablespoon lime juice
- 2 inches ginger, peeled, chopped
- 1/2 cup coconut milk, unsweetened
- 1/2 cup coconut water

Directions:
1. Place all the ingredients in the order in a food processor or blender and then pulse for 2 to 3 minutes at high speed until smooth.
2. Pour the smoothie into a glass and then serve.

Nutrition:
Calories: 331 Cal
Fat: 14 g
Carbs: 40 g
Protein: 16 g
Fiber: 9 g

136. Berry Beet Velvet Smoothie

Preparation Time: 5 minutes
Cooking Time: 0 minute
Servings: 1
Ingredients:
- 1/2 of frozen banana
- 1 cup mixed red berries
- 1 Medjool date, pitted
- 1 small beet, peeled, chopped
- 1 tablespoon cacao powder
- 1 teaspoon chia seeds
- 1/4 teaspoon vanilla extract, unsweetened
- 1/2 teaspoon lemon juice
- 2 teaspoons coconut butter
- 1 cup coconut milk, unsweetened

Directions:
1. Place all the ingredients in the order in a food processor or blender and then pulse for 2 to 3 minutes at high speed until smooth.
2. Pour the smoothie into a glass and then serve.

Nutrition:
Calories: 234 Cal
Fat: 5 g
Carbs: 42 g
Protein: 11 g
Fiber: 7 g

137. Spiced Strawberry Smoothie

Preparation Time: 5 minutes
Cooking Time: 0 minute
Servings: 1
Ingredients:
- 1 tablespoon goji berries, soaked
- 1 cup strawberries
- 1/8 teaspoon sea salt
- 1 frozen banana
- 1 Medjool date, pitted
- 1 scoop vanilla-flavored whey protein
- 2 tablespoons lemon juice
- ¼ teaspoon ground ginger
- ½ teaspoon ground cinnamon
- 1 tablespoon almond butter
- 1 cup almond milk, unsweetened

Directions:
1. Place all the ingredients in the order in a food processor or blender and then pulse for 2 to 3 minutes at high speed until smooth.
2. Pour the smoothie into a glass and then serve.

Nutrition:
Calories: 182 Cal
Fat: 1.3 g
Carbs: 34 g
Protein: 6.4 g
Fiber: 0.7 g

138. Banana Bread Shake With Walnut Milk

Preparation Time: 5 minutes
Cooking Time: 0 minute
Servings: 2
Ingredients:
- 2 cups sliced frozen bananas
- 3 cups walnut milk

- 1/8 teaspoon grated nutmeg
- 1 tablespoon maple syrup
- 1 teaspoon ground cinnamon
- 1/2 teaspoon vanilla extract, unsweetened
- 2 tablespoons cacao nibs

Directions:
1. Place all the ingredients in the order in a food processor or blender and then pulse for 2 to 3 minutes at high speed until smooth.
2. Pour the smoothie into two glasses and then serve.

Nutrition:
Calories: 339.8 Cal
Fat: 19 g
Carbs: 39 g
Protein: 4.3 g
Fiber: 1 g

139. Double Chocolate Hazelnut Espresso Shake

Preparation Time: 5 minutes
Cooking Time: 0 minute
Servings: 1
Ingredients:
- 1 frozen banana, sliced
- 1/4 cup roasted hazelnuts
- 4 Medjool dates, pitted, soaked
- 2 tablespoons cacao nibs, unsweetened
- 1 1/2 tablespoons cacao powder, unsweetened
- 1/8 teaspoon sea salt
- 1 teaspoon vanilla extract, unsweetened
- 1 cup almond milk, unsweetened
- 1/2 cup ice
- 4 ounces espresso, chilled

Directions:
1. Place all the ingredients in the order in a food processor or blender and then pulse for 2 to 3 minutes at high speed until smooth.
2. Pour the smoothie into a glass and then serve.

Nutrition:
Calories: 210 Cal
Fat: 5 g
Carbs: 27 g
Protein: 16.8 g
Fiber: 0.2 g

140. Strawberry, Banana And Coconut Shake

Preparation Time: 5 minutes
Cooking Time: 0 minute
Servings: 1
Ingredients:
- 1 tablespoon coconut flakes
- 1 1/2 cups frozen banana slices
- 8 strawberries, sliced
- 1/2 cup coconut milk, unsweetened
- 1/4 cup strawberries for topping

Directions:
1. Place all the ingredients in the order in a food processor or blender, except for topping and then pulse for 2 to 3 minutes at high speed until smooth.
2. Pour the smoothie into a glass and then serve.

Nutrition:
Calories: 335 Cal
Fat: 5 g
Carbs: 75 g
Protein: 4 g
Fiber: 9 g

141. Tropical Vibes Green Smoothie

Preparation Time: 5 minutes
Cooking Time: 0 minute
Servings: 1
Ingredients:
- 2 stalks of kale, ripped
- 1 frozen banana
- 1 mango, peeled, pitted, chopped
- 1/8 teaspoon sea salt
- ¼ cup of coconut yogurt
- ½ teaspoon vanilla extract, unsweetened
- 1 tablespoon ginger juice

- ½ cup of orange juice
- ½ cup of coconut water

Directions:
1. Place all the ingredients in the order in a food processor or blender and then pulse for 2 to 3 minutes at high speed until smooth.
2. Pour the smoothie into a glass and then serve.

Nutrition:
Calories: 197.5 Cal
Fat: 1.3 g
Carbs: 30 g
Protein: 16.3 g
Fiber: 4.8 g

142. Peanut Butter And Mocha Smoothie

Preparation Time: 5 minutes
Cooking Time: 0 minute
Servings: 1
Ingredients:
- 1 frozen banana, chopped
- 1 scoop of chocolate protein powder
- 2 tablespoons rolled oats
- 1/8 teaspoon sea salt
- ¼ teaspoon vanilla extract, unsweetened
- 1 teaspoon cocoa powder, unsweetened
- 2 tablespoons peanut butter
- 1 shot of espresso
- ½ cup almond milk, unsweetened

Directions:
1. Place all the ingredients in the order in a food processor or blender and then pulse for 2 to 3 minutes at high speed until smooth.
2. Pour the smoothie into a glass and then serve.

Nutrition:
Calories: 380 Cal
Fat: 14 g
Carbs: 29 g
Protein: 38 g
Fiber: 4 g

143. Tahini Shake With Cinnamon And Lime

Preparation Time: 5 minutes
Cooking Time: 0 minute
Servings: 1
Ingredients:
- 1 frozen banana
- 2 tablespoons tahini
- 1/8 teaspoon sea salt
- ¾ teaspoon ground cinnamon
- ¼ teaspoon vanilla extract, unsweetened
- 2 teaspoons lime juice
- 1 cup almond milk, unsweetened

Directions:
1. Place all the ingredients in the order in a food processor or blender and then pulse for 2 to 3 minutes at high speed until smooth.
2. Pour the smoothie into a glass and then serve.

Nutrition:
Calories: 225 Cal
Fat: 15 g
Carbs: 22 g
Protein: 6 g
Fiber: 8 g

144. Ginger And Greens Smoothie

Preparation Time: 5 minutes
Cooking Time: 0 minute
Servings: 1
Ingredients:
- 1 frozen banana
- 2 cups baby spinach
- 2-inch piece of ginger, peeled, chopped
- ¼ teaspoon cinnamon
- ¼ teaspoon vanilla extract, unsweetened
- 1/8 teaspoon salt
- 1 scoop vanilla protein powder
- 1/8 teaspoon cayenne pepper
- 2 tablespoons lemon juice

- 1 cup of orange juice

Directions:
1. Place all the ingredients in the order in a food processor or blender and then pulse for 2 to 3 minutes at high speed until smooth.
2. Pour the smoothie into a glass and then serve.

Nutrition:
Calories: 320 Cal
Fat: 7 g
Carbs: 64 g
Protein: 10 g
Fiber: 12 g

145. Two-Ingredient Banana Pancakes

Preparation time: 3 minutes
Cooking Time: 2 minutes
Ingredients:
- 5 min., 1 servings, 78 cals
- 1 ready banana
- 1 egg
- 1/2 teaspoon vanilla concentrate (discretionary
- Add all fixings to list

Bearings
1. Include a notePrint
2. Mix banana and egg together in a bowl until no bumps remain. Add vanilla concentrate to the hitter.
3. Heat a lubed skillet or frying pan over medium warmth. Empty hitter into the dish. Cooking Time: until bubbles show up, around 1 moment. Flip and Cooking Time: until brilliant, around brief more.

Nutrition: 78 calories; 5 g fat; 0.7 g starches; 6.3 g protein; 186 mg cholesterol; 70 mg sodium.

146. Vegan Smoothie Bowl With Carrot And Banana

Preparation time: 15 minutes
Ingredients:
- 2 pitted Medjool dates
- 1 solidified banana, cleaved
- 1 cup coarsely cleaved carrot
- 1/2 cup unsweetened vanilla-seasoned almond milk, or more to taste
- 1/2 teaspoon ground cinnamon
- 1/4 teaspoon ground ginger

Topping:
- 2 tablespoons chipped coconut
- 1 tablespoon goji berries
- Add all fixings to list

Bearings
1. Place dates in a little bowl and spread with cold water; let drench, around 5 minutes. Channel and cleave.
2. Place slashed dates, banana, carrot, almond milk, cinnamon, and ginger in a blender; puree until smoothie is thick and smooth. Fill a serving bowl.
3. Top smoothie bowl with chipped coconut and goji berries.

Sustenance Facts
Nutrition: 325 calories; 4.8 g fat; 71.6 g carbohydrates; 4.8 g protein; 0 mg cholesterol; 216 mg sodium.

147. Vanilla Chia Pudding

Preparation time: 15 minutes
Cooking Time: 20 minutes
Ingredients:
- 6 tablespoons chia seeds
- 2 cups almond milk
- 2 tablespoon maple syrup or agave
- 1 teaspoon vanilla concentrate
- 1/2 teaspoon cinnamon

Technique
1. Blend up the almond milk, vanilla, maple syrup, and cinnamon.
2. Pour fluid blend over the chia seeds and mix till seeds are uniformly blended in. Mix again five minutes after the fact, and five minutes after that. Let sit for an hour at any rate, or basically let it sit in the cooler medium-term. Serve, bested with

crisp product of decision. Pudding will keep in the ice chest for as long as four days.

3. *6 tablespoons vegan spread*
4. *2/3 cup So Delicious® Dairy Free Hazelnut Coconut Milk Creamer*
5. *1/3 cup dull chocolate chips*
6. *Add all fixings to list*

Bearings

1. *Preheat stove to 425 degrees F. Line a heating sheet with material paper. Filter together flour, sugar, preparing powder, salt, and heating soft drink in enormous bowl. Gather vegan spread and blend into a single unit with hands until blend frames enormous, coarse morsels the size of peas. Include chocolate chips and half and half, blend for a couple of more seconds until just dampened. Turn the mixture onto a daintily floured work surface and press together delicately until the batter sticks together in a ball. Pat into a hover around 2-inches thick and 6 creeps in width.*
2. *Let sit for 15 minutes at room temperature. Cut into 8 wedges. Sprinkle with outstanding tablespoon of sugar.*
3. *Bake for 15-20 minutes or until brilliant on top. Permit to cool for a couple of moments, before isolating wedges.*

Sustenance Facts
Nutrition: *256 calories; 8.9 g fat; 40 g carbohydrates;3.2 g protein; 0 mg cholesterol; 384 mg sodium.*

148. Orange Pancakes

Preparation time: 10 minutes
Cooking Time: 10 minutes
Ingredients:

- *2 cups white entire wheat flour*
- *2 tablespoons heating powder*
- *2 tablespoons ground flax meal*
- *17 liquid ounces squeezed orange*
- *1 teaspoon orange concentrate*

Add all fixings to list
Directions:

1. *Whisk flour, heating powder, and flax meal together in a bowl; mix squeezed orange and orange concentrate into flour blend until player is well-consolidated.*
2. *Heat a gently oiled frying pan over medium-high warmth, or an electric iron to 375 degrees F (190 degrees C). Drop hitter by huge spoonfuls onto the frying pan and Cooking Time: until bubbles structure and the edges are dry, 3 to 4 minutes. Flip and Cooking Time: until sautéed on the opposite side, 2 to 3 minutes. Rehash with outstanding hitter.*

Sustenance Facts
Nutrition: *304 calories; 2.7 g fat; 64.6 g carbohydrates;9.6 g protein; 0 mg cholesterol; 734 mg sodium.*

149. Oatmeal Energy Bars

Preparation time: 15 minutes
Cooking Time: 15 minutes
Ingredients:

- *40 min., 24 servings, 91 cals*
- *1/3 cups moved oats*
- *1/2 cup generally useful flour*
- *1/2 cup vegan semi-sweet chocolate chips*
- *1/2 cup ground unsalted cashews*
- *2 tablespoons shelled unsalted sunflower seeds*
- *1 tablespoon ground flax meal*
- *1 tablespoon wheat germinutes*
- *1/2 teaspoon ground cinnamon*
- *1/4 teaspoon ocean salt*
- *1/2 cup nectar, warmed*
- *1/3 cup almond spread*
- *1/2 teaspoon vanilla concentrate*

Add all fixings to list
Bearings

1. *Preheat stove to 350 degrees F (175 degrees C). Line a 9x11-inch preparing dish with aluminum foil.*

2. Whisk oats, flour, chocolate chips, ground cashews, sunflower seeds, flax meal, wheat germin., cinnamon, and ocean salt together in a huge shallow bowl.
3. Stir warmed nectar, almond spread, and vanilla concentrate together in a bowl until well-blended. Empty nectar blend into oat blend; mix until hitter is well-consolidated. Transform hitter out into prepared heating dish. Lay a sheet of waxed paper over player and press solidly to uniformly disseminate in the preparing dish. Expel and dispose of waxed paper.
4. Bake in the preheated stove until brilliant and fragrant, around 12 minutes. Pull aluminum foil from preparing dish and cool bars in the aluminum foil for 10 minutes; evacuate and dispose of aluminum foil. Cut into bars.

Nutrition: 91 calories; 4 g fat; 12.8 g starches; 2 g protein; 0 mg cholesterol; 50 mg sodium.

150. Orange Chia Smoothie

Preparation time: 10 minutes
Ingredients:
- 1 little orange, stripped
- 1/2 cup solidified mango pieces
- 1 tablespoon cashew spread
- 1 tablespoon unsweetened coconut pieces
- 1 teaspoon chia seeds
- 1 teaspoon ground flax seeds
- 1/2 cup squeezed orange
- water varying (discretionary

Add all fixings to list

Bearings
Layer orange, mango, cashew spread, coconut, chia seeds, and flax into a blender; include squeezed orange. Spread and mix blend until smooth, including water for a more slender smoothie.

Nutrition: 313 calories; 14.1 g fat; 45.8 g starches; 6.3 g protein; 0 mg cholesterol; 112 mg sodium.

151. Green Smoothie Bowl

Preparation time: 10 minutes
"Smoothie in a bowl, ideal for a fast and sound breakfast."
Ingredients:
Smoothie:
- 3 cups new spinach
- 1 banana
- 1/2 (14 ouncewould coconut be able to drain
- 1/2 cup solidified mango pieces
- 1/2 cup coconut water

Toppings:
- 1/3 cup new raspberries
- 1/4 cup new blueberries
- 2 tablespoons granola
- 1 tablespoon coconut chips
- 1/4 teaspoon cut almonds
- 1/4 teaspoon chia seeds (discretionary

Add all fixings to list

Bearings
Blend spinach, banana, coconut milk, mango, and coconut water in a blender until smooth. Empty smoothie into a bowl and top with raspberries, blueberries, granola, coconut chips, almonds, and chia seeds.

References

Cook's Note:
For thicker smoothie, include cut solidified banana.

Nutrition: 374 calories; 25.6 g fat; 37 g carbohydrates;6.3 g protein; 0 mg cholesterol; 116 mg sodium.

152. Mango Craze Juice Blend

Preparation time: 5 minutes
Ingredients:
- 5 min., 4 servings, 150 cals
- 3 cups diced mango
- 1/2 cups hacked crisp or solidified peaches
- 1/4 cup hacked orange portions

- 1/4 cup hacked and pitted nectarine
- 1/2 cup squeezed orange
- 2 cups ice

Add all fixings to list

Bearings

Place mango, peaches, orange, nectarine, squeezed orange, and ice into a blender. Mix for 1 moment, or until smooth.

Nutrition: 150 calories; 0.6 g fat; 38.4 g carbohydrates; 1.3 g protein; 0 mg cholesterol; 9 mg sodium.

153. Pumpkin Apple Pie Smoothie

Preparation time: 10 minutes
Cooking Time: 5 minutes
Ingredients:

- 2 h
- 1 apple - stripped, cored, and slashed
- 2 tablespoons water, or varying
- 2/3 cup unsweetened vanilla-enhanced almond milk
- 1/4 cup pumpkin puree
- 1/2 teaspoons darker sugar, or to taste
- 1/4 teaspoon pumpkin pie zest
- 2/3 cup squashed ice shapes

Add all fixings to list

Directions:

1. Place apple in a plastic microwave-safe bowl; pour in enough water to cover 1/4-inch of the base of bowl. Halfway spread bowl with a cover or paper towel. Microwave in brief interims until apple is mellowed, 2 to 3 minutes. Freeze apple in a similar holder with water until strong, 2 hours to medium-term.
2. Blend solidified apple, almond milk, and pumpkin puree in a blender until smooth; include dark colored sugar and pumpkin pie flavor. Mix until smooth. Include ice and mix until smooth.

References
Cook's Note:

Milk with a scramble of vanilla concentrate can be fill in for unsweetened vanilla almond milk if necessary.

Nutrition: 185 calories; 2.2 g fat; 42.6 g carbohydrates; 1.8 g protein; 0 mg cholesterol; 261 mg sodium.

154. Pina Colada Smoothie (Vegan

Preparation time: 10 minutes
Ingredients:

- 3 3D squares ice 3D squares, or varying
- 1 banana
- 1 cup new pineapple pieces
- 1/2 cup coconut milk
- 1/2 cup soy milk
- 1 tablespoon agave nectar
- 1 tablespoon ground flax seed
- 1 teaspoon unadulterated vanilla concentrate

Add all fixings to list

Bearings

Blend ice, banana, pineapple, coconut milk, soy milk, agave nectar, flax seed, and vanilla concentrate in a blender until smooth. Empty smoothie into a tall glass.

Sustenance Facts
Nutrition: 586 calories; 29.8 g fat; 78 g carbohydrates; 9.7 g protein; 0 mg cholesterol; 84 mg sodium.

155. Raw Mango Monster Smoothie

Preparation time: 10 minutes
Ingredients:

- 1 tablespoon flax seeds
- 2 tablespoons pepitas (crude pumpkin seeds
- 1 ready mango, cubed
- 1 solidified banana, quartered
- 1/3 cup water, or more to taste
- 3 ice 3D shapes
- 2 leaves kale, or more to taste

Add all fixings to list

Bearings

1. Blend flax seeds in a blender until finely ground; include pepitas and mix until ground, around 1 moment.
2. Place mango, banana, water, ice 3D shapes, and kale in the blender; mix until smooth, kale is completely joined, and the smoothie is uniform in shading, around 3 minutes. Slender with more water to arrive at wanted consistency.

Nutrition: 381 calories; 14.1 g fat; 63 g carbohydrates;9.8 g protein; 0 mg cholesterol; 32 mg sodium.

156. Acai Smoothie Bowl

Preparation time: 10 minutes
Ingredients:

On

- 1 huge banana, isolated
- 3 1/2 ounces acai berry mash, solidified, unsweetened
- 2 tablespoons soy milk, or more varying
- 2 tablespoons granola
- Add all fixings to list

Bearings
1. Combine acai mash, 2/3 of the banana, and 2 tablespoons of soy milk in a blender; mix until smooth, yet at the same time thick. Include more soy milk varying; smoothie ought to have the consistency of solidified yogurt.
2. Slice the rest of the banana. Empty thick smoothie into a bowl and top with granola and cut bananas.

Sustenance Facts
Nutrition: 282 calories; 9.6 g fat; 45.1 g carbohydrates;4.8 g protein; 0 mg cholesterol; 46 mg sodium.

157. Medium-Term Slow Cooker Apple Oatmeal

Preparation time: 5 minutes
Cooking Time: 8 h
Ingredients:

- 8 h 5 min., 6 servings, 180 cals
- spread seasoned cooking shower
- 2 medium apples, stripped and diced
- 2 cups antiquated moved oats
- 1/3 cup dark colored sugar
- 2 teaspoons ground cinnamon
- 2 teaspoons vanilla concentrate
- 1/2 teaspoon pumpkin pie flavor, or more to taste
- 4 cups water

Add all fixings to list

Bearings
1. Spray within a 4-quart moderate cooker with cooking splash.
2. Place diced apples into the moderate cooker; include oats, dark colored sugar, cinnamon, vanilla concentrate, pumpkin pie flavor, and water.
3. Cooking Time: on Low for 8 hours; change cooker to Warm until prepared to serve.
4. Commentaries
5. You can substitute milk for half of the fluid for creamier oatmeal; you can likewise substitute steel cut oats for the good old oatmeal.
6. Leftover oatmeal can be utilized to make biscuits or bread.

Sustenance Facts
Nutrition: 180 calories; 1.9 g fat; 37.5 g carbohydrates;3.7 g protein; 0 mg cholesterol; 11 mg sodium.

158. Simple Vegan French Toast

Preparation time: 5 minutes
Cooking Time: 5 minutes
Ingredients:

- 1/2 cups soy milk
- 2 tablespoons generally useful flour
- 1 teaspoon white sugar
- 1 teaspoon ground cinnamon
- 1 tablespoon vegetable oil
- 4 cuts bread, or more varying

Add all fixings to list

Bearings

1. Whisk soy milk, flour, sugar, and cinnamon together in a bowl until all around beaten. Fill a pie skillet or other wide, shallow dish.
2. Heat oil in a skillet over medium-high warmth.
3. Dip each cut of bread into the soy milk blend and spot into the skillet. Cooking Time: until brilliant dark colored and fresh on the two sides, 5 to 7 minutes.

Sustenance Facts

Nutrition: *331 calories; 11.7 g fat; 45.7 g sugars; 10.6 g protein; 0 mg cholesterol; 434 mg sodium.*

159. Blueberry Chia Pudding With Almond Milk

Preparation time: 10 minutes
Ingredients:

- 2 cups almond milk
- 6 tablespoons chia seeds, or more to taste
- 1/3 cup crisp blueberries
- 1 tablespoon maple syrup, or more to taste
- 1/2 teaspoon vanilla concentrate
- 1 squeeze ground cinnamon (discretionary)

Add all fixings to list
Directions:
Combine almond milk, chia seeds, blueberries, maple syrup, vanilla concentrate, and cinnamon in a blender; mix until smooth. Fill 3 ramekins or glasses. Chill until set, 8 hours to medium-term. Serve chilled.
Commentaries
Cook's Notes:

1. You can utilize solidified blueberries too or some other assortment of leafy foods.
2. For the sugar, you can utilize nearly anything you like and just improve to taste.

Sustenance Facts

Nutrition: *146 calories; 6.5 g fat; 19.4 g carbohydrates;3.2 g protein; 0 mg cholesterol; 110 mg sodium.*

160. Zucchini Smoothie

Preparation time: 5 minutes
Ingredients:

- 5 min., 1 servings, 118 cals
- 1/2 cup ice 3D squares, or varying (discretionary)
- 1/2 zucchini, destroyed
- 1/2 solidified banana
- 1/2 cup squeezed orange

Add all fixings to list
Bearings

1. Combine ice 3D squares, zucchini, banana, and squeezed orange in a blender. Mix until smooth.
2. References
3. Using overripe or dull green zucchini will make this smoothie not all that yummy.
4. You can include sugar or other sugar in the event that you have a sweet tooth, yet I discover it bounty sweet from the banana.

Nutrition: *118 calories; 0.5 g fat; 28.3 g carbohydrates;2.2 g protein; 0 mg cholesterol; 11 mg sodium.*

161. Cushioned Vegan Pumpkin Pancakes

Preparation time: 10 minutes
Cooking Time: 10 minutes
Ingredients:

- 1/4 cups universally handy flour
- 2 teaspoons heating powder
- 1 teaspoon pumpkin pie zest
- 1/2 teaspoon salt
- 1 cup soy milk
- 1 tablespoon darker sugar
- 3 tablespoons pumpkin puree
- 1 teaspoon vanilla concentrate
- 1/2 teaspoons vegetable oil
- 1/3 cup water

Add all fixings to list
Directions:

1. Combine flour, heating powder, pumpkin pie zest, and salt in a bowl.
2. Stir milk, darker sugar, pumpkin puree, vanilla concentrate, oil, and water together in a subsequent bowl; blend completely. Make a well in the flour blend, include milk blend, and blend until equally joined.
3. Heat a nonstick skillet over medium-high warmth. Drop 1/4 cup flapjack hitter onto the hot skillet and Cooking Time: until bubbles structure and edges are dry, 3 to 5 minutes. Flip and Cooking Time: until carmelized on the opposite side, 3 to 5 minutes. Rehash with residual hitter.

Nutrition: 284 calories; 4.3 g fat; 51.9 g carbohydrates; 8.2 g protein; 0 mg cholesterol; 794 mg sodium.

162. Oatmeal-Banana Pancakes

Preparation time: 5 minutes
Cooking Time: 10 minutes

"These fragile, crepe-like flapjacks are sans dairy and simple to make. Your children will cherish them! Present with cut bananas, syrup, and margarine."

Ingredients:

On

- 1/2 cup antiquated oatmeal
- 3/4 cup almond milk
- 1/2 cup almond flour
- 1 ready banana
- 2 tablespoons white sugar
- 1 teaspoon vanilla concentrate
- 1/2 teaspoon ground cinnamon
- 1/2 teaspoon preparing powder
- 1/4 teaspoon salt
- cooking splash

Add all fixings to list

Bearings

1. Place oats in a blender and mix into a fine powder. Include almond milk, almond flour, banana, sugar, vanilla concentrate, cinnamon, heating powder, and salt; mix until all around blended. Let player sit until thickened, around 10 minutes.
2. Heat a skillet over medium-high warmth and coat with cooking splash. Drop 1/4 cup player onto the hot skillet and Cooking Time: until bubbles structure and edges are dry, 3 to 4 minutes. Flip and Cooking Time: until carmelized on the opposite side, 2 to 3 minutes. Rehash with outstanding player.

Sustenance Facts
Nutrition: 340 calories; 17.9 g fat; 37.1 g sugars; 9.7 g protein; 0 mg cholesterol; 474 mg sodium.

163. Apple-Rosemary Steel-Cut Oats

Preparation time: 10 minutes
Cooking Time: 15 minutes

Ingredients:

- 1 cup steel-cut oats
- 2 cups water
- 1 cup unsweetened almond milk
- 1 huge apple - stripped, cored, and diced
- 1/3 cup dried pitted dates, diced
- 2 teaspoons finely hacked new rosemary
- 1 teaspoon vanilla concentrate
- 1/2 teaspoon ground cinnamon
- 1 squeeze salt
- 1 teaspoon hacked walnuts, or to taste (discretionary

Add all fixings to list

Bearings

1. Place oats into a multi-practical weight cooker, (for example, Instant Pot(R)). Include water, almond milk, apple, dates, rosemary, vanilla concentrate, cinnamon, and salt. Mix until fixings are simply joined. Close and lock the cover. Select high weight as per maker's directions; set clock for 4 minutes. Permit 10 to 15

minutes for strain to construct.
2. Let sit for 5 minutes before discharging pressure utilizing the brisk discharge technique as per maker's guidelines, around 5 minutes. Open and evacuate the top.
3. Stir cooked oatmeal and top with slashed walnuts.

Sustenance Facts

Nutrition: 232 calories; 3.6 g fat; 46 g carbohydrates; 5.6 g protein; 0 mg cholesterol; 43 mg sodium.

164. Mango Coconut Chia Pudding

Preparation time: 10 minutes
Ingredients:
- 1 h
- 1 mango, stripped and diced
- 2/3 cup unsweetened coconut milk drink, (for example, Silk®)
- 1 tablespoon maple syrup
- 2 tablespoons chia seeds
- 2 tablespoons unsweetened coconut chips, (for example, Bob's Red Mill®), partitioned

Add all fixings to list

Bearings
1. Mash portion of the mango in a bowl with a fork or puree in a nourishment processor to wanted consistency.
2. Whisk coconut milk drink and maple syrup into the crushed mango; mix in chia seeds and 1 tablespoon coconut pieces. Cover and refrigerate until thickened, in any event 60 minutes.
3. Divide pudding between 2 dishes and top with diced mango and remaining coconut pieces.

Nutrition: 210 calories; 9 g fat; 34.1 g starches; 2 g protein; 0 mg cholesterol; 9 mg sodium.

165. Healthy Pumpkin Spice Oatmeal

Preparation time: 5 minutes

Cooking Time: 13 minutes
"Delightful breakfast for fall."
Ingredients:
- 2 cups unsweetened almond milk
- 1/2 cup pumpkin puree
- 2 tablespoons maple syrup
- 1 teaspoon vanilla concentrate
- 1/4 teaspoon ground cinnamon
- 1/4 teaspoon ground nutmeg
- 1/4 teaspoon ground cloves
- 1 cup antiquated oats

Add all fixings to list

Bearings
1. Combine almond milk, pumpkin puree, maple syrup, vanilla concentrate, cinnamon, nutmeg, and cloves in a pot over medium warmth; heat to the point of boiling. Include oatmeal and cook, mixing much of the time, until chewy and delicate, 8 to 10 minutes.
2. References
3. Instead of utilizing 2 cups of almond milk, you can utilize 1 cup milk and 1 cup water.

Nutrition: 300 calories; 5.7 g fat; 55.2 g carbohydrates; 7.1 g protein; 0 mg cholesterol; 313 mg sodium.

166. Healthy Multigrain Seeded Bread

Preparation time: 20 minutes
Cooking Time: 30 minutes
Ingredients:
- 2 h 30 min., 12 servings, 124 cals
- 1 cup warm water
- 1/4 cup white sugar
- 1 (.25 ouncebundle dynamic dry yeast
- 2 cups bread flour
- 1 cup entire wheat flour
- 1/4 cup coconut oil
- 1 teaspoon salt
- 1 tablespoon chia seeds
- 1 tablespoon wheat germinutes

- *1 tablespoon flax seeds*
- *1 tablespoon millet*
- *2 tablespoons hulled hemp seeds, isolated*
- *2 tablespoons salted simmered sunflower seeds, isolated*
- *2 tablespoons antiquated oats, isolated*

Add all fixings to list

Bearings
1. *Mix warm water and sugar together in a bowl until sugar is broken up; mix in yeast. Put aside until a rich froth starts to formin., around 5 minutes.*
2. *Combine bread flour, entire wheat flour, coconut oil, and salt in a nourishment processor; beat multiple times. Include chia seeds, wheat germin., flax seeds, millet, 1 tablespoon hemp seeds, 1 tablespoon sunflower seeds, and 1 tablespoon oats; beat until fused.*
3. *Pour yeast blend over flour blend in the nourishment processor; process until a batter ball structures, around 1 moment.*
4. *Turn batter into a well-oiled huge bowl and spread with a clammy towel; permit to ascend in a warm zone until multiplied in size, around 60 minutes.*
5. *Punch batter down and massage a couple of times. Structure mixture into an elliptical shape and spot in a lubed bread dish. Daintily press the rest of the hemp seeds, sunflower seeds, and oats onto the portion. Spread with a sodden towel and let ascend in a warm territory for 30 minutes.*
6. *Preheat stove to 350 degrees F (175 degrees C).*
7. *Bake in the preheated stove until cooked through and outside layer is daintily sautéed, around 30 minutes. Cool bread in the search for gold minutes before moving to a wire rack to cool totally.*

Sustenance Facts
Nutrition: *124 calories; 6.9 g fat; 14.4 g carbohydrates;3.1 g protein; 0 mg cholesterol; 196 mg sodium.*

167. Warm Cinnamon Raisin Quinoa

Preparation time: 10 minutes
Cooking Time: 20 minutes
Ingredients:
- *2 cups almond milk*
- *1 cup quinoa*
- *1 teaspoon ground cinnamon*
- *5 vanilla beans*
- *1 cup raisins*
- *2 tablespoons chia seeds, or to taste*
- *2 tablespoons ground flax seeds, or to taste*

Add all fixings to list

Bearings
1. *Bring almond milk and quinoa to a bubble in a pot. Include cinnamon and vanilla beans; lessen warmth and stew, mixing every so often, until all fluid is assimilated, around 15 minutes. Expel vanilla beans from quinoa.*
2. *Spoon quinoa into bowls; top each with raisins, chia seeds, and ground flax seeds.*

Nutrition: *419 calories; 6.7 g fat; 84.6 g carbohydrates;9 g protein; 0 mg cholesterol; 88 mg sodium.*

168. Oatmeal Chia Hemp Chocolate Chip Vegan Bars

Preparation time: 15 minutes
Cooking Time: 15 minutes
Ingredients:
- *1 h 30 min., 10 servings, 276 cals*
- *1/3 cup bubbling water*
- *2 tablespoons ground flax seed*
- *3 cups fast cooking oats*
- *1/4 cup chia seeds*
- *2 tablespoons hemp seed hearts*

- 1/2 teaspoon preparing powder
- 1/2 teaspoon preparing pop
- 1/4 teaspoon salt
- 1/2 cup agave nectar
- 1/3 cup dissolved coconut oil
- 1/2 cup semisweet chocolate chips

Add all fixings to list

Bearings

1. Preheat stove to 350 degrees F (175 degrees C).
2. Mix bubbling water and flax seed meal together in a bowl; put aside to thicken.
3. Combine oats, chia seeds, hemp hearts, preparing powder, heating pop, and salt together in a huge bowl; mix in agave nectar, coconut oil, and flax blend until all around blended. Overlap chocolate chips into blend; press into a 9x11-inch heating container.
4. Bake in the preheated stove until cooked through, around 15 minutes. Cool to room temperature and cut into bars. Refrigerate before expelling from dish.

Nutrition: 276 calories; 13.8 g fat; 36.6 g starches; 4.9 g protein; 0 mg cholesterol; 149 mg sodium.

169. Duke Gray Chia Pudding

Preparation time: 10 minutes
Cooking Time: 5 minutes
"Brisk and simple."
Ingredients:

- 8 h 20 min., 4 servings, 73 cals
- 1 cup almond milk
- 1 Earl Gray tea pack
- 1/4 cup chia seeds
- 1 tablespoon vanilla concentrate
- 1/2 teaspoons darker sugar (discretionary
- 1 teaspoon maple syrup, or to taste (discretionary

Add all fixings to list
Directions:

1. Bring almond milk to a bubble in a pan; include tea sack. Expel pan from warm and permit tea to steep, around 5 minutes. Expel and dispose of tea sack.
2. Mix chia seeds, vanilla concentrate, and dark colored sugar together in a bowl; mix into the almond milk blend. Empty almond milk blend into little dishes and top each with maple syrup. Cover and refrigerate until set, 8 hours to medium-term.

Nutrition: 73 calories; 3 g fat; 8.6 g starches; 1.4 g protein; 0 mg cholesterol; 42 mg sodium.

170. Peanut Butter-Banana Green Smoothie

Ingredients:

- 1 cup unsweetened almond milk
- 2 cups of spinach, chopped
- 2 frozen ripe bananas
- 1 tbsp. peanut butter
- 2 ice cubes

Directions:
Place all ingredients in a blender and blend until smooth.

171. Raspberry Mango Green Smoothie

Ingredients:

- 3 cups fresh spinach
- 1 ripe banana, frozen
- 1 cup soy milk
- 1/2 cup mango, diced
- 1/3 cup fresh raspberries

Directions:
Blend all ingredients in a blender until smooth. Serve in cups.

172. Pineapple Orange Green Smoothie

Ingredients:

- 1 banana
- 1/3 cup kale, chopped
- 1/2 cup frozen banana

- *1 tablespoon pineapple*
- *1/3 cup orange juice*
- *1 tablespoon chia seeds*

Directions:
Blend all ingredients in a blender until smooth.

173. Blueberry Green Smoothie

Ingredients:
- *1 tablespoon flax seeds*
- *1 cup blueberries*
- *1 frozen ripe banana, quartered*
- *1/3 cup water, or more to taste*
- *3 ice cubes*
- *2 leaves kale*

Directions:
Blend all ingredients in a blender until smooth. If you would like a thinner smoothie add water.

174. Strawberry Green Smoothie

Ingredients:
- *2 cups coconut water*
- *1 cup spinach*
- *1 banana*
- *6 sliced fresh strawberries*

Directions:
Blend coconut water, spinach, banana and strawberries together in a blender until smooth.

175. Grape-Melon Green Smoothie

Ingredients:
- *3 cups melon, cubed*
- *3 cups ice cubes*
- *1 cup grapes*
- *1 cucumber, peeled and chopped*

Directions:
Blend all ingredients in a blender until smooth.

176. Raspberry Kale Smoothie

Ingredients:
- *1/2 cup raspberry, chopped*
- *2 leaves kale*
- *1/2 ripe banana*
- *1 cup cucumber*
- *3 ice cubes*

Directions:
Blend all ingredients in a blender until smooth. Serve in cups.

177. Banana Almond Green Smoothie

Ingredients:
- *3 ice cubes*
- *1 cup almond milk*
- *1 1/2 ripe bananas*
- *3 leaves kale, chopped*
- *1/4 cup flax seed, ground*
- *1 tablespoons vanilla extract*
- *1 tablespoon almond butter*

Directions:
Blend ice cubes, almond milk, banana, kale, flax seed, vanilla extract and almond butter, together in a blender until smooth.

178. Kiwi Coconut Green Smoothie

Ingredients:
- *3 ice cubes*
- *1 cup soy milk*
- *1 1/2 ripe bananas*
- *3 leaves kale, chopped*
- *½ cup kiwi*
- *¼ cup coconut, shredded*

Directions:
Blend all ingredients together in a blender until smooth.

179. Strawberry -Nectarine Green Smoothie

Ingredients:
- *3 ice cubes*
- *1 cup non-dairy milk*
- *1 1/2 ripe bananas*
- *2 leaves kale, chopped*
- *½ cup strawberry*
- *1/3 cup nectarines*

Directions:
Blend all ingredients together in a blender until smooth.

180. Triple Berry Green Smoothie

Ingredients:
- 1 banana
- ½ cups strawberries, chopped
- ½ cups blueberries
- ½ cups blackberry
- 1 1/2 cups chopped spinach
- 1/2 cup unsweetened soy milk
- 1 tablespoon chia seeds, ground
- 1 teaspoon agave nectar

Directions:
Place all ingredients in a blender. Cover, and puree until smooth. Serve over ice.

181. Orange Ginger Green Smoothie

Ingredients:
- 1/4 cucumber, chopped
- 1 frozen ripe banana, chopped
- 1 teaspoon ginger grated
- 1 teaspoon flax seeds
- 1/2 cup orange juice

Directions:
Add all ingredients to a blender, blend mixture until smooth.

182. Kale-Banana Power Smoothie

Ingredients:
- 1 cup non-dairy milk
- 3/4 cup chopped kale leaves
- 1 frozen ripe banana

Directions:
Blend non-dairy milk, banana and kale leaves together in a blender until smooth.

183. Cucumber-Apple Green Smoothie

Ingredients:
- 1 cucumber, chopped
- 1 tablespoon lime juice
- 2 apples, cored and chopped
- 1 cup old-fashioned rolled oats

Directions:
Combine the oats, cucumber, lime juice and apples in a blender; blend until smooth.

184. Blackcurrant-Peach Green Smoothie

Ingredients:
- 3 ice cubes
- 1 cup almond milk
- 1 1/2 ripe bananas
- 2 leaves kale, chopped
- ½ cup blackcurrants
- ¼ cup peach, chopped

Directions:
Blend all ingredients together in a blender until smooth.

185. Papaya-Banana Green Smoothie

Ingredients:
- 3 ice cubes
- 1 cup papaya
- ½ cup orange juice
- 2 ripe bananas
- 3 leaves kale, chopped
- 1/4 cup cucumber

Directions:
Blend all ingredients together in a blender until smooth.

186. Grape Mint Green Smoothie

Ingredients:
- 3 ice cubes
- 1 /4 cup mint leaves
- 1 cup grapes
- 2 leaves cucumber, chopped
- ½ cup kiwi

Directions:
Blend all ingredients together in a blender until smooth.

187. Tangerine Kale Smoothie

Ingredients:
- 3 ice cubes
- 1 cup tangerine, segmented
- 1 1/2 ripe bananas
- 2 leaves kale, chopped

Directions:
Blend all ingredients together in a blender until smooth.

188. Pear Cucumber Smoothie

Ingredients:
- 3 ice cubes
- 1 cup coconut water
- 1 cup pear, chopped
- ½ cup cucumber, chopped

Directions:
Blend all ingredients together in a blender until smooth.

189. Cherry-Kiwi Green Smoothie

Ingredients:
- 1 cup coconut water
- ½ cup cherries
- 1 cup broccoli, chopped
- ½ cup kiwi

Directions:
Blend all ingredients together in a blender until smooth.

190. Avocado-Kale Smoothie

Ingredients:
- ½ avocado, chopped
- 4 leaves kale, chopped
- ½ cup bananas, frozen

Directions:
Blend all ingredients together in a blender until smooth.

191. Coconut-Green Tea Smoothie

Ingredients:
- 2 leaves kale
- 1/2 cup coconut, shredded
- 1 teaspoon agave nectar
- 1/2 cup green tea
- 2 ice cubes

Directions:
Combine all ingredients in a blender, blend until smooth.

192. Orange-Carrot Green Smoothie

Ingredients:
- 2 cups kale, chopped
- 1 cup carrots, chopped
- 1 cup orange juice
- 3 ice cubes

Directions:
Add all ingredients to the blender and puree until smooth.

193. Pineapple-Coconut Green Smoothie

Ingredients:
- 4 cups pineapple, diced
- 2 cups coconut water
- 2 cups ice cubes
- 1 cup parsley, chopped
- ½ tablespoon agave nectar

Directions:
Blend pineapple, coconut water, ice cubes, dandelion greens, agave nectar in a blender until smooth and creamy.

194. Vanilla-Almond Green Smoothie

Ingredients:
- 1 cup water
- 1 banana, frozen
- 1 cup cucumber, chopped
- 1 tablespoon almonds
- 2 teaspoons almond butter
- 1 ½ teaspoons vanilla
- ¾ teaspoon ground cinnamon

Directions:
Add to your blender all the ingredients listed, then blend until smooth

195. Apple-Cucumber Smoothie

Ingredients:
- 1/2 teaspoon ground cinnamon
- 1/4 teaspoon vanilla extract
- pinch ground nutmeg
- 2 cups cucumber, chopped
- 1 apple, chopped and frozen
- 3 ice cubes

Directions:
Add all ingredients to a blender and blend until smooth.

196. Strawberry-Lemon Green Smoothie

Ingredients:
- 1 cup strawberries
- 1 cup non-dairy milk
- 3 tablespoons old-fashioned oats
- 1 tablespoon chia seed
- 1 tablespoon cashews
- 1 teaspoon lemon juice
- 1/2 teaspoon agave nectar

Directions:
Place all ingredients in a blender and blend until smooth.

197. Energy Smoothie

Ingredients:
- 1 cucumber, roughly chopped
- 2 cups lettuce, chopped
- 1 cup maca
- 1/4 cups lemon juice

Directions:
1. Add all ingredients to a blender and blend until smooth.

198. Pink Grapefruit Green Smoothie

Ingredients:
- ½ cup coconut water
- 1 cup watercress
- 1 cup pink grapefruit, segmented, chopped
- 1/4 cups lime juice

Directions:
Add all ingredients to a blender and blend until smooth.

199. Mint- Cocoa Smoothie

Ingredients:
- 1/2 cup soy milk
- 2 cups spinach
- 1 frozen ripe banana
- 2 tablespoon chia seeds
- 4 ice cubes
- 3 tablespoon vegan cocoa powder

Directions:
Add all ingredients to the blender and blend until smooth.

200. Cranberry-Raspberry Smoothie

Ingredients:
- ½ cup pitted fresh cranberries
- ½ cucumber, chopped
- ½ cup fresh raspberries
- 1 tablespoon hemp seeds
- ½ cup water
- 5 ice cubes

Directions:
Place in your blender and blend until smooth.

201. Plum Green Smoothie

Ingredients:
- 1 1/2 cup non-dairy milk
- 1 cup plums, pitted and chopped
- 1 cup celery
- ½ cu lettuce
- 1 teaspoon vanilla extract
- 1 tablespoon chia seed
- 3 ice cubes

Directions:
Add all ingredients to a blender and blend until smooth.

202. Pineapple Lemon Green Smoothie

Ingredients:
- 1/2 cup lemon juice
- 1/2 cup pineapples, diced

- *1 frozen ripe banana, quartered*
- *1 tablespoon lemon juice*
- *1 cup celery*
- *¼ cup kale*

Directions:
Add all ingredients to a blender and blend until smooth.

203. Blueberry Peach Green Smoothie

Ingredients:
- *1/2 peach, chopped*
- *1 cup blueberries*
- *1 cup kale*
- *1 cup watercress*
- *1 tablespoon flax seeds*
- *1 banana, frozen, quartered*

Directions:
Add all ingredients to a blender and puree until smooth.

204. Tropical Papaya Smoothie

Ingredients:
- *1 cup coconut water*
- *1 frozen ripe banana*
- *1 cup papaya, chopped*
- *½ cup cucumber, chopped*
- *1/2 cup celery*
- *1 tablespoon almond, sliced*

Directions:
Add ingredients to your blender and puree until smooth.

205. Pumpkin Banana Smoothie

Ingredients:
- *1 cup non-dairy milk*
- *1/2 cup canned pumpkin*
- *1/2 banana*
- *1 tablespoon raisins or 1/2 teaspoon maple syrup*
- *1/2 teaspoon pure vanilla extract*
- *1/4 teaspoon ground cinnamon*
- *1/8 teaspoon ground ginger*
- *pinch ground nutmeg*

Directions:
Add all ingredients to a blender and puree until smooth.

206. Almond Chia Green Smoothie

Ingredients:
- *1 cup almond milk*
- *3 tablespoon oats*
- *1 tablespoon chia seeds*
- *1 tablespoon almond butter*
- *1 cup kale, chopped*

Directions:
Add all ingredients to a blender and blend until smooth.

207. Basic Green Smoothie

Ingredients:
- *1 cup unsweetened non-dairy milk*
- *2 cups lettuce*
- *1 ripe banana*
- *3 ice cubes*

Directions:
Add all ingredients to a blender and puree until smooth.

208. Apple Cinnamon Green Smoothie

Ingredients:
- *1 cup non-dairy milk*
- *1 apple, chopped*
- *2 cups spinach*
- *1/8 teaspoon pure vanilla extract*
- *¼ teaspoon ground cinnamon*
- *2 ice cubes*

Directions:
Add all ingredients to a blender and puree until smooth.

209. Key Lime Green Smoothie

Ingredients:
- *2 tablespoons key lime juice*
- *1 ripe banana, frozen*
- *¼ teaspoon vanilla extract*
- *8 teaspoon maple syrup*

- 2 cups celery, chopped
- ½ cup oats
- 5 ice cubes

Directions:
Add all ingredients to a blender and puree until smooth.

210. Avocado-Banana Green Smoothie

Ingredients:
- 1 cup non-dairy milk
- 2 cups spinach
- 1/2 avocado, chopped
- 1/2 banana, frozen
- 2 tablespoon chia seeds
- 3 ice cubes

Directions:
Add all ingredients to a blender and puree until smooth.

211. Spirulina Green Smoothie

Ingredients:
- 1 cup unsweetened non-dairy milk
- 1 cup watercress
- 1 tablespoon cacao powder
- 1 tablespoon almonds, chopped
- 1 tablespoon coconut water
- 1 tablespoon agave nectar
- 1 teaspoon spirulina
- 4 ice cubes

Directions:
Add all ingredients to a blender and puree until smooth.

212. Raspberry Green Smoothie

Ingredients:
- 1 cup unsweetened non-dairy milk
- 2 cups celery
- 1 cup raspberries
- 2 tablespoon ground flax seed
- 1 tablespoon walnuts, chopped
- 3 ice cubes

Directions:
Add all ingredients to a blender and puree until smooth.

213. Mango-Orange Green Smoothie

Ingredients:
- 1 cup spinach leaves, packed
- 1 cup mango, cubed
- 1/2 medium banana, frozen
- ¼ cup coconut water
- 1/2 cup orange juice

Directions:
Add all ingredients to a blender and puree until smooth.

MAINS

214. Grilled tempeh with green beans

Preparation Time: 15 minutes
Serving: 4

If there is ever a dish that can replace the essence of BBQ, this would be it! Plus the extra ingredients of green beans.

Ingredients
- 1 tbsp plant butter, melted
- 1 lb tempeh, sliced into 4 pieces
- 1 lb green beans, trimmed
- Salt and black pepper to taste
- 2 sprigs thyme
- 2 tbsp olive oil
- 1 tbsp pure corn syrup
- 1 lemon, juiced

Directions
1. Preheat a grill pan over medium heat and brush with the plant butter.
2. Season the tempeh and green beans with the salt, black pepper, and place the thyme in the pan. Grill the tempeh and green beans on both sides until golden brown and tender, 10 minutes.
3. Transfer to serving plates.
4. In a small bowl, whisk the olive oil, corn syrup, lemon juice, and drizzle all over the food.
5. Serve warm.

Nutrition:
Calories 352
Fats 22.5g | Carbs 21.8g
Protein 22.6g

215. Tofu Fajita Bowl

Preparation Time: 5minutes
Cooking Time: 10minutes
Servings: 4

Ingredients:
- 2 tbsp olive oil
- 1½ lb tofu, cut into strips
- Salt and ground black pepper to taste
- 2 tbsp Tex-Mex seasoning
- 1 small iceberg lettuce, chopped
- 2 large tomatoes, deseeded and chopped
- 2 avocados, halved, pitted, and chopped
- 1 green bell pepper, deseeded and thinly sliced
- 1 yellow onion, thinly sliced
- 4 tbsp fresh cilantro leaves
- ½ cup shredded dairy-free parmesan cheese blend
- 1 cup plain unsweetened yogurt

Directions:
1. Heat the olive oil in a medium skillet over medium heat, season the tofu with salt, black pepper, and Tex-Mex seasoning. Fry in the oil on both sides until golden and cooked, 5 to 10 minutes. Transfer to a plate.
2. Divide the lettuce into 4 serving bowls, share the tofu on top, and add the tomatoes, avocados, bell pepper, onion, cilantro, and cheese.
3. Top with dollops of plain yogurt and serve immediately with low carb tortillas.

Nutrition:
Calories:263, Total Fat:26.4g, Saturated Fat:8.8g, Total Carbs:4g, Dietary Fiber:1g, Sugar:3g, Protein:4g, Sodium:826mg

216. Indian Style Tempeh Bake

Preparation Time: 10minutes
Cooking Time: 26minutes
Servings: 4

Ingredients:
- 3 tbsp unsalted butter
- 6 tempeh, cut into 1-inch cubes
- Salt and ground black pepper to taste
- 2 ½ tbsp garam masala

- 1 cup baby spinach, tightly pressed
- 1¼ cups coconut creaminutes
- 1 tbsp fresh cilantro, finely chopped

Directions:
1. Preheat the oven to 350 F and grease a baking dish with cooking spray. Set aside.
2. Heat the ghee in a medium skillet over medium heat, season the tempeh with salt and black pepper, and Cooking Time: in the oil on both sides until golden on the outside, 6 minutes.
3. Mix in half of the garam masala and transfer the tempeh (with juicesinto the baking dish.
4. Add the spinach, and spread the coconut cream on top. Bake in the oven for 20 minutes or until the cream is bubbly.
5. Remove the dish, garnish with cilantro, and serve with cauliflower couscous.

Nutrition:
Calories:598, Total Fat:56g, Saturated Fat:18.8g, Total Carbs12:g, Dietary Fiber:3g, Sugar:5g, Protein:15g, Sodium:762mg

217. Tofu- Seitan Casserole

Preparation Time: 10minutes
Cooking Time: 20minutes
Servings: 4
Ingredients:
- 1 tofu, shredded
- 7 oz seitan, chopped
- 8 oz dairy- free cream cheese (vegan
- 1 tbsp Dijon mustard
- 1 tbsp plain vinegar
- 10 oz shredded cheddar cheese
- Salt and ground black pepper to taste

Directions:
1. Preheat the oven to 350 F and grease a baking dish with cooking spray. Set aside.
2. Spread the tofu and seitan in the bottom of the dish.
3. In a small bowl, mix the cashew cream, Dijon mustard, vinegar, and two-thirds of the cheddar cheese. Spread the mixture on top of the tofu and seitan, season with salt and black pepper, and cover with the remaining cheese.
4. Bake in the oven for 15 to 20 minutes or until the cheese melts and is golden brown.
5. Remove the dish and serve with steamed collards.

Nutrition:
Calories475:, Total Fat:41.2g, Saturated Fat:12.3g, Total Carbs:6g, Dietary Fiber:3g, Sugar:2g, Protein:24g, Sodium:755mg

218. Ginger Lime Tempeh

Preparation Time: 10 minutes
Cooking Time: 40 minutes
Servings: 4
Ingredients:
- 5 kaffir lime leaves
- 1 tbsp cumin powder
- 1 tbsp ginger powder
- 1 cup plain unsweetened yogurt
- 2 lb tempeh
- Salt and ground black pepper to taste
- 1 tbsp olive oil
- 2 limes, juiced

Directions:
1. In a large bowl, combine the kaffir lime leaves, cumin, ginger, and plain yogurt. Add the tempeh, season with salt, and black pepper, and mix to coat well. Cover the bowl with a plastic wrap and marinate in the refrigerator for 2 to 3 hours.
2. Preheat the oven to 350 F and grease a baking sheet with cooking spray.
3. Take out the tempeh and arrange on the baking sheet. Drizzle with olive oil, lime juice, cover with aluminum foil, and slow-Cooking Time: in the oven for 1 to 1 ½ hours or until the

tempeh cooks within.

4. *Remove the aluminum foil, turn the broiler side of the oven on, and brown the top of the tempeh for 5 to 10 minutes.*
5. *Take out the tempeh and serve warm with red cabbage slaw.*

Nutrition:
Calories:285, Total Fat:25.6g, Saturated Fat:13.6g, Total Carbs:7g, Dietary Fiber:2g, Sugar:2g, Protein:11g, Sodium:772mg

219. Tofu Mozzarella

Preparation Time: 10minutes
Cooking Time: 35minutes
Servings: 4
Ingredients:

- *1½ lb tofu, halved lengthwise*
- *Salt and ground black pepper to taste*
- *2 eggs*
- *2 tbsp Italian seasoning*
- *1 pinch red chili flakes*
- *½ cup sliced Pecorino Romano cheese*
- *¼ cup fresh parsley, chopped*
- *4 tbsp butter*
- *2 garlic cloves, minced*
- *2 cups crushed tomatoes*
- *1 tbsp dried basil*
- *Salt and ground black pepper to taste*
- *½ lb sliced mozzarella cheese*

Directions:

1. *Preheat the oven to 400 F and grease a baking dish with cooking spray. Set aside.*
2. *Season the tofu with salt and black pepper; set aside.*
3. *In a medium bowl, whisk the eggs with the Italian seasoning, and red chili flakes. In a plate, combine the Pecorino Romano cheese with parsley.*
4. *Melt the butter in a medium skillet over medium heat.*
5. *Quickly dip the tofu in the egg mixture and then dredge generously in the cheese mixture. Place in the butter and fry on both sides until the cheese melts and is golden brown, 8 to 10 minutes. Place on a plate and set aside.*
6. *Sauté the garlic in the same pan and mix in the tomatoes. Top with the basil, salt, and black pepper, and Cooking Time: for 5 to 10 minutes. Pour the sauce into the baking dish.*
7. *Lay the tofu pieces in the sauce and top with the mozzarella cheese. Bake in the oven for 10 to 15 minutes or until the cheese melts completely.*
8. *Remove the dish and serve with leafy green salad.*

Nutrition:
Calories:140, Total Fat:13.2g, Saturated Fat:7.1g, Total Carbs:2g, Dietary Fiber:0g, Sugar:0g, Protein:3g, Sodium:78mg1

220. Seitan Meatza With Kale

Preparation Time: 10minutes
Cooking Time: 22minutes
Servings: 4
Ingredients:

- *1 lb ground seitan*
- *Salt and black pepper to taste*
- *2 cups powdered Parmesan cheese*
- *¼ tsp onion powder*
- *¼ tsp garlic powder*
- *½ cup unsweetened tomato sauce*
- *1 tsp white vinegar*
- *½ tsp liquid smoke*
- *¼ cup baby kale, chopped roughly*
- *1 cup mozzarella cheese*

Directions:

1. *Preheat the oven to 400 F and line a medium pizza pan with parchment paper and grease with cooking spray. Set aside.*
2. *In a medium bowl, combine the seitan, salt, black pepper, and parmesan cheese. Spread the mixture*

on the pizza pan to fit the shape of the pan. Bake in the oven for 15 minutes or until the meat cooks.
3. Meanwhile in a medium bowl, mix the onion powder, garlic powder, tomato sauce, vinegar, and liquid smoke. Remove the meat crust from the oven and spread the tomato mixture on top. Add the kale and sprinkle with the mozzarella cheese.
4. Bake in the oven for 7 minutes or until the cheese melts.
5. Take out from the oven, slice, and serve warm.

Nutrition:
Calories:601, Total Fat:51.8g, Saturated Fat:16.4g, Total Carbs:18g, Dietary Fiber:5g, Sugar:3g, Protein:23g, Sodium:398mg

221. Taco Tempeh Casserole

Preparation Time: 10minutes
Cooking Time: 20minutes
Servings: 4
Ingredients:
- 1 Tempeh, shredded
- 1/3 cup vegan mayonnaise
- 8 oz dairy- free cream cheese (vegan
- 1 yellow onion, sliced
- 1 yellow bell pepper, deseeded and chopped
- 2 tbsp taco seasoning
- ½ cup shredded cheddar cheese
- Salt and ground black pepper to taste

Directions:
1. Preheat the oven to 400 F and grease a baking dish with cooking spray.
2. Into the dish, put the tempeh, mayonnaise, cashew cream, onion, bell pepper, taco seasoning, and two-thirds of the cheese, salt, and black pepper. Mix the Ingredients and top with the remaining cheese.
3. Bake in the oven for 15 to 20 minutes or until the cheese melts and is golden brown.
4. Remove the dish, plate, and serve with lettuce leaves.

Nutrition:
Calories:132, Total Fat:11.5g, Saturated Fat4:4.3g, Total Carbs:7g, Dietary Fiber:4g, Sugar:2g, Protein:1g, Sodium:10mg

222. Broccoli Tempeh Alfredo

Preparation Time: 10minutes
Cooking Time: 15minutes
Servings: 4
Ingredients:
- 6 slices tempeh, chopped
- 2 tbsp butter
- 4 tofu, cut into 1-inch cubes
- Salt and ground black pepper to taste
- 4 garlic cloves, minced
- 1 cup baby kale, chopped
- 1 ½ cups full- fat heavy creaminutes
- 1 medium head broccoli, cut into florets
- ¼ cup shredded parmesan cheese

Directions:
1. Put the tempeh in a medium skillet over medium heat and fry until crispy and brown, 5 minutes. Spoon onto a plate and set aside.
2. Melt the butter in the same skillet, season the tofu with salt and black pepper, and Cooking Time: on both sides until goldern- brown. Spoon onto the tempeh's plate and set aside.
3. Add the garlic to the skillet, sauté for 1 minute.
4. Mix in the full- fat heavy cream, tofu, and tempeh, and kale, allow simmering for 5 minutes or until the sauce thickens.
5. Meanwhile, pour the broccoli into a large safe-microwave bowl, sprinkle with some water, season with salt, and black pepper, and microwave for 2 minutes or until the broccoli softens.
6. Spoon the broccoli into the sauce, top

with the parmesan cheese, stir and Cooking Time: until the cheese melts. Turn the heat off.

7. *Spoon the mixture into a serving platter and serve warm.*

Nutrition:
Calories:193, Total Fat:20.1g, Saturated Fat:12.5g, Total Carbs:3g, Dietary Fiber:0g, Sugar:2g, Protein:1g, Sodium:100mg

223. Avocado Seitan

Preparation Time: 10 minutes
Cooking Time: 2 hours 15 minutes
Servings: 4
Ingredients:

- *1 white onion, finely chopped*
- *¼ cup vegetable stock*
- *3 tbsp coconut oil*
- *3 tbsp tamari sauce*
- *3 tbsp chili pepper*
- *1 tbsp red wine vinegar*
- *Salt and ground black pepper to taste*
- *2 lb Seitan*
- *1 large avocado, halved and pitted*
- *½ lemon, juiced*

Directions:

1. *In a large pot, combine the onion, vegetable stock, coconut oil, tamari sauce, chili pepper, red wine vinegar, salt, black pepper. Add the seitan, close the lid, and Cooking Time: over low heat for 2 hours.*
2. *Scoop the avocado pulp into a bowl, add the lemon juice, and using a fork, mash the avocado into a puree. Set aside.*
3. *When ready, turn the heat off and mix in the avocado. Adjust the taste with salt and black pepper.*
4. *Spoon onto a serving platter and serve warm.*

Nutrition:
Calories:412, Total Fat:43g, Saturated Fat:37g, Total Carbs:9g, Dietary Fiber:3g, Sugar:0g, Protein:5g, Sodium:12mg

224. Seitan Mushroom Burgers

Preparation Time: 15 minutes
Cooking Time: 13 minutes
Servings: 4
Ingredients:

- *1 ½ lb ground seitan*
- *Salt and ground black pepper to taste*
- *1 tbsp unsweetened tomato sauce*
- *6 large Portobello caps, destemmed*
- *1 tbsp olive oil*
- *6 slices cheddar cheese*

For topping:

- *4 lettuce leaves*
- *4 large tomato slices*
- *¼ cup mayonnaise*

Directions:

1. *In a medium bowl, combine the seitan, salt, black pepper, and tomato sauce. Using your hands, mold the mixture into 4 patties, and set aside.*
2. *Rinse the mushrooms under running water and pat dry.*
3. *Heat the olive oil in a medium skillet; place in the Portobello caps and Cooking Time: until softened, 3 to 4 minutes. Transfer to a serving plate and set aside.*
4. *Put the seitan patties in the skillet and fry on both sides until brown and compacted, 8 minutes. Place the vegan cheddar slices on the food, allow melting for 1 minute and lift each patty onto each mushroom cap.*
5. *Divide the lettuce on top, then the tomato slices, and add some mayonnaise.*
6. *Serve immediately.*

Nutrition:
Calories:304, Total Fat:29g, Saturated Fat:23.5g, Total Carbs:8g, Dietary Fiber:3g, Sugar:1g, Protein:8g, Sodium:8mg

225. Taco Tempeh Stuffed Peppers

Preparation Time: 15 minutes
Cooking Time: 41 minutes
Servings: 6
Ingredients:

- 6 yellow bell peppers, halved and deseeded
- 1 ½ tbsp olive oil
- Salt and ground black pepper to taste
- 3 tbsp butter
- 3 garlic cloves, minced
- ½ white onion, chopped
- 2 lbs. ground tempeh
- 3 tsp taco seasoning
- 1 cup riced broccoli
- ¼ cup grated cheddar cheese
- Plain unsweetened yogurt for serving

Directions:

1. Preheat the oven to 400 F and grease a baking dish with cooking spray. Set aside.
2. Drizzle the bell peppers with the olive oil and season with some salt. Set aside.
3. Melt the butter in a large skillet and sauté the garlic and onion for 3 minutes. Stir in the tempeh, taco seasoning, salt, and black pepper. Cooking Time: until the meat is no longer pink, 8 minutes.
4. Mix in the broccoli until adequately incorporated. Turn the heat off.
5. Spoon the mixture into the peppers, top with the cheddar cheese, and place the peppers in the baking dish. Bake in the oven until the cheese melts and is bubbly, 30 minutes.
6. Remove the dish from the oven and plate the peppers. Top with the palin yogurt and serve warm.

Nutrition:
Calories:251, Total Fat:22.5g, Saturated Fat:3.8g, Total Carbs:13g, Dietary Fiber:9g, Sugar:2g, Protein:3g, Sodium:23mg

226. Tangy Tofu Meatloaf

Preparation Time: 10 minutes
Cooking Time: 40 minutes
Servings: 6
Ingredients:

- 2 ½ lb ground tofu
- Salt and ground black pepper to taste
- 3 tbsp flaxseed meal
- 2 large eggs
- 2 tbsp olive oil
- 1 lemon,1 tbsp juiced
- ¼ cup freshly chopped parsley
- ¼ cup freshly chopped oregano
- 4 garlic cloves, minced
- Lemon slices to garnish

Directions:

1. Preheat the oven to 400 F and grease a loaf pan with cooking spray. Set aside.
2. In a large bowl, combine the tofu, salt, black pepper, and flaxseed meal. Set aside.
3. In a small bowl, whisk the eggs with the olive oil, lemon juice, parsley, oregano, and garlic. Pour the mixture onto the mix and combine well.
4. Spoon the tofu mixture into the loaf pan and press to fit into the pan. Bake in the middle rack of the oven for 30 to 40 minutes.
5. Remove the pan, tilt to drain the meat's liquid, and allow cooling for 5 minutes.
6. Slice, garnish with some lemon slices and serve with braised green beans.

Nutrition:
Calories:238, Total Fat:26.3g, Saturated Fat:14.9g, Total Carbs:1g, Dietary Fiber:0g, Sugar:0g, Protein:1g, Sodium:183mg

227. Vegan Bacon Wrapped Tofu With Buttered Spinach

Preparation Time: 5 minutes
Cooking Time: 20 minutes
Servings: 4
Ingredients:

For the bacon wrapped tofu:
- 4 tofu
- 8 slices vegan bacon
- Salt and black pepper to taste
- 2 tbsp olive oil

For the buttered spinach:
- 2 tbsp butter
- 1 lb spinach
- 4 garlic cloves
- Salt and ground black pepper to taste

Directions:

For the bacon wrapped tofu:
1. Preheat the oven to 450 F.
2. Wrap each tofu with two vegan bacon slices, season with salt and black pepper, and place on the baking sheet. Drizzle with the olive oil and bake in the oven for 15 minutes or until the vegan bacon browns and the tofu cooks within.

For the buttered spinach:
1. Meanwhile, melt the butter in a large skillet, add and sauté the spinach and garlic until the leaves wilt, 5 minutes. Season with salt and black pepper.
2. Remove the tofu from the oven and serve with the buttered spinach.

Nutrition:
Calories:260, Total Fat:24.7g, Saturated Fat:14.3g, Total Carbs:4g, Dietary Fiber:0g, Sugar:2g, Protein:6g, Sodium:215mg

228. Veggie & Tofu Kebabs

Preparation Time: 15 minutes
Cooking Time: 12 minutes
Servings: 4
Ingredients:
- 2 cloves garlic, minced
- ¼ cup balsamic vinegar
- ¼ cup olive oil
- 1 tablespoon Italian seasoning
- Salt and pepper to taste
- 1 onion, sliced into quarters
- 12 medium mushrooms
- 16 cherry tomatoes
- 1 zucchini, sliced into rounds
- 1 cup tofu, cubed
- 4 cups cauliflower rice

Directions:
1. In a bowl, mix the garlic, vinegar, oil, Italian seasoning, salt and pepper.
2. Toss the vegetable slices and tofu in the mixture.
3. Marinate for 1 hour.
4. Thread into 8 skewers and grill for 12 minutes, turning once or twice.
5. Add cauliflower rice into 4 food containers.
6. Add 2 kebab skewers on top of each container of cauliflower rice.
7. Reheat kebabs in the grill before serving.

Nutritional Value:
Calories 58
Total Fat 2 g
Saturated Fat 0 g
Cholesterol 0 mg
Sodium 84 mg
Total Carbohydrate 9 g
Dietary Fiber 2 g
Total Sugars 5 g
Protein 2 g
Potassium 509 mg

229. Carrot And Radish Slaw With Sesame Dressing

Preparation Time: 10 minutes
Cooking Time: 0 minute
Servings: 4
Ingredients:
- 2 tablespoons sesame oil, toasted
- 3 tablespoons rice vinegar
- ½ teaspoon sugar
- 2 tablespoons low sodium tamari
- 1 cup carrots, sliced into strips
- 2 cups radishes, sliced
- 2 tablespoons fresh cilantro, chopped
- 2 teaspoons sesame seeds, toasted

Directions:

1. Mix the oil, vinegar, sugar and tamari in a bowl.
2. Add the carrots, radishes and cilantro.
3. Toss to coat evenly.
4. Let sit for 10 minutes.
5. Transfer to a food container.

Nutritional Value:
Calories 98
Total Fat 8 g
Saturated Fat 1 g
Cholesterol 0 mg
Sodium 336 mg
Total Carbohydrate 6 g
Dietary Fiber 2 g
Total Sugars 3 g
Protein 2 g
Potassium 241 mg

230. Spicy Snow Pea And Tofu Stir Fry

Preparation Time: 20 minutes
Cooking Time: 20 minutes
Servings: 4
Ingredients:

- 1 cup unsalted natural peanut butter
- 2 teaspoons brown sugar
- 2 tablespoons reduced-sodium soy sauce
- 2 teaspoons hot sauce
- 3 tablespoons rice vinegar
- 14 oz. tofu
- 4 teaspoons oil
- 1/4 cup onion, sliced
- 2 tablespoons ginger, grated
- 3 cloves garlic, minced
- 1/2 cup broccoli, sliced into florets
- 1/2 cup carrot, sliced into sticks
- 2 cups fresh snow peas, trimmed
- 2 tablespoons water
- 2 cups brown rice, cooked
- 4 tablespoons roasted peanuts (unsalted

Directions:
1. In a bowl, mix the peanut butter, sugar, soy sauce, hot sauce and rice vinegar.
2. Blend until smooth and set aside.
3. Drain the tofu and sliced into cubes.
4. Pat dry with paper towel.
5. Add oil to a pan over medium heat.
6. Add the tofu and Cooking Time: for 2 minutes or until brown on all sides.
7. Transfer the tofu to a plate.
8. Add the onion, ginger and garlic to the pan.
9. Cooking Time: for 2 minutes.
10. Add the broccoli and carrot.
11. Cooking Time: for 5 minutes.
12. Stir in the snow peas.
13. Pour in the water and cover.
14. Cooking Time: for 4 minutes.
15. Add the peanut sauce to the pan along with the tofu.
16. Heat through for 30 seconds.
17. In a food container, add the brown rice and top with the tofu and vegetable stir fry.
18. Top with roasted peanuts.

Nutritional Value:
Calories 514
Total Fat 27 g
Saturated Fat 4 g
Cholesterol 0 mg
Sodium 376 mg
Total Carbohydrate 49 g
Dietary Fiber 7 g
Total Sugars 12 g
Protein 22 g
Potassium 319 mg

231. Roasted Veggies In Lemon Sauce

Preparation Time: 15 minutes
Cooking Time: 20 minutes
Servings: 5
Ingredients:

- 2 cloves garlic, sliced
- 1 ½ cups broccoli florets
- 1 ½ cups cauliflower florets
- 1 tablespoon olive oil

- Salt to taste
- 1 teaspoon dried oregano, crushed
- ¾ cup zucchini, diced
- ¾ cup red bell pepper, diced
- 2 teaspoons lemon zest

Directions:
1. Preheat your oven to 425 degrees F.
2. In a baking pan, add the garlic, broccoli and cauliflower.
3. Toss in oil and season with salt and oregano.
4. Roast in the oven for 10 minutes.
5. Add the zucchini and bell pepper to the pan.
6. Stir well.
7. Roast for another 10 minutes.
8. Sprinkle lemon zest on top before serving.
9. Transfer to a food container and reheat before serving.

Nutritional Value:
Calories 52
Total Fat 3 g
Saturated Fat 0 g
Cholesterol 0 mg
Sodium 134 mg
Total Carbohydrate 5 g
Dietary Fiber 2 g
Total Sugars 2 g
Protein 2 g
Potassium 270 mg

232. Lunch Recipes

Potato Bean Quesadillas
Preparation time: 10 minutes
Cooking time: 10 minutes
Servings: 4
Ingredients:
- 4 whole-wheat tortillas
- 2 potatoes, boiled, cubed
- 200g refried beans
- 1 teaspoon chili powder
- ½ teaspoon dried oregano
- ¼ teaspoon garlic powder
- 120g spinach
- 1 onion, thinly sliced
- 2 cloves garlic, minced
- 30ml tamari sauce
- 45g nutritional yeast
- Salt and pepper, to taste

Directions:
1. Heat a splash of olive oil in a skillet.
2. Add onion and Cooking Time: over medium heat for 10 minutes, or until the onion is caramelized.
3. Add the garlic and Cooking Time: 1 minute.
4. Add spinach and toss gently.
5. Add tamari sauce and Cooking Time: 1 minutes.
6. Reheat the refried beans with nutritional yeast, chili, oregano, and garlic powder, in a microwave, on high for 1 minute.
7. Mash the potatoes and spread over tortilla.
8. Top the mashed potatoes with spinach mixture and refried beans.
9. Season to taste and place another tortilla on top.
10. Heat large skillet over medium-high heat.
11. Heat the tortilla until crispy. Flip and heat the other side.
12. Cut the tortilla in half and serve.

Nutrition:
Calories 232
Total Fat 2.1g
Total Carbohydrate 44.2g
Dietary Fiber 10.4g
Total Sugars 3g
Protein 12.4g

233. Lemon Pepper Pasta

Preparation time: 5 minutes
Cooking time: 20 minutes
Servings: 4
Ingredients:
- 300g pasta, any kind, without eggs
- 400ml unsweetened soy milk
- 100g soy cream cheese

- 45g blanched almonds
- 45g nutritional yeast
- 1 teaspoon lemon zest, finely grated
- ¼ teaspoon lemon pepper
- 30ml olive oil
- 2 clove garlic, minced
- 5 capers, rinsed, chopped
- 10g parsley, chopped

Directions:
1. Cooking Time: the pasta, according to the package directions, in a pot filled with salted boiling water.
2. Strain the pasta and reserve 230ml cooking liquid.
3. Combine soy milk, soy cheese, almonds, nutritional yeast, lemon zest, and pepper lemon in a food blender.
4. Blend until smooth. Place aside.
5. Heat olive oil in a skillet.
6. Add the garlic, and Cooking Time: until very fragrant, for 1 minute.
7. Pour in the soy milk mixture and reserved pasta cooking liquid.
8. Bring to a boil, and reduce heat.
9. Stir in chopped capers and simmer 6-8 minutes or until creamy. Remove from the heat and stir in cooked pasta.
10. Toss the pasta gently to coat with the sauce.
11. Serve pasta, garnished with chopped parsley.

Nutrition:
Calories 489
Total Fat 23g
Total Carbohydrate 53.5g
Dietary Fiber 5.9g
Total Sugars 2.4g
Protein 20.4g

234. Lentils Salad With Lemon Tahini Dressing

Preparation time: 10 minutes
Cooking time: 30 minutes
Servings: 4
Ingredients:

- 225g green lentils, picked, rinsed
- 1 clove garlic, minced
- ¼ teaspoon ground cumin
- 5ml olive oil
- 1 red onion, finely diced
- 75g dried apricots, chopped
- 1 small red bell pepper, seeded, chopped
- 1 small green bell pepper, seeded, chopped
- 1 small yellow bell pepper, seeded, chopped
- 1 small cucumber, diced
- 20g sunflower seeds
- Salt and pepper, to taste

Lemon dressing:
- 1 lemon, juiced
- 30g tahini
- 5g chopped coriander
- Salt, to taste

Directions:
1. Place rinsed lentils in a saucepan.
2. Add enough water to cover.
3. Bring to a boil and skim off any foam. Add garlic and cumin.
4. Reduce heat and simmer the lentils for 30 minutes.
5. In the meantime, make the dressing by combining all the ingredients together.
6. Heat olive oil in a skillet. Add onion and bell peppers. Cooking Time: stirring over medium-high heat for 5 minutes.
7. Remove from the heat.
8. Drain the lentils and toss in a large bowl with the cooked vegetables, apricots, cucumber, and sunflower seeds. Season to taste.
9. Drizzle with dressing and serve.

Nutrition:
Calories 318
Total Fat 7g
Total Carbohydrate 49.2g
Dietary Fiber 20.8g

Total Sugars 7.9g
Protein 18.1g

235. Spanish Chickpea Spinach Stew

Preparation time: 10 minutes
Cooking time: 25 minutes
Servings: 4
Ingredients:

- *1 splash olive oil*
- *1 small onion, chopped*
- *2 cloves garlic*
- *5g cumin powder*
- *5g smoked paprika*
- *¼ teaspoon chili powder*
- *235ml water*
- *670g can diced tomatoes*
- *165g cooked chickpeas (or can chickpeas*
- *60g baby spinach*
- *Salt, to taste*
- *A handful of chopped coriander, to garnish*
- *20g slivered almonds, to garnish*
- *4 slices toasted whole-grain bread, to serve with*

Directions:

1. *Heat olive oil in a saucepan over medium-high heat.*
2. *Add onion and Cooking Time: until browned, for 7-8 minutes.*
3. *Add garlic, cumin, paprika, and chili powder.*
4. *Cooking Time: 1 minute.*
5. *Add water and scrape any browned bits.*
6. *Add the tomatoes and chickpeas. Season to taste and reduce heat.*
7. *Simmer the soup for 10 minutes.*
8. *Stir in spinach and Cooking Time: 2 minutes.*
9. *Ladle soup in a bowl. Sprinkle with cilantro and almonds.*
10. *Serve with toasted bread slices.*

Nutrition:
Calories 369
Total Fat 9.7g
Total Carbohydrate 67.9g
Dietary Fiber 19.9g
Total Sugars 13.9g
Protein 18g

236. Lentils Bolognese With Soba Noodles

Preparation time: 10 minutes
Cooking time: 15 minutes (plus 25 for lentils
Servings: 4
Ingredients:

Bolognese:

- *100g red lentils*
- *1 bay leaf*
- *Splash of olive oil*
- *1 small onion, diced*
- *1 large stalk celery, sliced*
- *3 cloves garlic, minced*
- *230ml tomato sauce or fresh pureed tomatoes*
- *60ml red wine or vegetable stock (if you do not like wine*
- *1 tablespoon fresh basil, chopped*
- *Salt and pepper, to taste*

Soba noodles:

- *280g soba noodles*

Directions:

1. *Cooking Time: the lentils; place lentils and bay leaf in a saucepan.*
2. *Cover with water, so the water is 2-inches above the lentils.*
3. *Bring to a boil over medium-high heat.*
4. *Reduce heat and simmer the lentils for 25 minutes.*
5. *Drain the lentils and discard the bay leaf.*
6. *Heat a splash of olive oil in a saucepan.*
7. *Add onion, and Cooking Time: 6 minutes.*
8. *Add celery and Cooking Time: 2 minutes.*
9. *Add garlic and Cooking Time: 2*

minutes.
10. Add the tomatoes and wine. Simmer the mixture for 5 minutes.
11. Stir in the lentils and simmer 2 minutes.
12. Remove the Bolognese from the heat and stir in basil.
13. In the meantime, Cooking Time: the soba noodles according to package directions.
14. Serve noodles with lentils Bolognese.

Nutrition:
Calories 353
Total Fat 0.9g
Total Carbohydrate 74g
Dietary Fiber 9g
Total Sugars 4.2g
Protein 17.7g

237. Red Burgers

Preparation time: 10 minutes
Cooking time: 50 minutes
Servings: 4
Ingredients:
Patties:
- 2 large beets, peeled, cubed
- 1 red onion, cut into chunks
- 115g red kidney beans
- 85g red cooked quinoa
- 2 cloves garlic, minced
- 30g almond meal
- 20g ground flax
- 10ml lemon juice
- ½ teaspoon ground cumin
- ½ teaspoon red pepper flakes
- Salt, to taste
- 4 whole-meal burger buns

Tahini Guacamole:
- 1 avocado, pitted, peeled
- 45ml lime juice
- 30g tahini sauce
- 5g chopped coriander

Directions:
1. Preheat oven to 190C/375F.
2. Toss beet and onion with a splash of olive oil.
3. Season with salt. Bake the beets for 30 minutes.
4. Transfer the beets and onion into a food blender.
5. Add the beans and blend until coarse. You do not want a completely smooth mixture.
6. Stir in quinoa, garlic, almond meal, flax seeds, lemon juice, cumin, and red pepper flakes.
7. Shape the mixture into four patties.
8. Transfer the patties to a baking sheet, lined with parchment paper.
9. Bake the patties 20 minutes, flipping halfway through.
10. In the meantime, make the tahini guac; mash the avocado with lime juice in a bowl.
11. Stir in tahini and coriander. Season to taste.
12. To serve; place the patty in the bun, top with guacamole and serve.

Nutrition:
Calories 343
Total Fat 16.6g
Total Carbohydrate 49.1g
Dietary Fiber 14.4g
Total Sugars 8.1g
Protein 15g

238. Hemp Falafel With Tahini Sauce

Preparation time: 10 minutes
Cooking time: 10 minutes
Servings: 6
Ingredients:
- 80g raw hemp hearts
- 4g chopped cilantro
- 4g chopped basil
- 2 cloves garlic, minced
- 2g ground cumin seeds
- 3g chili powder
- 14g flax meal + 30ml filtered water
- Sea salt and pepper, to taste
- Avocado or coconut oil, to fry

Sauce:
- 115g tahini
- 60ml fresh lime juice
- 115ml filtered water
- 30ml extra-virgin olive oil
- Sea salt, to taste
- A good pinch ground cumin seeds

Directions:
1. Mix flax with filtered water in a small bowl.
2. Place aside for 10 minutes.
3. In meantime, combine raw hemp hearts, cilantro, basil, garlic, cumin, chili, and seasonings in a food processor.
4. Process until just comes together. Add the flax seeds mixture and process until finely blended and uniform.
5. Heat approximately 2 tablespoons avocado oil in a skillet. Shape 1 tablespoon mixture into balls and fry for 3-4 minutes or until deep golden brown.
6. Remove from the skillet and place on a plate lined with paper towels.
7. Make the sauce; combine all ingredients in a food blender. Blend until smooth and creamy.
8. Serve falafel with fresh lettuce salad and tahini sauce.

Nutrition:
Calories 347
Total Fat 29.9g
Total Carbohydrate 7.2g
Dietary Fiber 4.3g
Total Sugars 0.2g
Protein 13.8g

239. Tempeh Skewers With Dressing

Preparation time: 20 minutes
Cooking time: 10 minutes
Servings: 6

Ingredients:
- 445g tempeh, cut into fingers
- 155ml unsweetened almond milk
- 100g almond flour
- 8g paprika
- 4g garlic powder
- 3g dried basil
- Salt and pepper, to taste
- 15ml olive oil

Finger sauce:
- 60ml melted coconut oil
- 80g hot sauce
- 10 drops Stevia

Dressing:
- 230g vegan mayonnaise
- 115g vegan sour cream
- 1 clove garlic, minced
- 2g chopped dill
- 2g chopped chives
- 1g onion powder
- Salt and pepper, to taste

Directions:
1. Cut the tempeh into slices/fingers. Arrange onto bamboo skewers, soaked in water 30 minutes.
2. Bring a pot of water to a boil. Add tempeh and boil 15 minutes. Drain and place aside.
3. Heat oven to 200C/400F.
4. Pour almond milk into a bowl. Combine almond flour and spices into a separate bowl.
5. Dip the tempeh into almond milk, and coat with the almond flour mixture.
6. Grease baking sheet with coconut oil. Arrange the tempeh fingers onto a baking sheet.
7. Bake the tempeh 10 minutes. In the meantime, make the sauce.
8. Melt coconut oil in a saucepan. Add hot sauce and simmer 5 minutes. Add Stevia and remove from the heat.
9. Make the dressing by combining all ingredients together.
10. Toss the tempeh with hot sauce. Serve with prepared dressing.

Nutrition:

Calories 351
Total Fat 29.3g
Total Carbohydrate 9.9g
Dietary Fiber 1g
Total Sugars 0.2g
Protein 15.5g

240. White Bean Salad With Spicy Sauce

Preparation time: 15 minutes
Servings: 4
Ingredients:

- *450g can white beans, rinsed, drained or cooked beans*
- *1 avocado, peeled, chopped*
- *6 cherry tomatoes, quartered*
- *1 red onion, thinly sliced*

Sauce:

- *80g cashews, soaked in water 4 hours*
- *30ml extra-virgin olive oil*
- *30ml lemon juice*
- *70ml water*
- *10g Dijon mustard*
- *5g pure maple syrup*
- *1 clove garlic*
- *½ teaspoon cayenne pepper*
- *½ teaspoon paprika powder*
- *1 pinch salt*

Directions:

1. *Make the sauce; rinse and drain cashews and place in a food processor.*
2. *Add the remaining ingredients, olive oil, lemon juice, water, mustard, garlic, cayenne, paprika, and salt.*
3. *Process until smooth and creamy. Place aside.*
4. *Make the salad; prepared vegetables as described.*
5. *Toss the beans with avocado, cherry tomatoes, and red onion.*
6. *Drizzle with prepared dressing and toss once again.*
7. *Serve or refrigerate before serving.*

Nutrition:

Calories 366
Total Fat 24.2g
Total Carbohydrate 31.9g
Dietary Fiber 9.5g
Total Sugars 5.6g
Protein 11g

241. Stuffed Sweet Hummus Potatoes

Preparation time: 10 minutes
Cooking time: 15 minutes
Servings: 4
Ingredients:

- *4 large sweet potatoes*
- *10ml olive oil*
- *200g kale, stems removed, chopped*
- *300g can black beans, drained, rinsed*
- *240g hummus*
- *60ml water*
- *5g garlic powder*
- *Salt and pepper, to taste*
- *Sour cream:*
- *100g raw cashews, soaked in water for 4 hours*
- *80ml water*
- *15ml raw cider vinegar*
- *15ml lemon juice*
- *1 pinch salt*

Directions:

1. *Prick sweet potato with a fork or toothpick all over the surface.*
2. *Wrap the potato in a damp paper towel and place in a microwave.*
3. *Microwave the sweet potato 10 minutes or until fork tender.*
4. *In the meantime, heat olive oil in a skillet.*
5. *Add kale and Cooking Time: with a pinch of salt until wilted.*
6. *Add black beans and Cooking Time: 2 minutes.*
7. *Make the sour cream; combine all sour cream ingredients in a food processor.*
8. *Process until creamy. Chill briefly*

before serving.

9. Make a slit in each sweet potato.
10. Combine hummus, water, and garlic powder in a bowl.
11. Stuff potato with the kale-bean mixture. Top the sweet potato with hummus and a dollop of sour cream.
12. Serve.

Nutrition:
Calories 540
Total Fat 20.3g2
Total Carbohydrate 78.1g
Dietary Fiber 14.9g
Total Sugars 3g
Protein 16.6g

242. Crusted Tofu Steaks With Caramelized Onion

Preparation time: 15 minutes
Cooking time: 45 minutes
Servings: 4
Ingredients:
- 450g tofu, cut into 8 steaks/slices
- 100g graham crackers
- 80g raw cashews
- 230ml unsweetened soy milk
- 120g whole-wheat flour
- 10g garlic powder
- 10g onion powder
- 10g chili powder
- 5g lemon pepper
- 15ml olive oil
- Salt, to taste

Onion:
- 15ml grapeseed oil
- 1 large onion
- 15ml balsamic vinegar
- 15ml lemon juice
- 15ml water
- 15g maple sugar

Directions:
1. Make the tofu; preheat oven to 200C/400F and line a baking sheet with parchment paper.
2. Combine graham crackers and cashews in a food processor.
3. Process unto coarse crumbs form.
4. Transfer to a large bowl.
5. In a separate bowl, combine flour, garlic and onion powder, chili, and lemon pepper.
6. Pour the soy milk into a third bowl.
7. Coat tofu with flour, dip into milk and finally coat with the graham cracker crumbs.
8. Arrange the tofu steaks onto a baking sheet.
9. Bake the tofu for 15-20 minutes or until golden brown.
10. In the meantime, make the onion; heat grapeseed oil in a skillet.
11. Add onion and Cooking Time: over medium-high heat for 8 minutes.
12. Add balsamic, lemon juice, and maple sugar. Cooking Time: 2 minutes.
13. Add water and reduce heat. Simmer 15 minutes.
14. Serve tofu steaks with caramelized onions.

Nutrition:
Calories 617
Total Fat 29.5g
Total Carbohydrate 70.6g
Dietary Fiber 5.8g
Total Sugars 17g
Protein 23.6g

243. Spicy Beans And Rice

Preparation time: 10 minutes
Cooking time: 1 hour 10 minutes
Servings: 6
Ingredients:
- 450g dry red kidney beans, soaked overnight
- 15ml olive oil
- 1 onion, diced
- 1 red bell pepper, seeded, diced
- 1 large stalk celery, sliced
- 4 cloves garlic, minced
- 15ml hot sauce
- 5g paprika

- *2g dried thyme*
- *2 g parsley, chopped*
- *2 bay leaves*
- *900ml vegetable stock*
- *280g brown rice*
- *Salt and pepper, to taste*

Directions:
1. Drain the beans and place aside.
2. Heat olive oil in a saucepot.
3. Add onion and bell pepper. Cooking Time: 6 minutes.
4. Add celery and Cooking Time: 3 minutes.
5. Add garlic, hot sauce, paprika, and thyme. Cooking Time: 1 minute.
6. Add the drained beans, bay leaves, and vegetable stock.
7. Bring to a boil, and reduce heat.
8. Simmer the beans for 1 hour 15 minutes or until tender.
9. In the meantime, place rice in a small saucepot. Cover the rice with 4cm water.
10. Season to taste and Cooking Time: the rice until tender, for 25 minutes.
11. To serve; transfer ¼ of the beans into a food processor. Process until smooth.
12. Combine the processed beans with the remaining beans and ladle into a bowl.
13. Add rice and sprinkle with parsley before serving.

Nutrition:
Calories 469
Total Fat 6g
Total Carbohydrate 87.5g
Dietary Fiber 14.2g
Total Sugars 4.9g
Protein 21.1g

244. Chili Quinoa Stuffed Peppers

Preparation time: 15 minutes
Cooking time: 1 hour 5 minutes
Servings: 4

Ingredients:
- *160g quinoa*
- *460ml vegetable stock*
- *2 red bell peppers, cut in half, seeds and membrane removed*
- *2 yellow bell peppers, cut in half, seeds, and membrane removed*
- *120g salsa*
- *15g nutritional yeast*
- *10g chili powder*
- *5g cumin powder*
- *425g can black beans, rinsed, drained*
- *160g fresh corn kernels*
- *Salt and pepper, to taste*
- *1 small avocado, sliced*
- *15g chopped cilantro*

Directions:
1. Preheat oven to 190C/375F.
2. Brush the baking sheet with some cooking oil.
3. Combine quinoa and vegetable stock in a saucepan. Bring to a boil.
4. Reduce heat and simmer 20 minutes.
5. Transfer the quinoa to a large bowl.
6. Stir in salsa, nutritional yeast, chili powder, cumin powder, black beans, and corn. Season to taste with salt and pepper.
7. Stuff the bell pepper halves with prepared mixture.
8. Transfer the peppers onto a baking sheet, cover with aluminum foil, and bake for 30 minutes.
9. Increase heat to 200C/400F and bake the peppers for an additional 15 minutes.
10. Serve warm, topped with avocado slices, and chopped cilantro.

Nutrition:
Calories 456
Total Fat 15.4g
Total Carbohydrate 71.1g
Dietary Fiber 15.8g
Total Sugars 8.2g
Protein 17.4g

245. Spinach With Walnuts & Avocado

Preparation Time: 5 minutes
Cooking Time: 0 minute
Servings: 1

Ingredients:

- 3 cups baby spinach
- ½ cup strawberries, sliced
- 1 tablespoon white onion, chopped
- 2 tablespoons vinaigrette
- ¼ medium avocado, diced
- 2 tablespoons walnut, toasted

Directions:

1. Put the spinach, strawberries and onion in a glass jar with lid.
2. Drizzle dressing on top.
3. Top with avocado and walnuts.
4. Seal the lid and refrigerate until ready to serve.

Nutritional Value:
Calories 296
Total Fat 18 g
Saturated Fat 2 g
Cholesterol 0 mg
Sodium 195 mg
Total Carbohydrate 27 g
Dietary Fiber 10 g
Total Sugars 11 g
Protein 8 g
Potassium 103 mg

246. Vegan Tacos

Preparation Time: 20 minutes
Cooking Time: 10 minutes
Servings: 4

Ingredients:

- ½ teaspoon onion powder
- ½ teaspoon garlic powder
- 1 teaspoon chili powder
- 2 tablespoons tamari
- 16 oz. tofu, drained and crumbled
- 1 tablespoon olive oil
- 1 ripe avocado
- 1 tablespoon vegan mayonnaise
- 1 teaspoon lime juice
- Salt to taste
- 8 corn tortillas, warmed
- ½ cup fresh salsa
- 2 cups iceberg lettuce, shredded
- Pickled radishes

Directions:

1. Combine the onion powder, garlic powder, chili powder and tamari in a bowl.
2. Marinate the tofu in the mixture for 10 minutes.
3. Pour the oil in a pan over medium heat.
4. Cooking Time: the tofu mixture for 10 minutes.
5. In another bowl, mash the avocado and mix with mayo, lime juice and salt.
6. Stuff each corn tortilla with tofu mixture, mashed avocado, salsa and lettuce.
7. Serve with pickled radishes.

Nutritional Value:
Calories 360
Total Fat 21 g
Saturated Fat 3 g
Cholesterol 0 mg
Sodium 610 mg
Total Carbohydrate 33 g
Dietary Fiber 8 g
Total Sugars 4 g
Protein 17 g
Potassium 553 mg

247. Grilled Broccoli with Chili Garlic Oil

Preparation Time: 15 minutes
Cooking Time: 16 minutes
Servings: 4

Ingredients:

- 3 tablespoons olive oil, divided
- 2 tablespoons vegetable broth (unsalted
- 2 cloves garlic, sliced thinly
- 1 chili pepper, julienned
- 1 1/2 lb. broccoli, sliced into florets

- Salt and pepper to taste
- 2 lemons, sliced in half

Directions:
1. Preheat your grill to medium-high.
2. In a bowl, mix 1 tablespoon oil, garlic, broth and chili.
3. Heat in a pan over medium heat for 30 seconds.
4. In another bowl, toss the broccoli florets in salt, pepper and remaining oil.
5. Grill the broccoli florets for 10 minutes.
6. Grill the lemon slices for 5 minutes.
7. Toss the grilled broccoli and lemon in chili garlic oil.
8. Store in a food container and reheat before serving.

Nutritional Value:
Calories 164
Total Fat 11 g
Saturated Fat 1 g
Cholesterol 0 mg
Sodium 208 mg
Total Carbohydrate 12 g
Dietary Fiber 2 g
Total Sugars 4 g
Protein 6 g
Potassium 519 mg

248. Tomato Basil Pasta

Preparation Time: 5 minutes
Cooking Time: 10 minutes
Servings: 4
Ingredients:
- 2 cups low-sodium vegetable broth
- 2 cups water
- 8 oz. pasta
- 1 ½ teaspoons Italian seasoning
- 15 oz. canned diced tomatoes
- 2 tablespoons olive oil
- ½ teaspoon garlic powder
- ½ teaspoon onion powder
- ¼ teaspoon crushed red pepper
- ½ teaspoon salt
- 6 cups baby spinach
- ½ cup basil, chopped

Directions:
1. Add all the ingredients except spinach and basil in a pot over high heat.
2. Mix well.
3. Cover the pot and bring to a boil.
4. Reduce the heat.
5. Simmer for 5 minutes.
6. Add the spinach and Cooking Time: for 5 more minutes.
7. Stir in basil.
8. Transfer to a food container.
9. Microwave before serving.

Nutritional Value:
Calories 339
Total Fat 10 g
Saturated Fat 1 g
Cholesterol 0 mg
Sodium 465 mg
Total Carbohydrate 55 g
Dietary Fiber 8 g
Total Sugars 6 g
Protein 11 g
Potassium 308 mg

249. Risotto With Tomato & Herbs

Preparation Time: 10 minutes
Cooking Time: 20 minutes
Servings: 32
Ingredients:
- 2 oz. Arborio rice
- 1 teaspoon dried garlic, minced
- 3 tablespoons dried onion, minced
- 1 tablespoon dried Italian seasoning, crushed
- ¾ cup snipped dried tomatoes
- 1 ½ cups reduced-sodium chicken broth

Directions:
1. Make the dry risotto mix by combining all the ingredients except broth in a large bowl.
2. Divide the mixture into eight

resealable plastic bags. Seal the bag.
3. *Store at room temperature for up to 3 months.*
4. *When ready to serve, pour the broth in a pot.*
5. *Add the contents of 1 plastic bag of dry risotto mix.*
6. *Bring to a boil and then reduce heat.*
7. *Cover the pot and simmer for 20 minutes.*
8. *Serve with vegetables.*

Nutritional Value:
Calories 80
Total Fat 0 g
Saturated Fat 0 g
Cholesterol 0 mg
Sodium 276 mg
Total Carbohydrate 17 g
Dietary Fiber 2 g
Total Sugars 0 g
Protein 3 g
Potassium 320 mg

250. Tofu Shawarma Rice

Preparation Time: 15 minutes
Cooking Time: 15 minutes
Servings: 4
Ingredients:
- *4 cups cooked brown rice*
- *4 cups cooked tofu, sliced into small cubes*
- *4 cups cucumber, cubed*
- *4 cups tomatoes, cubed*
- *4 cups white onion, cubed*
- *2 cups cabbage, shredded*
- *1/2 cup vegan mayo*
- *1/8 cup garlic, minced*
- *Garlic salt to taste*
- *Hot sauce*

Directions:
1. *Add brown rice into 4 food containers.*
2. *Arrange tofu, cucumber, tomatoes, white onion and cabbage on top.*
3. *In a bowl, mix the mayo, garlic, and garlic salt.*
4. *Drizzle top with garlic sauce and hot sauce before serving.*

Nutritional Value:
Calories 667
Total Fat 12.6g
Saturated Fat 2.2g
Cholesterol 0mg
Sodium 95mg
Total Carbohydrate 116.5g
Dietary Fiber 9.9g
Total Sugars 9.4g
Protein 26.1g
Potassium 1138mg

251. Pesto Pasta

Preparation Time: 10 minutes
Cooking Time: 8 minutes
Servings: 2
Ingredients:
- *1 cup fresh basil leaves*
- *4 cloves garlic*
- *2 tablespoons walnut*
- *2 tablespoons olive oil*
- *1 tablespoon vegan Parmesan cheese*
- *2 cups cooked penne pasta*
- *2 tablespoons black olives, sliced*

Directions:
1. *Put the basil leaves, garlic, walnut, olive oil and Parmesan cheese in a food processor.*
2. *Pulse until smooth.*
3. *Divide pasta into 2 food containers.*
4. *Spread the basil sauce on top.*
5. *Top with black olives.*
6. *Store until ready to serve.*

Nutritional Value:
Calories 374
Total Fat 21.1g
Saturated Fat 2.6g
Cholesterol 47mg
Sodium 92mg
Total Carbohydrate 38.6g
Dietary Fiber 1.1g
Total Sugars 0.2g
Protein 10g
Potassium 215mg

252. "Cheesy" Spinach Rolls

Preparation Time: 20 minutes
Cooking Time: 15 minutes
Servings: 6
Ingredients:
- 18 spinach leaves
- 18 vegan spring roll wrappers
- 6 slices cheese, cut into 18 smaller strips
- Water
- 1 cup vegetable oil
- 6 cups cauliflower rice
- 3 cups tomato, cubed
- 3 cups cucumber, cubed
- 1 tablespoon olive oil
- 1 teaspoon balsamic vinegar

Directions:
1. Place one spinach leaf on top of each wrapper.
2. Add a small strip of vegan cheese on top of each spinach leaf.
3. Roll the wrapper and seal the edges with water.
4. In a pan over medium high heat, add the vegetable oil.
5. Cooking Time: the rolls until golden brown.
6. Drain in paper towels.
7. Divide cauliflower rice into 6 food containers.
8. Add 3 cheesy spinach rolls in each food container.
9. Toss cucumber and tomato in olive oil and vinegar.
10. Place the cucumber tomato relish beside the rolls.
11. Seal and reheat in the microwave when ready to serve.

Nutritional Value:
Calories 746
Total Fat 38.5g
Saturated Fat 10.1g
Cholesterol 33mg
Sodium 557mg
Total Carbohydrate 86.2g
Dietary Fiber 3.8g
Total Sugars 2.6g
Protein 18g
Potassium 364mg

253. Grilled Summer Veggies

Preparation Time: 15 minutes
Cooking Time: 6 minutes
Servings: 6
Ingredients:
- 2 teaspoons cider vinegar
- 1 tablespoon olive oil
- ¼ teaspoon fresh thyme, chopped
- 1 teaspoon fresh parsley, chopped
- ¼ teaspoon fresh rosemary, chopped
- Salt and pepper to taste
- 1 onion, sliced into wedges
- 2 red bell peppers, sliced
- 3 tomatoes, sliced in half
- 6 large mushrooms, stems removed
- 1 eggplant, sliced crosswise
- 3 tablespoons olive oil
- 1 tablespoon cider vinegar

Directions:
1. Make the dressing by mixing the vinegar, oil, thyme, parsley, rosemary, salt and pepper.
2. In a bowl, mix the onion, red bell pepper, tomatoes, mushrooms and eggplant.
3. Toss in remaining olive oil and cider vinegar.
4. Grill over medium heat for 3 minutes.
5. Turn the vegetables and grill for another 3 minutes.
6. Arrange grilled vegetables in a food container.
7. Drizzle with the herbed mixture when ready to serve.

Nutritional Value:
Calories 127
Total Fat 9 g
Saturated Fat 1 g
Cholesterol 0 mg
Sodium 55 mg
Total Carbohydrate 11 g

Dietary Fiber 5 g
Total Sugars 5 g
Protein 3 g
Potassium 464 mg

254. Superfood Buddha Bowl

Preparation Time: 10 minutes
Cooking Time: 10 minutes
Servings: 4
Ingredients:

- *8 oz. microwavable quinoa*
- *2 tablespoons lemon juice*
- *½ cup hummus*
- *Water*
- *5 oz. baby kale*
- *8 oz. cooked baby beets, sliced*
- *1 cup frozen shelled edamame (thawed*
- *¼ cup sunflower seeds, toasted*
- *1 avocado, sliced*
- *1 cup pecans*
- *2 tablespoons flaxseeds*

Directions:
1. *Cooking Time: quinoa according to directions in the packaging.*
2. *Set aside and let cool.*
3. *In a bowl, mix the lemon juice and hummus.*
4. *Add water to achieve desired consistency.*
5. *Divide mixture into 4 condiment containers.*
6. *Cover containers with lids and put in the refrigerator.*
7. *Divide the baby kale into 4 food containers with lids.*
8. *Top with quinoa, beets, edamame and sunflower seeds.*
9. *Store in the refrigerator until ready to serve.*
10. *Before serving add avocado slices and hummus dressing.*

Nutritional Value:
Calories 381
Total Fat 19 g
Saturated Fat 2 g

Cholesterol 0 mg
Sodium 188 mg
Total Carbohydrate 43 g
Dietary Fiber 13 g
Total Sugars 8 g
Protein 16 g
Potassium 1,066 mg

255. Burrito & Cauliflower Rice Bowl

Preparation Time: 15 minutes
Cooking Time: 10 minutes
Servings: 4
Ingredients:

- *1 cup cooked tofu cubes*
- *12 oz. frozen cauliflower rice*
- *4 teaspoons olive oil*
- *1 teaspoon unsalted taco seasoning*
- *1 cup red cabbage, sliced thinly*
- *½ cup salsa*
- *¼ cup fresh cilantro, chopped*
- *1 cup avocado, diced*

Directions:
1. *Prepare cauliflower rice according to directions in the package.*
2. *Toss cauliflower rice in olive oil and taco seasoning.*
3. *Divide among 4 food containers with lid.*
4. *Top with tofu, cabbage, salsa and cilantro.*
5. *Seal the container and chill in the refrigerator until ready to serve.*
6. *Before serving, add avocado slices.*

Nutritional Value:
Calories 298
Total Fat 20 g
Saturated Fat 3 g
Cholesterol 0 mg
Sodium 680 mg
Total Carbohydrate 15 g
Dietary Fiber 6 g
Total Sugars 5 g
Protein 15 g
Potassium 241 mg

256. Seitan Zoodle Bowl

Preparation Time: 15 minutes
Cooking Time: 13 minutes
Servings: 4
Ingredients:

- 5 garlic cloves, minced, divided
- ¼ tsp pureed onion
- Salt and ground black pepper to taste
- 2 ½ lb Seitan, cut into strips
- 2 tbsp avocado oil
- 3 large eggs, lightly beaten
- ¼ cup vegetable broth
- 2 tbsp coconut aminos
- 1 tbsp white vinegar
- ½ cup freshly chopped scallions
- 1 tsp red chili flakes
- 4 medium zucchinis, spiralized
- ½ cup toasted pine nuts, for topping

Directions:

1. In a medium bowl, combine the half of the pureed garlic, onion, salt, and black pepper. Add the seitan and mix well.
2. Heat the avocado oil in a large, deep skillet over medium heat and add the seitan. Cooking Time: for 8 minutes. Transfer to a plate.
3. Pour the eggs into the pan and scramble for 1 minute. Spoon the eggs to the side of the seitan and set aside.
4. Reduce the heat to low and in a medium bowl, mix the vegetable broth, coconut aminos, vinegar, scallions, remaining garlic, and red chili flakes. Mix well and simmer for 3 minutes.
5. Stir in the seitan, zucchini, and eggs. Cooking Time: for 1 minute and turn the heat off. Adjust the taste with salt and black pepper.
6. Spoon the zucchini food into serving plates, top with the pine nuts and serve warm.

Nutrition:
Calories:687, Total Fat:54.5g, Saturated Fat:27.4g, Total Carbs:9g, Dietary Fiber:2g, Sugar:4g, Protein:38g, Sodium:883mg

257. Tofu Parsnip Bake

Preparation Time: 5 minutes
Cooking Time: 44 minutes
Servings: 4
Ingredients:

- 6 vegan bacon slices, chopped
- 2 tbsp butter
- ½ lb parsnips, peeled and diced
- 2 tbsp olive oil
- 1 lb ground tofu
- Salt and ground black pepper to taste
- 2 tbsp butter
- 1 cup full-fat heavy creaminutes
- 2 oz dairy-free cream cheese (vegan), softened
- 1 ¼ cups grated cheddar cheese
- ¼ cup chopped scallions

Directions:

1. Preheat the oven to 300 F and lightly grease a baking dish with cooking spray. Set aside.
2. Put the vegan bacon in a medium pot and fry on both sides until brown and crispy, 7 minutes. Spoon onto a plate and set aside.
3. Melt the butter in a large skillet and sauté the parsnips until softened and lightly browned. Transfer to the baking sheet and set aside.
4. Heat the olive oil in the same pan and Cooking Time: the tofu (seasoned with salt and black pepper). Spoon onto a plate and set aside too.
5. Add the butter, full-fat heavy cream, cashew cream, two-thirds of the cheddar cheese, salt, and black pepper to the pot. Melt the Ingredients over medium heat with frequent stirring, 7 minutes.
6. Spread the parsnips in the baking dish, top with the tofu, pour the full-fat heavy cream mixture over, and

scatter the top with the vegan bacon and scallions.

7. Sprinkle the remaining cheese on top, and bake in the oven until the cheese melts and is golden, 30 minutes.
8. Remove the dish, spoon the food into serving plates, and serve immediately.

Nutrition:
Calories:534, Total Fat:56g, Saturated Fat:34.6g, Total Carbs:4g, Dietary Fiber:1g, Sugar:1g, Protein:7g, Sodium:430mg

258. Squash Tempeh Lasagna

Preparation Time: 15 minutes
Cooking Time: 40 minutes
Servings: 4
Ingredients:

- 2 tbsp butter
- 1 ½ lb ground tempeh
- Salt and ground black pepper to taste
- 1 tsp garlic powder
- 1 tsp onion powder
- 2 tbsp coconut flour
- 1 ½ cup grated mozzarella cheese
- 1/3 cup parmesan cheese
- 2 cups crumbled cottage cheese
- 1 large egg, beaten into a bowl
- 2 cups unsweetened marinara sauce
- 1 tbsp dried Italian mixed herbs
- ¼ tsp red chili flakes
- 4 large yellow squash, sliced
- ¼ cup fresh basil leaves

Directions:

1. Preheat the oven to 375 F and grease a baking dish with cooking spray. Set aside.
2. Melt the butter in a large skillet over medium heat and Cooking Time: the tempeh until brown, 10 minutes. Set aside to cool.
3. In a medium bowl, mix the garlic powder, onion powder, coconut flour, salt, black pepper, mozzarella cheese, half of the parmesan cheese, cottage cheese, and egg. Set aside.
4. In another bowl, combine the marinara sauce, mixed herbs, and red chili flakes. Set aside.
5. Make a single layer of the squash slices in the baking dish; spread a quarter of the egg mixture on top, a layer of the tempeh, then a quarter of the marinara sauce. Repeat the layering process in the same ingredient proportions and sprinkle the top with the remaining parmesan cheese.
6. Bake in the oven until golden brown on top, 30 minutes.
7. Remove the dish from the oven, allow cooling for 5 minutes, garnish with the basil leaves, slice and serve.

Nutrition:
Calories:194, Total Fat:17.4g, Saturated Fat:2.1g, Total Carbs:7g, Dietary Fiber:3g, Sugar:2g, Protein:7g, Sodium:72mg

259. Bok Choy Tofu Skillet

Preparation Time: 10 minutes
Cooking Time: 18 minutes
Servings: 4
Ingredients:

- 2 lb tofu, cut into 1-inch cubes
- Salt and ground black pepper to taste
- 4 vegan bacon slices, chopped
- 1 tbsp coconut oil
- 1 orange bell pepper, deseeded, cut into chunks
- 2 cups baby bok choy
- 2 tbsp freshly chopped oregano
- 2 garlic cloves, pressed

Directions:

1. Season the tofu with salt and black pepper, and set aside.
2. Heat a large skillet over medium heat and fry the vegan bacon until brown and crispy. Transfer to a plate.
3. Melt the coconut oil in the skillet

and Cooking Time: the tofu until golden-brown and cooked through, 10 minutes. Remove onto the vegan bacon plate and set aside.
4. Add the bell pepper and bok choy to the skillet and sauté until softened, 5 minutes. Stir in the vegan bacon, tofu, oregano, and garlic. Season with salt and black pepper and Cooking Time: for 3 minutes or until the flavors incorporate. Turn the heat off.
5. Plate the dish and serve with cauliflower rice.

Nutrition:
Calories:273, Total Fat:18.7g, Saturated Fat:7.9g, Total Carbs:15g, Dietary Fiber:4g, Sugar:8g, Protein:15g, Sodium:341mg

260. Quorn Sausage Frittata

Preparation Time: 10 minutes
Cooking Time: 33 minutes
Servings: 4
Ingredients:

- 12 whole eggs
- 1 cup plain unsweetened yogurt
- Salt and ground black pepper to taste
- 1 tbsp butter
- 1 celery stalk, chopped
- 12 oz quorn sausages
- ¼ cup shredded cheddar cheese

Directions:
1. Preheat the oven to 350 F.
2. In a medium bowl, whisk the eggs, plain yogurt, salt, and black pepper.
3. Melt the butter in a large (safe ovenskillet over medium heat. Sauté the celery until soft, 5 minutes. Transfer the celery into a plate and set aside.
4. Add the quorn sausages to the skillet and Cooking Time: until brown with frequent stirring to break the lumps that form, 8 minutes.
5. Flatten the quorn sausage in the bottom of the skillet using the spoon, scatter the celery on top, pour the egg mixture all over, and sprinkle with the cheddar cheese.
6. Put the skillet in the oven and bake until the eggs set and cheese melts, 20 minutes.
7. Remove the skillet, slice the frittata, and serve warm with kale salad.

Nutrition:
Calories:293, Total Fat:27.9g, Saturated Fat:2.9g, Total Carbs:11g, Dietary Fiber:4g, Sugar:2g, Protein:5g, Sodium:20mg

261. Jamaican Jerk Tempeh

Preparation Time: 15 minutes
Cooking Time: 45 minutes
Servings: 4
Ingredients:

- ½ cup plain unsweetened yogurt
- 2 tbsp melted butter
- 2 tbsp Jamaican jerk seasoning
- Salt and black pepper to taste
- 2 lb tempeh
- 3 tbsp tofu
- ¼ cup almond meal

Directions:
1. Preheat the oven to 350 F and grease a baking sheet with cooking spray.
2. In a large bowl, combine the plain yogurt, butter, Jamaican jerk seasoning, salt, and black pepper. Add the tempeh and toss to coat evenly. Allow marinating for 15 minutes.
3. In a food processor, blend the tofu with the almond meal until finely combined. Pour the mixture onto a wide plate.
4. Remove the tempeh from the marinade, shake off any excess liquid, and coat generously in the tofu mixture. Place on the baking sheet and grease lightly with cooking spray.
5. Bake in the oven for 40 to 45 minutes or until golden brown and crispy, turning once.

6. Remove the tempeh and serve warm with red cabbage slaw and parsnip fries.

Nutrition:
Calories:684, Total Fat:68g, Saturated Fat:12.1g, Total Carbs:13g, Dietary Fiber:4g, Sugar:1g, Protein:13g, Sodium:653mg

262. Zucchini Seitan Stacks

Preparation Time: 15 minutes
Cooking Time: 18 minutes
Servings: 4

Ingredients:

- 1 ½ lb seitan
- 3 tbsp almond flour
- Salt and black pepper to taste
- 2 large zucchinis, cut into 2-inch slices
- 4 tbsp olive oil
- 2 tsp Italian mixed herb blend
- ½ cup vegetable broth

Directions:

1. Preheat the oven to 400 F.
2. Cut the seitan into strips and set aside.
3. In a zipper bag, add the almond flour, salt, and black pepper. Mix and add the seitan slices. Seal the bag and shake to coat the seitan with the seasoning.
4. Grease a baking sheet with cooking spray and arrange the zucchinis on the baking sheet. Season with salt and black pepper, and drizzle with 2 tablespoons of olive oil.
5. Using tongs, remove the seitan from the almond flour mixture, shake off the excess flour, and put two to three seitan strips on each zucchini.
6. Season with the herb blend and drizzle again with olive oil.
7. Cooking Time: in the oven for 8 minutes; remove the sheet and carefully pour in the vegetable broth. Bake further for 5 to 10 minutes or until the seitan cooks through.
8. Remove from the oven and serve warm with low carb bread.

Nutrition:
Calories:582, Total Fat:49.7g, Saturated Fat:18.4g, Total Carbs:8g, Dietary Fiber:3g, Sugar:2g, Protein:31g, Sodium:385mg

263. Curried Tofu Meatballs

Preparation Time: 5 minutes
Cooking Time: 25 minutes
Servings: 4

Ingredients:

- 3 lb ground tofu
- 1 medium yellow onion, finely chopped
- 2 green bell peppers, deseeded and chopped
- 3 garlic cloves, minced
- 2 tbsp melted butter
- 1 tsp dried parsley
- 2 tbsp hot sauce
- Salt and ground black pepper to taste
- 1 tbsp red curry powder
- 3 tbsp olive oil

Directions:

1. Preheat the oven to 400 F and grease a baking sheet with cooking spray.
2. In a bowl, combine the tofu, onion, bell peppers, garlic, butter, parsley, hot sauce, salt, black pepper, and curry powder. With your hands, form 1-inch tofu ball from the mixture and place on the greased baking sheet.
3. Drizzle the olive oil over the meat and bake in the oven until the tofu ball brown on the outside and Cooking Time: within, 20 to 25 minutes.
4. Remove the dish from the oven and plate the tofu ball.
5. Garnish with some scallions and serve warm on a bed of spinach salad with herbed vegan paneer cheese dressing.

Nutrition:

Calories:506, Total Fat:45.6g, Saturated Fat:18.9g, Total Carbs:11g, Dietary Fiber:1g, Sugar:1g, Protein:19g, Sodium:794mg

264. Spicy Mushroom Collard Wraps

Preparation Time: 10 minutes
Cooking Time: 16 minutes
Servings: 4
Ingredients:

- 2 tbsp avocado oil
- 1 large yellow onion, chopped
- 2 garlic cloves, minced
- Salt and ground black pepper to taste
- 1 small jalapeño pepper, deseeded and finely chopped
- 1 ½ lb mushrooms, cut into 1-inch cubes
- 1 cup cauliflower rice
- 2 tsp hot sauce
- 8 collard leaves
- ¼ cup plain unsweetened yogurt for topping

Directions:

1. Heat 2 tablespoons of avocado oil in a large deep skillet; add and sauté the onion until softened, 3 minutes.
2. Pour in the garlic, salt, black pepper, and jalapeño pepper; Cooking Time: until fragrant, 1 minute.
3. Mix in the mushrooms and Cooking Time: both sides, 10 minutes.
4. Add the cauliflower rice, and hot sauce. Sauté until the cauliflower slightly softens, 2 to 3 minutes. Adjust the taste with salt and black pepper.
5. Lay out the collards on a clean flat surface and spoon the curried mixture onto the middle part of the leaves, about 3 tablespoons per leaf. Spoon the plain yogurt on top, wrap the leaves, and serve immediately.

Nutrition:
Calories:380, Total Fat:34.8g, Saturated Fat:19.9g, Total Carbs:10g, Dietary Fiber:5g, Sugar:5g, Protein:10g, Sodium:395mg

265. Pesto Tofu Zoodles

Preparation Time: 5 minutes
Cooking Time: 12 minutes
Servings size 4
Ingredients:

- 2 tbsp olive oil
- 1 medium white onion, chopped
- 1 garlic clove, minced
- 2 (14 oz blocks firm tofu, pressed and cubed
- 1 medium red bell pepper, deseeded and sliced
- 6 medium zucchinis, spiralized
- Salt and black pepper to taste
- ¼ cup basil pesto, olive oil based
- 2/3 cup grated parmesan cheese
- ½ cup shredded mozzarella cheese
- Toasted pine nuts to garnish

Directions:

1. Heat the olive oil in a medium pot over medium heat; sauté the onion and garlic until softened and fragrant, 3 minutes.
2. Add the tofu and Cooking Time: until golden on all sides then pour in the bell pepper and Cooking Time: until softened, 4 minutes.
3. Mix in the zucchinis, pour the pesto on top, and season with salt and black pepper. Cooking Time: for 3 to 4 minutes or until the zucchinis soften a little bit. Turn the heat off and carefully stir in the parmesan cheese.
4. Dish into four plates, share the mozzarella cheese on top, garnish with the pine nuts, and serve warm.

Nutrition:
Calories:79, Total Fat:6.2g, Saturated Fat:3.7g, Total Carbs:5g, Dietary Fiber:2g, Sugar:3g, Protein:2g, Sodium:54mg

266. Cheesy Mushroom Pie

Preparation Time: 12 minutes
Cooking Time: 43 minutes
Servings: 4
Ingredients:

For the piecrust:
- ¼ cup almond flour + extra for dusting
- 3 tbsp coconut flour
- ½ tsp salt
- ¼ cup butter, cold and crumbled
- 3 tbsp erythritol
- 1 ½ tsp vanilla extract
- 4 whole eggs

For the filling:
- 2 tbsp butter
- 1 medium yellow onion
- 2 garlic cloves, minced
- 2 cups mixed mushrooms, chopped
- 1 green bell pepper, deseeded and diced
- 1 cup green beans, cut into 3 pieces each
- Salt and black pepper to taste
- ¼ cup coconut creaminutes
- 1/3 cup vegan sour creaminutes
- ½ cup almond milk
- 2 eggs, lightly beaten
- ¼ tsp nutmeg powder
- 1 tbsp chopped parsley
- 1 cup grated parmesan cheese

Directions:

For the pastry crust:
1. Preheat the oven to 350 F and grease a pie pan with cooking spray
2. In a large bowl, mix the almond flour, coconut flour, and salt.
3. Add the butter and mix with an electric hand mixer until crumbly. Add the erythritol and vanilla extract until mixed in. Then, pour in the eggs one after another while mixing until formed into a ball.
4. Flatten the dough a clean flat surface, cover in plastic wrap, and refrigerate for 1 hour.
5. After, lightly dust a clean flat surface with almond flour, unwrap the dough, and roll out the dough into a large rectangle, ½ - inch thickness and fit into a pie pan.
6. Pour some baking beans onto the pastry and bake in the oven until golden. Remove after, pour the beans, and allow cooling.

For the filling:
1. Meanwhile, melt the butter in a skillet and sauté the onion and garlic until softened and fragrant, 3 minutes. Add the mushrooms, bell pepper, green beans, salt and black pepper; Cooking Time: for 5 minutes.
2. In a medium bowl, beat the coconut cream, vegan sour cream, milk, and eggs. Season with black pepper, salt, and nutmeg. Stir in the parsley and cheese.
3. Spread the mushroom mixture in the baked pastry and spread the cheese filling on top. Place the pie in the oven and bake for 30 to 35 minutes or until a toothpick inserted into the pie comes out clean and golden on top.
4. Remove, let cool for 10 minutes, slice, and serve with roasted tomato salad.

Nutrition:
Calories:120, Total Fat:9.2g, Saturated Fat:2.3g, Total Carbs:7g, Dietary Fiber:3g, Sugar:3g, Protein:5g, Sodium:17mg

267. Tofu Scallopini With Lemon

Preparation Time: 5 minutes
Cooking Time: 21 minutes
Servings: 4
Ingredients:
- 1½ lb thin cut tofu chops, boneless
- Salt and ground black pepper to taste
- 1 tbsp avocado oil

- *3 tbsp butter*
- *2 tbsp capers*
- *1 cup vegetable broth*
- *½ lemon, juiced + 1 lemon, sliced*
- *2 tbsp freshly chopped parsley*

Directions:
1. Heat the avocado oil in a large skillet over medium heat. Season the tofu chops with salt and black pepper; Cooking Time: in the oil on both sides until brown and cooked through, 12 to 15 minutes. Transfer to a plate, cover with another plate, and keep warm.
2. Add the butter to the pan to melt and Cooking Time: the capers until hot and sizzling stirring frequently to avoid burning, 3 minutes.
3. Pour in the vegetable broth and lemon juice, use a spatula to scrape any bits stuck to the bottom of the pan, and allow boiling until the sauce reduces by half.
4. Add the tofu back to the sauce, arrange the lemon slices on top, and sprinkle with half of the parsley. Allow simmering for 3 minutes.
5. Plate the food, garnish with the remaining parsley, and serve warm with creamy mashed cauliflower.

Nutrition:
Calories:214, Total Fat:15.6g, Saturated Fat:2.5g, Total Carbs:12g, Dietary Fiber:2g, Sugar:6g, Protein:9g, Sodium:280mg

268. Tofu Chops With Green Beans And Avocado Sauté

Preparation Time: 10minutes
Cooking Time: 22 minutes
Servings: 4
Ingredients:

For the tofu chops:
- *2 tbsp avocado oil*
- *4 slices firm tofu*
- *Salt and ground black pepper to taste*

For the green beans and avocado sauté:
- *2 tbsp avocado oil*
- *1 ½ cups green beans*
- *2 large avocados, halved, pitted, and chopped*
- *Salt and ground black pepper to taste*
- *6 green onions, chopped*
- *1 tbsp freshly chopped parsley*

Directions:

For the tofu chops:
Heat the avocado oil in a medium skillet, season the tofu with salt and black pepper, and fry in the oil on both sides until brown, and cooked through, 12 to 15 minutes. Transfer to a plate and set aside in a warmer for serving.

For the green beans and avocado sauté:
1. Heat the avocado oil in a medium skillet, add and sauté the green beans until sweating and slightly softened, 10 minutes. Mix in the avocados (don't worry if they mash up a bit), season with salt and black pepper, and the half of the green onions. Warm the avocados for 2 minutes. Turn the heat off.
2. Dish the sauté into serving plates, garnish with the remaining green onions and parsley, and serve with the tofu chops.

Nutrition:
Calories:503, Total Fat:41.9g, Saturated Fat:14.5g, Total Carbs:18g, Dietary Fiber:2g, Sugar:4g, Protein:19g, Sodium:314mg

269. Mexican Quinoa And Lima Bean Bowls

Preparation Time: 30 minutes
Serving: 4
A bowl filled with Mexican flavors with lima beans and quinoa for the perfect combo! Full of flavors and spices.

Ingredients
- *1 tbsp olive oil*
- *1 lb extra firm tofu, pressed and cut into 1-inch cubes*

- Salt and black pepper to taste
- 1 medium yellow onion, finely diced
- ½ cup cauliflower florets
- 1 jalapeño pepper, minced
- 2 garlic cloves, minced
- 1 tbsp red chili powder
- 1 tsp cumin powder
- 1 (8 oz) can sweet corn kernels, drained
- 1 (8 oz) can lima beans, rinsed and drained
- 1 cup quick-cooking quinoa
- 1 (14 oz) can diced tomatoes
- 2 ½ cups vegetable broth
- 1 cup grated homemade plant-based cheddar cheese
- 2 tbsp chopped fresh cilantro
- 2 limes, cut into wedges for garnishing
- 1 medium avocado, pitted, sliced and peeled

Directions
1. Heat olive oil in a pot and Cooking Time: the tofu until golden brown, 5 minutes. Season with salt, pepper, and mix in onion, cauliflower, and jalapeño pepper. Cooking Time: until the vegetables soften, 3 minutes. Stir in garlic, chili powder, and cumin powder; Cooking Time: for 1 minute.
2. Mix in sweet corn kernels, lima beans, quinoa, tomatoes, and vegetable broth. Simmer until the quinoa absorbs all the liquid, 10 minutes. Fluff quinoa. Top with the plant-based cheddar cheese, cilantro, lime wedges, and avocado. Serve warm.

Nutrition:
Calories 414
Fats 20.3g | Carbs 45.9g
Protein 20.8g

270. Creole Tempeh Rice Bowls

Preparation Time: 50 minutes
Serving: 4
Tempeh with vegetable over rice makes it delicious and healthy.

Ingredients
- 2 tbsp olive oil
- 1 ½ cups crumbled tempeh
- 1 tsp Creole seasoning
- 2 red bell peppers, deseeded and sliced
- 1 cup brown rice
- 2 cups vegetable broth
- Salt to taste
- 1 lemon, zested and juiced
- 1 (8 oz) can black beans, drained and rinsed
- 2 chives, chopped
- 2 tbsp freshly chopped parsley

Directions
1. Heat the olive oil in a medium pot and Cooking Time: in the tempeh until golden brown, 5 minutes.
2. Season with the Creole seasoning and stir in the bell peppers. Cooking Time: until the peppers slightly soften, 3 minutes.
3. Stir in the brown rice, vegetable broth, salt, and lemon zest.
4. Cover and Cooking Time: until the rice is tender and all the liquid is absorbed, 15 to 25 minutes.
5. Mix in the lemon juice, beans, and chives. Allow warming for 3 to 5 minutes and dish the food.
6. Garnish with the parsley and serve warm.

Nutrition:
Calories 216
Fats 13.9g | Carbs 13.8g
Protein 12.7g

271. Seitan Pesto Panini

Preparation Time: 15 minutes + 30 minutes refrigeration
Serving: 4
This is a delicious panini made from all plant sources.

Ingredients

For the seitan:
- 2/3 cup basil pesto
- ½ lemon, juiced
- 1 garlic clove, minced
- 1/8 tsp salt
- 1 cup chopped seitan

For the panini:
- 3 tbsp basil pesto
- 8 thick slices whole-wheat ciabatta
- Olive oil for brushing
- 8 slices plant-based mozzarella cheese
- 1 small yellow bell pepper, deseeded and chopped
- ¼ cup grated Parmesan cheese

Directions

For the seitan:
1. In a medium bowl, mix the pesto, lemon juice, garlic, and salt. Add the seitan and coat well with the marinade. Cover with a plastic wrap and marinate in the refrigerator for 30 minutes.
2. Preheat a large skillet over medium heat and remove the seitan from the fridge. Cooking Time: the seitan in the skillet until brown and cooked through, 2 to 3 minutes. Turn the heat off.

To make the panini:
1. Preheat a panini press to medium heat. In a small bowl, mix the pesto in the inner parts of two slices of bread. On the outer parts, apply some olive oil and place a slice with (the olive oil side downin the press.
2. Lay 2 slices of plant-based mozzarella cheese on the bread, spoon some seitan on top. Sprinkle with some bell pepper, and some plant-based Parmesan cheese. Cover with another bread slice.
3. Close the press and grill the bread for 1 to 2 minutes. Flip the bread, and grill further for 1 minute or until the cheese melts and golden brown on both sides. Serve warm.

Nutrition:
Calories 608
Fats 44.1g| Carbs 17g
Protein 37.6g

272. Creamy Fettucine With Peas

Preparation Time: 25 minutes
Serving: 4

This one is a dish made to taste fantastic. The tip for success is covering or coating the noodles in so much lushness.

Ingredients

- 16 oz whole-wheat fettuccine
- Salt and black pepper to taste
- ¾ cup flax milk
- ½ cup cashew butter, room temperature
- 1 tbsp olive oil
- 2 garlic cloves, minced
- 1 ½ cups frozen peas
- ½ cup chopped fresh basil

Directions

1. Add the fettuccine and 10 cups of water to a large pot, and Cooking Time: over medium heat until al dente, 10 minutes. Drain the pasta through a colander and set aside. In a bowl, whisk the flax milk, cashew butter, and salt until smooth. Set aside.
2. Heat the olive oil in a large skillet and sauté the garlic until fragrant, 30 seconds. Mix in the peas, fettuccine, and basil. Toss well until the pasta is well-coated in the sauce and season with some black pepper. Dish the food and serve warm.

Nutrition:
Calories 654
Fats 23.7g| Carbs 101.9g
Protein 18.2g

273. Buckwheat Cabbage Rolls

Preparation Time: 30 minutes

Serving: 4

Ingredients

- *2 tbsp plant butter*
- *2 cups extra firm tofu, pressed and crumbled*
- *½ medium sweet onion, finely chopped*
- *2 garlic cloves, minced*
- *Salt and black pepper to taste*
- *1 cup buckwheat groats*
- *1 ¾ cups vegetable stock*
- *1 bay leaf*
- *2 tbsp chopped fresh cilantro + more for garnishing*
- *1 head Savoy cabbage, leaves separated (scraps kept)*
- *1 (23 oz canned chopped tomatoes*

Directions

1. *Melt the plant butter in a large bowl and Cooking Time: the tofu until golden brown, 8 minutes. Stir in the onion and garlic until softened and fragrant, 3 minutes. Season with salt, black pepper and mix in the buckwheat, bay leaf, and vegetable stock.*
2. *Close the lid, allow boiling, and then simmer until all the liquid is absorbed. Open the lid; remove the bay leaf, adjust the taste with salt, black pepper, and mix in the cilantro.*
3. *Lay the cabbage leaves on a flat surface and add 3 to 4 tablespoons of the cooked buckwheat onto each leaf. Roll the leaves to firmly secure the filling.*
4. *Pour the tomatoes with juices into a medium pot, season with a little salt, black pepper, and lay the cabbage rolls in the sauce. Cooking Time: over medium heat until the cabbage softens, 5 to 8 minutes. Turn the heat off and dish the food onto serving plates. Garnish with more cilantro and serve warm.*

Nutrition:

Calories 1147
Fats 112.9g| Carbs 25.6g
Protein 23.8g

274. Bbq Black Bean Burgers

Preparation Time: 20 minutes
Serving: 4
Say hello to your new winning burger.

Ingredients

- *3 (15 oz cans black beans, drained and rinsed*
- *2 tbsp whole-wheat flour*
- *2 tbsp quick-cooking oats*
- *¼ cup chopped fresh basil*
- *2 tbsp pure barbecue sauce*
- *1 garlic clove, minced*
- *Salt and black pepper to taste*
- *4 whole-grain hamburger buns, split*

For topping:

- *Red onion slices*
- *Tomato slices*
- *Fresh basil leaves*
- *Additional barbecue sauce*

Directions

1. *In a medium bowl, mash the black beans and mix in the flour, oats, basil, barbecue sauce, garlic salt, and black pepper until well combined. Mold 4 patties out of the mixture and set aside.*
2. *Heat a grill pan to medium heat and lightly grease with cooking spray.*
3. *Cooking Time: the bean patties on both sides until light brown and cooked through, 10 minutes.*
4. *Place the patties between the burger buns and top with the onions, tomatoes, basil, and some barbecue sauce.*
5. *Serve warm.*

Nutrition:
Calories 589
Fats 17.7g| Carbs 80.9g
Protein 27.9g

275. Nutty Tofu Loaf

Preparation Time: 65 minutes
Serving: 4

Ingredients

- 2 tbsp olive oil + extra for brushing
- 2 white onions, finely chopped
- 4 garlic cloves, minced
- 1 lb firm tofu, pressed and crumbled
- 2 tbsp soy sauce
- ¾ cup chopped mixed nuts
- ¼ cup flaxseed meal
- 1 tbsp sesame seeds
- 1 cup chopped mixed bell peppers
- Salt and black pepper to taste
- 1 tbsp Italian seasoning
- ½ tsp pure date syrup
- ½ cup tomato sauce

Directions

1. Preheat the oven to 350 F and grease an 8 x 4-inch loaf pan with olive oil.
2. Heat 1 tbsp of olive oil in a small skillet and sauté the onion and garlic until softened and fragrant, 2 minutes.
3. Pour the onion mixture into a large bowl and mix with the tofu, soy sauce, nuts, flaxseed meal, sesame seeds, bell peppers, salt, black pepper, Italian seasoning, and date syrup until well combined.
4. Spoon the mixture into the loaf pan, press to fit and spread the tomato sauce on top.
5. Bake the tofu loaf in the oven for 45 minutes to 1 hour or until well compacted.
6. Remove the loaf pan from the oven, invert the tofu loaf onto a chopping board, and cool for 5 minutes. Slice and serve warm.

Nutrition:
Calories 544
Fats 39.2g | Carbs 30.4g
Protein 25g

276. Taco Rice Bowls

Preparation Time: 50 minutes
Serving: 4

Ingredients

- 2 tbsp olive oil
- 2 cups chopped soy chorizo
- 1 tsp taco seasoning
- 2 green bell peppers, deseeded and sliced
- 1 cup brown rice
- 2 cups vegetable broth
- Salt to taste
- ¼ cup salsa
- 1 lemon, zested and juiced
- 1 (8 oz can pinto beans, drained and rinsed
- 1 (7 oz can sweet corn kernels, drained
- 2 green onions, chopped
- 2 tbsp freshly chopped parsley

Directions

1. Heat the olive oil in a medium pot and Cooking Time: the soy chorizo until golden brown, 5 minutes.
2. Season with the taco seasoning and stir in the bell peppers; Cooking Time: until the peppers slightly soften, 3 minutes.
3. Stir in the brown rice, vegetable broth, salt, salsa, and lemon zest.
4. Close the lid and Cooking Time: the food until the rice is tender and all the liquid is absorbed, 15 to 25 minutes.
5. Mix in the lemon juice, pinto beans, corn kernels, and green onions. Allow warming for 3 to 5 minutes and dish the food.
6. Garnish with the parsley and serve warm.

Nutrition:
Calories 253
Fats 8.4g
Carbs 32.7g
Protein 15.5g

277. Red Sauce Mushroom Pizza

Preparation Time: 40 minutes
Serving: 4

Ingredients

For the crust:
- 2 tbsp flax seed powder + 6 tbsp water
- ½ cup tofu mayonnaise
- ¾ cup whole-wheat flour
- 1 tsp baking powder
- ½ tsp salt

For the topping:
- 1 cup sliced mixed mushrooms
- 2 tbsp olive oil
- 1 tbsp basil pesto
- Salt and black pepper
- ½ cup red pizza sauce
- ¾ cup shredded plant-based Parmesan cheese

Directions
1. Preheat the oven to 350 F.
2. In a medium bowl, mix the flax seed powder with water and allow thickening for 5 minutes to make the flax egg. Mix in the tofu mayonnaise, whole-wheat flour, baking powder, and salt until dough forms. Spread the dough on a pizza pan and bake in the oven for 10 minutes or until the dough sets.
3. In a medium bowl, mix the mushrooms, olive oil, basil pesto, salt, and black pepper.
4. Remove the pizza crust spread the pizza sauce on top. Scatter mushroom mixture on the crust and top with plant-based Parmesan cheese. Bake further until the cheese melts and the mushrooms soften, 10 to 15 minutes. Remove the pizza, slice and serve.

Nutrition:
Calories 515
Fats 35g | Carbs 35.9g
Protein 16.2g

278. Sweet Quinoa Veggie Burger

Preparation Time: 35 minutes
Serving: 4

Ingredients
- 1 cup quick-cooking quinoa
- 1 tbsp olive oil
- 1 shallot, chopped
- 2 tbsp chopped fresh celery
- 1 garlic clove, minced
- 1 (15 oz can pinto beans, drained and rinsed
- 2 tbsp whole-wheat flour
- ¼ cup chopped fresh basil
- 2 tbsp pure maple syrup
- Salt and black pepper to taste
- 4 whole-grain hamburger buns, split
- 4 small lettuce leaves for topping
- ½ cup tofu mayonnaise for topping

Directions
1. Cooking Time: the quinoa with 2 cups of water in a medium pot until liquid absorbs, 10 to 15 minutes.
2. Meanwhile, heat the olive oil in a medium skillet over medium heat and sauté the shallot, celery, and garlic until softened and fragrant, 3 minutes.
3. Transfer the quinoa and shallot mixture to a medium bowl and add the pinto beans, flour, basil, maple syrup, salt, and black pepper. Mash and mold 4 patties out of the mixture and set aside.
4. Heat a grill pan to medium heat and lightly grease with cooking spray. Cooking Time: the patties on both sides until light brown, compacted, and cooked through, 10 minutes. Place the patties between the burger buns and top with the lettuce and tofu mayonnaise. Serve warm.

Nutrition:
Calories 290
Fats 6.2g
Carbs 50.2g

Protein 12g

279. Green Bean And Mushroom Biryani

Preparation Time: 50 minutes
Serving: 4

Ingredients

- 1 cup brown rice
- 2 cups water
- Salt to taste
- 3 tbsp plant butter
- 3 medium white onions, chopped
- 6 garlic cloves, minced
- 1 tsp ginger puree
- 1 tbsp turmeric powder + more for dusting
- ¼ tsp cinnamon powder
- 2 tsp garam masala
- ½ tsp cardamom powder
- ½ tsp cayenne powder
- ½ tsp cumin powder
- 1 tsp smoked paprika
- 3 large tomatoes, diced
- 2 green chilies, deseeded and minced
- 1 tbsp tomato puree
- 1 cup chopped cremini mushrooms
- 1 cup chopped mustard greens
- 1 cup plant-based yogurt for topping

Directions

1. Melt the butter in a large pot and sauté the onions until softened, 3 minutes. Mix in the garlic, ginger, turmeric, cardamom powder, garam masala, cardamom powder, cayenne pepper, cumin powder, paprika, and salt. Stir-fry while cooking until the fragrant, 1 to 2 minutes.
2. Stir in the tomatoes, green chili, tomato puree, and mushrooms. Once boiling, mix in the rice and cover with water. Cover the pot and Cooking Time: over medium heat until the liquid absorbs and the rice is tender, 15-20 minutes.
3. Open the lid and fluff in the mustard greens and half of the parsley. Dish the food, top with the coconut yogurt, garnish with the remaining parsley, and serve warm.

Nutrition:
Calories 255
Fats 16.8g | Carbs 25.6g
Protein 5.8g

280. Cabbage & Bell Pepper Skillet

Preparation Time: 30 minutes
Serving: 4
Have a good benefit from my grandmum's kitchen.

Ingredients

- 1 can (28 oz whole plum tomatoes, undrained
- 1 lb crumbled tempeh
- 1 large yellow onion, chopped
- 1 can (8 oz tomato sauce
- 2 tbsp plain vinegar
- 1 tbsp pure date sugar
- 1 tsp dried mixed herbs
- 3 large tomatoes, chopped
- ½ tsp black pepper
- 1 small head cabbage, thinly sliced
- 1 medium green bell pepper, deseeded and cut into thin strips

Directions

1. Drain the tomatoes and reserve its liquid. Chop the tomatoes and set aside.
2. Add the tempeh to a large skillet and Cooking Time: until brown, 10 minutes. Mix in the onion, tomato sauce, vinegar, date sugar, mixed herbs, and chopped tomatoes. Close the lid and Cooking Time: until the liquid reduces and the tomato softens, 10 minutes.
3. Stir in the cabbage and bell pepper; Cooking Time: until softened, 5 minutes.
4. Dish the food and serve with cooked brown rice.

Nutrition:
Calories 403
Fats 16.9g
Carbs 44.1g
Protein 27.3g

281. Mixed Bean Burgers With Cashew Cheese

Preparation Time: 30 minutes
Serving: 4

Ingredients

- 1 (15 oz)can chickpea, drained and rinsed
- 1 (15 oz)can pinto beans, drained and rinsed
- 1 (15 oz)can red kidney beans, drained and rinsed
- 2 tbsp whole-wheat flour
- ¼ cup dried mixed herbs
- ¼ tsp hot sauce
- ½ tsp garlic powder
- Salt and black pepper to taste
- 4 slices cashew cheese
- 4 whole-grain hamburger buns, split
- 4 small lettuce leaves for topping

Directions

1. In a medium bowl, mash the chickpea, pinto beans, kidney beans and mix in the flour, mixed herbs, hot sauce, garlic powder, salt, and black pepper. Mold 4 patties out of the mixture and set aside.
2. Heat a grill pan to medium heat and lightly grease with cooking spray.
3. Cooking Time: the bean patties on both sides until light brown and cooked through, 10 minutes.
4. Lay a cashew cheese slice on each and allow slight melting, 2 minutes.
5. Remove the patties between the burger buns and top with the lettuce and serve warm.

Nutrition:
Calories 456
Fats 16.8g
Carbs 56.1g
Protein 24g

282. Beans, Tomato & Corn Quesadillas

Preparation Time: 35 minutes
Serving: 4

Ingredients

- 1 tsp olive oil
- 1 small onion, chopped
- ½ medium red bell pepper, deseeded and chopped
- 1 (7 oz)can chopped tomatoes
- 1 (7 oz)can black beans, drained and rinsed
- 1 (7 oz)can sweet corn kernels, drained
- 4 whole-wheat tortillas
- 1 cup grated plant-based cheddar cheese

Directions

1. Heat the olive oil in a medium skillet and sauté the onion and bell pepper until softened, 3 minutes.
2. Mix in the tomatoes, black beans, sweet corn, and Cooking Time: until the tomatoes soften, 10 minutes. Season with salt and black pepper.
3. Heat another medium skillet over medium heat and lay in one tortilla. Spread a quarter of the tomato mixture on top, scatter a quarter of the plant cheese on the sauce, and cover with another tortilla. Cooking Time: until the cheese melts. Flip and Cooking Time: further for 2 minutes.
4. Transfer to a plate and make one more piece using the remaining ingredients.
5. Cut each tortilla set into quarters and serve immediately.

Nutrition:
Calories 197
Fats 6.4g
Carbs 30.2g
Protein 6.6g

283. Bean & Rice Burritos

Preparation Time: 50 minutes
Serving: 4

Ingredients

- 1 cups brown rice
- Salt and black pepper to taste
- 1 tbsp olive oil
- 1 medium red onion, chopped
- 1 medium green bell pepper, deseeded and diced
- 2 garlic cloves, minced
- 1 tbsp chili powder
- 1 tsp cumin powder
- 1/8 tsp red chili flakes
- 1 (15 oz can black beans, rinsed and drained
- 4 (8-inch whole-wheat flour tortillas, warmed
- 1 cup salsa
- 1 cup coconut cream for topping
- 1 cup grated plant-based cheddar cheese for topping

Directions

1. Add 2 cups of water and brown rice to medium pot, season with some salt, and Cooking Time: over medium heat until the water absorbs and the rice is tender, 15 to 20 minutes.
2. Heat the olive oil in a medium skillet over medium heat and sauté the onion, bell pepper, and garlic until the softened and fragrant, 3 minutes.
3. Mix in the chili powder, cumin powder, red chili flakes, and season with salt and black pepper. Cooking Time: for 1 minute or until the food releases fragrance. Stir in the brown rice, black beans, and allow warming through, 3 minutes.
4. Lay the tortillas on a clean, flat surface and divide the rice mixture in the center of each. Top with the salsa, coconut cream, and plant cheddar cheese. Fold the sides and ends of the tortillas over the filling to secure. Serve immediately.

Nutrition:
Calories 421
Fats 29.1g
Carbs 37g
Protein 9.3g

284. Baked Sweet Potatoes With Corn Salad

Preparation Time: 35 minutes
Serving: 4

Ingredients

For the baked sweet potatoes:

- 3 tbsp olive oil
- 4 medium sweet potatoes, peeled and cut into ½-inch cubes
- 2 limes, juiced
- Salt and black pepper to taste
- ¼ tsp cayenne pepper
- 2 scallions, thinly sliced

For the corn salad:

- 1 (15 oz can sweet corn kernels, drained
- ½ tbsp, plant butter, melted
- 1 large green chili, deseeded and minced
- 1 tsp cumin powder

Directions

For the baked sweet potatoes:

1. Preheat the oven to 400 F and lightly grease a baking sheet with cooking spray.
2. In a medium bowl, add the sweet potatoes, lime juice, salt, black pepper, and cayenne pepper. Toss well and spread the mixture on the baking sheet. Bake in the oven until the potatoes soften, 20 to 25 minutes.
3. Remove from the oven, transfer to a serving plate, and garnish with the scallions.

For the corn salad:

In a medium bowl, mix the corn kernels, butter, green chili, and cumin powder. Serve the sweet potatoes with the corn salad.

Nutrition:
Calories 372
Fats 20.7g
Carbs 41.7g
Protein 8.9g

285. Cheesy Broccoli Casserole

Preparation Time: 50 minutes
Serving: 4

You can make this broccoli during the holidays or any occasion. It's fabulous and super delicious.

Ingredients

- 1 tbsp olive oil
- 2 cups broccoli florets
- 1 (10 oz can cream of mushroom soup
- 1 cup tofu mayonnaise
- Salt and black pepper to taste
- 3 tbsp coconut cream
- 1 medium red onion, chopped
- 2 cups grated plant-based cheddar cheese
- ¾ cup whole-wheat bread crumbs
- 3 tbsp plant butter, melted

Directions

1. Preheat the oven to 350 F.
2. Heat the olive oil in a medium skillet and sauté the broccoli florets until softened, 8 minutes.
3. Turn the heat off and mix in the mushroom soup, mayonnaise, salt, black pepper, coconut cream, and onion. Spread the mixture into the baking sheet.
4. In a small bowl, mix the breadcrumbs with the plant butter and evenly distribute the mixture on top. Add the cheddar cheese and bake the casserole in the oven until golden on top and the cheese melts.
5. Remove the casserole from the oven, allow cooling for 5 minutes, dish, and serve warm.

Nutrition:
Calories 412
Fats 38.14g
Carbs 13.19g
Protein 6.57g

286. Hummus & Vegetable Pizza

Preparation Time: 30 minutes
Serving: 4

If you like hummus, you will LOVE this hummus pizza with mushrooms, spinach and olives.

Ingredients

For the pizza crust:
- 3 ½ cups whole-wheat flour
- 1 tsp yeast
- 1 tsp salt
- 1 pinch sugar
- 3 tbsp olive oil
- 1 cup warm water

For the topping:
- 1 cup hummus
- 10 cremini mushrooms, sliced
- ½ cup fresh baby spinach
- ½ cup cherry tomatoes, halved
- ½ cup sliced Kalamata olives
- ½ medium onion, sliced
- 2 tsp dried oregano

Directions

1. Preheat the oven the 350 F and lightly grease a pizza pan with cooking spray.
2. In a medium bowl, mix the flour, nutritional yeast, salt, sugar, olive oil, and warm water until smooth dough forms. Allow rising for an hour or until the dough doubles in size.
3. Spread the dough on the pizza pan and apply the hummus on the dough. Add the mushrooms, spinach, tomatoes, olives, onion, and top with the oregano. Bake the pizza for 20 minutes or until the mushrooms soften.
4. Remove from the oven, cool for 5 minutes, slice, and serve.

Nutrition:
Calories 592
Fats 19.9g
Carbs 92.5g
Protein 18g

287. Chickpea Burgers With Guacamole

Preparation Time: *20 minutes*
Serving: *4*

Let's enjoy this burger meatless and it's the perfect time for a guacamole veggie burger!

Ingredients

For the guacamole:
- 1 large avocado, pitted and peeled
- 1 tomato, chopped
- 1 small red onion, chopped

For the burgers:
- 3 (15 oz cans chickpeas, drained and rinsed
- 2 tbsp almond flour
- 2 tbsp quick-cooking oats
- ¼ cup chopped fresh parsley
- 1 tbsp hot sauce
- 1 garlic clove, minced
- ¼ tsp garlic salt
- 1/8 tsp black pepper
- 4 whole-grain hamburger buns, split

Directions

1. In a medium bowl, mash avocados and mix in the tomato, onion, and parsley. Set aside.
2. In a medium bowl, mash the chickpeas and mix in the almond flour, oats, parsley, hot sauce, garlic, garlic salt, and black pepper. Mold 4 patties out of the mixture and set aside.
3. Heat a grill pan to medium heat and lightly grease with cooking spray. Cooking Time: the bean patties on both sides until light brown and cooked through, 10 minutes. Place each patty between each burger bun and top with the guacamole.

Nutrition:
Calories 369 kcal| Fats 12.7g
Carbs 52.7g
Protein 15.6g

288. Dark Bean And Quinoa Salad With Quick Cumin Dressing

Servings: 4

Ingredients

For the plate of mixed greens:
- 1 cup dry quinoa, washed
- Run salt
- 2 cups vegetable soup or water
- 1/2 huge cucumber, diced conveniently
- 1 little chime pepper, diced conveniently
- 1 can BPA free, natural dark beans
- 10-15 basil leaves, hacked into a chiffonade 1/4 cup crisp cilantro, slashed

For the vinaigrette:
- 2 tbsp additional virgin olive oil
- 1/4 cup apple juice vinegar
- 1 tbsp agave or maple syrup
- 1 tbsp dijon mustard
- 1 tsp cumin
- Salt and pepper to taste

Strategy

1. Rinse quinoa through a strainer till the water runs clear. Move it to a little or medium measured pot and include two cups of vegetable stock or water and run of salt. Heat to the point of boiling, at that point diminish to a stew. Spread the pot with the goal that the top is on, yet there's a little hole where water can get away. Stew till quinoa has consumed the entirety of the fluid and is soft (around 15-20 minutes).
2. Transfer cooked quinoa to a blending bowl. Include hacked vegetables, dark beans, and herbs.
3. Whisk dressing fixings. Add the dressing to the plate of mixed greens,

and serve. (In the event that you don't feel that you need all the dressing, simply include as much as you'd prefer to.
4. *Plate of mixed greens will keep for three days in the cooler.*
5. *Zucchini Pasta With Cherry Tomatoes, Basil, Sweet Potato, And Hemp*

289. Parmesan

Servings: 2
Ingredients:
- *2 huge zucchini*
- *1 red chime pepper, diced*
- *15 cherry tomatoes, quartered*
- *8 huge basil leaves, chiffonaded*
- *2 little sweet potato, prepared and afterward cut into blocks*
- *2 tbsp balsamic vinegar*
- *1 little avocado, cubed*
- *4 tbsp hemp parmesan (formula underneath*

Strategy
1. *Use a spiralizer or a julienne peeler to cut zucchini into long strips (taking after noodles).*
2. *Toss zucchini with every single outstanding fixing, and serve.*

290. Hemp Parmesan

Servings: 1/2 - 2/3 cup
Ingredients:
- *6 tbsp hemp seeds*
- *6 tbsp dietary yeast*
- *Run ocean salt*

Strategy
Consolidate all fixings in a nourishment processor, and heartbeat to separate and join. Store in the cooler for as long as about fourteen days.

291. Gluten Free White Bean And Summer Vegetable Pasta

Servings: 4
Ingredients:

- *1 little eggplant, cut into 1 inch 3D squares and softly salted for 30 minutes, at that point tapped dry 1 clove garlic, minced*
- *1 huge zucchini, cut*
- *1 would organic be able to fire simmered, diced tomatoes*
- *1 little can natural tomato sauce*
- *1 tsp agave*
- *1 tbsp dried basil*
- *1 tsp dried oregano*
- *1 tsp dried thyme*
- *1 can (or 2 cups newly cookedcannellini or naval force beans, depleted*
- *8 oz. dry dark colored rice or quinoa pasta (rigatoni, linguine, and penne are on the whole fine*

Strategy
1. *Heat a huge skillet with olive or coconut oil shower (or simply utilize a couple tbsp water). Sautee the eggplant with the garlic till the eggplant is getting decent and darker (around 8 minutes).*
2. *Add the zucchini and Cooking Time: it till delicate (an additional 5 minutes).*
3. *Add the canned tomatoes, tomato sauce, agave, basil, oregano, thyme. Warmth through. Test for flavoring, and include a greater amount of whatever herbs you like.*
4. *Add the white beans and warmth the entire sauce through. This is so delectable and straightforward, you could eat it all alone as a "cheater's" ratatouille.*
5. *While your sauce cooks, put a pot of salted water to bubble. Include pasta when it hits a moving bubble, and Cooking Time: pasta till delicate yet at the same time somewhat still somewhat firm.*
6. *Drain pasta, cover with sauce, and serve.*
7. *Remains will keep for three days in*

the ice chest.

292. Butternut Squash Curry

Servings: 4
Ingredients:
- *1 tablespoon dissolved coconut oil*
- *1 white or yellow onion, hacked*
- *1 clove garlic, minced*
- *1 tablespoon new ginger, minced*
- *3 tablespoons red curry glue*
- *1 tablespoon natural sugar or coconut sugar*
- *2/3 cups vegetable soup*
- *One 14-or 15-ounce would coconut be able to drain*
- *1 tablespoon soy sauce or tamari*
- *1 green or red chime pepper, slashed*
- *1 pound butternut squash*
- *2 cups green beans, cut into 2" pieces*
- *1 to 2 tablespoon lime juice*

Strategy
1. Heat the coconut oil in a huge pot or wok. Include the onion and Cooking Time: till it's delicate and translucent (5 to 8 minutes).
2. Add the garlic and ginger and let them Cooking Time: for about a moment. At that point, include the curry glue and sugar. Combine the fixings until the glue is uniformly consolidated.
3. Whisk in the stock, the coconut milk, and the tamari. Include the red pepper and butternut squash. Stew till the squash is absolutely delicate (25 to 30 minutes). On the off chance that you have to include additional juices as the blend cooks, do as such.
4. Stir in the green beans and let them Cooking Time: for a few minutes, or until delicate. Season the curry to taste with additional soy sauce or tamari and mix in the lime squeeze as wanted. Expel from warmth and serve over quinoa or darker basmati rice.

5. Remains will keep for four days.

293. Crude Zucchini Alfredo With Basil And Cherry Tomatoes

Servings: 2 (with remaining alfredo sauce
Ingredients:
- *Pasta*
- *2 huge zucchini*
- *1 cup cherry tomatoes, split*
- *1/4 cup basil, cut*
- *Crude alfredo sauce*
- *1 cup cashews, drenched for in any event three hours (or medium-termand depleted 1/3 cup water*
- *1 tsp agave or maple syrup*
- *1 clove garlic*
- *3-4 tbsp lemon juice (to taste*
- *1/4 cup wholesome yeast*
- *1/4 tsp ocean salt*

Strategy
1. Use a spiralizer or a julienne peeler to cut zucchini into long strips (looking like noodles).
2. Add tomatoes and basil to the zucchini noodles and put them with or without in an enormous blending bowl.
3. Blend the entirety of the alfredo sauce fixings together in a fast blender till smooth.
4. Cover the pasta in 1/2 cup sauce, and blend it in well, including extra sauce varying (you'll have some sauce remaining). Serve.

294. Dark Bean And Corn Burgers

Servings: 4 Burgers
Ingredients:
- *1 tablespoon coconut oil*
- *1 little yellow onion, cleaved*
- *1 cup crisp, solidified or canned natural corn pieces*
- *1 can natural, low sodium dark beans, depleted (or 1/2 cups cooked*

- dark beans 1 cup darker rice, cooked
- 1/4 cup oat flour (or ground, moved oats
- 1/4 cup tomato glue
- 2 tsp cumin
- 1 loading tsp paprika
- 1 loading tsp stew powder
- 1/2 - 1 tsp ocean salt (to taste
- Dark pepper or red pepper, to taste

Technique
1. Preheat your broiler to 350 F.
2. Heat the coconut oil in an enormous sauté dish. Include the onion and saute till onion is brilliant, delicate, and fragrant (around 5-8 minutes).
3. 2Add corn, beans and tomato glue to the container and warmth through.
4. 3Place cooked rice into the bowl of a nourishment processor. Include the beans, onion, tomato glue, and corn blend. Heartbeat to join. Include flavors, oat flour, and a bit of water, on the off chance that you need it. Heartbeat more, until you have a thick and clingy (yet malleableblend. In the event that the blend is excessively wet, include a tablespoon or two of extra oat flour.
5. 4Shape into 4 burgers and spot burgers on a foil lined heating sheet. Prepare for 25 - 30 minutes, or until burgers are delicately crisped, flipping once through. Present with crisp guacamole, whenever wanted!

295. Eggplant Rollatini With Cashew Cheese

Servings: 4

Ingredients

For rollatini:
- 2 enormous eggplant, cut the long way into 1/4 inch thick cuts
- Olive oil
- 1/4 cups cashews, drenched for in any event three hours (or medium-termand depleted 1/2 tsp ocean salt
- 1 small clove garlic, minced (discretionary
- 2 tbsp lemon juice
- 1/3-1/2 cup water
- 1/4 cup nourishing yeast
- 2 tsps dried basil
- 1 tsp dried oregano
- Dark pepper to taste
- 1/2 10 oz. bundle solidified spinach, defrosted and crushed completely to evacuate all abundance fluid (I press mine immovably through a strainer
- 1/2 cups natural, low sodium marinara sauce

Strategy
1. Preheat stove to 400 F. Cut eggplants the long way into strips around 1/2" thick. Spot eggplant cuts onto heating sheets and sprinkle well with ocean salt or fit salt. Let sit for 30 minutes; this abatements sharpness and expels abundance dampness. Pat the cuts dry, and splash them or brush them gently with olive oil.
2. Roast eggplant cuts till sautéing (around 20 min), flipping part of the way through.
3. While eggplant is cooking, make the cashew cheddar. Spot the cashews, ocean salt, garlic, lemon, and 1/3 cup water in a nourishment processor. Procedure till the blend is extremely smooth and delicate (you're focusing on a surface like velvety ricotta cheddar), halting to scratch the bowl down a couple of times and including some additional water as essential. Stop the engine, and include the wholesome yeast, basil, oregano, and dark pepper. Procedure again to fuse. Move the cashew cheddar to a bowl and blend in the cleaved spinach. Put the cheddar blend in a safe spot.
4. Remove the simmered eggplant from the stove and decrease warmth to 325 F. Permit the cuts to cool until they can be taken care of. Move them to a

cutting board and include around 3 tbsp of the cheddar blend as far as possible of one side. Move up from that side, and spot crease down in a little goulash dish. Rehash with every residual cut.
5. Smother the eggplant moves with tomato sauce, and heat, revealed, for around 20-25 minutes, or until hot. Present with sides of decision.

296. Ginger Lime Chickpea Sweet Potato Burgers

Servings: 4-6 Burgers
Ingredients:
- 3/4 cup cooked chickpeas
- 1/2 little onion
- 1 inch ginger, cleaved
- 1 tsp coconut oil
- 1 1/2 cups sweet potato, prepared or steamed and cubed
- 1/3 cup quinoa pieces or gluten free moved oats
- 2 heaping tbsp flax meal
- 2-3 tbsp lime juice (to taste
- 2 tbsp low sodium tamari
- 1/4 cup cilantro, slashed
- Run red pepper drops (discretionary
- Water varying

Strategy
1. Preheat stove to 350 F.
2. Heat coconut oil in a huge container or wok. Saute onion and ginger in 1 tsp coconut oil (or coconut oil splashtill delicate and fragrant (around 5 minutes). Include chickpeas and warmth through.
3. Place the chickpeas, onion, and ginger in a nourishment processor and include the sweet potato, quinoa chips or oats, flax seed, lime juice, cilantro, tamari or coconut aminos, and run of red pepper drops, if utilizing. Heartbeat to join, at that point run the engine and include some water until consistency is exceptionally thick yet simple to

form.
4. Shape blend into 4-6 burgers. Heat at 350 degrees for around 35 minutes, flipping part of the way through.

297. Sweet Potato And Black Bean Chili

Servings: 6
Ingredients:
- 1/2 cup dried dark beans
- 4 cups sweet potato, diced into 3/4 inch solid shapes
- 1 tablespoon olive oil
- 1 1/2 cups slashed white or yellow onion
- 2 cloves garlic, minced
- 1 chipotle pepper en adobo, slashed finely
- 2 teaspoons cumin powder
- 1/2 teaspoon smoked paprika
- 1 tablespoon ground bean stew powder
- 1 14 or 15 ounce container of natural, diced tomatoes (I like the Muir Glen brand
- 1 can natural, low sodium dark beans (or 1/2 cups cooked dark beans2 cups low sodium vegetable soup, Sea salt to taste

Strategy
1. Heat the tablespoon of oil in a dutch stove or a huge pot. Saute the onion for a couple of moments, at that point include the sweet potato and garlic. Keep sauteing until the onions are delicate, around 8-10 minutes.
2. Add the bean stew en adobo, the cumin, the stew powder, and the smoked paprika. Warmth until the flavors are exceptionally fragrant. Include the tomatoes, dark beans, and vegetable soup.
3. When juices is foaming, decrease to a stew and Cooking Time: for roughly 25-30 minutes, or until the sweet potatoes are delicate.

4. Add more juices varying, and season to taste with salt. Serve.
5. Extra stew can be solidified and will keep for as long as five days.

298. Crude Cauliflower Rice With Lemon, Mint, And Pistachios

Servings: 2
Ingredients:
- 5 cups crude cauliflower florets
- 1 oz pistachios
- 1/4 cup every basil and mint
- 2 tsp lemon get-up-and-go
- 1/2 tbsp lemon juice
- 1 tbsp olive oil
- 1/4 cup dried currants
- Ocean Salt And Dark Pepper To Taste

Strategy
1. Transfer 3 cups of the cauliflower to a nourishment processor. Procedure until the cauliflower is separated into pieces that are about the size of rice. Move to a huge blending bowl.
2. Transfer staying 2 cups of cauliflower to the nourishment processor. Include the pistachios. Procedure, by and by, until cauliflower is separated into rice estimated pieces. Heartbeat in the basil and mint till herbs are finely cleaved.
3. Add the extra hacked cauliflower, pistachios, and herbs to the blending bowl in with the principal bunch of cauliflower. Include the lemon juice, oil, and flows. Season to taste with salt and pepper. Serve.

299. Darker Rice And Lentil Salad

Servings: 4
Ingredients:
- 2 tablespoons olive oil
- 1 tablespoon apple juice vinegar
- 1 tablespoon lemon juice
- 1 tablespoon dijon mustard
- 1/2 tsp smoked paprika
- Ocean salt and dark pepper to taste
- 2 cups cooked dark colored rice
- 1 15-oz can natural, no sodium included lentils, flushed, or 1/cups cooked lentils
- 1 carrot, diced or ground
- 4 tbsp cleaved crisp parsley

Technique
1. Whisk oil, vinegar, lemon juice, mustard, paprika, salt and pepper together in a huge bowl.
2. Add the rice, lentils, carrot and parsley. Blend well and serve.

300. Crude "Nut" Noodles

Servings: 2
Ingredients:
For the dressing:
- 1 tablespoon ground ginger
- 1/2 cup olive oil
- 2 tsp sesame oil (toasted
- 2 tbsp smooth white miso
- 3 dates, pitted, or ¼ cup maple syrup
- 1 tbsp nama shoyu
- 1/4 cup water

For the noodles:
- 2 zucchinis
- 1 red chime pepper, cut into matchsticks
- 1 carrot, ground
- 1 little cucumber, stripped into slim strips
- 1 cup daintily cut, steamed snow peas
- 1/4 cup hacked scallions or green onion

Strategy
1. Blend dressing fixings in a rapid blender until all fixings are velvety and smooth.
2. Use a spiralizer or julienne peeler to cut the zucchini into long, slender "noodles." Combine the zucchini with the pepper, carrot, cucumber,

and scallions.
3. *Dress the noodles with enough dressing to cover them well. Serve.*

301. Simple Fried Rice And Vegetables

Servings: 2
Ingredients:
- *2 tsp toasted sesame oil*
- *1 tbsp ground ginger*
- *1/2 cups cooked dark colored rice*
- *2-3 cups solidified or new vegetables of decision*
- *1 tbsp low sodium tamari*
- *1 tbsp rice vinegar*
- *Vegetable Stock Varying*

Strategy
1. *Heat the sesame oil in a huge wok. Include the ground ginger and warmth it for a moment or two.*
2. *Add the dark colored rice and vegetables. Saute till the vegetables are delicate.*
3. *Add the tamari, rice vinegar, and a sprinkle of vegetable soup if the blend is dry. Serve.*

302. Arugula Salad With Roasted Butternut Squash, Goji Berries, And Cauliflower

Servings: 2
Ingredients

For the plate of mixed greens:
- *4 piling cups arugula (or other green*
- *1 lb butternut squash, stripped and hacked*
- *1 small head cauliflower, washed and hacked into little florets*
- *2 tbsp coconut or olive oil*
- *Ocean salt and pepper to taste*
- *1/4 cup crude pumpkin seeds*
- *1/4 cup goji berries*

For the dressing:
- *3 tbsp olive oil*
- *2 tbsp squeezed orange*
- *1 tbsp lemon juice*
- *1/2 tsp turmeric*
- *1/4 tsp ground ginger*
- *1 tbsp agave or maple syrup*
- *Ocean salt to taste*

Technique
1. *Toss the squash in 1 tbsp oil and season with salt and pepper. Hurl the cauliflower in the other tablespoon and season with salt and pepper. Broil the two veggies at 375 degrees for 2030 minutes (the cauliflower will Cooking Time: quicker), till brilliant dark colored and fragrant. Expel from stove and let cool.*
2. *Place the arugula, goji berries, and pumpkin seeds in an enormous bowl. Include broiled vegetables. Whisk together the olive oil, lemon juice, turmeric, maple syrup or agave, ginger, and ocean salt, and dress all the veggies.*
3. *Divide serving of mixed greens onto two plates, and serve.*

303. Simmered Vegetable Pesto Pasta Salad

Servings: 4
Ingredients:
- *3 cups zucchini, slashed into 3/4" pieces*
- *3 cups eggplant, slashed into 3/4" pieces*
- *1 large Jersey or legacy tomato, cleaved*
- *2 tbsp olive oil or softened coconut oil*
- *Ocean salt and dark pepper to taste*
- *8 oz darker rice or quinoa pasta (penne and fusilli function admirably*
- *1/2 - 2/3 cup pecan pesto (see: dressings*

Technique
1. *Preheat your broiler to 400 F.*
2. *Lay the zucchini, eggplant and*

tomato out on two material or foil fixed heating sheets and shower with the olive or coconut oil. Coat the vegetables with the oil and dish vegetables for thirty minutes, or until delicate and carmelizing.
3. While vegetables cook, carry a pot of salted water to bubble. Include the pasta and Cooking Time: till still somewhat firm (as indicated by bundle directions). Channel pasta and put aside in a huge blending bowl.
4. Add the simmered vegetables and to the pasta. Blend in the pesto, season to taste, and serve on the double.

304. Portobello "Steak" And Cauliflower "Pureed Potatoes"

Servings: 4
Ingredients:

For the mushrooms:
- 1/4 cup olive oil
- 3 tbsp balsamic vinegar
- 3 tbsp low sodium tamari or nama shoyu
- 3 tbsp maple syrup
- Sprinkle pepper
- 4 portobello mushroom tops, cleaned
- Submerge 4 Portobello tops in the marinade. 1 hour will be sufficient for them to be prepared, however medium-term in the refrigerator is far and away superior.

For the Cauliflower Mashed Potatoes:
- 1 cups cashews, crude
- 4 cups cauliflower, slashed into little florets and pieces
- 2 tbsp smooth white miso
- 3 tbsp dietary yeast
- 2 tbsp lemon juice
- Ocean salt and dark pepper to taste
- 1/3 cup (or lesswater

Strategy
1. Place cashews into the bowl of your nourishment processor, and procedure into a fine powder.
2. Add the miso, lemon juice, healthful yeast, pepper and cauliflower. Heartbeat to join. With the engine of the machine running, include water in a flimsy streamin., until the blend starts to take on a smooth, whipped surface. You may need to stop every now and again to clean the sides of the bowl and help it along.
3. When the blend looks like pureed potatoes, stop, scoop, and serve close by a Portobello top.

305. Quinoa Enchiladas

Adjusted from a formula in Food52
Servings: 6
Ingredients:
- 1 tbsp coconut oil
- 2 cloves garlic, minced
- 1 little yellow onion, cleaved
- 3/4 pounds infant bella mushrooms, hacked
- 1/2 cup diced green bean stews
- 1/2 teaspoon ground cumin
- 1/4 teaspoon ocean salt (or to taste)
- 1 can natural, low sodium dark beans or 1/2 cup cooked dark beans
- 1/2 cup cooked quinoa
- 10 6-inch corn tortillas
- 1/4 cup natural, low sodium tomato or enchilada sauce

Technique
1. Preheat broiler to 350 degrees.
2. In an enormous pot over medium warmth, heat coconut oil. Sautee onion and garlic till onion is translucent (around 5-8 min). Include mushrooms and Cooking Time: until fluid has been discharged and vanished (another 5 min).
3. Add the bean stews to the pot and give them a mix for 2 minutes. Include the cumin, ocean salt, dark beans and quinoa, and keep warming the blend until it's totally

warm.

4. Spread a flimsy layer (1/2 cup of marinara or enchilada sauce in the base of a goulash dish. Spot 33% of a cup of quinoa blend in the focal point of a corn tortilla and move it up. Spot the tortilla, crease down, in the goulash dish. Rehash with every outstanding tortilla and afterward spread them with 3/4 cup of extra sauce. Heat for 25 minutes, and serve.

306. Easy Flavored Potatoes Mix

Preparation time: 10 minutes
Cooking time: 25 minutes
Servings: 2
Ingredients:

- 4 potatoes, thinly sliced
- 2 tablespoons olive oil
- 1 fennel bulb, thinly sliced
- 1 tablespoon dill, chopped
- 8 cherry tomatoes, halved
- Salt and black pepper to the taste

Directions:

1. Preheat your air fryer to 365 degrees F and add the oil.
2. Add potato slices, fennel, dill, tomatoes, salt and pepper, toss, cover and Cooking Time: for 25 minutes.
3. Divide potato mix between plates and serve.
4. Enjoy!

Nutrition: calories 240, fat 3, fiber 2, carbs 5, protein 12

307. Eggplant Sandwich

Preparation time: 30 minutes
Cooking time: 30 minutes
Servings: 2
Ingredients:

- 1 eggplant, sliced
- 2 teaspoons parsley, dried
- Salt and black pepper to the taste
- ½ cup vegan breadcrumbs
- ½ teaspoon Italian seasoning
- ½ teaspoon garlic powder
- ½ teaspoon onion powder
- 2 tablespoons almond milk
- 4 vegan bread slices
- Cooking spray
- ½ cup avocado mayo
- ¾ cup tomato sauce
- A handful basil, chopped

Directions:

1. Season eggplant slices with salt and pepper, leave aside for 30 minutes and then pat dry them well.
2. In a bowl, mix parsley with breadcrumbs, Italian seasoning, onion and garlic powder, salt and black pepper and stir.
3. In another bowl, mix milk with vegan mayo and also stir well.
4. Brush eggplant slices with mayo mix, dip them in breadcrumbs mix, place them on a lined baking sheet, spray with cooking oil, introduce baking sheet in your air fryer's basket and Cooking Time: them at 400 degrees F for 15 minutes, flipping them halfway.
5. Brush each bread slice with olive oil and arrange 2 of them on a working surface.
6. Add baked eggplant slices, spread tomato sauce and basil and top with the other bread slices, greased side down.
7. Divide between plates and serve.
8. Enjoy!

Nutrition: calories 324, fat 16, fiber 4, carbs 19, protein 12

308. Veggie Salad

Preparation time: 10 minutes
Cooking time: 15 minutes
Servings: 6
Ingredients:

- 1 green bell pepper, cut into medium chunks
- 1 orange bell pepper, cut into medium chunks

- *1 zucchini, sliced*
- *1 red bell pepper, cut into medium chunks*
- *Salt and black pepper to the taste*
- *1 yellow squash, chopped*
- *1 red onion, roughly chopped*
- *4 ounces brown mushrooms, halved*
- *1 teaspoon Italian seasoning*
- *1 cups cherry tomatoes, halved*
- *½ cup kalamata olives, halved*
- *3 tablespoons balsamic vinegar*
- *2 tablespoons basil, chopped*
- *¼ cup olive oil*

Directions:

1. *In a bowl, mix all bell peppers with squash, zucchini, mushrooms, onion, half of the olive oil, salt, pepper and Italian seasoning, toss to coat, transfer to the air fryer, Cooking Time: at 380 degrees F for 15 minutes and shake them halfway.*
2. *In a bowl, mix the veggies with the olives, tomatoes, salt, pepper, vinegar and the rest of the oil, toss to coat and keep in the fridge until you serve.*
3. *Sprinkle basil on top, divide between plates and serve.*
4. *Enjoy!*

Nutrition: *calories 260, fat 8, fiber 4, carbs 14, protein 15*

309. Chickpeas Burgers

Preparation time: 10 minutes
Cooking time: 20 minutes
Servings: 2
Ingredients:

- *12 ounces canned chickpeas, drained and mashed*
- *2 teaspoons mustard*
- *Salt and black pepper to the taste*
- *3 tablespoons onion, chopped*
- *4 teaspoons tomato sauce*
- *8 dill pickle chips*

Directions:

1. *In a bowl, mix chickpeas with salt, pepper, tomato sauce, onion and mustard and stir well.*
2. *Divide this into 4 pieces, flatten them, top each with dill pickle chips, place burgers in your air fryer's basket and Cooking Time: at 370 degrees F and Cooking Time: for 20 minutes, flipping them after 10 minutes.*
3. *Divide burgers on vegan buns and serve.*
4. *Enjoy!*

Nutrition: *calories 251, fat 5, fiber 7, carbs 12, protein 4*

310. Potato Stew

Preparation time: 10 minutes
Cooking time: 25 minutes
Servings: 4
Ingredients:

- *2 carrots, chopped*
- *6 potatoes, chopped*
- *Salt and black pepper to the taste*
- *1 quart veggie stock*
- *½ teaspoon smoked paprika*
- *A handful thyme, chopped*
- *1 tablespoon parsley, chopped*

Directions:

1. *In your air fryer, mix carrots, potatoes, stock, salt, pepper, paprika, parsley and thyme, stir and Cooking Time: at 375 degrees F for 25 minutes.*
2. *Divide into bowls and serve right away.*
3. *Enjoy!*

Nutrition: *calories 200, fat 5, fiber 1, carbs 20, protein 14*

311. Greek Veggie Mix

Preparation time: 10 minutes
Cooking time: 20 minutes
Servings: 4
Ingredients:

- *A handful cherry tomatoes, halved*
- *Salt and black pepper to the taste*

- 1 parsnip, roughly chopped
- 1 zucchini, roughly chopped
- 1 green bell pepper, cut into strips
- 1 carrot, sliced
- 2 tablespoons stevia
- 1 tablespoon parsley, chopped
- 2 teaspoons garlic, minced
- 6 tablespoons olive oil
- 1 teaspoon mustard

Directions:
1. In your air fryer, mix zucchini with bell pepper, parsnip, carrot, tomatoes, half of the oil, salt and pepper and Cooking Time: at 360 degrees F for 15 minutes.
2. In a bowl, mix the rest of the oil with salt, pepper, stevia, mustard, parsley and garlic and whisk
3. Pour this over veggies, toss to coat, Cooking Time: for 5 minutes more at 375 degrees F, divide between plates and serve.
4. Enjoy!

Nutrition: calories 234, fat 2, fiber 4, carbs 12, protein 7

312. Herbed Mushrooms

Preparation time: 10 minutes
Cooking time: 12 minutes
Servings: 3
Ingredients:
- 10 oyster mushrooms, stems removed
- 1 tablespoon mixed oregano and basil dried
- 1 tablespoon cashew cheese, grated
- A drizzle of olive oil
- 1 tablespoon dill, chopped
- Salt and black pepper to the taste

Directions:
1. Season mushrooms with salt, pepper, mixed herbs, drizzle the oil over them, place them in your air fryer and Cooking Time: at 360 degrees F for 6 minutes.
2. Add cashew cheese and dill, Cooking Time: for 6 minutes more, divide between plates and serve.
3. Enjoy!

Nutrition: calories 210, fat 7, fiber 1, carbs 12, protein 6

313. Corn With Tofu

Preparation time: 10 minutes
Cooking time: 15 minutes
Servings: 4
Ingredients:
- 4 cups corn
- Salt and black pepper to the taste
- 1 tablespoon olive oil
- Juice of 2 limes
- 2 teaspoon smoked paprika
- ½ cup soft tofu, crumbled

Directions:
1. In your air fryer, mix oil with corn, salt, pepper, lime juice and paprika, toss well, cover and Cooking Time: at 400 degrees F for 15 minutes.
2. Divide between plates, sprinkle tofu crumbles all over and serve hot.
3. Enjoy!

Nutrition: calories 160, fat 2, fiber 2, carbs 12, protein 4

314. Garlicky Potatoes

Preparation time: 10 minutes
Cooking time: 40 minutes
Servings: 3
Ingredients:
- 3 big potatoes, peeled and cut into wedges
- Salt and black pepper to the taste
- 2 tablespoons olive oil
- 1 teaspoons sweet paprika
- 2 tablespoons garlic, minced
- 1 tablespoon parsley, chopped

Directions:
1. Put the potatoes in your air fryer's basket, add salt, pepper, garlic, parsley, paprika and oil, toss to coat and Cooking Time: at 392 degrees F for 40 minutes.
2. Divide them between plates and

serve hot.
3. Enjoy!

Nutrition: *calories 123, fat 1, fiber 2, carbs 21, protein 3*

315. Tasty Veggie Mix

Preparation time: 10 minutes
Cooking time: 15 minutes
Servings: 4
Ingredients:

- *2 red onions, cut into chunks*
- *2 zucchinis, cut into medium chunks*
- *3 tomatoes, cut into wedges*
- *¼ cup black olives, pitted and cut into halves*
- *¼ cup olive oil*
- *Salt and black pepper to the taste*
- *1 garlic clove, minced*
- *1 tablespoon mustard*
- *1 tablespoon lemon juice*
- *½ cup parsley, chopped*

Directions:
1. *In your air fryer's pan, mix onion with zucchini, olives, tomatoes, salt, pepper, oil, garlic, mustard and lemon juice, toss, cover and Cooking Time: at 370 degrees F for 15 minutes.*
2. *Add parsley, toss, divide between plates and serve.*
3. *Enjoy!*

Nutrition: *calories 210, fat 1, fiber 4, carbs 7, protein 11*

316. French Mushroom Mix

Preparation time: 10 minutes
Cooking time: 25 minutes
Servings: 4
Ingredients:

- *2 pounds mushrooms, halved*
- *2 teaspoons herbs de Provence*
- *½ teaspoon garlic powder*
- *1 tablespoon olive oil*

Directions:
1. *Heat up a pan with the oil over medium heat, add herbs and heat them up for 2 minutes.*
2. *Add mushrooms and garlic powder, stir, introduce pan in your air fryer's basket and Cooking Time: at 360 degrees F for 25 minutes.*
3. *Divide between plates and serve.*
4. *Enjoy!*

Nutrition: *calories 152, fat 2, fiber 4, carbs 9, protein 7*

317. Easy Broccoli Mix

Preparation time: 10 minutes
Cooking time: 20 minutes
Servings: 4
Ingredients:

- *2 broccoli heads, florets separated*
- *Juice of ½ lemon*
- *1 tablespoon olive oil*
- *2 teaspoons sweet paprika*
- *Salt and black pepper to the taste*
- *3 garlic cloves, minced*
- *1 tablespoon sesame seeds*

Directions:
1. *In a bowl, mix broccoli with lemon juice, olive oil, paprika, salt, pepper and garlic, toss to coat, transfer to your air fryer's basket, Cooking Time: at 360 degrees G for 15 minutes, sprinkle sesame seeds, Cooking Time: for 5 minutes more and divide between plates.*
2. *Serve right away.*
3. *Enjoy!*

Nutrition: *calories 156, fat 4, fiber 3, carbs 12, protein 5*

318. Zucchini And Squash Salad

Preparation time: 10 minutes
Cooking time: 25 minutes
Servings: 4
Ingredients:

- *6 teaspoons olive oil*
- *1 pound zucchinis, cut into half moons*
- *½ pound carrots, cubed*

- 1 yellow squash, cut into chunks
- Salt and white pepper to the taste
- 1 tablespoon tarragon, chopped
- 2 tablespoons tomato paste

Directions:
1. In your air fryer's pan, mix oil with zucchinis, carrots, squash, salt, pepper, tarragon and tomato paste, cover and Cooking Time: at 400 degrees F for 25 minutes.
2. Divide between plates and serve.
3. Enjoy!

Nutrition: calories 170, fat 2, fiber 2, carbs 12, protein 5

319. Indian Cauliflower Mix

Preparation time: 10 minutes
Cooking time: 20 minutes
Servings: 4
Ingredients:
- 3 cups cauliflower florets
- Salt and black pepper to the taste
- A drizzle of olive oil
- ½ cup veggie stock
- ¼ teaspoon turmeric powder
- 1 and ½ teaspoon red chili powder
- 1 tablespoon ginger paste
- 2 teaspoons lemon juice
- 2 tablespoons water

Directions:
1. In your air fryer's pan, mix stock with cauliflower, oil, salt, pepper, turmeric, chili powder, ginger paste, lemon juice and water, stir, cover and Cooking Time: at 400 degrees F for 10 minutes and at 360 degrees F for another 10 minutes.
2. Divide between bowls and serve.
3. Enjoy!

Nutrition: calories 150, fat 1, fiber 2, carbs 12, protein 3

320. "Baked" Potatoes

Preparation time: 10 minutes
Cooking time: 40 minutes
Servings: 3
Ingredients:
- 3 big baking potatoes
- 1 teaspoon dill, chopped
- 1 tablespoon garlic, minced
- Salt and black pepper to the taste
- 2 tablespoons olive oil

Directions:
1. Prick potatoes with a fork, season with salt and pepper to the taste, rub with the oil, garlic and dill, place them in your air fryer's basket and Cooking Time: at 392 degrees F for 40 minutes.
2. Divide them between plates and serve.
3. Enjoy!

Nutrition: calories 130, fat 2, fiber 3, carbs 23, protein 4

321. Squash Stew

Preparation time: 10 minutes
Cooking time: 30 minutes
Servings: 8
Ingredients:
- 2 carrots, chopped
- 1 yellow onion, chopped
- 2 celery stalks, chopped
- 2 green apples, cored, peeled and chopped
- 4 garlic cloves, minced
- 2 cups butternut squash, peeled and cubed
- 6 ounces canned chickpeas, drained
- 6 ounces canned black beans, drained
- 7 ounces canned coconut milk
- 2 teaspoons chili powder
- 1 teaspoon oregano, dried
- 1 tablespoon cumin, ground
- 2 cups veggie stock
- 2 tablespoons tomato paste
- Salt and black pepper to the taste
- 1 tablespoon cilantro, chopped

Directions:
1. In your air fryer, mix carrots with

onion, celery, apples, garlic, squash, chickpeas, black beans, coconut milk, chili powder, oregano, cumin, stock, tomato paste, salt and pepper, stir, cover and Cooking Time: at 370 degrees F for 30 minutes
2. Add cilantro, stir, divide into bowls and serve hot.
3. Enjoy!

Nutrition: calories 332, fat 6, fiber 8, carbs 12, protein 6

322. Chinese Green Beans Mix

Preparation time: 10 minutes
Cooking time: 30 minutes
Servings: 6
Ingredients:
- 1 pound green beans, halved
- 1 cup maple syrup
- 1 cup tomato sauce
- 4 tablespoons stevia
- ¼ cup tomato paste
- ¼ cup mustard
- ¼ cup olive oil
- ¼ cup apple cider vinegar
- 2 tablespoons coconut aminos

Directions:
1. In your air fryer, mix beans with maple syrup, tomato paste, stevia, tomato paste, mustard, oil, vinegar and aminos, stir, cover and Cooking Time: at 365 degrees F for 35 minutes.
2. Divide into bowls and serve hot.
3. Enjoy!

Nutrition: calories 23, fat 7, fiber 12, carbs 17, protein 13

323. Chinese Tofu Mix

Preparation time: 10 minutes
Cooking time: 20 minutes
Servings: 5
Ingredients:
- 2 pounds firm tofu, pressed and cut into medium cubes
- 1 tablespoons sesame oil
- 3 tablespoons coconut aminos
- ½ cup veggie stock
- 1 cup pineapple juice
- ¼ cup rice vinegar
- 2 tablespoons stevia
- 1 tablespoon ginger, grated
- 3 garlic cloves, minced
- 6 pineapple rings

Directions:
1. In your air fryer, mix tofu with sesame oil, coconut aminos, stock, pineapple juice, vinegar, stevia, ginger, garlic and pineapple rings, stir, cover and at 366 degrees F for 20 minutes
2. Divide into bowls and serve.
3. Enjoy!

Nutrition: calories 231, fat 5, fiber 7, carbs 16, protein 4

324. Tomato Stew

Preparation time: 10 minutes
Cooking time: 20 minutes
Servings: 6
Ingredients:
- 1 green bell pepper, chopped
- 1 cup okra
- 1 small yellow onion, chopped
- 2 garlic cloves, minced
- 3 celery ribs, chopped
- 16 ounces canned tomatoes, roughly chopped
- 1 and ½ cups veggie stock
- ½ teaspoon paprika
- A pinch of salt and black pepper

Directions:
1. In your air fryer, mix bell pepper with okra, onion, garlic, celery, tomatoes, stock, paprika, salt and pepper, stir, cover and Cooking Time: at 360 degrees F for 20 minutes
2. Divide into bowls and serve hot.
3. Enjoy!

Nutrition: calories 232, fat 4, fiber 6, carbs 12, protein 4

325. Ratatouille

Preparation time: 10 minutes
Cooking time: 20 minutes
Servings: 6
Ingredients:

- *2 yellow onions, chopped*
- *1 eggplant, sliced*
- *4 zucchinis, sliced*
- *2 garlic cloves, minced*
- *2 green bell peppers, cut into medium strips*
- *6 ounces tomato paste*
- *2 tomatoes, cut into medium wedges*
- *1 teaspoon oregano, dried*
- *1 teaspoon stevia*
- *1 teaspoon basil, dried*
- *Salt and black pepper to the taste*
- *2 tablespoons parsley, chopped*
- *2 tablespoons olive oil*

Directions:

1. In your air fryer, mix oil with onions, eggplant, zucchinis, garlic, bell peppers, tomato paste, basil, oregano, salt and pepper, don't stir, cover and Cooking Time: at 365 degrees F for 20 minutes.
2. Add parsley, stir gently, divide between plates and serve right away.
3. Enjoy!

Nutrition: *calories 189, fat 7, fiber 6, carbs 17, protein 4*

326. Exotic Black Beans Mix

Preparation time: 10 minutes
Cooking time: 25 minutes
Servings: 6
Ingredients:

- *1 yellow onion, chopped*
- *1 tablespoon olive oil*
- *1 red bell pepper, chopped*
- *1 jalapeno, chopped*
- *2 garlic cloves, minced*
- *1 teaspoon ginger, grated*
- *½ teaspoon cumin*
- *½ teaspoon allspice, ground*
- *½ teaspoon oregano, dried*
- *30 ounces canned black beans, drained*
- *½ teaspoon stevia*
- *1 cup water*
- *A pinch of salt and black pepper*
- *3 cups brown rice, cooked*
- *2 mangoes, peeled and chopped*

Directions:

1. In your air fryer's pan, combine onion with the oil, bell pepper, jalapeno, garlic, ginger, cumin, allspice, oregano, black beans, stevia, water, salt and pepper, stir, cover and Cooking Time: at 370 degrees F for 25 minutes.
2. Add rice and mangoes, toss, divide between plates and serve.
3. Enjoy!

Nutrition: *calories 260, fat 6, fiber 20, carbs 16, protein 17*

327. Creamy Beans Mix

Preparation time: 10 minutes
Cooking time: 25 minutes
Servings: 6
Ingredients:

- *2 tablespoons coconut oil*
- *28 ounces canned black beans, drained*
- *2 yellow onions, chopped*
- *4 garlic cloves, minced*
- *1 green bell pepper, chopped*
- *1 teaspoon thyme, dried*
- *2 teaspoons chili flakes*
- *1 tablespoon stevia*
- *4 potatoes, cut into medium cubes*
- *A pinch of salt and cayenne pepper*
- *28 ounces canned tomatoes, chopped*
- *1 cup veggie stock*
- *14 ounces coconut milk*

Directions:

1. In your air fryer's pan, combine oil with beans, onions, garlic, bell

pepper, thyme, chili, stevia, potatoes, salt, pepper, tomatoes, stock and coconut milk, stir, cover and Cooking Time: at 365 degrees F for 25 minutes.
2. Divide into bowls and serve.
3. Enjoy!

Nutrition: 275, fat 16, fiber 15, carbs 16, protein 14

328. Dark Bean And Quinoa Salad With Quick Cumin Dressing

Servings: 4

Ingredients

For the plate of mixed greens:
- 1 cup dry quinoa, washed
- Run salt
- 2 cups vegetable soup or water
- 1/2 huge cucumber, diced conveniently
- 1 little chime pepper, diced conveniently
- 1 can BPA free, natural dark beans
- 10-15 basil leaves, hacked into a chiffonade 1/4 cup crisp cilantro, slashed

For the vinaigrette:
- 2 tbsp additional virgin olive oil
- 1/4 cup apple juice vinegar
- 1 tbsp agave or maple syrup
- 1 tbsp dijon mustard
- 1 tsp cumin
- Salt and pepper to taste

Strategy
1. Rinse quinoa through a strainer till the water runs clear. Move it to a little or medium measured pot and include two cups of vegetable stock or water and run of salt. Heat to the point of boiling, at that point diminish to a stew. Spread the pot with the goal that the top is on, yet there's a little hole where water can get away. Stew till quinoa has consumed the entirety of the fluid and is soft (around 15-20 minutes).
2. Transfer cooked quinoa to a blending bowl. Include hacked vegetables, dark beans, and herbs.
3. Whisk dressing fixings. Add the dressing to the plate of mixed greens, and serve. (In the event that you don't feel that you need all the dressing, simply include as much as you'd prefer to.
4. Plate of mixed greens will keep for three days in the cooler.
5. Zucchini Pasta With Cherry Tomatoes, Basil, Sweet Potato, And Hemp

329. Parmesan

Servings: 2
Ingredients:
- 2 huge zucchini
- 1 red chime pepper, diced
- 15 cherry tomatoes, quartered
- 8 huge basil leaves, chiffonaded
- 2 little sweet potato, prepared and afterward cut into blocks
- 2 tbsp balsamic vinegar
- 1 little avocado, cubed
- 4 tbsp hemp parmesan (formula underneath

Strategy
1. Use a spiralizer or a julienne peeler to cut zucchini into long strips (taking after noodles).
2. Toss zucchini with every single outstanding fixing, and serve.

330. Hemp Parmesan

Servings: 1/2 - 2/3 cup
Ingredients:
- 6 tbsp hemp seeds
- 6 tbsp dietary yeast
- Run ocean salt

Strategy
Consolidate all fixings in a nourishment processor, and heartbeat to separate and join. Store in the cooler for as long as about fourteen days.

331. Gluten Free White Bean And Summer Vegetable Pasta

Servings: 4
Ingredients:
- 1 little eggplant, cut into 1 inch 3D squares and softly salted for 30 minutes, at that point tapped dry 1 clove garlic, minced
- 1 huge zucchini, cut
- 1 would organic be able to fire simmered, diced tomatoes
- 1 little can natural tomato sauce
- 1 tsp agave
- 1 tbsp dried basil
- 1 tsp dried oregano
- 1 tsp dried thyme
- 1 can (or 2 cups newly cookedcannellini or naval force beans, depleted
- 8 oz. dry dark colored rice or quinoa pasta (rigatoni, linguine, and penne are on the whole fine

Strategy
1. Heat a huge skillet with olive or coconut oil shower (or simply utilize a couple tbsp water). Sautee the eggplant with the garlic till the eggplant is getting decent and darker (around 8 minutes).
2. Add the zucchini and Cooking Time: it till delicate (an additional 5 minutes).
3. Add the canned tomatoes, tomato sauce, agave, basil, oregano, thyme. Warmth through. Test for flavoring, and include a greater amount of whatever herbs you like.
4. Add the white beans and warmth the entire sauce through. This is so delectable and straightforward, you could eat it all alone as a "cheater's" ratatouille.
5. While your sauce cooks, put a pot of salted water to bubble. Include pasta when it hits a moving bubble, and Cooking Time: pasta till delicate yet at the same time somewhat still somewhat firm.
6. Drain pasta, cover with sauce, and serve.
7. Remains will keep for three days in the ice chest.

332. Butternut Squash Curry

Servings: 4
Ingredients:
- 1 tablespoon dissolved coconut oil
- 1 white or yellow onion, hacked
- 1 clove garlic, minced
- 1 tablespoon new ginger, minced
- 3 tablespoons red curry glue
- 1 tablespoon natural sugar or coconut sugar
- 2/3 cups vegetable soup
- One 14-or 15-ounce would coconut be able to drain
- 1 tablespoon soy sauce or tamari
- 1 green or red chime pepper, slashed
- 1 pound butternut squash
- 2 cups green beans, cut into 2" pieces
- 1 to 2 tablespoon lime juice

Strategy
1. Heat the coconut oil in a huge pot or wok. Include the onion and Cooking Time: till it's delicate and translucent (5 to 8 minutes).
2. Add the garlic and ginger and let them Cooking Time: for about a moment. At that point, include the curry glue and sugar. Combine the fixings until the glue is uniformly consolidated.
3. Whisk in the stock, the coconut milk, and the tamari. Include the red pepper and butternut squash. Stew till the squash is absolutely delicate (25 to 30 minutes). On the off chance that you have to include additional juices as the blend cooks, do as such.
4. Stir in the green beans and let them Cooking Time: for a few minutes, or until delicate. Season the curry to

taste with additional soy sauce or tamari and mix in the lime squeeze as wanted. Expel from warmth and serve over quinoa or darker basmati rice.
5. Remains will keep for four days.

333. Crude Zucchini Alfredo With Basil And Cherry Tomatoes

Servings: 2 (with remaining alfredo sauce
Ingredients:
- Pasta
- 2 huge zucchini
- 1 cup cherry tomatoes, split
- 1/4 cup basil, cut
- Crude alfredo sauce
- 1 cup cashews, drenched for in any event three hours (or medium-termand depleted 1/3 cup water
- 1 tsp agave or maple syrup
- 1 clove garlic
- 3-4 tbsp lemon juice (to taste
- 1/4 cup wholesome yeast
- 1/4 tsp ocean salt

Strategy
1. Use a spiralizer or a julienne peeler to cut zucchini into long strips (looking like noodles).
2. Add tomatoes and basil to the zucchini noodles and put them with or without in an enormous blending bowl.
3. Blend the entirety of the alfredo sauce fixings together in a fast blender till smooth.
4. Cover the pasta in 1/2 cup sauce, and blend it in well, including extra sauce varying (you'll have some sauce remaining). Serve.

334. Dark Bean And Corn Burgers

Servings: 4 Burgers
Ingredients:
- 1 tablespoon coconut oil
- 1 little yellow onion, cleaved
- 1 cup crisp, solidified or canned natural corn pieces
- 1 can natural, low sodium dark beans, depleted (or 1/2 cups cooked dark beans1 cup darker rice, cooked
- 1/4 cup oat flour (or ground, moved oats
- 1/4 cup tomato glue
- 2 tsp cumin
- 1 loading tsp paprika
- 1 loading tsp stew powder
- 1/2 - 1 tsp ocean salt (to taste
- Dark pepper or red pepper, to taste

Technique
1. Preheat your broiler to 350 F.
2. Heat the coconut oil in an enormous sauté dish. Include the onion and saute till onion is brilliant, delicate, and fragrant (around 5-8 minutes).
3. 2Add corn, beans and tomato glue to the container and warmth through.
4. 3Place cooked rice into the bowl of a nourishment processor. Include the beans, onion, tomato glue, and corn blend. Heartbeat to join. Include flavors, oat flour, and a bit of water, on the off chance that you need it. Heartbeat more, until you have a thick and clingy (yet malleableblend. In the event that the blend is excessively wet, include a tablespoon or two of extra oat flour.
5. 4Shape into 4 burgers and spot burgers on a foil lined heating sheet. Prepare for 25 - 30 minutes, or until burgers are delicately crisped, flipping once through. Present with crisp guacamole, whenever wanted!

335. Eggplant Rollatini With Cashew Cheese

Servings: 4
Ingredients
For rollatini:
- 2 enormous eggplant, cut the long

way into 1/4 inch thick cuts
- Olive oil
- 1/4 cups cashews, drenched for in any event three hours (or medium-termand depleted 1/2 tsp ocean salt
- 1 small clove garlic, minced (discretionary
- 2 tbsp lemon juice
- 1/3-1/2 cup water
- 1/4 cup nourishing yeast
- 2 tsps dried basil
- 1 tsp dried oregano
- Dark pepper to taste
- 1/2 10 oz. bundle solidified spinach, defrosted and crushed completely to evacuate all abundance fluid (I press mine immovably through a strainer
- 1/2 cups natural, low sodium marinara sauce

Strategy
1. Preheat stove to 400 F. Cut eggplants the long way into strips around 1/2" thick. Spot eggplant cuts onto heating sheets and sprinkle well with ocean salt or fit salt. Let sit for 30 minutes; this abatements sharpness and expels abundance dampness. Pat the cuts dry, and splash them or brush them gently with olive oil.
2. Roast eggplant cuts till sautéing (around 20 min), flipping part of the way through.
3. While eggplant is cooking, make the cashew cheddar. Spot the cashews, ocean salt, garlic, lemon, and 1/3 cup water in a nourishment processor. Procedure till the blend is extremely smooth and delicate (you're focusing on a surface like velvety ricotta cheddar), halting to scratch the bowl down a couple of times and including some additional water as essential. Stop the engine, and include the wholesome yeast, basil, oregano, and dark pepper. Procedure again to fuse. Move the cashew cheddar to a bowl and blend in the cleaved spinach. Put the cheddar blend in a safe spot.
4. Remove the simmered eggplant from the stove and decrease warmth to 325 F. Permit the cuts to cool until they can be taken care of. Move them to a cutting board and include around 3 tbsp of the cheddar blend as far as possible of one side. Move up from that side, and spot crease down in a little goulash dish. Rehash with every residual cut.
5. Smother the eggplant moves with tomato sauce, and heat, revealed, for around 20-25 minutes, or until hot. Present with sides of decision.

336. Ginger Lime Chickpea Sweet Potato Burgers

Servings: 4-6 Burgers
Ingredients:
- 3/4 cup cooked chickpeas
- 1/2 little onion
- 1 inch ginger, cleaved
- 1 tsp coconut oil
- 1 1/2 cups sweet potato, prepared or steamed and cubed
- 1/3 cup quinoa pieces or gluten free moved oats
- 2 heaping tbsp flax meal
- 2-3 tbsp lime juice (to taste)
- 2 tbsp low sodium tamari
- 1/4 cup cilantro, slashed
- Run red pepper drops (discretionary)
- Water varying

Strategy
1. Preheat stove to 350 F.
2. Heat coconut oil in a huge container or wok. Saute onion and ginger in 1 tsp coconut oil (or coconut oil splashtill delicate and fragrant (around 5 minutes). Include chickpeas and warmth through.
3. Place the chickpeas, onion, and ginger in a nourishment processor and include the sweet potato, quinoa chips or oats, flax seed, lime juice,

cilantro, tamari or coconut aminos, and run of red pepper drops, if utilizing. Heartbeat to join, at that point run the engine and include some water until consistency is exceptionally thick yet simple to form.
4. Shape blend into 4-6 burgers. Heat at 350 degrees for around 35 minutes, flipping part of the way through.

337. Sweet Potato And Black Bean Chili

Servings: 6
Ingredients:
- 1/2 cup dried dark beans
- 4 cups sweet potato, diced into 3/4 inch solid shapes
- 1 tablespoon olive oil
- 1 1/2 cups slashed white or yellow onion
- 2 cloves garlic, minced
- 1 chipotle pepper en adobo, slashed finely
- 2 teaspoons cumin powder
- 1/2 teaspoon smoked paprika
- 1 tablespoon ground bean stew powder
- 1 14 or 15 ounce container of natural, diced tomatoes (I like the Muir Glen brand
- 1 can natural, low sodium dark beans (or 1/2 cups cooked dark beans 2 cups low sodium vegetable soup, Sea salt to taste

Strategy
1. Heat the tablespoon of oil in a dutch stove or a huge pot. Saute the onion for a couple of moments, at that point include the sweet potato and garlic. Keep sauteing until the onions are delicate, around 8-10 minutes.
2. Add the bean stew en adobo, the cumin, the stew powder, and the smoked paprika. Warmth until the flavors are exceptionally fragrant.

Include the tomatoes, dark beans, and vegetable soup.
3. When juices is foaming, decrease to a stew and Cooking Time: for roughly 25-30 minutes, or until the sweet potatoes are delicate.
4. Add more juices varying, and season to taste with salt. Serve.
5. Extra stew can be solidified and will keep for as long as five days.

338. Crude Cauliflower Rice With Lemon, Mint, And Pistachios

Servings: 2
Ingredients:
- 5 cups crude cauliflower florets
- 1 oz pistachios
- 1/4 cup every basil and mint
- 2 tsp lemon get-up-and-go
- 1/2 tbsp lemon juice
- 1 tbsp olive oil
- 1/4 cup dried currants
- Ocean Salt And Dark Pepper To Taste

Strategy
1. Transfer 3 cups of the cauliflower to a nourishment processor. Procedure until the cauliflower is separated into pieces that are about the size of rice. Move to a huge blending bowl.
2. Transfer staying 2 cups of cauliflower to the nourishment processor. Include the pistachios. Procedure, by and by, until cauliflower is separated into rice estimated pieces. Heartbeat in the basil and mint till herbs are finely cleaved.
3. Add the extra hacked cauliflower, pistachios, and herbs to the blending bowl in with the principal bunch of cauliflower. Include the lemon juice, oil, and flows. Season to taste with salt and pepper. Serve.

339. Darker Rice And Lentil Salad

Servings: 4
Ingredients:
- *2 tablespoons olive oil*
- *1 tablespoon apple juice vinegar*
- *1 tablespoon lemon juice*
- *1 tablespoon dijon mustard*
- *1/2 tsp smoked paprika*
- *Ocean salt and dark pepper to taste*
- *2 cups cooked dark colored rice*
- *1 15-oz can natural, no sodium included lentils, flushed, or 1/cups cooked lentils*
- *1 carrot, diced or ground*
- *4 tbsp cleaved crisp parsley*

Technique
1. *Whisk oil, vinegar, lemon juice, mustard, paprika, salt and pepper together in a huge bowl.*
2. *Add the rice, lentils, carrot and parsley. Blend well and serve.*

340. Crude "Nut" Noodles

Servings: 2
Ingredients:
For the dressing:
- *1 tablespoon ground ginger*
- *1/2 cup olive oil*
- *2 tsp sesame oil (toasted*
- *2 tbsp smooth white miso*
- *3 dates, pitted, or ¼ cup maple syrup*
- *1 tbsp nama shoyu*
- *1/4 cup water*

For the noodles:
- *2 zucchinis*
- *1 red chime pepper, cut into matchsticks*
- *1 carrot, ground*
- *1 little cucumber, stripped into slim strips*
- *1 cup daintily cut, steamed snow peas*
- *1/4 cup hacked scallions or green onion*

Strategy
1. *Blend dressing fixings in a rapid blender until all fixings are velvety and smooth.*
2. *Use a spiralizer or julienne peeler to cut the zucchini into long, slender "noodles." Combine the zucchini with the pepper, carrot, cucumber, and scallions.*
3. *Dress the noodles with enough dressing to cover them well. Serve.*

341. Simple Fried Rice And Vegetables

Servings: 2
Ingredients:
- *2 tsp toasted sesame oil*
- *1 tbsp ground ginger*
- *1/2 cups cooked dark colored rice*
- *2-3 cups solidified or new vegetables of decision*
- *1 tbsp low sodium tamari*
- *1 tbsp rice vinegar*
- *Vegetable Stock Varying*

Strategy
1. *Heat the sesame oil in a huge wok. Include the ground ginger and warmth it for a moment or two.*
2. *Add the dark colored rice and vegetables. Saute till the vegetables are delicate.*
3. *Add the tamari, rice vinegar, and a sprinkle of vegetable soup if the blend is dry. Serve.*

342. Arugula Salad With Roasted Butternut Squash, Goji Berries, And Cauliflower

Servings: 2
Ingredients

For the plate of mixed greens:
- *4 piling cups arugula (or other green)*
- *1 lb butternut squash, stripped and hacked*
- *1 small head cauliflower, washed and hacked into little florets*
- *2 tbsp coconut or olive oil*
- *Ocean salt and pepper to taste*

- 1/4 cup crude pumpkin seeds
- 1/4 cup goji berries

For the dressing:

- 3 tbsp olive oil
- 2 tbsp squeezed orange
- 1 tbsp lemon juice
- 1/2 tsp turmeric
- 1/4 tsp ground ginger
- 1 tbsp agave or maple syrup
- Ocean salt to taste

Technique

1. Toss the squash in 1 tbsp oil and season with salt and pepper. Hurl the cauliflower in the other tablespoon and season with salt and pepper. Broil the two veggies at 375 degrees for 2030 minutes (the cauliflower will Cooking Time: quicker), till brilliant dark colored and fragrant. Expel from stove and let cool.
2. Place the arugula, goji berries, and pumpkin seeds in an enormous bowl. Include broiled vegetables. Whisk together the olive oil, lemon juice, turmeric, maple syrup or agave, ginger, and ocean salt, and dress all the veggies.
3. Divide serving of mixed greens onto two plates, and serve.

343. Simmered Vegetable Pesto Pasta Salad

Note: Instead of utilizing darker rice or quinoa pasta right now, can likewise blend the broiled vegetables and pesto into an entire grain, similar to darker rice or millet or quinoa, for an increasingly healthy variety.

Servings: 4
Ingredients:

- 3 cups zucchini, slashed into 3/4" pieces
- 3 cups eggplant, slashed into 3/4" pieces
- 1 large Jersey or legacy tomato, cleaved
- 2 tbsp olive oil or softened coconut oil
- Ocean salt and dark pepper to taste
- 8 oz darker rice or quinoa pasta (penne and fusilli function admirably
- 1/2 - 2/3 cup pecan pesto (see: dressings

Technique

1. Preheat your broiler to 400 F.
2. Lay the zucchini, eggplant and tomato out on two material or foil fixed heating sheets and shower with the olive or coconut oil. Coat the vegetables with the oil and dish vegetables for thirty minutes, or until delicate and carmelizing.
3. While vegetables cook, carry a pot of salted water to bubble. Include the pasta and Cooking Time: till still somewhat firm (as indicated by bundle directions). Channel pasta and put aside in a huge blending bowl.
4. Add the simmered vegetables and to the pasta. Blend in the pesto, season to taste, and serve on the double.

344. Portobello "Steak" And Cauliflower "Pureed Potatoes"

Servings: 4
Ingredients:
For the mushrooms:

- 1/4 cup olive oil
- 3 tbsp balsamic vinegar
- 3 tbsp low sodium tamari or nama shoyu
- 3 tbsp maple syrup
- Sprinkle pepper
- 4 portobello mushroom tops, cleaned
- Submerge 4 Portobello tops in the marinade. 1 hour will be sufficient for them to be prepared, however medium-term in the refrigerator is far and away superior.

For the Cauliflower Mashed Potatoes:

- 1 cups cashews, crude

- 4 cups cauliflower, slashed into little florets and pieces
- 2 tbsp smooth white miso
- 3 tbsp dietary yeast
- 2 tbsp lemon juice
- Ocean salt and dark pepper to taste
- 1/3 cup (or less water

Strategy
1. Place cashews into the bowl of your nourishment processor, and procedure into a fine powder.
2. Add the miso, lemon juice, healthful yeast, pepper and cauliflower. Heartbeat to join. With the engine of the machine running, include water in a flimsy stream., until the blend starts to take on a smooth, whipped surface. You may need to stop every now and again to clean the sides of the bowl and help it along.
3. When the blend looks like pureed potatoes, stop, scoop, and serve close by a Portobello top.

345. Quinoa Enchiladas

Adjusted from a formula in Food52
Servings: 6
Ingredients:
- 1 tbsp coconut oil
- 2 cloves garlic, minced
- 1 little yellow onion, cleaved
- 3/4 pounds infant bella mushrooms, hacked
- 1/2 cup diced green bean stews
- 1/2 teaspoon ground cumin
- 1/4 teaspoon ocean salt (or to taste
- 1 can natural, low sodium dark beans or 1/2 cup cooked dark beans
- 1/2 cup cooked quinoa
- 10 6-inch corn tortillas
- 1/4 cup natural, low sodium tomato or enchilada sauce

Technique
1. Preheat broiler to 350 degrees.
2. In an enormous pot over medium warmth, heat coconut oil. Sautee onion and garlic till onion is translucent (around 5-8 min). Include mushrooms and Cooking Time: until fluid has been discharged and vanished (another 5 min).
3. Add the bean stews to the pot and give them a mix for 2 minutes. Include the cumin, ocean salt, dark beans and quinoa, and keep warming the blend until it's totally warm.
4. Spread a flimsy layer (1/2 cup of marinara or enchilada sauce in the base of a goulash dish. Spot 33% of a cup of quinoa blend in the focal point of a corn tortilla and move it up. Spot the tortilla, crease down, in the goulash dish. Rehash with every outstanding tortilla and afterward spread them with 3/4 cup of extra sauce. Heat for 25 minutes, and serve.

346. Greek Okra And Eggplant Stew

Preparation time: 10 minutes
Cooking time: 25 minutes
Servings: 10
Ingredients:
- 2 cups eggplant, cubed
- 1 butternut squash, peeled and cubed
- 2 cups zucchini, cubed
- 10 ounces tomato sauce
- 1 carrot, sliced
- 1 yellow onion, chopped
- ½ cup veggie stock
- 10 ounces okra
- 1/3 cup raisins
- 2 garlic cloves, minced
- ½ teaspoon turmeric powder
- ½ teaspoon cumin, ground
- ½ teaspoon red pepper flakes, crushed
- ¼ teaspoon sweet paprika
- ¼ teaspoon cinnamon powder

Directions:

1. In your air fryer, mix eggplant with squash, zucchini, tomato sauce, carrot, onion, okra, garlic, stock, raisins, turmeric, cumin, pepper flakes, paprika and cinnamon, stir, cover and Cooking Time: at 360 degrees F for 25 minutes.
2. Divide into bowls and serve.
3. Enjoy!

Nutrition: calories 260, fat 3, fiber 4, carbs 24, protein 3

347. Indian Chickpeas

Preparation time: 10 minutes
Cooking time: 25 minutes
Servings: 14
Ingredients:

- 6 cups canned chickpeas, drained
- 1 cup veggie stock
- 1 yellow onion, chopped
- 1 tablespoon ginger, grated
- 20 garlic cloves, minced
- 8 Thai peppers, chopped
- 2 tablespoons cumin, ground
- 2 tablespoons coriander, ground
- 1 tablespoons red chili powder
- 2 tablespoons garam masala
- 2 tablespoons vegan tamarind paste
- Juice of ½ lemon

Directions:

1. In your air fryer, mix chickpeas with stock, onion ginger, garlic, Thai peppers, cumin, coriander, chili powder, garam masala, tamarind paste and lemon juice, toss, cover and Cooking Time: at 365 degrees F for 25 minutes.
2. Divide between plates and serve hot.
3. Enjoy!

Nutrition: calories 255, fat 5, fiber 14, carbs 16, protein 17

348. White Beans Stew

Preparation time: 10 minutes
Cooking time: 20 minutes
Servings: 10
Ingredients:

- 2 pounds white beans, cooked
- 3 celery stalks, chopped
- 2 carrots, chopped
- 1 bay leaf
- 1 yellow onion, chopped
- 3 garlic cloves, minced
- 1 teaspoon rosemary, dried
- 1 teaspoon oregano, dried
- 1 teaspoon thyme, dried
- A drizzle of olive oil
- Salt and black pepper to the taste
- 28 ounces canned tomatoes, chopped
- 6 cups chard, chopped

Directions:

1. In your air fryer's pan, mix white beans with celery, carrots, bay leaf, onion, garlic, rosemary, oregano, thyme, oil, salt, pepper, tomatoes and chard, toss, cover and Cooking Time: at 365 degrees F for 20 minutes.
2. Divide into bowls and serve.
3. Enjoy!

Nutrition: calories 341, fat 8, fiber 12, carbs 20, protein 6

349. Squash Bowls

Preparation time: 10 minutes
Cooking time: 20 minutes
Servings: 5
Ingredients:

- 1 big butternut squash, peeled and roughly cubed
- 2 cups broccoli florets
- 1 tablespoon sesame seeds

For the salad dressing:

- 1 and ½ tablespoon stevia
- 3 tablespoons wine vinegar
- 3 tablespoons olive oil
- 1 tablespoon coconut aminos
- 1 tablespoon ginger, grated
- 2 garlic cloves, minced

- 1 teaspoon sesame oil

Directions:
1. In your blender, mix stevia with vinegar, oil, aminos, ginger, garlic and sesame oil, pulse really well and leave aside for now.
2. In your air fryer, mix squash with the dressing you've made, broccoli and sesame seeds, toss, cover and Cooking Time: at 370 degrees F for 20 minutes.
3. Divide salad into bowls and serve.
4. Enjoy!

Nutrition: calories 250, fat 4, fiber 6, carbs 26, protein 6

350. Cauliflower Stew

Preparation time: 10 minutes
Cooking time: 15 minutes
Servings: 4
Ingredients:
- 30 ounces canned cannellini beans, drained
- 4 cups cauliflower florets
- 1 yellow onion, chopped
- 28 ounces canned tomatoes and juice
- 4 ounces canned roasted green chilies, chopped
- ½ cup hot sauce
- 1 tablespoon stevia
- 2 teaspoons cumin, ground
- 1 tablespoon chili powder
- A pinch of salt and cayenne pepper

Directions:
1. In your air fryer's pan, mix cannellini beans with cauliflower, onion, tomatoes and juice, roasted green chilies, hot sauce, stevia, cumin, chili powder, salt and cayenne pepper, stir, cover and Cooking Time: at 360 degrees F for 15 minutes.
2. Divide into bowls and serve hot.
3. Enjoy!

Nutrition: calories 314, fat 6, fiber 6, carbs 29, protein 5

351. Simple Quinoa Stew

Preparation time: 10 minutes
Cooking time: 15 minutes
Servings: 6
Ingredients:
- ½ cup quinoa
- 30 ounces canned black beans, drained
- 28 ounces canned tomatoes, chopped
- 1 green bell pepper, chopped
- 1 yellow onion, chopped
- 2 sweet potatoes, cubed
- 1 tablespoon chili powder
- 2 tablespoons cocoa powder
- 2 teaspoons cumin, ground
- Salt and black pepper to the taste
- ¼ teaspoon smoked paprika

Directions:
1. In your air fryer, mix quinoa, black beans, tomatoes, bell pepper, onion, sweet potatoes, chili powder, cocoa, cumin, paprika, salt and pepper, stir, cover and Cooking Time: on High for 6 hours.
2. Divide into bowls and serve hot.
3. Enjoy!

Nutrition: calories 342, fat 6, fiber 7, carbs 18, protein 4

352. Green Beans Mix

Preparation time: 10 minutes
Cooking time: 12 minutes
Servings: 4
Ingredients:
- 1 pound green beans
- 1 yellow onion, chopped
- 4 carrots, chopped
- 4 garlic cloves, minced
- 1 tablespoon thyme, chopped
- 3 tablespoons tomato paste
- Salt and black pepper to the taste

Directions:
1. In your air fryer's pan, mix green beans with onion, carrots, garlic, tomato paste,, salt and pepper, stir,

cover and Cooking Time: at 365 degrees F for 12 minutes.
2. Add thyme, stir, divide between plates and serve.
3. Enjoy!

Nutrition: calories 231, fat 4, fiber 6, carbs 7, protein 5

353. Chickpeas And Lentils Mix

Preparation time: 10 minutes
Cooking time: 15 minutes
Servings: 6
Ingredients:

- 1 yellow onion, chopped
- 1 tablespoon olive oil
- 1 tablespoon garlic, minced
- 1 teaspoons sweet paprika
- 1 teaspoon smoked paprika
- Salt and black pepper to the taste
- 1 cup red lentils, boiled
- 15 ounces canned chickpeas, drained
- 29 ounces canned tomatoes and juice

Directions:
1. In your air fryer, mix onion with oil, garlic, sweet and smoked paprika, salt, pepper, lentils, chickpeas and tomatoes, stir, cover and Cooking Time: at 360 degrees F for 15 minutes.
2. Ladle into bowls and serve hot.
3. Enjoy!

Nutrition: calories 341, fat 5, fiber 8, carbs 19, protein 7

354. Creamy Corn

Preparation time: 10 minutes
Cooking time: 15 minutes
Servings: 6
Ingredients:

- 1 yellow onion, chopped
- A drizzle of olive oil
- 1 red bell pepper, chopped
- 3 cups gold potatoes, chopped
- 4 cups corn
- 2 tablespoons tomato paste
- ½ teaspoon smoked paprika
- 1 teaspoon cumin, ground
- Salt and black pepper to the taste
- ½ cup almond milk
- 2 scallions, chopped

Directions:
1. In your air fryer, mix onion with the oil, bell pepper, potatoes, corn, tomato paste, paprika, cumin, salt, pepper, scallions and almond milk, stir, cover and Cooking Time: at 365 degrees F for 15 minutes.
2. Divide between plates and serve
3. Enjoy!

Nutrition: calories 312, fat 4, fiber 6, carbs 12, protein 4

355. Spinach And Lentils Mix

Preparation time: 10 minutes
Cooking time: 15 minutes
Servings: 8
Ingredients:

- 10 ounces spinach
- 2 cups canned lentils, drained
- 1 tablespoon garlic, minced
- 15 ounces canned tomatoes, chopped
- 2 cups cauliflower florets
- 1 teaspoon ginger, grated
- 1 yellow onion, chopped
- 2 tablespoons curry paste
- ½ teaspoon cumin, ground
- ½ teaspoon coriander, ground
- 2 teaspoons stevia
- A pinch of salt and black pepper
- ¼ cup cilantro, chopped
- 1 tablespoon lime juice

Directions:
1. In a pan that fits your air fryer, mix spinach with lentils, garlic, tomatoes, cauliflower, ginger, onion, curry paste, cumin, coriander, stevia, salt, pepper and lime juice, stir, introduce in the fryer and Cooking Time: at 370 degrees F for 15 minutes.
2. Add cilantro, stir, divide into bowls and serve.

3. Enjoy!

Nutrition: calories 265, fat 1, fiber 7, carbs 12, protein 7

356. Cajun Mushrooms And Beans

Preparation time: 10 minutes
Cooking time: 15 minutes
Servings: 4
Ingredients:

- 2 tablespoons olive oil
- 1 green bell pepper, chopped
- 1 yellow onion, chopped
- 2 celery stalks, chopped
- 3 garlic cloves, minced
- 15 ounces canned tomatoes, chopped
- 8 ounces white mushrooms, sliced
- 15 ounces canned kidney beans, drained
- 1 zucchini, chopped
- 1 tablespoon Cajun seasoning
- Salt and black pepper to the taste

Directions:

1. In your air fryer's pan, mix oil with bell pepper, onion, celery, garlic, tomatoes, mushrooms, beans, zucchini, Cajun seasoning, salt and pepper, stir, cover and Cooking Time: on at 370 degrees F for 15 minutes.
2. Divide veggie mix between plates and serve.
3. Enjoy!

Nutrition: calories 312, fat 4, fiber 7, carbs 19, protein 4

357. Eggplant Stew

Preparation time: 10 minutes
Cooking time: 15 minutes
Servings: 4
Ingredients:

- 24 ounces canned tomatoes, chopped
- 1 red onion, chopped
- 2 red bell peppers, chopped
- 2 big eggplants, roughly chopped
- 1 tablespoon smoked paprika
- 2 teaspoons cumin, ground
- Salt and black pepper to the taste
- Juice of 1 lemon
- 1 tablespoons parsley, chopped

Directions:

1. In your air fryer's pan, mix tomatoes with onion, bell peppers, eggplant, smoked paprika, cumin, salt, pepper and lemon juice, stir, cover and Cooking Time: at 365 degrees F for 15 minutes
2. Add parsley, stir, divide between plates and serve cold.
3. Enjoy!

Nutrition: calories 251, fat 4, fiber 6, carbs 14, protein 3

358. Corn And Cabbage Salad

Preparation time: 10 minutes
Cooking time: 15 minutes
Servings: 4
Ingredients:

- 1 small yellow onion, chopped
- 1 tablespoon olive oil
- 2 garlic cloves, minced
- 1 and ½ cups mushrooms, sliced
- 3 teaspoons ginger, grated
- A pinch of salt and black pepper
- 2 cups corn
- 4 cups red cabbage, chopped
- 1 tablespoon nutritional yeast
- 2 teaspoons tomato paste
- 1 teaspoon coconut aminos
- 1 teaspoon sriracha sauce

Directions:

1. In your air fryer's pan, mix the oil with onion, garlic, mushrooms, ginger, salt, pepper, corn, cabbage, yeast and tomato paste, stir, cover and Cooking Time: at 365 degrees F for 15 minutes
2. Add sriracha sauce and aminos, stir, divide between plates and serve.
3. Enjoy!

Nutrition: calories 360, fat 4, fiber 4, carbs 10, protein 4

359. Okra And Corn Mix

Preparation time: 10 minutes
Cooking time: 15 minutes
Servings: 6
Ingredients:

- *1 green bell pepper, chopped*
- *1 small yellow onion, chopped*
- *3 garlic cloves, minced*
- *16 ounces okra, sliced*
- *2 cup corn*
- *12 ounces canned tomatoes, crushed*
- *1 and ½ teaspoon smoked paprika*
- *1 teaspoon marjoram, dried*
- *1 teaspoon thyme, dried*
- *1 teaspoon oregano, dried*
- *Salt and black pepper to the taste*

Directions:

1. *In your air fryer, mix bell pepper with onion, garlic, okra, corn, tomatoes, smoked paprika, marjoram, thyme, oregano, salt and pepper, stir, cover and Cooking Time: at 360 degrees F for 15 minutes.*
2. *Stir, divide between plates and serve.*
3. *Enjoy!*

Nutrition: *calories 243, fat 4, fiber 6, carbs 10, protein 3*

360. Potato And Carrot Mix

Preparation time: 10 minutes
Cooking time: 16 minutes
Servings: 6
Ingredients:

- *2 potatoes, cubed*
- *3 pounds carrots, cubed*
- *1 yellow onion, chopped*
- *Salt and black pepper to the taste*
- *1 teaspoon thyme, dried*
- *3 tablespoons coconut milk*
- *2 teaspoons curry powder*
- *3 tablespoons vegan cheese, crumbled*
- *1 tablespoon parsley, chopped*

Directions:

1. *In your air fryer's pan, mix onion with potatoes, carrots, salt, pepper, thyme and curry powder, stir, cover and Cooking Time: at 365 degrees F for 16 minutes.*
2. *Add coconut milk, sprinkle vegan cheese, divide between plates and serve.*
3. *Enjoy!*

Nutrition: *calories 241, fat 4, fiber 7, carbs 8, protein 4*

361. Winter Green Beans

Preparation time: 10 minutes
Cooking time: 16 minutes
Servings: 4
Ingredients:

- *1 and ½ cups yellow onion, chopped*
- *1 pound green beans, halved*
- *4 ounces canned tomatoes, chopped*
- *4 garlic cloves, chopped*
- *2 teaspoons oregano, dried*
- *1 jalapeno, chopped*
- *Salt and black pepper to the taste*
- *1 and ½ teaspoons cumin, ground*
- *1 tablespoons olive oil*

Directions:

1. *Preheat your air fryer to 365 degrees F, add oil to the pan, also add onion, green beans, tomatoes, garlic, oregano, jalapeno, salt, pepper and cumin, cover and Cooking Time: for 16 minutes.*
2. *Divide between plates and serve.*
3. *Enjoy!*

Nutrition: *calories 261, fat 5, fiber 8, carbs 10, protein 12*

362. Green Beans Casserole

Preparation time: 10 minutes
Cooking time: 20 minutes
Servings: 4
Ingredients:

- *1 teaspoon olive oil*
- *2 red chilies, dried*
- *¼ teaspoon fenugreek seeds*

- ½ teaspoon black mustard seeds
- 10 curry leaves, chopped
- ½ cup red onion, chopped
- 3 garlic cloves, minced
- 2 teaspoons coriander powder
- 2 tomatoes, chopped
- 2 cups eggplant, chopped
- ½ teaspoon turmeric powder
- ½ cup green bell pepper, chopped
- A pinch of salt and black pepper
- 1 cup green beans, trimmed and halved
- 2 teaspoons tamarind paste
- 1 tablespoons cilantro, chopped

Directions:

1. In a baking dish that fits your air fryer, combine oil with chilies, fenugreek seeds, black mustard seeds, curry leaves, onion, coriander, tomatoes, eggplant, turmeric, green bell pepper, salt, pepper, green beans, tamarind paste and cilantro, toss, put in your air fryer and Cooking Time: at 365 degrees F for 20 minutes.
2. Divide between plates and serve.

Nutrition: calories 251, fat 5, fiber 4, carbs 8, protein 12

363. Chipotle Green Beans

Preparation time: 10 minutes
Cooking time: 16 minutes
Servings: 6
Ingredients:

- 1 yellow onion, chopped
- 1 pound green beans, halved
- 2 teaspoons cumin, ground
- A drizzle of olive oil
- 12 ounces corn
- ¼ teaspoon chipotle powder
- 1 cup salsa

Directions:

1. In a pan that fits your air fryer, combine oil with onion, green beans, cumin, corn, chipotle powder and salsa, toss, introduce in your air fryer and Cooking Time: at 365 degrees F for 16 minutes.
2. Divide between plates and serve.
3. Enjoy!

Nutrition: calories 224, fat 2, fiber 12, carbs 14, protein 10

364. Cranberry Beans Pasta

Preparation time: 10 minutes
Cooking time: 15 minutes
Servings: 8
Ingredients:

- 2 cups canned cranberry beans, drained
- 2 celery ribs, chopped
- 1 yellow onion, chopped
- 7 garlic cloves, minced
- 1 teaspoon rosemary, chopped
- 26 ounces canned tomatoes, chopped
- ¼ teaspoon red pepper flakes
- 2 teaspoons oregano, dried
- 3 teaspoons basil, dried
- ½ teaspoon smoked paprika
- A pinch of salt and black pepper
- 10 ounces kale, roughly chopped
- 2 cups whole wheat vegan pasta, cooked

Directions:

1. In a pan that fits your air fryer, combine beans with celery, onion, garlic, rosemary, tomatoes, pepper flakes, oregano, basil, paprika, salt, pepper and kale, introduce in your air fryer and Cooking Time: at 365 degrees F for 15 minutes.
2. Divide vegan pasta between plates, add cranberry mix on top and serve.
3. Enjoy!

Nutrition: calories 251, fat 2, fiber 12, carbs 12, protein 6

365. Mexican Casserole

Preparation time: 10 minutes
Cooking time: 15 minutes
Servings: 4

Ingredients:
- 1 tablespoon olive oil
- 4 garlic cloves, minced
- 1 yellow onion, chopped
- 2 tablespoons cilantro, chopped
- 1 small red chili, chopped
- 2 teaspoons cumin, ground
- Salt and black pepper to the taste
- 1 teaspoon sweet paprika
- 1 teaspoon coriander seeds
- 1 pound sweet potatoes, cubed
- Juice of ½ lime
- 10 ounces green beans
- 2 cups tomatoes, chopped
- 1 tablespoon parsley, chopped

Directions:
1. Grease a pan that fits your air fryer with the oil, add garlic, onion, cilantro, red chili, cumin, salt, pepper, paprika, coriander, potatoes, lime juice, green beans and tomatoes, toss, place in your air fryer and Cooking Time: at 365 degrees F for 15 minutes.
2. Add parsley, divide between plates and serve.
3. Enjoy!

Nutrition: calories 223, fat 5, fiber 4, carbs 7, protein 8

366. Endives And Rice Casserole

Preparation time: 10 minutes
Cooking time: 20 minutes
Servings: 4
Ingredients:
- 1 tablespoon olive oil
- 2 scallions, chopped
- 3 garlic cloves chopped
- 1 tablespoon ginger, grated
- 1 teaspoon chili sauce
- A pinch of salt and black pepper
- ½ cup white rice
- 1 cup veggie stock
- 3 endives, trimmed and chopped

Directions:
1. Grease a pan that fits your air fryer with the oil, add scallions, garlic, ginger, chili sauce, salt, pepper, rice, stock and endives, place in your air fryer, cover and Cooking Time: at 365 degrees F for 20 minutes.
2. Divide casserole between plates and serve.
3. Enjoy!

Nutrition: calories 220, fat 5, fiber 8, carbs 12, protein 6

367. Cabbage And Tomatoes

Preparation time: 10 minutes
Cooking time: 12 minutes
Servings: 4
Ingredients:
- 1 tablespoon olive oil
- 1 green cabbage head, chopped
- Salt and black pepper to the taste
- 15 ounces canned tomatoes, chopped
- ½ cup yellow onion, chopped
- 2 teaspoons turmeric powder

Directions:
1. In a pan that fits your air fryer, combine oil with green cabbage, salt, pepper, tomatoes, onion and turmeric, place in your air fryer and Cooking Time: at 365 degrees F for 12 minutes.
2. Divide between plates and serve.
3. Enjoy!

Nutrition: calories 202, fat 5, fiber 8, carbs 9, protein 10

368. Simple Endive Mix

Preparation time: 10 minutes
Cooking time: 10 minutes
Servings: 4
Ingredients:
- 8 endives, trimmed
- Salt and black pepper to the taste
- 3 tablespoons olive oil
- Juice of ½ lemon
- 1 tablespoon tomato paste

- 2 tablespoons parsley, chopped
- 1 teaspoon stevia

Directions:
1. In a bowl, combine endives with salt, pepper, oil, lemon juice, tomato paste, parsley and stevia, toss, place endives in your air fryer's basket and Cooking Time: at 365 degrees F for 10 minutes.
2. Divide between plates and serve.
3. Enjoy!

Nutrition: calories 160, fat 4, fiber 7, carbs 9, protein 4

369. Eggplant And Tomato Sauce

Preparation time: 10 minutes
Cooking time: 12 minutes
Servings: 2
Ingredients:
- 4 cups eggplant, cubed
- 1 tablespoon olive oil
- 1 tablespoon garlic powder
- A pinch of salt and black pepper
- 3 garlic cloves, minced
- 1 cup tomato sauce

Directions:
1. In a pan that fits your air fryer, combine eggplant cubes with oil, garlic, salt, pepper, garlic powder and tomato sauce, toss, place in your air fryer and Cooking Time: at 370 degrees F for 12 minutes.
2. Divide between plates and serve.
3. Enjoy!

Nutrition: calories 250, fat 7, fiber 5, carbs 10, protein 4

370. Brown Rice And Mung Beans Mix

Preparation time: 10 minutes
Cooking time: 16 minutes
Servings: 2
Ingredients:
- ½ teaspoon olive oil
- ½ cup brown rice, cooked
- ½ cup mung beans
- ½ teaspoon cumin seeds
- ½ cup red onion, chopped
- 2 tomatoes, chopped
- 1 small ginger piece, grated
- 4 garlic cloves, minced
- 1 teaspoon coriander, ground
- ½ teaspoon turmeric powder
- A pinch of cayenne pepper
- ½ teaspoon garam masala
- 1 cup veggie stock
- Salt and black pepper to the taste
- 1 teaspoon lemon juice

Directions:
1. In your blender, mix tomato with garlic, onions, ginger, salt, pepper, garam masala, cayenne, coriander and turmeric and pulse really well.
2. In a pan that fits your air fryer, combine oil with blended tomato mix, mung beans, rice, stock, cumin and lemon juice, place in your air fryer and Cooking Time: at 365 degrees F for 16 minutes.
3. Divide everything between plates and serve.
4. Enjoy!

Nutrition: calories 200, fat 6, fiber 7, carbs 10, protein 8

371. Lentils And Spinach Casserole

Preparation time: 10 minutes
Cooking time: 16 minutes
Servings: 3
Ingredients:
- 1 teaspoon olive oil
- 1/3 cup canned brown lentils, drained
- 1 small ginger piece, grated
- 4 garlic cloves, minced
- 1 green chili pepper, chopped
- 2 tomatoes, chopped
- ½ teaspoon garam masala
- ½ teaspoon turmeric powder

- 2 potatoes, cubed
- Salt and black pepper to the taste
- ¼ teaspoon cardamom, ground
- ¼ teaspoon cinnamon powder
- 6 ounces spinach leaves

Directions:

1. In a pan that fits your air fryer combine oil with canned lentils, ginger, garlic, chili pepper, tomatoes, garam masala, turmeric, potatoes, salt, pepper, cardamom, cinnamon and spinach, toss, place in your air fryer and Cooking Time: at 356 degrees F for 16 minutes.
2. Divide casserole between plates and serve.
3. Enjoy!

Nutrition: calories 250, fat 3, fiber 11, carbs 16, protein 10

372. Red Potatoes And Tasty Chutney

Preparation time: 10 minutes
Cooking time: 14 minutes
Servings: 4
Ingredients:

- 2 pounds red potatoes, cubed
- 1 cup green beans
- 1 cup carrots, shredded
- 16 ounces canned chickpeas, drained
- 2 tablespoons olive oil
- 1 teaspoon coriander seeds
- 1 and ½ teaspoons cumin seeds
- 1 and ½ teaspoons garam masala
- ½ teaspoon mustard seeds
- 1 teaspoon garlic, minced

For the chutney:

- ¼ cup water
- ½ cup mint
- ½ cup cilantro
- 1 small ginger piece, grated
- 2 teaspoons lime juice
- A pinch of salt

Directions:

1. In a baking dish that fits your air fryer, combine oil with potatoes, green beans, carrots, chickpeas, coriander, cumin, garam masala, mustard seeds and garlic, place in your air fryer and Cooking Time: at 365 degrees F for 20 minutes.
2. In your blender, mix water with mint, cilantro, ginger, lime juice and salt and pulse really well.
3. Divide potato mix between plates, add mint chutney on top and serve.
4. Enjoy!

Nutrition: calories 241, fat 4, fiber 7, carbs 11, protein 6

373. Simple Veggie Salad

Preparation time: 10 minutes
Cooking time: 10 minutes
Servings: 8
Ingredients:

- 1 and ½ cups tomatoes, chopped
- 3 cups eggplant, chopped
- 2 teaspoons capers
- Cooking spray
- 3 garlic cloves, minced
- 2 teaspoons balsamic vinegar
- 1 tablespoon basil, chopped
- A pinch of salt and black pepper

Directions:

1. Grease a pan that fits your air fryer with cooking spray, add tomatoes, eggplant, capers, garlic, salt and pepper, place in your air fryer and Cooking Time: at 365 degrees F for 10 minutes.
2. Divide between plates, drizzle balsamic vinegar all over, sprinkle basil and serve cold.
3. Enjoy!

Nutrition: calories 171, fat 3, fiber 1, carbs 8, protein 12

374. Chickpea And Black Olive Stew

Preparation Time: 15 minutes
Serving: 4
Although this stew is eaten warmly with rice,

it's incredibly good cold too.

Ingredients

- 2 tbsp olive oil
- 2 cups chopped onion
- 2 garlic cloves, minced
- 2 carrots, peeled and cut into thick slices
- 1/3 cup white wine
- 3 cups cherry tomatoes
- 2/3 cup vegetable stock
- 1 1/3 cups canned chickpeas, drained and rinsed
- ½ cup pitted black olives
- 1 tbsp chopped fresh oregano

Directions

1. Heat the olive oil in a medium pot and sauté the onion, garlic, and carrots until softened, 5 minutes.
2. Mix in the white wine, allow reduction by one-third and mix in the tomatoes, and vegetable stock. Cover the lid and Cooking Time: until the tomatoes break, soften, and the liquid reduces by half.
3. Stir in the chickpeas, olives, oregano and season with salt and black pepper. Cooking Time: for 3 minutes to warm the chickpeas.
4. Dish the stew and serve warm.

Nutrition:
Calories 698 kcal| Fats 51.3g
Carbs 54.1g
Protein 12.1g

375. Chili Seitan Stew With Brown Rice

Preparation Time: 50 minutes
Serving: 4

The outcome is a spicy, slightly sweet, garlicky sauce, which can be used for tacos too.

Ingredients

For the stew:

- 2 tbsp olive oil
- 1 lb seitan, cut into cubes
- Salt and black pepper to taste
- 1 tsp chili powder
- 1 tsp onion powder
- 1 tsp cumin powder
- 1 tsp garlic powder
- 1 yellow onion, chopped
- 2 celery stalks, chopped
- 2 carrots diced
- 4-5 cloves garlic
- 1 cup vegetable broth
- 1 cup water
- 1 tsp oregano
- 1 cup chopped tomatoes
- 3 green chilies, deseeded and chopped
- 1 lime, juiced

For the brown rice:

- 1 cup brown rice
- 1 cup water
- Salt to taste

Directions

1. Heat the olive oil in a large pot, season the seitan with salt, black pepper, and Cooking Time: in the oil until brown, 10 minutes.
2. Stir in the chili powder, onion powder, cumin powder, garlic powder, and Cooking Time: until fragrant, 1 minute. Mix in the onion, celery, carrots, garlic, and Cooking Time: until softened. Pour in the vegetable broth, water, oregano, tomatoes, and green chilies.
3. Cover the pot and Cooking Time: until the tomatoes soften and the stew reduces by half, 10 to 15 minutes. Open the lid, adjust the taste with salt, black pepper, and mix in the lime juice. Dish the stew and serve warm with the brown rice.
4. Meanwhile, as the stew cooks, add the brown rice, water, and salt to a medium pot. Cooking Time: over medium heat until the rice is tender and the water absorbs, 15 to 20 minutes.

Nutrition:
Calories 1290
Fats 131.8g
Carbs 15.2g
Protein 24.4g

376. Potato And Pea Stir-Fry

Preparation Time: 21 minutes
Serving: 4

This potato pea stir-fry is absolutely tasty and more so if you like gingery tastes.

Ingredients
- 4 medium potatoes, peeled and diced
- 2 tbsp olive oil
- 1 medium onion, chopped
- 1 tsp red chili powder
- 1 tsp fresh ginger-garlic paste
- 1 tsp cumin powder
- ¼ tsp turmeric powder
- Salt and black pepper to taste
- 1 cup fresh green peas

Directions
1. Steam potatoes in a safe microwave bowl in the microwave for 8-10 minutes or until soften. Heat the olive oil in a wok and sauté the onion until softened, 3 minutes.
2. Mix in the chili powder, ginger-garlic paste, cumin powder, turmeric powder, salt, and black pepper. Cooking Time: until the fragrant releases, 1 minute. Stir in the green peas, potatoes, and Cooking Time: until softened, 2 to 3 minutes. Serve warm.

Nutrition:
Calories 394 kcal| Fats 7.7g
Carbs 73.9g
Protein 10.2g

377. Mongolian Seitan

Preparation Time: 20 minutes
Serving: 4

This recipe is the perfect swap for Mongolian beef, made by tossing crispy pan-fried seitan in slightly and sweet spicy inspired Asian sauce.

Ingredients
For the sauce:
- 2 tsp olive oil
- ½ tsp freshly grated ginger
- 3 garlic cloves, minced
- 1/3 tsp red chili flakes
- 1/3 tsp allspice
- 1/2 cup low-sodium soy sauce
- ½ cup + 2 tbsp pure date sugar
- 2 tsp cornstarch
- 2 tbsp cold water

For the crisped seitan:
- 1 ½ tbsp olive oil
- 1 lb seitan, cut into 1-inch pieces

For topping:
- 1 tbsp toasted sesame seeds
- 1 tbsp sliced scallions

Directions
1. Heat the olive oil in a wok and sauté the ginger and garlic until fragrant, 30 seconds.
2. Mix in the red chili flakes, Chinese all spice, soy sauce, and date sugar. Allow the sugar to melt and set aside.
3. In a small bowl, mix the cornstarch and water. Stir the cornstarch mixture into the sauce and allow thickening for 1 minute. Turn the heat off.
4. Heat the olive oil in a medium skillet over medium heat and fry the seitan on both sides until crispy on both sides, 10 minutes,
5. Mix the seitan into the sauce and warm over low heat. Dish the food, garnish with the sesame seeds and scallions. Serve warm with brown rice.

Nutrition:
Calories 354 kcal| Fats 20.8g
Carbs 17.7g
Protein 25.2g

378. Alfredo Pasta With Cherry Tomatoes

Preparation Time: 20 minutes
Serving: 4

Alfredo sauce is one of the easiest ways to turn an ordinary pasta into a gourmet experience, just put on some cherry tomatoes to make it more exciting.

Ingredients

- 2 cups almond milk
- 1 ½ cups vegetable broth
- 3 tbsp plant butter
- 1 large garlic clove, minced
- 16 oz whole-wheat fettuccine
- ½ cup coconut cream
- ¼ cup halved cherry tomatoes
- ¾ cup grated plant-based Parmesan cheese
- Salt and black pepper to taste
- Chopped fresh parsley to garnish

Directions

1. Bring almond milk, vegetable broth, butter, and garlic to a boil in a large pot, 5 minutes. Mix in the fettuccine and Cooking Time: until tender, while frequently tossing around, 10 minutes.
2. Mix in coconut cream, tomatoes, plant Parmesan cheese, salt, and pepper. Cooking Time: for 3 minutes or until the cheese melts. Garnish with some parsley and serve warm.

Nutrition:
Calories 698 kcal| Fats 26.1g
Carbs 101.8g
Protein 22.6g

379. Tempeh Tetrazzini With Garden Peas

Preparation Time: 50 minutes
Serving: 4

Let's make it vegan! This is a traditional recipe that is so delicious that has stood the test of time.

Ingredients

- 16 oz whole-wheat bow-tie pasta
- 2 tbsp olive oil, divided
- 2/3 lb tempeh, cut into 1-inch cubes
- Salt and black pepper to taste
- 1 medium yellow onion, chopped
- ½ cup sliced white mushrooms
- 2 tbsp whole-wheat flour
- ¼ cup white wine
- ¾ cup vegetable stock
- ¼ cup oats milk
- 2 tsp chopped fresh thyme
- ¼ cup chopped cauliflower
- ½ cup grated plant-based Parmesan cheese
- 3 tbsp whole-wheat breadcrumbs

Directions

1. Cooking Time: the pasta in 8 cups of slightly salted water for 10 minutes or until al dente. Drain and set aside.
2. Preheat the oven to 375 F.
3. Heat the 1 tbsp of olive oil in a skillet over medium heat, season the tempeh with salt, pepper, and Cooking Time: until golden brown all around. Mix in onion, mushrooms, and Cooking Time: until softened, 5 minutes. Stir in flour and Cooking Time: for 1 more minute. Mix in wine and add two-thirds of the vegetable stock. Cooking Time: for 2 minutes while occasionally stirring and then add milk; continue cooking until the sauce thickens, 4 minutes.
4. Season with the thyme, salt, black pepper, and half of the Parmesan cheese. Once the cheese melts, turn the heat off and allow cooling.
5. Add the rest of the vegetable stock and cauliflower to a food processor and blend until smooth. Pour the mixture into a bowl, pour in sauce, and mix in pasta until combined.
6. Grease a 2 quarts glass baking dish with cooking spray and spread the mixture in the baking dish. Drizzle the remaining olive oil on top, breadcrumbs, some more thyme, and the remaining cheese. Bake until the

cheese melts and is golden brown on top, 30 minutes. Remove the dish from the oven, allow cooling for 3 minutes, and serve.

Nutrition:
Calories 799 kcal| Fats 57.7g
Carbs 54.3g
Protein 27g

380. Portobello Kale Florentine

Preparation Time: 25 minutes
Serving: 4
Craving for something nice but plant-based? This one is a must try!

Ingredients

- 4 large portobello mushrooms, stems removed
- 1/8 tsp black pepper
- 1/8 tsp garlic salt
- ½ tsp olive oil
- 1 small onion, chopped
- 1 cup chopped fresh kale
- ¼ cup crumbled tofu cheese
- 1 tbsp chopped fresh basil

Directions

1. Preheat the oven to 350 F and grease a baking sheet with cooking spray.
2. Lightly oil the mushrooms with some cooking spray and season with the black pepper and garlic salt. Arrange the mushrooms on the baking sheet and bake in the oven until tender, 10 to 15 minutes.
3. Heat the olive oil in a medium skillet over medium heat and sauté the onion until tender, 3 minutes. Stir in the kale until wilted, 3 minutes. Turn the heat off. Spoon the mixture into the mushrooms and top with the tofu cheese and basil. Serve.

Nutrition:
Calories 65 kcal| Fats 1.6g
Carbs 10.1g
Protein 4.9g

381. Tempeh Oat Balls With Maple Asparagus

Preparation Time: 40 minutes
Serving: 4
Perfect meal for shifting from heartier winter foods to more refreshing spring foods, yet incredibly filling and nutritious.

Ingredients

For tempeh balls:

- 1 tbsp flax seed powder + 3 tbsp water
- 1 lb tempeh, crumbled
- ¼ cup chopped red bell pepper
- Salt and black pepper to taste
- 1 tbsp almond flour
- 1 tsp garlic powder
- 1 tsp onion powder
- 1 tsp tofu mayonnaise
- Olive oil for brushing

For maple asparagus:

- 2 tbsp plant butter
- 1 lb asparagus, hard part trimmed
- 2 tbsp pure maple syrup
- 1 tbsp freshly squeezed lemon juice

Directions

1. Preheat the oven to 400 F and line a baking sheet with parchment paper.
2. In a medium bowl, mix the flax seed powder with water and allow thickening for 5 minutes. Add the tempeh, bell pepper, salt, black pepper, almond flour, garlic powder, onion powder, and tofu mayonnaise. Mix well and form 1-inch balls from the mixture.
3. Arrange on the baking sheet, brush with cooking spray and bake in the oven for 15 to 20 minutes or until brown and compacted. Remove from the oven and set aside for serving.
4. Melt the butter in a large skillet and sauté the asparagus until softened with some crunch, 7 minutes. Mix in the maple syrup and lemon juice. Cooking Time: for 2 minutes and plate the asparagus. Serve warm with

the tempeh balls.

Nutrition:
Calories 365 kcal| Fats 22.1g
Carbs 24.5g
Protein 24.2g

382. Chili Mushroom Spaghetti With Watercress

Preparation Time: 30 minutes
Serving: 4
This recipe is so easy to make, which will charm you into amazing comfort.

Ingredients

- *1 lb whole-wheat spaghetti*
- *3 tbsp plant butter*
- *2 tbsp olive oil*
- *2 shallots, finely chopped*
- *2 garlic cloves, minced*
- *½ lb chopped white button mushrooms*
- *1 tbsp sake*
- *3 tbsp soy sauce*
- *1 tsp hot sauce*
- *A handful fresh watercress*
- *¼ cup chopped fresh parsley*
- *Black pepper to taste*

Directions

1. *Cooking Time: the spaghetti in slightly salted water in a large pot over medium heat until al dente, 10 minutes. Drain the spaghetti and set aside.*
2. *Heat the butter and olive oil in a large skillet over medium heat and sauté the shallots, garlic, and mushrooms until softened, 5 minutes.*
3. *Stir in the sake, soy sauce, and hot sauce. Cooking Time: further for 1 minute.*
4. *Toss the spaghetti in the sauce along with the watercress and parsley. Cooking Time: for 1 minute and season with the black pepper. Dish the food and serve warm.*

Nutrition:
Calories 393 kcal| Fats 22.2g
Carbs 42.9g
Protein 9.3g

383. Zucchini Rolls In Tomato Sauce

Preparation Time: 60 minutes
Serving: 4
Replace the zucchini lasagna noodles – it's LOW CARB and you're not going to miss the noodles! I promise This can even be done in advance – great for serving a party or preparing leftovers for the next day's work!

Ingredients

- *3 large zucchinis, sliced lengthwise into strips*
- *Salt and black pepper to taste*
- *1 tbsp olive oil*
- *¾ lb crumbled tempeh*
- *1 cup crumbled tofu cheese*
- *1/3 cup grated plant-based Parmesan cheese*
- *¼ cup chopped fresh basil leaves*
- *2 garlic cloves, minced*
- *1 ½ cups marinara sauce, divided*
- *2 cups shredded plant-based mozzarella, divided*

Directions

1. *Line a baking sheet with paper towels and lay the zucchini slices in a single layer on the sheet. Sprinkle each side with some salt and allow releasing of liquid for 15 minutes.*
2. *Heat the olive oil in a large skillet over medium heat and Cooking Time: the tempeh until browned, 10 minutes. Set aside.*
3. *In a medium bowl, mix the tempeh, tofu cheese, plant Parmesan cheese, basil and garlic; season with salt and black pepper.*
4. *Preheat the oven to 400 F.*
5. *Spread 1 cup of marinara sauce onto the bottom of a 10-inch oven-proof skillet and set aside.*
6. *Spread 1 tbsp of the cheese mixture evenly along each zucchini slice;*

sprinkle with 1 tbsp of plant mozzarella cheese. Roll up the zucchini slices over the filling and arrange in the skillet. Top with the remaining ½ cup of marinara sauce and sprinkle with the remaining plant mozzarella.
7. Bake in the oven for 25-30 minutes or until the zucchini rolls are heated through and the cheese begins to brown. Serve immediately.

Nutrition:
Calories 428 kcal| Fats 14.5g
Carbs 31.3g| Protein 40.3g

384. Paprika & Tomato Pasta Primavera

Preparation Time: 25 minutes
Serving: 4
Pasta Primavera is a straightforward and extremely light dish to prep.

Ingredients
- 2 tbsp olive oil
- 8 oz whole-wheat fidelini
- ½ tsp paprika
- 1 small red onion, sliced
- 2 garlic cloves, minced
- 1 cup dry white wine
- Salt and black pepper to taste
- 2 cups cherry tomatoes, halved
- 3 tbsp plant butter, cut into ½-in cubes
- 1 lemon, zested and juiced
- 1 cup packed fresh basil leaves

Directions
1. Heat the olive oil in a large pot and mix in the fidelini, paprika, onion, garlic, and stir-fry for 2-3 minutes.
2. Mix in the white wine, salt, and black pepper. Cover with water. Cooking Time: until the water absorbs and the fidelini al dente, 5 minutes. Mix in the cherry tomatoes, plant butter, lemon zest, lemon juice, and basil leaves.
3. Dish the food and serve warm.

Nutrition:
Calories 380 kcal| Fats 24.1g
Carbs 33.7g
Protein 11.2g

385. Green Lentil Stew With Brown Rice

Preparation Time: 50 minutes
Serving: 4
Easy one pot of lentil with veggies and rice. Convenient to Cooking Time: and the taste is flavorful.

Ingredients
For the stew:
- 2 tbsp olive oil
- 1 lb tempeh, cut into cubes
- Salt and black pepper to taste
- 1 tsp chili powder
- 1 tsp onion powder
- 1 tsp cumin powder
- 1 tsp garlic powder
- 1 yellow onion, chopped
- 2 celery stalks, chopped
- 2 carrots diced
- 4 garlic cloves, minced
- 2 cups vegetable broth
- 1 tsp oregano
- 1 cup green lentils, rinsed
- ¼ cup chopped tomatoes
- 1 lime, juiced

For the brown rice:
- 1 cup brown rice
- 1 cup water
- Salt to taste

Directions
1. Heat the olive oil in a large pot, season the tempeh with salt, black pepper, and Cooking Time: in the oil until brown, 10 minutes.
2. Stir in the chili powder, onion powder, cumin powder, garlic powder, and Cooking Time: until fragrant, 1 minute. Mix in the onion, celery, carrots, garlic, and Cooking Time: until softened. Pour

in the vegetable broth, oregano, green lentils, tomatoes, and green chilies.

3. Cover the pot and Cooking Time: until the tomatoes soften and the stew reduces by half, 10 to 15 minutes. Open the lid, adjust the taste with salt, black pepper, and mix in the lime juice. Dish the stew and serve warm with the brown rice.
4. Meanwhile, as the stew cooks, add the brown rice, water, and salt to a medium pot. Cooking Time: over medium heat until the rice is tender and the water absorbs, 15 to 25 minutes.

Nutrition:
Calories 1305 kcal| Fats 130.9g
Carbs 25.1g| Protein 24.3g

386. Cannellini Beans Bow Ties

Preparation Time: 35 minutes
Serving: 4
Seasoned pastas bowls during these cold nights are a great way to eat well. Try out this light-filled Cannellini Bowtie Pasta Salad.

Ingredients
- 2 ½ cups whole-wheat bow tie pasta
- 1 tbsp olive oil
- 1 medium zucchini, sliced
- 2 garlic cloves, minced
- 2 large tomatoes, chopped
- 1 (15 oz can cannellini beans, rinsed and drained
- 1 (2 ¼ oz can pitted green olives, sliced
- ½ cup crumbled tofu cheese

Directions
1. Cooking Time: the pasta in 8 cups of slightly salted water in a medium pot over medium heat until al dente, 10 minutes. Drain the pasta and set aside.
2. Heat olive oil in a skillet and sauté zucchini and garlic for 4 minutes. Stir in tomatoes, beans, and olives.

Cooking Time: until the tomatoes soften, 10 minutes. Mix in pasta. Allow warming for 1 minute. Stir in tofu cheese and serve warm.

Nutrition:
Calories 206 kcal| Fats 5.1g
Carbs 35.8g
Protein 7.6g

387. Fresh Puttanesca With Quinoa

Preparation Time: 30 minutes
Serving: 4
This dish is a quick, flavorful and super tasty quinoa puttanesca perfect for excellent health and comfort.

Ingredients
- 1 cup brown quinoa
- 2 cups water
- 1/8 tsp salt
- 4 cups plum tomatoes, chopped
- 4 pitted green olives, sliced
- 4 pitted Kalamata olives, sliced
- 1 ½ tbsp capers, rinsed and drained
- 2 garlic cloves, minced
- 1 tbsp olive oil
- 1 tbsp chopped fresh parsley
- ¼ cup chopped fresh basil
- 1/8 tsp red chili flakes

Directions
1. Add the quinoa, water, and salt to a medium pot and Cooking Time: covered over medium heat until tender and water absorbs, 10 to 15 minutes.
2. Meanwhile, in a medium bowl, mix the tomatoes, green olives, Kalamata olives, capers, garlic, olive oil, parsley, basil, and red chili flakes. Allow sitting for 5 minutes.
3. Serve the puttanesca with the quinoa.

Nutrition:
Calories 427 kcal| Fats 7.1g
Carbs 88.2g
Protein 7.2g

388. Quinoa Cherry Tortilla Wraps

Preparation Time: 25 minutes
Serving: 4
The ultimate example of flavor and convenience is a veggie wrap.

Ingredients

- ½ cup brown quinoa
- Salt and black pepper to taste
- 2 tsp olive oil
- 1 ½ cups shredded carrots
- 1 ¼ cups fresh cherries, pitted and halved
- 4 scallions, chopped
- 2 tbsp plain vinegar
- 2 tbsp low-sodium soy sauce
- 1 tbsp pure maple syrup
- 4 (8-inch tortilla wraps

Directions

1. Cooking Time: the quinoa in 1 cup of slightly salted water in a medium pot over medium heat until tender and the water absorbs, 10 minutes. Fluff and set aside to warm.
2. Heat the olive oil in a medium skillet and sauté the carrots, cherries, and scallions. While cooking, in a small bowl, mix the vinegar, soy sauce, and maple syrup. Stir the mixture into the vegetable mixture. Simmer for 5 minutes and turn the heat off.
3. Spread the tortillas on a flat surface, spoon the mixture at the center, fold the sides and ends to wrap in the filling.
4. Serve warm.

Nutrition:
Calories 282 kcal| Fats 6.5g
Carbs 48g
Protein 8.3g

389. Quinoa With Mixed Herbs

Preparation Time: 20 minutes
Serving: 4
This trick of comfort is creating moist, soft quinoa.

Ingredients

- 1 cup quinoa, well-rinsed
- 2 cups vegetable broth
- Salt to taste
- 2 garlic cloves, minced, divided
- ¼ cup chopped chives
- 2 tbsp finely chopped parsley
- 2 tbsp finely chopped basil
- 2 tbsp finely chopped mint
- 2 tbsp finely chopped soft sundried tomatoes
- 1 tbsp olive oil (optional)
- ½ tsp lemon zest
- 1 tbsp fresh lemon juice
- 2 tbsp minced walnuts
- Salt and black pepper to taste

Directions

1. In a medium pot, combine the quinoa, vegetable broth, ¼ tsp of salt and half of the garlic in a medium saucepan. Boil until the quinoa is tender and the liquid absorbs, 10-15 minutes.
2. Open the lid, fluff with a fork and stir in the chives, parsley, basil, mint, tomatoes, olive oil, zest, lemon juice, and walnuts. Warm for 5 minutes.
3. Dish the food and serve warm.

Nutrition:
Calories 393 kcal| Fats 17.1g
Carbs 31.9g| Protein 27.8g

390. Chickpea Avocado Pizza

Preparation Time: 40 minutes
Serving: 4
It's the perfect blend of healthy fats, proteins and carbs, plus it's tasty. Don't trust me? Try it on your own!

Ingredients

For the pizza crust:

- 3 ½ cups whole-wheat flour
- 1 tsp yeast
- 1 tsp salt
- 1 pinch sugar

- 3 tbsp olive oil
- 1 cup warm water

For the topping:
- 1 cup red pizza sauce
- 1 cup baby spinach
- Salt and black pepper to taste
- 1 (15 oz can chickpeas, drained and rinsed
- 1 medium avocado, pitted, peeled and chopped
- ¼ cup grated plant-based Parmesan cheese

Directions
1. Preheat the oven the 350 F and lightly grease a pizza pan with cooking spray.
2. In a medium bowl, mix the flour, nutritional yeast, salt, sugar, olive oil, and warm water until smooth dough forms. Allow rising for an hour or until the dough doubles in size.
3. Spread the dough on the pizza pan and apply the pizza sauce on top.
4. Top with the spinach, chickpeas, avocado, and plant Parmesan cheese.
5. Bake the pizza for 20 minutes or until the cheese melts.
6. Remove from the oven, cool for 5 minutes, slice, and serve.

Nutrition:
Calories 678 kcal| Fats 22.7g
Carbs 104.1g| Protein 23.5g

391. White Bean Stuffed Squash

Preparation Time: 60 minutes
Serving: 4

I've been battling crave of an endless summer, but these autumn flavors are coming in quick and strong, and I can't keep going anymore! So let's start with this dish.

Ingredients
- 2 pounds large acorn squash
- 2 tbsp olive oil
- 3 garlic cloves, minced
- 1 (15 oz can white beans, drained and rinsed
- 1 cup chopped spinach leaves
- ½ cup vegetable stock
- Salt and black pepper to taste
- ½ tsp cumin powder
- ½ tsp chili powder

Directions
1. Preheat the oven to 350 F.
2. Cut the squash into half and scoop out the seeds.
3. Season with salt and pepper and place face down on a sheet pan. Bake for 45 minutes.
4. While the squash cooks, heat the olive oil in a medium pot over medium heat.
5. Sauté the garlic until fragrant, 30 seconds and mix in the beans. Cooking Time: for 1 minute.
6. Stir in the spinach, allow wilting for 2 minutes and season with salt, black pepper, cumin powder, and chili powder. Cooking Time: for 2 minutes and turn the heat off.
7. When the squash is fork tender, remove from the oven and fill the holes with the bean and spinach mixture.
8. Serve warm.

Nutrition:
Calories 365 kcal| Fats 34.6g
Carbs 16.7g| Protein 2.3g

392. Grilled Zucchini And Spinach Pizza

Preparation Time: 30 minutes
Serving: 4

Fresh spinach, marinara sauce and plant Parmesan cheese on a roasted crust. A not so regular pizza but still delicious and flavorful.

Ingredients

For the pizza crust:
- 3 ½ cups whole-wheat flour

- 1 tsp yeast
- 1 tsp salt
- 1 pinch sugar
- 3 tbsp olive oil
- 1 cup warm water

For the topping:
- 1 cup marinara sauce
- 2 large zucchinis, sliced
- ½ cup chopped spinach
- ¼ cup pitted and sliced black olives
- ½ cup grated plant Parmesan cheese

Directions
1. Preheat the oven the 350 F and lightly grease a pizza pan with cooking spray.
2. In a medium bowl, mix the flour, nutritional yeast, salt, sugar, olive oil, and warm water until smooth dough forms. Allow rising for an hour or until the dough doubles in size. Spread the dough on the pizza pan and apply the pizza sauce on top.
3. Meanwhile, heat a grill pan over medium heat, season the zucchinis with salt, black pepper, and Cooking Time: in the pan until slightly charred on both sides.
4. Sit the cucumbers on the pizza crust and top with the spinach, olives, and plant Parmesan cheese. Bake the pizza for 20 minutes or until the cheese melts. Remove from the oven, cool for 5 minutes, slice, and serve.

Nutrition:
Calories 519 kcal| Fats 13.4g
Carbs 87.5g| Protein 19.6g

393. Crispy Tofu Burgers

Preparation Time: 20 minutes
Serving: 4
Fast food type tofu burgers sandwiched in a burger bun with thick slabs of crispy tofu is a must!

Ingredients
- 1 tbsp flax seed powder + 3 tbsp water
- 2/3 lb crumble tofu
- 1 tbsp quick-cooking oats
- 1 tbsp toasted almond flour
- ½ tsp garlic powder
- ½ tsp onion powder
- Salt and black pepper to taste
- ¼ tsp curry powder
- 3 tbsp whole-grain breadcrumbs
- 4 whole-wheat burger buns, halved

Directions
1. In a small bowl, mix the flax seed powder with water and allow thickening for 5 minutes to make the flax egg. Set aside.
2. In a medium bowl, mix the tofu, oats, almond flour, garlic powder, onion powder, salt, black pepper, and curry powder. Mold 4 patties out of the mixture and lightly brush both sides with the flax egg.
3. Pour the breadcrumbs onto a plate and coat the patties in the crumbs until well covered.
4. Heat a pan to medium heat and grease well with cooking spray.
5. Cooking Time: the patties on both sides until crispy, golden brown and cooked through, 10 minutes.
6. Place each patty between each burger bun and top with the guacamole.
7. Serve immediately.

Nutrition:
Calories 238 kcal| Fats 15.8g
Carbs 14.8g| Protein 14.1g

394. Bean Lentil Salad With Lime Dressing

Preparation time: 20 minute
Servings: 5

Ingredients
- 1 cup green lentils, uncooked
- 15 oz. Can black beans, rinsed, drained
- 2 roma tomatoes, finely diced
- 2/3 cup cilantro, stemmed, roughly

chopped
- ½ small red onion, finely diced
- 1 red bell pepper, finely diced

For the dressing:
- 1 lime, juiced
- 1 teaspoon dijon mustard
- 2 garlic cloves, minced
- ½ teaspoon oregano
- 1 teaspoon cumin
- 1/8 teaspoon salt

Direction
1. Cooking Time: lentils according to package direction. Drain.
2. Mix all dressing ingredients in a small bowl and set aside.
3. Add the black beans, lentils, tomatoes, bell pepper and onions into a bowl. Sprinkle the dressing on top and toss to coat. Add the cilantro and toss lightly. Enjoy!

395. Lentil Arugula Salad

Preparation time: 7 minutes
servings: 2

Ingredients
- 1 cup (15 oz brown lentils, cooked
- 1 handful arugula, washed
- ¾ cup (100g cashews
- 6 sun-dried tomatoes in oil, chopped
- 3 whole-wheat bread sliced, cut big pieces
- 2 tablespoons balsamic vinegar
- 3 tablespoons olive oil
- 1 onion
- 1 jalapeno pepper, chopped
- Pepper and salt, to taste

Direction
1. Place a frying pan over low heat and roast the cashews for 3 minutes. Transfer to a salad bowl.
2. Sauté onions in 1/3 olive oil for 3 minutes on low heat. Add jalapeno and dried tomatoes and Cooking Time: for about 2 minutes. Transfer to a bowl.
3. Add the remaining olive oil to the pan and fry the bread until crunchy. Sprinkle with pepper and salt. Set aside.
4. Add arugula to the bowl containing sautéed tomato mixture. Add lentils and toss to combine — season with pepper, salt and balsamic vinegar.
5. Serve with the crunchy bread.

396. Red Cabbage And Cucumber Salad With Seitan

Preparation time: 10 minutes
servings: 1-2

Ingredients

for the salad:
- ½ small head red cabbage, shredded
- 1 package (8 oz. Seitan, cut into strips
- 1 small cucumber, sliced
- 3 green onions, thinly sliced
- 1 tablespoon olive oil
- 3 garlic cloves, minced
- ¾ teaspoon mild curry powder

For the dressing:
- 1/3 cup mango chutney
- 1/3 cup peanut butter

Direction
1. Heat 2 teaspoons olive oil over medium heat in a pan. Sauté seitan for 7 minutes. Add remaining olive oil and garlic, then Cooking Time: for 30 seconds. Season with curry powder and Cooking Time: for extra 2 minutes. Turn off the heat and keep warm.
2. In a blender, combine peanut butter, chutney, and 1/3 cup water, process until smooth.
3. Place cabbage and cucumber into a bowl. Drizzle with the peanut butter mixture and toss properly. Top with seitan and green onions and serve.

397. Protein Packed Chickpeas And Kidney Beans Salad

Preparation time: 5 minute
Servings: 2

Ingredients

- *1 can chickpeas, drained, rinsed*
- *1 can red kidney beans, drained, rinsed*
- *½ cup feta cheese, crumbled*
- *1 cup parsley, chopped*
- *Olive oil*
- *1 lemon juice*
- *3 scallions, chopped*
- *1 small ginger, grated*
- *1 medium onion, diced*
- *2 garlic cloves, minced*
- *1 pinch red chili flakes*
- *Black pepper and salt*

Direction

1. *Sauté onions in 1 tablespoon olive oil until golden. Add ginger, garlic, and chili and sauté till garlic is fragrant. Set aside to cool.*
2. *In a salad bowl, combine chickpeas, kidney beans, feta cheese, scallions, parsley, lemon juice, pepper, salt, cooled garlic mixture, and some olive oil. Toss well to combine correctly and enjoy!*

398. Quick Chickpeas And Spinach Salad

Preparation time: 7 minutes
servings: 2

Ingredients

- *1 can chickpeas, drained, rinsed*
- *1 handful spinach*
- *1 small handful raisins*
- *3.5 oz. Feta cheese, chopped*
- *4 tablespoons olive oil*
- *3 teaspoons honey*
- *½ tablespoon lemon juice*
- *½ teaspoon chili flakes*
- *½ teaspoon cumin*
- *1 pinch salt*

Direction

1. *Add chickpeas, cheese, and spinach to a salad bowl.*
2. *In a separate bowl, mix honey, lemon juice, olive oil, and raisins. Stir in chili flakes, cumin, and salt. Drizzle over the salad and serve.*

399. Carrot Slaw And Tempeh Triangles

Preparation time: 5 minutes
servings: 4

Ingredients

- *8 oz tempeh, sliced into triangles*
- *4 cups carrots, shredded*
- *½ cup parsley, finely chopped*
- *1 tablespoon raw walnuts, crushed*
- *3 tablespoons grade b maple syrup*
- *1 teaspoon olive oil*
- *¼ cup lemon juice*
- *2 teaspoons soy sauce*
- *1 small onion, diced*
- *2 tablespoons tahini*
- *1/8 teaspoon black pepper*
- *1 tablespoon curry powder*
- *Pepper and salt, to taste*

Direction

1. *Heat olive oil in a skillet over high heat. Once hot, add tempeh, 1 ½ tbsp. Maple syrup and soy sauce. Cooking Time: for 5 minutes, flipping occasionally until the liquid is absorbed. Remove from heat and sprinkle with crushed walnut and pepper. Set aside and keep warm.*
2. *Toss carrots, tahini, lemon juice, remaining maple syrup, parsley, onions and spices in a mixing bowl for some minutes. Season with pepper and salt to taste.*
3. *Transfer to a serving bowl. Top with tempeh triangles and serve.*

400. Chili tofu

Preparation time: 50 minutes
servings: 8

Ingredients

- 1 package (14 oz. Firm tofu
- 1 can (28 oz. Kidney beans, drained
- 1 cup mushrooms, sliced
- 1 can (28 oz. Tomatoes with liquid, diced
- 1 can (14 oz. Tomato sauce
- 3 tablespoons vegetable oil
- 1 green bell pepper, diced
- 1 onion, diced
- ¼ teaspoon cayenne pepper
- 3 tablespoons chili powder
- ½ teaspoon cumin
- 3 garlic cloves, minced
- Pepper and salt, to taste

Direction
1. Sauté tofu in vegetable oil over medium-high heat for 3 minutes.
2. Add in the onions, green pepper, mushrooms, garlic, cayenne, cumin, chili powder, pepper, and salt and Cooking Time: for 5 minutes.
3. Stir in tomato sauce, kidney beans, diced tomatoes with the liquid, and bring everything to a simmer. Cover and Cooking Time: for an extra 45 minutes. Serve.

401. Lentil Soup (Vegan

Preparation time: 50 minutes
servings: 4

Ingredients
- 1 cup dry brown lentils
- 1 carrot, sliced
- 2 bay leaves
- 1 teaspoon vegetable oil
- 4 cups vegetable broth
- 1 onion, sliced
- ¼ teaspoon thyme, dried
- Pepper and salt, to taste

Direction
1. Sauté onions and carrots in vegetable oil for 5 minutes. Mix in vegetable broth, lentils, bay leaves, pepper, and salt, stir well to combine.
2. Lower the heat to a simmer. Cooking Time: for 45 minutes, covered. Discard the bay leaves and serve.

402. Hot Black Beans And Potato

Preparation time: 25 minute
Servings: 5

Ingredients
- 1 can (15 oz. Black beans
- 2 small sweet potatoes, peeled, chopped
- 2 medium carrots, sliced
- 1 can (15 oz. Tomato sauce
- 2 tablespoons olive oil
- ½ cup of water
- 1 small onion, diced
- 2 garlic cloves, minced
- 1/2 teaspoon cayenne
- ½ teaspoon garlic powder
- 1 tablespoon chili powder
- 1 teaspoon cumin
- ¼ teaspoon black pepper
- ½ teaspoon salt

Direction
1. Cooking Time: garlic and onions in olive oil for 2 minutes. Add potatoes and carrots and Cooking Time: for 6 minutes.
2. Lower the heat to medium-low and stir in the remaining ingredients. Cooking Time: for about 25 minutes, partially covered and stirring infrequently. Once done, serve.

403. Low-Fat Bean Soup

Preparation time: 10 minutes
servings: 4

Ingredients
- 2 cans (15 oz each black beans, undrained
- ½ cup of salsa
- 16 oz. Vegetable broth
- 1 tablespoon chili powder

Direction
1. Pulse 1 can beans in a food processor until almost smooth.
2. Pour the mixture into a saucepan. Add the remaining can beans, vegetable broth, salsa, and chili powder into the pan.
3. Bring to a boil, and remove from the heat. Serve and enjoy!

404. Protein Rich Vegetable Minestrone

Preparation time: 30 minutes
servings: 6

Ingredients
- ¼ cup white quinoa, uncooked
- 1 can (28 oz. Tomatoes, diced
- 1 cup carrots, sliced
- 1 ½ cups asparagus, chopped
- 1 cup packed kale, chopped
- ½ cup frozen peas
- 1 cup zucchini, chopped
- 2 bay leaves
- 1 tablespoon olive oil
- 4 cups of water
- 1 small white onion, diced
- 3 garlic cloves, minced
- 2 teaspoons italian seasoning
- Pepper and salt, to taste

Direction
1. Sauté onions, garlic and carrots in olive oil over medium-high heat for 3 minutes. Stir in water, tomatoes, quinoa, bay leaves, spices, pepper and salt and bring to a boil. Cover and simmer for 20 minutes.
2. Add the remaining vegetable and Cooking Time: for 10 minutes. Taste and adjust seasonings if needed and serve hot.

405. Quinoa Pumpkin Soup

Preparation time: 25 minutes
servings: 4

Ingredients
- ½ cup quinoa
- 20 oz. Can black beans, rinsed, drained
- 3 cups pumpkin, cubed
- 2 bay leaves
- 5 cups vegetable broth
- 1 tablespoon olive oil
- 1 onion, diced
- 5 garlic cloves, diced
- 1 red chili pepper, diced
- ½ teaspoon dried oregano
- 1 teaspoon ground cumin
- ½ teaspoon red pepper flakes, crushed

Direction
1. Sauté onions in olive oil over medium until translucent. Stir in red chili pepper and garlic and sauté until aromatic. Mix in the pumpkin and spices and Cooking Time: for a few minutes.
2. Pour in quinoa and 2 cups vegetable broth, then bring to a boil. Cooking Time: for extra 5 minutes, then add the remaining vegetable broth and Cooking Time: until boiled. Stir in beans and bay leaves. Lower the heat and simmer for 10 minutes. Serve with avocados.

406. Red Lentil Soup With Farro

Preparation time: 32 minutes
servings: 4

Ingredients
- ½ cup red lentils
- ½ cup quick-Cooking Time: farro
- 1 cup kale, stemmed, chopped
- 1 cup carrots, grated
- 2 tablespoons olive oil
- 5 cups vegetable broth
- 1 small onion, grated
- 1 small zucchini, grated
- 1 ½ teaspoon turmeric
- ½ teaspoon cumin
- ¼ teaspoon pepper

- 1 ½ teaspoons salt

For breadcrumbs:
- Eight slices french baguette, cubed
- Olive oil
- One garlic clove, minced
- Salt, to taste

Direction
1. Sauté onion, carrots, and zucchini in olive oil over medium heat for 2 minutes. Stir in turmeric, cumin, pepper, and salt, then Cooking Time: for 3 minutes.
2. Add the chicken broth and bring everything to a boil. Add lentils and farro and Cooking Time: for about 20 minutes over low heat.
3. In the meantime, pulse bread and garlic in a food processor until done. Transfer to a baking sheet and sprinkle with olive oil and salt — bake for 7 minutes.
4. Once the lentil soup has cooked for 15 minutes, add kale and Cooking Time: for 5 minutes. Serve topped with the breadcrumbs.

407. Broccoli & Black Beans Stir Fry

Preparation time 60 minutes
Servings: 6
Ingredients:
- 4 cups broccoli florets
- 2 cups cooked black beans
- 1 tablespoon sesame oil
- 4 teaspoons sesame seeds
- 2 cloves garlic, finely minced
- 2 teaspoons ginger, finely chopped
- A large pinch red chili flakes
- A pinch turmeric powder
- Salt to taste
- Lime juice to taste (optional

Direction:
1. Steam broccoli for 6 minutes. Drain and set aside.
2. Warm the sesame oil in a large frying pan over medium heat. Add sesame seeds, chili flakes, ginger, garlic, turmeric powder, and salt. Sauté for a couple of minutes.
3. Add broccoli and black beans and sauté until thoroughly heated.
4. Sprinkle lime juice and serve hot.

408. Stuffed peppers

Preparation time 40 minutes
Servings: 8
Ingredients:
- 2 cans (15 ounces eachblack beans, drained, rinsed
- 2 cups tofu, pressed, crumbled
- 3/4 cup green onion s, thinly sliced
- 1/2 cup fresh cilantro, chopped
- 1/4 cup vegetable oil
- 1/4 cup lime juice
- 3 cloves garlic, finely chopped
- 1/2 teaspoon salt
- 1/2 teaspoon chili powder
- 8 large bell peppers, halved lengthwise, deseeded
- 3 roma tomatoes, diced

Direction:
1. Mix together in a bowl all the ingredients except the bell peppers to make the filling.
2. Fill the peppers with this mixture.
3. Cut 8 aluminum foils of size 18 x 12 inches. Place 2 halves on each aluminum foil. Seal the peppers such that there is a gap on the sides.
4. Grill under direct heat for about 15 minutes.
5. Sprinkle with some cilantro and serve.

409. Sweet 'N Spicy Tofu

Preparation time 45 minutes
servings: 8
Ingredients:
- 14 ounces extra firm tofu; press the excess liquid and chop into cubes.
- 3 tablespoons olive oil
- 2 2-3 cloves garlic, minced

- *4 tablespoons sriracha sauce or any other hot sauce*
- *2 tablespoons soy sauce*
- *1/4 cup sweet chili sauce*
- *5-6 cups mixed vegetables of your choice (like carrots, cauliflower, broccoli, potato, etc.*
- *Salt to taste (optional*

Direction:

1. Place a nonstick pan over medium-high heat. Add 1 tablespoon oil. When oil is hot, add garlic and mixed vegetables and stir-fry until crisp and tender. Remove and keep aside.
2. Place the pan back on heat. Add 2 tablespoons oil. When oil is hot, add tofu and sauté until golden brown. Add the sautéed vegetables. Mix well and remove from heat.
3. Make a mixture of sauces by mixing together all the sauces in a small bowl.
4. Serve the stir fried vegetables and tofu with sauce.

410. Eggplant & Mushrooms In Peanut Sauce

Preparation time 32 minutes
servings: 6
Ingredients:

- *4 Japanese eggplants cut into 1-inch thick round slices*
- *3/4 pounds of shiitake mu shrooms, stems discarded, halved*
- *3 tablespoons smooth peanut butter*
- *2 1/2 tablespoons rice vinegar*
- *1 1/2 tablespoons soy sauce*
- *1 1/2 tablespoons, peeled, fresh ginger, finely grated*
- *1 1/2 tablespoons light brown sugar*
- *Coarse salt to taste*
- *3 scallions, cut into 2-inch lengths, thinly sliced lengthwise*

Direction:

1. Place the eggplants and mushroom in a steamer. Steam the eggplant and mushrooms until tender. Transfer to a bowl.
2. To a small bowl, add peanut butter and vinegar and whisk.
3. Add rest of the ingredients and whisk well. Add this to the bowl of eggplant slices. Add scallions and mix well.
4. Serve hot.

411. Green Beans Stir Fry

Preparation time 30 minutes
servings: 6-8
Ingredients:

- *1 1/2 pounds of green beans, stringed, chopped into 1 ½-inch pieces*
- *1 large onion, thinly sliced*
- *4 star anise (optional*
- *3 tablespoons avocado oil*
- *1 1/2 tablespoons tamari sauce or soy sauce*
- *Salt to taste*
- *3/4 cup water*

Direction:

1. Place a wok over medium heat. Add oil. When oil is heated, add onions and sauté until onions are translucent.
2. Add beans, water, tamari sauce, and star anise and stir. Cover and Cooking Time: until the beans are tender.
3. Uncover, add salt and raise the heat to high. Cooking Time: until the water dries up in the wok. Stir a couple of times while cooking.

412. Collard Greens 'N Tofu

Preparation time 15 minutes
Servings: 4
Ingredients:

- *2 pounds of collard greens, rinsed, chopped*
- *1 cup water*
- *1/2 pound of tofu, chopped*

- Salt to taste
- Pepper powder to taste
- Crushed red chili to taste

Direction:
1. Place a large skillet over medium-high heat. Add oil. When the oil is heated, add tofu and Cooking Time: until brown.
2. Add rest of the ingredients and mix well.
3. Cooking Time: until greens wilts and almost dry.

413. Cassoulet

Preparation time: 35 minutes
Servings: 4
Protein: 22 g

Ingredients
- ¼ cup (60 ml olive oil, divided
- 4 ounces (113 g quit-the-cluck seitan, chopped
- 1/3 of a smoky sausage, chopped
- 1½ cups (240 g chopped onion
- 2 ounces (57 g minced shiitake mushrooms
- 2 large carrots, peeled, sliced into ¼-inch (6 mm rounds
- 2 stalks celery, chopped
- 1½ cups (355 ml vegetable broth, divided
- 1 teaspoon liquid smoke
- 3 cans (each 15 ounces, or 425 g white beans of choice, drained and rinsed
- 1 can (14.5 ounces, or 410 g diced tomatoes, undrained
- 2 tablespoons (32 g tomato paste 1 tablespoon (15 ml tamari
- 1 tablespoon (18 g no chicken bouillon paste, or 2 bouillon cubes, crumbled
- 2 tablespoons (8 g minced fresh parsley
- 2 teaspoons dried thyme
- ½ teaspoon dried rosemary salt and pepper
- 2 cups (200 g fresh bread crumbs
- ½ cup (40 g panko crumbs

Direction
1. Preheat the oven to 375°f (190°c, or gas mark 5).
2. Heat 1 tablespoon (15 ml of olive oil in a large skillet over medium heat.
3. Add the seitan and sausage. Cooking Time: for 4 to 6 minutes, occasionally stirring, until browned. Transfer to a plate and set aside.
4. Add the onion and a pinch of salt to the same skillet. Cooking Time: for 5 to 7 minutes until translucent. Transfer to the same plate. Add the shiitakes, carrots, and celery to the skillet and Cooking Time: for 2 minutes. Add 1 tablespoon (15 ml vegetable broth and the liquid smoke. Cooking Time: for 2 to 3 minutes, stirring until the liquid is absorbed or evaporated.
5. Return the seitan and onions to the skillet and add the beans, tomatoes, tomato paste, tamari, bouillon, parsley, thyme, rosemary, and remaining broth. Cooking Time: for 3 to 4 minutes, stirring to combine. Season with salt and pepper to taste and transfer to a large casserole pan.
6. Toss together the fresh bread crumbs, panko crumbs, and the remaining 3 tablespoons (45 ml olive oil in a small bowl. Spread evenly over the bean mixture. Bake for 30 to 35 minutes until the crumbs are browned.

414. Double-Garlic Bean And Vegetable Soup

Preparation time: 25 minutes
Servings: 4
Protein: 21 g

Ingredients
- 1 tablespoon (15 ml olive oil
- 1 teaspoon fine sea salt
- 1 (240 g minced onion 5 cloves garlic, minced

- 2 cups (220 g) chopped red potatoes
- 2/3 cup (96 g) sliced carrots
- Protein content per serving cup (60 g) chopped celery
- 1 teaspoon italian seasoning blend
- Protein content per serving teaspoon red pepper flakes, or to taste
- Protein content per serving teaspoon celery seed
- 4 cups water (940 ml), divided
- 1 can (14.5 ounces, or 410 g) crushed tomatoes or tomato puree
- 1 head roasted garlic
- 2 tablespoons (30 g) prepared vegan pesto, plus more for garnish
- 2 cans (each 15 ounces, or 425 g) different kinds of white beans, drained and rinsed
- Protein content per serving cup (50 g)
- 1-inch (2.5 cm) pieces green beans
- Salt and pepper

Direction
1. Heat the oil and salt in a large soup pot over medium heat. Add the onion, garlic, potatoes, carrots, and celery. Cooking Time: for 4 to 6 minutes, occasionally stirring, until the onions are translucent. Add the seasoning blend, red pepper flakes, and celery seed and stir for 2 minutes. Add 3 cups (705 ml) of the water and the crushed tomatoes.
2. Combine the remaining 1 cup (235 ml) water and the roasted garlic in a blender. Process until smooth. Add to the soup mixture and bring to a boil. Reduce the heat to simmer and Cooking Time: for 30 minutes.
3. Stir in the pesto, beans, and green beans. Simmer for 15 minutes. Taste and adjust the seasonings. Serve each bowl with a dollop of pesto, if desired.

415. Mean Bean Minestrone

Preparation time: 45 minutes
Servings: 6

Protein: 9g

Ingredients
- 1 tablespoon (15 ml) olive oil
- 1/3 cup (80 g) chopped red onion
- 4 cloves garlic, grated or pressed
- 1 leek, white and light green parts, trimmed and chopped (about 4 ounces, or 113 g
- 2 carrots, peeled and minced (about 4 ounces, or 113 g
- 2 ribs of celery, minced (about 2 ounces, or 57 g
- 2 yellow squashes, trimmed and chopped (about 8 ounces, or 227 g
- 1 green bell pepper, trimmed and chopped (about 8 ounces, or 227 g
- 1 tablespoon (16 g) tomato paste
- 1 teaspoon dried oregano
- 1 teaspoon dried basil
- 1/3 teaspoon smoked paprika
- 1/4 To 1/4 teaspoon cayenne pepper, or to taste
- 2 cans (each 15 ounces, or 425 g) diced fire-roasted tomatoes
- 4 cups (940 ml) vegetable broth, more if needed
- 3 cups (532 g) cannellini beans, or other white beans
- 2 cups (330 g) cooked farro, or other whole grain or pasta
- Salt, to taste
- Nut and seed sprinkles, for garnish, optional and to taste

Direction
1. In a large pot, add the oil, onion, garlic, leek, carrots, celery, yellow squash, bell pepper, tomato paste, oregano, basil, paprika, and cayenne pepper. Cooking Time: on medium-high heat, stirring often until the vegetables start to get tender, about 6 minutes.
2. Add the tomatoes and broth. Bring to a boil, lower the heat, cover with a lid, and simmer 15 minutes.

3. Add the beans and simmer another 10 minutes. Add the farro and simmer 5 more minutes to heat the farro.
4. Note that this is a thick minestrone. If there are leftovers (which taste even better, by the way), the soup will thicken more once chilled.
5. Add extra broth if you prefer a thinner soup and adjust seasoning if needed. Add nut and seed sprinkles on each portion upon serving, if desired.
6. Store leftovers in an airtight container in the refrigerator for up to 5 days. The minestrone can also be frozen for up to 3 months.

416. Sushi Rice And Bean Stew

Preparation time: 45 minutes
Servings: 6

Ingredients

For the sushi rice:
- 1 cup (208 g dry sushi rice, thoroughly rinsed until water runs clear and drained
- 1¾ cups (295 ml water
- 1 tablespoon (15 ml fresh lemon juice
- 1 teaspoon toasted sesame oil
- 1 teaspoon sriracha
- 1 teaspoon tamari
- 1 teaspoon agave nectar or brown rice syrup

For the stew:
- 1 tablespoon (15 ml toasted sesame oil
- 9 ounces (255 g minced carrot (about 4 medium carrots
- 1/3 cup (80 g chopped red onion or ¼ cup (40 g minced shallot
- 2 teaspoons grated fresh ginger or ⅓ teaspoon ginger powder 4 cloves garlic, grated or pressed
- 1½ cups (246 g cooked chickpeas
- 1 cup (155 g frozen, shelled edamame
- 3 tablespoons (45 ml seasoned rice vinegar
- 2 tablespoons (30 ml tamari
- 2 teaspoons sriracha, or to taste
- 1 cup (235 ml mushroom-soaking broth
- 2 cups (470 ml vegetable broth
- 2 tablespoons (36 g white miso
- 2 tablespoons (16 g toasted white sesame seeds

Direction

To make the sushi rice:
1. combine the rice and water in a rice cooker, cover with the lid, and Cooking Time: until the water is absorbed without lifting the lid. (alternatively, Cooking Time: the rice on the stove top, following the directions on the package. While the rice is cooking, combine the remaining sushi rice ingredients in a large bowl.
2. Let the rice steam for 10 minutes in the rice cooker with the lid still on. Gently fold the cooked rice into the dressing. Set aside.

To make the stew:
1. heat the oil in a large pot on medium-high heat. Add the carrots, onion, ginger, and garlic. Lower the temperature to medium and Cooking Time: until the vegetables start to get tender, stirring often about 4 minutes.
2. Add the chickpeas, edamame, vinegar, tamari, and sriracha. Stir and Cooking Time: for another 4 minutes. Add the broths, and bring back to a slow boil. Cover with a lid, lower the heat, and simmer for 10 minutes.
3. Place the miso in a small bowl and remove 3 tablespoons (45 ml of the broth from the pot. Stir into the miso to thoroughly combine. Stir the miso mixture back into the pan, and remove from the heat.
4. Divide the rice among 4 to 6 bowls, depending on your appetite. Add

approximately 1 cup (235 ml of the stew on top of each portion of rice. Add 1 teaspoon of sesame seeds on top of each serving, and serve immediately.

5. If you do not plan on eating this dish in one shot, keep the rice and stew separated and store in the refrigerator for up to 4 days.
6. When reheating the stew, do not bring to a boil. Slowly warm the rice with the stew on medium heat in a small saucepan until heated through.

417. Giardiniera Chili

Preparation time: 35 minutes
Servings: 6
Protein: 28 g

Ingredients

- *1 tablespoon (15 ml neutral-flavored oil*
- *1 medium red onion, chopped*
- *4 carrots, peeled and minced (9 ounces, or 250 g*
- *2 zucchini, trimmed and minced (11 ounces, or 320 g*
- *4 roma tomatoes, diced (14 ounces, or 400 g*
- *4 cloves garlic, grated or pressed*
- *1 tablespoon (8 g mild to medium chili powder*
- *1 teaspoon ground cumin*
- *½ teaspoon smoked paprika*
- *½ teaspoon liquid smoke*
- *¼ teaspoon fine sea salt, or to taste*
- *¼ teaspoon cayenne pepper, or to taste*
- *2 tablespoons (32 g tomato paste*
- *1 can (15 ounces, or 425 g diced fire-roasted tomatoes*
- *½ cup (120 ml vegetable broth*
- *½ cup (120 ml mushroom-soaking broth or extra vegetable broth*
- *1 can (15 ounces, or 425 g pinto beans, drained and rinsed*
- *1 can (15 ounces, or 425 g black beans, drained and rinsed*
- *½ cup (60 g nutritional yeast*

Direction

1. Heat the oil on medium-high in a large pot and add the onion, carrots, zucchini, tomatoes, and garlic. Cooking Time: for 6 minutes, stirring occasionally until the carrots start to get tender. Add the chili powder, cumin, paprika, liquid smoke, salt, cayenne pepper, and tomato paste, stirring to combine. Cooking Time: another 2 minutes. Add the diced tomatoes, broths, beans, and nutritional yeast. Bring to a low boil. Lower the heat, cover with a lid, and simmer 15 minutes, stirring occasionally. Remove the lid and simmer for another 5 minutes.
2. Serve on top of a cooked whole grain of choice or with your favorite chili accompaniments.
3. Leftovers can be stored in an airtight container in the refrigerator for up to 4 days or frozen for up to 3 months.

418. Shorba (Lentil Soup

Preparation time: 30 minutes
Servings: 6
Protein: 10 g

Ingredients

- *1 tablespoon (15 ml olive oil*
- *1 medium onion, minced*
- *1 large carrot, peeled and chopped*
- *1 fist-size russet potato, cut into small cubes (about 7 ounces, or 198 g*
- *4 large cloves garlic, minced*
- *2 teaspoons grated fresh ginger root*
- *1 to 2 teaspoons berbere, to taste*
- *1/3 teaspoon turmeric*
- *1 cup (192 g brown lentils, picked over and rinsed*
- *6 cups (1.4 l water, more if desired*
- *1 tablespoon (16 g tomato paste*
- *1 tablespoon (18 g vegetable bouillon paste, or 2 bouillon cubes*

- Salt and pepper

Direction

Heat the oil in a large soup pot over medium heat. Add the onion, carrot, and potato. Cooking Time: for 5 to 7 minutes, stirring occasionally until the onions are translucent. Stir in the garlic, ginger, berbere, turmeric, and lentils and Cooking Time: and stir for 1 minute until fragrant. Add the water, tomato paste, and bouillon. Bring to a boil, and then reduce the heat to a simmer. Cooking Time: for 30 minutes, stirring occasionally until the lentils are tender. Taste and adjust the seasonings.

419. The Whole Enchilada

Preparation time: 20 minutes
Servings: 6
Protein content per enchilada: 6 g

Ingredients

For the sauce:

- 2 tablespoons (30 ml olive oil 1/3 cup (80 g chopped red onion 4 ounces (113 g tomato paste
- 1 tablespoon (15 ml adobo sauce
- 1 tablespoon (8 g mild to medium chili powder
- 1 teaspoon ground cumin
- 3 cloves garlic, grated or pressed
- ⅓ teaspoon fine sea salt, or to taste
- 2 tablespoons (15 g whole wheat pastry flour or (16 g all-purpose flour
- 2 cups (470 ml water

For the filling:

- 1 protein content per serving teaspoons olive oil
- ⅓ cup (53 g chopped red onion
- 1 sweet potato, trimmed and peeled, chopped (about 8.8 ounces, or 250 g
- 1 yellow squash, trimmed and chopped (about 5.3 ounces, or 150 g
- 2 cloves garlic, grated or pressed
- 1 tablespoon (8 g nutritional yeast
- 1 smoked paprika
- ¼ teaspoon liquid smoke
- Pinch of fine sea salt, or to taste
- 1 (258 g cooked black beans
- 3 tablespoons (45 ml enchilada sauce
- 12 to 14 corn tortillas
- 1 recipe creamy cashew sauce
- Chopped fresh cilantro, to taste hot sauce, to taste

Direction

1. To make the sauce: heat the oil on medium heat in a large skillet. Add the onion and Cooking Time: until fragrant while occasionally stirring, about 2 minutes. Add the tomato paste, adobo sauce, chili powder, cumin, garlic, and salt. Saute for 2 minutes, stirring frequently. Sprinkle the flour on top and Cooking Time: 2 minutes, stirring frequently. Slowly whisk in the water and Cooking Time: until slightly thickened, about 6 minutes, frequently whisking to prevent clumps. Remove from the heat and set aside.

2. To make the filling: heat the oil in a large skillet on medium heat. Add the onion and sweet potato and Cooking Time: 6 minutes or until the potato starts to get tender, stirring occasionally. Add the squash and garlic and Cooking Time: for 4 minutes, stirring occasionally. Add the nutritional yeast, paprika, liquid smoke, and salt, stir to combine, and Cooking Time: for another minute. Add the beans and enchilada sauce and stir to combine. Cover the pan and simmer until the vegetables are completely tender about 4 minutes. Add a little water if the plants stick to the skillet. Adjust the seasonings if needed.

3. Preheat the oven to 350°f (180°c, or gas mark 4).

4. Place the sauce in a large shallow bowl. If you aren't using pre-shaped, uncooked tortillas, follow the direction in the recipe notes to soften the tortillas so that they are easier to

work with. Ladle about 1/3 cup (80 mlof enchilada sauce on the bottom of a 9 x 13-inch (23 x 33 cmbaking dish. Dip each tortilla in the sauce to coat only lightly. Don't be too generous and gently scrape off the excess sauce with a spatula; otherwise, you will run out of sauce. Add a scant ¼ cup (about 45 gof the filling in each tortilla. Fold the tortilla over the filling, rolling like a cigar. Place the enchiladas in the pan, seam side down. Make sure to squeeze them in tight so that there's room in the dish for all of them. Top evenly with the remaining enchilada sauce. Add the creamy cashew sauce consistently on top.

5. Bake for 20 to 25 minutes or until the top is set, and the enchiladas are heated through. Garnish with cilantro and serve with hot sauce.

420. Black Bean And Avocado Salad

Preparation time: 45 minutes
Servings: 6
Protein: 8 g.

Ingredients

- *1 cup (172 gcooked black beans*
- *⅓ cup (82 gfrozen corn (run under hot water, drained*
- *3 tablespoons (15 gminced scallion*
- *6 cherry tomatoes, cut into quarters*
- *2 cloves garlic, minced*
- *1 teaspoon minced fresh cilantro, or to taste*
- *Pinch of dried oregano 1 chipotle in adobo*
- *1 tablespoon (15 mlfresh lemon juice*
- *1 tablespoon (15 mlapple cider vinegar 1 tablespoon (15 mlvegetable broth*
- *1 teaspoon nutritional yeast*
- *2 tablespoons (15 groasted salted pepitas (hulled pumpkin seeds*
- *2 avocados, pitted, peeled, and chopped*
- *Salt and pepper*

Direction

Combine the beans, corn, scallion, cherry tomatoes, garlic, cilantro, and oregano in a medium-size bowl. Using a small blender or a mortar and pestle, thoroughly combine the chipotle, lemon juice, vinegar, broth, and nutritional yeast to form a dressing. Pour over the bean mixture and stir in the pepitas. Gently stir in the avocados. Season to taste with salt and pepper. Serve promptly so that the avocado doesn't discolor.

421. Mediterranean Quinoa And Bean Salad

Preparation time: 35 minutes
Servings: 6
Protein: 6 g

Ingredients

- *1¾ cups (213 gdry ivory quinoa, rinsed*
- *2 (590 mlvegetable broth*
- *2 tablespoons (30 mlapple cider vinegar*
- *2 tablespoons (30 mlfresh lemon juice*
- *3 tablespoons (45 mlextra-virgin olive oil*
- *⅔ cup (40 gfinely chopped red onion*
- *2 to 3 cloves garlic, minced, or to taste*
- *Protein content per serving teaspoon red pepper flakes, or to taste*
- *Salt and pepper*
- *1 (266 gcooked cannellini beans*
- *24 jumbo pitted kalamata olives, minced*
- *Half of red bell pepper, cored and diced*
- *Half of yellow bell pepper, cored and diced*
- *8 ounces (227 gmini heirloom tomatoes, halved or quartered depending on size*
- *6 tablespoons (24 gminced fresh*

parsley
- 15 leaves fresh basil, cut in chiffonade

Direction

1. Combine the quinoa with the broth in a medium saucepan. Bring to a boil and then reduce the heat to a simmer. Cover and Cooking Time: until all liquid is absorbed, 12 to 15 minutes. The quinoa should be tender and translucent, and the germ ring should be visible along the outside edge of the grain. Set aside to cool completely.
2. In a large bowl, combine the vinegar, lemon juice, oil, onion, garlic, red pepper flakes, salt, and pepper. Stir the beans into the dressing. Add the cooled quinoa, olives, bell peppers, tomatoes, and parsley into the bowl with the beans. Fold with a rubber spatula to thoroughly yet gently combine.
3. Cover and chill for an hour to let the flavors meld. Garnish with basil upon serving. Leftovers can be stored in an airtight container in the refrigerator for up to 4 days.

422. Tabbouleh verde

Preparation time: 40 minutes
Servings: 6
Protein: 9 g

Ingredients

- 1 cup (186 gdry whole-wh eat couscous
- ⅓ cup (120 mlvegetable broth, brought to a boil
- 3 tablespoons (45 mlextra-virgin olive oil
- 2 tablespoons (30 mlfresh lemon juice
- 2 tablespoons (30 mlfresh lime juice
- 1½ cups (258 gcooked black beans
- 1½ cups (225 gdiced heirloom green tomato (any other color will do.
- 1 cup (150 gdiced green bell pepper (any different color will do.
- ⅓ cup (5 gloosely packed fresh cilantro leaves, minced
- ⅓ cup (20 gminced scallion
- 1 small jalapeno, seeded and minced
- ⅓ teaspoon toasted cumin seeds
- Salt and pepper, optional
- Roasted pepitas (hulled pumpkin seeds), for garnish
- 1 lemon, cut into 4 to 6 wedges
- 1 lime, cut into 4 to 6 wedges

Direction

1. Mix the couscous with the broth in a large glass bowl. Add the oil, lemon juice, and lime juice. Stir well. Cover and let stand 5 minutes until the liquids are absorbed. Fluff with a fork.
2. Add the beans, tomato, bell pepper, cilantro, scallion, and jalapeno on top. Rub the cumin seeds between your fingers while adding them to release the flavor. Fold to combine with a rubber spatula. Adjust the seasonings to taste. Refrigerate for at least 30 minutes to chill and to let the flavors meld.
3. Serve and garnish each portion with a small handful of pepitas and a wedge of lemon and lime to drizzle before eating.
4. Leftovers can be stored in an airtight container in the refrigerator for up to 4 days.

423. Curried Bean And Corn Salad

Preparation time: 15 minutes
Servings: 6
Protein: 27 g

Ingredients

- Protein content per servi ng cup (90 gwhole freekeh
- 3 cups (705 mlsalted water
- 1 can (15 ounces, or 425 gchickpeas, drained and rinsed

- 1 cup (164 g fresh or frozen corn (run under hot water, drained
- ¼ cup (40 g minced red onion
- ¼ cup (32 g minced celery
- ¼ cup (38 g minced bell pepper (any color
- 3 tablespoons (12 g minced fresh parsley
- 1 tablespoon (6 g curry powder (mild or hot
- 1 teaspoon ground cumin
- 1 teaspoon garam masala
- 1 teaspoon ginger powder
- 1 teaspoon fine sea salt
- 1 clove garlic
- 2 tablespoons (30 ml seasoned rice vinegar
- 3 tablespoons (45 ml olive oil

Direction

1. Bring the freekeh and salted water to a boil in a medium-size saucepan. Reduce to simmer and Cooking Time: for 45 minutes, occasionally stirring, until tender. Drain and run under cold water, draining again. Transfer to a medium-size bowl. Add the chickpeas, corn, onion, celery, bell pepper, and parsley.
2. Heat the curry powder, cumin, and garam masala in a small skillet over medium heat. Stir and Cooking Time: for 3 to 4 minutes until fragrant. Do not burn. Transfer to a small blender and add the ginger powder, salt, garlic, and vinegar. Blend until smooth. Add the olive oil and blend again to emulsify. Pour the dressing (to taste over the bean mixture. Stir to coat and let sit for 15 minutes for the flavors to meld. The salad can also be covered and refrigerated for up to 3 days.

424. Eggplant balela

Preparation time: 45 minutes
Servings: 6

Ingredients

For the marinated eggplant:
- 1 tablespoon (16 g tahini
- 1 tablespoon (15 ml olive oil
- 1 tablespoon (15 ml fresh lemon juice
- 1 tablespoon (15 ml white balsamic vinegar
- 1 protein content per serving teaspoons nutritional yeast protein content per serving teaspoon onion powder protein content per serving teaspoon harissa paste, or to taste 1 clove garlic, grated or pressed protein content per serving teaspoon ground cumin salt, to taste 1 small eggplant (a little over 10 ounces, or 280 g), trimmed, cut in two widthwise and then length¬wise in protein content per serving-inch (1.3 cm slices

For the balela:
- 1 tablespoon (15 ml extra-virgin olive oil
- 2 tablespoons (30 ml fresh lemon juice
- 2 tablespoons (30 ml white balsamic vinegar
- ⅓ cup (53 g minced red onion
- 2 cloves garlic, grated or pressed
- 1 (246 g cooked chickpeas
- 1 (258 g cooked black beans
- 1 of a roasted red or yellow bell pepper, chopped
- 1 small tomato, seeded if desired, minced
- 3 tablespoons (18 g minced fresh mint leaves
- 3 tablespoons (11 g minced fresh parsley
- Salt and pepper
- Red pepper flakes, to taste

Direction

To make the marinated eggplant:

1. combine the tahini, oil, lemon juice, vinegar, nutritional yeast, onion powder, harissa paste, garlic, cumin, and salt in a shallow pan. Brush a generous amount of this mixture on

both sides and edges of each piece of eggplant and place in the shallow pan. Place the container in the refrigerator for 1 hour to marinate.
2. Preheat the oven to 450°f (230°c, or gas mark 8). Place the slices of eggplant on a large rimmed baking sheet.
3. Bake for 8 minutes, flip the slices, and bake for another 6 to 8 minutes until tender and golden brown. Remove from the oven and set aside. Once cool enough to handle, cut the eggplant slices into ^-inch (8 mmcubes.

To make the balela:

in a large bowl, combine the oil, lemon juice, vinegar, onion, and garlic. Add the chick-peas, black beans, roasted bell pepper, tomato, mint, parsley, cubed eggplant, salt, ground pepper, and red pepper flakes to taste. Chill overnight and serve cold or brought back to room temperature. Leftovers can be stored in an airtight container for up to 4 days, and they get even better with each passing day.

425. Carrot and radish slaw with sesame dressing

Preparation time: 10 minutes
Cooking time: 0 minute
Servings: 4
Ingredients:
- 2 tablespoons sesame oil, toasted
- 3 tablespoons rice vinegar
- ½ teaspoon sugar
- 2 tablespoons low sodium tamari
- 1 cup carrots, sliced into strips
- 2 cups radishes, sliced
- 2 tablespoons fresh cilantro, chopped
- 2 teaspoons sesame seeds, toasted

Directions
1. Mix the oil, vinegar, sugar and tamari in a bowl.
2. Add the carrots, radishes and cilantro.
3. Toss to coat evenly.
4. Let sit for 10 minutes.
5. Transfer to a food container.

426. Roasted veggies in lemon sauce

Preparation time: 15 minutes
Cooking time: 20 minutes
servings: 5
Ingredients:
- 2 cloves garlic, sliced
- 1 ½ cups broccoli florets
- 1 ½ cups cauliflower florets
- 1 tablespoon olive oil
- Salt to taste
- 1 teaspoon dried oregano, crushed
- ¾ cup zucchini, diced
- ¾ cup red bell pepper, diced
- 2 teaspoons lemon zest

Directions
1. Preheat your oven to 425 degrees f.
2. In a baking pan, add the garlic, broccoli and cauliflower.
3. Toss in oil and season with salt and oregano.
4. Roast in the oven for 10 minutes.
5. Add the zucchini and bell pepper to the pan.
6. Stir well.
7. Roast for another 10 minutes.
8. Sprinkle lemon zest on top before serving.
9. Transfer to a food container and reheat before serving.

427. Spinach with walnuts & avocado

Preparation time: 5 minutes
Cooking time: 0 minute
Servings: 1
Ingredients:
- 3 cups baby spinach
- ½ cup strawberries, sliced
- 1 tablespoon white onion, chopped
- 2 tablespoons vinaigrette
- ¼ medium avocado, diced

- 2 tablespoons walnut, toasted

Directions
1. Put the spinach, strawberries and onion in a glass jar with lid.
2. Drizzle dressing on top.
3. Top with avocado and walnuts.
4. Seal the lid and refrigerate until ready to serve.

296 calories; 18 g fat(2 g sat); 10 g fiber; 27 g carbohydrates; 8 g protein;
63 mcg folate; 0 mg cholesterol; 11 g sugars; 0 g added sugars; 11,084 iu vitamin a; 103 mg
Vitamin c; 192 mg calcium; 7 mg iron; 195 mg sodium; 385 mg

428. Vegan tacos

Preparation time: 20 minutes
Cooking time: 10 minutes
servings: 4
Ingredients:
- ½ teaspoon onion powder
- ½ teaspoon garlic powder
- 1 teaspoon chili powder
- 2 tablespoons tamari
- 16 oz. Tofu, drained and crumbled
- 1 tablespoon olive oil
- 1 ripe avocado
- 1 tablespoon vegan mayonnaise
- 1 teaspoon lime juice
- Salt to taste
- 8 corn tortillas, warmed
- ½ cup fresh salsa
- 2 cups iceberg lettuce, shredded
- Pickled radishes

Directions
1. Combine the onion powder, garlic powder, chili powder and tamari in a bowl.
2. Marinate the tofu in the mixture for 10 minutes.
3. Pour the oil in a pan over medium heat.
4. Cooking Time: the tofu mixture for 10 minutes.
5. In another bowl, mash the avocado and mix with mayo, lime juice and salt.
6. Stuff each corn tortilla with tofu mixture, mashed avocado, salsa and lettuce.
7. Serve with pickled radishes.

429. Grilled broccoli with chili garlic oil

Preparation time: 15 minutes
Cooking time: 16 minutes
servings: 4
Ingredients:
- 3 tablespoons olive oil, divided
- 2 tablespoons vegetable broth (unsalted
- 2 cloves garlic, sliced thinly
- 1 chili pepper, julienned
- 1 1/2 lb. Broccoli, sliced into florets
- Salt and pepper to taste
- 2 lemons, sliced in half

Directions
1. Preheat your grill to medium-high.
2. In a bowl, mix 1 tablespoon oil, garlic, broth and chili.
3. Heat in a pan over medium heat for 30 seconds.
4. In another bowl, toss the broccoli florets in salt, pepper and remaining oil.
5. Grill the broccoli florets for 10 minutes.
6. Grill the lemon slices for 5 minutes.
7. Toss the grilled broccoli and lemon in chili garlic oil.
8. Store in a food container and reheat before serving.

430. Tomato basil pasta

Preparation time: 5 minutes
Cooking time: 10 minutes
servings: 4
Ingredients:
- 2 cups low-sodium vegetable broth
- 2 cups water

- 8 oz. Pasta
- 1 ½ teaspoons italian seasoning
- 15 oz. Canned diced tomatoes
- 2 tablespoons olive oil
- ½ teaspoon garlic powder
- ½ teaspoon onion powder
- ¼ teaspoon crushed red pepper
- ½ teaspoon salt
- 6 cups baby spinach
- ½ cup basil, chopped

Directions
1. Add all the ingredients except spinach and basil in a pot over high heat.
2. Mix well.
3. Cover the pot and bring to a boil.
4. Reduce the heat.
5. Simmer for 5 minutes.
6. Add the spinach and Cooking Time: for 5 more minutes.
7. Stir in basil.
8. Transfer to a food container.
9. Microwave before serving.

431. Risotto with tomato & herbs

Preparation time: 10 minutes
Cooking time: 20 minutes
servings: 32
Ingredients:
- 2 oz. Arborio rice
- 1 teaspoon dried garlic, minced
- 3 tablespoons dried onion, minced
- 1 tablespoon dried italian seasoning, crushed
- ¾ cup snipped dried tomatoes
- 1 ½ cups reduced-sodium chicken broth

Directions
1. Make the dry risotto mix by combining all the ingredients except broth in a large bowl.
2. Divide the mixture into eight resealable plastic bags. Seal the bag.
3. Store at room temperature for up to 3 months.
4. When ready to serve, pour the broth in a pot.
5. Add the contents of 1 plastic bag of dry risotto mix.
6. Bring to a boil and then reduce heat.
7. Cover the pot and simmer for 20 minutes.
8. Serve with vegetables.

432. Tofu shawarma rice

Preparation time: 15 minutes
Cooking time: 15 minutes
servings: 4
Ingredients:
- 4 cups cooked brown rice
- 4 cups cooked tofu, sliced into small cubes
- 4 cups cucumber, cubed
- 4 cups tomatoes, cubed
- 4 cups white onion, cubed
- 2 cups cabbage, shredded
- 1/2 cup vegan mayo
- 1/8 cup garlic, minced
- Garlic salt to taste
- Hot sauce

Directions
1. Add brown rice into 4 food containers.
2. Arrange tofu, cucumber, tomatoes, white onion and cabbage on top.
3. In a bowl, mix the mayo, garlic, and garlic salt.
4. Drizzle top with garlic sauce and hot sauce before serving.

433. Garlic pea shoots

Preparation time: 5 minutes
Cooking time: 5 minutes
servings: 6
Ingredients:
- 2 tablespoons canola oil
- 2 tablespoons sesame oil
- 3 tablespoons garlic, minced
- 1 lb. Pea shoots
- ¼ cup rice wine

- *Salt and pepper to taste*

Directions
1. Heat both of the oils in a pot over medium high heat.
2. Add garlic and Cooking Time: for 30 seconds, stirring frequently.
3. Add pea shoots and rice wine.
4. Season with salt and pepper.
5. Cooking Time: for 3 minutes.
6. Place in a food container and heat in the microwave when ready to eat.

434. Pesto pasta

Preparation time: 10 minutes
Cooking time: 8 minutes
servings: 2
Ingredients:
- *1 cup fresh basil leaves*
- *4 cloves garlic*
- *2 tablespoons walnut*
- *2 tablespoons olive oil*
- *1 tablespoon vegan parmesan cheese*
- *2 cups cooked penne pasta*
- *2 tablespoons black olives, sliced*

Directions
1. Put the basil leaves, garlic, walnut, olive oil and parmesan cheese in a food processor.
2. Pulse until smooth.
3. Divide pasta into 2 food containers.
4. Spread the basil sauce on top.
5. Top with black olives.
6. Store until ready to serve.

435. Tomato Mint Salad with Rice Wine Vinaigrette

Ingredients:
- *2 medium beets*
- *8 ounces green beans, trimmed and cut into 2-inch pieces*
- *1 (15-ounce can chickpeas, rinsed and drained*
- *3 tablespoons finely chopped shallots*
- *2 tablespoons chopped fresh mint*
- *1 tablespoon chopped fresh tarragon*
- *3 tablespoons olive oil*
- *2 tablespoons rice wine vinegar*
- *1 tablespoon fresh lemon juice*
- *1 1/2 teaspoons Dijon mustard*
- *1/4 teaspoon salt*
- *1/8 teaspoon freshly ground black pepper*
- *2 medium tomatoes, each cut into 8 wedges*
- *1/2 cup nutritional yeast*

Directions:
1. Preheat oven to 350° F.
2. Leave root and 1-inch stem on beets; scrub with a brush. Wrap beets in heavy-duty foil. Bake at 350° F for 1 hour and 15 minutes or until tender. Remove from oven; cool. Trim off beet roots and stems; rub off skins. Cut each beet into 8 wedges.
3. Cooking Time: beans in boiling water 4 minutes or until crisp-tender. Drain and plunge beans into ice water; drain well. Combine beans and chickpeas in a medium bowl.
4. Combine shallots, mint, lemon juice, tarragon, olive oil, rice wine vinegar, mustard, salt and pepper in a small bowl, stirring with a whisk. Add 2 tablespoons dressing to beets; toss well. Combine 2 tablespoons dressing and tomatoes in a bowl; toss gently to coat. Add the remaining 1/4 cup dressing to bean mixture; tossing well to combine. Place 3/4 cup bean mixture on each of 4 plates. Arrange 4 pieces each of beets and tomatoes around bean mixture. Sprinkle each serving with 2 tablespoons nutritional yeast.

436. Greek Style Salad Wraps

Ingredients:
- *2 tablespoons olive oil, divided*
- *1 (8-ounce package tempeh, cut into 24 pieces*
- *1 cup water*
- *3 tablespoons lemon juice, divided*

- 2 tablespoons plain soy yogurt
- 1 1/2 teaspoons dried Italian seasoning, divided
- 1 teaspoon grated lemon rind
- 1/2 teaspoon paprika
- 1/4 teaspoon salt
- 1 garlic clove, minced
- 2 cups bagged baby spinach
- 1 cup shredded romaine lettuce
- 2/3 cup sliced cherry tomato
- 2/3 cup sliced English cucumber
- 1/4 cup (1 ounce feta vegan cheese
- 1/4 teaspoon freshly ground black pepper
- 4 (8-inch whole-wheat tortillas

Directions:

1. Heat a 10-inch skillet over medium-high heat. Add 1 tablespoon oil; swirl to coat. Add tempeh; sauté 4 minutes or until lightly browned, turning once. Add 1 cup water and 2 tablespoons juice to pan; reduce heat to medium, and simmer 10 minutes, stirring once.
2. Combine 2 tablespoons yogurt, 1/2 teaspoon Italian seasoning, lemon rind, paprika, salt and garlic in a small bowl.
3. Combine 1 tablespoon olive oil, 1 tablespoon lemon juice, 1 teaspoon Italian seasoning, spinach, lettuce, tomato, cucumber, vegan cheese and black pepper in a bowl.
4. Warm tortillas per the package directions. Spread 2 teaspoons yogurt mixture over each tortilla. Top each tortilla with 3/4 cup spinach mixture and 6 pieces tempeh; roll up. Cut each rolled tortilla in half crosswise.

437. Roasted Asparagus With Penne Salad

Ingredients:

- 2 cups uncooked penne
- 12 asparagus spears
- 12 cherry tomatoes
- 4 tablespoons extra-virgin olive oil, divided
- 3/8 teaspoon salt, divided
- 1/2 teaspoon black pepper, divided
- 1 tablespoon minced shallots
- 2 tablespoons fresh lemon juice
- 1 tablespoon Dijon mustard
- 1 teaspoon dried herbes de Provence
- 1 1/2 teaspoons agave nectar
- 1/2 cup pitted Kalamata olives, halved
- 2 cups baby arugula
- 1/2 cup nutritional yeast

Directions:

1. Preheat oven to 400° F.
2. Cooking Time: pasta per package directions, drain and set aside.
3. Place asparagus and tomatoes on a jelly-roll pan. Drizzle with 1 tablespoon olive oil; sprinkle with 1/4 teaspoon salt and 1/4 teaspoon black pepper. Toss gently to coat; arrange asparagus and tomato mixture in a single layer. Bake at 400° F for 6 minutes or until asparagus is crisp-tender. Remove asparagus from pan. Place pan back in oven, and bake tomatoes an additional 4 minutes. Remove tomatoes from pan; let asparagus and tomatoes stand 10 minutes. Cut asparagus into 1-inch lengths; halve tomatoes.
4. Combine shallots, lemon juice, mustard, herbes de Provence and agave nectar in a small bowl, stirring with a whisk. Gradually add remaining 3 tablespoons oil, stirring constantly with a whisk. Stir in remaining 1/8 teaspoon salt and 1/4 teaspoon black pepper.
5. Place pasta, asparagus, tomato, olives, and arugula in a large bowl; toss. Drizzle juice mixture over pasta mixture; toss. Sprinkle with nutritional yeast.

438. Grilled Eggplant Sandwiches

Ingredients:

- 2 tablespoons olive oil, divided
- 8 (1/2-inch-thickslices eggplant
- 2 (1/2-inch-thickslices red onion
- 1 large zucchini, cut lengthwise into 4 pieces
- 2 teaspoons chopped fresh rosemary
- 1/4 teaspoon black pepper
- 1/8 teaspoon salt
- 1 tablespoon white balsamic vinegar
- 4 (2 1/2-ounceciabatta bread portions, cut in half horizontally
- Cooking spray
- 1 ounce nutritional yeast, halved
- 8 (1/4-inch-thickslices tomato
- 8 basil leaves

Directions:

1. Preheat grill to medium-high.
2. Brush 1 tablespoon olive oil evenly over both sides of flax eggplant, onion, and zucchini. Sprinkle with rosemary, pepper, and salt.
3. Combine 1 tablespoon oil and vinegar in a bowl. Brush vinegar mixture over cut sides of bread.
4. Place onion on grill rack coated with cooking spray, and grill for 6 minutes on each side or until tender. Remove from grill, and separate into rings. Grill eggplant and zucchini 4 minutes on each side or until tender. Cut zucchini pieces in half crosswise.
5. Place bread, cut sides down, on grill rack; grill 2 minutes. Remove from grill. Place 1 piece of nutritional yeast on bottom halves bread portions; top each serving with 1 eggplant slice, 1 tomato slice, 1 basil leaf, 2 pieces zucchini, one-fourth of onion rings, 1 eggplant slice, 1 tomato slice, 1 basil leaf, 1 piece of nutritional yeast, and top half of bread. Place sandwiches on grill rack; grill 2 minutes, covered, or until nutritional yeast melts.

139. Vegan Paella

Ingredients:

- 6 ounces meatless soy chorizo
- 2 tablespoons extra-virgin olive oil
- 2 1/4 cups chopped yellow onion
- 1/4 teaspoon saffron threads, crushed
- 4 garlic cloves, minced
- 1 cup medium-grain rice
- 1 cup (1/2-inchpieces red bell pepper
- 1/2 cup dry white wine
- 2 cups organic vegetable broth
- 1/4 teaspoon salt
- 1 1/2 cups frozen shelled green soybeans, thawed
- 1/4 cup coarsely chopped fresh flat-leaf parsley
- 1/4 cup chopped green onions

Directions:

1. Heat a large nonstick skillet over medium heat. Add soy chorizo to pan, and Cooking Time: for 12 minutes or until browned, crumbling and stirring occasionally. Place in a small bowl, and set aside.
2. Return pan to medium heat. Add olive oil, swirling to coat. Add yellow onion; cover and Cooking Time: for 10 minutes or until tender, stirring occasionally. Add saffron and garlic; Cooking Time: for 1 minute, stirring constantly. Add 1 cup rice and bell pepper; Cooking Time: for 2 minutes, stirring frequently. Stir in white wine, and Cooking Time: for 2 minutes or until liquid is nearly absorbed, stirring frequently. Add vegetable broth and salt; bring to a simmer. Cover, reduce heat, and simmer for 20 minutes or until rice is tender and liquid is absorbed.
3. Return soy chorizo to pan, and stir in edamame. Cooking Time: for 5 minutes or until edamame is thoroughly heated, stirring

occasionally. Sprinkle with chopped parsley and 1/4 cup green onions.

440. Tofu Vietnamese Style Sandwich

Ingredients:

- 1 (14-ouncepackage water-packed extra-firm tofu, drained
- 2 tablespoons finely chopped lemongrass
- 2 tablespoons water
- 1 tablespoon soy sauce
- 2 teaspoons sesame oil, divided
- 1/4 cup rice vinegar
- 1/4 cup water
- 1 tablespoon sugar
- 1/4 teaspoon salt
- 1 1/4 cups julienne-cut carrot
- 1 1/4 cups julienne-cut peeled daikon radish
- 1 1/2 tablespoons chopped fresh cilantro
- 3 tablespoons vegan mayonnaise
- 1 1/2 teaspoons Sriracha
- 1 (12-ounceFrench bread baguette, halved lengthwise and toasted
- Cooking spray
- 1 cup thinly sliced English cucumber

Directions:

1. Cut tofu crosswise into 6 slices. Arrange tofu on several layers of paper towels. Cover with additional paper towels; top with a cast-iron skillet or another heavy pan. Let stand 15 minutes. Remove tofu from paper towels.
2. Combine 2 tablespoons lemongrass, 2 tablespoons water, soy sauce, and 1 teaspoon sesame oil in a 13 x 9-inch glass or ceramic baking dish. Arrange tofu slices in a single layer in soy mixture, turning to coat. Let stand for 15 minutes.
3. Combine vinegar, water, sugar and salt in a medium bowl, stirring until sugar and salt dissolve. Add carrot and radish; toss well. Let stand for 30 minutes, stirring occasionally. Drain; stir in cilantro.
4. Combine remaining 1 teaspoon sesame oil, vegan mayonnaise, and Sriracha in a small bowl, stirring with a whisk. Cut bread horizontally. Spread mayonnaise mixture evenly on cut sides of bread.
5. Heat a large nonstick skillet over medium-high heat. Coat pan with cooking spray. Remove tofu from marinade, and discard marinade. Pat tofu slices dry with paper towels. Add tofu slices to pan, and Cooking Time: for 4 minutes on each side or until crisp and golden. Arrange tofu slices on bottom half of bread; top tofu slices with carrot mixture and cucumber slices. Cut loaf crosswise into equal pieces.

441. Artichoke And Nutritional Yeast Strata

Ingredients:

- 1 teaspoon olive oil
- 1/2 cup finely chopped shallots
- 1 (10-ouncepackage frozen artichoke hearts, thawed
- 2 garlic cloves, minced
- 1/2 teaspoon dried herbes de Provence
- 1 3/4 cups soy milk
- 1/2 teaspoon freshly ground black pepper
- 1/4 teaspoon salt
- 1 cup flax eggs
- 1/3 cup nutritional yeast
- 1/2 (1-poundloaf bread, cut into 1-inch cubes
- Cooking spray

Directions:

1. Heat a large nonstick skillet over medium heat. Add olive oil to pan; swirl to coat. Add shallots, and Cooking Time: for 2 minutes, stirring frequently. Stir in artichoke

hearts and garlic; Cooking Time: for 8 minutes or until artichoke hearts begin to brown, stirring occasionally. Remove from heat, and stir in herbes de Provence. Cool 10 minutes.
2. Combine soy milk, black pepper, salt, and flax eggs in a large bowl, stirring with a whisk. Add nutritional yeast and bread; toss gently to combine. Stir in artichoke mixture, and let stand for 20 minutes.
3. Preheat oven to 375°F.
4. Spoon half of bread mixture into an 8-inch square glass or ceramic baking dish coated with cooking spray. Sprinkle with half of nutritional yeast, and top with remaining bread mixture. Sprinkle remaining half of nutritional yeast over top. Bake at 375° F for 50 minutes or until browned and bubbly.

442. Tofu Crisps With Greens

Ingredients:
- 1/3 cup white miso
- 1/3 cup mirin
- 1/3 cup rice vinegar
- 1 tablespoon finely grated peeled fresh ginger
- 1/2 cup chopped dry-roasted peanuts, divided
- 5 tablespoons canola oil, divided
- 2 (14-ounce packages water-packed firm tofu, drained
- 5 cups salad greens

Directions:
1. Combine miso, mirin, vinegar, ginger, 1/4 cup peanuts, and 3 tablespoons oil in a small bowl; stir with a whisk.
2. Cut each tofu block crosswise into 8 (1/2-inch-thick slices. Arrange tofu on several layers of paper towels. Top with several more layers of paper towels; top with a cast-iron skillet or another heavy pan. Let stand 30 minutes. Remove tofu from paper towels.
3. Heat 1 tablespoon oil in a large nonstick skillet over medium-high heat. Add 8 tofu slices to pan; sauté 4 minutes on each side or until crisp and golden. Remove from pan, and drain tofu on paper towels. Repeat procedure with remaining 1 tablespoon oil and remaining 8 tofu slices. Place 1 cup greens on each of 8 plates. Top each serving with 2 tofu slices, 3 tablespoons miso mixture, and 1 1/2 teaspoons chopped peanuts.

443. Polenta And Mushrooms

Ingredients:
- 2 tablespoons olive oil
- 2 (4-ounce packages exotic mushroom blend, chopped
- 1 (8-ounce package presliced cremini mushrooms
- 1 teaspoon minced fresh thyme
- 1/2 teaspoon minced fresh oregano
- 3 garlic cloves, chopped
- 1/3 cup vegetable broth
- 2 teaspoons fresh lemon juice
- 1/8 teaspoon salt
- 1/8 teaspoon black pepper
- 2 cups almond milk
- 1 1/2 cups vegetable broth
- 3/4 cup polenta
- 1 cup nutritional yeast, divided
- 1/4 teaspoon salt

Directions:
1. Heat oil in a skillet over high heat. Add mushrooms; sauté 4 minutes. Add herbs and garlic; sauté 1 minute. Stir in 1/3 cup broth, juice, 1/8 teaspoon salt, and pepper.
2. Bring milk and 1 1/2 cups broth to a boil. Stir in polenta; Cooking Time: 4 minutes, stirring constantly. Stir in half of nutritional yeast and 1/4 teaspoon salt. Place polenta in gratin dishes, top with remaining

nutritional yeast. Broil 5 minutes. Top each serving with mushrooms.

444. Roasted Cauliflower Penne With Olives

Ingredients:

- *2 tablespoons vegan margarine*
- *2 tablespoons olive oil*
- *2 medium shallots, peeled and cut into wedges*
- *1 (1 1/2-poundhead cauliflower, trimmed and cut into florets*
- *1/3 cup sliced Spanish olives*
- *3/8 teaspoon salt*
- *1/2 teaspoon crushed red pepper*
- *5 garlic cloves, crushed*
- *12 ounces uncooked penne*
- *3 tablespoons coarsely chopped fresh parsley*
- *1 ounce nutritional yeast*

Directions:

1. *Place a small heavy roasting pan in oven. Preheat oven to 450°F.*
2. *Remove preheated pan from oven. Add vegan margarine and oil to pan; swirl to coat. Add shallots and cauliflower to pan; toss to coat. Bake at 450° F for 10 minutes. Add olives, salt, red pepper and garlic to pan; toss to combine. Bake an additional 7 minutes or until cauliflower is tender and browned.*
3. *Cooking Time: pasta in boiling water 7 minutes or until almost tender. Drain pasta through a sieve over a bowl, reserving 1/2 cup pasta cooking liquid. Return pasta to pan over medium-high heat. Add reserved cooking liquid and cauliflower mixture; toss. Cooking Time: 2 minutes or until pasta is al dente, stirring occasionally. Remove from heat; sprinkle with parsley, and garnish with shaved nutritional yeast.*

445. Grilled Vegetable Ratatouille With Tofu

Ingredients:

- *1 cup vegetable broth*
- *1/2 cup fresh orange juice*
- *1/2 cup red wine vinegar*
- *2 teaspoons dried herbes de Provence*
- *2 tablespoons olive oil*
- *1 tablespoon olive paste*
- *1/2 teaspoon salt*
- *1/4 teaspoon freshly ground black pepper*
- *4 garlic cloves, minced*
- *1 (14-ouncepackage extra-firm tofu, sliced*
- *3 small eggplants, each cut lengthwise into 4 slices*
- *3 small zucchinis, cut lengthwise*
- *1 sweet onion, chopped*
- *1 large red bell pepper, cut into 8 wedges*
- *4 tomatoes*
- *Cooking spray*
- *2 tablespoons chopped fresh basil*
- *1 tablespoon chopped fresh parsley*
- *1 tablespoon chopped fresh thyme*

Directions:

1. *Preheat grill to medium-high heat.*
2. *Place vegetable broth, orange juice, red wine vinegar, dried herbes de Provence in a medium saucepan over medium-high heat; bring to a boil. Cooking Time: until slightly syrupy about 10 minutes. Remove from heat; cool. Stir in olive oil, olive paste, salt, black pepper and garlic.*
3. *Place tofu and vegetables on grill rack coated with cooking spray. Brush half of juice mixture over tofu and vegetables; grill for 4 minutes. Turn tofu and vegetables over; brush with remaining juice mixture. Cooking Time: for 3 minutes or until vegetables are golden brown and tender.*
4. *Combine basil, parsley, and thyme. Divide vegetables and tofu equally among 4 plates. Sprinkle each*

serving with 1 tablespoon herb mixture.

446. Pasta With Lemon Cream Sauce, Asparagus, And Peas

Ingredients:

- *8 ounces uncooked long fusilli*
- *1 3/4 cups (1 1/2-inch slices asparagus (about 1/2 pound*
- *1 cup frozen green peas, thawed*
- *1 tablespoon vegan margarine*
- *1 garlic clove, minced*
- *1 cup vegetable broth*
- *1 teaspoon cornstarch*
- *1/3 cup heavy cream*
- *3 tablespoons fresh lemon juice (about 1 lemon*
- *1/2 teaspoon salt*
- *1/4 teaspoon freshly ground black pepper*
- *Dash of ground red pepper*
- *Coarsely ground black pepper (optional*
- *Lemon slices (optional*

Directions:

1. *Cooking Time: pasta per package directions, omitting salt and fat. Add asparagus during last minute of cooking time. Place peas in a colander. Drain pasta mixture over peas; set aside.*
2. *Melt vegan margarine in a skillet over medium-high heat. Add garlic to pan; sauté 1 minute. Combine broth and cornstarch in a small bowl; stir until well blended. Add broth mixture to pan; bring to a boil. Cooking Time: 1 minute or until thick, stirring constantly. Remove from heat. Stir in cream, juice, salt, 1/4 teaspoon black pepper, and red pepper. Add pasta mixture to broth mixture; toss gently to coat. Garnish with coarsely ground black pepper and lemon slices, if desired. Serve immediately.*

447. Leek Chickpea And Quinoa

Ingredients:

- *2 teaspoons extra-virgin olive oil*
- *1 garlic clove, minced*
- *1 cup vegetable broth*
- *1 cup water*
- *1 cup uncooked quinoa*
- *1 1/2 teaspoons chopped fresh thyme*
- *1/4 teaspoon salt*
- *2 teaspoons extra-virgin olive oil, divided*
- *2 cups thinly sliced leek*
- *4 garlic cloves, chopped*
- *2 1/2 cups sliced fennel bulb*
- *1 3/4 cups sliced carrot*
- *1/2 teaspoon fennel seeds*
- *1/2 cup white wine*
- *1 cup vegetable broth*
- *4 teaspoons chopped fresh thyme, divided*
- *1 (14 1/2-ounce can chickpeas, rinsed and drained*
- *1 tablespoon fresh lemon juice*
- *1/4 teaspoon salt*
- *1/4 teaspoon freshly ground black pepper*
- *1 (5-ounce package baby spinach*

Directions:

1. *To prepare quinoa, heat 2 teaspoons oil in a large saucepan over medium-high heat. Add 1 garlic clove to pan; sauté 1 minute. Add 1 cup broth, water, quinoa, lime and salt; cover, reduce heat, and simmer 15 minutes or until liquid is absorbed and quinoa is tender.*
2. *To prepare chickpea mixture, heat 1 teaspoon oil in a Dutch oven over medium-high heat. Add leek and 4 garlic cloves to pan; sauté 5 minutes or until tender. Add remaining 1 teaspoon oil, fennel bulb, carrot, and fennel seeds; sauté 10 minutes or until vegetables are golden. Add*

wine; Cooking Time: 3 minutes or until liquid almost evaporates. Stir in 1 cup broth, 2 teaspoons thyme, and chickpeas; Cooking Time: 1 minute or until thoroughly heated. Remove from heat; stir in juice, 1/4 teaspoon salt, pepper, and spinach.
3. Place about 2/3 cup quinoa in each of 4 bowls; top each serving with about 1 1/2 cups chickpea mixture. Sprinkle each serving with 1/2 teaspoon thyme.

448. Spaghetti With Roasted Cherry Tomato

Ingredients:
- 4 quarts water
- 2 teaspoons salt
- 8 ounces uncooked spaghetti
- 2 2/3 cups cherry tomatoes
- 2 tablespoons extra-virgin olive oil, divided
- 2 teaspoons red wine vinegar
- 3/8 teaspoon sea salt
- 1/8 teaspoon crushed red pepper
- 2 1/2 tablespoons chopped basil leaves
- 2 1/2 tablespoons chopped parsley
- 1/2 cup nutritional yeast

Directions:
1. Preheat oven to 450° F.
2. Bring 4 quarts water to a boil in a large Dutch oven. Add 1 tablespoon salt and spaghetti to boiling water; Cooking Time: 10 minutes or until spaghetti is al dente. Drain spaghetti in a colander over a bowl, reserving 1/3 cup cooking water. Return spaghetti to pan; set aside, and keep warm.
3. While spaghetti cooks, combine tomatoes, 1 tablespoon olive oil, vinegar, 3/8 teaspoon salt, and pepper on a jelly-roll pan, tossing well to coat. Bake tomato mixture at 450° F for 10 minutes or until tomatoes are soft and lightly charred in places.
4. Add tomatoes and any tomato juice to spaghetti in Dutch oven. Add 3 tablespoons reserved cooking water to jelly-roll pan, scraping pan to loosen browned bits; carefully pour water mixture and remaining 1 tablespoon oil into spaghetti mixture. Place Dutch oven over medium heat. Add remaining reserved cooking water, 1 tablespoon at a time, until spaghetti mixture is moist, tossing frequently. Stir in basil and parsley. Sprinkle with nutritional yeast. Serve immediately.

449. Vegetable Curry Samosas With Chutney

Ingredients:
- 1/2 cup fresh cilantro leaves
- 1/2 cup fresh mint leaves
- 1/4 cup chopped red onion
- 2 tablespoons fresh lemon juice
- 1 tablespoon water
- 1/4 teaspoon salt
- 1/8 teaspoon sugar
- 1 serrano chile, coarsely chopped
- 1 (1/2-inch piece peeled fresh ginger
- 1 1/4 cups mashed cooked peeled baking potatoes
- 1/4 cup cooked yellow lentils
- 1 tablespoon minced fresh mint
- 1 teaspoon curry powder
- 1 teaspoon vegan margarine, softened
- 1/4 teaspoon salt
- 1/4 teaspoon ground cumin
- 1/2 cup green peas
- 10 egg roll wrappers
- 1/4 cup flax egg
- Cooking spray

Directions:
1. To prepare chutney, combine first 9 ingredients in a blender; process until smooth. Set aside.

2. *To prepare samosas, combine potatoes, lentils, mint, curry powder, 1 teaspoon vegan margarine, 1/4 teaspoon salt, and cumin. Gently fold in peas.*
3. *Working with 1 flax egg roll wrapper at a time (cover remaining wrappers to prevent drying), cut down middle to form 2 long rectangles. Moisten edges of wrapper with flax egg. Spoon 1 tablespoon potato mixture near bottom edge of wrapper. Fold up from 1 corner to the opposite outer edge of the wrapper, making a triangle. Fold over to opposite side again as if folding up a flag. Repeat fold to opposite side to form a triangle. Repeat with remaining wrappers and filling.*
4. *Heat a large cast-iron skillet over medium-high heat. Coat pan with cooking spray. Lightly coat samosas with cooking spray. Add samosas to pan, and Cooking Time: 1 minute on each side. Drain on paper towels. Serve with chutney.*

450. Lentil Burgers With Salsa

Ingredients:
- *1/4 cup finely chopped pineapple*
- *1/4 cup finely chopped mango*
- *1/4 cup finely chopped tomatillo*
- *1/4 cup halved grape tomatoes*
- *1 tablespoon fresh lime juice*
- *1 serrano chile, minced*
- *1 1/2 cups water*
- *1/2 cup dried lentils*
- *Cooking spray*
- *1 cup chopped onion*
- *1/4 cup grated carrot*
- *2 teaspoons minced garlic*
- *2 tablespoons tomato paste*
- *1 1/2 teaspoons ground cumin*
- *3/4 teaspoon dried oregano*
- *1/2 teaspoon chili powder*
- *3/4 teaspoon salt, divided*
- *3/4 cup cooked pearl barley*
- *1/2 cup panko (Japanese breadcrumbs*
- *1/4 cup finely chopped fresh parsley*
- *1/2 teaspoon coarsely ground black pepper*
- *3/4 cup flax egg*
- *3 tablespoons canola oil, divided*

Directions:
1. *To prepare salsa, combine pineapple, mango, tomatillo, grape tomatoes, fresh lime juice, serrano chile, minced cover and refrigerate.*
2. *To prepare burgers, combine 1 1/2 cups water and lentils in a saucepan; bring to a boil. Cover, reduce heat, and simmer 25 minutes or until lentils are tender. Drain. Place half of lentils in a large bowl. Place remaining lentils in a food processor; process until smooth. Add processed lentils to whole lentils in bowl.*
3. *Heat a large nonstick skillet over medium-high heat. Coat pan with cooking spray. Add onion and carrot; sauté 6 minutes or until tender, stirring occasionally. Add garlic; Cooking Time: 1 minute, stirring constantly. Add tomato paste, cumin, oregano, chili powder, and 1/4 teaspoon salt; Cooking Time: 1 minute, stirring constantly. Add onion mixture to lentils. Add remaining 1/2 teaspoon salt, barley, and next 5 ingredients (through flax egg); stir well. Cover and refrigerate 1 hour or until firm.*
4. *Divide mixture into 8 portions, shaping each into a 1/2-inch-thick patty. Heat 1 1/2 tablespoons oil in a large nonstick skillet over medium-high heat. Add 4 patties; Cooking Time: 3 minutes on each side or until browned. Repeat procedure with remaining 1 1/2 tablespoons oil and 4 patties. Serve with salsa.*

Baked Tofu Zucchini And Oregano Lasagna

Ingredients:
- 3 tablespoons olive oil, divided
- 1/2 cup chopped white onion
- 2 garlic cloves, minced
- 1 teaspoon salt, divided
- 1 teaspoon sugar
- 1/4 teaspoon freshly ground black pepper, divided
- 1/4 teaspoon crushed red pepper
- 1 (28-ounce can crushed tomatoes
- 1/2 cup chopped fresh basil
- 1 tablespoon chopped fresh oregano
- 2 cups nutritional yeast
- 1 (14-ounce package water-packed firm tofu, drained
- 1/4 cup flax egg
- 1/2 cup thinly sliced green onions
- 3 cups finely chopped red bell pepper
- 2 medium zucchinis, quartered lengthwise and thinly sliced
- 1/3 cup finely chopped fresh parsley
- Cooking spray
- 12 cooked lasagna noodles

Directions:
1. Preheat oven to 375° F.
2. Heat 2 tablespoons oil in a medium saucepan over medium-high heat. Add white onion; sauté 5 minutes or until tender. Add garlic; sauté 1 minute or until golden. Add 1/2 teaspoon salt, sugar, 1/8 teaspoon black pepper, crushed red pepper, and tomatoes. Cover, reduce heat to low, and simmer 15 minutes or until thoroughly heated. Remove from heat; stir in basil and oregano. Cool.
3. Combine 1 ½ cup nutritional yeast, tofu, flax egg, and 1/4 teaspoon salt in a food processor; process for 10 seconds or until blended. Stir in green onions. Set aside.
4. Heat remaining 1 tablespoon olive oil in a large nonstick skillet over medium-high heat. Add bell pepper, zucchini, and remaining 1/4 teaspoon salt to pan; sauté 10 minutes or until vegetables are tender and liquid evaporates. Remove from heat; stir in parsley and remaining 1/8 teaspoon black pepper.
5. Spread 1/2 cup tomato mixture in the bottom of a 13 x 9–inch baking dish coated with cooking spray; top with 3 noodles. Spread 3/4 cup tomato mixture over noodles; top with 1 cup tofu mixture and 1 cup zucchini mixture. Repeat layers twice, ending with noodles. Spread remaining 3/4 cup tomato mixture over top. Bake at 375° for 35 minutes; top with remaining nutritional yeast. Bake an additional 5 minutes or until nutritional yeast melts. Let stand 10 minutes.

452. Potato And Turnip French-Style Casserole

Ingredients:
- 1 tablespoon margarine
- 1 pound sliced mushroom caps
- 1 teaspoon minced garlic
- 1 cup white wine
- 2 tablespoons chopped fresh flat-leaf parsley
- 1 large thyme sprig
- 3/4 teaspoon freshly ground black pepper, divided
- 2 tablespoons nutritional yeast
- Cooking spray
- 2 onions, sliced
- 1 (8-ounce Yukon gold potato, peeled and sliced
- 2 cups packed baby spinach leaves
- 1/2 teaspoon salt, divided
- 1 turnip, peeled and cut into slices
- 1 1/2 teaspoons chopped fresh tarragon

- *1/4 cup coconut milk*
- *1/2 cup nutritional yeast*

Directions:
1. Preheat oven to 350° F.
2. Melt vegan margarine in a large nonstick skillet over medium-high heat. Add mushrooms to pan, and sauté 2 minutes or until lightly browned. Stir in garlic; sauté 30 seconds. Add wine; Cooking Time: 2 minutes. Add parsley, thyme, and 1/4 teaspoon pepper. Cover, reduce heat, and simmer 10 minutes. Uncover and Cooking Time: 6 minutes or until liquid almost evaporates. Remove from heat; discard thyme. Add nutritional yeast, stirring until nutritional yeast melts. Remove mushroom mixture from pan. Wipe pan clean with paper towels.
3. Heat pan over medium-high heat. Coat pan with cooking spray. Add onion; sauté for 5 minutes, stirring frequently. Reduce heat to medium; continue cooking for 15 minutes or until deep golden brown, stirring frequently. Set aside.
4. Coat a 6-cup baking dish with cooking spray. Arrange potato slices in dish, and top with spinach. Sprinkle 1/4 teaspoon salt and 1/4 teaspoon black pepper evenly over spinach. Spoon the mushroom mixture over black pepper, and arrange turnip slices over mushroom mixture. Top with caramelized onions; sprinkle with remaining 1/4 teaspoon salt, remaining 1/4 teaspoon black pepper, and tarragon. Pour coconut milk over tarragon, and sprinkle evenly with nutritional yeast. Cover and bake at 350°F for 40 minutes. Uncover and bake an additional 20 minutes or until vegetables are tender and nutritional yeast begins to brown.

453. Chipotle Bean Burritos

Ingredients:
- *1 tablespoon olive oil*
- *1 garlic clove, minced*
- *1/2 teaspoon chipotle chile powder*
- *1/4 teaspoon salt*
- *1/3 cup water*
- *1 (15-ouncecan black beans, drained*
- *1 (15-ouncecan kidney beans, drained*
- *3 tablespoons salsa*
- *6 (10-inchflour tortillas*
- *1 cup (4 ouncesnutritional yeast*
- *1 1/2 cups chopped plum tomato*
- *1 1/2 cups shredded lettuce*
- *6 tablespoons thinly sliced green onions*
- *6 tablespoons soy yogurt*

Directions:
1. Heat oil in a large nonstick skillet over medium heat. Add garlic to pan; Cooking Time: 1 minute, stirring frequently. Stir in chile powder and salt; Cooking Time: 30 seconds, stirring constantly. Stir in 1/3 cup water and beans; bring to a boil. Reduce heat, and simmer 10 minutes. Remove from heat; stir in salsa. Partially mash bean mixture with a fork.
2. Warm tortillas per package directions. Spoon about 1/3 cup bean mixture into center of each tortilla. Top each serving with about 2 1/2 tablespoons nutritional yeast, 1/4 cup tomato, 1/4 cup lettuce, 1 tablespoon onions, and 1 tablespoon soy yogurt; roll up.

454. Corn Quesadillas With Chile

Ingredients:
- *2 Anaheim chiles*
- *2 teaspoons olive oil*
- *1 cup thinly sliced mushroom caps*
- *1 cup whole-kernel corn, thawed*
- *1/4 cup chopped green onions*

- 1/8 teaspoon ground black pepper
- 4 (8-inch flour tortillas
- 3/4 cup nutritional yeast
- Cooking spray
- 1/2 cup salsa

Directions:
1. Preheat broiler.
2. Cut chiles in half lengthwise; discard seeds and membranes. Place chile halves, skin sides up, on a foil-lined baking sheet; flatten with hand. Broil 8 minutes or until blackened. Place in a plastic bag; seal. Let stand 15 minutes. Peel and chop. Reduce oven temperature to 200° F.
3. Heat oil in a large nonstick skillet over medium-high heat. Add mushrooms; sauté 2 minutes. Add corn, onions, and pepper; sauté 2 minutes. Place mixture in a bowl; stir in chopped chiles. Wipe pan clean.
4. Place about 1/4 cup mushroom mixture and 1/4 cup nutritional yeast over half of 1 tortilla. Repeat procedure with remaining 1 1/4 cups mushroom mixture, remaining 3/4 cup nutritional yeast, and remaining 3 tortillas. Heat pan over medium heat. Coat pan with cooking spray. Place 1 tortilla in pan; Cooking Time: 2 minutes or until nutritional yeast melts and bottom is golden. Fold tortilla in half; place on a baking sheet. Place in 200° F oven to keep warm. Repeat procedure with remaining tortillas. Cut each quesadilla into wedges; serve with salsa.

455. Sautéed Tofu

Ingredients:
- 2 tablespoons rice vinegar
- 2 tablespoons agave nectar
- 1 tablespoon low-sodium soy sauce
- 1 teaspoon dark sesame oil
- 1/8 teaspoon kosher salt
- 1/4 teaspoon ground red pepper, divided
- 1 (14-ounce package water-packed soft tofu, drained
- 2 tablespoons canola oil, divided
- 1 ounce fresh ginger, peeled and julienne-cut
- 3 tablespoons diagonally sliced green onions
- 1 teaspoon minced fresh garlic
- 1/4 teaspoon kosher salt
- 1 teaspoon sesame seeds

Directions:
1. Combine vinegar, agave nectar, soy sauce, sesame oil, 1/8 teaspoon salt, and 1/8 teaspoon red pepper in a medium bowl; stir with a whisk.
2. Cut tofu crosswise into 8 (1/2-inch-thick slices. Arrange tofu on several layers of paper towels. Top with several more layers of paper towels; top with a cast-iron skillet or another heavy pan. Let stand 30 minutes. Remove tofu from paper towels. Cut tofu into (1-inch cubes. Sprinkle tofu with remaining 1/8 teaspoon red pepper.
3. Heat 1 tablespoon canola oil in a large nonstick skillet over medium-high heat. Add tofu to pan; sauté 8 minutes or until crisp, carefully turning to brown on all sides. Remove tofu from pan; keep warm. Heat remaining 1 tablespoon canola oil in pan. Add ginger and green onions to pan; sauté 30 seconds. Add garlic to pan; sauté 30 seconds or just until golden. Add ginger mixture to vinegar mixture; stir well. Pour vinegar mixture over tofu; sprinkle evenly with 1/4 teaspoon salt and sesame seeds.

456. Lentil-Rice Cakes With Salsa

Ingredients:
- 3 cups finely chopped plum tomato
- 1/4 cup chopped fresh basil

- *1 tablespoon balsamic vinegar*
- *2 teaspoons capers*
- *1/4 teaspoon salt*
- *5 cups water, divided*
- *1 cup dried small red lentils*
- *1/2 cup uncooked basmati rice*
- *2 tablespoons olive oil, divided*
- *1/2 cup finely chopped red bell pepper*
- *1/2 cup finely chopped red onion*
- *1/2 teaspoon fennel seeds, crushed*
- *2 garlic cloves, minced*
- *3/4 cup mozzarella nutritional yeast*
- *1/4 cup dry breadcrumbs*
- *1 tablespoon chopped fresh basil*
- *1 teaspoon salt*
- *1/4 teaspoon freshly ground black pepper*
- *1/2 cup vegan egg replacer*

Directions:
1. To prepare salsa, tomatoes, basil, capers, vinegar and salt; set aside at room temperature.
2. To prepare cakes, bring 4 cups water and lentils to a boil in a medium saucepan. Reduce heat, and simmer for 20 minutes or until tender. Drain and rinse with cold water; drain. Place lentils in a large bowl.
3. Combine remaining 1 cup water and rice in pan; bring to a boil. Cover, reduce heat, and simmer 18 minutes or until liquid is absorbed. Cool 10 minutes. Add rice to lentils.
4. Heat 1 teaspoon oil in a large nonstick skillet over medium-high heat. Add bell pepper, onion, fennel seeds, and garlic to pan; sauté 2 minutes or until tender. Cool 10 minutes. Add to rice mixture. Add mozzarella nutritional yeast, breadcrumbs, basil, salt, black pepper and vegan egg replacer stirring until well combined. Let stand for 10 minutes.
5. Wipe skillet clean with paper towels. Heat 2 teaspoons olive oil in skillet over medium heat. Spoon half of rice mixture by 1/3-cupfuls into pan, spreading to form circles; Cooking Time: 5 minutes or until lightly browned. Carefully turn cakes over; Cooking Time: 5 minutes on other side. Remove cakes from pan. Repeat procedure with remaining 1 tablespoon olive oil and remaining rice mixture. Serve with salsa.

457. Nutritional Yeast Tamales

Ingredients:
- *10 dried corn husks*
- *1/2 cup sliced green onions*
- *1/4 cup soy yogurt*
- *1/4 teaspoon salt*
- *6 olives, chopped*
- *1/2 cup flax egg*
- *6 ounces' nutritional yeast*
- *2 cups Masa dough*
- *2 cups hot water*

Directions:
1. Place corn husks in a large bowl; cover with water. Weight husks down with a can; soak 30 minutes. Drain husks.
2. Preheat oven to 450° F.
3. Combine onions, yogurt, salt, flax eggs and nutritional yeast stirring well to combine. Working with one husk at a time, place 3 tablespoons Masa dough in the center of husk about 1/2 inch from top of husk; press dough into a 4-inch wide. Spoon about 1 tablespoon nutritional yeast mixture down one side of dough. Using the corn husk as your guide, fold husk over tamale, being sure to cover filling with dough; fold over 1 more time. Fold bottom end of husk under. Place tamale, seam side down, on the rack of a broiler pan lined with a damp towel. Repeat procedure with remaining husks, Masa dough, and filling. Cover filled tamales with another damp towel.

Pour 2 cups hot water in the bottom of a broiler pan; top with prepared rack.
4. Steam tamales at 450°F for 55 minutes, adding water as necessary to maintain a depth of about 1/2 inch. Let tamales stand 10 minutes.

458. Arugula Pizza

Ingredients:
- 1 (11-ounce package pizza crust dough
- Cooking spray
- 1 cup nutritional yeast
- 1 (5-ounce package baby arugula
- 4 teaspoons extra-virgin olive oil
- 1/2 teaspoon grated fresh lemon rind
- 1 tablespoon fresh lemon juice
- 1/8 teaspoon salt
- 1/4 teaspoon freshly ground black pepper

Directions:
1. Preheat oven to 450° F.
2. Unroll pizza dough on a baking sheet lightly coated with cooking spray; place in preheating oven. Bake as oven heats for 7 minutes.
3. Remove pan from oven. Spread nutritional yeast mixture over dough. Return pan to oven, and bake for 5 minutes.
4. Combine arugula, nutritional yeast, arugula, olive oil, lemon rind, lemon juice and salt in a large bowl; toss well. Top pizza with arugula mixture; sprinkle with pepper. Slice.

459. Rice Noodle Salad

Ingredients:
- 8 ounces uncooked wide rice sticks
- 2 tablespoons plus 1 teaspoon sesame oil, divided
- 1/2 cup vegetable broth
- 6 tablespoons ketchup
- 2 tablespoons lime juice
- 2 tablespoons soy sauce
- 1 teaspoon hot chile sauce
- 8 ounces tempeh, cut into 1/2-inch cubes
- 6 garlic cloves, minced
- 2 shallots, thinly sliced
- 1/2 cup liquid vegan egg replacer
- 2 cups fresh bean sprouts
- 1 1/2 cups thinly sliced cucumber
- 5 thinly sliced green onions
- 1 1/2 cups matchstick-cut carrots
- 1/2 cup fresh basil leaves
- 1/2 cup fresh mint leaves
- 1/2 cup chopped fresh cilantro

Directions:
1. Cooking Time: the noodles per package directions. Drain and toss with 1 teaspoon sesame oil.
2. Combine broth and ketchup, lime juice, soy sauce and chile sauce stirring with a whisk.
3. Heat remaining 2 tablespoons oil in a large nonstick skillet over medium-high heat; swirl to coat. Add tempeh, and stir-fry 3 minutes or until lightly browned. Add garlic and shallots; stir-fry 1 minute or until shallots begin to soften. Add flax eggs; stir-fry for 30 seconds or until soft-scrambled, stirring constantly. Add soy sauce mixture, and bring to a boil. Add noodles and bean sprouts; toss gently to coat. Cooking Time: 1 minute or until sauce is thickened.
4. Remove from heat, and top with cucumber, onions, carrots, basil leaves, mint leaves and cilantro.

460. Gemelli Salad With Almonds And Lime Vinaigrette

Ingredients:
- 8 ounces uncooked gemelli
- 1 cup (1 1/2-inch cut haricots verts
- 1/2 cup chopped almonds
- 2 tablespoons fresh thyme leaves,

- *divided*
- *2 tablespoons grated lime rind, divided*
- *1 tablespoon minced shallots*
- *2 tablespoons rice vinegar*
- *3 garlic cloves, crushed*
- *5 tablespoons extra-virgin olive oil*
- *1/2 teaspoon salt*
- *1/2 teaspoon freshly ground black pepper*
- *1 ounce Parmesan nutritional yeast*

Directions:
1. Cooking Time: the pasta per package directions. Add haricots verts during the final 2 minutes of cooking. Drain and rinse pasta mixture under cold water; drain well.
2. Place the pasta mixture, almonds, 1 tablespoon thyme, and 1 tablespoon lime rind in a large bowl; toss gently to combine.
3. Combine remaining 1 tablespoon thyme, remaining 1 tablespoon lime rind, shallots, rice vinegar, and garlic in a small bowl, stirring well with a whisk. Gradually add olive oil, stirring constantly with a whisk. Add salt and black pepper; stir with a whisk. Drizzle over pasta mixture, and toss gently to coat. Top each serving with Parmesan nutritional yeast.

461. Grilled Portobello Tacos

Ingredients:
- *1 1/2 cups chopped seeded plum tomato*
- *1/2 cup julienne-cut jicama*
- *2 tablespoons chopped fresh cilantro*
- *2 tablespoons fresh lime juice*
- *1/8 teaspoon crushed red pepper*
- *1 minced serrano chile*
- *1/2 teaspoon salt, divided*
- *4 Portobello mushroom caps*
- *1/2 onion, sliced*
- *1 whole poblano chile*
- *Cooking spray*
- *4 teaspoons olive oil*
- *3 garlic cloves, thinly sliced*
- *1/2 teaspoon ground cumin*
- *6 corn tortillas*
- *1 cup sliced peeled avocado*
- *1 cup   nutritional yeast*

Directions:
1. Preheat grill to medium-high heat.
2. Combine tomato, jicama, cilantro, lime juice, red pepper and chile and 1/8 teaspoon salt in a small bowl.
3. Place mushrooms, onion, and poblano on a grill rack coated with cooking spray, and grill mushrooms and poblano for 5 minutes on each side or until tender. Grill onion 6 minutes on each side or until tender. Remove from heat. Seed poblano and remove stem, and cut mushrooms and poblano into thin strips. Chop onion, and combine vegetables in a bowl.
4. Heat olive oil in a large nonstick skillet over medium-high heat. Add garlic; sauté for 1 minute or until lightly browned. Add mushroom mixture, remaining 3/8 teaspoon salt, and cumin; Cooking Time: 2 minutes or until thoroughly heated.
5. Heat tortillas per package directions. Divide mushroom mixture, pico de gallo, and avocado evenly among tortillas. Top each with 2 tablespoons nutritional yeast.

462. Potato Hash With Beets And Vegan Eggs

Ingredients:
- *2 tablespoons extra-virgin olive oil*
- *2 cups sliced leek*
- *12 ounces potatoes, cut in half lengthwise*
- *2 garlic cloves, minced*
- *1 1/4 teaspoons paprika, divided*
- *1/2 teaspoon salt, divided*
- *1/2 teaspoon coarsely ground black*

pepper, divided
- 4 cups thinly sliced trimmed beets
- ¾ cup vegan eggs
- 1/4 cup nutritional yeast

Directions:
1. Heat a large skillet over medium heat. Add oil to pan. Add leek; Cooking Time: 8 minutes, stirring frequently. Add potatoes and garlic; Cooking Time: 15 minutes or until potatoes are tender, stirring occasionally. Stir in 1 teaspoon paprika, 1/4 teaspoon salt, and 1/4 teaspoon pepper. Add beets; Cooking Time: 4 minutes, stirring constantly. Using a spoon, push potato mixture aside to make 4 spaces for vegan eggs.
2. Add a vegan egg into each space; sprinkle remaining 1/4 teaspoon salt, remaining 1/4 teaspoon pepper, and remaining 1/4 teaspoon paprika over vegan eggs. Cover and Cooking Time: 3 minutes; sprinkle nutritional yeast over potato mixture. Cover and Cooking Time: 2 minutes or until vegan eggs are cooked.

463. Bean Chili

Ingredients:
- 1 (15-ounce can white beans, rinsed, drained, and divided
- 1 tablespoon olive oil
- 1 (4-ounce vegan sausage
- 1 1/2 cups chopped white onion
- 3 garlic cloves, minced
- 2 poblano chiles, seeded and chopped
- 2 teaspoons chili powder
- 1 teaspoon ground cumin
- 1 1/2 cups water
- 2 tablespoons chopped fresh oregano
- 2 teaspoons hot pepper sauce
- 1/2 teaspoon salt
- 1 (15.5-ounce can white hominy, rinsed and drained
- 2 tablespoons thinly sliced green onions
- 2 tablespoons chopped fresh cilantro
- 4 lime wedges

Directions:
1. Mash 2/3 cup beans with a fork.
2. Heat a large Dutch oven over medium heat. Add oil to pan; swirl to coat. Add vegan sausage, and sauté for 4 minutes. Add onion, garlic, and poblanos; sauté 6 minutes. Add chili powder and cumin; Cooking Time: 30 seconds, stirring constantly. Add mashed beans, whole beans, 1 1/2 cups water, oregano, pepper sauce, salt and hominy. Bring to a boil. Cover, reduce heat, and simmer for 20 minutes or until slightly thickened. Stir in green onions and cilantro. Serve with lime wedges.

464. Sweet Potato Tamales

Ingredients:
- 6 dried cornhusks

Filling:
- 1 (1-pound sweet potato
- 2 teaspoons extra-virgin olive oil
- 1 cup chopped onion
- 1 teaspoon ground cumin
- 1/2 teaspoon ground cinnamon
- 1 (15-ounce can black beans, rinsed and drained
- 1 (4-ounce can chopped green chiles, drained
- 1 1/4 cups (5 ounces nutritional yeast
- 1/4 cup chopped fresh cilantro

Masa Dough:
- 2 cups organic vegetable broth
- 1 1/2 cups frozen corn kernels, thawed
- 3 3/4 cups masa harina
- 1 1/2 teaspoons baking powder
- 1/4 teaspoon salt
- 1/4 cup vegan margarine, melted

Sauce:

- 2 teaspoons extra-virgin olive oil
- 1 cup chopped onion
- 1 jalapeño pepper, seeded and chopped
- 3 garlic cloves, minced
- 1 pound fresh tomatillos, husked and rinsed
- 1/3 cup organic vegetable broth
- 2 tablespoons chopped fresh oregano
- 1 teaspoon ground cumin
- 1 teaspoon chipotle chile powder
- 1/4 teaspoon salt
- 1/2 cup cilantro leaves

Directions:

1. Place corn husks in a large bowl; cover with water. Weight husks down with a can; soak 30 minutes. Drain.
2. Preheat oven to 400° F.
3. To prepare filling, pierce potato with a fork; wrap in foil. Bake at 400° for 1 hour or until tender. Peel potato; mash. Heat 2 teaspoons oil in a skillet over medium-high heat. Add 1 cup onion; sauté 4 minutes. Add 1 teaspoon cumin and cinnamon; sauté 30 seconds. Add beans and green chiles; sauté 2 minutes. Remove from heat. Combine potato, bean mixture, nutritional yeast, and chopped cilantro.
4. Increase oven temperature to 450° F.
5. To prepare masa dough, combine 2 cups broth and corn in a blender; process until smooth.
6. Lightly spoon masa harina into dry measuring cups; level with a knife. Combine masa harina, baking powder, and salt. Add broth mixture and vegan margarine to masa mixture; stir until a soft dough forms. Cover.
7. To prepare a tomatillo sauce, heat 2 teaspoons oil in a medium saucepan over medium-high heat. Add 1 cup onion, jalapeño, and garlic; sauté 2 minutes. Add tomatillos, vegetable broth, oregano, chile powder, cumin and salt; bring to a boil. Cover, reduce heat, and simmer 10 minutes. Cool slightly.
8. Place tomatillo mixture and cilantro leaves in a blender. Remove center piece of blender lid; secure blender lid on blender. Place a clean towel over opening in blender lid. Blend until smooth.
9. To assemble, working with 1 husk at a time, place 3 tablespoons masa dough in center of husk about 1/2 inch from top, and press dough into a 4 x 3-inch rectangle. Spoon 2 tablespoons bean mixture down 1 side of dough. Fold husk over tamale, being sure to cover the filling with dough; fold over 1 more time. Fold bottom end of husk under. Place the tamale, seam side down, on the rack of a broiler pan lined with a damp towel. Repeat the procedure with remaining husks, dough, and bean mixture. Cover filled tamales with another damp towel. Pour 2 cups hot water in the bottom of a broiler pan; top with prepared rack.
10. Steam at 450° F for 1 hour, adding water as necessary to maintain a depth of about 1/2 inch. Let stand 10 minutes. Serve with sauce.

465. Beet Penne

Ingredients:

- 8 ounces uncooked penne
- 2 (8-ounce golden beets with greens
- 2 tablespoons extra-virgin olive oil, divided
- 3/4 cup water, divided
- 1/3 cup vegetable broth
- 1/2 teaspoon sea salt
- 1/2 teaspoon freshly ground black pepper
- 2 cups loosely packed fresh basil leaves
- 1/4 cup dry-roasted unsalted almonds

- 3 garlic cloves, chopped
- 2 ounces fresh nutritional yeast
- 1 tablespoon fresh lemon juice

Directions:
1. Cooking Time: pasta per the package directions, omitting salt and fat. Drain.
2. Remove greens and stems from beets; rinse and drain. Coarsely chop greens and stems to measure 4 cups. Peel beets, cut in half vertically, and cut into 1/8-inch slices.
3. Heat a large skillet over medium-high heat. Add 1 tablespoon oil to pan; swirl to coat. Add beets; sauté 3 minutes. Add beet greens and stems, 1/2 cup water, broth, salt, and pepper; cover. Reduce heat to medium; simmer 8 minutes or until beets are tender.
4. Combine remaining 1 tablespoon oil, basil, almonds, and garlic in a food processor; process until smooth. Add nutritional yeast and remaining 1/4 cup water; process until blended. Add pasta, pesto, and lemon juice to beet mixture; toss to combine.

466. Spinach-Feta Casserole

Ingredients:
- 2 1/4 teaspoons dry yeast
- 3/4 cup warm water
- 1 teaspoon olive oil
- 2 cups all-purpose flour
- 1/2 teaspoon salt
- Cooking spray

Filling:
- 1 tablespoon olive oil, divided
- 5 garlic cloves, thinly sliced and divided
- 2 cups thinly vertically sliced onion
- 1/4 teaspoon salt
- 1/4 teaspoon crushed red pepper
- 2 pounds coarsely chopped fresh spinach
- 3/4 cup vegan feta nutritional yeast

Directions:
1. To prepare dough, dissolve yeast in 3/4 cup warm water in a small bowl; let stand 5 minutes. Stir in 1 teaspoon oil. Lightly spoon flour into dry measuring cups; level with a knife. Combine flour and 1/2 teaspoon salt in a large bowl; add yeast mixture, stirring until dough forms. Turn dough out onto a lightly floured surface. Knead until smooth and elastic (about 6 minutes). Place dough in a large bowl coated with cooking spray, turning to coat top. Cover and let rise in a warm place until doubled in size.
2. Punch dough down; cover and let rest 5 minutes. Roll dough into a 12-inch square; fit dough into an 8-inch square baking pan coated with cooking spray, allowing excess dough to hang over edges of dish.
3. Preheat oven to 425° F.
4. To prepare filling, combine 1 teaspoon oil and 2 garlic cloves; set aside.
5. Heat remaining 2 teaspoons oil in a Dutch oven over medium-high heat. Add remaining 3 garlic cloves and onion; sauté 5 minutes or until onion is tender and lightly browned. Spoon onion mixture into a large bowl. Stir in 1/4 teaspoon salt and pepper; keep warm. Add half of spinach to pan; Cooking Time: 1 minute or until spinach begins to wilt, stirring frequently. Add remaining spinach; Cooking Time: 5 minutes or until spinach wilts. Place spinach in a colander; press until barely moist. Add spinach and vegan feta cheese to onion mixture, stirring until well combined.
6. Brush dough with half of garlic-oil mixture; top with spinach mixture. Fold excess dough over filling to cover; brush with remaining garlic-oil mixture. Bake at 425° for 30 minutes or until golden. Let stand

for 10 minutes.

467. Curried Vegetables

Ingredients:

- *1 1/2 teaspoons olive oil*
- *1 cup diced peeled sweet potato*
- *1 cup small cauliflower florets*
- *1/4 cup thinly sliced yellow onion*
- *2 teaspoons curry powder*
- *1/2 cup vegetable broth*
- *1/4 teaspoon salt*
- *1 (15-ounce can chickpeas, rinsed and drained*
- *1 (14.5-ounce can diced tomatoes, undrained*
- *2 tablespoons chopped fresh cilantro*

Directions:

1. *Heat olive oil in a large nonstick skillet over medium-high heat. Add sweet potato to pan; sauté 3 minutes. Decrease heat to medium.*
2. *Add cauliflower, onion, and curry powder; Cooking Time: 1 minute, stirring mixture constantly. Add broth, salt, chickpeas and tomatoes; bring to a boil.*
3. *Cover, reduce heat, and simmer 10 minutes or until vegetables are tender, stirring occasionally. Sprinkle with cilantro.*

468. Nutritional Yeast Stuffed Shells With Marinara Sauce

Ingredients:

- *2 cups jumbo shell pasta*
- *Cooking spray*
- *1 cup nutritional yeast*
- *2 tablespoons chopped fresh chives*
- *2 tablespoons chopped fresh parsley*
- *1/4 teaspoon black pepper*
- *1/4 teaspoon salt*
- *1 (10-ounce package frozen chopped spinach, thawed and drained*
- *6 cups marinara*

Directions:

1. *Cooking Time: pasta per package directions. Drain and set aside.*
2. *Preheat oven to 375° F.*
3. *Coat 2 (13 x 9-inch baking dishes with cooking spray; set aside.*
4. *Place nutritional yeast a food processor; process until smooth. Add chives, parsley, black pepper, salt and spinach.*
5. *Spoon or pipe 1 tablespoon nutritional yeast mixture into each shell. Arrange half of stuffed shells, seam sides up, in one prepared dish. Pour 3 cups marinara over stuffed shells. Sprinkle with ½ cup nutritional yeast. Cover with foil. Bake at 375° F for 30 minutes or until thoroughly heated.*

SIDES AND SALADS

469. Squash & Pomegranate Salad

Preparation time: 10 minutes
Cooking time: 0 minutes
Total time: 10 minutes
Servings: 04
Ingredients:

Vegetables:
- 5 cups butternut squash, boiled, peeled, and cubed
- 1 tablespoon coconut oil, melted
- 1 tablespoon coconut sugar
- 1 pinch cayenne pepper
- 1 healthy pinch salt
- ½ teaspoon ground cinnamon
- 2 tablespoons maple syrup

Nuts:
- 1 cup raw pecans
- 2 teaspoons coconut oil
- 1 tablespoon maple syrup
- 1 tablespoon coconut sugar
- 1 pinch cayenne pepper
- 1 pinch salt
- ½ teaspoon ground cinnamon

Pomegranate Dressing:
- ¼ cup pomegranate molasses
- 2 cups mixed greens
- Juice from ½ a medium lemon
- 2 teaspoons olive oil
- 1 pinch salt
- Black pepper, to taste
- ½ cup pomegranate arils
- ¼ cup red onion, sliced

How to Prepare:
1. In a salad bowl, add butternut cubes and all the salad ingredients.
2. In a separate bowl, toss all the nuts together.
3. Prepare the dressing by mixing all the dressing ingredients in a different bowl.
4. Add nuts and dressing to the squash and mix well.
5. Serve.

Nutritional Values:
Calories 210.6
Total Fat 10.91 g
Saturated Fat 7.4 g
Sodium 875 mg
Potassium 604 mg
Carbohydrates 25.6 g
Fiber 4.3 g
Sugar 7.9 g
Protein 2.1 g

470. French Style Potato Salad

Preparation time: 10 minutes
Cooking time: 0 minutes
Total time: 10 minutes
Servings: 04
Ingredients:

Potatoes:
- 2 pounds baby yellow potatoes, boiled, peeled, and diced
- 1 pinch salt and black pepper
- 1 tablespoon apple cider vinegar
- 1 cup green onion, diced
- ¼ cup fresh parsley, chopped

Dressing:
- 2½ tablespoons brown mustard
- 3 cloves garlic, minced
- ¼ teaspoon salt and black pepper
- 3 tablespoons red wine vinegar
- 1 tablespoon apple cider vinegar
- 3 tablespoons olive oil
- ¼ cup dill, chopped

How to Prepare:
1. Combine all the dressing ingredients in a salad bowl.
2. In a salad bowl, toss in all the vegetables, seasonings, and dressing.
3. Mix them well then refrigerate to chill.

4. Serve.

Nutritional Values:
Calories 197
Total Fat 4 g
Saturated Fat 0.5 g
Cholesterol 135 mg
Sodium 790 mg
Total Carbs 31 g
Fiber 12.2 g
Sugar 2.5 g
Protein 11 g

471. Mango Salad With Peanut Dressing

Preparation time: 10 minutes
Cooking time: 0 minutes
Total time: 10 minutes
Servings: 04
Ingredients:

Salad:
- 1 head butter lettuce, washed and chopped
- 1½ cups carrot, shredded
- 1¼ cups red cabbage, shredded
- 1 large ripe mango, cubed
- ½ cup fresh cilantro, chopped

Dressing:
- ⅓ cup creamy peanut butter
- 2½ tablespoons lime juice
- 1½ tablespoons maple syrup
- 2 teaspoon chili garlic sauce
- 3 tablespoons coconut aminos

How to Prepare:
1. Combine all the dressing ingredients in a small bowl.
2. In a salad bowl, toss in all the vegetables, seasonings, and dressing.
3. Mix them well then refrigerate to chill.
4. Serve.

Nutritional Values:
Calories 305
Total Fat 11.8 g
Saturated Fat 2.2 g
Cholesterol 56 mg
Sodium 321 mg
Total Carbs 34.6 g
Fibers 0.4 g
Sugar 2 g
Protein 7 g

472. Loaded Kale Salad

Preparation time: 10 minutes
Cooking time: 0 minutes
Total time: 10 minutes
Servings: 04
Ingredients:

Quinoa:
- ¾ cups quinoa, cooked and drained

Vegetables:
- 4 large carrots, halved and chopped
- 1 whole beet, sliced
- 2 tablespoons water
- 1 pinch salt
- ½ teaspoon curry powder
- 8 cups kale, chopped
- ½ cups cherry tomatoes, chopped
- 1 ripe avocado, cubed
- ¼ cup hemp seeds
- ½ cup sprouts

Dressing:
- ⅓ cup tahini
- 3 tablespoons lemon juice
- 1-2 tablespoons maple syrup
- 1 pinch salt
- ¼ cup water

How to Prepare:
1. Combine all the dressing ingredients in a small bowl.
2. In a salad bowl, toss in all the vegetables, quinoa, and dressing.
3. Mix them well then refrigerate to chill.
4. Serve.

Nutritional Values:
Calories 72
Total Fat 15.4 g
Saturated Fat 4.2 g
Cholesterol 168 mg
Sodium 203 mg

Total Carbs 28.5 g
Sugar 1.1 g
Fiber 4 g
Protein 7.9 g

473. Cauliflower & Lentil Salad

Preparation time: 10 minutes
Cooking time: 25 minutes
Total time: 35 minutes
Servings: 04
Ingredients:

Cauliflower:
- 1 head cauliflower, florets
- 1½ tablespoons melted coconut oil
- 1½ tablespoons curry powder
- ¼ teaspoon salt

Salad:
- 5 cups mixed greens
- 1 cup cooked lentils
- 1 cup red or green grapes, halved
- Fresh cilantro

Tahini Dressing:
- 4½ tablespoons green curry paste
- 2 tablespoons tahini
- 2 tablespoons lemon juice
- 1 tablespoon maple syrup
- 1 pinch salt
- 1 pinch black pepper
- Water to thin

How to Prepare:
1. Preheat your oven to 400 degrees F.
2. On a greased baking sheet, toss cauliflower with salt, curry powder, and oil.
3. Bake the cauliflower for 25 minutes in the oven.
4. Combine all the dressing ingredients in a small bowl.
5. In a salad bowl, toss in all the vegetables, roasted cauliflower, and dressing.
6. Mix them well then refrigerate to chill.
7. Serve.

Nutritional Values:

Calories 212
Total Fat 7 g
Saturated Fat 1.3 g
Cholesterol 25 mg
Sodium 101 mg
Total Carbs 32.5 g
Sugar 5.7 g
Fiber 6 g
Protein 4 g

474. Sweet Potato & Avocado Salad

Preparation time: 10 minutes
Cooking time: 20 minutes
Total time: 30 minutes
Servings: 50
Ingredients:

Sweet potato:
- 1 large organic sweet potato, cubed
- 1 tablespoon avocado or coconut oil
- 1 pinch salt

Dressing:
- ¼ cup tahini
- 2 tablespoons lemon juice
- 1 tablespoon maple syrup
- 1 pinch salt
- Water

Salad:
- 5 cups greens of choice
- 1 medium ripe avocado, chopped
- 2 tablespoons hemp seeds

How to Prepare:
1. Preheat your oven to 375 degrees.
2. On a greased baking sheet, toss sweet potato with salt and oil.
3. Bake the potatoes for 20 minutes in the oven, toss halfway through.
4. Combine all the dressing ingredients in a small bowl.
5. In a salad bowl, toss in all the vegetables, roasted potato, and dressing.
6. Mix them well then refrigerate to chill.
7. Serve.

Nutritional Values:
Calories 119
Total Fat 14 g
Saturated Fat 2 g
Cholesterol 65 mg
Sodium 269 mg
Total Carbs 19 g
Fiber 4 g
Sugar 6 g
Protein 5g

475. Broccoli Sweet Potato Chickpea Salad

Preparation time: 10 minutes
Cooking time: 22 minutes
Total time: 32 minutes
Servings: 06
Ingredients:
Vegetables:
- *1 large sweet potato, peeled and diced*
- *1 head broccoli*
- *2 tablespoons olive or grapeseed oil*
- *1 pinch each salt and black pepper*
- *1 teaspoon dried dill*
- *1 medium red bell pepper*

Chickpeas:
- *1 (15 ouncecan chickpeas, drained*
- *1 tablespoon olive or grapeseed oil*
- *1 tablespoon tandoori masala spice*
- *1 pinch salt*
- *1 teaspoon coconut sugar*
- *1 pinch cayenne pepper*

Garlic dill sauce:
- *⅓ cup hummus*
- *3 large cloves garlic, minced*
- *1 teaspoon dried dill*
- *2 tablespoons lemon juice*
- *Water*

How to Prepare:
1. *Preheat your oven to 400 degrees F.*
2. *In a greased baking sheet, toss sweet potato with salt and oil.*
3. *Bake the sweet potatoes for 15 minutes in the oven.*
4. *Toss all chickpea ingredients and spread in a tray.*
5. *Bake them for 7 minutes in the oven.*
6. *Combine all the sauce ingredients in a small bowl.*
7. *In a salad bowl, toss in all the vegetables, roasted potato, chickpeas, and sauce.*
8. *Mix them well then refrigerate to chill.*
9. *Serve.*

Nutritional Values:
Calories 231
Total Fat 20.1 g
Saturated Fat 2.4 g
Cholesterol 110 mg
Sodium 941 mg
Total Carbs 20.1 g
Fiber 0.9 g
Sugar 1.4 g
Protein 4.6 g

476. Penne Pasta Salad

Preparation time: 30 minutes
Cooking time: 0 minutes
Total time: 30 minutes
Servings: 04
Ingredients:
Salad:
- *2 cups roasted tomatoes*
- *12 ounces penne pasta*

Pesto:
- *2 cups fresh basil*
- *4 cloves garlic, minced*
- *¼ cup toasted pine nuts*
- *1 medium lemon, juice*
- *¼ cup vegan cheese, shredded*
- *1 pinch salt*
- *¼ cup olive oil*

How to Prepare:
1. *In a blender, add all the pesto ingredients.*
2. *Blend them well until it is lump free.*
3. *In a salad bowl toss in pasta, roasted tomatoes, and pesto.*

4. Mix them well then refrigerate to chill.
5. Serve.

Nutritional Values:
Calories 361
Total Fat 16.3 g
Saturated Fat 4.9 g
Cholesterol 114 mg
Sodium 515 mg
Total Carbs 29.3 g
Fiber 0.1 g
Sugar 18.2 g
Protein 3.3 g

477. Roasted Fennel Salad

Preparation time: 10 minutes
Cooking time: 20 minutes
Total time: 30 minutes
Servings: 4
Ingredients:
Fennel:
- *1 bulb fennel fronds, sliced*
- *1 tablespoon curry powder*
- *1 tablespoon avocado oil*
- *1 pinch salt*

Salad:
- *5 cups salad greens*
- *1 red bell pepper, sliced*

Dressing:
- *¼ cup tahini*
- *1½ tablespoons lemon juice*
- *1½ teaspoons apple cider vinegar*
- *1 tablespoon freshly minced rosemary*
- *3 cloves garlic, minced*
- *1½ tablespoons coconut aminos*
- *5 tablespoons water to thin*
- *1 pinch salt*

How to Prepare:
1. Preheat your oven at 375 degrees F.
2. On a greased baking sheet, toss fennel with salt, curry powder, and oil.
3. Bake the curried fennel for 20 minutes in the oven.
4. Combine all the dressing ingredients in a small bowl.
5. In a salad bowl, toss in all the vegetables, roasted fennel, and dressing.
6. Mix them well then refrigerate to chill.
7. Serve.

Nutritional Values:
Calories 205
Total Fat 22.7 g
Saturated Fat 6.1 g
Cholesterol 4 mg
Sodium 227 mg
Total Carbs 26.1 g
Fiber 1.4 g
Sugar 0.9 g
Protein 5.2 g

478. Kale Salad With Tahini Dressing

Preparation time: 10 minutes
Cooking time: 20 minutes
Total time: 30 minutes
Servings: 04
Ingredients:

Roasted vegetables:
- *1 medium zucchini, chopped*
- *1 medium sweet potato, chopped*
- *1 cup red cabbage, chopped*
- *1 tablespoon melted coconut oil*
- *1 pinch salt*
- *½ teaspoon curry powder*

Dressing:
- *⅓ cup tahini*
- *½ teaspoon garlic powder*
- *1 tablespoon coconut aminos*
- *1 pinch salt*
- *1 large clove garlic, minced*
- *¼ cup water*

Salad:
- *6 cups mixed greens*
- *4 small radishes, sliced*
- *3 tablespoons hemp seeds*
- *2 tablespoons lemon juice*

- ½ ripe avocado, to garnish
- 2 tablespoons vegan feta cheese, crumbled
- Pomegranate seeds, to garnish
- Pecans, to garnish

How to Prepare:
1. Preheat your oven at 375 degrees F.
2. On a greased baking sheet, toss zucchini, sweet potato, and red cabbage with salt, curry powder, and oil.
3. Bake the zucchini cabbage mixture for 20 minutes in the oven.
4. Combine all the dressing ingredients in a small bowl.
5. In a salad bowl, toss in all the vegetables, roasted vegetables, and dressing.
6. Mix them well then refrigerate to chill.
7. Garnish with feta cheese, pecans, pomegranate seeds and avocado.
8. Serve.

Nutritional Values:
Calories 201
Total Fat 8.9 g
Saturated Fat 4.5 g
Cholesterol 57 mg
Sodium 340 mg
Total Carbs 24.7 g
Fiber 1.2 g
Sugar 1.3 g
Protein 15.3 g

479. Roasted Squash Salad

Preparation time: 10 minutes
Cooking time: 20 minutes
Total time: 30 minutes
Servings: 04
Ingredients:

Squash:
- 1 medium acorn squash, peeled and cubed
- 1 tablespoon avocado oil
- 1 pinch each salt and black pepper

Dressing:
- 1 cup balsamic vinegar

Salad:
- ¼ cup macadamia nut cheese
- 2 tablespoons roasted pumpkin seeds
- 5 cups arugula
- 2 tablespoons dried currants

How to Prepare:
1. Preheat your oven to 425 degrees F.
2. On a greased baking sheet, toss squash with salt, black pepper, and oil.
3. Bake the seasoned squash for 20 minutes in the oven.
4. Combine all the dressing ingredients in a small bowl.
5. In a salad bowl, toss in the squash, salad ingredients, and dressing.
6. Mix them well then refrigerate to chill.
7. Serve.

Nutritional Values:
Calories 119
Total Fat 14 g
Saturated Fat 2 g
Cholesterol 65 mg
Sodium 269 mg
Total Carbs 19 g
Fiber 4 g
Sugar 6 g
Protein 5g

480. Vegetable Salad With Chimichurri

Preparation time: 10 minutes
Cooking time: 25 minutes
Total time: 35 minutes
Servings: 04
Ingredients:

Roasted vegetables:
- 1 large sweet potato (chopped
- 6 red potatoes, quartered
- 2 whole carrots, chopped
- 2 tablespoons melted coconut oil
- 2 teaspoons curry powder
- ½ teaspoon salt

- 1 cup chopped broccolini
- 2 cups red cabbage, chopped
- 1 medium red bell pepper, sliced

Chimichurri:
- 5 cloves garlic, chopped
- 1 medium serrano pepper
- 1 cup packed cilantro
- 1 cup parsley
- 3 tablespoons ripe avocado
- ¼ teaspoon salt
- 3 tablespoons lime juice
- 1 tablespoon maple syrup
- Water to thin

Salad:
- 4 cups hearty greens
- 1 medium ripe avocado, chopped
- 3 tablespoons hemp seeds
- Fresh herbs
- 5 medium radishes, sliced
- ¼ cup macadamia nut cheese

How to Prepare:
1. Preheat your oven to 400 degrees F.
2. In a suitable bowl, toss all the vegetables for roasting with salt, curry powder and oil.
3. Divide these vegetables into two roasting pans.
4. Bake the vegetables for 25 minutes in the oven.
5. Meanwhile, in a blender, blend all chimichurri sauce ingredients until smooth.
6. In a salad bowl, toss in all the roasted vegetables, chimichurri sauce and salad ingredients.
7. Mix them well then refrigerate to chill.
8. Serve.

Nutritional Values:
Calories 231
Total Fat 20.1 g
Saturated Fat 2.4 g
Cholesterol 110 mg
Sodium 941 mg
Total Carbs 20.1 g
Fiber 0.9 g
Sugar 1.4 g
Protein 4.6 g

481. Thai Salad With Tempeh

Preparation time: 10 minutes
Cooking time: 0 minutes
Total time: 10 minutes
Servings: 04
Ingredients:

Salad:
- 6 ounces vermicelli noodles, boiled
- 2 medium whole carrots, ribboned
- 2 stalks green onions, chopped
- ¼ cup cilantro, chopped
- 2 tablespoons mint, chopped
- 1 cup packed spinach, chopped
- 1 cup red cabbage, sliced
- 1 medium red bell pepper, sliced

Dressing:
- ⅓ cup creamy peanut butter
- 3 tablespoons tamari
- 3 tablespoons maple syrup
- 1 teaspoon chili garlic sauce
- 1 medium lime, juiced
- ¼ cup water

How to Prepare:
1. Combine all the dressing ingredients in a small bowl.
2. In a salad bowl, toss in the noodles, salad, and dressing.
3. Mix them well then refrigerate to chill.
4. Serve.

Nutritional Values:
Calories 361
Total Fat 16.3 g
Saturated Fat 4.9 g
Cholesterol 114 mg
Sodium 515 mg
Total Carbs 29.3 g
Fiber 0.1 g
Sugar 18.2 g
Protein 3.3 g

482. Niçoise Salad

Preparation time: 10 minutes
Cooking time: 15 minutes
Total time: 25 minutes
Servings: 04
Ingredients:
Salad:

- 6 small red potatoes, peeled, boiled, and diced
- 1 cup green beans, chopped
- 1 head lettuce, chopped
- ½ cup pitted kalamata olives
- ½ cup tomato, sliced
- ½ medium red beet

Chickpeas:

- 1 (15 ounce can chickpeas
- 1 teaspoon Dijon mustard
- 1 teaspoon maple syrup
- 1 teaspoon dried dill
- 1 pinch salt
- 1 tablespoon roasted sunflower seeds

Dressing:

- 3 tablespoons minced shallot
- 1 heaping teaspoon Dijon mustard
- 1 teaspoon fresh thyme, chopped
- ⅓ cup red wine vinegar
- ¼ teaspoon salt and black pepper
- ¼ cup olive oil

How to Prepare:
1. Preheat your oven to 400 degrees F.
2. In a greased baking sheet, toss chickpeas with salt and all the chickpea ingredients.
3. Bake the chickpeas for 15 minutes in the oven.
4. Combine all the dressing ingredients in a small bowl.
5. In a salad bowl, toss in all the vegetables, roasted chickpeas, and dressing.
6. Mix them well then refrigerate to chill.
7. Serve.

Nutritional Values:
Calories 205
Total Fat 22.7 g
Saturated Fat 6.1 g
Cholesterol 4 mg
Sodium 227 mg
Total Carbs 26.1 g
Fiber 1.4 g
Sugar 0.9 g
Protein 5.2 g

483. Avocado Kale Salad

Preparation time: 10 minutes
Cooking time: 0 minutes
Total time: 10 minutes
Servings: 04
Ingredients:
Dressing:

- ⅓ cup tahini
- 2 teaspoons garlic, chopped
- 1 medium lemon juiced
- 1½ tablespoons maple syrup
- Water

Salad:

- 1 large bundle kale, chopped
- 1 tablespoon grapeseed oil
- 1 tablespoon lemon juice
- 1 medium beet

How to Prepare:
1. Combine all the dressing ingredients in a small bowl.
2. In a salad bowl, toss in all the salad ingredients and dressing.
3. Mix them well then refrigerate to chill.
4. Serve.

Nutritional Values:
Calories 201
Total Fat 8.9 g
Saturated Fat 4.5 g
Cholesterol 57 mg
Sodium 340 mg
Total Carbs 24.7 g
Fiber 1.2 g
Sugar 1.3 g
Protein 15.3 g

484. Sesame Seed Simple Mix

Preparation Time: 5 minutes
Servings: 2

Ingredients
- Frozen peas: 1 cup can washed and drained
- Corn kernel: 2 cups can
- Salt: as per your taste
- Sesame seeds: 2 tbsp
- Pepper: as per your taste
- Cashew cream: ½ cup

Directions:
1. Combine all the ingredients
2. Serve as the side dish

Nutrition:
Carbs: 44.5g
Protein: 11.5g
Fats: 11.4g
Calories: 306Kcal

485. Cherry Tomato Salad With Soy Chorizo

Preparation Time: 5 minutes
Cooking Time: 5 minutes
Serving Size: 4

Ingredients:
- 2 ½ tbsp olive oil
- 4 soy chorizo, chopped
- 2 tsp red wine vinegar
- 1 small red onion, finely chopped
- 2 ½ cups cherry tomatoes, halved
- 2 tbsp chopped cilantro
- Salt and freshly ground black pepper to taste
- 3 tbsp sliced black olives to garnish

Directions:
1. Over medium fire, heat half tablespoon of olive oil in a skillet and fry soy chorizo until golden. Turn heat off.
2. In a salad bowl, whisk remaining olive oil and vinegar. Add onion, cilantro, tomatoes, and soy chorizo. Mix with dressing and season with salt and black pepper.
3. Garnish with olives and serve.

Nutrition:
Calories 138, Total Fat 8.95g, Total Carbs 5.63g, Fiber 0.4g, Net Carbs 5.23g, Protein 7.12g

486. Roasted Bell Pepper Salad With Olives

Preparation Time: 10 minutes
Cooking Time: 20 minutes
Serving Size: 4

Ingredients:
- 8 large red bell peppers, deseeded and cut in wedges
- ½ tsp erythritol
- 2 ½ tbsp olive oil
- 1/3 cup arugula
- 1 tbsp mint leaves
- 1/3 cup pitted Kalamata olives
- 3 tbsp chopped almonds
- ½ tbsp balsamic vinegar
- Crumbled feta cheese for topping
- Toasted pine nuts for topping

Directions:
1. Preheat oven to 400o F.
2. Pour bell peppers on a roasting pan; season with erythritol and drizzle with half of olive oil. Roast in oven until slightly charred, 20 minutes. Remove from oven and set aside.
3. Arrange arugula in a salad bowl, scatter bell peppers on top, mint leaves, olives, almonds, and drizzle with balsamic vinegar and remaining olive oil. Season with salt and black pepper.
4. Toss; top with feta cheese and pine nuts and serve.

Nutrition:
Calories 163, Total Fat 13.3g, Total Carbs 6.53g, Fiber 2.2g, Net Carbs 4.33g, Protein 3.37g

487. Tofu-Dulse-Walnut Salad

Preparation Time: 10 minutes
Cooking Time: 15 minutes
Serving Size: 4

Ingredients:

- 1 (7 oz block extra firm tofu
- 2 tbsp olive oil
- 2 tbsp butter
- 1 cup asparagus, trimmed and halved
- 1 cup green beans, trimmed
- 2 tbsp chopped dulse
- Salt and freshly ground black pepper to taste
- ½ lemon, juiced
- 4 tbsp chopped walnuts

Directions:

1. Place tofu in between two paper towels and allow soaking for 5 minutes. After, remove towels and chop into small cubes.
2. Heat olive oil in a skillet and fry tofu until golden, 10 minutes. Remove onto a paper towel-lined plate and set aside.
3. Melt butter in skillet and sauté asparagus and green beans until softened, 5 minutes. Add dulse, season with salt and black pepper, and Cooking Time: until softened. Mix in tofu and stir-fry for 5 minutes.
4. Plate, drizzle with lemon juice, and scatter walnuts on top.
5. Serve warm.

Nutrition:
Calories 237, Total Fat 19.57g, Total Carbs 5.9g, Fiber 2.1g, Net Carbs 3.89, Protein 12.75g

488. Almond-Goji Berry Cauliflower Salad

Preparation Time: 10 minutes
Cooking Time: 2 minutes
Serving Size: 4

Ingredients:

- 1 small head cauliflower, cut into florets
- 8 sun-dried tomatoes in olive oil, drained
- 12 pitted green olives, roughly chopped
- 1 lemon, zested and juiced
- 3 tbsp chopped green onions
- A handful chopped almonds
- ¼ cup goji berries
- 1 tbsp sesame oil
- ½ cup watercress
- 3 tbsp chopped parsley
- Salt and freshly ground black pepper to taste
- Lemon wedges to garnish

Directions:

1. Pour cauliflower into a large safe-microwave bowl, sprinkle with some water, and steam in microwave for 1 to 2 minutes or until softened.
2. In a large salad bowl, combine cauliflower, tomatoes, olives, lemon zest and juice, green onions, almonds, goji berries, sesame oil, watercress, and parsley. Season with salt and black pepper, and mix well.
3. Serve with lemon wedges.

Nutrition:
Calories 203, Total Fat 15.28g, Total Carbs 9.64g, Fiber 3.2g, Net Carbs 6.44g, Protein 6.67g, Protein 2.54g

489. Warm Mushroom And Orange Pepper Salad

Preparation Time: 10 minutes
Cooking Time: 8 minutes
Serving Size: 4

Ingredients:

- 2 tbsp avocado oil
- 1 cup mixed mushrooms, chopped
- 2 orange bell peppers, deseeded and finely sliced
- 1 garlic clove, minced
- 2 tbsp tamarind sauce
- 1 tsp maple (sugar-free syrup
- ½ tsp hot sauce
- ½ tsp fresh ginger paste
- Sesame seeds to garnish

Directions:

1. Over medium fire, heat half of avocado oil in a large skillet, sauté mushroom and bell peppers until slightly softened, 5 minutes.
2. In a small bowl, whisk garlic, tamarind sauce, maple syrup, hot sauce, and ginger paste. Add mixture to vegetables and stir-fry for 2 to 3 minutes.
3. Turn heat off and dish salad. Drizzle with remaining avocado oil and garnish with sesame seeds.
4. Serve with grilled tofu.

Nutrition:
Calories 289, Total Fat 26.71g, Total Carbs 9g, Fiber 3.8g, Net Carbs 5.2g, Protein 4.23g

490. Broccoli, Kelp, And Feta Salad

Preparation Time: 15 minutes
Serving Size: 4
Ingredients:
- 2 tbsp olive oil
- 1 tbsp white wine vinegar
- 2 tbsp chia seeds
- Salt and freshly ground black pepper to taste
- 2 cups broccoli slaw
- 1 cup chopped kelp, thoroughly washed and steamed
- 1/3 cup chopped pecans
- 1/3 cup pumpkin seeds
- 1/3 cup blueberries
- 2/3 cup ricotta cheese

Directions:
1. In a small bowl, whisk olive oil, white wine vinegar, chia seeds, salt, and black pepper. Set aside.
2. In a large salad bowl, combine the broccoli slaw, kelp, pecans, pumpkin seeds, blueberries, and ricotta cheese.
3. Drizzle dressing on top, toss, and serve.

Nutrition:
Calories 397, Total Fat 3.87g, Total Carbs 8.4g, Fiber 3.5g, Net Carbs 4.9g, Protein 8.93g

491. Roasted Asparagus With Feta Cheese Salad

Preparation Time: 10 minutes
Cooking Time: 20 minutes
Serving Size: 4
Ingredients:
- 1 lb asparagus, trimmed and halved
- 2 tbsp olive oil
- ½ tsp dried basil
- ½ tsp dried oregano
- Salt and freshly ground black pepper to taste
- ½ tsp hemp seeds
- 1 tbsp maple (sugar-freesyrup
- ½ cup arugula
- 4 tbsp crumbled feta cheese
- 2 tbsp hazelnuts
- 1 lemon, cut into wedges

Directions:
1. Preheat oven to 350oF.
2. Pour asparagus on a baking tray, drizzle with olive oil, basil, oregano, salt, black pepper, and hemp seeds. Mix with your hands and roast in oven for 15 minutes.
3. Remove, drizzle with maple syrup, and continue cooking until slightly charred, 5 minutes.
4. Spread arugula in a salad bowl and top with asparagus. Scatter with feta cheese, hazelnuts, and serve with lemon wedges.

Nutrition:
Calories 146, Total Fat 12.87g, Total Carbs 5.07g, Fiber 1.6g, Net Carbs 3.47g, Protein 4.44g

492. Spicy Avocado Bites

Preparation Time: 25 minutes
Servings: 4
Ingredients
- Avocado mashed:1
- Cucumbers:2cut into thick slices
- Lemon: 1 tsp
- Salt and pepper: as per your taste

- Vegan chipotle mayo: 2 tbsp
- Spicy roasted chickpeas: ½ pack
- Fresh herbs: 3 tbsp

Directions:
1. Add lemon and seasoning to the mashed avocado
2. Place on each cucumber slice and press using chickpeas
3. Top with herbs and mayo and serve

Nutrition:
Carbs: 5 g
Protein: 1 g
Fats: 10 g
Calories: 110 Kcal

493. Spicy Broccoli Salad

Preparation Time: 45 minutes
Servings: 2

Ingredients
- Broccoli: 2 cups cut in big florets
- Hot sauce: 2 tbsp
- Rice vinegar: 1 tbsp
- Salt: as per your taste
- Pepper: as per your taste
- Sliced red pepper: 1 cup sliced
- Olive oil: 1 tbsp

Directions:
1. Preheat the oven 200C
2. Add broccoli to the baking sheet and sprinkle seasoning and brush with olive oil
3. Roast for 25 minutes till it turns golden and soft
4. Take a small bowl and combine hot sauce, vinegar, salt, and pepper
5. Remove broccoli from oven and brush with this dressing and Cooking Time: in the oven again for 10 minutes
6. Add to the serving bowl and serve with red pepper
7. Serve as the side dish

Nutrition:
Carbs: 10.5 g
Protein: 2.6 g
Fats: 7.5 g
Calories: 133Kcal

494. Spinach Hummus

Preparation Time: 10 minutes
Servings: 4 as a side dish

Ingredients
- Chickpeas: 2 cups tin drained and rinsed
- Baby spinach: 1 cup
- Tahini: 3 tbsp
- Garlic: 1 clove
- Lemon: 2 tbsp
- Extra-virgin olive oil: 3 tbsp, plus extra to serve
- Salt: as per your need

Directions:
- Blend baby spinach, chickpeas, tahini, olive oil, salt, and garlic together in a blender
- Add in lemon juice and mix
- Add to the serving bowl and top with extra olive oil

Nutrition:
Carbs: 25.8g
Protein: 10.7g
Fats: 18.6g
Calories: 296Kcal

495. Stir Fry Turmeric Butternut Squash

Preparation Time: 30 minutes
Servings: 2

Ingredients
- Olive oil: 2 tbsp
- Butternut squash: 2 cups
- Turmeric: 1 tsp
- Salt: as per your taste
- Red pepper: ½ tsp

Directions:
1. Take a pan and heat olive oil
2. Take a bowl and add butternut squash, salt, turmeric, pepper and mix well and add to the pan
3. Fry on low heat for 20 minutes and turn in between

4. Serve as a salad with the main dish

Nutrition:
Carbs: 22g
Protein: 1.9g
Fats: 14.2g
Calories: 201Kcal

496. Rainbow Vegetable Bowl

Preparation Time: 25 minute
Servings: 4

Ingredients
- Red bell Pepper: 1
- Yellow bell pepper: 1
- Smoked Paprika: ½ tsp
- Potatoes: 3 medium
- Mushrooms: 8 oz
- Yellow Onion: 1
- Zucchini: 1
- Cumin Powder: ½ tsp
- Garlic Powder: ½ tsp
- Salt and Pepper: as per your taste
- Cooking oil: 2 tbsp (optional

Directions:
1. Heat a large pan on medium flame, add oil and put the sliced potatoes
2. Cooking Time: the potatoes till they change color
3. Cut the rest of the vegetables and add all the spices
4. Cooked till veggies are soften

Nutrition:
Carbs: 29.9g
Protein: 5.9g
Fats: 10g
Calories: 227 Kcal

497. Red Bell Pepper Hummus

Preparation Time: 10 minutes
Servings: 4 as a side dish

Ingredients
- Chickpeas: 2 cups can rinsed and drained
- Red bell pepper: 1 cup diced
- Tahini: 3 tbsp
- Garlic: 1 clove
- Lemon: 2 tbsp
- Extra-virgin olive oil: 3 tbsp, plus extra to serve
- Salt: as per your need
- Cayenne pepper: 1 tsp

Directions:
1. Blend red bell pepper, chickpeas, tahini, olive oil, salt, and garlic together in a blender
2. Add in lemon juice and mix
3. Add to the serving bowl and top with extra olive oil and cayenne pepper

Nutrition:
Carbs: 27.1g
Protein: 9.8g
Fats: 18.7g
Calories: 302Kcal

498. Simple Peas Mix

Preparation Time: 5 minutes
Servings: 2

Ingredients
- Frozen peas: 1 cup can washed and drained
- Salt: as per your taste
- Pepper: as per your taste
- Cashew cream: ½ cup

Directions:
1. Combine all the ingredients
2. Serve as the side dish

Nutrition:
Carbs: 10g
Protein: 5g
Fats: 6.5g
Calories: 133Kcal

499. Spinach Green Hummus

Preparation Time: 10 minutes
Servings: 4 as a side dish

Ingredients
- Chickpeas: 2 cups drained and rinsed
- Spinach: 1 cup
- Pistachios: 1 cup finely shredded
- Tahini: 3 tbsp

- Garlic: 1 clove
- Lemon juice: 2 tbsp
- Salt: as per your need
- Sesame seed: ½ tsp
- Water: 3 tbsp

Directions:
1. Blend spinach, chickpeas, tahini, water, salt, and garlic together in a blender
2. Add in lemon juice and mix
3. Add to the serving bowl and top with sesame seeds and pistachios

Nutrition:
Carbs: 34.2g
Protein: 16.9g
Fats: 22.7g
Calories: 295Kcal

500. Stir-Fry Greens

Preparation Time: 30 minutes
Servings: 2

Ingredients
- Long-stemmed broccoli: 1 cup
- Kale: 1 cup
- Olive oil: 1 tbsp
- Peas: 1 cup
- Salt: as per your taste
- Smoked paprika: ½ tsp

Directions:
1. Take a pan and heat olive oil
2. Take a bowl and add broccoli, peas, salt, paprika and mix well and add to the pan
3. Fry on low heat for 20 minutes and turn in between
4. Add kale at the last minutes
5. Serve as a salad with the main dish

Nutrition:
Carbs: 21.5g
Protein: 9.4g
Fats: 9.55g
Calories: 127.2Kcal
Rice Milk

501. Preparation Time: 20 minutes plus overnight soaking

Servings: 400ml

Ingredients
- Rice: 250g
- Maple syrup: 2 tsp
- Water: 500 ml

Directions:
1. Toast rice in the pan lightly and soak overnight in 250ml water
2. Add maple syrup, rice, and 250ml water to the blender and blend till smoothen
3. Strain and discard the puree
4. Shake before serving

Nutrition:
Carbs: 7.5g
Protein: 0.4g
Fats: 0.1g
Calories: 33Kcal

502. Roasted Chili Potatoes

Preparation Time: 35 minutes
Servings: 2

Ingredients
- Olive oil: 1 tbsp
- Potatoes: 2 cups cut like fries
- Salt: as per your taste
- Pepper: as per your taste
- Red chili flakes: 1 tsp

Directions:
1. Preheat the oven 200C
2. Add potatoes to the baking sheet and sprinkle seasoning and brush with olive oil
3. Roast for 25 minutes till it turns golden and soft
4. Remove from the oven and sprinkle red chili flakes
5. Serve as the side dish

Nutrition:
Carbs: 26 g
Protein: 3g
Fats: 7.2g
Calories: 178Kcal

503. Roasted Parsnips With

Zhoug

Preparation Time: 35 minutes
Servings: 4

Ingredients
- Parsnips: 4 thickly sliced
- Salt and pepper: as per your taste
- Olive oil: 1 tbsp

For the Zhoug:
- Flat-leaf parsley: ½ cup chopped
- Coriander: ½ cup chopped
- Vinegar: 1 tbsp
- Green chili: 1 chopped
- Garlic: ½ clove chopped
- Ground cumin: ½ tsp

Directions:
1. Preheat the oven to 200C
2. Take a baking sheet and place parsnips
3. Brush oil and sprinkle salt and pepper
4. Bake for 25-30 minutes till they tender
5. In the meanwhile, add all the zhoug ingredients to the food processor and blend
6. Add 3-4 tablespoons of water if needed
7. Serve roasted parsnips with zhoug

Nutrition:
Carbs: 24g
Protein: 1.6g
Fats: 3.9g
Calories: 141Kcal

504. Roasted Broccoli With Peanuts And Kecap Manis

Preparation Time: 40 minutes
Servings: 4

Ingredients
- Broccoli: a large head diced
- Vegetable oil: 1 tbsp
- Kecap manis: 4 tbsp
- Spring onions: 2 sliced
- Grated garlic: 2 cloves
- Sesame oil: 2 tbsp
- Ginger: 1 tbsp grated
- Dried chili flakes: a pinch
- Salted peanuts: a handful roughly chopped
- Rice vinegar: 3 tbsp
- Coriander: ½ cup chopped
- Ready-made crispy onions: 3 tbsp
- Water: 50ml
- Cooked jasmine rice to serve

Directions:
1. Preheat the oven to 180C
2. Take a large pan and add oil and fry broccoli in batches and spread on baking sheet
3. In the same pan, fry garlic, ginger, and chili flakes for a minute and then add rice vinegar, manis, sesame oil, and water
4. Pour all of this mixture over broccoli and cover with foil
5. Roast the broccoli for 20 minutes in the oven
6. Mix crispy onion and salted peanuts together and sprinkle over cooked broccoli
7. Top with coriander and serve with rice

Nutrition:
Carbs: 22.5 g
Protein: 9.4 g
Fats: 12.8 g
Calories: 258 Kcal

505. Roasted Red Cabbage Pesto

Preparation Time: 10 minutes
Servings: 4 as a side dish

Ingredients
- Red cabbage: 1 head small
- Garlic: 2 cloves
- Lemon juice: 3 tbsp
- Ground almonds: 2 tbsp
- Extra-virgin olive oil: 3 tbsp
- Salt: as per your need

- Chili sauce: 1 tbsp

Directions:
1. Roast cabbage in the oven for 10 minutes at 160C
2. Take a blender and add all the ingredients including roasted cabbage
3. Blend them well
4. Serve with crispy chips

Nutrition:
Carbs: 11.8g
Protein: 10.4g
Fats: 34.2g
Calories: 366Kcal

506. Roasted Garlic Toasts

Preparation Time: 45 minutes
Servings: 4

Ingredients
- Whole bulbs garlic: 4
- Olive oil: 400ml
- Cherry tomatoes: 300g halved
- Sprigs thyme: 6
- Toasted sourdough: 4 slices

Directions:
1. Preheat the oven to medium heat
2. Cut the garlic horizontally and sprinkle thyme and salt, and add to the bowl filled with oil
3. Place in the oven and Cooking Time: for 25 minutes till garlic becomes soft
4. Remove from the oven and spread on the toasted sourdough
5. Top with cherry tomatoes and serve

Nutrition:
Carbs: 38 g
Protein: 8.8 g
Fats: 18.2 g
Calories: 358 Kcal

507. Roasted Olive Oil Tomatoes

Preparation Time: 1 hour 50 minutes
Servings: 5

Ingredients
- Cherry tomatoes on the vine: 4-6 bunches
- Bay leaves: 6
- Olive oil: 200ml
- Garlic: 1 whole bulb cut in ½
- Crusty bread warmed to serve

Directions:
1. Heat the oven to 150C
2. Put the garlic and tomatoes in a baking dish, now add bay leaves and season
3. Pour the olive oil on a baking dish and cover it with foil
4. Let it bake for 1 ½ hour and then serve it with crusty bread

Nutrition:
Carbs: 4.6g
Protein: 1.3g
Fats: 33.6g
Calories: 328Kcal

508. Rocket Chickpeas Salad

Preparation Time: 15 minutes
Servings: 2

Ingredients
- Avocado: 1 cut into small pieces
- Chickpeas: 400g can drained and rinsed
- Red chili: 1 chopped
- Cumin seeds: 1 tsp
- Red onion: 1/2 finely chopped
- Roasted red peppers: 3 chopped
- Olive oil
- Lime: 1 plus wedges to serve
- Rocket: 2 handfuls
- Pitta bread: 2 warmed

Directions:
1. Mix onion, avocado, peppers, chickpeas, and chili in a bowl
2. Take two tablespoons of olive oil and whisk it with lime juice while adding seasoning and cumin seeds
3. Put it in the bowl and mix well
4. Add the chickpeas mixture to the rocket pile into 2 plates

5. Best served with warm pittas

Nutrition:
Carbs: 60.4g
Protein: 18.3g
Fats: 26.4g
Calories: 586Kcal

509. Savory Broccoli Mash

Preparation Time: 30 minutes
Servings: 4 as a side dish

Ingredients
- Broccoli: 2 cups florets
- Spinach: 1 cup
- Tahini: 2 tbsp
- Garlic: 1 clove
- Vinegar: 1 tbsp
- Pepper: as per your need
- Salt: as per your need

Directions:
1. Take a pan and boil salt and water
2. Add broccoli in the salted water and cover and Cooking Time: for 20 minutes and add spinach at the end
3. Drain and mash using a potato masher and add to the bowl
4. Mix tahini, olive oil, vinegar, salt, pepper, and garlic together
5. Add this dressing to the broccoli mixture and combine well

Nutrition:
Carbs: 5.5g
Protein: 4.07g
Fats: 14.5g
Calories: 178Kcal

510. Savory Mango Chat

Preparation Time: 5 minutes
Servings: 4

Ingredients
- Mango: 4 peeled and diced into bite-sized chunks
- Chaat masala: 2 tsp
- Lime: 1 juiced
- Sea salt: ½ tsp
- Coconut yogurt to serve

Directions:

1. Place all the ingredients in a large bowl and shake them well
2. Now serve it with some coconut yogurt if you desire

Nutrition:
Carbs: 50 g
Protein: 2.8 g
Fats: 1.3 g
Calories: 201Kcal

511. Som Tam Salad

Preparation Time: 20 minutes and marinating as well
Servings: 2

Ingredients
- Green beans: 110g cooked and divided
- Courgettes: 2
- Cherry tomatoes: 120g halved
- Carrot: 1 shredded
- Lime: 1 juiced
- Palm sugar: 1 tbsp
- Tamari: 1 tbsp
- Coriander: ¼ cup chopped
- Mint: ¼ cup chopped
- Chili: 1 finely sliced
- Roasted peanuts: 1 tbsp chopped

Directions:
1. With the spiraliser, create thin strands of courgette
2. Add green beans, cherry tomatoes, carrots, lime juice, palm sugar, and chili and give pulse in the blender or crush in pestle and mortar
3. Add the mixture to the courgette and mix for 15 minutes
4. Top with chopped peanuts, mint, and coriander, combine well and serve

Nutrition:
Carbs: 20.6 g
Protein: 8.9 g
Fats: 5.2 g
Calories: 178 Kcal

512. Steamed Brinjal With Peanut Dressing

Preparation Time: 20 minutes
Servings: 4

Ingredients
- Baby brinjals: 360g pack halved
- Rice vinegar: 1 tbsp
- Peanut butter: 1 tbsp
- Soy sauce: 1 tbsp
- Chilli oil: 1 tbsp
- Spring onions: 2 thinly sliced
- Caster sugar: 1 tbsp
- Sesame seeds: 2 tsp toasted
- Coriander: 2 tbsp chopped

Directions:
1. Add brinjals to the steamer and steam for 15 minutes
2. In a bowl, add peanut butter and a splash of boiling water then include soy sauce, sugar, vinegar, and chili oil
3. Take a serving tray and place brinjals and top with the sauce
4. Sprinkle sesame seeds, coriander, and spring onions from above

Nutrition:
Carbs: 4.8 g
Protein: 2.8 g
Fats: 6.2 g
Calories: 89 Kcal

515. Sticky Seeds And Nuts

Time: 30 minutes
Servings: make 6 portions

Ingredients
- Whole almonds: 100g
- Cashew nuts: 100g
- Black or white sesame seeds: 3 tbsp
- Black peppercorns: ¼ tsp
- Peanuts: 100g
- Granulated sugar: 100g
- Brown miso paste: 2 tbsp
- Toasted sesame oil: 2 tsp
- Pumpkin seeds: 25g
- Sunflower seeds: 25g

Directions:
1. Preheat the oven to 180C
2. Take a baking sheet and place the nuts
3. Bake for 15 minutes till they turn golden brown
4. Take a pan and add sugar with 4 tbsp water
5. Let the sugar to melt on the low heat and stir in between
6. Allow it to turn golden and remove from heat and add in sesame oil
7. Add in miso while stirring gently
8. Take a large bowl and add nuts, seeds, and black pepper
9. Pour caramel from the top and stir continuously to coat the seeds and nuts evenly
10. Line a tray with a baking paper and add nuts and seeds and allow to cool
11. Divide and eat right away or store for a week in a sterilized airtight jar

Nutrition:
Carbs: 25.1g
Protein: 16.1g
Fats: 32.7g
Calories: 462Kcal

514. Sweet Potato Salad With Salad And Green Dip

Preparation Time: 45 minutes
Servings: 4

Ingredients
- Gram flour: 120g
- Sweet potato: 1 large
- Olive oil
- Middle eastern wraps to serve
- Ground cumin: 1 tsp
- Coriander: 1 tbsp chopped
- Ginger grated to make: 1 tsp
- Garlic: 1 clove crushed
- Mild chili powder: ½ tsp

For the Coriander Chutney
- Coriander: a bunch chopped
- Shallot: 1 small chopped
- Green chili: 1 chopped
- Ginger: a chunk peeled and chopped

- Lemon: ½ juiced

For the Carrot Salad
- Carrots: 2 peeled and grated
- Lemon:: ½ juiced
- Cumin seeds: 1 tsp toasted
- Coriander leaves: ½ small bunch chopped

Directions:
1. Heat the oven to 200C
2. Prick sweet potatoes with the fork and bake for 10 minutes
3. Allow to cool and add to the bowl and add the remaining falafel ingredients and mix
4. Make the mixture into 12 flattish balls with your hands
5. Now cover the balls with oiled baking sheet and let it bake for 10-15 minutes till they are dry and golden
6. Add the ingredients of coriander chutney into a blender and add water if necessary, blend till its smooth then season and put in a bowl
7. Put the carrot salad ingredients with some seasoning and add 1 teaspoon of oil on top
8. Now serve falafels with coriander chutney, wraps, and carrot salad

Nutrition:
Carbs: 55g
Protein: 10g
Fats: 3.7g
Calories: 313Kcal

515. Sweet Potato Spicy Bites

Preparation Time: 30 minutes
Servings: 4

Ingredients
- Sweet potato: 3 peeled and sliced
- Olive oil: 1 tbsp
- Salt and pepper: as per your taste

For the dressing:
- Lemon: 1 tsp
- Salt and pepper: as per your taste
- Vegan chipotle mayo: 2 tbsp
- Chili: 1 tbsp finely chopped
- Hot sauce: 1 tbsp
- Fresh herbs: 3 tbsp

Directions:
1. Preheat the oven 200C
2. Add sweet potatoes to the baking sheet and olive oil
3. Roast for 25 minutes till it turns golden and soft
4. Add all the dressing together and pour on to the sweet potatoes
5. Serve as the side dish

Nutrition:
Carbs: 166g
Protein: 11g
Fats: 16g
Calories: 211Kcal

516. Tarragon Cauli Salad

Preparation Time: 45 minutes
Servings: 2

Ingredients
- Cauliflower: 1 cup florets
- Salt: as per your need
- Pepper: as per your need
- Olive oil: 1 tbsp

For The Tarragon Dressing:
- Tarragon: ½ bunch
- Baby spinach: ½ cup
- Dijon mustard: 1 tsp
- Lemon juice: 1 tbsp
- Capers: 2 tsp
- Salt: ½ tsp
- Olive oil: 2 tbsp

Directions:
1. Preheat the oven to 200C
2. Take a baking sheet and place cauliflower florets
3. Brush oil and sprinkle salt and pepper
4. Bake for 25-30 minutes till they tender
5. Add all the tarragon dressing ingredients into the bowl with water
6. Add to the blender and blend and

make smooth and thick
7. Add cauliflower to the bowl and top with the dressing
8. Serve as the side dish

Nutrition:
Carbs: 3.45g
Protein: 2.42g
Fats: 14.22g
Calories: 177.75Kcal

517. Tarragon Spinach Cauliflower Salad

Preparation Time: 45 minutes
Servings: 3

Ingredients
- Cauliflower: 2 cups
- olive oil: 2 tbsp
- Garlic powder: 1 tbsp
- Baby spinach: 1 cup
- Tarragon: ½ a bunch
- Salt: as per your taste
- Pepper: as per your taste
- Lemon juice: 1 tbsp

Directions:
1. Preheat the oven 200C
2. Add cauliflowers to the baking sheet and sprinkle seasoning and brush with olive oil
3. Roast for 25 minutes till turn golden and soft
4. Remove from the oven and sprinkle spinach, tarragon, salt, pepper, garlic powder, and lemon juice on top
5. Serve as a side dish

Nutrition:
Carbs: 4.6g
Protein: 3.23g
Fats: 9.6g
Calories: 105Kcal

518. Temaki

Preparation Time: 1 hour
Servings: 3

Ingredients
- Brown sushi rice: 150g
- Avocado: ½ thinly sliced
- Carrot: 1 small shredded
- Cucumber: ¼ cut into small pieces
- Rice vinegar: 1 tbsp
- Nori sheets: 3
- Roasted red pepper: 1 cut into strips

For a Dipping Sauce:
- Red chili: ½ deseeded and chopped
- Light soy sauce: 2 tbsp
- Sesame seeds: 2 tsp toasted
- Rice vinegar: 2 ts

Directions:
1. Wash the rice and drain and add into the pan with salt and water
2. Boil the mixture, cover and Cooking Time: for 30 minutes
3. Add in rice vinegar and stir and leave to cool for 5 minutes
4. Cut nori sheets diagonally to create six triangles
5. Add the rice to the triangles leaving behind the corners
6. Mix carrot, cucumber, pepper, and avocado to the bowl and add to the rice
7. Create cones
8. Add all the ingredients of the sauce in the bowl and serve with the cones

Nutrition:
Carbs: 45.2 g
Protein: 6.7 g
Fats: 7.8 g
Calories: 278 Kcal

519. Tomato Chickpeas Salad

Preparation Time: 20 minutes
Servings: 2

Ingredients
- Chickpeas: 2 cups can
- Cherry tomatoes: 4 halved
- Salt: as per your need
- Lemon juice: 2 tbsp
- Rose harissa 2 tsp
- Olive oil: 2 tbsp
- Flat-leaf parsley: 2 tbsp chopped
- Garlic: 1 clove crushed

Directions:
1. Preheat the oven to 180C
2. Add tomatoes to the baking sheet and sprinkle seasoning and brush with olive oil
3. Roast for 10 minutes
4. Add garlic, lemon juice, harissa, and olive oil in a bowl and whisk
5. Take a serving bowl and combine chickpeas, tomatoes, and the sauce you made
6. Add parsley from the top and serve

Nutrition:
Carbs: 45.3g
Protein: 8.65g
Fats: 18.8g
Calories: 431Kcal

520. Tomato Salsa

Preparation Time: 25 minutes
Servings: 4

Ingredients
- Red onion: 1 small chopped
- Lime juice: 4 tbsp
- Vine tomatoes: 4 large
- Fresh jalapeño chilies: 3
- Sugar: 1 tsp
- Sea salt flakes: 1 tsp
- Coriander: ½ cup chopped
- Plain tortilla chips to serve

Directions:
1. Take a bowl and add onion, lime juice, salt, and sugar and mix together
2. Take a griddle pan and grill tomatoes and chilies
3. Remove the skin of tomatoes and chilies and discard
4. Chop chilies and tomatoes and add to the bowl
5. Combine and leave for 30 minutes
6. Add in flavors and serve with tortilla chips

Nutrition:
Carbs: 5.47g
Protein: 2.4g
Fats: 0.5g
Calories: 55Kcal

521. Tex-Mex Salad

Preparation Time: 15 minutes
Servings: 2

Ingredients
- Avocado: 1 cut into small pieces
- Black beans: 400g can drained and rinsed
- Red chili: 1 chopped
- Cumin seeds: 1 tsp
- Red onion: 1/2 finely chopped
- Roasted red peppers: 3 chopped
- Olive oil
- Lime: 1 plus wedges to serve
- Rocket: 2 handfuls
- Pitta bread: 2 warmed

Directions:
1. Mix onion, avocado, peppers, beans and chili in a bowl
2. Take two tablespoons of olive oil and whisk it with lime juice while adding seasoning and cumin seeds
3. Put it in the bowl and mix well
4. Add the bean mixture to the rocket pile into 2 plates
5. Best served with warm pittas

Nutrition:
Carbs: 61.4g
Protein: 19.4g
Fats: 27.4g
Calories: 596Kcal

522. Treviso Walnut Salad

Preparation Time: 30 minutes
Servings: 4

Ingredients
- Treviso: 1 head leaves separated
- Walnuts: 100g
- Pomegranate seeds: 50g
- Lemon juice: 1 tbsp
- Mint: ¼ cup leaves torn

For the Dressing:
- Mustard: 1 tbsp

- Vinegar: 2 tsp
- Garlic: 1 clove crushed
- Extra-virgin olive oil: 100ml
- Lemon: 1 zest and juice
- Salt: as per your need

Directions:
1. Take a pan and add walnut to roast them dry and crush using hand
2. Prepare the dressing by adding all the ingredients except oil and combine it slowly at the end whisking to gain the correct consistency
3. Coat Treviso in the dressing and place on the serving tray
4. Top with pomegranate seeds and walnuts
5. Sprinkle mint leaves and pour lemon juice and serve

Nutrition:
Carbs: 5.6 g
Protein: 6 g
Fats: 42.6 g
Calories: 437 Kcal

523. Turmeric Butternut Squash With Peas

Preparation Time: 30 minutes
Servings: 2

Ingredients
- Peas: 2 cups
- Olive oil: 2 tbsp
- Butternut squash: 2 cups
- Turmeric: 1 tsp
- Salt: as per your taste
- Red pepper: ½ tsp

Directions:
1. Take a pan and heat olive oil
2. Take a bowl and add butternut squash, peas, salt, turmeric, pepper and mix well and add to the pan
3. Fry on low heat for 20 minutes and turn in between
4. Serve hot

Nutrition:
Carbs: 62g
Protein: 6.9g
Fats: 14.2g
Calories: 268Kcal

524. Vegan Orzo Salad

Preparation Time: 20 minutes
Servings: 2

Ingredients
- Orzo: 120g
- Red onion: ½ finely sliced
- Roasted red peppers: 2 chopped
- Kalamata olives: 12 halved and pitted
- Artichoke hearts: ½ jar drained and cut into wedges
- Vinegar: 2 tbsp
- Tomatoes: 6 chopped
- Caster sugar: a pinch
- Olive oil: 2 tbsp
- Basil: ¼ cup shredded

Directions:
1. Take a bowl and add sugar and vinegar and leave till you prepare pasta
2. Prepare orzo as per the instruction and drain
3. Now include salt, pepper, and olive oil to the onions and add orzo
4. Include remaining vegetables and mix well
5. Top with basil and serve

Nutrition:
Carbs: 22 g
Protein: 8.9 g
Fats: 16.8 g
Calories: 270 Kcal

525. White Bean Tamari Salad

Preparation Time: 20 minutes
Servings: 2

Ingredients
- White beans: 1 cup
- Cherry tomatoes: 1
- Carrot: 1 shredded
- Lime: 1 juiced

- Palm sugar: 1 tbsp
- Tamari: 1 tbsp
- Coriander: ¼ cup chopped
- Mint: ¼ cup chopped
- Chili: 1 finely sliced

Directions:
1. Add beans, cherry tomatoes, carrots, lime juice, palm sugar, and chili together and toss
2. Top with chopped mint, and coriander, combine well and serve

Nutrition:
Carbs: 31.1 g
Protein: 10.15g
Fats: 7.9g
Calories: 243Kcal

526. White Protein Pesto

Preparation Time: 20 minutes
Servings: 4 as a side dish

Ingredients
- Cauliflower: 1 small
- White beans: 1 cup
- Garlic: 2 cloves
- Lemon juice: 3 tbsp
- Extra-virgin olive oil: 1 tbsp
- Salt: as per your need
- Pepper: 1 tbsp

Directions:
1. Boil cauliflower in salted water and add white beans at the end
2. Take a blender and add all the ingredients including beans and cauliflower
3. Blend them well
4. Serve with crispy chips

Nutrition:
Carbs: 13g
Protein: 9.52g
Fats: 3.32g
Calories: 100.25Kcal

527. Black Bean Taco Salad Bowl

Preparation Time: 15 Minutes
Cooking Time: 5 Minutes
Servings: 3

Ingredients

For The Black Bean Salad
- 1 (14-ouncecan black beans, drained and rinsed, or 1½ cups cooked
- 1 cup corn kernels, fresh and blanched, or frozen and thawed
- ¼ cup fresh cilantro, or parsley, chopped
- Zest and juice of 1 lime
- 1 to 2 teaspoons chili powder
- Pinch sea salt
- 1½ cups cherry tomatoes, halved
- 1 red bell pepper, seeded and chopped
- 2 scallions, chopped

For 1 Serving Of Tortilla Chips
- 1 large whole-grain tortilla or wrap
- 1 teaspoon olive oil
- Pinch sea salt
- Pinch freshly ground black pepper
- Pinch dried oregano
- Pinch chili powder

For 1 Bowl
- 1 cup fresh greens (lettuce, spinach, or whatever you like
- ¾ cup cooked quinoa, or brown rice, millet, or other whole grain
- ¼ cup chopped avocado, or Guacamole
- ¼ cup Fresh Mango Salsa

Directions
Preparing the Ingredients.

To Make The Black Bean Salad
Toss all the ingredients together in a large bowl.

To Make The Tortilla Chips
1. Brush the tortilla with olive oil, then sprinkle with salt, pepper, oregano, chili powder, and any other seasonings you like. Slice it into eighths like a pizza.
2. Transfer the tortilla pieces to a small baking sheet lined with parchment

paper and put in the oven or toaster oven to toast or broil for 3 to 5 minutes, until browned. Keep an eye on them, as they can go from just barely done to burned very quickly.

To Make The Bowl

1. Lay the greens in the bowl, top with the cooked quinoa, 1/3 of the black bean salad, the avocado, and salsa.
2. Nutrition: Calories: 589; Total fat: 14g; Carbs: 101g; Fiber: 20g; Protein: 21g

528. Romaine And Grape Tomato Salad With Avocado And Baby Peas

Preparation Time: 15 Minutes
Cooking Time: 0 Minutes
Servings: 4

Ingredients

- *1 garlic clove, chopped*
- *1 tablespoon chopped shallot*
- *1/2 teaspoon dried basil*
- *1/2 teaspoon salt*
- *1/8 teaspoon freshly ground black pepper*
- *1/4 teaspoon brown sugar (optional*
- *3 tablespoons white wine vinegar*
- *1/3 cup olive oil*
- *1 medium head romaine lettuce, cut into 1/4-inch strips*
- *12 ripe grape tomatoes, halved*
- *1/2 cup frozen baby peas, thawed*
- *8 kalamata olives, pitted*
- *1 ripe Hass avocado*

Directions

1. In a blender or food processor, combine the garlic, shallot, basil, salt, pepper, sugar, and vinegar until smooth. Add the oil and blend until emulsified. Set aside.
2. In a large bowl, combine the lettuce, tomatoes, peas, and olives. Pit and peel the avocado and cut into 1/2-inch dice. Add to the bowl, along with enough dressing to lightly coat.

Toss gently to combine and serve.

529. Warm Vegetable "Salad"

Preparation Time: 10 Minutes
Cooking Time: 15 Minutes
Servings: 4

Ingredients

- *Salt for salting water, plus 1/2 teaspoon (optional*
- *4 red potatoes, quartered*
- *1 pound carrots, sliced into 1/4-inch-thick rounds*
- *1 tablespoon extra-virgin olive oil (optional*
- *2 tablespoons lime juice*
- *2 teaspoons dried dill*
- *1/4 teaspoon freshly ground black pepper*
- *1 cup Cashew Cream or Parm-y Kale Pesto*

Directions

1. Preparing the Ingredients.
2. In a large pot, bring salted water to a boil. Add the potatoes and Cooking Time: for 8 minutes. Add the carrots and continue to boil for another 8 minutes, until both the potatoes and carrots are crisp tender. Drain and return to the pot. Add the olive oil (if using), lime juice, dill, remaining 1/2 teaspoon of salt (if using), and pepper, and stir to coat well.
3. Divide the vegetables evenly among 4 single-compartment storage containers or wide-mouth pint glass jars, and spoon 1/4 cup of cream or pesto over the vegetables in each. Let cool before sealing the lids.

Nutrition: Calories: 393; Fat: 15g; Protein: 10g; Carbohydrates: 52g; Fiber: 9g; Sugar: 8g; Sodium: 343mg

530. Puttanesca Seitan And Spinach Salad

Preparation Time: 5 Minutes
Cooking Time: 6 Minutes
Servings: 4

Ingredients

- 4 tablespoons olive oil
- 8 ounces seitan, homemade or store-bought, cut into 1/2-inch strips
- 3 garlic cloves, minced
- 1/2 cup kalamata olives, pitted and halved
- 1/2 cup green olives, pitted and halved
- 2 tablespoons capers
- 3 cups fresh baby spinach, cut into strips
- 1 1/2 cups ripe cherry tomatoes, halved
- 2 tablespoons balsamic vinegar
- 1/4 teaspoon salt (optional)
- 1/4 teaspoon freshly ground black pepper
- 2 tablespoons torn fresh basil leaves
- 2 tablespoons minced fresh parsley

Directions

1. In a large skillet, heat 1 tablespoon of the oil over medium heat. Add the seitan and Cooking Time: until browned on both sides, about 5 minutes. Add the garlic and Cooking Time: until fragrant, about 30 seconds. Transfer to a large bowl and set aside to cool, about 15 minutes.
2. When the seitan has cooled to room temperature, add the kalamata and green olives, capers, spinach, and tomatoes. Set aside.
3. In a small bowl, combine the remaining 3 tablespoons oil with the vinegar, salt, and pepper. Whisk until blended, then pour the dressing over the salad. Add the basil and parsley, toss gently to combine, and serve.

531. Rice Salad With Cashews And Dried Papaya

Preparation Time: 15 Minutes
Cooking Time: 0 Minutes
Servings: 4

Ingredients

- 3 1/2 cups cooked brown rice
- 1/2 cup chopped roasted cashews
- 1/2 cup thinly sliced dried papaya
- 4 green onions, chopped
- 3 tablespoons fresh lime juice
- 2 teaspoons agave nectar
- 1 teaspoon grated fresh ginger
- 1/3 cup grapeseed oil
- Salt and freshly ground black pepper

Directions

1. In a large bowl, combine the rice, cashews, papaya, and green onions. Set aside.
2. In a small bowl, combine the lime juice, agave nectar, and ginger. Whisk in the oil and season with the salt and pepper to taste. Pour the dressing over the rice mixture, mix well, and serve.

532. Spinach Salad With Orange-Dijon Dressing

Preparation Time: 10 Minutes
Cooking Time: 0 Minutes
Servings: 4

Ingredients

- 2 tablespoons Dijon mustard
- 2 tablespoons olive oil
- 1/4 cup fresh orange juice
- 1 teaspoon agave nectar
- 1/2 teaspoon salt
- 1/4 teaspoon freshly ground black pepper
- 2 tablespoons minced fresh parsley
- 1 tablespoon minced green onions
- 5 cups fresh baby spinach, torn into bite-size pieces
- 1 navel orange, peeled and segmented
- 1/2 small red onion, sliced paper thin

Directions

1. In a blender or food processor combine the mustard, oil, orange juice, agave nectar, salt, pepper,

parsley, and green onions. Blend well and set aside.
2. In a large bowl, combine the spinach, orange, and onion. Add the dressing, toss gently to combine, and serve.

533. Caramelized Onion And Beet Salad

Preparation Time: 10 Minutes
Cooking Time: 40 Minutes
Servings: 4

Ingredients
- *3 medium golden beets*
- *2 cups sliced sweet or Vidalia onions*
- *1 teaspoon extra-virgin olive oil or no-beef broth*
- *Pinch baking soda*
- *¼ to ½ teaspoon salt, to taste*
- *2 tablespoons unseasoned rice vinegar, white wine vinegar, or balsamic vinegar*

Directions
1. *Preparing the Ingredients.*
2. *Cut the greens off the beets, and scrub the beets.*
3. *In a large pot, place a steamer basket and fill the pot with 2 inches of water.*
4. *Add the beets, bring to a boil, then reduce the heat to medium, cover, and steam for about 35 minutes, until you can easily pierce the middle of the beets with a knife.*
5. *Meanwhile, in a large, dry skillet over medium heat, sauté the onions for 5 minutes, stirring frequently.*
6. *Add the olive oil and baking soda, and continuing cooking for 5 more minutes, stirring frequently. Stir in the salt to taste before removing from the heat. Transfer to a large bowl and set aside.*
7. *When the beets have cooked through, drain and cool until easy to handle. Rub the beets in a paper towel to easily remove the skins. Cut into wedges, and transfer to the bowl with the onions. Drizzle the vinegar over everything and toss well.*
8. *Divide the beets evenly among 4 wide-mouth jars or storage containers. Let cool before sealing the lids.*

Nutrition: *Calories: 104; Fat: 2g; Protein: 3g; Carbohydrates: 20g; Fiber: 4g; Sugar: 14g; Sodium: 303mg*

534. Treasure Barley Salad

Preparation Time: 10 Minutes
Cooking Time: 30 Minutes
Servings: 4 To 6

Ingredients
- *1 cup pearl barley*
- *1 1/2 cups cooked or 1 (15.5-ouncecan navy beans, drained and rinsed*
- *1 celery rib, finely chopped*
- *1 medium carrot, shredded*
- *3 green onions, minced*
- *1/2 cup chopped pitted kalamata olives*
- *1/2 cup dried cherries or sweetened dried cranberries*
- *1/2 cup toasted pecans pieces, coarsely chopped*
- *1/2 cup minced fresh parsley*
- *1 garlic clove, pressed*
- *3 tablespoons sherry vinegar*
- *Salt and freshly ground black pepper*
- *1/4 cup grapeseed oil*

Directions
1. *In a large saucepan, bring 2 1/2 cups salted water to boil over high heat. Add the barley and return to a boil. Reduce heat to low, cover, and simmer until the barley is tender, about 30 minutes. Transfer to a serving bowl.*
2. *Add the beans, celery, carrot, green onions, olives, cherries, pecans, and parsley. Set aside.*
3. *In a small bowl, combine the garlic, vinegar, and salt and pepper to taste. Whisk in the oil until well blended. Pour the dressing over the salad, toss*

535. Golden Couscous Salad

Preparation Time: 5 Minutes
Cooking Time: 12 Minutes
Servings: 4

Ingredients

- 1/4 cup olive oil
- 1 medium shallot, minced
- 1/2 teaspoon ground coriander
- 1/2 teaspoon turmeric
- 1/4 teaspoon ground cayenne
- 1 cup couscous
- 2 cups vegetable broth, homemade or store-bought, or water
- Salt
- 1 medium yellow bell pepper, chopped
- 1 medium carrot, shredded
- 1/2 cup chopped dried apricots
- 1/4 cup golden raisins
- 1/4 cup chopped unsalted roasted cashews
- 1 1/2 cups cooked or 1 (15.5-ouncecan chickpeas, drained and rinsed
- 2 tablespoons minced fresh cilantro leaves
- 2 tablespoons fresh lemon juice

Directions

1. In a large saucepan, heat 1 tablespoon of the oil over medium heat. Add the shallot, coriander, turmeric, cayenne, and couscous and stir until fragrant, about 2 minutes, being careful not to burn. Stir in the broth and salt to taste. Bring to a boil, then remove from the heat, cover, and let stand for 10 minutes.
2. Transfer the cooked couscous to a large bowl. Add the bell pepper, carrot, apricots, raisins, cashews, chickpeas, and cilantro. Toss gently to combine and set aside.
3. In a small bowl, combine the remaining 3 tablespoons of oil with the lemon juice, stirring to blend. Pour the dressing over the salad, toss gently to combine, and serve.

536. Chopped Salad

Preparation Time: 15 Minutes
Cooking Time: 0 Minutes
Servings: 4

Ingredients

- ¾ cup olive oil
- 1/4 cup white wine vinegar
- 2 teaspoons Dijon mustard
- 1 garlic clove
- 1 tablespoon minced green onions
- 1/2 teaspoon salt (optional
- 1/4 teaspoon ground black pepper
- 1/2 small head romaine lettuce, chopped
- 1/2 small head iceberg lettuce, chopped
- 1 1/2 cups cooked or 1 (15.5-ouncecan chickpeas, drained and rinsed
- 2 ripe tomatoes, cut into 1/2-inch dice
- 1 medium English cucumber, peeled, halved lengthwise, and chopped
- 2 celery ribs, chopped celery
- 1 medium carrot, chopped
- 1/2 cup halved pitted kalamata olives
- 3 small red radishes, chopped
- 2 tablespoons chopped fresh parsley
- 1 ripe Hass avocado, pitted, peeled, and cut into 1/2-inch dice

Directions

1. In a blender or food processor, combine the oil, vinegar, mustard, garlic, green onions, salt, and pepper. Blend well and set aside.
2. In a large bowl, combine the romaine and iceberg lettuces. Add the chickpeas, tomatoes, cucumber, celery, carrot, olives, radishes, parsley, and avocado. Add enough dressing to lightly coat. Toss gently to combine and serve.

537. Warm Lentil Salad With Red Wine Vinaigrette

Preparation Time: 10 Minutes
Cooking Time: 50 Minutes
Servings: 4

Ingredients
- 1 teaspoon olive oil plus ¼ cup, divided, or 1 tablespoon vegetable broth or water
- 1 small onion, diced
- 1 garlic clove, minced
- 1 carrot, diced
- 1 cup lentils
- 1 tablespoon dried basil
- 1 tablespoon dried oregano
- 1 tablespoon red wine or balsamic vinegar (optional
- 2 cups water
- ¼ cup red wine vinegar or balsamic vinegar
- 1 teaspoon sea salt
- 2 cups chopped Swiss chard
- 2 cups torn red leaf lettuce
- 4 tablespoons Cheesy Sprinkle

Directions
1. Preparing the Ingredients.
2. Heat 1 teaspoon of the oil in a large pot on medium heat, then sauté the onion and garlic until they are translucent, about 5 minutes.
3. Add the carrot and sauté until it is slightly cooked, about 3 minutes. Stir in the lentils, basil, and oregano, then add the wine or balsamic vinegar (if using).
4. Pour the water into the pot and turn the heat up to high to bring to a boil.
5. Turn the heat down to a simmer and let the lentils cook, uncovered, 20 to 30 minutes, until they are soft but not falling apart.
6. While the lentils are cooking, whisk together the red wine vinegar, olive oil, and salt in a small bowl and set aside. Once the lentils have cooked, drain any excess liquid and stir in most of the red wine vinegar dressing. Set a little bit of dressing aside. Add the Swiss chard to the pot and stir it into the lentils. Leave the heat on low and cook, stirring, for at least 10 minutes. Toss the lettuce with the remaining dressing. Place some lettuce on a plate, and top with the lentil mixture. Finish the plate off with a little Cheesy Sprinkle and enjoy.

Per Serving Calories: 387; Total fat: 17g; Carbs: 42g; Fiber: 19g; Protein: 18g

538. Carrot And Orange Salad With Cashews And Cilantro

Preparation Time: 15 Minutes
Cooking Time: 0 Minutes
Servings: 4

Ingredients
- 1 pound carrots, shredded
- 2 oranges, peeled, segmented, and chopped
- 1/2 cup unsalted roasted cashews
- 1/4 cup chopped fresh cilantro
- 2 tablespoons fresh orange juice
- 2 tablespoons fresh lime juice
- 2 teaspoons brown sugar(optional
- Salt (optionaland freshly ground black pepper
- 1/3 cup olive oil

Directions
1. In a large bowl, combine the carrots, oranges, cashews, and cilantro and set aside.
2. In a small bowl, combine the orange juice, lime juice, sugar, and salt and pepper to taste. Whisk in the oil until blended. Pour the dressing over the carrot mixture, stirring to lightly coat. Taste, adjusting seasonings if necessary. Toss gently to combine and serve.

539. Not-Tuna Salad

Preparation Time: 5 Minutes
Cooking Time: 0 Minutes • Total: 5 Minutes
Servings: 4

Ingredients

- 1 (15.5-ounce can chickpeas, drained and rinsed
- 1 (14-ounce can hearts of palm, drained and chopped
- ½ cup chopped yellow or white onion
- ½ cup diced celery
- ¼ cup vegan mayonnaise, plus more if needed
- ½ teaspoon salt
- ¼ teaspoon freshly ground black pepper

Directions

1. Preparing the Ingredients.
2. In a medium bowl, use a potato masher or fork to roughly mash the chickpeas until chunky and "shredded." Add the hearts of palm, onion, celery, vegan mayonnaise, salt, and pepper.
3. Combine and add more mayonnaise, if necessary, for a creamy texture. Into each of 4 single-serving containers, place ¾ cup of salad. Seal the lids.

Nutrition: *Calories: 214; Fat: 6g; Protein: 9g; Carbohydrates: 35g; Fiber: 8g; Sugar: 1g; Sodium: 765mg*

540. Dazzling Vegetable Salad

Preparation Time: 15 Minutes
Cooking Time: 0 Minutes
Servings: 4

Ingredients

- 1 medium carrot, shredded
- 1 cup finely shredded red cabbage
- 1 cup ripe grape or cherry tomatoes, halved
- 1 medium yellow bell pepper, cut into matchsticks
- 1½ cups cooked or 1 (15.5-ounce can chickpeas, rinsed and drained
- ¼ cup halved pitted kalamata olives
- 1 ripe Hass avocado, pitted, peeled, and cut into ½-inch dice
- ¼ cup olive oil
- 1½ tablespoons fresh lemon juice
- ½ teaspoon salt
- ⅛ teaspoon freshly ground black pepper
- Pinch sugar (optional

Directions

1. In a large bowl, combine the watercress, carrot, cabbage, tomatoes, bell pepper, chickpeas, olives, and avocado and set aside.
2. In a small bowl, combine the oil, lemon juice, salt, black pepper, and sugar. Blend well and add to the salad. Toss gently to combine and serve.

541. Red Bean And Corn Salad

Preparation Time: 15 Minutes
Cooking Time: 0 Minutes
Servings: 4

Ingredients

- ¼ cup Cashew Cream or other salad dressing
- 1 teaspoon chili powder
- 2 (14.5-ounce cans kidney beans, rinsed and drained
- 2 cups frozen corn, thawed, or 2 cups canned corn, drained
- 1 cup cooked farro, barley, or rice (optional
- 8 cups chopped romaine lettuce

Directions

1. Preparing the Ingredients.
2. Line up 4 wide-mouth glass quart jars.
3. In a small bowl, whisk the cream and chili powder. Pour 1 tablespoon of cream into each jar. In each jar, add ¾ cup kidney beans, ½ cup corn, ¼ cup cooked farro (if using), and 2 cups romaine, punching it down to fit it into the jar. Close the lids tightly.

Nutrition: *Calories: 303; Fat: 9g; Protein: 14g; Carbohydrates: 45g; Fiber: 15g; Sugar: 6g; Sodium: 654mg*

542. Mango And Snow Pea Salad

Preparation Time: 15 Minutes
Cooking Time: 0 Minutes
Servings: 4

Ingredients

- *1/2 teaspoon minced garlic*
- *1/2 teaspoon grated fresh ginger*
- *1/4 cup creamy peanut butter*
- *1 tablespoon plus 1 teaspoon light brown sugar*
- *1/4 teaspoon crushed red pepper*
- *3 tablespoons rice vinegar*
- *3 tablespoons water*
- *1 tablespoon soy sauce*
- *2 cups snow peas, trimmed and lightly blanched*
- *2 ripe mangos, peeled, pitted, cut into 1/2-inch dice*
- *1 large carrot, shredded*
- *1 medium cucumber, peeled, halved lengthwise, and seeded*
- *3 cups shredded romaine lettuce*
- *1/2 cup chopped unsalted roasted peanuts, for garnish*

Directions

1. *In a small bowl, combine the garlic, ginger, peanut butter, sugar, and crushed red pepper. Stir in the vinegar, water, and soy sauce. Taste, adjusting seasonings, if necessary, and set aside.*
2. *Cut the snow peas diagonally into a thin matchsticks and place in a large bowl. Add the mangos and carrot. Cut the cucumber into 1/4-inch slices and add to the bowl.*
3. *Pour the dressing onto the salad and toss gently to combine. Spoon the salad onto a bed of shredded lettuce, sprinkle with peanuts, and serve.*

543. Cucumber-Radish Salad With Tarragon Vinaigrette

Preparation Time: 15 Minutes
Cooking Time: 0 Minutes
Servings: 4

Ingredients

- *2 medium English cucumbers, peeled, halved, seeded, cut into 1/4-inch slices*
- *6 small red radishes, cut into 1/8-inch slices*
- *2 1/2 tablespoons tarragon vinegar*
- *1/2 teaspoon dried tarragon*
- *1/4 teaspoon sugar*
- *Salt and freshly ground black pepper*
- *1/4 cup olive oil*

Directions

1. *In a large bowl, combine the cucumbers and the radishes and set aside.*
2. *In a small bowl, combine the vinegar, tarragon, sugar, and salt and pepper to taste. Whisk in the oil until well blended, then add the dressing to the salad. Toss gently to combine and serve.*

544. Italian-Style Pasta Salad

Preparation Time: 5 Minutes
Cooking Time: 10 Minutes
Servings: 4 To 6

Ingredients

- *8 ounces penne, rotini, or other small pasta*
- *1 1/2 cups cooked or 1 (15.5-ounce can chickpeas, drained and rinsed*
- *1/2 cup pitted kalamata olives*
- *1/2 cup minced oil-packed sun-dried tomatoes*
- *1 (6-ounce jar marinated artichoke hearts, drained*
- *2 jarred roasted red peppers, chopped*
- *1/2 cup frozen peas, thawed*
- *1 tablespoon capers*
- *2 teaspoons dried chives*
- *1/2 cup olive oil*
- *1/4 cup white wine vinegar*
- *1/2 teaspoon dried basil*
- *1 garlic clove, minced*

- Salt and freshly ground black pepper

Directions

1. In a pot of boiling salted water, Cooking Time: the pasta, stirring occasionally, until al dente, about 10 minutes. Drain well and transfer to a large bowl. Add the chickpeas, olives, tomatoes, artichoke hearts, roasted peppers, peas, capers, and chives. Toss gently and set aside.
2. In a small bowl, combine the oil, vinegar, basil, garlic, sugar, and salt and black pepper to taste. Pour the dressing onto the pasta salad and toss to combine. Serve chilled or at room temperature.

545. Tabbouleh Salad

Preparation Time: 15 Minutes
Cooking Time: 10 Minutes
Servings: 4

Ingredients

- 1 cup whole-wheat couscous
- 1 cup boiling water
- Zest and juice of 1 lemon
- 1 garlic clove, pressed
- Pinch sea salt
- 1 tablespoon olive oil, or flaxseed oil (optional
- ½ cucumber, diced small
- 1 tomato, diced small
- 1 cup fresh parsley, chopped
- ¼ cup fresh mint, finely chopped
- 2 scallions, finely chopped
- 4 tablespoons sunflower seeds (optional

Directions

1. Preparing the Ingredients.
2. Put the couscous in a medium bowl, and cover with boiling water until all the grains are submerged. Cover the bowl with a plate or wrap. Set aside.
3. Put the lemon zest and juice in a large salad bowl, then stir in the garlic, salt, and the olive oil (if using).
4. Put the cucumber, tomato, parsley, mint, and scallions in the bowl, and toss them to coat with the dressing. Take the plate off the couscous and fluff with a fork.
5. Add the cooked couscous to the vegetables, and toss to combine.
6. Serve topped with the sunflower seeds (if using).

Per Serving Calories: 304; Total fat: 11g; Carbs: 44g; Fiber: 6g; Protein: 10g

546. Tuscan White Bean Salad

Preparation Time: 10 Minutes • **Marinating Time:** 30 Minutes •
Servings: 2

Ingredients

For The Dressing

- 1 tablespoon olive oil
- 2 tablespoons balsamic vinegar
- 1 teaspoon minced fresh chives, or scallions
- 1 garlic clove, pressed or minced
- 1 tablespoon fresh rosemary, chopped, or 1 teaspoon dried
- 1 tablespoon fresh oregano, chopped, or 1 teaspoon dried
- Pinch sea salt

For The Salad

- 1 (14-ouncecan cannellini beans, drained and rinsed, or 1½ cups cooked
- 6 mushrooms, thinly sliced
- 1 zucchini, diced
- 2 carrots, diced
- 2 tablespoons fresh basil, chopped

Directions

1. Preparing the Ingredients.
2. Make the dressing by whisking all the dressing ingredients together in a large bowl.
3. Toss all the salad ingredients with the dressing. For the best flavor, put the salad in a sealed container, shake it vigorously, and leave to marinate 15 to 30 minutes.

Per Serving Calories: 360; Total fat: 8g; Carbs: 68g; Fiber: 15g; Protein: 18g

547. Indonesian Green Beansalad With Cabbage And Carrots

Preparation Time: 15 Minutes
Cooking Time: 0 Minutes
Servings: 4

Ingredients

- 2 cups green beans, trimmed and cut into 1-inch pieces
- 2 medium carrots, cut into 1/4-inch slices
- 2 cups finely shredded cabbage
- 1/3 cup golden raisins
- 1/4 cup unsalted roasted peanuts
- 1 garlic clove, minced
- 1 medium shallot, chopped
- 1 1/2 teaspoons grated fresh ginger
- 1/3 cup creamy peanut butter
- 2 tablespoons soy sauce
- 2 tablespoons fresh lemon juice
- 1 teaspoon sugar(optional
- 1/4 teaspoon salt(optional
- 1/8 teaspoon ground cayenne
- 3/4 cup unsweetened coconut milk

Directions

1. Lightly steam the green beans, carrots, and cabbage for about 5 minutes, then place them in a large bowl. Add the raisins and peanuts and set aside to cool.
2. In a food processor or blender, puree the garlic, shallot, and ginger. Add the peanut butter, soy sauce, lemon juice, sugar, salt, and cayenne, and process until blended. Add the coconut milk and blend until smooth. Pour the dressing over the salad, toss gently to combine, and serve.

548. Cucumber And Onion Quinoa Salad

Preparation Time: 15 Minutes
Cooking Time: 20 Minutes
Servings: 4

Ingredients

- 1½ cups dry quinoa, rinsed and drained
- 2¼ cups water
- 1/3 cup white wine vinegar
- 2 tablespoons extra-virgin olive oil
- 1 tablespoon chopped fresh dill
- 1½ teaspoons vegan sugar
- 2 pinches salt
- 1/4 teaspoon freshly ground black pepper
- 2 cups sliced sweet onions
- 2 cups diced cucumber
- 4 cups shredded lettuce

Directions

1. Preparing the Ingredients.
2. In a medium pot, combine the quinoa and water. Bring to a boil.
3. Cover, reduce the heat to medium-low, and simmer for 15 to 20 minutes, until the water is absorbed. Remove from the stove and let stand for 5 minutes. Fluff with a fork and set aside.
4. Meanwhile, in a small bowl, mix the vinegar, olive oil, dill, sugar, salt, and pepper. Set aside. Into each of 4 wide-mouth jars, add 2 tablespoons of dressing, ½ cup of onions, ½ cup of cucumber, 1 cup of cooked quinoa, and 1 cup of shredded lettuce. Seal the lids tightly.

Nutrition: *Calories: 369; Fat: 11g; Protein: 10g; Carbohydrates: 58g; Fiber: 6g; Sugar: 12g; Sodium: 88mg*

549. Moroccan Aubergine Salad

Preparation Time: 30 Minutes
Cooking Time: 15 Minutes
Servings: 2

Ingredients

- 1 teaspoon olive oil
- 1 eggplant, diced

- ½ teaspoon ground cumin
- ½ teaspoon ground ginger
- ¼ teaspoon turmeric
- ¼ teaspoon ground nutmeg
- Pinch sea salt
- 1 lemon, half zested and juiced, half cut into wedges
- 2 tablespoons capers
- 1 tablespoon chopped green olives
- 1 garlic clove, pressed
- Handful fresh mint, finely chopped
- 2 cups spinach, chopped

Directions
1. Preparing the Ingredients.
2. Heat the oil in a large skillet on medium heat, then sauté the eggplant. Once it has softened slightly, about 5 minutes, stir in the cumin, ginger, turmeric, nutmeg, and salt. Cooking Time: until the eggplant is very soft, about 10 minutes.
3. Add the lemon zest and juice, capers, olives, garlic, and mint. Sauté for another minute or two, to blend the flavors. Put a handful of spinach on each plate, and spoon the eggplant mixture on top.
4. Serve with a wedge of lemon, to squeeze the fresh juice over the greens.
5. To tenderize the eggplant and reduce some of its naturally occurring bitter taste, you can sweat the eggplant by salting it. After dicing the eggplant, sprinkle it with salt and let it sit in a colander for about 30 minutes. Rinse the eggplant to remove the salt, then continue with the recipe as written.

Per Serving Calories: 97; Total fat: 4g; Carbs: 16g; Fiber: 8g; Protein: 4g

550. Potato Salad With Artichoke Hearts

Preparation Time: 15 Minutes
Cooking Time: 15 Minutes
Servings: 4 To 6

Ingredients
- 1 1/2 pounds Yukon Gold potatoes, peeled and cut into 1-inch dice
- 1 (10-ouncepackage frozen artichoke hearts, cooked
- 2 cups halved ripe grape tomatoes
- 1/2 cup frozen peas, thawed
- 3 green onions, minced
- 1 tablespoon minced fresh parsley
- 1/3 cup olive oil
- 2 tablespoons fresh lemon juice
- 1 garlic clove, minced
- Salt and freshly ground black pepper

Directions
1. In a large pot of boiling salted water, Cooking Time: the potatoes until just tender but still firm, about 15 minutes. Drain well and transfer to a large bowl.
2. Quarter the artichokes and add them to the potatoes. Add the tomatoes, peas, green onions, and parsley and set aside.
3. In a small bowl, combine the oil, lemon juice, garlic, and salt and pepper to taste. Mix well, pour the dressing over potato salad, and toss gently to combine. Set aside at room temperature to allow flavors to blend, about 20 minutes. Taste, adjusting seasonings if necessary, and serve.

551. Giardiniera

Preparation Time: 15 Minutes
Cooking Time: 0 Minutes • Total: 15 minutes
Servings: 6

Ingredients
- 1 medium carrot, cut into 1/4-inch rounds
- 1 medium red bell pepper, cut into 1/2-inch dice
- 1 cup small cauliflower florets
- 2 celery ribs, finely chopped
- 1/2 cup chopped onion

- 2 tablespoons salt (optional
- 1/4 cup sliced pimiento-stuffed green olives
- 1 garlic clove, minced
- 1/2 teaspoon sugar (optional
- 1/2 teaspoon crushed red pepper
- 1/4 teaspoon freshly ground black pepper
- 3 tablespoons white wine vinegar
- 1/3 cup olive oil

Directions

1. In a large bowl, combine the carrot, bell pepper, cauliflower, celery, and onion. Stir in the salt and add enough cold water to cover. Tightly cover the bowl and refrigerate for 4 to 6 hours.
2. Drain and rinse the vegetables and place them in a large bowl. Add the olives and set aside.
3. In a small bowl, combine the garlic, sugar, crushed red pepper, black pepper, vinegar, and oil, and mix well. Pour the dressing over the vegetables and toss gently to combine. Cover and refrigerate overnight before serving.

552. Creamy Avocado-Dressed Kale Salad

Preparation Time: 10 Minutes
Cooking Time: 20 Minutes
Servings: 4

Ingredients

For The Dressing

- 1 avocado, peeled and pitted
- 1 tablespoon fresh lemon juice, or 1 teaspoon lemon juice concentrate and 2 teaspoons water
- 1 tablespoon fresh or dried dill1 small garlic clove, pressed
- 1 scallion, chopped
- Pinch sea salt
- 1/4 cup water

For The Salad

- 8 large kale leaves
- 1/2 cup chopped green beans, raw or lightly steamed
- 1 cup cherry tomatoes, halved
- 1 bell pepper, chopped
- 2 scallions, chopped
- 2 cups cooked millet, or other cooked whole grain, such as quinoa or brown rice
- Hummus (optional

Directions

To Make The Dressing

Put all the ingredients in a blender or food processor. Purée until smooth, then add water as necessary to get the consistency you're looking for in your dressing. Taste for seasoning, and add more salt if you need to.

To Make The Salad

Chop the kale, removing the stems if you want your salad less bitter, and then massage the leaves with your fingers until it wilts and gets a bit moist, about 2 minutes. You can use a pinch salt if you like to help it soften. Toss the kale with the green beans, cherry tomatoes, bell pepper, scallions, millet, and the dressing. Pile the salad onto plates, and top them off with a spoonful of hummus (if using).

Per Serving Calories: 225; Total fat: 7g; Carbs: 37g; Fiber: 7g; Protein: 7g

553. Indonesian-Style Potato Salad

Preparation Time: 10 Minutes
Cooking Time: 30 Minutes
Servings: 4 To 6

Ingredients

- 1 1/2 pounds small white potatoes, unpeeled
- 1 cup frozen peas, thawed
- 1/2 cup shredded carrot
- 4 green onions, chopped
- 1 tablespoon grapeseed oil
- 1 garlic clove, minced
- 1/3 cup creamy peanut butter
- 1/2 teaspoon Asian chili paste

- 2 tablespoons soy sauce
- 1 tablespoon rice vinegar
- ¾ cup unsweetened coconut milk
- 3 tablespoons chopped unsalted roasted peanuts, for garnish

Directions
1. In a large pot of boiling salted water, Cooking Time: the potatoes until tender, 20 to 30 minutes. Drain well and set aside to cool.
2. When cool enough to handle, cut the potatoes into 1-inch chunks and transfer to a large bowl. Add the peas, carrot, and green onions, and set aside.
3. In a small saucepan, heat the oil over medium heat. Add the garlic and Cooking Time: until fragrant, about 30 seconds. Stir in the peanut butter, chili paste, soy sauce, vinegar, and about half of the coconut milk. Simmer over medium heat for 5 minutes, stirring frequently to make a smooth sauce. Add as much of the remaining coconut milk as needed for a creamy consistency. Pour the dressing over the salad and toss well to combine. Garnish with peanuts and serve.

554. Roasted Beet And Avocado Salad

Preparation Time: 10 Minutes
Cooking Time: 30 minutes
Servings: 2

Ingredients
- 2 beets, peeled and thinly sliced
- 1 teaspoon olive oil
- Pinch sea salt
- 1 avocado
- 2 cups mixed greens
- 3 to 4 tablespoons Creamy Balsamic Dressing
- 2 tablespoons chopped almonds, pumpkin seeds, or sunflower seeds (raw or toasted

Directions
1. Preparing the Ingredients.
2. Preheat the oven to 400°F.
3. Put the beets, oil, and salt in a large bowl, and toss the beets with your hands to coat. Lay them in a single layer in a large baking dish, and roast them in the oven 20 to 30 minutes, or until they're softened and slightly browned around the edges.
4. While the beets are roasting, cut the avocado in half and take the pit out. Scoop the flesh out, as intact as possible, and slice it into crescents.
5. Once the beets are cooked, lay slices out on two plates and top each beet slice with a similar-size avocado slice.
6. Top with a handful of mixed greens. Drizzle the dressing over everything, and sprinkle on a few chopped almonds.

Per Serving Calories: 167; Total fat: 13g; Carbs: 15g; Fiber: 5g; Protein: 4g

555. Creamy Coleslaw

Preparation Time: 10 Minutes
Cooking Time: 0 Minutes
Servings: 4

Ingredients
- 1 small head green cabbage, finely shredded
- 1 large carrot, shredded
- ¾ cup vegan mayonnaise, homemade or store-bought
- 1/4 cup soy milk
- 2 tablespoons cider vinegar
- 1/2 teaspoon dry mustard
- 1/4 teaspoon celery seeds
- 1/2 teaspoon salt (optional
- Freshly ground black pepper

Directions
1. In a large bowl, combine the cabbage and carrot and set aside.
2. In a small bowl, combine the mayonnaise, soy milk, vinegar, mustard, celery seeds, salt, and

pepper to taste. Mix until smooth and well blended. Add the dressing to the slaw and mix well to combine. Taste, adjusting seasonings if necessary, and serve.

SOUPS AND STEWS

556. Herby Cheddar Soup

Preparation Time: 12 minutes
Cooking Time: 23 minutes
Serving Size: 4
Ingredients:

- 5 tbsp butter
- 6 slices vegan bacon, chopped
- 1 small yellow onion, roughly chopped
- 3 garlic cloves, minced
- 2 tbsp finely chopped rosemary
- 1 tbsp chopped fresh oregano
- 1 tbsp chopped fresh tarragon
- 2 cups peeled and cubed parsnips
- 3 ½ cups vegetable broth
- Salt and freshly ground black pepper to taste
- 1 cup unsweetened almond milk
- 1 cup grated cheddar cheese
- 2 tbsp chopped scallions for garnishing

Directions:

1. Over medium heat, melt 1 tablespoon of butter in a large saucepan. Fry in vegan bacon until browned and crispy, 5 minutes. Transfer to a paper towel-lined plate and set aside.
2. Melt remaining butter in the same pot and sauté onion, garlic, rosemary, oregano, and tarragon until fragrant, 3 minutes.
3. Stir in parsnips and vegetable broth, season with salt and black pepper, and Cooking Time: (covereduntil parsnips soften, 10 to 12 minutes.
4. Using an immersion blender, process ingredients until smooth. Stir in almond milk and cheddar cheese; simmer with frequent stirring until cheese melts, 3 minutes.
5. Divide soups into serving bowls, top with vegan bacon, and garnish with scallions.
6. Serve warm with low carb bread.

Nutrition:
Calories 775, Total Fat 57.42g, Total Carbs 8.63g, Fiber 2.1g, Net Carbs 6.53g, Protein 18.2g

557. Creamy Onion Soup

Preparation Time: 15 minutes
Cooking Time: 1 hour 5 minutes
Serving Size: 4
Ingredients:

- 1 tbsp olive oil
- 2 tbsp butter
- 3 cups thinly sliced white onions
- 2 garlic cloves, pressed
- ½ cup dry white wine
- 2 tsp almond flour
- 3 tbsp freshly chopped rosemary
- Salt and freshly ground black pepper to taste
- 2 cups hot vegetable broth
- 2 cups unsweetened almond milk
- 1 cup grated Pecorino Romano cheese

Directions:

1. Over medium fire, heat olive oil and butter in a large pot. Sauté onions until softened, 10 minutes, stirring regularly to avoid browning. Reduce heat to low and continue cooking for 15 minutes.
2. Add garlic; Cooking Time: further until onions caramelize while still stirring, 10 minutes.
3. Stir in white wine, almond flour, and increase heat. Season with rosemary, salt, and black pepper, and pour in vegetable broth. Cover pot, allow boiling, and then simmer for 30 minutes.
4. Pour in almond milk and half of Pecorino Romano cheese. Stir until cheese melts; adjust taste with salt and black pepper.
5. Spoon soup into serving bowls, top with remaining cheese, and serve

warm.

Nutrition:
Calories 340, Total Fat 23.43g, Total Carbs 7.24g, Fiber 1.6g, Net Carbs 5.64g, Protein 15.15g

558. Creamy Tofu Mushroom Soup

Preparation Time: 10 minutes
Cooking Time: 14 minutes
Serving Size: 4
Ingredients:

- *1 tbsp olive oil*
- *2/3 cup sliced white button mushrooms*
- *1 large white onion, finely chopped*
- *1 garlic clove, minced*
- *1 tsp ginger puree*
- *1 cup vegetable broth*
- *2 turnips, peeled and chopped*
- *Salt and freshly ground black pepper to taste*
- *2 (14 oz silken tofu, drained and rinsed*
- *2 cups unsweetened almond milk*
- *1 tbsp freshly chopped oregano*
- *1 tbsp freshly chopped parsley to garnish*
- *1 tbsp chopped walnuts for topping*

Directions:

1. *Over medium fire, heat olive oil in a large saucepan and Cooking Time: mushrooms until softened, 5 minutes. Remove onto a plate and set aside.*
2. *Add and sauté onion, garlic, and ginger puree until fragrant and soft.*
3. *Pour in vegetable broth, turnips, salt, and black pepper. Cooking Time: until turnips soften, 6 minutes.*
4. *Add silken tofu and using an immersion blender, puree ingredients until very smooth.*
5. *Stir in mushrooms and simmer until mushrooms heat through, 2 to 3 minutes. Make sure to stir soup frequently to prevent tofu from curdling.*
6. *Add almond milk and adjust taste with salt and black pepper. Stir in oregano and dish soup.*
7. *Garnish with parsley and serve with soy chorizo chips.*

Nutrition:
Calories 923, Total Fat 8.59g, Total Carbs 12.23g, Fiber 4.8g, Net Carbs 7.43g, Protein 23.48g

559. Kale-Ginger Soup With Poached Eggs

Preparation Time: 10 minutes
Cooking Time: 16 minutes
Serving Size: 4
Ingredients:

- *1 tbsp butter*
- *½ tbsp sesame oil + extra for topping*
- *1 small onion, finely sliced*
- *3 garlic cloves, minced*
- *2 tsp ginger paste*
- *2 cups chopped baby kale*
- *2 cups chopped green beans*
- *3 tbsp freshly chopped parsley + extra for garnish*
- *4 cups vegetable stock*
- *Salt and freshly ground black pepper to taste*
- *3 cups water*
- *4 eggs*

Directions:

1. *Over medium heat, melt butter and sesame oil in a large pot. Sauté onion and garlic until softened and fragrant, 3 minutes. Stir in ginger and Cooking Time: for 2 minutes.*
2. *Add kale, allowing wilting, and pour in green beans, parsley, and vegetable stock. Season with salt and black pepper. Cover and allow boiling; reduce heat, and simmer for 7 to 10 minutes.*
3. *Meanwhile, bring water to simmer in a medium pot over medium heat.*

Swirl water with a spoon and poach eggs in water one after another, 4 minutes. Remove onto a paper towel-lined plate to drain water.
4. Turn soup's heat off and pour ingredients into a blender. Puree until very smooth and divide into four bowls.
5. Top each with an egg, sesame oil, and parsley.

Nutrition:
Calories 463, Total Fat 30.05g, Total Carbs 8.5g, Fiber 2.7g, Net Carbs 5.8g, Protein 23.69g

560. Broccoli And Collard Soup

Preparation Time: 15 minutes
Cooking Time: 18 minutes
Serving Size: 4
Ingredients:

- 1 tbsp olive oil
- 2 tbsp butter
- 1 medium brown onion, thinly sliced
- 3 garlic cloves, finely sliced
- 1 large head broccoli, cut into florets
- 4 cups vegetable stock
- 2 cups collards
- ¼ cup freshly chopped parsley
- Salt and freshly ground black pepper to taste
- 1 tbsp fresh dill leaves for garnishing
- 1 cup grated Parmesan cheese for topping

Directions:
1. Over medium fire, heat olive oil and butter in a large saucepan and sauté onion and garlic until softened and fragrant, 3 minutes.
2. Stir in broccoli and Cooking Time: until softened, 5 minutes.
3. Add vegetable stock, salt, and black pepper. Cover pot and allow boiling. Reduce heat and simmer until broccoli is very soft, 10 minutes.
4. Open lid and use an immersion blender to puree soup until completely smooth. Stir in collards, parsley, and adjust taste with salt and black pepper.
5. Dish soup, garnish with dill leaves and Parmesan cheese; serve warm.

Nutrition:
Calories 515, Total Fat 33.89g, Total Carbs 9.1g, Fiber 4.6g, Net Carbs 4.5g, Protein 38.33g

561. Chilled Lemongrass And Avocado Soup

Preparation Time: 5 minutes
Cooking Time: 5 minutes + 1 hour refrigeration
Serving Size: 4
Ingredients:

- 2 stalks lemongrass, chopped
- 2 cups chopped avocado pulp
- 2 cups vegetable broth
- 2 lemons, juiced
- 3 tbsp chopped mint leaves + extra to garnish
- Salt and freshly ground black pepper to taste
- 2 cups heavy cream

Directions:
1. In a large pot, add lemongrass, avocado, and vegetable broth; bring to a slow boil over low heat until lemongrass softens and avocado warms through, 5 minutes.
2. Stir in lemon juice, mint leaves, salt, black pepper, and puree ingredients with an immersion blender.
3. Stir in heavy cream and turn heat off.
4. Dish soup into serving bowls, chill for 1 hour, and garnish with some mint leaves. Serve.

Nutrition:
Calories 339, Total Fat 33.3g, Total Carbs 6.58g, Fiber 3g, Net Carbs 3.58g, Protein 3.59g

562. Turnip-Tomato Soup

Preparation Time: 15 minutes
Cooking Time: 33 minutes

Serving Size: 6
Ingredients*:*
- *1 tbsp butter*
- *1 tbsp olive oil*
- *1 large yellow onion, chopped*
- *4 garlic cloves, minced*
- *6 red bell peppers, deseeded and sliced*
- *2 turnips, peeled and chopped*
- *3 cups chopped tomatoes*
- *4 cups vegetable stock*
- *Salt and freshly ground black pepper to taste*
- *3 cups coconut milk*
- *2 cups toasted chopped almonds*
- *1 cup grated Parmesan cheese*

Directions*:*
1. *Over medium fire, heat butter and olive oil in a medium pot, and sauté onion and garlic until fragrant and soft, 3 minutes.*
2. *Stir in bell pepper and turnips; Cooking Time: until sweaty, 10 minutes.*
3. *Mix in tomatoes, vegetable stock, salt, and black pepper. Cover lid and Cooking Time: over low heat for 20 minutes.*
4. *Turn heat off and using an immersion blender, puree ingredients until smooth. Stir in coconut milk.*
5. *Pour soup into serving bowls and garnish with almonds and Parmesan cheese.*
6. *Serve immediately with low carb cheese bread.*

Nutrition*:*
Calories 955, Total Fat 86.65g, Total Carbs 10.5g, Fiber 6.5g, Net Carbs 4g, Protein 19.11g

563. Spring Vegetable Soup

Preparation Time: 8 minutes
Cooking Time: 12 minutes
Serving Size: 4
Ingredients*:*
- *4 cups vegetable stock*
- *3 cups green beans, chopped*
- *2 cups asparagus, chopped*
- *1 cup pearl onions, peeled and halved*
- *2 cups seaweed mix (or spinach*
- *1 tbsp garlic powder*
- *Salt and freshly ground white pepper to taste*
- *2 cups grated Parmesan cheese, for serving*

Directions*:*
1. *In a large pot, add vegetable stock, green beans, asparagus, and pearl onions. Season with garlic powder, salt and white pepper.*
2. *Cover pot and Cooking Time: over low heat until vegetables soften, 10 minutes.*
3. *Stir in seaweed mix and adjust taste with salt and white pepper.*
4. *Dish into serving bowls and top with plenty of Parmesan cheese.*
5. *Serve with low carb bread.*

Nutrition*:*
Calories 196, Total Fat 11.9g, Total Carbs 10.02g, Fiber 5.7g, Net Carbs 4.32g

564. Zucchini-Dill Bowls With Ricotta Cheese

Preparation Time: 10 minutes
Cooking Time: 25 minutes
Serving Size: 4
Ingredients*:*
- *4 zucchinis, spiralized and chopped roughly*
- *Salt and freshly ground black pepper to taste*
- *¼ tsp Dijon mustard*
- *1 tbsp olive oil*
- *1 tbsp freshly squeezed lemon juice*
- *½ cup baby spinach*
- *1 tbsp freshly chopped tarragon*
- *2/3 cup ricotta cheese*
- *2 tbsp toasted pine nuts*

Directions*:*

1. Place zucchinis in a medium bowl and season with salt and black pepper.
2. In a small bowl, whisk mustard, olive oil, and lemon juice. Pour mixture over zucchini and toss well.
3. Add spinach, tarragon, ricotta cheese, and pine nuts. Mix with two ladles and serve.

Nutrition:
Calories 857, Total Fat 36.33g, Total Carbs 12.46g, Fiber 2.4g, Net Carbs 10.06g, Protein 26.13g

565. Cauliflower Soup

Preparation time: 10 minutes
Cooking time: 4 hours 5 minutes
Total time: 4 hours 15 minutes
Servings: 04
Ingredients:

- 2 tablespoons olive oil
- 1½ cups sweet white onion, chopped
- 2 large cloves of garlic, chopped
- 1 head cauliflower, cut into florets
- 1 cup coconut milk
- 1 cup filtered water
- 1 teaspoon vegetable stock paste
- 2 tablespoons nutritional yeast
- Dash of olive oil
- Fresh cracked pepper
- Parsley, to serve

How to prepare:
1. Add olive oil and onion to a slow cooker.
2. Sauté for 5 minutes then add the rest of the ingredients.
3. Put on the slow cooker's lid and Cooking Time: for 4 hours on low heat.
4. Once done, blend the soup with a hand blender.
5. Garnish with parsley, and cracked pepper
6. Serve.

Nutritional Values:
Calories 119
Total Fat 14 g
Saturated Fat 2 g
Cholesterol 65 mg
Sodium 269 mg
Total Carbs 19 g
Fiber 4 g
Sugar 6 g
Protein 5g

566. Greek Lentil Soup

Preparation time: 10 minutes
Cooking time: 6 hours 2 minutes
Total time: 6 hours 12 minutes
Servings: 04
Ingredients:

Soup:
- 1 cup lentils
- 1 medium sweet onion, chopped
- 2 large carrots, chopped
- 2 sticks of celery, chopped
- 4 cups veggie broth
- Olive oil to sauté
- 4 tablespoons tomato sauce
- 3 cloves garlic
- 3 bay leaves
- Salt, to taste
- Black pepper, to taste
- Dried oregano, to taste

Toppings:
- Vinegar
- Lemon juice
- Hot sauce

How to Prepare:
1. In a slow cooker, add olive oil and onion.
2. Sauté for 2 minutes then add the rest of the soup ingredients.
3. Put on the slow cooker's lid and Cooking Time: for 6 hours on low heat.
4. Serve warm with the vinegar, lemon juice, and hot sauce.

Nutritional Values:
Calories 231
Total Fat 20.1 g

Saturated Fat 2.4 g
Cholesterol 110 mg
Sodium 941 mg
Total Carbs 20.1 g
Fiber 0.9 g
Sugar 1.4 g
Protein 4.6 g

567. Broccoli White Bean Soup

Preparation time: 10 minutes
Cooking time: 4 hrs. 32 minutes
Total time: 4 hrs. 42 minutes
Servings: 04
Ingredients:
- *1 large bunch broccoli*
- *3 cloves garlic*
- *1 medium white potato*
- *¼ cup carrot, chopped*
- *2 cups almond milk*
- *1½ cups white beans, cooked*
- *1 white onion, chopped*
- *¾ teaspoon black pepper*
- *¼ teaspoon salt*
- *½ teaspoon smoky paprika*
- *⅓ cup nutritional yeast*
- *1 bay leaf*
- *1 cup cooked pasta*

How to Prepare:
1. *In a slow cooker, add olive oil and onion.*
2. *Sauté for 2 minutes then toss in the rest of the ingredients except pasta and beans.*
3. *Put on the slow cooker's lid and Cooking Time: for 4 hours on low heat.*
4. *Once done, add pasta and beans to the soup and mix gently.*
5. *Cover the soup and remove it from the heat then leave it for another 30 minutes.*
6. *Serve warm.*

Nutritional Values:
Calories 361
Total Fat 16.3 g
Saturated Fat 4.9 g

Cholesterol 114 mg
Sodium 515 mg
Total Carbs 29.3 g
Fiber 0.1 g
Sugar 18.2 g
Protein 3.3 g

568. African Lentil Soup

Preparation time: 10 minutes
Cooking time: 20 minutes
Total time: 30 minutes
Servings: 4
Ingredients:
- *1 teaspoon oil*
- *½ medium onion, chopped*
- *2 juicy tomatoes, chopped*
- *4 garlic cloves, chopped*
- *1-inch piece of ginger, chopped*
- *1 tablespoon Sambal Oelek*
- *1 tablespoon tomato paste*
- *1½ teaspoons ground cumin*
- *2 teaspoons ground coriander*
- *1 teaspoon Harissa Spice Blend*
- *¼ teaspoon black pepper*
- *¼ cup nut butter*
- *2 tablespoons peanuts*
- *½ cup red lentils*
- *2½ cups vegetable stock*
- *¾ teaspoon salt*
- *1 teaspoon lemon juice*
- *½ cup packed baby spinach*

How to Prepare:
1. *In a slow cooker, add olive oil and onion.*
2. *Sauté for 5 minutes then toss in rest of the ingredients except peanuts.*
3. *Put on the slow cooker's lid and Cooking Time: for 5 hours on low heat.*
4. *Once done, garnish with peanuts.*
5. *Serve.*

Nutritional Values:
Calories 205
Total Fat 22.7 g
Saturated Fat 6.1 g

Cholesterol 4 mg
Sodium 227 mg
Total Carbs 26.1 g
Fiber 1.4 g
Sugar 0.9 g
Protein 5.2 g

569. Artichoke Bean Soup

Preparation time: 10 minutes
Cooking time: 20 minutes
Total time: 30 minutes
Servings: 04
Ingredients:

- 1 (15 ouncecan artichoke hearts
- ½ bunch kale, chopped
- 2 cups vegetable broth
- 1 tablespoon dried basil
- 1 tablespoon dried oregano
- 1 teaspoon salt
- ½ teaspoon red pepper flakes
- Black pepper, to taste
- 2 (14 ouncecans roasted tomatoes, diced
- 1 (15 ouncecan white beans, drained

How to Prepare:
1. Add all ingredients to a saucepan.
2. Put on the saucepan's lid and Cooking Time: for 20 minutes on a simmer.
3. Serve warm.

Nutritional Values:
Calories 201
Total Fat 8.9 g
Saturated Fat 4.5 g
Cholesterol 57 mg
Sodium 340 mg
Total Carbs 24.7 g
Fiber 1.2 g
Sugar 1.3 g
Protein 15.3 g

570. Chinese Rice Soup

Preparation time: 10 minutes
Cooking time: 3 hrs.
Total time: 3hrs. 10 minutes
Servings: 04

Ingredients:
Congee:

- 1 cup of white rice (uncooked)
- 2-inch piece fresh ginger, minced
- 4 cloves garlic, minced
- 10 cups water
- 14 dried shiitake mushrooms

Toppings:

- Green onions
- Cilantro
- Sesame seeds
- Hot sauce
- Toasted sesame oil
- Soy sauce
- Peanuts
- Chili oil
- Shelled edamame

How to Prepare:
1. Add all the ingredients to a slow cooker.
2. Put on the slow cooker's lid and Cooking Time: for 3 hours on low heat.
3. Once done, garnish with desired toppings.
4. Serve warm.

Nutritional Values:
Calories 210.6
Total Fat 10.91g
Saturated Fat 7.4g
Sodium 875 mg
Potassium 604 mg
Carbohydrates 25.6g
Fiber 4.3g
Sugar 7.9g
Protein 2.1g

571. Black-Eyed Pea Soup With Greens

Preparation time: 10 minutes
Cooking time: 5 hrs.
Total time: 5 hrs. 10 minutes
Servings: 04
Ingredients:

- ½ cup black eyed peas

- ½ cup brown lentils
- 1 teaspoon oil
- ½ teaspoon cumin seeds
- ½ cup onions, chopped
- 5 cloves garlic, chopped
- 1-inch piece of ginger chopped
- 1 teaspoon ground coriander
- ½ teaspoon ground cumin
- ½ teaspoon turmeric
- ¼ teaspoon black pepper
- ½ teaspoon cayenne powder
- 2 tomatoes, chopped
- ½ teaspoon lemon juice
- 1 teaspoon salt
- 2 ½ cups water
- ½ cup chopped spinach
- ½ cup small chopped green beans

How to Prepare:
1. Add olive oil and cumin seeds to a slow cooker.
2. Sauté for 1 minute then toss in the rest of the ingredients.
3. Put on the slow cooker's lid and Cooking Time: for 5 hours on low heat.
4. Once done, garnish as desired
5. Serve warm.

Nutritional Values:
Calories 197
Total Fat 4 g
Saturated Fat 0.5 g
Cholesterol 135 mg
Sodium 790 mg
Total Carbs 31 g
Fiber 12.2 g
Sugar 2.5 g
Protein 11 g

572. Beanless Garden Soup

Preparation time: 10 minutes
Cooking time: 4 hrs. 5 minutes
Total time: 4 hrs. 15 minutes
Servings: 04
Ingredients:

- 1 medium onion, diced
- 2 cloves garlic, minced
- 1 green bell pepper, diced
- 1 red bell pepper, diced
- 2 carrots, peeled and diced
- 1 medium zucchini, diced
- 1 small eggplant, diced
- 1 hot banana pepper, seeded and minced
- 1 jalapeño pepper, seeded and minced
- 1 can (28 ouncediced tomatoes
- 3 cups vegetable broth
- 1½ tablespoon chili powder
- 2 teaspoons smoked paprika
- 1 tablespoon cumin
- 2 tablespoons fresh oregano, chopped
- 2 tablespoons fresh cilantro, chopped
- Salt and black pepper to taste
- A few dashes of liquid smoke

How to Prepare:
1. In a slow cooker, add olive oil and onion.
2. Sauté for 5 minutes then toss in the rest of the ingredients.
3. Put on the slow cooker's lid and Cooking Time: for 4 hours on low heat.
4. Once done mix well.
5. Serve warm.

Nutritional Values:
Calories 305
Total Fat 11.8 g
Saturated Fat 2.2 g
Cholesterol 56 mg
Sodium 321 mg
Total Carbs 34.6 g
Fibers 0.4 g
Sugar 2 g
Protein 7 g

573. Black-Eyed Pea Soup With Olive Pesto

Preparation time: 10 minutes
Cooking time: 3 hrs. 5 minutes
Total time: 3 hrs. 15 minutes

Servings: 04
Ingredients:
Soup:
- 1 leek, trimmed
- 1 tablespoon olive oil
- 1 clove garlic, chopped
- 1 small carrot, chopped
- 1 stem fresh thyme, chopped
- 1 (15 ounce can black-eyed peas, drained and rinsed
- 2½ cups vegetable broth
- ½ teaspoon salt
- ¼ teaspoon black pepper

Pesto:
- 1¼ cups pitted green olives
- ¼ cup parsley leaves
- 1 clove garlic
- 1 teaspoon capers, drained
- 1 tablespoon olive oil

How to Prepare:
1. In a slow cooker, add olive oil, carrot, leek, and garlic.
2. Sauté for 5 minutes then toss in the rest of the soup ingredients.
3. Put on the slow cooker's lid and Cooking Time: for 3 hours on low heat.
4. Meanwhile, blend the pesto ingredients in a blender until smooth.
5. Blend the soup in the slow cooker with a hand mixer.
6. Top with prepared pesto.
7. Serve warm.

Nutritional Values:
Calories 72
Total Fat 15.4 g
Saturated Fat 4.2 g
Cholesterol 168 mg
Sodium 203 mg
Total Carbs 28.5 g
Sugar 1.1 g
Fiber 4 g
Protein 7.9 g

574. Spinach Soup With Basil

Preparation time: 10 minutes
Cooking time: 5 hrs. 5 minutes
Total time: 5 hrs. 15 minutes
Servings: 06
Ingredients:
- 8 ounces potatoes, diced
- 1 medium onion, chopped
- 1 large clove of garlic, chopped
- 1 teaspoon powdered mustard
- 3 cups water
- ¼ teaspoon salt
- Ground cayenne pepper
- ½ cup packed fresh dill
- 10 ounces frozen spinach

How to Prepare:
1. In a low cooker, add olive oil and onion.
2. Sauté for 5 minutes then toss in rest of the soup ingredients.
3. Put on the slow cooker's lid and Cooking Time: for 5 hours on low heat.
4. Once done, puree the soup with a hand blender.
5. Serve warm.

Nutritional Values:
Calories 162
Total Fat 4 g
Saturated Fat 1.9 g
Cholesterol 25 mg
Sodium 101 mg
Total Carbs 17.8 g
Sugar 2.1 g
Fiber 6 g
Protein 4 g

575. Red Lentil Salsa Soup

Preparation time: 10 minutes
Cooking time: 17 minutes
Total time: 27 minutes
Servings: 06
Ingredients:
- 1¼ cups red lentils, rinsed
- 4 cups of water
- ½ cup diced red bell pepper

- *1¼ cups red salsa*
- *1 tablespoon chili powder*
- *1 tablespoon dried oregano*
- *1 teaspoon smoked paprika*
- *¼ teaspoon black pepper*
- *¾ cup frozen sweet corn*
- *Salt to taste*
- *2 tablespoons lime juice*

How to Prepare:
1. In a saucepan, add all the ingredients except the corn.
2. Put on saucepan's lid and Cooking Time: for 15 minutes at a simmer.
3. Stir in corn and Cooking Time: for another 2 minutes.
4. Serve.

Nutritional Values:
Calories 119
Total Fat 14 g
Saturated Fat 2 g
Cholesterol 65 mg
Sodium 269 mg
Total Carbs 19 g
Fiber 4 g
Sugar 6 g
Protein 5g

576. Caldo Verde A La Mushrooms

Preparation time: 10 minutes
Cooking time: 5 hrs. 5 minutes
Total time: 5 hrs. 15 minutes
Servings: 08
Ingredients:

- *¼ cup olive oil*
- *10 ounces button mushrooms, cleaned, and sliced*
- *1½ teaspoons smoked paprika*
- *1 pinch ground cayenne pepper*
- *1 teaspoon salt*
- *1 large onion, diced*
- *2 cloves garlic, minced*
- *2 pounds russet potatoes, peeled and diced*
- *7 cups vegetable broth*
- *8 ounces kale, sliced*
- *½ teaspoon black pepper*

How to Prepare:
1. In a pan, heat cooking oil and sauté mushrooms for 12 minutes.
2. Season the mushrooms with salt, cayenne pepper, and paprika.
3. Add olive oil and onion to a slow cooker.
4. Sauté for 5 minutes then toss in rest of the soup ingredients.
5. Put on the slow cooker's lid and Cooking Time: for 5 hours on low heat.
6. Once done, puree the soup with a hand blender.
7. Stir in sautéed mushrooms.
8. Serve.

Nutritional Values:
Calories 231
Total Fat 20.1 g
Saturated Fat 2.4 g
Cholesterol 110 mg
Sodium 941 mg
Total Carbs 20.1 g
Fiber 0.9 g
Sugar 1.4 g
Protein 4.6 g

577. Shiitake Mushroom Split Pea Soup

Preparation time: 10 minutes
Cooking time: 6 hours
Total time: 6 hours 10 minutes
Servings: 12
Ingredients:

- *1 cup dried, green split peas*
- *2 cups celery, chopped*
- *2 cups sliced carrots*
- *1½ cups cauliflower, chopped*
- *2 ounces dried shiitake mushrooms, chopped*
- *9 ounces frozen artichoke hearts*
- *11 cups water*
- *1 teaspoon garlic powder*
- *1½ teaspoon onion powder*

- ½ teaspoon black pepper
- 1 tablespoon parsley
- ½ teaspoon ginger
- ½ teaspoon ground mustard seed
- ½ tablespoon brown rice vinegar

How to Prepare:
1. Add all the ingredients to a slow cooker.
2. Put on the slow cooker's lid and Cooking Time: for 6 hours on low heat.
3. Once done, garnish as desired.
4. Serve warm.

Nutritional Values:
Calories 361
Total Fat 16.3 g
Saturated Fat 4.9 g
Cholesterol 114 mg
Sodium 515 mg
Total Carbs 29.3 g
Fiber 0.1 g
Sugar 18.2 g
Protein 3.3 g

578. Velvety Vegetable Soup

Preparation time: 10 minutes
Cooking time: 2hrs 2 minutes
Total time: 2 hrs. 12 minutes
Servings: 4
Ingredients:

- ½ sweet onion, chopped
- 4 garlic cloves, chopped
- 1 small head broccoli, chopped
- 2 stalks celery, chopped
- 1 cup green peas
- 3 green onions, chopped
- 2¾ cups vegetable broth
- 4 cups leafy greens
- 1 (15 ounce can of cannellini beans
- Juice from 1 lemon
- 2 tablespoons fresh dill, chopped
- 5 fresh mint leaves
- 1 teaspoon salt
- ½ cup coconut milk
- Fresh herbs and peas, to garnish

How to Prepare:
1. In a slow cooker, add olive oil and onion.
2. Sauté for 2 minutes then toss in the rest of the soup ingredients.
3. Put on the slow cooker's lid and Cooking Time: for 2 hours on low heat.
4. Once done, blend the soup with a hand blender.
5. Garnish with fresh herbs and peas.
6. Serve warm.

Nutritional Values:
Calories 205
Total Fat 22.7 g
Saturated Fat 6.1 g
Cholesterol 4 mg
Sodium 227 mg
Total Carbs 26.1 g
Fiber 1.4 g
Sugar 0.9 g
Protein 5.2 g

579. Sweet Potato And Peanut Soup

Preparation time: 10 minutes
Cooking time: 4 hrs. 5 minutes
Total time: 4 hrs. 15 minutes
Servings: 06
Ingredients:

- 1 tablespoon water
- 6 cups sweet potatoes, peeled and chopped
- 2 cups onions, chopped
- 1 cup celery, chopped
- 4 large cloves garlic, chopped
- 1 teaspoon salt
- 2 teaspoons cumin seeds
- 3½ teaspoons ground coriander
- 1 teaspoon paprika
- ½ teaspoon crushed red pepper flakes
- 2 cups vegetable stock
- 3 cups water

- *4 tablespoons fresh ginger, grated*
- *2 tablespoons natural peanut butter*
- *2 cups cooked chickpeas*
- *4 tablespoons lime juice*
- *Fresh cilantro, chopped*
- *Chopped peanuts, to garnish*

How to Prepare:
1. *In a slow cooker, add olive oil and onion.*
2. *Sauté for 5 minutes then toss in the rest of the soup ingredients except chickpeas.*
3. *Put on the slow cooker's lid and Cooking Time: for 4 hours on low heat.*
4. *Once done, blend the soup with a hand blender.*
5. *Stir in chickpeas and garnish with cilantro and peanuts.*
6. *Serve warm.*

Nutritional Values:
Calories 201
Total Fat 8.9 g
Saturated Fat 4.5 g
Cholesterol 57 mg
Sodium 340 mg
Total Carbs 24.7 g
Fiber 1.2 g
Sugar 1.3 g
Protein 15.3 g

580. 3-Ingredient Carrot And Red Lentil Soup

Preparation Time: 40 minutes
Servings: 3

Ingredients
- *Split red lentils: 1 cup*
- *Carrots: 1 cup grated*
- *Water: 6 cups*
- *Onion: 1 large coarsely chopped*
- *Fine sea salt: as per your taste*

Directions:
1. *Take a large saucepan and add water and bring to boil*
2. *Add the chopped onions, carrots, lentils and salt and bring to boil*
3. *Lower the heat to medium and Cooking Time: for 20 minutes with partial cover*
4. *Add the mixture to the high-speed blender to make a puree*
5. *Whisk in water if desired*
6. *Add again to the pan and slowly heat on a low flame for 10-15 minutes*
7. *Add herbs or spices in between to augment the taste*

Nutrition:
Carbs: 15.3 g
Protein: 6.2 g
Fats: 0.3 g
Calories: 90 Kcal

581. 3-Ingredient Enchilada Soup

Preparation Time: 25 minutes
Servings: 3

Ingredients
- *Tomatoes: 1 cup crushed*
- *Vegan red enchilada sauce: 1.5 cups*
- *Black beans: 2 cups can rinsed and drained*

Directions:
1. *Take a medium-sized saucepan and add crushed tomatoes and enchilada sauce*
2. *Heat on a medium flame to thicken it for 6-8 minutes*
3. *Add beans to the pan and lower the heat to a minimum*
4. *Cooking Time: for 8-10 minutes*
5. *Serve with any toppings if you like*

Nutrition:
Carbs: 27.4 g
Protein: 11g
Fats: 1 g
Calories: 166.4 Kcal

582. 3- Ingredient Lentil Soup

Preparation Time: 50 minutes
Servings: 2

Ingredients
- *Brown lentils: 1 ¼ cups*

- Fresh rosemary leaves: 2 ½ tbsp minced
- Onion: 1 large chopped
- Sea salt: as per your taste
- Black pepper: ¼ tsp
- Water: 6 cups

Directions:
1. Take a large saucepan and add 1/3 cup of water and bring to boil
2. Add the chopped onions and lower the heat to medium
3. Stir with intervals for 10 minutes till onion changes color
4. Add salt, pepper, and rosemary and continue to stir for a minutes
5. Add lentils and remaining water to the pan and cover and Cooking Time: for 20 minutes
6. Lower the heat and continue simmering for 15 more minutes
7. Stir and break some lentils in the final minutes
8. Blend the soup if you like a creamy texture
9. Add more salt and pepper if needed and serve

Nutrition:
Carbs: 20 g
Protein: 8.5 g
Fats: 0.4 g
Calories: 150 Kcal

583. All Spices Lentils Bean Soup

Preparation Time: 45 minutes
Servings: 4

Ingredients
- Red lentils: 1 cup washed and drained
- Carrot: 2 medium chopped
- Beans: 1 cup drained
- Water: 3 cups
- Garlic: 3 cloves minced
- Onion: 1 medium finely chopped
- Ground cumin: 1 tsp
- Nutmeg: 1 tsp
- Ground coriander: 1 tsp
- Ground allspice: 1 tsp
- Ground cinnamon: 1 tsp
- Ground cayenne: ½ tsp
- Black pepper: as per your taste
- Extra virgin olive oil: 2 tbsp
- Salt: as per your taste
- Cilantro: 1 tbsp chopped

Directions:
1. Take a soup pot and heat oil in it on a medium flame
2. Add onion and fry for 4-5 minutes
3. Add carrot and garlic and stir for 5 minutes
4. Wash lentils and add them to the pot
5. Add water and bring to boil
6. Lower the heat and Cooking Time: and cover for 15 minutes till lentil softens
7. Add the remaining ingredients except for cilantro and Cooking Time: for an additional 15 minutes
8. Serve warm with cilantro on top

Nutrition:
Carbs: 425 g
Protein: 8.17 g
Fats: 4 g
Calories: 148.75 Kcal

584. Asparagus Cashew Cream Soup

Preparation Time: 30 minutes
Servings: 2

Ingredients
- Asparagus: 2 cups
- Vegetable stock: 4 cups
- Sesame seed: 2 tbsp
- Lemon juice: 1 tbsp
- Garlic: 4 cloves crushed
- Cashew cream: ½ cup
- Onion: 1 chopped
- Olive oil: 2 tbsp
- Salt & pepper: as per your taste

Preparation
1. Take a large saucepan and add olive

oil to it
2. Fry onion and garlic till it turns golden brown
3. Chop asparagus and add to the pan along with the vegetable stock
4. Let it boil and then Cooking Time: on low heat for 20 minutes
5. When ready, add sesame seeds, lemon juice, and salt and pepper as per your taste
6. Serve with cashew cream on top

Nutrition:
Carbs: 11 g
Protein: 9.4 g
Fats: 18.3 g
Calories: 243.5 Kcal

585. Artichoke Spinach Soup

Preparation Time: 20 minutes
Servings: 3

Ingredients
- Cannellini beans: 1 cup rinsed and drained
- Artichoke hearts: 2 cups drained and chopped
- Frozen chopped spinach: 2 cups
- Water: 3 cups + 1 cup
- Garlic: 4 cloves chopped
- Onion: 1 medium chopped
- Italian herb blend: 2 tsp
- Sea salt: as per your taste
- Black pepper: as per your taste

Directions:
1. Take a blender and add onion, garlic, drained beans, salt, herb blend, and pepper and add water
2. Blend to give a smooth texture
3. Add this puree to a large pan and Cooking Time: on medium-high heat
4. When it initiates to boil, lower the heat and stir in between
5. Let the mixture to thicken a bit
6. Add one cup of water and spinach and blend
7. Also, add artichokes and heat for 5 minutes
8. Season with salt and pepper if desired and serve

Nutrition:
Carbs: 29.86 g
Protein: 12.9 g
Fats: 1.2 g
Calories: 144 Kcal

586. Beans With Garam Masala Broth

Preparation Time: 40 minutes
Servings: 2

Ingredients
- Red lentils: 1 cups
- Tomatoes: 1 cup can diced
- Beans: 1 cup can rinsed and drained
- Garam masala: 1 tbsp
- Vegetable oil: 2 tbsp
- Onion: 1 cup chopped
- Garlic: 3 cloves minced
- Ground cumin: 2 tbsp
- Smoked paprika: 1 tsp
- Celery: 1 cup chopped
- Sea salt: 1 tsp
- Lime juice and zest: 3 tbsp
- Fresh cilantro: 3 tbsp chopped
- Water: 2 cups

Directions:
1. Take a large pot and add oil to it
2. On the medium flame, add garlic, celery and onion
3. Add salt, garam masala, and cumin to them and stir for 5 minutes till they turn brown
4. Add water, lentils, and tomatoes with the juice and bring to boil
5. Bring to boil and heat for 25-30 minutes on low flame
6. Add in lime juice and zest and beans of your choice and stir
7. Serve with cilantro on top

Nutrition:
Carbs: 51.5 g
Protein: 19.1 g

Fats: 15.3 g
Calories: 420 Kcal

587. Black Beans And Potato Soup

Preparation Time: 50 minutes
Servings: 4

Ingredients

- *Potatoes: 2 cups peeled and diced*
- *Black beans can: 2 cups rinsed and drained*
- *Kale: 1 cup chopped*
- *Onion: 1 medium finely chopped*
- *Garlic: 4 cloves minced*
- *Olive oil: 2 tsp*
- *Fresh rosemary leaves: 2 tbsp minced*
- *Vegetable broth: 4 cups*
- *Salt and ground black pepper: as per your taste*

Directions:

1. *Take a large saucepan and add oil*
2. *On a medium heat, add onions and Cooking Time: for 6-8 minutes*
3. *Add rosemary and garlic and stir for a minute*
4. *Add potatoes with salt and pepper and sauté for two minutes*
5. *Pour vegetable broth and bring to boil*
6. *Lower the heat and Cooking Time: for 30 minutes till potatoes become soft*
7. *By using the back of spoon mash a few potatoes*
8. *Add kale and beans to the soup and again Cooking Time: for 5 minutes till they tender*
9. *Remove the soup from heat and season with salt and pepper*

Nutrition:
Carbs: 45.25 g
Protein: 10.4 g
Fats: 8.7 g
Calories: 264 Kcal

588. Black Bean Cashew Soup

Preparation Time: 35 minutes
Servings: 3

Ingredients

- *Black beans: 1 cup can*
- *Cashew nuts: ½ cup*
- *Spinach: 2 cups chopped*
- *Onion: 1 medium*
- *Freshly grated ginger: 2 tbsp*
- *Curry powder: 1 tbsp mild*
- *Vegetable broth: 2 cups*
- *Olive oil: 2 tbsp*
- *Lemon juice: as per your taste*
- *Garlic: 3 cloves*
- *Salt: as per your taste*
- *Fresh coriander: 2 tbsp*

Directions:

1. *Take a large pan and add olive oil*
2. *Add onion and garlic and fry for a minute and add curry powder and ginger*
3. *Continue frying for 5 minutes to make onion soft*
4. *Add spinach and vegetable broth and Cooking Time: on a medium flame for 10 minutes*
5. *Now blend with the hand blender*
6. *Add sliced cashews and black beans*
7. *Add water if needed and simmer for 5 minutes*
8. *Serve with lemon juice and fresh coriander on top*

Nutrition:
Carbs: 44.5g
Protein: 21.7g
Fats: 20.26g
Calories: 312.66Kcal

589. Black Beans Veggie Soup

Preparation Time: 45 minutes
Servings: 4

Ingredients

- *Potatoes: 3 cups chopped*
- *Black beans: 1 cup can rinsed and drained*
- *Celery: 4 stalks sliced*

- *Fresh rosemary: 3 sprigs*
- *Carrots: 4 large sliced*
- *Vegetable oil: 2 tbsp*
- *Garlic: 2 cloves minced*
- *Shallots: 2 small diced*
- *Vegetable broth: 4 cups*
- *Broccoli: 1 cup florets*
- *Kale: 1 cup chopped*
- *Salt and black pepper: as per your need*

Directions:
1. Take a large pot and add oil to it
2. On the medium flame, add shallots, garlic, celery and onion
3. Add salt and pepper to them and stir for 5 minutes till they turn brown
4. Now add potatoes and broccoli and again season with salt and pepper and sauté for two minutes
5. Pour vegetable broth and add rosemary and bring the mixture to boil
6. Lower the heat now and let it Cooking Time: for 20 minutes till potatoes soften
7. Include kale and black beans; stir, cover, and Cooking Time: for 5 minutes
8. Adjust the overall seasoning and add salt and pepper if needed

Nutrition:
Carbs: 43.5g
Protein: 7.72g
Fats: 8.6g
Calories: 248.5 Kcal

590. Broccoli Corn Soup

Preparation Time: 40 minutes
Servings: 2

Ingredients
- *Corns: 2 cups can*
- *Broccoli: 1 cup*
- *Potato: 1 cup*
- *Spinach: 3 cups*
- *Garlic: 4 cloves*
- *Ginger root: 1 tbsp grated*
- *Spring onion: 4*
- *Turmeric: 1 tsp*
- *Lemon juice: 2 tbsp*
- *Coriander: ¼ cup chopped*
- *Ground coriander: 1 tsp*
- *Ground cumin: 1 tsp*
- *Salt and pepper: as per your taste*
- *Olive oil: 2 tbsp*
- *Vegetable broth: 4 cups*

Directions:
1. In a large saucepan and heat olive oil
2. Crush garlic and chop white part of the green onion and sauté for a minute
3. Add coriander, cumin, ginger and turmeric and fry for a minute
4. Peel and dice potatoes, wash spinach, and separate broccoli florets and add to the pan
5. Sauté them for 5 minutes and add vegetable broth
6. Boil, and heat on low flame for 20 minutes
7. Blend the soup well and season with salt and pepper
8. Top with corns, lemon juice, and coriander leaves

Nutrition:
Carbs: 24.35g
Protein: 4.7g
Fats: 7.95g
Calories: 167.5Kcal

591. Brown Lentils Tomato Soup

Preparation Time: 40 minutes
Servings: 2

Ingredients
- *Brown lentils: 1 cup*
- *Crushed tomatoes: 2 cups*
- *Onion: 1 diced*
- *Ginger: 1 tbsp paste*
- *Garlic: 1 tbsp paste*
- *Vegetable oil: 2 tbsp*

- Water: 4 cups
- Italian herb seasoning: 1 tbsp
- Salt & pepper: as per your taste

Directions:
1. Take a large saucepan and add oil on a medium flame
2. Add onion and ginger and garlic paste and sauté for 3-4 minutes
3. Pour water and bring to boil
4. Add lentils and salt and bring to boil
5. Lower the heat to medium and Cooking Time: for 20 minutes with partial cover
6. Now add crushed tomatoes to the lentils along with herb seasoning and pepper
7. Cooking Time: on low flame for 15 minutes
8. Add the mixture to the high speed blender to make puree
9. Add salt and pepper to augment taste

Nutrition:
Carbs: 30.8g
Protein: 12.7g
Fats: 15.2g
Calories: 323.2Kcal

592. Brown Lentils Green Veggies Combo Soup

Preparation Time: 1 hour
Servings: 4-6

Ingredients
- Brown lentils: 150g
- Chickpeas: 400g can drained and rinsed
- Onion: 1 large finely chopped
- Leek: 2 diced
- Parsnips: 2 large finely diced
- Kale: 85g leaves shredded
- Olive oil: 2 tbsp
- Garlic: 2 cloves crushed
- Cayenne pepper: 1 tsp
- Coriander: a small bunch finely sliced
- Ground cinnamon: 1 tsp
- Ground turmeric: 1 tsp
- Ground coriander: 2 tsp
- Vegetable stock: 1 liter
- Lemons juice: 2 tbsp
- Salt: as per your need

Directions:
1. Take a large pan and heat olive oil in it
2. Add onions and parsnips and Cooking Time: them for 10 minutes
3. Then add coriander stalks and garlic and Cooking Time: for a minute and mix well
4. Next add spices and stir in lentils
5. Pour the stock and boil and then cover and Cooking Time: for 20 minutes and add leek at 10 minutes
6. Remove the lid and add in kale and chickpeas and stir
7. Sprinkle salt and pour in lemon juice
8. Top with coriander and serve

Nutrition:
Carbs: 29.4 g
Protein: 12.8 g
Fats: 7.2 g
Calories: 258 Kcal

593. Cannellini Beans Tomato Soup

Preparation Time: 30 minutes
Servings: 2

Ingredients
- Cannellini beans: 1 cup can
- Tomatoes: 1 cup chunks
- Tomatoes: 1 cup can
- Tomato paste: 2 tbsp
- Oregano: 2 tbsp dried
- Onion: 1 (finely chopped
- Garlic: 3 cloves (crushed
- Fresh basil: 1 small bunch
- Vegetable broth: 4 cups
- Salt & pepper: as per your taste
- Olive oil: 2 tbsp

Directions:

1. Take a large saucepan, heat olive oil in it
2. Add onion and garlic in it
3. Include tomato chunks, can chopped tomatoes, and tomato paste and combine them all together
4. Now add vegetable broth, oregano and fresh basil
5. Bring the mixture to boil and then lower the heat to medium and Cooking Time: for 15 minutes
6. Use the hand blender to blend the soup content and season with salt and pepper
7. Rinse, dry, and roast the cannellini beans
8. Add these beans on top of the soup and serve hot

Nutrition:
Carbs: 40g
Protein: 13.87g
Fats: 18.05g
Calories: 385.7Kcal

594. Cashew Chickpeas Soup

Preparation Time: 25 minutes
Servings: 2

Ingredients
- Chickpeas: 1 cup can
- Cashew nuts: ½ cup
- Spinach: 2 cups chopped
- Onion: 1 medium
- Freshly grated ginger: 2 tbsp
- Curry powder: 1 tbsp mild
- Vegetable broth: 2 cups
- Olive oil: 2 tbsp
- Lemon juice: as per your taste
- Garlic: 3 cloves
- Salt: as per your taste
- Fresh coriander: 2 tbsp

Directions:
1. Take a large pan and add olive oil
2. Add onion and garlic and fry for a minute and add curry powder and ginger
3. Continue frying for 5 minutes to make onion soft
4. Add spinach and vegetable broth and Cooking Time: on a medium flame for 10 minutes
5. Now blend with the hand blender and add sliced cashews and chickpeas
6. Add water if needed and simmer for 5 minutes
7. Serve with lemon juice and fresh coriander on top

Nutrition:
Carbs: 24.03g
Protein: 12.16g
Fats: 21.26g
Calories: 309 Kcal

595. Charred Mexican Sweetcorn Soup

Preparation Time: 45 minutes
Servings: 4

Ingredients
- Corn on the cob: 2
- Dried ancho chili: 1
- Onion: 1 finely chopped
- Vegetable stock: 1 liter
- Celery: 2 sticks finely chopped
- Ground cumin: 2 tsp
- Roasted red peppers: 4 chopped
- Garlic: 3 cloves finely chopped
- Sweet smoked paprika: 2 tsp
- Limes: 2 - 1 juice and other wedged to serve
- Vegetable oil: 2 tbsp
- Coriander: a small bunch chopped

Directions:
1. Take a bowl and add ancho chili and pour boiling water from the top
2. Leave the mixture for 10 minutes and then remove stem and seed
3. Take a pan and heat oil in it and add celery and onion and Cooking Time: for 10 minutes with a pinch of salt
4. Add all the spices and Cooking Time: for a minute

5. Include now ancho chili, vegetable stock, and pepper and Cooking Time: for 15 minutes
6. Season with salt and blend the mixture
7. In the meanwhile, on a light heat Cooking Time: corns in the pan lightly brushed with salt, pepper, and oil
8. Cooking Time: the cobs for 10 minutes and then remove from heat
9. Use a sharp knife to remove corns and add to the soup
10. Sprinkle coriander on top and serve with lime juice

Nutrition:
Carbs: 12.9 g
Protein: 5.6 g
Fats: 8.5 g
Calories: 162 Kcal

596. Chickpeas And Root Vegetable Soup

Preparation Time: 45 minutes
Servings: 2

Ingredients
- *Chickpeas: 1 cup can*
- *Almonds: ½ cup*
- *Potatoes: 1 cup*
- *Carrots: 1 cup*
- *Parsnips: 1 cup*
- *Onion: 1 large*
- *Curry powder: 1 tbsp mild*
- *Tomato paste: 1 tbsp*
- *Garlic: 3 cloves crushed*
- *Grated ginger: 2 tbsp*
- *Turmeric: 1 tsp*
- *Ground coriander: 1 tsp*
- *Ground cumin: 1 tsp*
- *Vegetable broth: 3 cups*
- *Lemon juice: 2 tbsp*
- *Fresh coriander: 3 tbsp*
- *Olive oil: 2 tbsp*
- *Salt & pepper: as per your taste*

Directions:

1. In a large saucepan, add olive oil and heat on medium flame
2. Add the chopped onion, garlic, grated ginger, ground cumin, ground coriander, curry powder, turmeric, and tomato paste
3. Sauté for a minute or two
4. Peel the veggies and dice them and add to the pan and stir for 5 minutes
5. Now add vegetable broth and bring the mixture to boil and cover and heat for 20 minutes
6. With the hand blender, blend the soup and season with salt and pepper
7. Rinse and drain chickpeas and add to the soup
8. Add fresh coriander, almonds, and lemon juice on top and serve hot

Nutrition:
Carbs: 38.32g
Protein: 10.89g
Fats: 18.83g
Calories: 346Kcal

597. Chickpeas Mushroom Broth

Preparation Time: 25 minutes
Servings: 2

Ingredients
- *Chickpeas: 1 cup can rinsed and drained*
- *Mushrooms: 2 cups*
- *Spring onions: 6*
- *Tomato sauce: 2 tbsp*
- *Garlic: 2 cloves crushed*
- *Ginger root: 2 tbsp crushed*
- *Sesame seeds: 4 tbsp*
- *Sesame oil: 1 tbsp*
- *Salt: as per your need*
- *Pepper: as per your need*
- *Tamari: 2 tbsp*
- *Water: 2 cups*

Preparation
1. Chop spring onion and reserve its green part and cut mushrooms in

half
2. Take a large saucepan and add sesame oil
3. Add the white part of the spring onion to the pan and sauté for a minute
4. Add tomato paste, ginger and garlic and fry again for a minute
5. Add water and fresh mushrooms and chickpeas
6. Cooking Time: for 10 minutes on medium flame and season with salt and pepper
7. Add sesame seeds and tamari sauce and boil for two minutes
8. Serve hot with spring onion sprinkled on top

Nutrition:
Carbs: 27g
Protein: 10.2g
Fats: 11.2g
Calories: 188Kcal

598. Chickpeas Puree Pumpkin Soup

Preparation Time: 40 minutes
Servings: 4

Ingredients
- Chickpeas: 2 cups can rinsed and drained
- Pumpkin puree: 1 cup can unsweetened
- Onion: 1 cup finely chopped
- Tomatoes: 1 cup can diced not drained
- Water: 3 cups
- Olive oil: 2 tbsp
- Ground cumin: 1 tbsp
- Garlic powder: 2 tsp
- Chili powder: 1 tsp
- Dried oregano: 2 tsp
- Fresh cilantro: 2 tbsp chopped
- Fine sea salt: 1 tsp
- Fresh lime juice: 2 tbsp

Directions:
1. Take a food processor and add tomatoes and chickpeas and make their puree and set aside
2. Take a large saucepan and add oil on the medium heat
3. Add onion and sauté till it turns brown
4. Add chili powder, cumin, garlic powder, salt, and oregano and stir for a minute
5. Add in the pumpkin, chickpeas puree, and water and mix well
6. Lower the heat and simmer uncover for 25-30 minutes and stir after regular intervals
7. When ready, serve with lime juice and season with salt, pepper, and add cilantro on the top

Nutrition:
Carbs: 30.8g
Protein: 9.25g
Fats: 9.4g
Calories: 242.55Kcal

599. Chickpeas Stew

Preparation Time: 40 minutes
Servings: 2

Ingredients
- Chickpeas: 1 cup
- Vegetable broth: 2 cups
- Olive oil: 1 tbsp
- Garlic: 2 cloves minced
- Red bell pepper: ½ cup chopped
- Onion: 1 medium minced
- Tomatoes: 1 cup chopped
- Cayenne pepper: ¼ tsp
- Carrot: 1 diced
- Dried basil: ½ tsp
- Dried parsley: ½ tsp
- Tomato paste: 1 tbsp
- Salt: as per your need

Directions:
1. Cooking Time: chickpeas by soaking them overnight and boiling them for two hours on medium heat
2. Take a large saucepan and heat oil on medium flame

3. Add onions and Cooking Time: for 3-4 minutes
4. Add garlic and Cooking Time: for a minute and stir
5. Add tomatoes, bell pepper, carrot, chickpeas, basil, oregano, tomato sauce, and parsley
6. Stir for around a minute or two
7. Add vegetable broth, cover, and boil
8. Simmer for 20-25 minutes until thickened
9. To give a better texture, mash some chickpeas with the back of the spoon
10. Season with cayenne pepper, salt, and pepper
11. Serve with bread or rice

Nutrition:
Carbs: 35.4g
Protein: 10.47g
Fats: 16.7g
Calories: 332.6Kcal

600. Corns And Kale Potato Soup

Preparation Time: 30 minutes
Servings: 4

Ingredients
- Potatoes: 2 cups peeled and diced
- Corns can: 2 cups rinsed and drained
- Kale: 3 cup chopped
- Onion: 1 medium finely chopped
- Garlic: 4 cloves minced
- Olive oil: 2 tbsp
- Ground cumin: ½ tsp
- Smoked paprika: ¼ tsp
- Fresh rosemary leaves: 2 tbsp minced
- Vegetable broth: 4 cups
- Salt and ground black pepper: as per your taste

Directions:
1. Take a large saucepan and add oil
2. On medium heat, add onions and Cooking Time: for 6-8 minutes
3. Add rosemary, smoked paprika, and garlic and stir for a minute
4. Add potatoes with salt and pepper and sauté for two minutes
5. Pour vegetable broth and bring to boil
6. Lower the heat and Cooking Time: for 30 minutes till potatoes become soft
7. By using the back of spoon mash a few potatoes
8. Add kale and corns to the soup and again Cooking Time: for 5 minutes till they tender
9. Remove the soup from heat and season with salt and pepper

Nutrition:
Carbs: 53.15g
Protein: 6,25g
Fats: 11.25g
Calories: 234.3Kcal

601. Creamy Broccoli Soup

Preparation Time: 30 minutes
Servings: 2

Ingredients
- Broccoli: 2 cups
- Vegetable broth: 2 cups
- Sesame seed: 2 tbsp
- Lemon juice: 1 tbsp
- Garlic: 4 cloves crushed
- Cashew cream: ½ cup
- Onion: 1 chopped
- Olive oil: 2 tbsp
- Salt & pepper: as per your taste

Preparation
1. Take a large saucepan and add olive oil to it
2. Fry onion and garlic till it turns golden brown
3. Slice broccoli florets and add to the pan along with the vegetable broth
4. Let it boil and then Cooking Time: on low heat for 20 minutes
5. When ready, add sesame seeds, lemon juice, and salt and pepper as per your taste
6. Serve with cashew cream on top

Nutrition:

Carbs: 23.1g
Protein: 7.45g
Fats: 25g
Calories: 344Kcal

602. Easy Black Bean Stew

Preparation Time: 40 minutes
Servings: 2

Ingredients

- *Black beans: 1 cup*
- *Vegetable broth: 2 cups*
- *Olive oil: 1 tbsp*
- *Garlic: 2 cloves minced*
- *Red bell pepper: ¼ cup chopped*
- *Onion: 1 medium minced*
- *Tomatoes: 1 cup chopped*
- *Cayenne pepper: ¼ tsp*
- *Dried basil: ½ tsp*
- *Dried parsley: ½ tsp*
- *Tomato paste: 1 tbsp*
- *Salt: as per your need*

Directions:

1. *Cooking Time: black beans by soaking them overnight and boiling them for two hours on medium heat*
2. *Take a large saucepan and heat oil on medium flame*
3. *Add onions and Cooking Time: for 3-4 minutes*
4. *Add garlic and Cooking Time: for a minute and stir*
5. *Add tomatoes, bell pepper, black beans, basil, oregano, tomato sauce, and parsley*
6. *Stir for around a minute or two*
7. *Add vegetable broth, cover, and boil*
8. *Simmer for 20-25 minutes until thickened*
9. *To give a better texture, mash some black beans with the back of the spoon*
10. *Season with cayenne pepper, salt, and pepper*
11. *Serve with bread or rice*

Nutrition:
Carbs: 25.9g

Protein: 9.37g
Fats: 7.85g
Calories: 220.1Kcal

603. Easy Split Pea Soup

Preparation Time: 40 minutes
Servings: 2

Ingredients

- *Split peas: 1 cup*
- *Garlic: 4 cloves*
- *Ground cinnamon: ¼ tsp*
- *Ground turmeric: 1 tsp*
- *Sea salt: ½ tsp*
- *Smoked paprika: ¼ tsp*
- *Freshly cracked pepper: ¼ tsp*
- *Parsley leaves: ¼ cup chopped*
- *Water: 4 cups*

Directions:

1. *Take a large saucepan and add water and bring to boil*
2. *Add split peas, turmeric, pepper, garlic, cinnamon, smoked paprika, and salt and bring to boil*
3. *Lower the heat to medium and Cooking Time: for 25 minutes with partial cover*
4. *With the back of the stirring spoon, mash the split peas*
5. *Serve hot and top with parsley leaves*

Nutrition:
Carbs: 20g
Protein: 8.9g
Fats: 0.4g
Calories: 115Kcal

604. Every Day One-Pot Lentil Soup

Preparation Time: 40 minutes
Servings: 4

Ingredients

- *Baby potatoes: 3 cups chopped*
- *Green lentils: 1 cup rinsed and drained*
- *Celery: 4 stalks sliced*
- *Fresh rosemary: 3 sprigs*

- Coconut oil: 2 tbsp
- Garlic: 2 cloves minced
- Shallots: 2 small diced
- Vegetable broth: 4 cups
- Kale: 2 cups chopped
- Salt and black pepper: as per your need

Directions:
1. Take a large pot and add oil to it
2. On the medium flame, add shallots, garlic, celery and onion
3. Add salt and pepper to them and stir for 5 minutes till they turn brown
4. Now add potatoes and again season with salt and pepper and sauté for two minutes
5. Pour vegetable broth and add rosemary and bring the mixture to boil
6. Add lentils now and stir and let it simmer
7. Lower the heat now and let it Cooking Time: for 20 minutes till potatoes and lentils soften
8. Include kale, stir, cover, and Cooking Time: for 5 minutes
9. Adjust the overall seasoning and add salt and pepper if needed
10. Serve with your favorite bread or rice

Nutrition:
Carbs: 42.5g
Protein: 8g
Fats: 2.55g
Calories: 162.7Kcal

605. Garam Masala Lentil Stew

Preparation Time: 40 minutes
Servings: 2

Ingredients
- Tomatoes: 1 cup can diced
- Red lentils: 1cup rinsed and drained
- Garam masala: 1 tbsp
- Vegetable oil: 2 tbsp
- Onion: 1 cup chopped
- Garlic: 3 cloves minced
- Ground cumin: 2 tbsp
- Celery: 1 cup chopped
- Sea salt: 1 tsp
- Lime juice and zest: 3 tbsp
- Fresh cilantro: 3 tbsp chopped
- Water: 4 cups

Directions:
1. Take a large pot and add oil to it
2. On the medium flame, add garlic, celery, and onion
3. Add salt, garam masala, and cumin to them and stir for 5 minutes till they turn brown
4. Add water, lentils, and tomatoes with the juice and bring to boil
5. Bring to boil and heat for 25-30 minutes
6. Add in lime juice and zest and stir
7. Serve with cilantro on top

Nutrition:
Carbs: 39.5g
Protein: 14.2g
Fats: 17.7g
Calories: Kcal

606. Green Chickpeas Soup

Preparation Time: 30 minutes
Servings: 3

Ingredients
- Broccoli: 1 cup
- Potato: 1 cup
- Spinach: 3 cups
- Mustard seeds: 2 tbsp
- Garlic: 4 cloves
- Ginger root: 1 tbsp grated
- Spring onion: 4
- Turmeric: 1 tsp
- Chickpeas: 1 cup can
- Lemon juice: 2 tbsp
- Coriander: ¼ cup chopped
- Ground coriander: 1 tsp
- Ground cumin: 1 tsp
- Salt and pepper: as per your taste
- Olive oil: 2 tbsp
- Vegetable broth: 3 cups

Directions:
1. In a large saucepan and heat olive oil
2. Crush garlic and chop the white part of the green onion and sauté for a minute
3. Add coriander, cumin, mustard seeds, ginger, and turmeric and fry for a minute
4. Peel and dice potatoes, wash spinach, and separate broccoli florets and add to the pan
5. Sauté them for 5 minutes and add vegetable broth
6. Boil, and heat on low flame for 20 minutes
7. Blend the soup well and season with salt and pepper
8. Top with chickpeas, lemon juice, and coriander leaves

Nutrition:
Carbs: 29.46g
Protein: 11.93g
Fats: 11.2g
Calories: 293Kcal

607. Green Lentils Tomato Soup

Preparation Time: 25 minutes
Servings: 2

Ingredients
- Green Lentils: 1 cup
- Tomatoes: 1 cup chunks
- Tomatoes: 1 cup can
- Tomato paste: 2 tbsp
- Oregano: 2 tbsp dried
- Onion: 1 finely chopped
- Garlic: 3 cloves crushed
- Fresh basil: 1 small bunch
- Vegetable broth: 4 cups
- Salt & pepper: as per your taste
- Olive oil: 2 tbsp

Directions:
1. Take a large saucepan, heat olive oil in it
2. Add onion and garlic in it
3. Include tomato chunks, can chopped tomatoes, and tomato paste and combine them all together
4. Stir for a minute and add lentils to the pan
5. Now add vegetable broth, oregano, and fresh basil
6. Bring the mixture to boil and then lower the heat to medium and Cooking Time: for 15 minutes
7. Use the hand blender to blend the soup content and season with salt and pepper

Nutrition:
Carbs: 30.8g
Protein: 13.2g
Fats: 15.2g
Calories: 323.2Kcal

608. Green Peas Tomato Soup

Preparation Time: 30 minutes
Servings: 2

Ingredients
- Green Peas: 2 cups
- Tomatoes: 1 cup chunks
- Tomatoes: 1 cup can
- Tomato paste: 2 tbsp
- Oregano: 2 tbsp dried
- Onion: 1 (finely chopped
- Garlic: 3 cloves (crushed
- Fresh basil: 1 small bunch
- Vegetable broth: 4 cups
- Salt & pepper: as per your taste
- Olive oil: 2 tbsp

Directions:
1. Take a large saucepan, heat olive oil in it
2. Add onion and garlic in it
3. Include tomato chunks, can chopped tomatoes, and tomato paste and combine them all together
4. Stir for a minute and add peas to the pan
5. Now add vegetable broth, oregano, and fresh basil
6. Bring the mixture to boil and then

lower the heat to medium and Cooking Time: for 15 minutes
7. Use the hand blender to blend the soup content and season with salt and pepper

Nutrition:
Carbs: 21.8g
Protein: 9.25g
Fats: 15.2g
Calories: 275.2Kcal

609. Groundnut Sweet Potato Soup

Preparation Time: 40 minutes
Servings: 4

Ingredient
- Sweet potato: 2 medium cut into small pieces
- Plum tomatoes: 2 diced
- Vegetable stock: 1 liter
- Chili: 1 seeded and chopped
- Onion: 1 diced
- Celery: 2 sticks finely diced
- Ginger: 2 tbsp grated
- Garlic: 2 cloves sliced
- Salt: as per your taste
- Peanut butter: 2 tbsp
- Groundnut oil: 2 tsp
- Coriander: 2 tbsp

Directions:
1. Take a large pan and heat oil
2. Add onion, sweet potato, and celery and Cooking Time: for 10 minutes
3. Add ginger, garlic, chili, and salt and stir for 2 minutes
4. Add tomatoes and stock and bring the mixture to boil
5. Cooking Time: for 20 minutes on the medium flame
6. Add in peanut butter and grind the mixture to give a smooth consistency
7. Serve hot with coriander leaves on the top

Nutrition:
Carbs: 32.5 g
Protein: 5.6 g
Fats: 6.8 g
Calories: 226 Kcal

610. Harissa Lentil Soup

Preparation Time: 1 hour
Servings: 4-6

Ingredients
- Green lentils: 160g
- Chickpeas: 400g can drained and rinsed
- Onion: 1 large finely chopped
- Leeks: 2 diced
- Parsnips: 2 large finely diced
- Kale: 85g leaves shredded
- Celery: 2 sticks finely diced
- Olive oil: 2 tbsp
- Harissa: 1 tbsp
- Garlic: 2 cloves crushed
- Coriander: a small bunch finely sliced
- Ground cinnamon: 1 tsp
- Ground turmeric: 1 tsp
- Ground coriander: 2 tsp
- Vegetable stock: 1 liter
- Lemons juice: 2 tbsp
- Salt: as per your need
- Pepper: as per your need
- Warmed flatbreads for serving

Directions:
1. Take a large pan and heat olive oil in it
2. Add onion, parsnips, and celery and Cooking Time: them for 10 minutes
3. Then add coriander stalks and garlic and Cooking Time: for a minute and mix well
4. Next add harissa and spices and stir in lentils
5. Pour the stock and boil and then cover and Cooking Time: for 20 minutes and add leeks at 10 minutes
6. Remove the lid and add in kale and chickpeas and stir
7. Sprinkle salt and pepper and pour in lemon juice

8. Top with coriander and serve with warm flatbread

Nutrition:
Carbs: 29.8 g
Protein: 12.4 g
Fats: 7 g
Calories: 253 Kcal

611. Healthy Split Peas Spinach Soup

Preparation Time: 50minutes
Servings: 2

Ingredients
- Split peas: 1 cup
- Spinach: 1 cup
- Water: 6 cups
- Onion: 1 large coarsely chopped
- Garlic: 1 tbsp paste
- Fine sea salt: as per your taste

Directions:
1. Take a large saucepan and add water and bring to boil
2. Add the chopped onions, garlic paste, spinach, split peas and salt and bring to boil
3. Lower the heat to medium and Cooking Time: for 30-35 minutes with partial cover
4. Add the mixture to the high speed blender to make puree
5. Whisk in water if desired
6. Add again to the pan and slowly heat on a low flame for 10-15 minutes
7. Add herbs or spices in between to augment taste

Nutrition:
Carbs: 42.9g
Protein: 18.95g
Fats: 0.95g
Calories: 242.5Kcal

612. Kale And Kidney Beans Soup

Preparation Time: 40 minutes
Servings: 4

Ingredients
- Potatoes: 2 cups peeled and diced
- Kidney beans can: 1 cup rinsed and drained
- Kale: 3 cup chopped
- Onion: 1 medium finely chopped
- Garlic: 4 cloves minced
- Olive oil: 2 tsp
- Ground cumin: ½ tsp
- Ground cinnamon: ½ tsp
- Cayenne pepper: ¼ tsp
- Fresh rosemary leaves: 2 tbsp minced
- Vegetable broth: 4 cups
- Salt and ground black pepper: as per your taste

Directions:
1. Take a large saucepan and add oil
2. On a medium heat, add onions and Cooking Time: for 6-8 minutes
3. Add rosemary, cayenne pepper, and garlic and stir for a minute
4. Add potatoes with salt and pepper and sauté for two minutes
5. Pour vegetable broth and bring to boil
6. Lower the heat and Cooking Time: for 30 minutes till potatoes become soft
7. By using the back of spoon mash a few potatoes
8. Add kale and kidney beans to the soup and again Cooking Time: for 5 minutes till they tender
9. Remove the soup from heat and season with salt and pepper

Nutrition:
Carbs: 48g
Protein: 7.8g
Fats: 10.7g
Calories: 224.8Kcal

613. Kidney Beans Soup

Preparation Time: 30 minutes
Servings: 2

Ingredients
- Kidney beans: 1 cup

- Potato: 1 cup diced
- Vegetable broth: 2 cups
- Olive oil: 1 tbsp
- Garlic: 2 cloves minced
- Onion: 1 medium minced
- Tomatoes: 1 cup chopped
- Cayenne pepper: ¼ tsp
- Carrot: 1 diced
- Dried basil: ½ tsp
- Dried parsley: ½ tsp
- Tomato paste: 1 tbsp
- Salt: as per your need

Directions:
1. Cooking Time: kidney beans by soaking them overnight and boiling them for two hours on medium heat
2. Take a large saucepan and heat oil on medium flame
3. Add onions and Cooking Time: for 3-4 minutes
4. Add garlic and Cooking Time: for a minute and stir
5. Add tomatoes, carrot, kidney beans, basil, oregano, tomato sauce and parsley
6. Stir for around a minute or two
7. Add vegetable broth, cover, and boil
8. Simmer for 20-25 minutes until thicken
9. To give a better texture, mash some kidney beans with the back of the spoon
10. Season with cayenne pepper, salt, and pepper

614. Serve with bread or rice

Nutrition:
Carbs: 47.15g
Protein: 11.95g
Fats: 8.05g
Calories: 312.6Kcal
Pumpkin Chili
Preparation time: 10 minutes
Cooking time: 5 hours
Servings: 6
Ingredients:

- 1 cup pumpkin puree
- 30 ounces canned kidney beans, drained
- 30 ounces canned roasted tomatoes, chopped
- 2 cups water
- 1 cup red lentils, dried
- 1 cup yellow onion, chopped
- 1 jalapeno pepper, chopped
- 1 tablespoon chili powder
- 1 tablespoon cocoa powder
- ½ teaspoon cinnamon powder
- 2 teaspoons cumin, ground
- A pinch of cloves, ground
- Salt and black pepper to the taste
- 2 tomatoes, chopped

Directions:
1. In your slow cooker, mix pumpkin puree with kidney beans, roasted tomatoes, water, lentils, onion, jalapeno, chili powder, cocoa, cinnamon, cumin, cloves, salt and pepper, stir, cover and Cooking Time: on High for 5 hours.
2. Divide into bowls, top with chopped tomatoes and serve hot.
3. Enjoy!

Nutrition: calories 266, fat 6, fiber 4, carbs 12, protein 4

615. 3 Bean Chili

Preparation time: 10 minutes
Cooking time: 8 hours
Servings: 6
Ingredients:

- 15 ounces canned kidney beans, drained
- 30 ounces canned chili beans in sauce
- 15 ounces canned black beans, drained
- 2 green bell peppers, chopped
- 30 ounces canned tomatoes, crushed
- 2 tablespoons chili powder
- 2 yellow onions, chopped
- 2 garlic cloves, minced

- *1 teaspoon oregano, dried*
- *1 tablespoon cumin, ground*
- *Salt and black pepper to the taste*

Directions:
1. In your slow cooker, mix kidney beans with chili beans, black beans, bell peppers, tomatoes, chili powder, onion, garlic, oregano, cumin, salt and pepper, stir, cover and Cooking Time: on Low for 8 hours.
2. Divide into bowls and serve.
3. Enjoy!

Nutrition: *calories 314, fat 6, fiber 5, carbs 14, protein 4*

616. Root Vegetable Chili

Preparation time: 10 minutes
Cooking time: 6 hours
Servings: 12
Ingredients:
- *2 cups turnips, cubed*
- *2 cups rutabagas, cubed*
- *2 cups sweet potatoes, cubed*
- *2 cups parsnips, cubed*
- *1 cup beets, cubed*
- *1 cup carrots, cubed*
- *1 and ½ cups yellow onion, chopped*
- *8 ounces tempeh, rinsed and cubed*
- *28 ounces canned tomatoes, chopped*
- *1 cup veggie stock*
- *15 ounces canned black beans, drained*
- *15 ounces canned kidney beans, drained*
- *Salt and black pepper to the taste*
- *1 teaspoon cumin, ground*
- *1 teaspoon chili powder, ground*
- *A pinch of cayenne pepper*
- *½ teaspoon nutmeg, ground*
- *½ teaspoon sweet paprika*
- *½ cup parsley, chopped*

Directions:
1. In your slow cooker, mix turnips with rutabagas, sweet potatoes, parsnips, beets, carrots, onion, tempeh, tomatoes, stock, black and kidney beans, salt, pepper, cumin, chili powder, cayenne, nutmeg and paprika, stir, cover and Cooking Time: on Low for 6 hours.
2. Add parsley, stir, divide into bowls and serve.
3. Enjoy!

Nutrition: *calories 311, fat 6, fiber 6, carbs 16, protein 6*

617. Brown Rice Soup

Preparation time: 10 minutes
Cooking time: 8 hours
Servings: 6
Ingredients:
- *70 ounces canned black beans, drained*
- *1 cup yellow onion, chopped*
- *1 tablespoon olive oil*
- *2 carrots, chopped*
- *1 jalapeno pepper, chopped*
- *3 garlic cloves, minced*
- *1 teaspoon cumin, ground*
- *1 teaspoon chili powder*
- *1 teaspoon oregano, dried*
- *Salt and black pepper to the taste*
- *2 tablespoons tomato paste*
- *4 cups veggie stock*
- *A splash of Tabasco sauce*
- *2 cups brown rice, already cooked*
- *1 tablespoon cilantro, chopped*

Directions:
1. Drizzle the olive oil on the bottom of your slow cooker.
2. Add black beans, onion, carrots, jalapeno, garlic, cumin, chili, oregano, tomato paste, stock, Tabasco, salt, pepper and rice, stir, cover and Cooking Time: on Low for 8 hours.
3. Add cilantro, stir, ladle into bowls and serve.
4. Enjoy!

Nutrition: *calories 314, fat 5, fiber 8, carbs 18, protein 4*

618. Butternut Squash Soup

Preparation time: 10 minutes
Cooking time: 8 hours
Servings: 6
Ingredients:
- 3 pounds butternut squash, peeled and cubed
- 1 yellow onion, chopped
- 4 cups veggie stock
- 14 ounces coconut milk
- Salt and black pepper to the taste
- 3 tablespoons red curry paste
- 1 tablespoon cilantro, chopped

Directions:
1. In your slow cooker, mix squash with onion, stock, milk, curry paste, salt and pepper, stir, cover and Cooking Time: on Low for 8 hours
2. Blend using an immersion blender, ladle soup into bowls, sprinkle cilantro on top and serve.
3. Enjoy!

Nutrition: calories 237, fat 5, fiber 6, carbs 19, protein 6

619. Green Beans Soup

Preparation time: 10 minutes
Cooking time: 4 hours
Servings: 4
Ingredients:
- 1 pound green beans
- 1 yellow onion, chopped
- 4 carrots, chopped
- 4 garlic cloves, minced
- 1 tablespoon thyme, chopped
- 7 cups veggie stock
- Salt and black pepper to the taste

Directions:
1. In your slow cooker, mix green beans with onion, carrots, garlic, stock, salt and pepper, stir, cover and Cooking Time: on High for 4 hours.
2. Add thyme, stir, ladle soup into bowls and serve.
3. Enjoy!

Nutrition: calories 231, fat 4, fiber 6, carbs 7, protein 5

620. Rich Chickpeas And Lentils Soup

Preparation time: 10 minutes
Cooking time: 5 hours
Servings: 6
Ingredients:
- 1 yellow onion, chopped
- 1 tablespoon olive oil
- 1 tablespoon garlic, minced
- 1 teaspoons sweet paprika
- 1 teaspoon smoked paprika
- Salt and black pepper to the taste
- 1 cup red lentils
- 15 ounces canned chickpeas, drained
- 4 cups veggie stock
- 29 ounces canned tomatoes and juice

Directions:
1. In your slow cooker, mix onion with oil, garlic, sweet and smoked paprika, salt, pepper, lentils, chickpeas, stock and tomatoes, stir, cover and Cooking Time: on High for 5 hours.
2. Ladle into bowls and serve hot.
3. Enjoy!

Nutrition: calories 341, fat 5, fiber 8, carbs 19, protein 3

621. Chard And Sweet Potato Soup

Preparation time: 10 minutes
Cooking time: 8 hours
Servings: 6
Ingredients:
- 1 yellow onion, chopped
- 1 tablespoon olive oil
- 1 carrot, chopped
- 1 celery stalk, chopped
- 1 bunch Swiss chard, leaves torn
- 2 garlic cloves, minced
- 4 sweet potatoes, cubed
- 1 cup brown lentils, dried

- 6 cups veggie stock
- 1 tablespoon coconut aminos
- Salt and black pepper to the taste

Directions:
1. In your slow cooker, mix oil with onion, carrot, celery, chard, garlic, potatoes, lentils, stock, salt, pepper and aminos, stir, cover and Cooking Time: on Low for 8 hours.
2. Ladle soup into bowls and serve right away.
3. Enjoy!

Nutrition: calories 312, fat 5, fiber 7, carbs 10, protein 5

622. Chinese Soup And Ginger Sauce

Preparation time: 10 minutes
Cooking time: 8 hours
Servings: 6
Ingredients:

- 2 celery stalks, chopped
- 1 yellow onion, chopped
- 1 cup carrot, chopped
- 8 ounces water chestnuts
- 8 ounces canned bamboo shoots, drained
- 2 teaspoons garlic, minced
- 2 teaspoons ginger paste
- ½ teaspoon red pepper flakes
- 3 tablespoons coconut aminos
- 1-quart veggie stock
- 2 bunches bok choy, chopped
- 5 ounces white mushrooms, sliced
- 8 ounces tofu, drained and cubed
- 1 ounce snow peas, cut into small pieces
- 6 scallions, chopped

For the ginger sauce:
- 1 teaspoon sesame oil
- 2 tablespoons ginger paste
- 2 tablespoons agave syrup
- 2 tablespoon coconut aminos

Directions:

1. In your slow cooker, mix onion with carrot, celery, chestnuts, bamboo shoots, garlic paste, 2 teaspoons ginger paste, pepper flakes, 3 tablespoons coconut aminos, stock, bok choy, mushrooms, tofu, snow peas and scallions, stir, cover and Cooking Time: on Low for 8 hours.
2. In a bowl, mix 2 tablespoons ginger paste with agave syrup, 2 tablespoons coconut aminos and sesame oil and whisk well.
3. Ladle Chinese soup into bowls, add ginger sauce on top and serve.
4. Enjoy!

Nutrition: calories 300, fat 4, fiber 6, carbs 19, protein 4

623. Corn Cream Soup

Preparation time: 10 minutes
Cooking time: 8 hours and 10 minutes
Servings: 6
Ingredients:

- 1 yellow onion, chopped
- 2 tablespoons olive oil
- 1 red bell pepper, chopped
- 3 cups gold potatoes, chopped
- 4 cups corn kernels
- 4 cups veggie stock
- ½ teaspoon smoked paprika
- 1 teaspoon cumin, ground
- Salt and black pepper to the taste
- 1 cup almond milk
- 2 scallions, chopped

Directions:

1. Heat up a pan with the oil over medium high heat, add onion, stir and Cooking Time: for 5-6 minutes.
2. Transfer this to your slow cooker, add bell pepper, potatoes, 3 cups corn, stock, paprika, cumin, salt and pepper, stir, cover and Cooking Time: on Low for 7 hours and 30 minutes.
3. Blend soup using an immersion blender, add almond milk and blend again.

4. Add the rest of the corn, cover pot and Cooking Time: on Low for 30 minutes more.
5. Ladle soup into bowls, sprinkle scallions on top and serve.
6. Enjoy!

Nutrition: calories 312, fat 4, fiber 6, carbs 12, protein 4

624. Veggie Medley

Preparation time: 10 minutes
Cooking time: 4 hours
Servings: 6
Ingredients:
- 1 tablespoon ginger, grated
- 3 garlic cloves, minced
- 1 date, pitted and chopped
- 1 and ½ teaspoon coriander, ground
- ½ teaspoon dry mustard
- 1 and ¼ teaspoon cumin, ground
- A pinch of salt and black pepper
- ½ teaspoon turmeric powder
- 1 tablespoon white wine vinegar
- ¼ teaspoon cardamom, ground
- 2 carrots, chopped
- 1 yellow onion, chopped
- 4 cups cauliflower florets
- 1 and ½ cups kidney beans, cooked
- 2 zucchinis, chopped
- 6 ounces tomato paste
- 1 green bell pepper, chopped
- 1 cup green peas

Directions:
1. In your slow cooker, mix ginger with garlic, date, coriander, dry mustard, cumin, salt, pepper, turmeric, vinegar, cardamom, carrots, onion, cauliflower, kidney beans, zucchinis, tomato paste, bell pepper and peas, stir, cover and Cooking Time: on High for 4 hours.
2. Divide into bowls and serve hot.
3. Enjoy!

Nutrition: calories 165, fat 2, fiber 10, carbs 32, protein 9

625. Lentils Curry

Preparation time: 10 minutes
Cooking time: 6 hours
Servings: 8
Ingredients:
- 10 ounces spinach
- 2 cups red lentils
- 1 tablespoon garlic, minced
- 15 ounces canned tomatoes, chopped
- 2 cups cauliflower florets
- 1 teaspoon ginger, grated
- 1 yellow onion, chopped
- 4 cups veggie stock
- 2 tablespoons curry paste
- ½ teaspoon cumin, ground
- ½ teaspoon coriander, ground
- 2 teaspoons stevia
- A pinch of salt and black pepper
- ¼ cup cilantro, chopped
- 1 tablespoon lime juice

Directions:
1. In your slow cooker, mix spinach with lentils, garlic, tomatoes, cauliflower, ginger, onion, stock, curry paste, cumin, coriander, stevia, salt, pepper and lime juice, stir, cover and Cooking Time: on Low for 6 hours.
2. Add cilantro, stir, divide into bowls and serve.
3. Enjoy!

Nutrition: calories 105, fat 1, fiber 7, carbs 22, protein 7

626. Lentils Dal

Preparation time: 10 minutes
Cooking time: 5 hours
Servings: 12
Ingredients:
- 6 cups water
- 3 cups red lentils
- 28 ounces canned tomatoes, chopped
- 1 yellow onion, chopped
- 4 garlic cloves, minced

- *1 tablespoon turmeric powder*
- *2 tablespoons ginger, grated*
- *3 cardamom pods*
- *1 bay leaf*
- *2 teaspoons mustard seeds*
- *2 teaspoons onion seeds*
- *2 teaspoons fenugreek seeds*
- *1 teaspoon fennel seeds*
- *Salt and black pepper to the taste*

Directions:

1. In your slow cooker, mix water with lentils, tomatoes, onion, garlic, turmeric, ginger, cardamom, bay leaf, mustard seeds, onion seeds, fenugreek seeds, fennel seeds, salt and pepper, stir, cover and Cooking Time: on High for 5 hours.
2. Divide into bowls and serve.
3. Enjoy!

Nutrition: calories 283, fat 4, fiber 8, carbs 12, protein 4

627. Rich Jackfruit Dish

Preparation time: 10 minutes
Cooking time: 6 hours
Servings: 4
Ingredients:

- *½ cup tamari*
- *40 ounces canned young jackfruit, drained*
- *¼ cup coconut aminos*
- *1 cup mirin*
- *½ cup agave nectar*
- *8 garlic cloves, minced*
- *2 tablespoons ginger, grated*
- *1 yellow onion, chopped*
- *4 tablespoons sesame oil*
- *1 green pear, cored and chopped*
- *½ cup water*

Directions:

1. In your slow cooker, mix tamari with jackfruit, aminos, mirin, agave nectar, garlic, ginger, onion, sesame oil, water and pear, stir, cover and Cooking Time: on Low for 6 hours.
2. Divide into bowls and serve.
3. Enjoy!

Nutrition: calories 160, fat 4, fiber 1, carbs 20, protein 4

628. Vegan Gumbo

Preparation time: 10 minutes
Cooking time: 8 hours
Servings: 4
Ingredients:

- *2 tablespoons olive oil*
- *1 green bell pepper, chopped*
- *1 yellow onion, chopped*
- *2 celery stalks, chopped*
- *3 garlic cloves, minced*
- *15 ounces canned tomatoes, chopped*
- *2 cups veggie stock*
- *8 ounces white mushrooms, sliced*
- *15 ounces canned kidney beans, drained*
- *1 zucchini, chopped*
- *1 tablespoon Cajun seasoning*
- *Salt and black pepper to the taste*

Directions:

1. In your slow cooker, mix oil with bell pepper, onion, celery, garlic, tomatoes, stock, mushrooms, beans, zucchini, Cajun seasoning, salt and pepper, stir, cover and Cooking Time: on Low for 8 hours
2. Divide into bowls and serve hot.
3. Enjoy!

Nutrition: calories 312, fat 4, fiber 7, carbs 19, protein 4

629. Eggplant Salad

Preparation time: 10 minutes
Cooking time: 8 hours
Servings: 4
Ingredients:

- *24 ounces canned tomatoes, chopped*
- *1 red onion, chopped*
- *2 red bell peppers, chopped*
- *1 big eggplant, roughly chopped*
- *1 tablespoon smoked paprika*

- 2 teaspoons cumin, ground
- Salt and black pepper to the taste
- Juice of 1 lemon
- 1 tablespoons parsley, chopped

Directions:
1. In your slow cooker, mix tomatoes with onion, bell peppers, eggplant, smoked paprika, cumin, salt, pepper and lemon juice, stir, cover and Cooking Time: on Low for 8 hours
2. Add parsley, stir, divide into bowls and serve cold as a dinner salad.
3. Enjoy!

Nutrition: calories 251, fat 4, fiber 6, carbs 8, protein 3

630. Corn And Cabbage Soup

Preparation time: 10 minutes
Cooking time: 7 hours
Servings: 4
Ingredients:
- 1 small yellow onion, chopped
- 1 tablespoon olive oil
- 2 garlic cloves, minced
- 1 and ½ cups mushrooms, sliced
- 3 teaspoons ginger, grated
- A pinch of salt and black pepper
- 2 cups corn kernels
- 4 cups red cabbage, chopped
- 4 cups water
- 1 tablespoon nutritional yeast
- 2 teaspoons tomato paste
- 1 teaspoon sesame oil
- 1 teaspoon coconut aminos
- 1 teaspoon sriracha sauce

Directions:
1. In your slow cooker, mix olive oil with onion, garlic, mushrooms, ginger, salt, pepper, corn, cabbage, water, yeast and tomato paste, stir, cover and Cooking Time: on Low for 7 hours.
2. Add sriracha sauce and aminos, stir, leave soup aside for a few minutes, ladle into bowls, drizzle sesame oil all over and serve.
3. Enjoy!

Nutrition: calories 300, fat 4, fiber 4, carbs 10, protein 4

631. Okra Soup

Preparation time: 10 minutes
Cooking time: 5 hours
Servings: 6
Ingredients:
- 1 green bell pepper, chopped
- 1 small yellow onion, chopped
- 3 cups veggie stock
- 3 garlic cloves, minced
- 16 ounces okra, sliced
- 2 cup corn
- 29 ounces canned tomatoes, crushed
- 1 and ½ teaspoon smoked paprika
- 1 teaspoon marjoram, dried
- 1 teaspoon thyme, dried
- 1 teaspoon oregano, dried
- Salt and black pepper to the taste

Directions:
1. In your slow cooker, mix bell pepper with onion, stock, garlic, okra, corn, tomatoes, smoked paprika, marjoram, thyme, oregano, salt and pepper, stir, cover and Cooking Time: on High for 5 hours.
2. Ladle into bowls and serve.
3. Enjoy!

Nutrition: calories 243, fat 4, fiber 6, carbs 10, protein 3

632. Carrot Soup

Preparation time: 10 minutes
Cooking time: 5 hours
Servings: 6
Ingredients:
- 2 potatoes, cubed
- 3 pounds carrots, cubed
- 1 yellow onion, chopped
- 1-quart veggie stock
- Salt and black pepper to the taste
- 1 teaspoon thyme, dried

- *3 tablespoons coconut milk*
- *2 teaspoons curry powder*
- *3 tablespoons vegan cheese, crumbled*
- *A handful pistachios, chopped*

Directions:
1. *In your slow cooker, mix onion with potatoes, carrots, stock, salt, pepper, thyme and curry powder, stir, cover, Cooking Time: on High for 1 hour and on Low for 4 hours.*
2. *Add coconut milk, stir, blend soup using an immersion blender, ladle soup into bowls, sprinkle vegan cheese and pistachios on top and serve.*
3. *Enjoy!*

Nutrition: *calories 241, fat 4, fiber 7, carbs 10, protein 4*

633. Baby Carrots And Coconut Soup

Preparation time: *10 minutes*
Cooking time: *7 hours*
Servings: *6*
Ingredients:

- *1 sweet potato, cubed*
- *2 pounds baby carrots, peeled*
- *2 teaspoons ginger paste*
- *1 yellow onion, chopped*
- *4 cups veggie stock*
- *2 teaspoons curry powder*
- *Salt and black pepper to the taste*
- *14 ounces coconut milk*

Directions:
1. *In your slow cooker, mix sweet potato with baby carrots, ginger paste, onion, stock, curry powder, salt and pepper, stir, cover and Cooking Time: on High for 7 hours.*
2. *Add coconut milk, blend soup using an immersion blender, divide soup into bowls and serve.*
3. *Enjoy!*

Nutrition: *calories 100, fat 2, fiber 4, carbs 18, protein 3*

634. Chinese Carrot Cream

Preparation time: *10 minutes*
Cooking time: *5 hours*
Servings: *6*
Ingredients:

- *1 tablespoon coconut oil*
- *3 garlic cloves, minced*
- *1 yellow onion, chopped*
- *1 pound carrots, chopped*
- *2 cups veggie stock*
- *2 cups water*
- *Salt and black pepper to the taste*
- *1/3 cup peanut butter*
- *2 teaspoons chili sauce*

Directions:
1. *In your slow cooker, mix oil with garlic, onion, carrots, stock, water, salt, pepper and chili sauce, stir, cover and Cooking Time: on High for 4 hours and 30 minutes.*
2. *Add peanut butter, stir, cover, Cooking Time: soup for 30 minutes more, blend using an immersion blender, divide soup into bowls and serve.*
3. *Enjoy!*

Nutrition: *calories 224, fat 14, fiber 6, carbs 18, protein 7*

SOUPS, STEWS & CHILIES

635. Cheesy Broccoli And Potato Soup

Preparation Time: 40 Minutes
Servings: 2
Ingredients:

- 2½ lb of potatoes, peeled and then chopped
- 3 carrots, chopped
- 1 broccoli head, chopped
- 4 cups water
- 2 tsp chili powder
- 1 tsp garlic powder
- ½ tsp smoked paprika
- 1 tsp turmeric
- 2 tsp salt
- 1/3 cup nutritional yeast
- ½ lemon, squeezed

Directions:

1. Place broccoli head on a trivet in iPot along with 1 cup water. Cover the pot with lid, switch on manual button and set the timer for 3 minutes. Once done, immediately release the steam. Remove broccoli, chop into small pieces.
2. Clean inner pot. Add potatoes to Instant Pot. Add carrots and remaining ingredients except for lemon juice and nutritional yeast.
3. Switch on manual button for 10 minutes over high pressure. Set steam release handle to 'sealing'. Once timer beeps, allow pressure to release naturally for 10 minutes and set handle to 'venting' to release any remaining steam.
4. Using an immersion blender, blend the soup until smooth. Add lemon juice and nutritional yeast and blend it again quickly.
5. Add in chopped broccoli now and just mix with a spoon and serve this!

636. Split Peas & Carrot Soup

Preparation Time: 35 Minutes
Servings: 3
Ingredients:

- 2 cups of green split peas
- 3-4 medium-sized carrots, chopped
- 1/2 of a large yellow onion, chopped
- 2 garlic cloves, minced
- 1/2 tsp of ground black pepper
- 4 cups of water
- 1 tbsp of veggie base or 1 bouillon cube (or 3 cups water with 3 cups veggie broth

Directions:

1. Add onion and garlic to Instant Pot along with 1/3 cup water and Switch the sautée button. Allow it to sautée for about 5 minutes till onions turn translucent.
2. Combine rest of the ingredients (except pepperin Instant Pot. Cover the pot with lid and switch manual button to 7 minutes over high pressure. Set steam release handle to 'sealing'.
3. When time is up, allow pressure to release naturally for 15 minutes. Let the soup cool down for some time. Add black pepper and using an immersion blender blend the soup so that still some chunks are left.
4. Add an additional ½ cup of water, if the soup is too thick.
5. Serve hot and enjoy.

637. Black Beans Soup

This black bean soup can be used as a delicious topping over steamed potatoes or rice.
Preparation Time: 70 Minutes
Servings: 2
Ingredients:

- 3 cups dry black beans, rinsed
- 1 carrot, chopped
- 1 yellow onion, diced

- *3 celery stalks, minced*
- *4½ cups water*
- *2 tsp vegetable base (or use 2 cups water with 2 cups veggie broth*
- *6 garlic cloves, minced*
- *1 tbsp cumin*
- *1 tsp cayenne pepper*
- *1 tsp chili powder*
- *Juice of 1 lime*
- *¼ cup cilantro*

Directions:
1. Rinse and drain beans.
2. Except for cilantro and lime juice, add all ingredients to Instant Pot and stir well. Set the vent on top to 'sealing' and cover with lid. Switch on manual button for 30 minutes over high pressure.
3. Once done, allow the steam to release naturally for about 15-20 minutes. Set the steam release handle to 'venting'.
4. Add cilantro and lime juice. use an immersion blender to lightly blend the soup.
5. Optionally some avocado, salsa or tortilla chips can be added to accompany this great soup!

638. Lentil And Mixed Vegetable Soup

Preparation Time: 40 Minutes
Servings: 3
Ingredients:
- *1 cup green lentils*
- *5 potatoes, chopped*
- *2 celery ribs, chopped*
- *2 carrots, chopped*
- *1 yellow onion, chopped*
- *2 bay leaves*
- *1 can (14.5 fl oz of diced tomatoes*
- *1 cup green peas (frozen or canned*
- *1 cup kale or spinach, finely chopped (fresh or frozen*
- *3½ cups water*
- *2 tsp black pepper*
- *3 garlic cloves, minced*
- *2 tsp vegetable base (or use 2 cups water with 2 cups veggie broth*

Directions:
1. Chop potatoes, celery, carrots, onion and mince garlic and add them to Instant Pot along with rest of ingredients except for green peas and kale or spinach.
2. Cover with lid and set iPot manual for 10 minutes over high pressure. Once done allow steam to release naturally for about 15 minutes. Then release remaining steam using steam release handle. Open the lid.
3. Add green peas and kale or spinach. Stir the whole thing well. Let Instant Pot stay in 'Keep Warm' setting for around 10 minutes.
4. Remove bay leaves and serve the soup. When serving, add some salt or pepper to taste.

639. Pumpkin Stew

Preparation Time: 45 Minutes
Servings: 4
Ingredients:
- *21 oz sweet pumpkin, chopped*
- *2 medium-sized onions, peeled and finely chopped*
- *1 garlic clove*
- *1 red pepper, finely chopped*
- *1 tbsp of fresh tomato sauce*
- *½ tbsp of chili powder*
- *2 bay leaves*
- *2 cups of red wine*
- *1 cup of water*
- *1 tsp of thyme, dry*
- *Salt and pepper to taste*
- *Oil for frying*

Directions:
1. Plug in your instant pot and press "Sautee" button. Add chopped onions and stir-fry for 2 minutes. Add finely chopped red pepper,

tomato sauce, and chili powder.
2. Continue to Cooking Time: until the pepper has softened.
3. Add the remaining ingredients and securely lock the lid. Adjust the steam release handle and set the timer for 8 minutes. Cooking Time: on high pressure.
4. When done, press "Cancel" button and release the steam naturally.
5. Enjoy!

640. Bean Onion Stew

Preparation Time: 30 Minutes
Servings: 6
Ingredients:
- 1 pound of fresh beans
- 1 large onion, chopped
- 4 cloves of garlic, finely chopped
- 3 ½ oz of olives, pitted
- 1 tbsp of ginger powder
- 1 tbsp of turmeric
- 1 tbsp of salt
- 4 cups of water

Directions:
1. Plug in your instant pot and press "Sautee" button. Heat up the oil and add onions and garlic. Stir-fry for 5 minutes, or until onions translucent.
2. Now, add the remaining ingredients and close the lid. Press "Manual" button and set the timer for 15 minutes. Adjust the steam release and Cooking Time: on high pressure.
3. When done, press "Cancel" button and release the pressure naturally.
4. Open the pot and serve warm.
5. Enjoy!

641. Curried Carrot Kale Soup

Preparation Time: 40 Minutes
Servings: 2
Ingredients:
- 2 cups kale, finely chopped (frozen or fresh
- 8 carrots, chopped
- 5 potatoes, chopped
- ½ yellow onion, chopped
- 3 garlic cloves, minced
- ¼ cup peanut butter, powdered
- 1 tsp cayenne pepper
- 1 tbsp curry powder
- 4 cups water
- 2 tsp of vegetable base (or use 2 cups water with 2 cups veggie broth

Directions:
1. Add garlic and onion to Instant Pot along with ¼ cup water and Switch on 'Sautée' button. Sauté garlic and onions for 5 minutes.
2. Add peanut butter, cayenne and curry powder and stir. Add bit water if needed. Sauté this for 2 more minutes.
3. Except for the kale, add remaining ingredients, cover with lid and switch on manual button for 8 minutes on high pressure.
4. When timer beeps, allow natural pressure release for 10-15 minutes. Set steam release handle to 'venting'. Open the lid.
5. Using an immersion blender, blend the soup until desired consistency.
6. Add chopped kale and stir again.

642. Italian Plum Tomato Soup

Preparation Time: 10 Minutes
Servings: 6
Ingredients:
- 1 (28-ouncecan Italian plum tomatoes
- ½ cup nondairy milk
- 1 large yellow onion, chopped
- 1 teaspoon dried marjoram
- 1 (14-ouncecan crushed tomatoes
- 1 cup vegetable broth
- 2 tablespoons tomato paste
- 1 teaspoon dried basil
- 1 teaspoon brown sugar
- ¼ cup oil-packed sun-dried tomatoes, chopped

- 2 garlic cloves, minced
- Salt and freshly ground black pepper

Directions:
1. In an instant pot add the oil with garlic, onion and tomato paste.
2. Cooking Time: for 1 minute and add the marjoram, basil, brown sugar and Cooking Time: for another minute.
3. Add the rest of the ingredients and mix well.
4. Add the lid and Cooking Time: for about 5 minutes.
5. Transfer the mix to a blender.
6. Blend until smooth and serve warm.

643. Balsamic Hatchet Soup

Preparation Time: 20 Minutes
Servings: 4

A hatchet soup is one where you combine any number of different ingredients, and is great for using up a medley of vegetables.

Ingredients:
- 3 shallots, halved
- 3 garlic cloves, minced
- 6 ounces green beans, trimmed and halved
- 1 red or yellow bell pepper, seeded and cut into ¼-inch strips
- 8 ounces mushrooms, halved, quartered, or sliced
- 3 small zucchini, halved lengthwise and cut into ¼-inch slices
- 2 small yellow summer squash, halved lengthwise and cut into ¼-inch slices
- 1½ cups cherry tomatoes, halved
- ½ cup balsamic reduction
- 3 tablespoons chopped fresh basil
- 2 tablespoons chopped fresh flat-leaf parsley
- 2 teaspoons olive oil
- Salt and freshly ground black pepper

Directions:
1. Put the oil in your instant pot and warm.
2. Add the shallots and soften for 3 minutes.
3. Add the garlic and Cooking Time: another minute.
4. Add the green beans, bell pepper, mushrooms, zucchini, and yellow squash.
5. Seal and Cooking Time: on Stew for 10 minutes.
6. Depressurize quickly, add the tomato, basil, and parsley.
7. Reseal and Cooking Time: on Stew 2 minutes.
8. Depressurize naturally and serve drizzled with balsamic reduction.

644. Pearl Barley Tomato Mushroom Soup

Preparation Time: 6 Minutes
Servings: 6

Ingredients:
- 1(14-ouncecan crushed tomatoes
- ½cup pearl barley
- ½ounce dried porcini mushrooms, rinsed
- 1ounces cremini mushrooms, sliced
- 2teaspoons olive oil (optional
- 1large carrot, chopped
- 5cups vegetable broth
- 1large yellow onion, chopped
- Salt and freshly ground black pepper
- 1teaspoon dried thyme
- 4ounces shiitake mushrooms, stemmed and sliced
- 2tablespoons soy sauce

Directions:
1. Add the oil in your instant pot.
2. Toss the onion and make it caramelized.
3. Add the remaining ingredients.
4. Mix well and Cooking Time: for 5 minutes with the lid on.
5. Serve warm.

645. Sweet Potato Soup

Preparation Time: 20 Minutes

Servings: 2
Ingredients:
- *2 large sweet potatoes, peeled and chopped*
- *1 medium carrot, sliced*
- *1 medium onion, finely chopped*
- *2 cups vegetable broth*
- *2 garlic cloves, finely chopped*
- *1 tsp salt*
- *½ tsp black pepper, freshly ground*
- *1 tbsp olive oil*

Directions:
1. *Plug in your instant pot and press "Sautee" button. Grease the stainless steel insert and add potatoes, onions, and garlic. Stir-fry for 3-4 minutes, or until onions translucent.*
2. *Now, add the remaining ingredients and stir well until combined. Close the lid and adjust the steam release handle. Press "Manual" button and set the timer for 7 minutes. Cooking Time: on high pressure.*
3. *When done, press "Cancel" button and perform a quick release. Let it stand for 10 minutes before opening.*
4. *Enjoy!*

646. Corn Chowder

Preparation Time: 5 Minutes
Servings: 4
Ingredients:
- *4cups fresh corn kernels*
- *1onion, chopped*
- *2chipotle chilies in adobo, minced*
- *Salt and black pepper*
- *1celery rib, chopped*
- *4cups vegetable broth*
- *1Potato, peeled and diced*

Directions:
1. *Add the corn kernels, onion, chiles in adobo, seasoning, celery rib, and potato in your instant pot.*
2. *Pour in the broth and mix well.*
3. *Cooking Time: for 10 minutes.*
4. *Use a hand blender to blend the mixture.*
5. *Serve warm.*

647. Onion Soup

Preparation Time: 5 Minutes
Servings: 6
Ingredients:
- *4slices French or Italian bread, cubed*
- *1teaspoon vegan Worcestershire sauce*
- *2tablespoons olive oil*
- *½teaspoon dried thyme*
- *5cups vegetable broth*
- *5onions, sliced*
- *Salt and black pepper*

Directions:
1. *Add the oil in your instant pot.*
2. *Add the onion and toss for 30 seconds.*
3. *Add the rest of the ingredients.*
4. *Cover and Cooking Time: for about 3 minutes.*
5. *Serve hot.*

648. Baby Spinach Coconut Soup

Preparation Time: 5 Minutes
Servings: 4
Ingredients:
- *2jalapeños, seeded and minced*
- *8ounces baby spinach*
- *1onion, chopped*
- *½teaspoon fresh thyme*
- *3garlic cloves, chopped*
- *1red bell pepper, seeded and chopped*
- *4cups vegetable broth*
- *¼teaspoon ground allspice*
- *Salt and black pepper*
- *1(14.5-ouncecan diced tomatoes, drained*
- *1(13.5-ouncecan coconut milk*
- *1½cups cooked dark red kidney beans*
- *2potatoes, peeled and diced*

Directions:

1. Toss the garlic and onion in an instant pot for 30 seconds.
2. Add the vegetables, kidney beans, coconut milk, broth, spices, and herbs.
3. Mix well and Cooking Time: for 4 minutes with the lid on.
4. Serve hot.

649. Cabbage Carrot Beet Soup

Preparation Time: 10 Minutes
Servings: 6
Ingredients:

- 1carrot, shredded
- 5cups vegetable broth
- 2tablespoons fresh lemon juice
- ¼cup minced fresh dill
- 1teaspoon light brown sugar
- ½teaspoon caraway seeds
- 1onion, minced
- 1Potato, peeled and minced
- Salt and black pepper
- 3cups shredded cabbage
- 4beets, peeled and minced
- 1teaspoon dried thyme

Directions:

1. Add the cabbage, carrot, potato, beets in your instant pot.
2. Add the sugar, dill, and the rest of the ingredients.
3. Cooking Time: for 6 minutes with the lid on.
4. Serve hot.

650. Tomato Tortilla Soup

Preparation Time: 5 Minutes
Servings: 4
Ingredients:

- 1jalapeño chile, seeded and minced
- 1onion, minced
- ½cup chopped fresh cilantro leaves
- 2tablespoons tomato paste
- 3cups lightly crushed tortilla chips
- 3garlic cloves, minced
- 1(14-ouncecan diced tomatoes
- 1teaspoon ground cumin
- 5cups vegetable broth
- Salt and black pepper
- 3teaspoons chipotle chiles in adobo, minced

Directions:

1. Add all the ingredients in an instant pot except the chips.
2. Cover and Cooking Time: for 3 minutes.
3. Add the chips and Cooking Time: for another 2 minutes.
4. Serve hot.

651. Basil Marjoram Tomato Soup

Preparation Time: 10 Minutes
Servings: 6
Ingredients:

- ¼cup oil-packed sun-dried tomatoes, chopped
- 1(28-ouncecan tomatoes
- 1teaspoon dried marjoram
- 2teaspoons olive oil (optional
- 2tablespoons tomato paste
- 2garlic cloves, minced
- 1teaspoon dried basil
- 1 cup vegetable broth
- 1(14-ouncecan crushed tomatoes
- 1onion, chopped
- 1teaspoon brown sugar
- Salt and black pepper

Directions:

1. In your instant pot add all the ingredients one by one.
2. Mix well using a wooden spoon.
3. Cooking Time: for 10 Minutes with the lid on.
4. Add the mixture to a blender and blend until smooth.
5. Serve hot.

652. Porcini Mushroom And Barley Soup

Preparation Time: 10 Minutes
Servings: 6

Ingredients:
- 4 ounces shiitake mushrooms, stemmed and sliced
- ½ cup pearl barley
- ½ ounce dried porcini mushrooms, rinsed
- 1 onion, chopped
- 1 (14-ounce can crushed tomatoes
- 1 large carrot, chopped
- 1 teaspoon dried thyme
- 5 cups vegetable broth
- 8 ounces mushrooms, sliced
- 2 tablespoons soy sauce
- 2 teaspoons olive oil (optional
- Salt and black pepper

Directions:
1. In your instant pot add the mushroom, broth, seasoning, herbs, spices, and vegetables.
2. Add the pearl barley and mix well.
3. Cover with lid and Cooking Time: for about 8 minutes.
4. Serve hot.

653. Tofu Mushroom Kombu Soup

Preparation Time: 10 Minutes
Servings: 4

Ingredients:
- 1 pound cabbage, thinly sliced
- 8 ounces extra-firm tofu, cut into ½-inch dice
- 4 cups water
- 4 ounces shiitake mushrooms, sliced
- 1 (1-inch piece peeled fresh ginger
- ½ cup soy sauce
- 1 ounce enoki mushrooms, trimmed
- 1 (3-inch piece kombu sea vegetable
- 1 bunch scallions, sliced
- 2 ounces cellophane noodles
- ½ cup mirin
- 1 carrot, sliced
- Salt
- 8 ounces seitan, sliced

Directions:
1. In your instant pot add ginger, water, soy sauce, kombu, and mirin.
2. Mix well and Cooking Time: for 2 minutes.
3. Discard the ginger and kombu and add the rest of the ingredients.
4. Mix well and cover with lid.
5. Cooking Time: for 5 minutes with the lid on.
6. Use a hand blender to blend well.
7. Serve hot.

654. Basmati Rice Coconut Milk Soup

Preparation Time: 10 Minutes
Servings: 6

Ingredients:
- 3 cups cooked brown basmati rice
- 1 sweet potato, peeled and diced
- 1 (13-ounce can coconut milk
- 1 red bell pepper, seeded and chopped
- 1 onion, chopped
- 4 cups vegetable broth
- 1 tablespoon curry powder
- ½ teaspoon cayenne pepper, or to taste
- 3 garlic cloves, minced
- 1½ cups cooked chickpeas
- 2 teaspoons grated fresh ginger
- 1 teaspoon ground coriander
- 1 Apple, peeled, cored, and chopped
- 2 tablespoons fresh lemon juice
- Salt and black pepper
- 1 green bell pepper, seeded and chopped

Directions:
1. In your instant pot add the ginger, garlic and onion and toss for a minute.
2. Add the spices, and vegetables. Add the rest of the ingredients and stir well.
3. Cover and Cooking Time: for about 5 minutes.
4. Transfer the mixture to a blender

and blend until smooth.
5. *Serve hot.*

655. Rice Noodle Soup

Preparation Time: 10 Minutes
Servings: 4
Ingredients:

- 8ounces dried rice noodles
- 6cups vegetable broth
- 1½tablespoons fresh lime juice
- 3whole cloves
- 2tablespoons barley miso paste
- 3whole star anise
- 1fresh ginger, minced
- 1small yellow onion, minced
- 3garlic cloves, minced
- 6ounces seitan, sliced
- 3tablespoons hoisin sauce
- 3tablespoons soy sauce

Directions:
1. *In a cloth add the ginger, cloves, star anise and tie it tightly.*
2. *Add all the ingredients in your instant pot.*
3. *Add the ginger cloth to the pot.*
4. *Cover with lid and Cooking Time: for 7 minutes.*
5. *Discard the ginger cloth and serve hot.*

656. Indian Red Split Lentil Soup

Preparation Time: 5 Minutes
Cooking Time: 50 Minutes
Servings: 4
Ingredients

- 1 cup red split lentils
- 2 cups water
- 1 teaspoon curry powder plus 1 tablespoon, divided, or 5 coriander seeds (optional
- 1 teaspoon coconut oil, or 1 tablespoon water or vegetable broth
- 1 red onion, diced
- 1 tablespoon minced fresh ginger
- 2 cups peeled and cubed sweet potato
- 1 cup sliced zucchini
- Freshly ground black pepper
- Sea salt
- 3 to 4 cups vegetable stock, or water
- 1 to 2 teaspoons toasted sesame oil
- 1 bunch spinach, chopped
- Toasted sesame seeds

Directions
1. *Preparing the Ingredients.*
2. *Put the lentils in a large pot with 2 cups water, and 1 teaspoon of the curry powder. Bring the lentils to a boil, then reduce the heat and simmer, covered, for about 10 minutes, until the lentils are soft.*
3. *Meanwhile, heat a large pot over medium heat. Add the coconut oil and sauté the onion and ginger until soft, about 5 minutes. Add the sweet potato and leave it on the heat about 10 minutes to soften slightly, then add the zucchini and Cooking Time: until it starts to look shiny, about 5 minutes. Add the remaining 1 tablespoon curry powder, pepper, and salt, and stir the vegetables to coat.*
4. *Add the vegetable stock, bring to a boil, then turn down to simmer and cover. Let the vegetables slowly Cooking Time: for 20 to 30 minutes, or until the sweet potato is tender.*
5. *Add the fully cooked lentils to the soup. Add another pinch salt, the toasted sesame oil, and the spinach. Stir, allowing the spinach to wilt before removing the pot from the heat.*
6. *Serve garnished with toasted sesame seeds.*

Nutrition: *Calories: 319; Protein: 16g; Total fat: 8g; Carbohydrates: 50g; Fiber: 10g*

657. Light Vegetable Broth

Preparation Time: 10 Minutes
Cooking Time: Time:1 Hour 30 Minutes
Servings: About 6 Cups

Ingredients

- 1 tablespoon olive oil
- 2 medium onions, quartered
- 2 medium carrots, chopped
- 1 celery rib, chopped
- 2 garlic cloves, unpeeled and crushed
- 8 cups water
- 2 teaspoons soy sauce
- 1/3 cup coarsely chopped fresh parsley
- 1 bay leaf
- 1 teaspoon salt
- 1/2 teaspoon black peppercorns

Directions

1. In a large stockpot, heat the oil over medium heat. Add the onions, carrots, celery, and garlic. Cover and Cooking Time: until softened, about 10 minutes. Stir in the water, soy sauce, parsley, bay leaf, salt, and peppercorns. Bring to a boil and then reduce heat to low and simmer, uncovered, for 1 1/2 hours.
2. Set aside to cool, then strain through a fine-mesh sieve into a large bowl or pot, pressing against the solids with the back of a spoon to release all the liquid. Discard solids. Cool broth completely, then portion into tightly covered containers and refrigerate for up to 4 days or freeze for up to 3 months.

658. Roasted Vegetable Broth

Preparation Time: 5 Minutes
Cooking Time: 1 hour 30 Minutes •
Servings: About 6 Cups

Ingredients

- 1 large onion, thickly sliced
- 2 large carrots, chopped
- 1 celery rib, chopped
- 1 large potato, unpeeled and chopped
- 3 garlic cloves, unpeeled and crushed
- 2 tablespoons olive oil
- Salt and freshly ground black pepper
- 8 cups water
- 1/2 cup coarsely chopped fresh parsley
- 2 bay leaves
- 1/2 teaspoon black peppercorns
- 1 tablespoon soy sauce

Directions

1. Preheat the oven to 425°F. In a lightly oiled 9 x 13-inch baking pan, place the onion, carrots, celery, potato, and garlic. Drizzle with the oil and sprinkle with salt and pepper to taste. Roast the vegetables until they are slightly browned, turning once, about 30 minutes total. Set aside for 10 minutes to cool slightly.
2. Place the roasted vegetables in a large stockpot. Add the water, parsley, bay leaves, peppercorns, soy sauce, and salt to taste. Bring to a boil and then reduce heat to low and simmer, uncovered, until the broth has reduced slightly and is a deep golden color, about 1 hour.
3. Set aside to cool, then strain through a fine-mesh sieve into a large bowl or pot, pressing against the solids with the back of a spoon to release all the liquid. Discard solids. Cool broth completely, then portion into tightly covered containers and refrigerate for up to 4 days or freeze for up to 3 months.

659. Root Vegetable Broth

Preparation Time: 5 Minutes • Cooking Time: Time:1 Hour 38 Minutes •
Servings: About 6 Cups

Ingredients

- 1 tablespoon olive oil
- 1 large onion, coarsely chopped
- 2 medium carrots, coarsely chopped
- 2 medium parsnips, coarsely chopped
- 1 medium turnip, coarsely chopped
- 8 cups water
- 1 medium white potato, unpeeled and quartered
- 3 garlic cloves, unpeeled and crushed
- ¾ cup coarsely chopped fresh parsley

- 2 bay leaves
- 1/2 teaspoon black peppercorns
- 1 teaspoon salt

Directions

1. In a large stockpot, heat the oil over medium heat. Add the onion, carrots, parsnips, and turnip. Cover and Cooking Time: until softened, about 8 minutes. Stir in the water. Add the potato, garlic, parsley, bay leaves, peppercorns, and salt. Bring to a boil and then reduce heat to low and simmer, uncovered, for 1 1/2 hours.
2. Set aside to cool, then strain through a fine-mesh sieve into a large bowl or pot, pressing against the solids with the back of a spoon to release all the liquid. Discard solids. Cool broth completely, then portion into tightly covered containers and refrigerate for up to 4 days or freeze for up to 3 months.

660. Mushroom Vegetable Broth

Preparation Time: 5 Minutes • Cooking Time: Time:1 Hour 37 Minutes • Servings: About 6 Cups

Ingredients

- 1 tablespoon olive oil
- 1 medium onion, unpeeled and quartered
- 1 medium carrot, coarsely chopped
- 1 celery rib with leaves, coarsely chopped
- 8 ounces white mushrooms, lightly rinsed, patted dry, and coarsely chopped
- 5 dried shiitake or porcini mushrooms, soaked in 2 cups hot water, drained, soaking liquid strained and reserved
- 3 garlic cloves, unpeeled and crushed
- 1/2 cup coarsely chopped fresh parsley
- 2 bay leaves
- 1/2 teaspoon black peppercorns

- 1 teaspoon salt
- 5 cups water

Directions

1. In a large stockpot, heat the oil over medium heat. Add the onion, carrot, celery, and white mushrooms. Cover and Cooking Time: until softened, about 7 minutes. Stir in the softened dried mushrooms and the reserved soaking liquid, along with the garlic, parsley, bay leaves, peppercorns, salt, and water. Bring to a boil and then reduce heat to low and simmer, uncovered, for 1 1/2 hours.
2. Set aside to cool, then strain through a fine-mesh sieve into a large bowl or pot, pressing against the solids with the back of a spoon to release all the liquid. Discard solids. Cool broth completely, then portion into tightly covered containers and refrigerate for up to 4 days or freeze for up to 3 months.

661. Jamaican Red Bean Stew

Preparation Time: 10 Minutes
Cooking Time: 40 Minutes
Servings: 4

Ingredients

- 1 tablespoon olive oil
- 1 medium yellow onion, chopped
- 2 large carrots, cut into 1/4-inch slices
- 2 garlic cloves, minced
- 1 large sweet potato, peeled and cut into 1/4-inch dice
- 1/4 teaspoon crushed red pepper
- 3 cups cooked or 2 (15.5-ouncecans dark red kidney beans, drained and rinsed
- 1 (14.5-ouncecan diced tomatoes, drained
- 1 teaspoon hot or mild curry powder
- 1 teaspoon dried thyme
- 1/4 teaspoon ground allspice
- 1/2 teaspoon salt
- 1/4 teaspoon freshly ground black

pepper
- 1/2 cup water
- 1 (13.5-ounce can unsweetened coconut milk

Directions
1. In a large saucepan, heat the oil over medium heat. Add the onion and carrots, cover, and Cooking Time: until softened, 5 minutes.
2. Add the garlic, sweet potato, and crushed red pepper. Stir in the kidney beans, tomatoes, curry powder, thyme, allspice, salt, and black pepper.
3. Stir in the water, cover, and simmer until the vegetables are tender, about 30 minutes. Stir in the coconut milk and simmer, uncovered, for 10 minutes to blend flavors and thicken the sauce. If a thicker sauce is desired, puree some of the vegetables with an immersion blender. Serve immediately.

662. Greens And Beans Soup

Preparation Time: 15 Minutes
Cooking Time: 0 Minutes
Servings: 4

Ingredients
- 1 tablespoon olive oil
- 1 medium onion, chopped
- 3 large garlic cloves, minced
- 1 1/2 cups cooked or 1 (15.5-ounce can cannellini beans, drained and rinsed
- 1 1/2 cups cooked or 1 (15.5-ounce can dark red kidney beans, drained and rinsed
- 5 cups vegetable broth, homemade (see Light Vegetable Broth or store-bought, or water
- 1/4 teaspoon crushed red pepper
- Salt and freshly ground black pepper
- 3 cups coarsely chopped stemmed Swiss chard
- 3 cups coarsely chopped stemmed kale

Directions
1. In a large soup pot, heat the oil over medium heat. Add the onion, cover, and Cooking Time: until softened, about 5 minutes. Add the garlic and cook, uncovered, 1 minute.
2. Stir in the beans, broth, crushed red pepper, and salt and black pepper to taste and bring to a boil. Reduce heat to a simmer, uncovered, and stir in the greens. Continue to Cooking Time: until the greens are tender, 15 to 20 minutes. Serve hot.

663. Hearty Chili

Preparation Time: 10 Minutes
Cooking Time: 15 Minutes
Servings: 4

Ingredients
- 1 onion, diced
- 2 to 3 garlic cloves, minced
- 1 teaspoon olive oil, or 1 to 2 tablespoons water, vegetable broth, or red wine
- 1 (28-ounce can tomatoes
- 1/4 cup tomato paste, or crushed tomatoes
- 1 (14-ounce can kidney beans, rinsed and drained, or 1 1/2 cups cooked
- 2 to 3 teaspoons chili powder
- 1/4 teaspoon sea salt
- 1/4 cup fresh cilantro, or parsley leaves

Directions
1. Preparing the Ingredients.
2. In a large pot, sauté the onion and garlic in the oil, about 5 minutes. Once they're soft, add the tomatoes, tomato paste, beans, and chili powder. Season with the salt.
3. Let simmer for at least 10 minutes, or as long as you like. The flavors will get better the longer it simmers, and it's even better as leftovers.
4. Garnish with cilantro and serve.

Nutrition: Calories: 160; Protein: 8g; Total fat: 3g; Saturated fat: 11g; Carbohydrates:

29g; Fiber: 7g

664. Golden Beet Soup With A Twist

Preparation Time: 5 Minutes
Cooking Time: 50 Minutes
Servings: 6

Ingredients

- *2 tablespoons olive oil*
- *1 medium yellow onion, finely chopped*
- *1 medium carrot, finely chopped*
- *4 medium golden beets, peeled and diced*
- *1 small yellow bell pepper, chopped*
- *1 medium Yukon Gold potato, diced*
- *5 cups vegetable broth, homemade (see Light Vegetable Broth or store-bought, or water*
- *1 teaspoon dried thyme*
- *Salt and freshly ground black pepper*
- *1 tablespoon fresh lemon juice*
- *2 tablespoons minced fresh dillweed or 1 1/2 teaspoons dried, for garnish*

Directions

1. *In a large soup pot, heat the oil over medium heat. Add the onion and carrot. Cover and Cooking Time: until softened, 5 minutes. Add the beets, bell pepper, and potato and cook, uncovered, stirring, for 1 minute. Stir in the broth, sugar, and thyme and season with salt and black pepper to taste. Cooking Time: until the vegetables are tender, about 45 minutes.*
2. *Serve hot or, alternately, set aside to cool, then refrigerate until chilled. Just before serving, stir in the lemon juice and garnish with the dill.*

665. Asian-Inspired Chili

Preparation Time: 15 Minutes
Cooking Time: 20 Minutes
Servings: 4

Ingredients

- *1 teaspoon sesame oil or 2 teaspoons vegetable broth or water*
- *1 cup diced onion*
- *3 teaspoons minced garlic (about 3 cloves*
- *1 cup chopped carrots*
- *2 cups shredded green or napa cabbage*
- *1 (14.5-ouncecan small red beans or adzuki beans, drained and rinsed*
- *1 (14.5-ouncefire-roasted diced tomatoes*
- *2 cups vegetable broth*
- *2 tablespoons red miso paste or tomato paste*
- *2 tablespoons hot water*
- *1 tablespoon hot sauce*
- *2 teaspoons to 1 tablespoon tamari or soy sauce (optional*

Directions

1. *Preparing the Ingredients.*
2. *In a large pot, over medium-high heat, heat the sesame oil. Add the onion, garlic, and carrot. Sauté for 5 minutes, until the onions are translucent. Add the cabbage, beans, tomatoes, and broth, and stir well. Bring to a boil.*
3. *Cover, reduce the heat to low, and simmer for 15 minutes.*
4. *In a measuring cup, whisk the miso paste and hot water. Set aside.*
5. *After 15 minutes, remove the chili from the stove, add the miso mixture and hot sauce, and stir well. Taste before determining how much tamari to add (if using).*
6. *Divide the chili evenly among 4 single-serving containers or large glass jars. Let cool before sealing the lids.*
7. *Place the containers in the refrigerator for up to 5 days or freeze for up to 3 months. To thaw, refrigerate overnight. Reheat in the microwave for 2 to 3 minutes.*

Nutrition: Calories: 177; Protein: 9g; Total fat: 2g; Carbohydrates: 33g; Fiber: 191g

666. African-Inspired Red Bean Stew

Preparation Time: 5 Minutes
Cooking Time: 45 Minutes
Servings: 4

Ingredients

- 1 tablespoon olive oil
- 1 medium yellow onion, chopped
- 2 medium carrots, cut into 1/4-inch slices
- 3 garlic cloves, minced
- 1 teaspoon grated fresh ginger
- 1/2 teaspoon ground cumin
- 1/8 teaspoon ground cayenne
- 2 large Yukon Gold or russet potatoes, peeled and cut into 1/2-inch dice
- 3 cups cooked dark red kidney beans or 2 (15.5-ouncecans, drained and rinsed
- 1 (14.5-ouncecan crushed tomatoes
- 1 (4-ouncecan diced mild green chiles, drained
- 1 1/2 cups vegetable broth, or water
- Salt and freshly ground black pepper
- 1/4 cup creamy peanut butter
- 3 cups fresh baby spinach
- 1/3 cup chopped unsalted roasted peanuts

Directions

1. In a large saucepan, heat the oil over medium heat. Add the onion and carrots. Cover and Cooking Time: until softened, about 10 minutes. Stir in the garlic and ginger. Cook, uncovered, until fragrant, about 1 minute.
2. Add the cumin, cayenne, potatoes, beans, tomatoes, chiles, and 1 cup of the broth. Season with salt and pepper to taste. Cover and bring to a boil, then reduce heat to low and simmer until the vegetables are soft, about 30 minutes.
3. In a small bowl, combine the peanut butter and the remaining 1/2 cup of broth, stirring until blended, then add it to the stew. Add the spinach and cook, stirring, until wilted, about 3 minutes. Taste, adjusting seasonings if necessary. Sprinkle with peanuts and serve immediately.

667. Chile-Lime Tortilla Soup

Preparation Time: 5 Minutes
Cooking Time: 25 Minutes
Servings: 4

Ingredients

- 1 tablespoon olive oil
- 1 medium red onion, chopped
- 3 garlic cloves, minced
- 2 serrano chiles, seeded and cut into 1/4-inch slices
- 6 cups vegetable broth, homemade (see Light Vegetable Brothor store-bought, or water
- 8 ounces seitan, homemade or store-bought, cut into 1/4-inch strips
- 1 (14.5-ouncecan diced tomatoes, drained
- 1 (4-ouncecan mild chopped green chiles, drained
- Salt and freshly ground black pepper
- 1/4 cup chopped fresh cilantro
- 3 tablespoons fresh lime juice
- 3 to 4 (6-inchcorn tortillas, cut into strips
- 1 ripe Hass avocado

Directions

1. Preheat the oven to 350°F. In a large pot, heat the oil over medium heat. Add the onion, cover, and Cooking Time: until softened, about 5 minutes. Add the garlic and serrano chiles, then stir in the broth, seitan, tomatoes, canned chiles, and salt and pepper to taste. Bring to a boil, then reduce heat to low and simmer, uncovered, for 20 minutes. Stir in the cilantro and lime juice and taste, adjusting seasonings if necessary.
2. While the soup simmers, spread the

tortilla strips on a baking sheet and bake until crisp, about 8 minutes. Pit, peel, and dice the avocado. Ladle the soup into bowls and top with the tortilla strips and diced avocado and serve.

668. Weeknight Chickpea Tomato Soup

Preparation Time: 10 Minutes
Cooking Time: 20 Minutes
Servings: 2

Ingredients

- 1 to 2 teaspoons olive oil, or vegetable broth
- ½ cup chopped onion
- 3 garlic cloves, minced
- 1 cup mushrooms, chopped
- ⅛ to ¼ teaspoon sea salt, divided
- 1 tablespoon dried basil
- ½ tablespoon dried oregano
- 1 to 2 tablespoons balsamic vinegar, or red wine
- 1 (19-ounce can diced tomatoes
- 1 (14-ounce can chickpeas, drained and rinsed, or 1½ cups cooked
- 2 cups water
- 1 to 2 cups chopped kale

Directions
1. Preparing the Ingredients.
2. In a large pot, warm the olive oil and sauté the onion, garlic, and mushrooms with a pinch salt until softened, 7 to 8 minutes. Add the basil and oregano and stir to mix. Then add the vinegar to deglaze the pan, using a wooden spoon to scrape all the browned, savory bits up from the bottom. Add the tomatoes and chickpeas. Stir to combine, adding enough water to get the consistency you want. Add the kale and the remaining salt. Cover and simmer for 5 to 15 minutes, until the kale is as soft as you like it.
3. This is delicious topped with a tablespoon of toasted walnuts and a sprinkle of nutritional yeast, or the Cheesy Sprinkle.

Nutrition: Calories: 343; Protein: 17g; Total fat: 9g; Carbohydrates: 61g; Fiber: 15g

669. Shiitake Mushroom Soup With Sake

Preparation Time: 5 Minutes
Cooking Time: 20 Minutes
Servings: 4

Ingredients

- 1 tablespoon canola or grapeseed oil
- 2 leeks, white parts only, well rinsed and chopped
- 2 celery ribs with leaves, chopped
- 8 ounces fresh shiitake mushrooms, lightly rinsed, patted dry, stemmed, and sliced
- 3 tablespoons sake
- 2 tablespoons soy sauce
- 6 cups vegetable broth, homemade (see Light Vegetable Broth or store-bought, or water
- Salt and freshly ground black pepper
- 2 tablespoons minced fresh parsley

Directions
1. In a large soup pot, heat the oil over medium heat. Add the leeks and celery. Cover and Cooking Time: until softened, about 5 minutes.
2. Stir in the mushrooms, sake, soy sauce, and broth and season with salt and pepper to taste. Bring to a boil, then reduce heat to low and simmer, uncovered, until the mushrooms are tender, about 15 minutes. Stir in the parsley, taste, adjusting seasonings if necessary, and serve.

670. Potato And Kale Soup

Preparation Time: 5 Minutes
Cooking Time: 50 Minutes
Servings: 4

Ingredients

- 1 tablespoon olive oil
- 1 medium onion, chopped

- 2 garlic cloves, minced
- 6 cups vegetable broth, homemade (see Light Vegetable Broth or store-bought, or water
- 2 large russet potatoes, peeled and cut into 1/2-inch dice
- 1/2 teaspoon dried oregano
- 1/4 teaspoon crushed red pepper
- 1 bay leaf
- Salt
- 4 cups chopped stemmed kale
- 1 1/2 cups cooked or 1 (15.5-ouncecan Great Northern beans, drained and rinsed

Directions

1. In a large pot, heat the oil over medium heat. Add the onion and garlic, cover, and Cooking Time: until softened, about 5 minutes. Add the broth, potatoes, oregano, crushed red pepper, bay leaf, and salt to taste, and bring to a boil. Reduce heat to low and simmer, uncovered, for 30 minutes.
2. Stir in the kale and the beans and Cooking Time: until the vegetables are tender, 15 to 20 minutes longer. Remove, discard the bay leaf, and serve.

671. Coconut Watercress Soup

Preparation Time: 10 Minutes
Cooking Time: 20 Minutes
Servings: 4

Ingredients

- 1 teaspoon coconut oil
- 1 onion, diced
- 2 cups fresh or frozen peas
- 4 cups water, or vegetable stock
- 1 cup fresh watercress, chopped
- 1 tablespoon fresh mint, chopped
- Pinch sea salt
- Pinch freshly ground black pepper
- ¾ cup coconut milk

Directions

1. Preparing the Ingredients.
2. Melt the coconut oil in a large pot over medium-high heat. Add the onion and Cooking Time: until soft, about 5 minutes, then add the peas and the water. Bring to a boil, then lower the heat and add the watercress, mint, salt, and pepper.
3. Cover and simmer for 5 minutes. Stir in the coconut milk, and purée the soup until smooth in a blender or with an immersion blender.
4. Try this soup with any other fresh, leafy green—anything from spinach to collard greens to arugula to Swiss chard.

Nutrition: *Calories: 178; Protein: 6g; Total fat: 10g; Carbohydrates: 18g; Fiber: 5g*

672. Roasted Red Pepper And Butternut Squash Soup

Preparation Time: 10 Minutes
Cooking Time: 45 Minutes
Servings: 6

Ingredients

- 1 small butternut squash
- 1 tablespoon olive oil
- 1 teaspoon sea salt
- 2 red bell peppers
- 1 yellow onion
- 1 head garlic
- 2 cups water, or vegetable broth
- Zest and juice of 1 lime
- 1 to 2 tablespoons tahini
- Pinch cayenne pepper
- ½ teaspoon ground coriander
- ½ teaspoon ground cumin
- Toasted squash seeds (optional

Directions

1. Preparing the Ingredients.
2. Preheat the oven to 350°F.
3. Prepare the squash for roasting by cutting it in half lengthwise, scooping out the seeds, and poking some holes in the flesh with a fork. Reserve the seeds if desired.

4. Rub a small amount of oil over the flesh and skin, then rub with a bit of sea salt and put the halves skin-side down in a large baking dish. Put it in the oven while you prepare the rest of the vegetables.
5. Prepare the peppers the exact same way, except they do not need to be poked.
6. Slice the onion in half and rub oil on the exposed faces. Slice the top off the head of garlic and rub oil on the exposed flesh.
7. After the squash has cooked for 20 minutes, add the peppers, onion, and garlic, and roast for another 20 minutes. Optionally, you can toast the squash seeds by putting them in the oven in a separate baking dish 10 to 15 minutes before the vegetables are finished.
8. Keep a close eye on them. When the vegetables are cooked, take them out and let them cool before handling them. The squash will be very soft when poked with a fork.
9. Scoop the flesh out of the squash skin into a large pot (if you have an immersion blenderor into a blender.
10. Chop the pepper roughly, remove the onion skin and chop the onion roughly, and squeeze the garlic cloves out of the head, all into the pot or blender. Add the water, the lime zest and juice, and the tahini. Purée the soup, adding more water if you like, to your desired consistency. Season with the salt, cayenne, coriander, and cumin. Serve garnished with toasted squash seeds (if using).

Nutrition: *Calories: 156; Protein: 4g; Total fat: 7g; Saturated fat: 11g; Carbohydrates: 22g; Fiber: 5g*

673. Mushroom Medley Soup

Preparation Time: *5 Minutes*
Cooking Time: *40 Minutes*
Servings: *4 To 6*

Ingredients
- 1 tablespoon olive oil
- 1 medium onion, chopped
- 1 large carrot, chopped
- 1 celery rib, chopped
- 8 ounces fresh shiitake mushrooms, lightly rinsed, patted dry, stemmed and cut into 1/4-inch slices
- 8 ounces cremini mushrooms, lightly rinsed, patted dry, and quartered
- 8 ounces white mushrooms, lightly rinsed, patted dry, and quartered
- 6 cups vegetable broth, mushroom broth, homemade
- 1/4 cup chopped fresh parsley
- 1 teaspoon minced fresh thyme or 1/2 teaspoon dried
- Salt and freshly ground black pepper

Directions
1. In a large pot, heat the oil over medium heat. Add the onion, carrot, and celery. Cover and Cooking Time: until softened, about 10 minutes. Stir in all the mushrooms and broth, and bring to boil.
2. Reduce heat to low, add the parsley and thyme, and season with salt and pepper to taste. Simmer, uncovered, until the vegetables are tender, about 30 minutes. Serve hot.

674. Tofu Coconut Indonesian Soup

Preparation Time: *10 Minutes*
Servings: *4*

Ingredients:
- 8ounces extra-firm tofu, cut into ½-inch dice
- 6ounces dried rice noodles
- 1(14-ouncecan coconut milk
- ½teaspoon paprika
- 1onion, chopped
- 2teaspoons grated fresh ginger
- 3teaspoons curry powder
- 1teaspoon Asian chili paste

- 2 teaspoons ground coriander
- 1 teaspoon sugar
- 4 cups vegetable broth
- 1 teaspoon salt
- ¼ teaspoon cayenne pepper
- ¼ teaspoon black pepper
- 3 scallions, chopped
- ¼ teaspoon ground turmeric
- 1 tablespoon fresh lime juice
- Lime wedges, for serving

Directions:
1. Add the coconut milk, tofu, all the vegetables, lemon juice, spices, and herbs in an instant pot.
2. Mix well and Cooking Time: with the lid on for 8 minutes.
3. Serve hot.

675. Cabbage Scallion And Potato Soup

Preparation Time: 5 Minutes
Servings: 4
Ingredients:

- ¼ cup chopped scallions
- 1 onion, minced
- 2 potatoes, peeled and diced
- 6 cups water
- ¼ cup white miso paste
- 3 tablespoons soy sauce
- ½ teaspoon salt
- 4 cups chopped napa cabbage
- ¼ teaspoon black pepper

Directions:
1. Add the scallions, onion, cabbage, and potatoes in your instant pot.
2. Add the seasoning, sauce, miso paste and water.
3. Stir well and cover.
4. Cooking Time: for about 4 minutes.
5. Serve hot.

676. Lentil Soup

Preparation Time: 10 Minutes
Servings: 6
Ingredients:

- 1 cup dried red lentils
- 4 cups water
- 1 cup dried brown lentils
- 1 bell pepper, seeded and chopped
- 2 jalapeño chiles, seeded and minced
- 1 onion, chopped
- 4 garlic cloves, minced
- 3 tablespoons chili powder
- 1 teaspoon dried oregano
- 1 (28-ounce can crushed tomatoes
- 1 teaspoon unsweetened cocoa powder
- 1 teaspoon ground cumin
- 1 tablespoon soy sauce
- 1 teaspoon natural sugar
- Salt and black pepper

Directions:
1. Add the lentil in your instant pot.
2. Add the garlic, onion, chiles, vegetables, sugar, sauce, and seasoning.
3. Pour in the water and mix well.
4. Cover and Cooking Time: for about 5 minutes.
5. Use a hand blender to blend well.
6. Serve hot.

677. Black Bean Soup

Preparation Time: 6 Minutes
Servings: 6
Ingredients:

- 4 cups cooked black beans
- 2 tablespoons minced chipotle chiles in adobo
- 1 butternut squash, peeled, seeds removed, diced
- 1 onion, chopped
- 1 teaspoon ground cumin
- 1 bell pepper, seeded and chopped
- 1 tablespoon tomato paste
- 3 tablespoons chili powder, or to taste
- ½ teaspoon dried oregano
- 1 teaspoon ground coriander
- 4 garlic cloves, minced
- 1½ cups water

- 1 (14.5-ounce can tomatoes
- Salt and black pepper

Directions:
1. Add the black beans, tomatoes, garlic, onion, squash, chipotle chiles and the rest of the ingredients.
2. Mix well and Cooking Time: for 6 minutes.
3. Serve hot.

678. Pepper Stew With Fire Roasted Tomatoes

Preparation Time: 25 Minutes
Servings: 4
Ingredients:
- 1 cup fire-roasted tomatoes, diced
- 6 red bell peppers, sliced
- 1 tsp dried basil
- 4 cup beef stock
- 6 tbsp tomato paste
- 3 large celery stalks, chopped
- 3 large carrots, sliced
- 1/4 cup olive oil
- 1 large onion, finely chopped
- 3 garlic cloves, crushed
- ½ cup button mushrooms
- ½ tsp salt
- ¼ tsp black pepper

Directions:
1. Combine the ingredients in your instant pot and seal the lid.
2. Press the 'Stew' button and set the steam release handle.
3. When you hear the cooker's end signal, release the pressure naturally and open the lid.
4. Serve warm.

679. Lentil Curry

Preparation Time: 45 Minutes
Servings: 5
Ingredients:
- 1 cup brown lentils
- 2 medium-sized potatoes
- ½ cup green peas
- 1 cup fire-roasted tomatoes, diced
- 2 large onions, finely chopped
- 3 garlic cloves, crushed
- 2 celery stalks, chopped
- 3 tbsp olive oil
- 1 tsp cayenne pepper
- ½ tsp garam masala
- 1 tsp salt
- ¼ tsp black pepper
- ¼ tsp chili flakes
- 3 cups vegetable stock

Directions:
1. Plug in your instant pot and press the 'Sauté' button. Grease the stainless steel insert with olive oil and add onions, celery stalk, and garlic. Cooking Time: for 10 minutes, stirring occasionally.
2. Now add potatoes and season with cayenne, salt, pepper, and chili flakes. Give it a good stir and continue to Cooking Time: for another 10 minutes.
3. Finally, add the remaining ingredients and pour in the vegetable stock. Seal the lid and press the 'Stew' button.
4. When you hear the cooker's end signal, release the pressure naturally and open the lid.
5. Optionally, sprinkle with chopped parsley leaves and serve warm.

680. Vegetarian Broth

Preparation Time: 10 Minutes
Servings: 8 cups
Ingredients:
- 1 onion, sliced
- ½ teaspoon black peppercorns
- 1 tablespoon soy sauce
- 1 celery rib, diced
- 2 large carrots, diced
- 3 garlic cloves, crushed
- ⅓ cup chopped parsley
- ½ teaspoon salt

- 1 Potato, peeled and diced
- 2 bay leaves
- 8 cups water
- 3 dried mushrooms

Directions:
1. In an instant pot add all the ingredients one by one.
2. Stir well and cover with the lid.
3. Cooking Time: for about 8 minutes.
4. Serve hot.

681. Spicy Black Bean Soup

Preparation Time: 5 Minutes
Servings: 8 cups
Ingredients:

- 1 jalapeño pepper, seeded and minced
- 1 onion, chopped
- 4 cups water
- ¼ teaspoon chili powder
- 1 green bell pepper, seeded and chopped
- 1 tablespoon dried oregano
- 3 garlic cloves, minced
- 2 bay leaves
- 2 teaspoons ground cumin
- 1 teaspoon smoked paprika
- 1 teaspoon liquid smoke
- ¼ teaspoon black pepper
- 6 cups cooked black beans, drained
- 1 teaspoon salt
- 1 teaspoon cider vinegar
- ½ cup chopped fresh cilantro, for garnish

Directions:
1. Add the vegetables, spices, herbs in your instant pot.
2. Mix well and add the lid.
3. Cooking Time: for about 5 minutes.
4. Serve hot with the cilantro on top.

682. Kale And Cannellini Bean Soup

Preparation Time: 5 Minutes
Servings: 4-6
Ingredients:

- 8 ounces kale, chopped
- 1 onion, chopped
- 3 large garlic cloves, minced
- ¼ teaspoon red pepper flakes
- 6 cups vegetable broth
- 1 Potato, peeled and chopped
- Salt and black pepper

Directions:
1. In an instant pot sauté the onion and garlic for 30 seconds.
2. Add the vegetables, seasoning, and broth and mix well.
3. Cover and Cooking Time: for 3 minutes.
4. Serve hot.

683. Tomato Lentil Soup

Preparation Time: 10 Minutes
Servings: 6
Ingredients:

- 1 cup dried brown lentils
- 1 (14-ounce can diced tomatoes
- 1 onion, chopped
- 1 tablespoon soy sauce
- 3 carrots, chopped
- 6 cups water
- ½ teaspoon dried thyme
- 3 garlic cloves, minced
- 1 cup baby lima beans
- Salt and black pepper
- 2 celery ribs, chopped
- 1 cup chopped spinach
- 1 teaspoon dried basil

Directions:
1. Add the lentils, tomatoes, carrots, water, lima beans and the rest of the ingredients in your instant pot.
2. Stir well and add the lid.
3. Cooking Time: for about 10 minutes.
4. Serve hot.

684. Spicy Chickpea Soup

Preparation Time: 10 Minutes
Servings: 6

Ingredients:

- 3cups cooked chickpeas
- 1onion, chopped
- 6cups vegetable broth
- 1teaspoon ground coriander
- 2carrots, chopped
- 1teaspoon ground cumin
- 1tablespoon fresh lemon juice
- 3garlic cloves, chopped
- 1(14-ouncecan diced tomatoes, drained
- ½teaspoon cayenne pepper
- Salt and black pepper
- 1teaspoon grated fresh ginger
- ¼cup chopped parsley

Directions:

1. In your instant pot sauté the onion, ginger, garlic for 30 seconds.
2. Add the rest of the ingredients one by one.
3. Mix well and cover with the lid.
4. Cooking Time: for nearly 4 minutes.
5. Serve hot.
6. Drain the tomatoes and add to a blender.

685. Vegan Sausage Bean Soup

Preparation Time: 5 Minutes
Servings: 4

Ingredients:

- 1bell pepper, seeded and chopped
- 3cups cooked dark red kidney beans
- 4cups vegetable broth
- 1(14-ouncecan diced fire-roasted tomatoes
- ½ cooked Vegan Sausage
- ½teaspoon liquid smoke
- 1onion, chopped
- 1teaspoon dried thyme
- 1cup sliced okra
- 1teaspoon Tabasco sauce
- 3garlic cloves, minced
- 2celery ribs, chopped
- Salt and black pepper
- 1tablespoon beurre manié

Directions:

1. Add the sausage, vegetables, kidney beans, sauce, herbs and spices in your instant pot.
2. Add the broth and seasoning and cover with lid.
3. Cooking Time: for 3 minutes and add the beurre manie.
4. Mix well and Cooking Time: for one minute.
5. Serve hot.

686. Instant Pot Corn Chowder

Preparation Time: 45 Minutes
Servings: 4

Ingredients:

For Chowder:

- 5 potatoes (2 lbs), peeled and chopped
- 3 cups (1 lbof corn (fresh or frozen
- 3 cloves of garlic, minced
- 1 red pepper, chopped
- 1 yellow onion, chopped
- 2 tsp smoked paprika
- 2 cups of vegetable broth (or 2 cups of water with 2 tsp of vegetable base
- 1 can (13.5 fl ozof coconut milk

For Garnishing (Optional):

- Salt and pepper, to taste
- Green onion and cilantro, chopped
- Red pepper, corn (reserved from above ingredients

Directions:

1. Place onion and garlic in Instant Pot. Chop up the potatoes and red pepper and leave aside.
2. Set Instant Pot to 'sautée' and add around 1/2 cup of broth (or water). Using a wooden spatula, stir onion and garlic for 5 minutes and add in rest of ingredients.
3. Mix and cover the pot. Set the vent to 'sealing'. Switch on manual button and set timer to 8 minutes over high pressure. When the timer

beeps, allow a 10-minute natural pressure release.
4. Using immersion blender give short zaps till the soup thickens.
5. Serve this chowder over rice if desired and garnished with corn, cilantro, green onion, red pepper, salt and pepper.

687. Carrot Split Pea Soup

Preparation Time: 5 Minutes
Servings: 6
Ingredients:
- 1Potato, peeled and diced
- 1onion, chopped
- 1teaspoon liquid smoke
- 7cups water
- 1carrot, chopped
- 1teaspoon ground coriander
- 1celery rib, chopped
- ½teaspoon ground cumin
- ¼teaspoon black pepper
- 1pound green split peas
- 1bay leaf
- 1teaspoon salt

Directions:
1. Add the onion, carrot, celery rib, bay leaf in your instant pot.
2. Cooking Time: for 1 minute and add the remaining ingredients.
3. Stir well and cover using the lid.
4. Cooking Time: for 4 minutes.
5. Serve hot.

688. Bread Cabbage Soup

Preparation Time: 5 Minutes
Servings: 6
Ingredients:
- 5cups vegetable broth
- 1onion, chopped
- 2cups Italian bread cubes, crusts removed
- 3carrots, chopped
- 1(28-ouncecan Italian plum tomatoes, chopped
- 6cups chopped cabbage
- 1potato, peeled and chopped
- 5garlic cloves, minced
- 2celery ribs, chopped
- 3cups cooked cannellini beans
- ½teaspoon dried basil
- ½teaspoon dried marjoram
- ¼teaspoon red pepper flakes
- ½cup chopped fresh basil leaves
- Salt and black pepper

Directions:
1. Add the carrot, cabbage, beans, broth, basil, and the rest of the ingredients in your instant pot.
2. Mix well and add the lid.
3. Cooking Time: for about 5 minutes.
4. Serve hot with fresh basil on top.

689. Cannellini Potato Bean Soup

Preparation Time: 5 Minutes
Servings: 6
Ingredients:
- 3cups chopped chard
- 6cups vegetable broth
- 2potato, scrubbed and diced
- 1½cups cooked cannellini
- 1celery rib, chopped
- 1small zucchini, diced
- 2tablespoons chopped fresh basil
- 4ounces green beans, diced
- 2garlic cloves, minced
- 2carrots, chopped
- 1onion, chopped
- Salt and black pepper
- 1large ripe tomato, diced
- 2tablespoons parsley

Directions:
1. Add the tomato, onion, carrots, garlic, green beans, cannellini, potato, broth, celery, chard, zucchini, seasoning, parsley and basil.
2. Mix well and cover.
3. Cooking Time: for only 3 minutes.

4. Serve hot.

690. Vegan Gazpacho

Preparation Time: 40 Minutes
Servings: 5
Ingredients:

- 2 lbs of medium-sized tomatoes, diced
- 1 cup of white beans, pre-cooked
- 1 small onion, diced
- 2 garlic cloves, crushed
- 1 cup of cashews, blended
- 1 cup of vegetable broth
- 2 tbsp of fresh parsley, finely chopped
- ¼ tsp of black pepper, ground
- 2 tbsp of extra virgin olive oil
- 1 tsp of sugar
- ½ tsp of salt

Directions:

1. Plug in your instant pot and grease the bottom of the stainless steel insert with olive oil. Press "Sautee" button and add chopped onion and garlic. Briefly, stir-fry for 2 minutes.
2. Now, add tomatoes, beans, broth, parsley, salt, and pepper. Pour in two cups of water and add sugar to balance the bitterness. Close the lid and set the steam release handle. Press "Manual" button and set the timer for 30 minutes. Cooking Time: on high pressure.
3. When done, press "Cancel" button and turn off the pot. Release the pressure naturally. Let it stand for 10 minutes covered before opening.
4. Top with one tablespoon of cashew cream and garnish with some parsley.
5. Enjoy!

691. Chickpeas Zucchini Pasta Soup

Preparation Time: 5 Minutes
Servings: 4
Ingredients:

- ⅓ cup uncooked soup pasta
- 1 (28-ounce can diced tomatoes
- 1 onion, minced
- 2 small zucchini, diced
- 2 carrots, chopped
- 1 cup chopped celery
- ½ teaspoon dried marjoram
- 1½ cups cooked chickpeas
- 4 cups vegetable broth
- ¼ cup parsley
- 1 bay leaf
- 3 garlic cloves, minced
- ¼ cup chopped fresh basil
- Salt and black pepper

Directions:

1. Take an instant pot and add the cooked chickpeas, onion, marjoram, broth, garlic, basil, seasoning, parsley, bay leaf, carrots, zucchini, soup pasta and tomatoes.
2. Mix well and Cooking Time: with the lid on for 3 minutes.
3. Serve hot with basil on top.

692. Brown Rice Herbes De Provence Soup

Preparation Time: 5 Minutes
Servings: 6
Ingredients:

- 2 parsnips, peeled and chopped
- ⅓ cup uncooked brown rice
- 1 onion, chopped
- 1 medium-size Potato, peeled and diced
- 1 (14-ounce can diced tomatoes, drained
- 3 garlic cloves, chopped
- 4 cups vegetable broth
- 1 turnip, peeled and diced
- 2 teaspoons dried herbes de Provence
- Salt and black pepper
- 2 carrots, coarsely chopped
- 2 tablespoons parsley, for garnish

Directions:

1. Add all the vegetables to your

instant pot.
2. Add the herbs, seasoning, and spices.
3. Pour in the broth, and brown rice.
4. Mix well and cover with the lid.
5. Cooking Time: for 4 minutes.
6. Serve hot with parsley on top.

693. Milky Potato Soup

Preparation Time: 5 Minutes
Servings: 6
Ingredients:
- 5Potatoes, peeled and diced
- 1onion, chopped
- 4cups vegetable broth
- 3garlic cloves, minced
- 2teaspoons salt
- 1cup nondairy milk
- ½teaspoon black pepper
- ½cup vegan sour cream

Directions:
1. Add the potatoes, broth, onion, garlic, salt, milk, and pepper in your instant pot.
2. Cover and Cooking Time: for 3 minutes.
3. Add the sour cream and mix well.
4. Serve warm.

694. Hard Cider Harvest Soup

Preparation Time: 15 Minutes
Servings: 6
Ingredients:
- 1 package (12 ouncesvegan sausage links
- 1 1/2 cups hard cider
- 1 small head cabbage, chopped
- 1 small apple, peeled, and diced
- 1 shallot, chopped
- 3 cloves garlic, minced
- 2 medium-size carrots, sliced
- 2 tablespoons olive oil
- 2 tablespoons vegan chicken-flavored bouillon
- 1 sprig rosemary
- 1/4 teaspoon nutmeg
- 1 teaspoon dried thyme
- 1/4 teaspoon salt
- 1/4 teaspoon pepper

Directions:
1. Heat the olive oil on the sauté setting and Cooking Time: the shallot for 5 minutes. Add the garlic and Cooking Time: an additional minute.
2. Add the rest of the ingredients to the instant pot, seal the lid, and Cooking Time: on high 3 minutes.
3. Discard the rosemary sprig and serve.

695. Homestyle Beet & Cabbage Borscht

Preparation Time: 20 Minutes
Servings: 6
Ingredients:
- 2 cups chopped cabbage
- 2 potatoes, peeled and diced
- 3 large yellow beets, peeled and chopped
- 2 carrots, cut into half-coins
- 2 tablespoons vegan chicken-flavored bouillon
- 4 teaspoons tomato paste
- 2 cloves garlic, minced
- 1 teaspoon dried dill
- 1 teaspoon dried thyme
- 1/2 teaspoon salt
- 1 teaspoon maple syrup
- 1 to 2 tablespoons apple cider vinegar
- 1 teaspoon pepper
- Vegan sour cream
- 6 cups water
- Zest and juice of one lemon

Directions:
1. Oil the instant pot and add the beets, potatoes, carrots, water, tomato paste, bouillon, and thyme. Seal the lid and Cooking Time: on high for 11 minutes.

2. Add the dill, maple syrup, vinegar, lemon juice and zest and Cooking Time: on the sauté setting for 5 minutes.
3. Serve in bowls with a scoop of vegan sour cream to garnish.

696. Pureed Turnip & Carrot Soup

Preparation Time: 10 Minutes
Servings: 6
Ingredients:

- 6 cups water
- 6 baby turnips, quartered
- 2 pounds carrots, chopped
- 1 clove crushed garlic
- 5 sprigs fresh thyme
- 2 sprigs fresh rosemary
- 1 teaspoon onion powder
- 1/2 teaspoon salt
- 1/2 teaspoon fresh ground pepper
- 2 tablespoons vegan chicken-flavored bouillon

Directions:

1. Add all the ingredients to the instant pot, seal the lid, and Cooking Time: on high for 4 minutes.
2. Discard the sprig of thyme and rosemary.
3. Transfer contents to a food processor and puree. Add extra salt and pepper if needed and serve hot in bowls.

PASTA

697. 5-Ingredients Pasta

Preparation Time: 25 minutes
Servings: 6

Ingredients
- Dry pasta: 1 pound
- Different vegetables: 1 pound (tomatoes, zucchini, and red onion)
- Vegan marinara sauce: 125 oz. jar
- Hummus: ¼ cup
- Olive oil
- Salt: as per your need

Directions:
1. Preheat the oven to 400F
2. Add water and salt to the pot and boil and Cooking Time: pasta as per packet instruction
3. Chop all the vegetables and spread on the baking sheet and brush with olive oil and salt
4. Roast the vegetables for 15 minutes
5. Prepare the sauce by combining hummus and marinara sauce together in a pan and put on medium heat
6. Add vegetables and pasta to the sauce and combine well
7. Serve warm

Nutrition:
Carbs: 65 g
Protein: 14 g
Fats: 2 g
Calories: 329 Kcal

698. Brussels Sprout Penne

Preparation Time: 20 minutes
Servings: 2

Ingredients
- Penne: 1 cup
- Brussels Sprout: 320g roasted halved
- Garlic: 2 cloves thinly sliced
- Olive oil: 2 tbsp
- Chili flakes: 1 tsp
- Salt: as per your taste
- Pepper: as per your taste
- Lemon: 1 juice and zest

Directions:
1. Cooking Time: the pasta as per the packet instruction
2. Take a large pan and heat oil
3. Add in garlic and Cooking Time: for two minutes
4. Add in chili flakes and Cooking Time: for a minutes
5. Add pasta, lemon juice and zest, salt, pepper, and roasted Brussels sprouts
6. Mix everything well and serve

Nutrition:
Carbs:24.7 g
Protein:5.75 g
Fats:14.9 g
Calories: 245Kcal

699. Bang Bang Sauce With Pasta

Preparation Time: 40 minutes
Servings: 4

Ingredients
- Pasta: 4 cups cooked

For the cauliflower:
- Cauliflower:1 head diced
- Rice crisp cereal:3 cups
- Rice flour:1/4 cup
- Garlic powder:1/4 tsp
- Ground black pepper:1/4 tsp
- Salt:1/4 tsp
- Neutral oil:1 tbsp
- Water:6 tbsp

For the bang bang sauce:
- Vegan mayonnaise:1/4 cup
- Rice vinegar:1 tsp
- Sweet chili sauce:3 tbsp
- Hot sauce:1 tbsp

Directions:

1. Cooking Time: pasta as per packet instruction
2. Preheat the oven to 400F
3. Line parchment paper on the baking sheet and spray with oil
4. Make crumbs of the rice crisp cereal by pulsing in the food processor
5. Mix the crumbs with black pepper, garlic powder, and salt
6. Make a thin batter of the rice flour using water
7. Now take a single cauliflower floret and dip in the rice flour mixture
8. Then add it to the cereal crumbs to coat it
9. Place them to the baking sheet one by one
10. Oil spray from the top and bake for 25 minutes
11. Add all the sauce ingredients and mix well
12. Serve the sauce and cauliflower together with pasta

Nutrition:
Carbs: 97 g
Protein: 13.5g
Fats: 5.6 g
Calories: 497 Kcal

700. Beans And Pasta

Preparation Time: 30 minutes
Servings: 2

Ingredients

- Pasta: 1 cup cooked
- Beans: 1 cup rinsed and drained well
- Onion: 1 cup finely diced
- Tomato: 2 cups diced
- Lemon juice: 2 tbsp
- Harissa 2 tsp
- Olive oil: 2 tbsp
- Fresh coriander: 2 tbsp chopped
- Garlic: 1 clove crushed

Directions:

1. Cooking Time: pasta as per packet instructions
2. Add garlic, lemon juice, harissa, and olive oil in a bowl and whisk
3. Take a serving bowl and combine pasta, beans, onion, tomatoes, and the sauce you made
4. Add fresh coriander from the top and serve

Nutrition:
Carbs: 64.3g
Protein: 16.5
Fats: 20.6
Calories: 459Kcal

701. Broccoli Elbow Macaroni

Preparation Time: 40 minutes
Servings: 2

Ingredients

- Elbow macaroni: 1 cup (after cooked
- Broccoli florets: 1 cup
- Spinach: 1 cup chopped
- Onion: 1 chopped
- Garlic: 2 tsp paste
- Ginger: 2 tsp paste
- Cumin: 1 tsp
- Cayenne pepper: ¼ tsp
- Cooking oil: 2 tbsp
- Dried oregano: ½ tsp
- Salt and pepper: as per your taste
- Cilantro: 2 tbsp
- Almond milk: ¼ cup
- Water: as per your need

Directions:

1. Take a saucepan and heat oil in it
2. Add garlic, ginger, and onion to it and make them tender
3. Add salt, cayenne pepper, cumin, and pepper and bring to boil
4. Now add broccoli florets and spinach and mix for a minute
5. Lower the heat to medium and Cooking Time: for 10 minutes
6. In the meanwhile, Cooking Time: elbow macaroni as per packet instructions
7. Add macaroni to the broccoli pan and mix well
8. Add almond milk from the top and

mix well
9. Remove from heat and add to the serving bowl
10. Garnish with cilantro and sprinkle oregano from the top and serve

Nutrition:
Carbs: 34.15g
Protein: 8.8g
Fats: 11.3g
Calories: 232Kcal

702. Broccoli Pasta

Preparation Time: 45 minutes
Servings: 2

Ingredients
- Pasta: 1 cup cooked
- Broccoli: 2 cups cut in big florets
- Hot sauce: 2 tbsp
- Rice vinegar: 1 tbsp
- Salt: as per your taste
- Pepper: as per your taste
- Sliced red pepper: 1 cup sliced
- Olive oil: 1 tbsp

Directions:
1. Cooking Time: pasta as per packet instruction
2. Preheat the oven 200C
3. Add broccoli to the baking sheet and sprinkle seasoning and brush with olive oil
4. Roast for 25 minutes till it turns golden and soft
5. Take a small bowl and combine hot sauce, vinegar, salt, and pepper
6. Remove broccoli from oven and brush with this dressing and Cooking Time: in the oven again for 10 minutes
7. Add to the serving bowl and serve with red pepper
8. Serve at the top of pasta

Nutrition:
Carbs: 28.5 g
Protein: 6.6g
Fats: 8.5g
Calories: 223Kcal

703. Caponata Pasta

Preparation Time: 55 minutes
Servings: 4

Ingredients
- Wholewheat spaghetti: 300g
- Aubergines: 2 cut into 3cm cubes
- Red onion: ½ sliced
- Vegetable oi:l 4 tsp
- Raisins: 2 tbsp heaped
- Celery: 2 sticks sliced
- Garlic: 2 cloves sliced
- Dried oregano:1 tsp
- Chopped tomatoes:400g tin
- Capers: 1 tsp
- Vinegar: 2 tbsp
- Kalamata olives: a handful chopped
- Flat-leaf parsley a small bunch, chopped

Directions:
1. Preheat the oven to 200C
2. Take a bowl and add 2 tablespoons oil and seasoning and add the aubergine
3. Place them to the baking sheet and Cooking Time: for 20 minutes
4. Take a large pan and heat the remaining oil
5. Add in celery, red onion, and salt and Cooking Time: for 10 minutes
6. Add oregano and garlic and stir and then add tomatoes and 100ml water
7. Add in aubergine and Cooking Time: for 15 minutes and allow the sauce to thicken
8. Add vinegar, capers, and raisins and lower the heat
9. Cooking Time: the pasta as per packet instruction and drain
10. Add pasta to the caponata and top with parsley
11. Mix well and serve

Nutrition:
Carbs: 61g
Protein: 13.8g
Fats: 6.7g

Calories: 387Kcal

704. Carbonara With Pine Nuts

Preparation Time: 45 minutes
Servings: 6

Ingredients

- Spaghetti: 450g
- Cauliflower: 1 small with leaves separated and reserved
- Salt: as per your taste
- Garlic 2 cloves, peeled
- White pepper
- Olive oil: 3 tbsp
- Vegetable stock: 750ml
- Pine nuts: 4 tbsp toasted

Directions:

1. Preheat the oven to 200C
2. Take a bowl and add 1 tablespoon oil and seasoning and add cauliflower leaves
3. Place them to the baking sheet and Cooking Time: for 12 minutes
4. Break the cauliflower and separate florets and stalk
5. Take a pan and add the stock, garlic, and 2 tablespoons oil and add the cauliflower
6. Cover and Cooking Time: for 20 minutes
7. Remove cauliflower and garlic from the pan and blend together
8. Make the sauce by adding a small amount of water
9. Add back to the pan and mix in salt and pepper
10. Cooking Time: pasta and add to the sauce
11. Serve with pine nuts and cauliflower leaves on the top

Nutrition:
Carbs: 61.4g
Protein: 13.7g
Fats: 14.4g
Calories: 441Kcal

705. Casarecce With Raw Tomato Sauce

Preparation Time: 15 minutes
Servings: 2

Ingredients

- Casarecce: 200g
- Cherry tomatoes: 250g, halved
- Spring onions: 3 chopped
- Vinegar: 3 tbsp
- Olive oil: 4 tbsp
- Tabasco: 4-5 dashes
- Salt: as per your taste
- Pepper: as per your taste
- Basil: 2 tbsp torn

Directions:

1. Take a bowl and add in cherry tomatoes, olive oil, vinegar, Tabasco, spring onion, and a lot of salt and pepper
2. Cooking Time: casarecce as per packet instructions
3. Drain the pasta but keep 2 tablespoons of water and add to the sauce
4. Add pasta to the sauce
5. Top with torn basil and serve

Nutrition:
Carbs: 74.8g
Protein: 14.5g
Fats: 24.3g
Calories: 595Kcal

706. Cauli Cabbage Pasta

Preparation Time: 30 minutes
Servings: 4

Ingredients

- Pasta: 2 cups (after cooked)
- Olive oil: 1 tbsp
- Cauliflower: 2 cups diced
- Garlic: 3 cloves minced
- Red onion: 1 small diced
- Cabbage: 1 cup diced
- Soy sauce: 1 tbsp
- Salt: 1 tsp
- Black pepper: ½ tsp
- Green onions: 2 tbsp

Directions:

1. Cooking Time: pasta as per packet instructions
2. Take a large saucepan and add olive oil and heat on medium flame
3. Include onion and garlic to the pan and Cooking Time: for a minute
4. Now add cabbage, cabbage, salt, pepper, and soy sauce and stir for 5 minutes
5. Then add cooked pasta and mix well
6. Then cover and Cooking Time: for 2 minutes on low flame and remove from heat
7. Sprinkle green onion on top and serve

Nutrition:
Carbs: 22.6g
Protein: 5.2g
Fats: 4.4g
Calories: 148Kcal

707. Chickpeas Pasta

Preparation Time: 30 minutes
Servings: 4

Ingredients
- Pasta: 1 ½ cup (after cooking
- Olive oil: 2 tbsp
- Garlic: 2 cloves minced
- Chickpeas: 1 cup can
- Red onion: 1 small diced
- Bell pepper: 1 cup diced
- Zucchini: 1 cup diced
- Tomatoes: 1 cup diced
- Chili powder: 1 tsp
- Cumin: 1 tsp
- Salt: 1 tsp
- Black pepper: ½ tsp
- Green onions: 2 tbsp chopped

Directions:
1. Cooking Time: pasta as per packet instructions
2. Take a large saucepan and add olive oil and heat on medium flame
3. Include onion and garlic to the pan and Cooking Time: for a minute
4. Now add bell pepper, zucchini, tomatoes, chickpeas, cumin, salt, pepper, and chili powder and stir
5. Cooking Time: for 10 minutes
6. Stir the spoon and add cooked pasta
7. Then cover and Cooking Time: for 5 minutes on low flame and remove from heat
8. Sprinkle green onion on top and serve

Nutrition:
Carbs: 36g
Protein: 9.8g
Fats: 5.9g
Calories: 234Kcal

708. Chili Pasta With Chickpeas Gravy

Preparation Time: 30 minutes
Servings: 4

Ingredients
- Pasta: 2 cups (after cooking
- Olive oil: 2 tbsp
- Jalapeño: 1 diced
- Green chili: 2 finely diced
- Salt: as per your need
- Garlic: 2 cloves minced
- Red onion: 1 small diced
- Dried oregano: 2 tbsp
- For the gravy:
- Vegetable oil 2 tsp
- Chickpeas: 1 cup rinsed and drained
- Onions: 2 thinly sliced
- Plain flour 1 tbsp
- Water: 250 ml
- Boiled water: 600 ml
- Vegan gravy granules: 2 tbsp

Directions:
1. Cooking Time: pasta as per packet instructions
2. Take a large saucepan and add olive oil and heat on medium flame
3. Include onion and garlic to the pan and Cooking Time: for a minute
4. Add pasta, chili, and jalapeño and

sprinkle salt and mix well
5. For the gravy, take a pan and heat oil
6. Add in onions and stir then add salt and water
7. Allow the water to evaporate so that onion caramelized
8. Add in flour and Cooking Time: for a minute and then add gravy granules and boiled water
9. Cooking Time: till the gravy becomes thick and then add chickpeas and simmer for 5 minutes
10. Spread pasta on the serving tray and serve with the chickpeas gravy on top
11. Sprinkle dried oregano from top

Nutrition:
Carbs: 47.5g
Protein: 14.8g
Fats: 12.4g
Calories: 304Kcal

709. Chickpeas Tomato Garlic Sauce Macaronis

Preparation Time: 30 minutes
Servings: 2

Ingredients
- Macaronis: 1 cup (after cooking
- Chickpeas: 1 cup rinsed and drained
- Cherry tomatoes: 1 cup diced
- Onions: 1 chopped
- Garlic: 2 cloves
- Vinegar: 3 tbsp
- Olive oil: 2 tbsp
- Tabasco: 4-5 dashes
- Salt: as per your taste
- Pepper: as per your taste
- Spring onion greens: 3 tbsp chopped

Directions:
1. Take a pan and heat oil
2. Add onion and sauté for 5 minutes
3. Add tomatoes and whole garlic cloves and sauté for 5 minutes and stir
4. Add in vinegar, Tabasco, and a lot of salt and pepper
5. Cooking Time: macaroni as per packet instructions and add chickpeas near the end and stir
6. Drain the pasta but keep 2 tablespoons of water and add to tomatoes
7. Add the tomato mixture to the blender and blend
8. Add pasta to the serving tray and mix in tomato sauce
9. Top with spring onion

Nutrition:
Carbs: 52g
Protein: 26.9g
Fats: 17.4g
Calories: 312Kcal

710. Chinese Style Pasta

Preparation Time: 30 minutes
Servings: 4

Ingredients
- Pasta: 2 cups (after cooking
- Olive oil: 2 tbsp
- Garlic: 2 cloves minced
- Red onion: 1 small diced
- Bell pepper: 1 cup diced
- Cabbage: 1 cup diced
- Carrot: 1 cup diced
- Soy sauce: 1 tbsp
- Hot sauce: 1 tbsp
- Salt: 1 tsp
- Black pepper: ½ tsp
- Green onions: 2 tbsp

Directions:
1. Cooking Time: pasta as per packet instructions
2. Take a large saucepan and add olive oil and heat on medium flame
3. Include onion and garlic to the pan and Cooking Time: for a minute
4. Now add bell pepper, cabbage, carrot, salt, soy sauce, hot sauce, and pepper and stir for 5 minutes
5. Then add pasta and mix well
6. Then cover and Cooking Time: for 2 minutes on low flame and remove

from heat
7. Sprinkle green onion on top and serve

Nutrition:
Carbs: 29.5g
Protein: 5.4g
Fats: 8.05g
Calories: 205Kcal

711. Cold Szechuan Noodles

Preparation Time: 15 minutes
Servings: 2

Ingredients
- Wholewheat noodles: 275g pack
- Sugar snap peas: a handful halved
- Toasted sesame seeds: 1 tbsp
- Cucumber: ½ peeled seeded and chopped
- Sesame oil: 1 tsp
- Red pepper: ½ sliced
- Roughly chopped coriander: a small bunch

For the Dressing:
- Soy sauce: 2 tsp
- Vinegar: 2 tbsp
- Ginger: 3cm piece grated
- Garlic: 1/2 clove crushed
- Peanut butter: 1 tbsp smooth
- Chili oil: 1 tbsp

Directions:
1. Cooking Time: noodles as per packet instructions
2. Take a bowl and add cooked noodles and pour some sesame oil
3. Add red pepper, cucumber and sugar snaps and mix well
4. Mix all dressing ingredients well, ladle over the noodles
5. Sprinkle some sesame seeds and coriander

Nutrition:
Carbs: 46.8g
Protein: 13g
Fats: 17.3g
Calories: 408Kcal

712. Creamy Garlic Pasta

Preparation Time: 30 minutes
Servings: 2

Ingredients
- All-purpose flour: 4 tbsp
- Whole wheat pasta: 1 ¼ cup
- Garlic: 8 large cloves
- Grape tomatoes: 3 cups half
- Shallots: 2 medium diced
- Olive oil
- Salt: as per your taste
- Black pepper: as per your taste
- Unsweetened plain almond milk: 2 ½ cup

Directions:
1. Preheat the oven to 204C
2. Add half tomatoes to the baking sheet lined with parchment paper
3. Brush with olive oil and sprinkle salt on top and bake for 20 minutes
4. Cooking Time: pasta as per packet instructions
5. Prepare sauce side by side, take a pan and add 1 tablespoon of olive oil
6. Add shallot and garlic and stir
7. Sprinkle salt and pepper and mix and Cooking Time: for 4 minutes till it softens
8. Add in flour and mix and add almond milk and again add a pinch of salt and pepper
9. Cooking Time: until thicken and add in garlic
10. Blend the sauce to make it creamier and back to the pan to heat up
11. Now add pasta and top with tomatoes and mix
12. Serve immediately when hot

Nutrition:
Carbs: 63.8 g
Protein: 11.8 g
Fats: 8.9 g
Calories: 378 Kcal

713. Fried Green Pasta

Preparation Time: 30 minutes

Servings: 2

Ingredients

- *Pasta: 1 cup cooked*
- *Long-stemmed broccoli: 1 cup*
- *Kale: 1 cup*
- *Olive oil: 1 tbsp*
- *Peas: 1 cup*
- *Salt: as per your taste*
- *Smoked paprika: ½ tsp*

Directions:

1. *Cooking Time: pasta as per packet instructions*
2. *Take a pan and heat olive oil*
3. *Take a bowl and add broccoli, peas, salt, paprika and mix well and add to the pan*
4. *Fry on low heat for 20 minutes and turn in between*
5. *Add kale at the last minutes*
6. *Mix pasta and season*

Nutrition:
Carbs: 42.5g
Protein:13.4g
Fats: 10.5g
Calories:227.2Kcal

714. Gazpacho Spaghetti

Preparation Time: 15 minutes
Servings: 2

Ingredients

- *Spaghetti : 160g*
- *Red onion: ½ roughly chopped*
- *Green pepper: 1 chopped*
- *Cherry tomatoes:250g*
- *Tabasco: a good dash*
- *Garlic: ½ clove*
- *Vinegar: 1 tbsp*
- *Basi l a small bunch*

Directions:

1. *Cooking Time: pasta as per packet instructions*
2. *In the meanwhile, take a blender and add tomatoes, garlic, onion, and pepper, and blend*
3. *Add in salt, Tabasco, and vinegar and combine well*
4. *Add the sauce to the paste*
5. *Top with basil and serve*

Nutrition:
Carbs: 69g
Protein: 12.7g
Fats: 2.3g
Calories: 364sKcal

715. Garlic Vegetable Pasta

Preparation Time: 40 minutes
Servings: 2

Ingredients

- *Pasta: 1 cup (after cooking*
- *Olive oil: 2 tbsp*
- *Garlic: 2 cloves minced*
- *Chickpeas: 1 cup can*
- *Red onion: 1 small diced*
- *Bell pepper: 1 cup diced*
- *Tomatoes: 1 cup diced*
- *Chili powder: 1 tsp*
- *Cumin: 1 tsp*
- *Salt: 1 tsp*
- *Black pepper: ½ tsp*
- *Garlic whole: 1*
- *Cashew cream: ½ cup*
- *Cilantro: 2 tbsp chopped*

Directions:

1. *Cooking Time: pasta as per packet instructions*
2. *Roast garlic in the oven by brushing oil for 30 minutes*
3. *Take a large saucepan and add olive oil and heat on medium flame*
4. *Include onion and garlic to the pan and Cooking Time: for a minute*
5. *Now add bell pepper, tomatoes, chickpeas, cumin, salt, pepper, and chili powder and stir*
6. *Cooking Time: for 10 minutes*
7. *Stir the spoon and add cooked pasta*
8. *Slice roasted garlic and add to the pasta and mix in the cream*
9. *Cover and Cooking Time: for 2 minutes on low flame and remove*

from heat

10. *Sprinkle cilantro on top and serve*

Nutrition:
Carbs: 60g
Protein: 15.4g
Fats: 19.6g
Calories: 543Kcal

716. Gochujang Cauliflower Spaghetti

Preparation Time: 45 minutes
Servings: 2

Ingredients

- Spaghetti: 2 cups
- Olive oil: 2 tbsp
- Cauliflower: 2 cups cut in big florets
- Gochujang: 2 tbsp
- Rice vinegar: 1 tbsp
- Sliced red pepper: 1 cup sliced
- Carrot: 2 sliced
- Salt: as per your taste
- Pepper: as per your taste
- Coriander: 1/2 cup chopped

Directions:

1. Cooking Time: spaghetti as per packet instructions
2. Preheat the oven 200C
3. Add cauliflowers to the baking sheet and sprinkle seasoning and brush with olive oil
4. Roast for 25 minutes till it turns golden and soft
5. Remove from oven and brush with gochujang and Cooking Time: in the oven again for 10 minutes
6. Add to the bowl and mix with carrots and red bell pepper
7. Season with salt, coriander, and pepper and pour vinegar from top
8. Spread spaghetti on the serving tray and top with the cauliflower

Nutrition:
Carbs: 52.5g
Protein: 10.9g
Fats: 15.5g
Calories: 404Kcal

717. Kale Chickpeas Pasta

Preparation Time: 30 minutes
Servings: 2

Ingredients

- Pasta: 1 cup cooked
- Chickpeas: 1 cup rinsed and drained well
- Onion: 1 cup finely diced
- Tomato: 2 cups diced
- Lemon juice: 2 tbsp
- Kale: 1 cup
- Olive oil: 2 tbsp
- Tamari: 1 tbsp
- Coriander: 2 tbsp chopped
- Garlic: 1 clove crushed

Directions:

1. Cooking Time: pasta as per packet instructions
2. Add garlic, lemon juice, tamari, and olive oil in a bowl and whisk
3. Take a serving bowl and combine kale, pasta, chickpeas, onion, tomatoes, and the sauce you made
4. Add coriander from the top and serve

Nutrition:
Carbs: 54g
Protein: 14.6g
Fats: 18g
Calories: 442Kcal

718. Lemon Fusilli With Cauli

Preparation Time: 20 minutes
Servings: 2

Ingredients

- Fusilli: 1 cup cooked
- Cauliflower: 1 cup roughly chopped
- Garlic: 2 cloves thinly sliced
- Olive oil: 1 tbsp
- Chili flakes: 1 tsp
- Salt: as per your taste
- Pepper: as per your taste
- Lemon: 1 juice and zest

Directions:

1. Cooking Time: the pasta as per the packet instruction
2. Add cauliflower when the pasta is about to be done
3. Drain but keep one cup of the water
4. Take a large pan and heat oil
5. Add in garlic and Cooking Time: for two minutes
6. Add in chili and Cooking Time: for a minutes
7. Add pasta, lemon juice and zest, salt, pepper, and cauliflower with the pasta water
8. Mix everything well and serve

Nutrition:
Carbs: 21.6g
Protein: 4.85g
Fats: 7.9g
Calories: 172Kcal

719. Lemony Pasta With Kidney Beans

Preparation Time: 30 minutes
Servings: 4

Ingredients
- Pasta: 2 cups (after cooking
- Onion: 1 chopped
- Garlic: 1 ½ tsp minced
- Cumin: 1 tsp
- Frozen corn: 1 cup
- Cayenne pepper: ¼ tsp
- Kidney beans: 1 cup drained and rinsed
- Fresh cilantro: 2 tsp
- Lemon juice: 3 tbsp
- Cooking oil: 2 tbsp
- Salt: as per your taste

Directions:
1. Cooking Time: pasta as per packet instructions
2. Take a saucepan and heat oil in it
3. Add garlic and onion to it and make them tender
4. Add salt, cayenne pepper, and cumin
5. Now add corns and beans and mix well
6. Cover and Cooking Time: for 5 minutes
7. Add in pasta and stir and remove from heat after 5 minutes
8. Pour lemon juice on top
9. Garnish with cilantro and serve

Nutrition:
Carbs: 41.98g
Protein: 9.3g
Fats: 8.4g
Calories: 274Kcal

720. Lentils Soup Savory Spaghetti

Time: 45 minutes
Servings: 2

Ingredients
- Spaghetti: 1 cup cooked
- Red lentils: 1 cup
- Potato: 1 cup diced
- Crushed tomatoes: 2 cups
- Onion: 1 diced
- Ginger: 1 tbsp paste
- Garlic: 1 tbsp paste
- Vegetable oil: 2 tbsp
- Water: 4 cups
- Italian herb seasoning: 1 tbsp
- Salt & pepper: as per your taste

Directions:
1. Cooking Time: spaghetti as per packet instructions
2. Take a large saucepan and heat oil on a medium flame
3. Add onion and ginger and garlic paste and sauté for 3-4 minutes
4. Pour water and bring to boil
5. Add lentils, potatoes, and salt and bring to boil
6. Lower the heat to medium and Cooking Time: for 20 minutes with partial cover
7. Now add crushed tomatoes to the lentils along with Italian herb seasoning and pepper
8. Cooking Time: on low flame for 15 minutes

9. Add the mixture to the high-speed blender to make a puree
10. Add in spaghetti pasta and mix well
11. Add salt and pepper to augment the taste

Nutrition:
Carbs: 33.33g
Protein: 13.3g
Fats: 15.1g
Calories: 335.2Kcal

721. Long-Stemmed Broccoli With Spaghetti

Preparation Time: 20 minutes
Servings: 2

Ingredients
- Wholewheat spaghetti: 150g
- Long-stemmed broccoli: 320g roughly chopped
- Garlic: 2 cloves thinly sliced
- Olive oil: 2 tbsp
- Chili flakes: 1 tsp
- Salt: as per your taste
- Pepper: as per your taste
- Lemon: 1 juice and zest

Directions:
1. Cooking Time: the spaghetti as per the packet instruction
2. Add the broccoli when the pasta is about to be done
3. Drain but keep one cup of the water
4. Take a large pan and heat oil
5. Add in garlic and Cooking Time: for two minutes
6. Add in chili and Cooking Time: for a minutes
7. Add pasta, lemon juice and zest, salt, pepper, and broccoli with the pasta water
8. Mix everything well and serve

Nutrition:
Carbs: 32.6g
Protein: 24.7g
Fats: 28.3g
Calories: 498Kcal

722. Pasta With Beans

Preparation Time: 30 minutes
Servings: 2

Ingredients
- Pasta: 1 cup (after cooking
- Olive oil: 1 tbsp
- Beans: 1 cup can rinsed and drained
- Garlic: 2 cloves minced
- Tomato paste: ¼ cup
- Red onion: 1 small diced
- Red chili flakes: 1 tsp
- Salt: 1 tsp
- Black pepper: ½ tsp
- Parsley: ½ cup

Directions:
1. Cooking Time: pasta as per packet instructions
2. Take a saucepan and heat oil in it
3. Add minced garlic and onion to it and make them tender
4. Add beans, salt, pepper, tomato paste, and red chili flakes and mix well
5. Add cooked pasta and stir
6. Lower the heat and cover and Cooking Time: for 5 minutes and then remove from heat
7. Sprinkle parsley on top and serve

Nutrition:
Carbs: 39.2g
Protein: 11.3g
Fats: 8.2g
Calories: 272Kcal

723. Peas Tomatoes Macaroni

Preparation Time: 40 minutes
Servings: 2

Ingredients
- Macaroni: 1 cup (after cooking
- Frozen peas: 1 cup rinsed and drained
- Cherry tomatoes: 1 cup diced
- Onions: 1 chopped
- Garlic: 2 cloves
- Vinegar: 3 tbsp
- Olive oil: 2 tbsp

- Tahini: 2 tbsp
- Salt: as per your taste
- Pepper: as per your taste
- Spring onion greens: 3 tbsp chopped

Directions:
1. Take a pan and heat oil
2. Add onion and sauté for 5 minutes
3. Add tomatoes and whole garlic cloves and sauté for 5 minutes and stir
4. Add in vinegar, tahini, and a lot of salt and pepper
5. Cooking Time: macaroni as per packet instructions and add peas at the end
6. Drain the pasta but keep 2 tablespoons of water and add to tomatoes
7. Add the tomato mixture to the blender and blend
8. Combine pasta and tomato mixture
9. Serve with spring onions on top

Nutrition:
Carbs: 37.5g
Protein: 8.9g
Fats: 15.4g
Calories: 320Kcal

724. Penne Bean Pasta With Roasted Tomato Sauce

Preparation Time: 15 minutes
Servings: 2

Ingredients
- Penne: 1 cup (after cooking
- Beans: 1 cup washed and drained
- Cherry tomatoes: 1 cup halved
- Spring onions: 3 chopped
- Vinegar: 3 tbsp
- Olive oil: 3 tbsp
- Tabasco: 4-5 dashes
- Salt: as per your taste
- Pepper: as per your taste
- Basil: 2 tbsp torn

Directions:
1. Roast tomatoes in the oven for 8 minutes
2. Take a bowl and add in roasted tomatoes, olive oil, vinegar, Tabasco, spring onion, and a lot of salt and pepper and mix well
3. Cooking Time: penne as per packet instructions and add bean when it is about to be cooked
4. Drain the pasta but keep 2 tablespoons of water and add to the sauce
5. Add pasta to the sauce
6. Top with torn basil and serve

Nutrition:
Carbs: 49.9g
Protein: 13.9g
Fats: 22.7g
Calories: 490Kcal

725. Protein-Rich Chickpeas Pasta

Preparation Time: 30 minutes
Servings: 2

Ingredients
- Pasta: 1 cup
- Olive oil: 1 tbsp
- Chickpeas: 1 cup can
- Garlic: 2 cloves minced
- Garlic: 1 tbsp minced
- Red onion: 1 small diced
- Cumin: 1 tsp
- Salt: 1 tsp
- Pepper: ½ tsp
- Hummus: ½ cup

Directions:
1. Cooking Time: pasta as per packet instructions
2. Take a large saucepan and add olive oil and heat on medium flame
3. Include onion, ginger, and garlic to the pan and Cooking Time: for 2-4 minutes
4. Now add chickpeas, cumin, salt, and pepper
5. Stir the spoon and add pasta
6. Lower the heat and cover and

Cooking Time: for 2 minutes and mix in hummus and serve

Nutrition:
Carbs: 61.8g
Protein: 18.9g
Fats: 18.9g
Calories: 488Kcal

726. Protein-Rich Zucchini Pasta

Preparation Time: 30 minutes
Servings: 2

Ingredients
- Pasta: 1 cup (after cooked
- Olive oil: 1 tbsp
- Vegetable broth: ½ cup
- Black beans: 1 cup
- Garlic: 2 cloves minced
- Zucchini: 1 cup diced
- Red onion: 1 small diced
- Chili powder: 1 tsp
- Cumin: 1 tsp
- Salt: 1 tsp
- Black pepper: ½ tsp
- Fresh cilantro: 2 tbsp

Directions:
1. Take a large saucepan and add olive oil and heat on medium flame
2. Include onion and garlic to the pan and Cooking Time: for a minute
3. Now add zucchini, black beans, cumin, salt, chili powder, and broth
4. Stir the spoon and let them boil
5. Lower the heat and cover and Cooking Time: for 10 minutes
6. In the meanwhile, Cooking Time: pasta as per packet instructions
7. When done, add to the beans
8. Sprinkle salt, pepper, and cilantro on top and serve

Nutrition:
Carbs: 28.15g
Protein: 12.35g
Fats: 8.5g
Calories: 287Kcal

727. Raw Garlic Tomato Sauce Spaghetti

Preparation Time: 15 minutes
Servings: 2

Ingredients
- Spaghetti: 1 cup (after cooking
- Cherry tomatoes: 4 halved
- Spring onions: 3 chopped
- Garlic: 3 cloves minced
- Vinegar: 3 tbsp
- Olive oil: 2 tbsp
- Tabasco: 5 dashes
- Salt: as per your taste
- Pepper: as per your taste
- Basil: 2 tbsp torn

Directions:
1. Take a bowl and add in cherry tomatoes, minced garlic, olive oil, vinegar, Tabasco, spring onion, and a lot of salt and pepper
2. Cooking Time: spaghetti as per packet instructions
3. Drain the pasta but keep 2 tablespoons of water and add to the sauce
4. Blend the sauce by removing tomatoes
5. Add pasta to the sauce and mix in tomatoes
6. Top with basil and serve

Nutrition:
Carbs: 21.8g
Protein: 8.45g
Fats: 15.95g
Calories: 379Kcal

728. Red Pesto Pasta

Preparation Time: 10 minutes
Servings: 4

Ingredients
- Pasta: 4 cups cooked
- Red cabbage: 1 head small
- Garlic: 2 cloves
- Lemon juice: 3 tbsp
- Pepper: ½ tsp

- Ground almonds: 2 tbsp
- Extra-virgin olive oil: 3 tbsp
- Salt: as per your need
- Chili sauce: 1 tbsp

Directions:
1. Prepare pasta as per packet instructions
2. Roast cabbage in the oven for 10 minutes at 160C
3. Take a blender and add all the ingredients including roasted cabbage
4. Blend them well
5. Mix pasta to the paste and season with more salt and pepper

Nutrition:
Carbs: 31.8g
Protein: 13.8g
Fats: 35.2g
Calories: 468Kcal

729. Roasted Broccoli With Pasta

Preparation Time: 30 minutes
Servings: 2

Ingredients
- Pasta: 1 cup (after cooking
- Broccoli florets: 1 cup
- Olive oil: 1 tbsp
- Cashew cream: ½ cup
- Green onion: 1 chopped
- Salt and pepper: as per your taste

Directions:
1. Cooking Time: pasta as per packet instructions
2. Preheat the oven to 400F
3. In a bowl, add broccoli and season with pepper and salt and brush with oil
4. Add them to the baking sheet and roast for 20 minutes
5. In a serving tray, spread pasta and top with roasted broccoli
6. Spread cashew cream on top
7. Sprinkle green onions on top and serve

Nutrition:
Carbs: 26.2g
Protein: 6.7g
Fats: 9.65g
Calories: 204Kcal

730. Roasted Veggie Lemon Salad

Preparation Time: 30 minutes
Servings: 4

Ingredients
- Macaroni pasta: 4 cups
- Carrots: 1 cup sliced
- Broccoli: 1 cup sliced
- Cauliflower: 1 cup sliced
- Olive oil: 1 tbsp
- Salt: as per your taste
- Pepper: as per your taste

For the Dressing:
- Lemon: 2 zest and juice
- Mustard: 1 tbsp
- Vinegar: 2 tsp
- Garlic: 1 clove crushed
- Extra-virgin olive oil: 2 tbsp
- Salt: as per your need

Directions:
1. Cooking Time: pasta as per packet instructions
2. Add all the vegetables to the baking tray, sprinkle salt and pepper, brush with olive oil and bake for 20 minutes
3. Prepare the dressing by adding all the ingredients except oil and combine it slowly at the end whisking to gain the correct consistency
4. Add pasta to the tray, and spread vegetables to the tray and pour dressing from the top and serve

Nutrition:
Carbs: 41.5g
Protein: 10.7g
Fats: 8.1g
Calories: 399Kcal

731. Savory Chickpeas Pasta

Preparation Time: 40 minutes
Servings: 2

Ingredients
- Pasta: 1 cup cooked
- Chickpeas: 1 cup
- Vegetable broth: 2 cups
- Olive oil: 1 tbsp
- Garlic: 2 cloves minced
- Red bell pepper: ½ cup chopped
- Onion: 1 medium minced
- Tomatoes: 1 cup chopped
- Black pepper: ¼ tsp
- Carrot: 1 diced
- Dried parsley: ½ tsp
- Tomato paste: 1 tbsp
- Salt: as per your need

Directions:
1. Cooking Time: pasta as per packet instructions
2. Cooking Time: chickpeas by soaking them overnight and boiling them for two hours on medium heat
3. Take a large saucepan and heat oil on medium flame
4. Add onions and Cooking Time: for 3-4 minutes
5. Add garlic and Cooking Time: for a minute and stir
6. Add tomatoes, bell pepper, carrot, chickpeas, oregano, tomato sauce, and parsley
7. Stir for around a minute or two
8. Add vegetable broth, cover, and boil
9. Simmer for 20-25 minutes until thickened
10. To give a better texture, mash some chickpeas with the back of the spoon
11. Add pasta to the chickpeas soup
12. Season with salt, and pepper

Nutrition:
Carbs: 56.4g
Protein: 14.47g
Fats: 17.7g
Calories: 442Kcal

732. Saucy Brussels Macaroni

Preparation Time: 30 minutes
Servings: 2

Ingredients
- Macaroni: 1 cup (after cooking
- Brussels sprout: 1 cup halved
- Olive oil: 1 tbsp
- Almond milk: ½ cup
- Flour: 2 tbsp
- Green onion: 1 chopped
- Salt and pepper: as per your taste
- Dried oregano: 2 tbsp

Directions:
1. Cooking Time: pasta as per packet instructions
2. Preheat the oven to 400F
3. In a bowl, add Brussels sprouts and season with pepper and salt and brush with oil
4. Add them to the baking sheet and roast for 20 minutes
5. In a serving tray, spread pasta and top with roasted sprouts
6. In a small pan, heat almond milk and stir in flour
7. Add pasta and sprouts to them and stir to thicken
8. Serve with oregano on top

Nutrition:
Carbs: 49.75g
Protein: 6.75g
Fats: 9.65g
Calories: 204Kcal

733. Simple Pasta With Chili Garlic Tarka

Preparation Time: 25 minutes
Servings: 2

Ingredients
- Pasta: 1 cup (after cooking
- Chickpeas: 1 cup can rinsed and drained
- Olive oil: 1 tbsp
- Garlic: 2 cloves minced
- Garlic: 3 cloves sliced

- Red onion: 1 small diced
- Parsley: ½ cup chopped
- Red chili flakes: 1 tsp
- Salt: 1 tsp
- Black pepper: ½ tsp
- Vegetable oil: 2 tbsp
- Cumin: 2 tbsp

Directions:
1. Cooking Time: pasta as per packet instructions
2. Take a saucepan and heat oil in it
3. Add minced garlic and onion to it and make them tender
4. Add salt and black pepper, stir
5. Add pasta and chickpeas and mix well
6. Lower the heat and cover and Cooking Time: for 5 minutes
7. In a separate small pan, pour vegetable oil and add sliced garlic and cumin
8. When garlic turn golden add red chili flakes and pour this mixture immediately on the top of the pasta

Nutrition:
Carbs: 41.2g
Protein: 11.25g
Fats: 23.6
Calories: 412Kcal

734. Spaghetti With Roasted Cauliflower

Preparation Time: 30 minutes
Servings: 2

Ingredients
- Spaghetti Pasta: 1 cup (after cooking
- Cauliflower florets: 1 cup
- Olive oil: 1 tbsp
- Salt and pepper: as per your taste

Directions:
1. Cooking Time: pasta as per packet instructions
2. Preheat the oven to 400F
3. In a bowl, add cauliflower and season with pepper and salt and brush with oil
4. Add them to the baking sheet and roast for 20 minutes
5. In a serving tray, spread pasta and top with roasted cauliflower
6. Serve with your favorite sauce

Nutrition:
Carbs: 21.2g
Protein: 4.8g
Fats: 17.9g
Calories: 172Kcal

735. Spicy Bean Pasta

Preparation Time: 30 minutes
Servings: 2

Ingredients
- Pasta: 1 cup (after cooking
- Spinach: 1 cup
- Beans: 1 cup can
- Green chili: 2 sliced
- Cayenne pepper: 1 tsp
- Garlic powder: ¼ tsp
- Tahini: 2 tbsp
- Onion: 1 small diced
- Salt: as per your taste
- Oil: 2 tbsp

Directions:
1. Cooking Time: pasta as per packet instructions
2. Take a pan and heat oil in it and add onion and green chili
3. Stir and Cooking Time: for 3-4 minutes
4. Now add spinach and beans and add salt, cayenne pepper, tahini, and garlic powder
5. Mix them all well and add pasta
6. Then reduce the heat and cover and Cooking Time: for 5 minutes
7. Remove from heat and serve hot

Nutrition:
Carbs: 51g
Protein: 15.4g
Fats: 25g
Calories: 389Kcal

736. Split Peas Pasta

Preparation Time: 50 minutes
Servings: 2
Ingredients
- Pasta: 1 cup cooked
- Split peas: 1 cup
- Spinach: 1 cup
- Water: 6 cups
- Onion: 1 large coarsely chopped
- Garlic: 1 tbsp paste
- Fine sea salt: as per your taste

Directions:
1. Cooking Time: pasta as per packet instructions
2. Take a large saucepan and add water and bring to boil
3. Add the chopped onions, garlic paste, spinach, split peas, and salt and bring to boil
4. Lower the heat to medium and Cooking Time: for 30-35 minutes with partial cover
5. Add the mixture to the high-speed blender to make a puree
6. Whisk in water if desired
7. Add again to the pan and slowly heat on a low flame for 10-15 minutes
8. Add in pasta during the last minutes
9. Add herbs or spices in between to augment the taste

Nutrition:
Carbs: 64.9g
Protein: 21.95g
Fats: 1.95g
Calories: 352Kcal

737. Stir-Fry Veggies With Pasta

Preparation Time: 45 minutes
Servings: 4
Ingredients
For the stir-fry vegetable:
- Purple cabbage: 1 chopped
- Broccoli: 1 cut into florets
- Bell pepper: 1 cut into strips
- Carrots: 1 cup sliced
- Onion: 1 sliced
- Garlic powder: 1 tsp
- Onion powder: 1 tsp
- Ginger: 1 tbsp minced
- Garlic: 1 tbsp minced
- Salt: as per your taste
- Pepper: as per your taste
- Oil: 2 tbsp
- Pasta: 2 cups (after cooked

For the sauce:
- Vinegar: 1 tbsp
- Vegan sugar: ½ tsp
- Soy sauce: ¼ cup
- Lime juice: 2 tbsp

Directions:
1. Take a large pot and add oil and heat
2. Add minced ginger and garlic and Cooking Time: for 30 seconds
3. Add onion, bell pepper, cabbage, broccoli and carrot, and stir
4. Sprinkle salt, pepper, onion powder, and ginger powder and mix well
5. Cooking Time: till the vegetable changes color
6. Cooking Time: pasta as per packet instructions
7. Spread pasta on the serving plate, top with fried vegetables
8. Pour the sauce and serve

Nutrition:
Carbs: 63 g
Protein: 12 g
Fats: 7 g
Calories: 355 Kcal

738. Stuffed Veggie Balls With Pasta

Preparation Time: 50 minutes
Servings: 4
Ingredients
- Pasta: 4 cups cooked
- Cauliflower: 1 cup florets
- Broccoli: 1 cup florets
- Spinach: 1 cup

- Potato: 1 cup
- Tahini: 2 tbsp
- Garlic: 1 clove
- Vinegar: 1 tbsp
- Pepper: as per your need
- Salt: as per your need

Directions:
1. Cooking Time: pasta as per packet instructions
2. Take a pan and boil salted water
3. Add broccoli, cauliflower, garlic, and potato in the salted water and cover and Cooking Time: for 30 minutes and add spinach at the end
4. Drain and mash using a potato masher and add to the bowl
5. Mix tahini, olive oil, vinegar, salt, pepper, and garlic together
6. Add this dressing to the broccoli mixture and combine well
7. Make small golf ball sized balls from this mixture
8. Preheat the oven to 200C
9. Add these ball to the baking sheet and brush with olive oil
10. Bake for 20 minutes or till they turn golden
11. Serve with pasta and top with your favorite dressing

Nutrition:
Carbs: 48.8g
Protein: 11.4g
Fats: 6.3g
Calories: 304Kcal

739. Tomato Sauce Pasta

Preparation Time: 30 minutes
Servings: 2

Ingredients
- Pasta: 1 cup cooked
- Green Peas: 2 cups
- Tomatoes: 1 cup chunks
- Tomatoes: 1 cup can
- Tomato paste: 2 tbsp
- Oregano: 2 tbsp dried
- Onion: 1 finely chopped
- Garlic: 3 cloves crushed
- Fresh basil: 1 small bunch
- Vegetable broth: 4 cups
- Salt & pepper: as per your taste
- Olive oil: 2 tbsp

Directions:
1. Cooking Time: pasta as per packet instructions and add peas at the end to heat theminutes
2. Take a large saucepan, heat olive oil in it
3. Add onion and garlic in it
4. Include tomato chunks, can chopped tomatoes, and tomato paste and combine them all together
5. Stir for a minute
6. Now add vegetable broth, oregano, and fresh basil
7. Bring the mixture to boil and then lower the heat to medium and Cooking Time: for 15 minutes
8. Use the hand blender to blend the soup contents
9. Add pasta and peas to the bowl and mix in tomato sauce
10. Season with salt and pepper and serve

Nutrition:
Carbs: 42.8g
Protein: 12.25g
Fats: 20.2g
Calories: 385.2Kcal

740. Two Beans Spaghetti

Preparation Time: 30 minutes
Servings: 2

Ingredients
- Spaghetti: 1 cup (after cooking
- Olive oil: 1 tbsp
- White Beans: ½ cup can
- Black Beans: ½ cup can
- Garlic: 2 cloves minced
- Garlic: 1 tbsp minced
- Red onion: 1 small diced
- Cumin: 1 tsp
- Salt: 1 tsp

- Black pepper: ½ tsp

Directions:
1. Cooking Time: pasta as per packet instructions
2. Take a large saucepan and add olive oil and heat on medium flame
3. Include onion, ginger, and garlic to the pan and Cooking Time: for a minute
4. Now add beans, cumin, salt, and pepper
5. Stir the spoon
6. Lower the heat and cover and Cooking Time: for 5 minutes and serve

Nutrition:
Carbs: 46.7g
Protein: 24.8g
Fats: 8.4g
Calories: 319Kcal

741. Vegetable Pasta With Tahini Dressing

Preparation Time: 45 minutes
Servings: 4

Ingredients
- Cauliflower: 1 small divided into florets
- Small carrots: 4 thickly sliced
- Red cabbage: 1 small shredded
- Vinegar: 3 tbsp
- Olive oil: 2 tbsp
- Ginger: 1 tbsp minced
- Garlic: 1 tbsp minced
- Salt: as per your taste
- Pepper: as per your taste
- Pasta: 2 cups (after cooked

For the Tahini Dressing:
- Tahini: 2 tbsp
- Almond milk: 4 tbsp
- Cumin seeds: ½ tsp dry roasted
- Garlic: ½ clove crushed
- Lemon juice: 2 tbsp
- Salt: ¼ tsp
- Boiling water: as per your need

Directions:
1. Take a large pot and add oil and heat
2. Add minced ginger and garlic and Cooking Time: for 30 seconds
3. Add all the vegetables and stir
4. Sprinkle salt and pepper and mix well
5. Cooking Time: till the vegetable changes color
6. Combine all the dressing ingredients and add boiling water bit by bit
7. Cooking Time: pasta as per packet instructions
8. Add pasta to the serving bowl and top with vegetables and pour dressing from the top

Nutrition:
Carbs: 23g
Protein: 4.7g
Fats: 7.9g
Calories: 177Kcal

742. Veggies Spaghetti

Preparation Time: 30 minutes
Servings: 4

Ingredients
- Spaghetti: 2 cups (after cooking
- Olive oil: 2 tbsp
- Garlic: 2 cloves minced
- Red onion: 1 small diced
- Bell pepper: 1 cup diced
- Cabbage: 1 cup diced
- Carrot: 1 cup diced
- Soy sauce: 1 tbsp
- Hot sauce: 1 tbsp
- Salt: 1 tsp
- Black pepper: ½ tsp
- Green onions: 2 tbsp

Directions:
1. Cooking Time: pasta as per packet instructions
2. Take a large saucepan and add olive oil and heat on medium flame
3. Include onion and garlic to the pan and Cooking Time: for a minute

4. Now add bell pepper, cabbage, carrot, salt, soy sauce, hot sauce, and pepper and stir for 5 minutes
5. Then add spaghetti and mix well
6. Then cover and Cooking Time: for 2 minutes on low flame and remove from heat
7. Sprinkle green onion on top and serve

Nutrition:
Carbs: 32g
Protein: 5.5g
Fats: 7.6g
Calories: 217Kcal

743. White Bean Pasta

Preparation Time: 30 minutes
Servings: 2

Ingredients
- Pasta: 1 cup (after cooking
- Olive oil: 1 tbsp
- Beans: 1 cup can
- Garlic: 2 cloves minced
- Garlic: 1 tbsp minced
- Red onion: 1 small diced
- Cumin: 1 tsp
- Salt: 1 tsp
- Black pepper: ½ tsp

Directions:
1. Cooking Time: pasta as per packet instructions
2. Take a large saucepan and add olive oil and heat on medium flame
3. Include onion, ginger, and garlic to the pan and Cooking Time: for a minute
4. Now add beans, cumin, salt, and pepper
5. Stir the spoon
6. Lower the heat and cover and Cooking Time: for 5 minutes and serve

Nutrition:
Carbs: 49.7g
Protein: 25.8g
Fats: 8.4g
Calories: 318Kcal

744. Instant Pot Spaghetti

Preparation time: 20 minutes
Cooking Time: 10 Minutes
Servings: 2

Ingredients
- 1 tablespoon coconut oil
- ½ cup tofu
- ½ onion, diced
- ½ teaspoon garlic powder
- ¼ teaspoon dried thyme
- ¼ teaspoon dried basil
- ¼ teaspoon salt
- Freshly ground black pepper
- ½ cup jarred spaghetti sauce
- 2 tablespoons tomato paste
- 1 cups vegetable broth
- 2 tablespoon goat cheese, plus extra for serving
- 6 ounces spaghetti noodles

Directions:
1. Press Saute on your Instant Pot .Add the coconut oil and tofu to the Instant Pot.
2. Cooking Time: for about 3 minutes, stirring and breaking up with a spoon occasionally.
3. Next, add the chopped onion. Stir, and Cooking Time: for about 4 minutes.
4. Next, stir in the garlic powder, thyme, basil, salt, pepper, spaghetti sauce, tomato paste broth and goat cheese. Stir very well.
5. Turn off the instant pot.
6. Break the noodles in half, and layer them in the tomato mixture, ensuring they are covered by the liquid. Press PRESSURE COOKING TIME: and set the timer for 8 minutes.
7. Place the lid on the Instant Pot, and turn the valve to 'sealing.'
8. When the timer goes off, very carefully do a forced pressure release

Cover your hand with a kitchen towel, and gently release the steam. When you hear the float valve drop down, all of the pressure is released.
9. Open the lid to the instant pot. It may look like there is a bit too much liquid, but just stir until it all comes together.
10. If it's still too much liquid for you, press SAUTE and Cooking Time: to reduce for 2 minutes. My family likes a lot of sauce on their pasta.
11. Divide into bowl, and serve topped with more goat cheese.

Nutrition:
Calories 522, Total Fat 22.3g, Saturated Fat 13.9g, Cholesterol 92mg, Sodium 817mg, Total Carbohydrate 54.9g, Dietary Fiber 2g 7%, Total Sugars 4.6g, Protein 27g

745. Mushrooms Creamed Noodles

Preparation time: 05 minutes
Cooking Time: 20 Minutes
Servings: 2

Ingredients
- ½ cup heavy creaminutes
- 2 cups vegetable broth
- ½ teaspoon dried oregano
- ½ teaspoon garlic minced
- ½ teaspoon red pepper flakes
- 1 cup noodles
- 1 cup mushrooms

Directions:
1. Put ¼ cup of the heavy cream in an Instant Pot. Stir in the broth, oregano, garlic and red pepper flakes until smooth. Stir in the noodles, then set the block of mushrooms right on top. Lock the lid onto the Instant pot.
2. Press Pressure Cooking Time: on Max pressure for 3 minutes with the Keep Warm setting off.
3. When the Instant pot has finished cooking, turn it off and let its pressure return to normal naturally for 1 minute. Then use the quick--release Directions to get rid of any residual pressure in the pot.
4. Unlatch the lid and open the cooker. Stir in the remaining 1/4 cup heavy cream. Set the lid askew over the pot and let sit for a couple of minutes so the noodles continue to absorb some of the liquid. Serve hot.

Nutrition:
Calories182, Total Fat 5.3g, Saturated Fat 1.6g, Cholesterol 31mg, Sodium 850mg, Total Carbohydrate 23.9g, Dietary Fiber 1.9g, Total Sugars 2g, Protein 10.2g

746. Pasta With Peppers

Preparation time: 05 minutes
Cooking Time: 10 Minutes
Servings: 2

Ingredients
- 1-1/2 cups spaghetti sauce
- 1 cup vegetable broth
- ½ tablespoon dried Italian seasoning blend
- 1 cup bell pepper strips
- 1 cup dried pasta
- 1 cup shredded Romano cheese

Directions:
1. Press the button SAUTÉ. Set it for HIGH, MORE, and set the time for 10 minutes.
2. Mix the broth, and seasoning blend in an Instant Pot. Cook, Turn off the SAUTÉ function; stir in the bell pepper strips and pasta. Lock the lid onto the pot.
3. Press Pressure Cooking Time: on Max pressure for 5 minutes with the Keep Warm setting off.
4. Use the quick--release Directions to bring the pot's pressure back to normal. Unlatch the lid and open the cooker. Stir in the shredded Romano cheese. Set the lid askew over the pot and set aside for 5 minutes to melt the cheese and let the pasta continue to absorb excess liquid. Serve by the big spoonful.

Nutrition:
Calories 291, Total Fat 6.2g, Saturated Fat 2.9g, Cholesterol 61mg, Sodium 994mg, Total Carbohydrate 43.7g, Dietary Fiber 1g, Total Sugars 3.5g, Protein 15.1g

747. Tofu & Dumplings

Preparation time: 05 minutes
Cooking Time: 20 Minutes
Servings: 2

Ingredients

- *2 tablespoons butter*
- *1 small onion, diced*
- *1 carrot, peeled and diced*
- *1 stalk green onion, sliced into 1/4" pieces*
- *½ teaspoon garlic powder*
- *2 cups vegetable broth*
- *1 bay leaves*
- *Salt*
- *Black pepper*
- *1/2 teaspoon basil*
- *½ teaspoon dried thyme*
- *½ teaspoon dried parsley*
- *1 cup tofu*
- *1 tablespoon corn-starch*
- *1/4 cup coconut cream*

The Dumplings:

- *1 cup coconut flour*
- *1 teaspoon baking powder*
- *½ teaspoon salt*
- *1 tablespoon salted butter*
- *½ cup coconut milk*

Directions:

1. Press "Sauté" on the Instant Pot and add in the butter and once melted, add in the onion, carrots and green onion and sauté for 5 minutes. Add the garlic and sauté for 1 minute longer
2. Then, pour in the broth and stir well. Add the tofu and make sure it's all covered by the broth. Toss the in the bay leaves and secure the lid
3. Hit "Keep Warm/Cancel" and then hit "Manual" or "Pressure Cook" High Pressure for 10 minutes
4. When the tofu is done cooking, perform a quick release. Discard the bay leaves and remove the tofu from pot with tongs. Set tofu aside in a bowl to cool
5. Add the seasoned salt, pepper, rubbed basil, thyme parsley, leafy tops from green onion to the pot and stir well. Let the pot rest for the time being
6. While the tofu's cooling down, make the dumplings by mixing together all the dumpling Ingredients. Begin by placing the flour, baking powder and salt in a mixing bowl and whisk together. Then, place the butter and milk in and microwave for 40 seconds.
7. Pour the milk/butter mixture into the flour and lightly mix with a fork until totally blended so a warm dough forms. From there, let your hands take over and lightly knead the dough. Then, on a clean surface covered with flour, take a flour-coated rolling pin and roll the dough to be 1/8" thick max Then, using a pizza cutter or knife, slice the into the dough vertically into strips about 1" wide and then slice horizontally about 2" wide, forming little rectangular strips. Dust with additional flour so they don't stick to each other
8. Now give the Instant pot some heat again by hitting "Sauté" and adjust so it's on the "More" or "High" setting. Once it bubbles, stir in the corn-starch slurry followed by adding the dumpling strips one-by-one and then give them a good stir making sure none are sticking to each other. Then, allow them to simmer for 10 minutes With The Lid On The Pot.
9. After 10 minutes of the dumplings boiling in the pot, hit "Keep Warm/Cancel" so the bubbles die

down
10. Add in the heavy cream and give everything a final stir until well combined.

Nutrition:
Calories 376, Total Fat 26.4g, Saturated Fat 16.1g, Cholesterol 31mg, Sodium 983mg, Total Carbohydrate 20.8g, Dietary Fiber 6.2g, Total Sugars 6.2g, Protein 17.9g

748. Fresh Tomato Mint Pasta

Preparation time: 05 minutes
Cooking Time: 10 Minutes
Servings: 2

Ingredients
- 1 cup pasta
- 1 tablespoon coconut oil
- ½ teaspoon garlic powder
- 1 tomato
- ½ tablespoon butter
- ¼ cup fresh mint
- ¼ cup coconut milk
- Salt & pepper to taste

Directions:
1. Add the coconut oil to the Instant Pot hit "Sauté", add in the garlic and stir. Add the tomatoes and a pinch of salt. Then add mint and pepper.
2. Next, add in coconut milk, butter and water a minute. Stir well, lastly, add in the pasta.
3. Secure the lid and hit "Keep Warm/Cancel" and then hit "Manual" or "Pressure Cook" High Pressure for 6 minutes. Quick release when done.
4. Enjoy

Nutrition:
Calories 350, Total Fat 18.5g, Saturated Fat 14.3g, Cholesterol 54mg, Sodium 47mg, Total Carbohydrate 39.4g, Dietary Fiber 1.9g, Total Sugars 2g, Protein 8.7g

749. Lemon Garlic Broccoli Macaroni

Preparation time: 05 minutes
Cooking Time: 10 Minutes
Servings: 2

Ingredients
- 1 cup macaroni
- ½ cup broccoli
- 1 tablespoon butter
- ½ teaspoon garlic powder
- 1 lemon
- Salt and Pepper to taste

Directions:
Add macaroni, butter, water, broccoli, lemon, garlic powder and salt to Instant Pot. Place lid on pot and lock into place to seal. Pressure Cooking Time: on High Pressure for 4 minutes. Use Quick Pressure Release.

Nutrition:
Calories 254, Total Fat 7.4g, Saturated Fat 3.9g, Cholesterol 62mg, Sodium 66mg, Total Carbohydrate 39.8g, Dietary Fiber 1.5g, Total Sugars 1.3g, Protein 8.4g

750. Spinach Pesto Pasta

Preparation time: 05 minutes
Cooking Time: 10 Minutes
Servings: 2

Ingredients
- 1 cup pasta
- 2 cups spinach, chopped,
- ¼ cup coconut oil
- ½ large lemon
- ¼ teaspoon garlic powder
- 1/8 cup chopped pecans
- ¼ cup goat cheese, grated
- ¼ teaspoon salt
- Freshly cracked pepper to taste
- 2 oz. mozzarella (optional

Directions:
1. Add the chopped and washed spinach to a food processor along with the coconut oil, 1/4 cup juice from the lemon, garlic powder, pecans, goat cheese, salt, and pepper. Purée the mixture until smooth and bright green. Add more oil if needed to allow the mixture to become a thick, smooth sauce. Taste the pesto

and adjust the salt, pepper, or lemon juice to your liking. Set the pesto aside.
2. Add pasta, water, and pesto, coconut oil into Instant Pot. Place lid on Instant pot and lock into place to seal. Pressure Cooking Time: on High Pressure for 4 minutes. Use Quick Pressure Release.
3. Add mozzarella cheese and serve.

Nutrition:
Calories 534, Total Fat 35.8g, Saturated Fat 27.7g, Cholesterol 65mg, Sodium 514mg, Total Carbohydrate 39g, Dietary Fiber 1.2g, Total Sugars 0.7g, Protein 17.5g

751. Paprika Pumpkin Pasta

Preparation time: 05 minutes
Cooking Time: 10 Minutes
Servings: 2

Ingredients
- ½ onion
- ½ tablespoon butter
- ½ teaspoon garlic
- ¼ teaspoon paprika
- 1 cup pumpkin purée
- 1.5 cups vegetable broth
- ¼ teaspoon salt
- Freshly cracked pepper
- 1 cup pasta
- 1/8 cup coconut creaminutes
- 1/4 cup grated mozzarella cheese

Directions:
1. Add the coconut oil to the Instant Pot hit "Sauté", Add butter and onion is soft and transparent. Add the paprika to the onion and sauté for about one minute more. Finally, add the pumpkin purée, vegetable broth, salt, and pepper to the instant pot and stir until the Ingredients are combined and smooth.
2. Add pasta Place lid on Instant pot and lock into place to seal. Pressure Cooking Time: on High Pressure for 4 minutes. Use Quick Pressure Release.
3. Add coconut cream and mozzarella cheese .

Nutrition:
Calories 327, Total Fat 8.9g, Saturated Fat 4.4g, Cholesterol 67mg, , Sodium 931mg, Total Carbohydrate 49g , Dietary Fiber 4.7g , Total Sugars 5.7g, Protein 13.5g

752. Creamy Mushroom Herb Pasta

Preparation time: 05 minutes
Cooking Time: 10 Minutes
Servings: 2

Ingredients
- ½ cup mushrooms
- ½ teaspoon garlic powder
- 1-1/2 tablespoon butter
- 1-1/2 tablespoon coconut flour
- 1 cup vegetable broth
- 1 spring fresh thyme
- ½ teaspoon basil
- Salt and pepper to taste

Directions:
1. Add the coconut oil to the Instant Pot hit "Sauté" add butter when butter melt then add garlic powder, add the sliced mushrooms and continue to Cooking Time: until the mushrooms have turned dark brown and all of the moisture they release has evaporated.
2. Add the flour, Whisk the vegetable broth into the Instant pot with the flour and mushrooms. Add the thyme, basil, and some freshly cracked pepper. Then add pasta Place lid on pot and lock into place to seal. Pressure Cooking Time: on High Pressure for 4 minutes. Use Quick Pressure Release.
3. Serve and enjoy.

Nutrition:
Calories 107, Total Fat 7.5g, Saturated Fat 4.8g, Cholesterol 15mg , Sodium 439mg, Total Carbohydrate 5.7g, Dietary Fiber 2.8g , Total Sugars 1.3g, Protein 4.2g

753. Cabbage And Noodles

Preparation time: 05 minutes
Cooking Time: 05 Minutes
Servings: 2

Ingredients

- *1 cup wide egg noodles*
- *1-1/2 tablespoon butter*
- *1small onion*
- *1/2 head green cabbage, shredded*
- *Salt and pepper to taste*

Directions:

1. *Add egg noodles, butter, water, onion, green cabbage, pepper and salt to Instant Pot. Place lid on Instant pot and lock into place to seal. Pressure Cooking Time: on High Pressure for 4 minutes. Use Quick Pressure Release.*
2. *Serve and enjoy*

Nutrition:
Calories183, Total Fat 6.8g, Saturated Fat 3.9g, Cholesterol 31mg, Sodium 78mg, Total Carbohydrate 27.2g, Dietary Fiber 5.9g, Total Sugars 7.6g, Protein 5.4g

754. Basil Spaghetti Pasta

Preparation time: 05 minutes
Cooking Time: 05 Minutes
Servings: 2

Ingredients

- *½ teaspoon garlic powder*
- *1 cup spaghetti*
- *2 large eggs*
- *¼ cup grated Parmesan cheese*
- *Freshly cracked pepper*
- *Salt to taste*
- *Handful fresh basil*

Directions:

1. *In a medium bowl, whisk together the eggs, 1/2 cup of the Parmesan cheese, and a generous dose of freshly cracked pepper.*
2. *Add spaghetti, water, basil, pepper and salt to Instant Pot. Place lid on Instant pot and lock into place to seal. Pressure Cooking Time: on High Pressure for 4 minutes. Use Quick Pressure Release.*
3. *Pour the eggs and Parmesan mixture over the hot pasta.*

Nutrition:
Calories216, Total Fat 2.3g, Saturated Fat 0.7g, Cholesterol 49mg, Sodium 160mg, Total Carbohydrate 36g, Dietary Fiber 0.1g, Total Sugars 0.4g, Protein 12.2g

755. Parsley Hummus Pasta

Preparation time: 05 minutes
Cooking Time: 05 Minutes
Servings: 2

Ingredients

- *½ cup chickpeas*
- *1/8 cup coconut oil*
- *½ fresh lemon*
- *1/8 cup tahini*
- *½ teaspoon garlic powder*
- *1/8 teaspoon cumin*
- *1/4 teaspoon salt*
- *1 green onions*
- *1/8 bunch fresh parsley, or to taste*
- *1 cup pasta*

Directions:

1. *Drain the chickpeas and add them to a food processor along with the olive oil, juice from the lemon, tahini, garlic powder, cumin, and salt. Pulse the Ingredients, adding a small amount of water if needed to keep it moving, until the hummus is smooth.*
2. *Slice the green onion (both white and green endsand pull the parsley leaves from the stems. Add the green onion and parsley to the hummus in the food processor and process again until only small flecks of green remain. Taste the hummus and adjust the salt, lemon, or garlic if needed.*
3. *Add pasta, water, into Instant Pot. Place lid on pot and lock into place to seal. Pressure Cooking Time: on High Pressure for 4 minutes. Use Quick Pressure Release.*

4. In sauté mode add hummus to pasta. When it mix turn off the switch of Instant pot.
5. Serve and enjoy

Nutrition:
Calories 582, Total Fat 26.3g, Saturated Fat 13.5g, Cholesterol 47mg, Sodium 338mg, Total Carbohydrate 71g, Dietary Fiber 10.8g, Total Sugars 6.1g, Protein 19.9g

756. Creamy Spinach Artichoke Pasta

Preparation time: 05 minutes
Cooking Time: 05 Minutes
Servings: 2

Ingredients
- 1 tablespoon butter
- ¼ teaspoon garlic powder
- 1 cup vegetable broth
- 1 cup coconut milk
- ¼ teaspoon salt
- Freshly cracked pepper
- ½ cup pasta
- 1/4 cup fresh baby spinach
- ½ cup quartered artichoke hearts
- 1/8 cup grated Parmesan cheese

Directions:
1. Instant Pot hit "Sauté" add butter when its melt add garlic powder just until it's tender and fragrant.
2. Add the vegetable broth, coconut milk, salt, some freshly cracked pepper, and the pasta. Place lid on pot and lock into place to seal. Pressure Cooking Time: on High Pressure for 4 minutes. Use Quick Pressure Release.
3. Instant pot in sauté mode add the spinach, a handful at a time, to the hot pasta and sauce and toss it in the pasta until it wilts. Stir the chopped artichoke hearts into the pasta. Sprinkle grated Parmesan over the pasta, then stir slightly to incorporate the Parmesan. Top with an additional Parmesan then serve.

Nutrition:
Calories 457, Total Fat 36.2g, Saturated Fat 29.6g, Cholesterol 40mg, Sodium 779mg, Total Carbohydrate 27.6g, Dietary Fiber 4g, Total Sugars 4.7g, Protein 10.3g

757. Easy Spinach Ricotta Pasta

Preparation time: 05 minutes
Cooking Time: 05 Minutes
Servings: 2

Ingredients
- 1/2 lb. uncooked Tagliatelle
- 1 tablespoon coconut oil
- ½ teaspoon garlic powder
- ¼ cup almond milk
- ½ cup whole milk ricotta
- 1/8 teaspoon salt
- Freshly cracked pepper
- ¼ cup chopped spinach

Directions:
1. Add the vegetable broth, spinach, salt, some freshly cracked pepper, and the pasta. Place lid on Instant pot and lock into place to seal. Pressure Cooking Time: on High Pressure for 4 minutes. Use Quick Pressure Release.
2. Prepare the ricotta sauce. Mince the garlic and add it to a large skillet with the olive oil. Cooking Time: over medium-low heat for 1-2 minutes, or just until soft and fragrant (but not browned). Add the almond milk and ricotta, then stir until relatively smooth (the ricotta may be slightly grainy). Allow the sauce to heat through and come to a low simmer. The sauce will thicken slightly as it simmers. Once it's thick enough to coat the spoon (3-5 minutes), season with salt and pepper.
3. Add the cooked and drained pasta to the sauce and toss to coat. If the sauce becomes too thick or dry, add a small amount of the reserved pasta cooking water. Serve warm.

Nutrition:

Calories277, Total Fat 18.9g, Saturated Fat 15.2g, Cholesterol 16mg, Sodium 191mg, Total Carbohydrate 23.8g, Dietary Fiber 1.2g, Total Sugars 1.4g, Protein 5.1g

758. Roasted Red Pepper Pasta

Preparation time: 05 minutes
Cooking Time: 05 Minutes
Servings: 2

Ingredients

- 2 cups vegetable broth
- ½ cup Spaghetti
- 1 small onion
- ½ teaspoon garlic minced
- ½ cup roasted red peppers
- ½ cup roasted diced tomatoes
- ¼ tablespoon dried mint
- 1/8 teaspoon crushed red pepper
- Freshly cracked black pepper
- ½ cup goat cheese

Directions:

1. In an Instant pot, combine the vegetable broth, onion, garlic, red pepper slices, diced tomatoes, mint, crushed red pepper, and some freshly cracked black pepper. Stir these Ingredients to combine. Add spaghetti to the Instant pot.
2. Place lid on Instant pot and lock into place to seal. Pressure Cooking Time: on High Pressure for 4 minutes. Use Quick Pressure Release.
3. Divide the goat cheese into tablespoon sized pieces, then add them to the Instant pot. Stir the pasta until the cheese melts in and creates a smooth sauce. Serve hot.

Nutrition:
Calories198, Total Fat 4.9g, Saturated Fat 2.2g, Cholesterol 31mg, Sodium 909mg, Total Carbohydrate 26.8g, Dietary Fiber 1.9g, Total Sugars 5.6g, Protein 11.9g

759. Cheese Beetroot Greens Maccheroni

Preparation time: 05 minutes
Cooking Time: 05 Minutes
Servings: 2

Ingredients

- 1 tablespoon butter
- 1 clove garlic minced
- 1 cup button mushrooms
- ½ bunch beetroot greens
- ½ cup vegetable broth
- ½ cup maccheroni
- ¼ teaspoon salt
- ½ cup grated Parmesan cheese
- Freshly cracked pepper

Directions:

1. Instant Pot hit "Sauté" add butter, Garlic and slice the mushrooms. Add the beetroot greens to the pot along with 1/2 cup vegetable broth. Stir the beetroot greens as it cooks until it is fully wilted.
2. Add vegetable broth, maccheroni, salt and pepper, Place lid on Instant pot and lock into place to seal. Pressure Cooking Time: on High Pressure for 4 minutes. Use Quick Pressure Release. Add grated parmesan cheese.

Nutrition:
Calories 147, Total Fat 8g, Saturated Fat 4.8g, Cholesterol 23mg, Sodium 590mg, Total Carbohydrate 12.7g, Dietary Fiber 1g, Total Sugars 1.5g, Protein 6.5g

760. Pastalaya

Preparation time: 05 minutes
Cooking Time: 05 Minutes
Servings: 2

Ingredients

- ½ tablespoon avocado oil
- 1 cup cottage cheese
- ½ teaspoon garlic powder
- 1 diced tomato
- ¼ teaspoon dried basil
- ¼ teaspoon smoked paprika
- ¼ teaspoon dried rosemary
- Freshly cracked pepper

- 1 cup vegetable broth
- ½ cup water
- 1 cup orzo pasta
- 1 tablespoon coconut creaminutes
- ½ bunch fresh coriander
- ½ bunch leek

Directions:

1. In the Instant Pot, place the garlic powder and avocado oil, Sauté for 15 seconds, or until the garlic is fragrant. Add diced tomatoes, basil, smoked paprika, rosemary, freshly cracked pepper, and orzo pasta to the Instant pot. Finally, add the vegetable broth and ½ cup of water, and stir until everything is evenly combined.
2. Place the lid on the Instant Pot, and bringing the toggle switch into the "seal" position. Press Manual Or Pressure Cooking Time: and adjust time for 5 minutes.
3. When the five minutes are up, do a natural release for 5 minutes and then move the toggle switch to "Vent" to release the rest of the pressure in the pot.
4. Remove the lid. If the mixture looks watery, press "Sauté", and bring the mixture up to a boil and let it boil for a few minutes. It will thicken as it boils. Add the coconut cream and leek to the Instant pot, stir and let warm through for a few minutes.
5. Serve and garnish with coriander toast. Enjoy!

Nutrition:
Calories 351, Total Fat 6.8g, Saturated Fat 3.5g, Cholesterol 56mg, , Sodium 869mg, Total Carbohydrate 45.5g, Dietary Fiber 1.5g , Total Sugars 2.9g, Protein 26.3g

761. Corn And Chiles Fusilli

Preparation time: 05 minutes
Cooking Time: 05 Minutes
Servings: 2

Ingredients

- ½ tablespoon butter
- 1 tablespoon garlic minced
- 2 oz. can green chills
- ½ cup frozen corn kernels
- ¼ teaspoon cumin
- 1/8 teaspoon paprika
- 1 cup fusilli
- 1 cup vegetable broth
- ¼ cup coconut creaminutes
- 2 leeks, sliced
- 1/8 bunch parsley
- 1 oz. shredded mozzarella cheese

Directions:

1. Add In the Instant Pot, add butter when butter melt place minced garlic, salt and pepper press SAUTE on the Instant pot. Add the can of green chills (with juices), frozen corn kernels, cumin, and red pepper.
2. Add the uncooked fusilli and vegetable broth to the Instant pot.
3. Place the lid on the Instant Pot, and bringing the toggle switch into the "seal" position. Press Manual Or Pressure Cooking Time: and adjust time for 5 minutes.
4. When the five minutes are up, do a natural release for 5 minutes and then move the toggle switch to "Vent" to release the rest of the pressure in the pot.
5. Remove the lid. If the mixture looks watery, press "Sauté", and bring the mixture up to a boil and let it boil for a few minutes. Then add the coconut cream and stir until it has fully coated the pasta. Stir in most of the sliced leek and parsley, reserving a little to sprinkle over top. mozzarella on top of the pasta.

Nutrition:
Calories 399, Total Fat 14.4g, Saturated Fat 10g, Cholesterol 15mg , Sodium 531mg, Total Carbohydrate 56.2g, Dietary Fiber 4.9g , Total Sugars 7.2g, Protein 15.4g

Creamy Penne With Vegetables

Preparation time: 05 minutes

Cooking Time: 10 Minutes
Servings: 2

Ingredients

- ½ tablespoon butter
- 1 cup penne
- 1 small onion
- ½ teaspoon garlic powder
- 1 carrot
- ½ red bell pepper
- ½ pumpkin
- 2 cups vegetable broth
- 2 oz. coconut creaminutes
- 1/8 cup grated Parmesan
- 1/8 teaspoon salt or to taste
- Freshly cracked black pepper
- Dash hot sauce, optional
- ¼ cup cauliflower florets

Directions:

1. Set Instant Pot to SAUTE. Add the butter and allow it to melt. Add the onions and garlic powder Cooking Time: for 2 minutes. Stir regularly. Add the carrots, red pepper and pumpkin and cauliflower in the pot.
2. Add vegetable broth and coconut cream then add hot sauce. Add penne salt and pepper.
3. Set Instant Pot to MANUAL or PRESSURE COOKING TIME: on HIGH PRESSURE for 20 minutes. Lock lid and make sure vent is closed. When cooking time ends, release pressure and wait for steam to completely stop before opening lid.
4. Stir in cheese, sprinkle a bit on top of the pasta when you serve it.

Nutrition:
Calories 381, Total Fat 13.2g, Saturated Fat 8.7g, Cholesterol 56mg, Sodium 1006mg, Total Carbohydrate 52.3g, Dietary Fiber 4.7g, Total Sugars 8.6g, Protein 15.3g

763. Pasta With Eggplant Sauce

Preparation time: 05 minutes
Cooking Time: 10 Minutes

Servings: 2

Ingredients

- 1 tablespoon coconut oil
- 2 cloves garlic
- 1 small onion
- 1 med eggplant,
- 1 cup diced tomatoes
- 1 tablespoon tomato sauce
- ¼ teaspoon dried thyme
- ½ teaspoon honey
- Pinch paprika,
- Freshly cracked pepper
- ¼ salt or to taste
- 6 oz. Spaghetti
- Handful fresh coriander, chopped
- 2 tablespoon grated goat cheese

Directions:

1. Set Instant Pot to SAUTE. Add the coconut oil and allow it to melt. Add the onions and garlic powder Cooking Time: for 2 minutes or until the onion is soft and transparent.
2. Add eggplant, diced tomatoes, tomato sauce, thyme, honey, paprika, and freshly cracked pepper. Stir well to combine, Add Spaghetti, and vegetable broth salt and pepper.
3. Set Instant Pot to Manual Or Pressure Cooking Time: on High Pressure for 20 minutes. Lock lid and make sure vent is closed. When cooking time ends, release pressure and wait for steam to completely stop before opening lid.
4. Top each serving with grated goat and a sprinkle of fresh coriander.

Nutrition:
Calories 306, Total Fat 18g, Saturated Fat 12.9g, Cholesterol 30mg, Sodium 188mg, Total Carbohydrate 27g, Dietary Fiber 12.6g 45%, Total Sugars 13.9g, Protein 14.2g

764. Creamy Pesto Pasta With Tofu & Broccoli

Preparation time: 05 minutes

Cooking Time: 10 Minutes
Servings: 2

Ingredients

- 4 oz. Farfalline pasta
- 4 oz. frozen broccoli florets
- ½ tablespoon coconut oil
- ½ cup tofu
- ¼ cup basil pesto
- ¼ cup vegetable broth
- 2 oz. heavy creaminutes

Directions:

1. In Instant pot add Farfalline pasta, broccoli, coconut oil, tofu, basil pesto, vegetable broth. Cover the Instant pot and lock it in.
2. Set the manual or pressure Cooking Time: timer for 10 minutes. Make sure the timer is set to "sealing".
3. Once the timer reaches zero, quick release the pressure. Add heavy cream.
4. Enjoy.

Nutrition:
Calories 383, Total Fat 17.8g, Saturated Fat 10.1g, Cholesterol 39mg, Sodium 129mg, Total Carbohydrate 44g, Dietary Fiber 2.4g, Total Sugars 3.2g, Protein 13.6g

765. Chili Cheese Cottage Cheese Mac

Preparation time: 05 minutes
Cooking Time: 10 Minutes
Servings: 2

Ingredients

- ½ tablespoon butter
- 1 cup cottage cheese
- ½ teaspoon garlic powder
- 1 small onion
- 1 tablespoon coconut flour
- ½ tablespoon chili powder
- ¼ teaspoon smoked paprika
- ¼ teaspoon dried basil
- 1 cup tomato paste
- 2 cups vegetable broth
- 1 cup dry macaroni
- ½ cup shredded sharp cheddar

Directions:

1. Set the Instant Pot to sauté. Add butter and wait one minute to heat up.
2. Add the cottage cheese. sauté for one minute. Stir often. Add onion and garlic powder.
3. Add the chili powder, smoked paprika, basil, tomato paste, and 2 cups of vegetable broth. Add the dry macaroni, cottage cheese. Stir well. Cover the Instant pot and lock it in.
4. Set the manual or pressure Cooking Time: timer for 10 minutes. Make sure the timer is set to "sealing".
5. Once the timer reaches zero, quick release the pressure.
6. Add shredded sharp cheddar cheese and enjoy.

Nutrition:
Calories 509, Total Fat 11.3g, Saturated Fat 6.4g, Cholesterol 23mg, Sodium 1454mg, Total Carbohydrate 70.3g, Dietary Fiber 10.8g, Total Sugars 20.5g, Protein 34.8g

76. Spicy Cauliflower Pasta

Preparation time: 05 minutes
Cooking Time: 10 Minutes
Servings: 2

Ingredients

- 1 tablespoon coconut oil
- 1 teaspoon garlic powder
- ¼ teaspoon paprika
- ½ cup cauliflower florets
- ½ cup broccoli florets
- 1 cup bow tie pasta
- ¼ cup shredded goat cheese
- Salt & pepper
- 1 cup vegetable broth

Directions:

1. In the Instant Pot set saute button add coconut oil when oil is hot, place garlic powder, paprika, cauliflower florets, broccoli florets, salt and pepper and press SAUTE on the IP.

2. Sauté the mixture until it's cooked through.
3. Add the vegetable broth, and dry bow tie pasta, salt and pepper.
4. Mix every well and place the lid on the Instant Pot, and bringing the toggle switch into the "seal" position.
5. Press MANUAL or PRESSURE COOKING TIME: and adjust time for 5 minutes.
6. When the five minutes are up, do a natural release for 5 minutes and then move the toggle switch to "Vent" to release the rest of the pressure in the pot.
7. Remove the lid. If the mixture looks watery, press "Sauté", and bring the mixture up to a boil and let it boil for a few minutes. It will thicken as it boils.
8. Serve and garnish with garlic toast. Enjoy!

Nutrition:
Calories298, Total Fat 10.4g, Saturated Fat 7.2g, Cholesterol 50mg, Sodium 426mg, Total Carbohydrate 39.6g, Dietary Fiber 1.5g, Total Sugars 1.8g, Protein 12.2g

767. Tasty Mac And Cheese

Preparation time: 05 minutes
Cooking Time: 10 Minutes
Servings: 2

Ingredients
- ½ cup soy milk
- 1 cup dry macaroni
- ½ cup shredded mozzarella cheese
- ¼ teaspoon salt
- ¼ teaspoon Dijon mustard
- 1/8 teaspoon red chilli
- 5 fresh cracked pepper, optional

Directions:
Add macaroni, soy milk, water, and salt, chilli powder, Dijon mustard to the Instant Pot. Place lid on Instant pot and lock into place to seal. Pressure Cooking Time: on High Pressure for 4 minutes. Use Quick Pressure Release. Stir cheese into macaroni and then stir in the cheeses until melted and combined.

Nutrition:
Calories 210, Total Fat 3g, Saturated Fat 1g, Cholesterol 4mg, Sodium 374mg, Total Carbohydrate 35.7g, Dietary Fiber 1.8g, Total Sugars 3.6g, Protein 9.6g

768. Jackfruit And Red Pepper Pasta

Preparation time: 05 minutes
Cooking Time: 10 Minutes
Servings: 2

Ingredients
- ½ cup Gnocchi
- 1/8 cup avocado oil
- ½ tablespoon garlic powder
- 1/2 teaspoon crushed red pepper
- ½ bunch fresh mint
- ½ cup jackfruit
- Salt and pepper

Directions:
1. Set Instant Pot to SAUTE. Add the avocado oil and allow it to sizzle. Add the garlic powder Cooking Time: for 2 minutes. Stir regularly.
2. Add jackfruit and Cooking Time: until about 4 - 5 minutes. Add gnocchi, water, fresh mint, salt and red pepper into Instant Pot.
3. Set Instant Pot to MANUAL or PRESSURE COOKING TIME: on HIGH PRESSURE for 20 minutes. Lock lid and make sure vent is closed. When cooking time ends, release pressure and wait for steam to completely stop before opening lid.
4. Enjoy.

Nutrition:
Calories 110, Total Fat 2.3g, Saturated Fat 0.4g, Cholesterol 0mg, Sodium 168mg, Total Carbohydrate 21.5g, Dietary Fiber 2.5g, Total Sugars 0.6g, Protein 2.3g

769. Creamy Mushroom Pasta With Broccoli

Preparation time: 05 minutes
Cooking Time: 10 Minutes

Servings: 2

Ingredients

- 1 tablespoon coconut oil
- 1 small onion
- ½ teaspoon garlic powder
- 1 cup mushrooms
- 1 tablespoon coconut flour
- 1 cup water
- ¼ cup red wine
- 1/8 cup coconut cream
- ¼ teaspoon dried basil
- Salt and pepper
- 1/8 bunch fresh cilantro
- ½ cup mozzarella
- 4 oz. pasta
- ½ cup broccoli

Directions:

1. Set Instant Pot to SAUTE. Add the coconut oil allow it to sizzle. Add coconut flour and mushrooms sauté for 2 minutes. Stir regularly. It will coat the mushrooms and will begin to turn golden in colour. Just make sure to keep stirring so that the flour does not burn.
2. Combine water along with the red wine and basil. Whisk until no flour lumps remain.
3. Add pasta, broccoli, and onion and garlic powder. Set Instant Pot to MANUAL or PRESSURE COOKING TIME: on HIGH PRESSURE for 20 minutes. Lock lid and make sure vent is closed. When cooking time ends, release pressure and wait for steam to completely stop before opening lid.
4. Stir in cheese and coconut cream.
5. Serve hot and enjoy.

Nutrition:

Calories 363, Total Fat 14.2g, Saturated Fat 11g, Cholesterol 45mg, Sodium 91mg, Total Carbohydrate 43.4g, Dietary Fiber 4.6g, Total Sugars 3.9g, Protein 12.1g

SAUCES, AND CONDIMENTS

770. Green Goddess Hummus

Preparation time: 5 minutes
Cooking time: 0 minute
Servings: 6

Ingredients:

- ¼ cup tahini
- ¼ cup lemon juice
- 2 tablespoons olive oil
- ½ cup chopped parsley
- ¼ cup chopped basil
- 3 tablespoons chopped chives
- 1 large clove of garlic, peeled, chopped
- ½ teaspoon salt
- 15-ounce cooked chickpeas
- 2 tablespoons water

Directions:

1. Place all the ingredients in the order in a food processor or blender and then pulse for 3 to 5 minutes at high speed until the thick mixture comes together.
2. Tip the hummus in a bowl and then serve.

Nutrition Value:

Calories: 110.4 Cal
Fat: 6 g
Carbs: 11.5 g
Protein: 4.8 g
Fiber: 2.6 g

771. Garlic, Parmesan And White Bean Hummus

Preparation time: 5 minutes
Cooking time: 0 minute
Servings: 6

Ingredients:

- 4 cloves of garlic, peeled
- 12 ounces cooked white beans
- 1/8 teaspoon salt
- ½ lemon, zested

- 1 tablespoon lemon juice
- 1 tablespoon olive oil
- 3 tablespoon water
- 1/4 cup grated Parmesan cheese

Directions:
1. Place all the ingredients in the order in a food processor or blender and then pulse for 3 to 5 minutes at high speed until the thick mixture comes together.
2. Tip the hummus in a bowl and then serve.

Nutrition Value:
Calories: 90 Cal
Fat: 7 g
Carbs: 5 g
Protein: 2 g
Fiber: 1 g

772. Tomato Jam

Preparation time: 10 minutes
Cooking time: 20 minutes
Servings: 16
Ingredients:
- 2 pounds tomatoes
- ¼ teaspoon. ground black pepper
- ½ teaspoon. salt
- ¼ cup coconut sugar
- ½ teaspoon. white wine vinegar
- ¼ teaspoon. smoked paprika

Directions:
1. Place a large pot filled with water over medium heat, bring it to boil, then add tomatoes and boil for 1 minute.
2. Transfer tomatoes to a bowl containing chilled water, let them stand for 2 minutes, and then peel them by hand.
3. Cut the tomatoes, remove and discard seeds, then chop tomatoes and place them in a large pot.
4. Sprinkle sugar over coconut, stir until mixed and let it stand for 10 minutes.
5. Then place the pot over medium-high heat, Cooking Time: for 15 minutes, then add remaining ingredients except for vinegar and Cooking Time: for 10 minutes until thickened.
6. Remove pot from heat, stir in vinegar and serve.

Nutrition Value:
Calories: 17.6 Cal
Fat: 1.3 g
Carbs: 1.5 g
Protein: 0.2 g
Fiber: 0.3 g

773. Kale And Walnut Pesto

Preparation time: 5 minutes
Cooking time: 10 minutes
Servings: 4
Ingredients:
- 1/2 bunch kale, leaves chop
- 1/2 cup chopped walnuts
- 2 cloves of garlic, peeled
- 1/4 cup nutritional yeast
- ½ of lemon, juiced
- 1/4 cup olive oil
- ¼ teaspoon. ground black pepper
- 1/3 teaspoon. salt

Directions:
1. Place a large pot filled with water over medium heat, bring it to boil, then add kale and boil for 5 minutes until tender.
2. Drain kale, then transfer it in a blender, add remaining ingredients and then pulse for 5 minutes until smooth.
3. Serve straight away.

Nutrition Value:
Calories: 344 Cal
Fat: 29 g
Carbs: 16 g
Protein: 9 g
Fiber: 6 g

774. Buffalo Chicken Dip

Preparation time: 5 minutes
Cooking time: 15 minutes

Servings: 4
Ingredients:
- 2 cups cashews
- 2 teaspoons garlic powder
- 1 1/2 teaspoons salt
- 2 teaspoons onion powder
- 3 tablespoons lemon juice
- 1 cup buffalo sauce
- 1 cup of water
- 14-ounce artichoke hearts, packed in water, drained

Directions:
1. Switch on the oven, then set it to 375 degrees F and let it preheat.
2. Meanwhile, pour 3 cups of boiling water in a bowl, add cashews and let soak for 5 minutes.
3. Then drain the cashew, transfer them into the blender, pour in water, add lemon juice and all the seasoning and blend until smooth.
4. Add artichokes and buffalo sauce, process until chunky mixture comes together, and then transfer the dip to an ovenproof dish.
5. Bake for 20 minutes and then serve.

Nutrition Value:
Calories: 100 Cal
Fat: 100 g
Carbs: 100 g
Protein: 100 g
Fiber: 100 g

775. Barbecue Tahini Sauce

Preparation time: 5 minutes
Cooking time: 0 minute
Servings: 8
Ingredients:
- 6 tablespoons tahini
- 3/4 teaspoon garlic powder
- 1/8 teaspoon red chili powder
- 2 teaspoons maple syrup
- 1/4 teaspoon salt
- 3 teaspoons molasses
- 3 teaspoons apple cider vinegar
- 1/4 teaspoon liquid smoke
- 10 teaspoons tomato paste
- 1/2 cup water

Directions:
1. Place all the ingredients in the order in a food processor or blender and then pulse for 3 to 5 minutes at high speed until smooth.
2. Tip the sauce in a bowl and then serve.

Nutrition Value:
Calories: 86 Cal
Fat: 5 g
Carbs: 7 g
Protein: 2 g
Fiber: 0 g

776. Vegan Ranch Dressing

Preparation time: 5 minutes
Cooking time: 0 minute
Servings: 16
Ingredients:
- 1/4 teaspoon. ground black pepper
- 2 teaspoon. chopped parsley
- 1/2 teaspoon. garlic powder
- 1 tablespoon chopped dill
- 1/2 teaspoon. onion powder
- 1 cup vegan mayonnaise
- 1/2 cup soy milk, unsweetened

Directions:
1. Take a medium bowl, add all the ingredients in it and then whisk until combined.
2. Serve straight away

Nutrition Value:
Calories: 16 Cal
Fat: 9 g
Carbs: 0 g
Protein: 0 g
Fiber: 0 g

777. Cashew Yogurt

Preparation time: 12 hours and 5 minutes
Cooking time: 0 minute
Servings: 8
Ingredients:

- 3 probiotic supplements
- 2 2/3 cups cashews, unsalted, soaked in warm water for 15 minutes
- 1/4 teaspoon sea salt
- 4 tablespoon lemon juice
- 1 1/2 cup water

Directions:
1. Drain the cashews, add them into the food processor, then add remaining ingredients, except for probiotic supplements, and pulse for 2 minutes until smooth.
2. Tip the mixture in a bowl, add probiotic supplements, stir until mixed, then cover the bowl with a cheesecloth and let it stand for 12 hours in a dark and cool room.
3. Serve straight away.

Nutrition Value:
Calories: 252 Cal
Fat: 19.8 g
Carbs: 14.1 g
Protein: 8.3 g
Fiber: 1.5 g

778. Nacho Cheese Sauce

Preparation time: 15 minutes
Cooking time: 5 minutes
Servings: 12
Ingredients:
- 2 cups cashews, unsalted, soaked in warm water for 15 minutes
- 2 teaspoons salt
- 1/2 cup nutritional yeast
- 1 teaspoon garlic powder
- 1/2 teaspoon smoked paprika
- 1/2 teaspoon red chili powder
- 1 teaspoon onion powder
- 2 teaspoons Sriracha
- 3 tablespoons lemon juice
- 4 cups water, divided

Directions:
1. Drain the cashews, transfer them to a food processor, then add remaining ingredients, reserving 3 cups water, and, and pulse for 3 minutes until smooth.
2. Tip the mixture in a saucepan, place it over medium heat and Cooking Time: for 3 to 5 minutes until the sauce has thickened and bubbling, whisking constantly.
3. When done, taste the sauce to adjust seasoning and then serve.

Nutrition Value:
Calories: 128 Cal
Fat: 10 g
Carbs: 8 g
Protein: 5 g
Fiber: 1 g

779. Thai Peanut Sauce

Preparation time: 10 minutes
Cooking time: 10 minutes
Servings: 4
Ingredients:
- 2 tablespoons ground peanut, and more for topping
- 2 tablespoons Thai red curry paste
- ½ teaspoon salt
- 1 tablespoon sugar
- 1/2 cup creamy peanut butter
- 2 tablespoons apple cider vinegar
- 3/4 cup coconut milk, unsweetened

Directions:
1. Take a saucepan, place it over low heat, add all the ingredients, whisk well until combined, and then bring the sauce to simmer.
2. Then remove the pan from heat, top with ground peanuts, and serve.

Nutrition Value:
Calories: 397 Cal
Fat: 50 g
Carbs: 16 g
Protein: 26 g
Fiber: 4 g

780. Garlic Alfredo Sauce

Preparation time: 10 minutes
Cooking time: 5 minutes
Servings: 4

Ingredients:
- 1 1/2 cups cashews, unsalted, soaked in warm water for 15 minutes
- 6 cloves of garlic, peeled, minced
- 1/2 medium sweet onion, peeled, chopped
- 1 teaspoon salt
- 1/4 cup nutritional yeast
- 1 tablespoon lemon juice
- 2 tablespoons olive oil
- 2 cups almond milk, unsweetened
- 12 ounces fettuccine pasta, cooked, for serving

Directions:
1. Take a small saucepan, place it over medium heat, add oil and when hot, add onion and garlic, and Cooking Time: for 5 minutes until sauté.
2. Meanwhile, drain the cashews, transfer them into a food processor, add remaining ingredients including onion mixture, except for pasta, and pulse for 3 minutes until very smooth.
3. Pour the prepared sauce over pasta, toss until coated and serve.

Nutrition Value:
Calories: 439 Cal
Fat: 20 g
Carbs: 52 g
Protein: 15 g
Fiber: 4 g

781. Spicy Red Wine Tomato Sauce

Preparation time: 5 minutes
Cooking time: 1 hour
Servings: 4

Ingredients:
- 28 ounces puree of whole tomatoes, peeled
- 4 cloves of garlic, peeled
- 1 tablespoon dried basil
- 1/4 teaspoon ground black pepper
- 1 tablespoon dried oregano
- 1/4 teaspoon red pepper flakes
- 1 tablespoon dried sage
- 1 tablespoon dried thyme
- 3 teaspoon coconut sugar
- 1/2 of lemon, juice
- 1/4 cup red wine

Directions:
1. Take a large saucepan, place it over medium heat, add tomatoes and remaining ingredients, stir and simmer for 1 hour or more until thickened and cooked.
2. Serve sauce over pasta.

Nutrition Value:
Calories: 110 Cal
Fat: 2.5 g
Carbs: 9 g
Protein: 2 g
Fiber: 2 g

782. Vodka Cream Sauce

Preparation time: 5 minutes
Cooking time: 5 minutes
Servings: 1

Ingredients:
- 1/4 cup cashews, unsalted, soaked in warm water for 15 minutes
- 24-ounce marinara sauce
- 2 tablespoons vodka
- 1/4 cup water

Directions:
1. Drain the cashews, transfer them in a food processor, pour in water, and blend for 2 minutes until smooth.
2. Tip the mixture in a pot, stir in pasta sauce and vodka and simmer for 3 minutes over medium heat until done, stirring constantly.
3. Serve sauce over pasta.

Nutrition Value:
Calories: 207 Cal
Fat: 16 g
Carbs: 9.2 g
Protein: 2.4 g
Fiber: 4.3 g

783. Hot Sauce

Preparation time: 10 minutes
Cooking time: 15 minutes
Servings: 6
Ingredients:

- 4 Serrano peppers, destemmed
- 1/2 of medium white onion, chopped
- 1 medium carrot, chopped
- 10 habanero chilies, destemmed
- 6 cloves of garlic, unpeeled
- 2 teaspoons sea salt
- 1 cup apple cider vinegar
- 1/2 teaspoon brown rice syrup
- 1 cup of water

Directions:

1. Take a skillet pan, place it medium heat, add garlic, and Cooking Time: for 15 minutes until roasted, frequently turning garlic, set aside to cool.
2. Meanwhile, take a saucepan, place it over medium-low heat, add remaining ingredients in it, except for salt and syrup, stir and Cooking Time: for 12 minutes until vegetables are tender.
3. When the garlic has roasted and cooled, peel them and add them to a food processor.
4. Then add cooked saucepan along with remaining ingredients, and pulse for 3 minutes until smooth.
5. Let sauce cool and then serve straight away

Nutrition Value:
Calories: 137 Cal
Fat: 0 g
Carbs: 30 g
Protein: 4 g
Fiber: 10 g

784. Hot Sauce

Preparation time: 5 minutes
Cooking time: 0 minute
Servings: 16
Ingredients:

- 4 cloves of garlic, peeled
- 15 Hot peppers, de-stemmed, chopped
- 1/2 teaspoon. coriander
- 1/2 teaspoon. sea salt
- 1/2 teaspoon. red chili powder
- 1/2 of lime, zested
- 1/4 teaspoon. cumin
- 1/2 lime, juiced
- 1 cup apple cider vinegar

Directions:

1. Place all the ingredients in the order in a food processor or blender and then pulse for 3 to 5 minutes at high speed until smooth.
2. Tip the sauce in a bowl and then serve.

Nutrition Value:
Calories: 5 Cal
Fat: 0 g
Carbs: 1 g
Protein: 0 g
Fiber: 0.3 g

785. Barbecue Sauce

Preparation time: 5 minutes
Cooking time: 0 minute
Servings: 16
Ingredients:

- 8 ounces tomato sauce
- 1 teaspoon garlic powder
- ¼ teaspoon ground black pepper
- 1/2 teaspoon. sea salt
- 2 Tablespoons Dijon mustard
- 3 packets stevia
- 1 teaspoon molasses
- 1 Tablespoon apple cider vinegar
- 2 Tablespoons tamari
- 1 teaspoon liquid aminos

Directions:

1. Take a medium bowl, place all the ingredients in it, and stir until combined.
2. Serve straight away

Nutrition Value:
Calories: 29 Cal

Fat: 0.1 g
Carbs: 7 g
Protein: 0.1 g
Fiber: 0.1 g

786. Bolognese Sauce

Preparation time: 10 minutes
Cooking time: 45 minutes
Servings: 8

Ingredients:

- ½ of small green bell pepper, chopped
- 1 stalk of celery, chopped
- 1 small carrot, chopped
- 1 medium white onion, peeled, chopped
- 2 teaspoons minced garlic
- 1/2 teaspoon crushed red pepper flakes
- 3 tablespoons olive oil
- 8-ounce tempeh, crumbled
- 8 ounces white mushrooms, chopped
- 1/2 cup dried red lentils
- 28-ounce crushed tomatoes
- 28-ounce whole tomatoes, chopped
- 1 teaspoon dried oregano
- 1/2 teaspoon fennel seed
- 1/2 teaspoon ground black pepper
- 1/2 teaspoon salt
- 1 teaspoon dried basil
- 1/4 cup chopped parsley
- 1 bay leaf
- 6-ounce tomato paste
- 1 cup dry red wine

Directions:

1. Take a Dutch oven, place it over medium heat, add oil, and when hot, add the first six ingredients, stir and Cooking Time: for 5 minutes until sauté.
2. Then switch heat to medium-high level, add two ingredients after olive oil, stir and Cooking Time: for 3 minutes.
3. Switch heat to medium-low level, stir in tomato paste, and continue cooking for 2 minutes.
4. Add remaining ingredients except for lentils, stir and bring the mixture to boil.
5. Switch heat to the low level, simmer sauce for 10 minutes, covering the pan partially, then add lentils and continue cooking for 20 minutes until tender.
6. Serve sauce with cooked pasta.

Nutrition Value:
Calories: 208.8 Cal
Fat: 12 g
Carbs: 17.8 g
Protein: 10.6 g
Fiber: 3.8 g

787. Alfredo Sauce

Preparation time: 5 minutes
Cooking time: 0 minute
Servings: 4

Ingredients:

- 1 cup cashews, unsalted, soaked in warm water for 15 minutes
- 1 teaspoon minced garlic
- 1/4 teaspoon ground black pepper
- 1/3 teaspoon salt
- 1/4 cup nutritional yeast
- 2 tablespoons tamari
- 2 tablespoons olive oil
- 4 tablespoons water

Directions:

1. Drain the cashews, transfer them into a food processor, add remaining ingredients in it, and pulse for 3 minutes until thick sauce comes together.
2. Serve straight away.

Nutrition Value:
Calories: 105.7 Cal
Fat: 5.3 g
Carbs: 11 g
Protein: 4.7 g
Fiber: 2 g

788. Garden Pesto

Preparation time: 5 minutes
Cooking time: 0 minute
Servings: 10
Ingredients:
- 1/4 cup pistachios, shelled
- 3/4 cup parsley leaves
- 1 cup cilantro leaves
- ½ teaspoon minced garlic
- 1/4 cup mint leaves
- 1 cup basil leaves
- ¼ teaspoon ground black pepper
- 1/3 teaspoon salt
- 1/2 cup olive oil
- 1 1/2 teaspoons miso
- 2 teaspoons lemon juice

Directions:
1. Place all the ingredients in the order in a food processor or blender and then pulse for 3 to 5 minutes at high speed until smooth.
2. Tip the pesto in a bowl and then serve.

Nutrition Value:
Calories: 111.5 Cal
Fat: 11.5 g
Carbs: 2.8 g
Protein: 1.2 g
Fiber: 1.4 g

789. Cilantro And Parsley Hot Sauce

Preparation time: 5 minutes
Cooking time: 0 minute
Servings: 4
Ingredients:
- 2 cups of parsley and cilantro leaves with stems
- 4 Thai bird chilies, destemmed, deseeded, torn
- 2 teaspoons minced garlic
- 1 teaspoon salt
- 1/4 teaspoon coriander seed, ground
- 1/4 teaspoon ground black pepper
- 1/2 teaspoon cumin seeds, ground
- 3 green cardamom pods, toasted, ground
- 1/2 cup olive oil

Directions:
1. Take a spice blender or a food processor, place all the ingredients in it, and process for 5 minutes until the smooth paste comes together.
2. Serve straight away.

Nutrition Value:
Calories: 130 Cal
Fat: 14 g
Carbs: 2 g
Protein: 1 g
Fiber: 1 g

790. Potato Carrot Gravy

Preparation Time: 20 Minutes
Servings: 2 cups of gravy
Ingredients:
- 1 potato, peeled and chopped
- ½ lb (about 4 carrots, chopped
- 2 cups water
- 1 tsp garlic powder
- 1 tsp onion powder
- 1 tsp salt
- 1/2 tsp turmeric
- 2 tbsp nutritional yeast
- 2 tsp soy sauce

Directions:
1. Add potato and carrot to Instant Pot along with water.
2. Cover the pot with lid. Set steam release handle to 'sealing' and switch on manual button for 7 minutes over high-pressure.
3. When the timer beeps, allow it to naturally release steam for 5 minutes and then change stem handle to 'venting' to release any remaining steam.
4. Add in rest of the ingredients to Instant Pot® and using an immersion blender, make gravy directly in Instant Pot.
5. To make the gravy thinner just add a bit more water.

791. Instant Pot Sriracha Sauce

Preparation Time: 30 Minutes
Servings: 2 cups of Sriracha
Ingredients:

- 1 lb red chili peppers (jalapeno, Fresno, etc.
- 6 garlic cloves, peeled
- ½ cup distilled vinegar
- 3 tbsp brown sugar
- 1/3 cup water
- 1 tbsp salt

Directions:

1. Chop chili peppers and put them into a blender.
2. Add remaining ingredients into the blender and blend over high until smooth.
3. Pour this mixture into Instant Pot. Switch on sautée button. Then set 'Adjust' button two times to change heat setting to 'Less'.
4. Let the mixture sauté for about 15 minutes stirring occasionally. After 15 minutes, allow the sauce to cool for about 15 minutes.
5. Store the sriracha in glass containers and keep it in the fridge for 2 weeks.

792. Healthy One-Pot Hummus

Preparation Time: 1 HR 15 Minutes
Servings: 2
Ingredients:

- 1 cup dry garbanzo beans
- 2 cups water
- ½ tsp salt
- 1 tsp cumin
- 2 garlic cloves
- Juice of ½ lemon

Directions:

1. Rinse and drain garbanzo beans. Add beans and water to Instant Pot and Cooking Time: for 1 hour over manual setting, high pressure. Set steam release handle to 'sealing'.
2. When the timer beeps, using quick release Directions, release the steam immediately.
3. Place garbanzo beans along with remaining ingredients in a blender. Use the reserved water after cooking beans.
4. Blend the mixture over high until creamy smooth and serve.

793. Mushroom Gravy

Preparation Time: 20 Minutes
Servings: 10
Ingredients:

- 2 cups sliced fresh mushrooms
- 1½ cups plus 2 tablespoons vegetable or mushroom broth
- 2 tablespoons dry red or white wine
- ¼ cup minced yellow onion
- ½ teaspoon ground dried thyme
- ¼ teaspoon ground sage
- Salt and freshly ground black pepper
- ½ to 1 teaspoon vegan gravy browner

Directions:

1. Combine the onion and 2 tablespoons of broth in the open instant pot on low and simmer until the onion softens.
2. Add the mushrooms and soften more before adding the sage, thyme, and wine.
3. Add half the broth and boil.
4. Reduce the heat and simmer 5 minutes.
5. Add the remaining broth, then put into a blender and make smooth.
6. Put back into the instant pot, salt and pepper, then seal and Cooking Time: on Stew for 10 minutes.
7. Depressurize naturally and serve hot.

794. Creamy Cheesy Sauce

Preparation Time: 6 Minutes
Servings: 2 cups
Ingredients:

- 1 cup cashews, soaked
- ½ teaspoon vegetable broth powder

- 1 teaspoon Dijon mustard
- ½ teaspoon paprika
- ½ teaspoon garlic powder
- 2 tablespoons fresh lemon juice
- ½ teaspoon salt
- ½ cup nutritional yeast
- 1 cup almond milk
- ½ teaspoon onion powder

Directions:
1. Add the cashews in a blender.
2. Add the mustard, lemon juice, yeast, onion, salt, garlic, paprika, broth powder and blend into a smooth paste.
3. Serve with curry.

795. Homemade Cashew Cream Cheese

Preparation Time: 15 Minutes
Servings: 2 cups
Ingredients:
- 1 cup raw cashews, soaked for 4 hours
- 1 teaspoon white miso paste
- 1 tablespoon apple cider vinegar
- ½ teaspoon salt
- 1 teaspoon agave nectar
- 6 ounces firm silken tofu
- 2 tablespoons fresh lemon juice

Directions:
1. Drain the cashew and add to a blender.
2. Add the agave, salt, miso, vinegar and lemon juice.
3. Blend again into a smooth paste.
4. Add the tofu and blend again.
5. Store in the fridge.

796. Sunflower Seed, Potato & Brown Lentil Pâté

Preparation Time: 15 Minutes
Servings: 6-8
Ingredients:
- 1 cup unsalted sunflower seeds, soaked overnight
- ½ cup nutritional yeast
- 1 onion, chopped
- 1 potato, peeled and chopped
- 1½ cups brown lentils, cooked
- ⅓ cup whole-grain flour
- ¾ cup walnut pieces
- 2 tablespoons vital wheat gluten
- 1 tablespoon olive oil
- 1 teaspoon dried thyme
- 3 garlic cloves, chopped
- 2 tablespoons soy sauce
- ½ teaspoon black pepper
- 1 teaspoon sweet paprika
- 1 teaspoon salt
- 2 tablespoons chopped parsley
- ⅛ teaspoon ground allspice
- ½ teaspoon ground sage
- ⅛ teaspoon cayenne pepper

Directions:
1. In an instant pot toss the garlic, onion with some water for 1 minute.
2. Drain the lentils and sunflower seeds.
3. Add the walnuts and sunflower seeds in a blender.
4. Blend into a smooth mix and add the onion mix.
5. Add the lentils, potato and blend again.
6. Add the rest of the ingredients one by one.
7. Blend well to make a smooth paste.
8. Add the mixture to a baking pan.
9. Cover the top using aluminum foil. Make some holes on top.
10. Add to the instant pot and Cooking Time: for 8 minutes.
11. Serve at room temperature.

797. Chickpea & Artichoke Mushroom Pâté

Preparation Time: 15 Minutes
Servings: 6-8
Ingredients:
- 2 cups canned artichoke hearts,

- drained
- 1½ cups cooked chickpeas
- 3 garlic cloves, chopped
- 1 tablespoon fresh lemon juice
- 1 teaspoon dried basil
- ½ cup raw cashews, soaked overnight and drained
- 1 cup chopped mushrooms
- Shredded fresh basil leaves, for garnish
- 1 cup crumbled extra-firm tofu
- Salt and black pepper
- Paprika, for garnish

Directions:
1. In an instant pot add some oil and toss the garlic, mushroom and artichokes for 1 minute.
2. Drain them to get rid of excess liquid.
3. Add the cashews, tofu in a blender and blend until smooth.
4. Add the artichoke mixture, lemon juice, salt, chickpeas, basil and pepper.
5. Blend again and pour into a loaf pan.
6. Cover with aluminum foil and poke some holes on top.
7. Add to your instant pot and Cooking Time: for about 3 minutes.
8. Let it cool down and refrigerate until served.
9. Garnish using basil, paprika.

798. Vegan Sauce

Preparation Time: 5 Minutes
Servings: 1 ¾ cups
Ingredients:

- 2 tablespoons yeast extract
- 2 tablespoons salt
- 1½ cups vegetarian broth
- 2 tablespoons vegan gravy browner

Directions:
1. Combine the yeast, vegetarian broth and salt in a bowl.
2. Mix well and add the gravy browner.
3. Mix well and store in a container.

799. Pumpkin Butter

Preparation Time: 30 Minutes
Servings: 2 Cups
Ingredients:

- 1 15 Ounce Can Pure Pumpkin
- 1 Tablespoon Lemon Juice
- 1/4 Teaspoon Cinnamon
- 1/8 Teaspoon Ground Cloves
- 1/4 Cup Maple Syrup or Agave
- 2/3 Cup Coconut Sugar, muscovado sugar, or maple sugar
- 1 Cup Water- For bottom of instant pot

Directions:
1. Mix pumpkin, lemon juice, cinnamon, cloves, and syrup or agave in an oven-safe bowl.
2. Add coconut sugar or other sugar and cover bowl with foil.
3. Place the steam rack into the instant pot and fill with water.
4. Place the oven safe bowl on the steam rack. On manual setting, Cooking Time: for 25 minutes on high pressure.
5. Quick release or let pressure dissolve on its own.
6. Remove foil and stir. Add more spices if needed.
7. For thicker butter spread, remove steam rack and in the empty instant pot, pour in contents and saute on low setting, stirring occasionally until it thickens.
8. Use as a spread for breads, pancakes, or oatmeal topping. Enjoy!

800. Vegan Cheese Dip

Preparation Time: 30 Mins
Servings: 10
Ingredients:

- 1 7.1 Ounce Daiya Medium Cheddar Style Block or other block vegan cheese, cubed

- 1 8 Ounce Bag Daiya Pepperjack Style Shreds
- 1 Tablespoon Vegan Butter
- 1 Tub Daiya Plain Cream Cheeze Style Spread, Tofu Cream Cheese, or other vegan cream cheese spread
- 1 Tablespoon Garlic Powder
- 1 Teaspoon Turmeric
- 1 Tablespoon Unsweetened Plain Almond Milk
- 1 Tablespoon Dried Oregano
- 1 Cup Water

Directions:
1. Place all ingredients in the instant pot and seal.
2. Use the manual setting and set to 5 minutes.
3. Quick release and remove lid when done cooking.
4. Whisk immediately until smooth. Enjoy!

801. Artichoke Spinach Dip

Preparation Time: 5 Minutes
Servings: 3 ½ cups
Ingredients:

- 1(10-ouncepackage spinach, chopped
- ⅓cup nutritional yeast
- 2(8-ouncejars marinated artichoke hearts
- ½teaspoon Tabasco sauce
- 3scallions, minced
- 1tablespoon fresh lemon juice
- 1cup vegan cream cheese
- ½teaspoon salt

Directions:
1. Drain the artichoke hearts and chop them finely.
2. Add the scallions, lemon juice, salt, artichoke hearts, sauce, spinach and yeast in an instant pot.
3. Cover and Cooking Time: for about 3 minutes.
4. Add the cheese and stir well.
5. Serve warm.

802. Chipotle Bean Cheesy Dip

Preparation Time: 10 Minutes
Servings: 3 cups
Ingredients:

- 2cups pinto beans, cooked, mashed
- 1tablespoon chipotle chiles in adobo, minced
- ¼cup water
- ½cup shredded vegan cheddar cheese
- ¾cup tomato salsa
- 1teaspoon chili powder
- Salt

Directions:
1. In a bowl combine the mashed beans, chipotle chile, salsa, chili powder and water in an instant pot.
2. Mix well and cover with lid.
3. Cooking Time: for about 5 minutes.
4. Add the cheddar cheese and salt and serve warm.
5. Drain the tomatoes and add to a blender.

803. Pasta Sauce From Bologna

Preparation Time: 5 Minutes
Servings: 6
Ingredients:

- 2 tablespoons olive oil
- 2 14oz. can crushed tomatoes
- ¼ cup basil leaves
- ¼ cup chopped parsley
- 1 onion, chopped
- 3 tablespoons lemon juice
- 2 celery stalks, diced
- 2 carrots, grated
- 2 cloves garlic, minced
- Salt and pepper, to taste

Directions:
1. Heat olive oil into Instant pot.
2. Add onion, carrots, and celery. Cooking Time: 3 minutes.
3. Add garlic and Cooking Time: 2 minutes.
4. Add remaining ingredients and lock

the lid into place.
5. *High-pressure 2 minutes.*
6. *Use a natural pressure release Directions.*
7. *Open the lid and transfer into a bowl.*
8. *Serve with pasta.*

804. Delicious Bbq Sauce

Preparation Time: 7 Minutes
Servings: 6
Ingredients:
- ¼ cup coconut oil
- 1 tablespoon molasses
- 1 cup raw cider vinegar
- 2 teaspoons vegan Worcestershire sauce
- 1 teaspoon coconut aminos
- 1 tablespoon Dijon mustard
- 1 good pinch Cayenne pepper
- 1/3 cup coconut sugar

Directions:
1. *Heat coconut oil into Instant pot on Sauté.*
2. *Add remaining ingredients and lock lid into place.*
3. *Select Manual and high-pressure 5 minutes.*
4. *Release the pressure with a quick-pressure release Directions.*
5. *Open the lid and transfer into bowl.*
6. *Serve or store into fridge.*

805. Thai Curry Sauce

Preparation Time: 7 Minutes
Servings: 6
Ingredients:
- 1 teaspoon coconut oil
- 2 ½ cup full-fat coconut milk
- 1 tablespoon mild curry sauce
- 1 cup vegetable stock
- 1 teaspoon coconut aminos
- 2 cloves garlic, minced
- 1 lemongrass stalk, bruised
- 1 tablespoon lime juice
- 4 tablespoons chopped cilantro

Directions:
1. *Heat coconut oil in instant pot on Sauté.*
2. *Add garlic and curry paste and Cooking Time: 30 seconds.*
3. *Add remaining ingredients, and lock lid into place.*
4. *Select Manual and High-pressure 4 minutes.*
5. *Use a natural pressure release Directions.*
6. *Open the lid and strain into a bowl.*
7. *Serve or store into a fridge.*

806. Sweet Peanut Sauce

Preparation Time: 35 Minutes
Servings: 4
Ingredients:
- 1 cup peanut butter, organic
- ½ cup peanut oil
- 1 teaspoon garlic powder
- 4 tablespoons maple syrup or coconut nectar
- 2 cups water
- 1 teaspoon chili flakes
- 1 tablespoon lime juice
- 1 teaspoon ground cumin
- ½ teaspoon ground fennel
- Salt, to taste

Directions:
1. *Combine all ingredients into a food blender.*
2. *Blend until smooth.*
3. *Transfer the ingredients into Instant pot.*
4. *Lock lid into place and select Manual.*
5. *Low-pressure 30 minutes.*
6. *Use a natural pressure release Directions.*
7. *Open the lid and serve sauce.*

807. Fast Hollandaise Sauce

Preparation Time: 5 Minutes
Servings: 4

Ingredients:

- ¼ cup fresh lemon juice
- 1 tablespoon nutritional yeast
- 1/3 cup Vegan mayonnaise
- 1 ½ tablespoons Dijon mustard
- 3 tablespoons almond milk
- 1 pinch salt
- 1 pinch black pepper
- 2 cups water

Directions:

1. Pour water into Instant pot and insert trivet.
2. Combine all ingredients into food blender.
3. Blend until smooth. Transfer into heat-proof bowl.
4. Place the bowl onto trivet and lock lid.
5. Select Sauté and adjust heat to More.
6. Steam 3 minutes.
7. Remove from the Instant pot and whisk with a wire whisk until fluffy.
8. Serve.

808. Red Pepper Sauce

Preparation Time: 25 Minutes
Servings: 4

Ingredients:

- 2 red bell peppers, sliced
- 1 tablespoon olive oil
- ¾ cup vegetable stock
- 4 tablespoons unsweetened almond milk
- Salt and pepper, to taste
- 2 shallots, sliced
- 2 cloves garlic, minced
- ½ teaspoon dried basil

Directions:

1. Heat oil in Instant pot on Sauté.
2. Add shallots and bell peppers.
3. Cooking Time: 4 minutes.
4. Add remaining ingredients and lock the lid.
5. Adjust heat to More, and Cooking Time: 20 minutes.
6. Open the lid and puree the bell peppers with immersion blender.
7. Serve or store into fridge.

809. Divine Green Sauce

Preparation Time: 25 Minutes
Servings: 4

Ingredients:

- 1 green chili pepper, seeded, chopped
- 12 tomatillos
- 2 shallots, diced
- 2 cloves garlic, peeled
- Salt and pepper, to taste
- 1 tablespoon cilantro, chopped
- ½ tablespoon parsley, chopped

Directions:

1. Place tomatillos into Instant pot.
2. Cover with water.
3. Lock the lid and Select Sauté. Adjust heat to More.
4. Cooking Time: tomatillos 20 minutes or until tender.
5. Open the lid and drain the tomatillos.
6. Place them into food processor, along with remaining ingredients.
7. Blend until smooth.
8. Pour back the mixture into the Instant pot. Cooking Time: on Sauté 5 minutes.
9. Serve or store in a fridge.

810. Smokey Tomato Sauce

Preparation Time: 8 Minutes
Servings: 4

Ingredients:

- 2 tablespoons coconut oil
- 3 cups can-fire roasted tomatoes
- 2 cups can crushed tomatoes
- 1 teaspoon liquid smoke
- 2 teaspoons coconut sugar
- 1 shallot, sliced
- 2 cloves garlic, chopped
- 3 tablespoons lemon juice
- 1 tablespoon chopped parsley

- *1 teaspoon dried basil*
- *Salt and pepper, to taste*

Directions:

1. Heat olive oil into Instant pot on Sauté.
2. Add shallots and garlic. Cooking Time: 1 minute.
3. Stir in remaining ingredients and lock lid into place.
4. High-pressure on Manual, for 2 minutes.
5. Use a quick pressure release Directions and open the lid.
6. Transfer sauce into a bowl,
7. Serve or store in a fridge.

811. Perfect Tomato Sauce

Preparation Time: 5 Minutes
Servings: 6
Ingredients:

- *2 tablespoons olive oil*
- *1 tablespoon balsamic vinegar*
- *½ teaspoon coconut nectar*
- *1.5lb. ripe tomatoes, peeled, chopped*
- *Salt and pepper, to taste*
- *3 heads garlic, roasted, pulp removed*
- *1 teaspoon dried basil*
- *1 teaspoon dried oregano*

Directions:

1. Heat oil into Instant pot on Sauté.
2. Add herbs and fry 20 seconds.
3. Add remaining ingredients and stir to coat with herbed oil.
4. Lock the lid and select Manual.
5. High-pressure 3 minutes.
6. Use a quick pressure release and open the lid.
7. Serve or store in a fridge.

812. Merlot Sauce

Preparation Time: 20 Minutes
Servings: 4
Ingredients:

- *1 cup Merlot wine*
- *¼ cup almond butter*
- *1 tablespoon olive oil*
- *2 cloves garlic, minced*
- *1 cup vegetable stock*
- *1 shallot, sliced*
- *1 pinch nutmeg*

Directions:

1. Heat olive oil into Instant pot on Sauté.
2. Add shallots and garlic. Cooking Time: 2 minutes.
3. Add remaining ingredients, and stir gently.
4. Select Manual, and Cooking Time: 15 minutes.
5. Open the lid stir once again.
6. If you desire you can simmer sauce on Sauté until reduced as you desire.
7. Serve.

813. Italian Gourmet Sauce

Preparation Time: 12 Minutes
Servings: 6
Ingredients:

- *¼ cup coconut oil*
- *4 cup unsweetened almond milk*
- *Salt and pepper, to taste*
- *¼ cup all-purpose flour*
- *1 tablespoon coconut aminos*
- *1 cup sun-dried tomatoes, drained*
- *1 teaspoon dried basil*
- *1 teaspoon Cayenne pepper*

Directions:

1. Heat coconut oil into Instant pot on Sauté.
2. When melted, stir in all-purpose flour.
3. Cook, stirring until flour starts to smell like popcorns.
4. Once you sense it, whisk in almond milk.
5. Gently fold in remaining ingredients, and lock lid into place.
6. Select Manual and Cooking Time: 10 minutes.
7. Open the lid and puree the sauce with an immersion blender.
8. Serve.

814. Cashew Alfredo

Preparation Time: 10 Minutes
Servings: 8
Ingredients:
- 3 cups vegetable stock
- 1 cup cashews, soaked 2 hours, rinsed and drained
- ½ cup nutritional yeast
- 2 tablespoons lemon juice
- ¾ cup water
- 2 cloves garlic, minced
- ½ cup unsweetened almond milk
- Salt and pepper, to taste
- 1 teaspoon finely grated lemon peel

Directions:
1. Place cashews into food blender, along with lemon juice, peel, water, and almond milk.
2. Blend until smooth.
3. Transfer the mixture into Instant pot and add remaining ingredients.
4. Lock lid into place.
5. Select Manual and set time to 8 minutes.
6. When the time is up, remove the lid.
7. Serve with pasta.

815. Aromatic Wine Sauce

Preparation Time: 8 Minutes
Servings: 6
Ingredients:
- ¼ cup white wine
- ¼ cup coconut oil
- ¼ cup all-purpose flour
- 1 tablespoon dill weed, chopped
- 3 ½ cups unsweetened almond milk
- 1 tablespoon lemon juice
- Salt and pepper, to taste

Directions:
1. Heat coconut oil in Instant pot on Sauté.
2. Once the oil is melted, whisk in all-purpose flour.
3. Cooking Time: the flour until starts to change color and smell like popcorns.
4. Stir in almond milk and whisk until you have a smooth mixture. Season to taste.
5. Add wine, lemon juice, and dill.
6. Lock lid into place.
7. Select Manual and Cooking Time: 3 minutes.
8. Serve sauce with pasta or seitan.

816. Sweet And Sour Meatball Sauce

Preparation Time: 15 Minutes
Servings: 12
Ingredients:
- 12 ounces fresh blueberries
- 1/2 cup balsamic vinegar
- 1/2 cup red wine
- 1 tablespoon tomato paste
- 2 tablespoons agave nectar
- 1 teaspoon lemon zest
- 1/2 teaspoon thyme
- 2 sprigs fresh rosemary
- 1 clove garlic, minced
- 1/2 cup water

Directions:
1. Puree all the ingredients except for the rosemary in a food processor.
2. Spray the instant pot with nonstick spray and add the puree and the rosemary.
3. Seal the lid and Cooking Time: on high 4 minutes, then let the pressure release naturally.
4. Remove the lid and the rosemary sprigs. Serve over vegan meatballs or as a dipping sauce.

817. Brandy Nutmeg Cranberry Sauce

Preparation Time: 20 Minutes
Servings: 2 Cups
Ingredients:
- 1/2 cup orange juice
- 12 ounces of fresh cranberries
- 1/2 cup agave nectar

- *1 teaspoon lemon juice*
- *1/4 cup brandy*
- *1/4 teaspoon nutmeg*

Directions:
1. Combine the ingredients in your oiled pressure cooker.
2. Seal the lid and Cooking Time: on high for 10 minutes, then remove the lid and Cooking Time: an additional 5-10 minutes using the sauté setting to Cooking Time: down the alcohol and give the sauce a thicker consistency.

818. Instant Roasted Garlic

Preparation Time: 15 Minutes
Servings: 4
Ingredients:

- *4 to 6 heads garlic*

Directions:
1. Slice the top off the head of garlic to expose the cloves. Place into the instant pot cut side facing up.
2. Seal the lid and Cooking Time: for 3 minutes on high.
3. After it's cooked, remove the skins by hand or using a knife. Eat by itself or use as a healthy spread or a flavorful addition to pastas.

819. Spiced Rum & Orange Barbecue Sauce

Preparation Time: 18 Minutes
Servings: 4 Cups
Ingredients:

- *1/2 cup spiced ruminutes*
- *1/2 cup orange juice*
- *2 tablespoons maple syrup*
- *2 tablespoons apple cider vinegar*
- *2 tablespoons olive oil*
- *1 can tomato sauce*
- *Juice from ½ lime*
- *Zest from 1 lime*
- *3 tablespoons brown sugar*
- *1 onion, minced*
- *2 cloves garlic, minced*
- *6 ounces tomato paste*
- *1 teaspoon dried thyme*
- *1/4 teaspoon nutmeg*
- *1/4 teaspoon cinnamon*
- *1/2 teaspoon paprika*
- *Pinch of ground cloves*

Directions:
1. Add olive oil to the instant pot and heat using the sauté setting. Sauté the onions for 3 minutes.
2. Add the remaining ingredients, seal the lid, and Cooking Time: on high for 5 minutes.
3. If the sauce is too thin, turn back to the sauté setting and simmer until the sauce thickens. Sauce can be stored in the fridge for up to one week and the rest can be frozen in ice cube trays and thawed as needed.

820. Balsamic Onion Marmalade

Preparation Time: 10 Minutes
Servings: 3 Cups
Ingredients:

- *1/4 cup balsamic vinegar*
- *2 tablespoons maple syrup*
- *2 tablespoons olive oil*
- *4 large onions, sliced*
- *1/2 cup water*
- *1 teaspoon ground rosemary*
- *1 teaspoon ground thyme*
- *1 teaspoon salt*

Directions:
1. Stir ingredients together in an oiled instant pot.
2. Seal the lid and Cooking Time: on high for 3 minutes.
3. Allow the marmalade to cool before using. Can be stored in the fridge for up to one week or can be froze.
4. Works great as a condiment or in pasta.

821. Chipotle Ketchup

Preparation Time: 10 Minutes

Servings: 2 Cups

Ingredients:
- 1 can crushed tomatoes
- 2 tablespoons tomato paste
- 1/2 cup apple cider vinegar
- 2 tablespoons olive oil
- 1/2 cup packed brown sugar
- 1/2 small onion, minced
- 2 cloves garlic, minced
- 1/2 teaspoon salt
- 1/2 teaspoon chipotle chili powder
- 1/4 teaspoon celery seed
- 1/8 teaspoon dry mustard
- 1/8 teaspoon ground ginger
- 1/8 teaspoon ground nutmeg
- 1/8 teaspoon ground cloves
- 1/8 teaspoon ground oregano

Directions:
1. Add olive oil to the instant pot and heat using the sauté setting. Sauté the onions for 3 minutes. Add the garlic and Cooking Time: until fragrant.
2. Stir in the remaining ingredients. Seal, then Cooking Time: on high for 3 minutes.
3. Remove the lid and continue cooking on the sauté setting if the sauce is not thick enough. You are only as limited as your imagination.
4. Ketchup will store in the fridge for one week or in the freezer for up to 6 months. Freeze unused ketchup in ice cube trays, then store in a freezer bag and thaw when needed.

822. Classic Spinach Party Dip

Preparation Time: 30 Minutes
Servings: 8

Ingredients:
- 1 can artichoke hearts in water
- 8 cups fresh baby spinach
- 1 small onion, minced
- 1 clove garlic, minced
- 2 tablespoons olive oil
- 1/2 cup cashews
- Juice from 1/2 lemon
- 1/4 teaspoon smoked paprika
- 1/3 cup nutritional yeast
- 1/4 teaspoon salt
- 1/2 teaspoon fresh ground pepper
- 1/2 cup water

Directions:
1. Add olive oil to the instant pot and heat using the sauté setting. Sauté the onions for 3 minutes, then add the spinach and garlic. Sauté an additional 5 minutes to wilt the spinach.
2. Make the sour cream by pureeing the water, lemon juice, and cashews in a food processor. Set aside.
3. Spray the instant pot with nonstick spray and add the sour cream and the rest of the ingredients to the pot. Seal the lid and Cooking Time: on high 4 minutes, the let the pressure reduce naturally. Stir and serve warm with tortilla chips or pumpernickel bread.

823. Cheesy Chili Sausage Dip

Preparation Time: 15 Minutes
Servings: 4

Ingredients:
- 6 ounces vegan sausage
- 1 can black beans, drained and rinsed
- 1 can fire roasted diced tomatoes
- 1/4 teaspoon cumin
- 1/2 teaspoon chili powder
- 1 1/4 cups shredded vegan cheddar cheese
- 1/4 teaspoon salt
- 1/2 teaspoon fresh ground pepper

Directions:
1. Spray the instant pot with nonstick spray. Seal the lid and Cooking Time: on high 4 minutes, then let the pressure release naturally.
2. Serve hot with tortilla chips for

dipping.

824. Salsa Bean Dip

Preparation Time: 15 Minutes
Servings: 8
Ingredients:
- *1 can vegan refried beans*
- *1/2 cup shredded vegan cheddar cheese*
- *1/2 cup spicy salsa*
- *2 drops liquid smoke*
- *1/2 teaspoon cumin*
- *1/8 teaspoon coriander*
- *1/8 teaspoon chipotle chili powder*
- *1/4 teaspoon salt*

Directions:
1. *Spray the instant pot with nonstick spray. Seal the lid and Cooking Time: on high 4 minutes, then let the pressure release naturally.*
2. *Serve hot with tortilla chips for dipping, or use as a burrito filling.*

825. Cinnamon Ginger Syrup

Preparation Time: 15 Minutes
Servings: 1 CUP
Ingredients:
- *1 cup packed brown sugar*
- *4 whole cinnamon sticks*
- *6 whole cloves*
- *1/8 teaspoon allspice*
- *1/8 teaspoon nutmeg*
- *1/4 teaspoon ginger*
- *1 cup water*

Directions:
1. *Whisk together all the ingredients in the instant pot. Seal the lid and Cooking Time: on low 4 minutes.*
2. *Let the pressure release naturally, then remove the lid. Use a slotted spoon to scoop out the cinnamon sticks and cloves.*
3. *Use as a flavoring for tea, coffee, or cocoa. Can be stored up to 2 weeks in the fridge.*

826. Chai Green Tea Flavoring

Preparation Time: 25 Minutes
Servings: 6 CUP
Ingredients:
- *10 green tea bags*
- *6 cups water*
- *1 teaspoons ground ginger*
- *1/4 teaspoon cardamom seeds*
- *7 whole cinnamon sticks*
- *10 whole peppercorns*
- *10 whole cloves*
- *1/2 teaspoon ground allspice*
- *1/8 teaspoon ground nutmeg*
- *1 cup agave nectar*

Directions:
1. *Combine everything except for the tea bags and agave in the instant pot.*
2. *Seal the lid and Cooking Time: on high 4 minutes. Let the pressure release naturally, then remove the lid and switch to sauté setting.*
3. *Add the tea bags and let the mixture simmer for 5 to 10 minutes, until the tea is as dark as you'd like.*
4. *Stir in the agave. Take out the cinnamon sticks, and then strain the rest of the seasonings out using cheesecloth.*
5. *To use the flavoring, mix the concentrate with an equal amount of almond milk or water. Can be served warm or added to a blender with ice to make an iced chai tea!*

827. Spiced Apple Spread

Preparation Time: 15 Minutes
Servings: 6-8 Cups
Ingredients:
- *2 cups cubed fresh pumpkin*
- *1/2 cup packed brown sugar*
- *6 pears*
- *4 apples*
- *Juice of 2 lemons*
- *1/2 teaspoon allspice*
- *1 teaspoon cinnamon*
- *1/2 teaspoon ground ginger*

- 1/4 teaspoon nutmeg
- 1/4 teaspoon ground cloves

Directions:

1. Peel, core, and chop the pear and the apple.
2. Combine the ingredients in an oiled instant pot, seal, and Cooking Time: on high for 5 minutes.
3. If the mixture still has a lot of liquid, Cooking Time: longer using the sauté setting to evaporate some of the liquid.
4. Once most of the moisture has evaporated, transfer the mixture a batch at a time to a food processor and blend until smooth.
5. Allow the mixture to cool before using. You can also freeze in batches in small freezer bags. Goes great on a bagel or English muffin for breakfast!

828. Balsamic Reduction 10

Preparation Time: 20 Minutes
Servings: ½ cup
Ingredients:

- 1 cup balsamic vinegar
- 2 tablespoons brown sugar
- 1 teaspoon margarine

Directions:

1. Bring the vinegar to a boil in your Instant Pot on a medium heat with the lid off.
2. Simmer for 10 minutes.
3. Add the sugar and simmer another five minutes.
4. Add in the margarine at the very end and stir before taking off the heat.

829. Butternut Squash Spread.

Preparation Time: 55 Minutes
Servings: 3 cups
Ingredients:

- 1 large butternut squash, peeled, cleaned, and diced
- 1 cup packed light brown sugar or granulated natural sugar
- 1 cup apple juice
- ¼ cup maple syrup
- ½ teaspoon salt
- ½ teaspoon ground cinnamon
- ¼ teaspoon ground allspice
- ⅛ teaspoon ground ginger
- ⅛ teaspoon ground nutmeg

Directions:

1. Oil the inside of your Instant Pot and put all the ingredients in it, mix them well.
2. Seal and Cooking Time: on Stew for 45 minutes.
3. Depressurize naturally. If still watery Cooking Time: another 10 minutes with the lid off, stirring continually, to reduce the water.
4. When cool, use a blender to make sure it is extra smooth.

830. Quick Apple Butter.

Preparation Time: 75 Minutes
Servings: 4 cups
Ingredients:

- 3 pounds cooking apples washed, cored, and finely sliced
- 1¼ cups natural sugar
- ⅓ cup apple juice
- 1 tablespoon ground cinnamon
- ¼ teaspoon ground allspice
- ¼ teaspoon ground ginger
- ¼ teaspoon ground nutmeg
- Juice of 1 lemon

Directions:

1. Mix all the ingredients in your Instant Pot, stir well, and seal.
2. Cooking Time: on Stew for 70 minutes.
3. Release the pressure naturally.
4. When cool, blend to remove any chunky bits that may remain.

831. Spiced Applesauce.

Preparation Time: 30 Minutes
Servings: 3 cups
Ingredients:

- 2½ pounds apples, peeled, cored, and diced
- ½ cup apple juice
- ⅓ cup granulated natural sugar
- 1 tablespoon freshly squeezed lemon juice
- 1 teaspoon ground cinnamon
- Pinch of salt

Directions:
1. Combine all the ingredients in your Instant Pot and mix well.
2. Seal and Cooking Time: on Stew for 25 minutes.
3. Depressurize naturally and allow to cool.
4. Mash to create the desired texture.

832. Cranberry Apple Chutney.

Preparation Time: 35 Minutes
Servings: 4 cups
Ingredients:

- 1 12-ounce bag fresh cranberries, rinsed and picked over
- 1¼ cups packed light brown sugar or granulated natural sugar
- ½ cup sweetened dried cranberries
- ¼ cup cider vinegar
- 2 large apples, cored and finely chopped
- 2 shallots, minced
- 1½ teaspoons grated fresh ginger
- 1 teaspoon chopped crystallized ginger
- Grated zest of 1 lemon or orange

Directions:
1. Combine all the ingredients in your Instant Pot and mix well.
2. Seal and Cooking Time: on Stew for 25 minutes.
3. Release the pressure naturally.
4. Simmer for another 5 minutes with the lid off to thicken.

833. Spicy Sweet Chutney.

Preparation Time: 30 Minutes
Servings: 4 cups
Ingredients:

- 5 large apples peeled, cored, and coarsely chopped
- 2 cups dried fruit (any kind), chopped
- 1 cup granulated natural sugar
- ½ cup cider vinegar
- ⅓ cup golden raisins
- 2 shallots, minced
- 2 teaspoons grated fresh ginger
- ¼ teaspoon salt
- ¼ teaspoon red pepper flakes

Directions:
1. Combine all the ingredients in your Instant Pot and mix well.
2. Cooking Time: on Stew for 25 minutes.
3. Release the pressure naturally.
4. Simmer with the lid off for another 5 minutes.

834. Apple & Tomato Chutney.

Preparation Time: 30 Minutes
Servings: 3 cups
Ingredients:

- 5 large green tomatoes, peeled (see Note), seeded, and chopped
- 2 large Granny Smith apples, peeled, cored, and chopped
- 1 cup raisins
- ¾ cup granulated natural sugar
- ¼ cup cider vinegar
- 2 shallots, chopped
- 2 teaspoons grated fresh ginger
- 1 teaspoon salt
- ¼ teaspoon red pepper flakes
- ¼ teaspoon ground cloves or allspice

Directions:
1. Mix all the ingredients in your Instant Pot.
2. Seal and Cooking Time: on Stew for 25 minutes.
3. Release the pressure naturally.
4. If any liquid remains, simmer it off with the lid open.

835. Blueberry Peach Chutney.

Preparation Time: 35 Minutes
Servings: 3 cups
Ingredients:

- 5 large under ripe peaches, peeled, pitted, and chopped
- 1 cup packed light brown sugar or granulated natural sugar
- ¾ cup dried blueberries
- ⅓ cup cider vinegar
- 3 tablespoons minced onion
- 1 teaspoon grated fresh ginger
- ½ teaspoon salt
- ¼ teaspoon red pepper flakes

Directions:

1. Combine all the ingredients in your Instant Pot.
2. Seal and Cooking Time: on Stew for 30 minutes.
3. Release the pressure naturally.
4. If any liquid remains, simmer it off with the lid open.

836. Mango Chutney.

Preparation Time: 30 Minutes
Servings: 3 cups
Ingredients:

- 3 large ripe mangoes, peeled, pitted, and chopped
- 8 ounces pitted dates, chopped
- 1 cup firmly packed light brown sugar or granulated natural sugar
- ½ cup cider vinegar
- 2 limes, washed, quartered, and chopped
- 2 large shallots, minced
- 2 teaspoons grated fresh ginger
- ½ teaspoon ground cinnamon
- ½ teaspoon red pepper flakes
- ½ teaspoon ground coriander

Directions:

1. Mix all the ingredients in your Instant Pot.
2. Seal and Cooking Time: on Stew for 25 minutes.
3. Release the pressure naturally.
4. If any liquid remains, simmer it off with the lid open.

837. Pear Confit.

Preparation Time: 60 Minutes
Servings: 3 cups
Ingredients:

- 3 pounds under ripe pears, peeled, cored, and chopped
- 1 cup packed light brown sugar
- 1 cup apple juice
- ½ cup golden raisins
- 1 teaspoon grated fresh ginger
- ½ teaspoon ground cinnamon
- Juice and zest of 2 lemons
- Pinch of salt

Directions:

1. Combine the pears, sugar, apple juice, raisins, ginger, cinnamon, and salt in the Instant Pot.
2. Seal and Cooking Time: on Stew for 45 minutes.
3. Depressurize naturally and leave to simmer for 15 minutes, stirring continually.
4. Add the lemon juice and allow to cool.

838. Cranberry Sauce.

Preparation Time: 20 Minutes
Servings: 2 cups
Ingredients:

- 12 ounces fresh cranberries, rinsed and picked over
- 1 cup natural sugar
- 1 tablespoon freshly squeezed lemon juice
- Finely grated zest of 1 lemon

Directions:

1. Combine the cranberries, sugar, and juice and mix well.
2. Seal and Cooking Time: on Stew for 15 minutes.
3. Release the pressure quickly. If the

cranberries are still whole, reseal and Cooking Time: another 5 minutes.
4. Once the cranberries are falling apart, add the zest and allow to cool.

839. Peach Jam.

Preparation Time: 2H 45 Minutes
Servings: 4 cups
Ingredients:

- 2 pounds fresh firm peaches, pitted, and chopped
- 1 pound fresh firm apricots, pitted, and chopped
- 3 cups sugar, or to taste
- 1 (1.75-ouncepackage pectin
- 3 tablespoons freshly squeezed lemon juice

Directions:
1. Combine the peaches, apricots, and lemon in your Instant Pot and mix well.
2. Add the pectin and let the whole lot stand for 20 minutes.
3. Add the sugar, seal your Instant Pot, and Cooking Time: on Stew for 20 minutes.
4. Release the pressure naturally and allow to simmer over a low heat for 2 hours, until it thickens.
5. Cool.

840. Strawberry Jam

Preparation Time: 6 Minutes
Servings: 2 Pints
Ingredients:

- 1 Pound Organic Strawberries, diced
- 1 Cup Agave

Directions:
1. On saute mode add agave, when warm add strawberries.
2. Allow to boil about 3-4 minutes.
3. Cover the instant pot and seal. Turn pot to manual setting and Cooking Time: on high pressure for 3 minutes.
4. When done cooking, allow pressure to release naturally.
5. Mash strawberries with a potato masher.
6. Turn on saute mode and Cooking Time: off remaining liquid.
7. Store jam in a glass jar. When cool cover with lid and store in the refrigerator.

841. Tomato Jam

Preparation Time: 23 Minutes
Servings: 1 Pint
Ingredients:

- 4 Pounds Cherry Tomatoes (or any tomatoes
- 1 1/4 Cups Organic Cane Sugar
- 1 Teaspoon Sea Salt
- 1/4 Teaspoon Ground Black Pepper
- 1 Teaspoon Smoked Paprika

Directions:
1. Add tomatoes to the instant pot with sugar, sea salt, pepper, and smoked paprika.
2. Close the lid and seal.
3. Cooking Time: at high pressure for 1 minute.
4. When it is done cooking, let the pressure release for 15 minutes. It will thicken as it cools.
5. Serve with toast or biscuits.
6. Enjoy!

842. Ginger Syrup

Preparation Time: 22 Minutes
Servings: 3 Cups
Ingredients:

- 3 Tablespoons Fresh Ginger, peeled and grated
- 1/3 Cup Organic Cane Sugar
- 2 Cups Spring Water

Directions:
1. Add ginger, sugar and water to the instant pot.
2. Cover and seal.
3. Select manual and pressure Cooking Time: on high for 12 minutes.
4. When done, quick release. Uncover when all of the pressure has been

released.

5. *Turn on saute mode and simmer for 10 minutes until liquid has been reduced by half.*
6. *Allow to cool before transferring to a container.*
7. *Serve as a sweetener for drinks, oatmeals or yogurt. Enjoy!*

843. Citrus Marmalade.

Preparation Time: 45 Minutes
Servings: 4 cups
Ingredients:

- *2lbs oranges, washed*
- *4 cups sugar*
- *3½ cups water*
- *Juice and zest of 1 lemon*

Directions:

1. *Use a grater to remove the zest from the oranges in thick strips. Make sure to avoid getting too much pith.*
2. *Quarter the oranges and get rid of the remaining pith and the seeds.*
3. *Chop the orange pieces finely.*
4. *Put the orange pieces and zest in your Instant Pot and add the remaining ingredients.*
5. *Stir well, seal, and set to Stew.*
6. *Cooking Time: for 35 minutes.*
7. *Release the pressure naturally, then chill or can your marmalade.*

844. Ketchup.

Preparation Time: 45 Minutes
Servings: 3 cups
Ingredients:

- *2 (28-ouncecans tomato puree*
- *⅓ cup cider vinegar*
- *⅓ cup packed light brown sugar*
- *1 small yellow onion, quartered*
- *½ teaspoon dry mustard*
- *¼ teaspoon ground allspice*
- *¼ teaspoon ground cloves or mace*
- *¼ teaspoon ground cinnamon*
- *¼ teaspoon ground ginger*
- *Salt and freshly ground black pepper*

Directions:

1. *Mince the onion finely and combine with sugar and vinegar. Blend until smooth.*
2. *Mix all the ingredients in your Instant Pot and seal.*
3. *Cooking Time: on Stew for 12 minutes.*
4. *Release the pressure naturally and simmer with the lid off to thicken for 30 minutes.*
5. *Allow to cool.*

845. Bbq.

Preparation Time: 37 Minutes
Servings: 3 cups
Ingredients:

- *1 (8-ouncecan tomato sauce*
- *1 cup ketchup*
- *⅓ cup apple cider vinegar*
- *¼ cup water*
- *1 medium-size yellow onion, minced*
- *2 garlic cloves, minced*
- *1 chipotle chile in adobo, minced*
- *3 tablespoons light brown sugar*
- *1 tablespoon vegan Worcestershire sauce*
- *1 tablespoon soy sauce*
- *2 teaspoons olive oil*
- *1 teaspoon smoked paprika*
- *1 teaspoon liquid smoke*
- *½ teaspoon chilli powder*
- *½ teaspoon ground coriander*
- *½ teaspoon ground cumin*
- *¼ teaspoon cayenne pepper*
- *¼ teaspoon dry mustard*
- *Salt and freshly ground black pepper*

Directions:

1. *Warm the oil in your Instant Pot with the lid off.*
2. *When the oil is hot soften the onion in it for 5 minutes.*
3. *Add the garlic and Cooking Time: another minute.*
4. *Add the chipotle, ketchup, tomato*

sauce, sugar, Worcestershire sauce, soy sauce, paprika, chili powder, cumin, mustard, coriander, cayenne, salt and pepper.

5. *Mix in the water and stir well.*
6. *Seal and Cooking Time: on Stew for 25 minutes.*
7. *Release the pressure naturally.*
8. *Stir in the vinegar and liquid smoke.*
9. *When cool, blend everything until smooth.*

846. Pumpkin Sauce.

Preparation Time: 5 Minutes
Servings: 1 cup
Ingredients:

- *½ cup soy creamer or a thick non-dairy milk, plus more if needed*
- *¼ cup reserved pumpkin puree*
- *1 tablespoon rum or bourbon or 1 teaspoon rum extract*
- *1 teaspoon light brown sugar*
- *⅛ teaspoon ground nutmeg*
- *⅛ teaspoon ground cinnamon*
- *⅛ teaspoon ground ginger*

Directions:

1. *Combine all the ingredients in your Instant Pot with the lid off.*
2. *Cooking Time: for 4 minutes.*

SNACKS

847. Butter Carrots

Preparation time: 10 minutes
Cooking time: 10 minutes
Total time: 20 minutes
Servings: 04
Ingredients:
- 2 cups baby carrots
- 1 tablespoon brown sugar
- ½ tablespoon vegan butter, melted
- A pinch each salt and black pepper

How to Prepare:
1. Take a baking dish suitable to fit in your air fryer.
2. Toss carrots with sugar, butter, salt and black pepper in the baking dish.
3. Place the dish in the air fryer basket and seal the fryer.
4. Cooking Time: the carrots for 10 minutes at 350 degrees F on air fryer mode.
5. Enjoy.

Nutritional Values:
Calories 119
Total Fat 14 g
Saturated Fat 2 g
Cholesterol 65 mg
Sodium 269 mg
Total Carbs 19 g
Fiber 4 g
Sugar 6 g
Protein 5g

848. Leeks With Butter

Preparation time: 10 minutes
Cooking time: 7 minutes
Total time: 17 minutes
Servings: 04
Ingredients:
- 1 tablespoon vegan butter, melted
- 1 tablespoon lemon juice
- 4 leeks, washed and halved
- Salt and black pepper to taste

How to Prepare:
1. Take a baking dish suitable to fit in your air fryer.
2. Toss the leeks with butter, salt, and black pepper in the dish.
3. Place the dish in the air fryer basket.
4. Seal the fryer and Cooking Time: the carrots for 7 minutes at 350 degrees F on air fryer mode.
5. Add a drizzle of lemon juice.
6. Mix well then serve.

Nutritional Values:
Calories 231
Total Fat 20.1 g
Saturated Fat 2.4 g
Cholesterol 110 mg
Sodium 941 mg
Total Carbs 20.1 g
Fiber 0.9 g
Sugar 1.4 g
Protein 4.6 g

849. Juicy Brussel Sprouts

Preparation time: 10 minutes
Cooking time: 10 minutes
Total time: 20 minutes
Servings: 04
Ingredients:
- 1-pound brussels sprouts, trimmed
- ¼ cup green onions, chopped
- 6 cherry tomatoes, halved
- 1 tablespoon olive oil
- Salt and black pepper to taste

How to Prepare:
1. Take a baking dish suitable to fit in your air fryer.
2. Toss brussels sprouts with salt and black pepper in the dish.
3. Place this dish in the air fryer and seal the fryer.
4. Cooking Time: the sprouts for 10 minutes at 350 degrees F on air fryer mode.
5. Toss these sprouts with green onions, tomatoes, olive oil, salt, and pepper

in a salad bowl.
6. Devour.

Nutritional Values:
Calories 361
Total Fat 16.3 g
Saturated Fat 4.9 g
Cholesterol 114 mg
Sodium 515 mg
Total Carbs 29.3 g
Fiber 0.1 g
Sugar 18.2 g
Protein 3.3 g

850. Parsley Potatoes

Preparation time: 10 minutes
Cooking time: 10 minutes
Total time: 20 minutes
Servings: 4
Ingredients:

- 1-pound gold potatoes, sliced
- 2 tablespoons olive oil
- ¼ cup parsley leaves, chopped
- Juice from ½ lemon
- Salt and black pepper to taste

How to Prepare:
1. Take a baking dish suitable to fit in your air fryer.
2. Place the potatoes in it and season them liberally with salt, pepper, olive oil, and lemon juice.
3. Place the baking dish in the air fryer basket and seal it.
4. Cooking Time: the potatoes for 10 minutes at 350 degrees F on air fryer mode.
5. Serve warm with parsley garnishing.
6. Devour.

Nutritional Values:
Calories 205
Total Fat 22.7 g
Saturated Fat 6.1 g
Cholesterol 4 mg
Sodium 227 mg
Total Carbs 26.1 g
Fiber 1.4 g
Sugar 0.9 g
Protein 5.2 g

851. Fried Asparagus

Preparation time: 10 minutes
Cooking time: 8 minutes
Total time: 18 minutes
Servings: 04
Ingredients:

- 2 pounds fresh asparagus, trimmed
- ½ teaspoon oregano, dried
- 4 ounces vegan feta cheese, crumbled
- 4 garlic cloves, minced
- 2 tablespoons parsley, chopped
- ¼ teaspoon red pepper flakes
- ¼ cup olive oil
- Salt and black pepper to the taste
- 1 teaspoon lemon zest
- 1 lemon, juiced

How to Prepare:
1. Combine lemon zest with oregano, pepper flakes, garlic and oil in a large bowl.
2. Add asparagus, salt, pepper, and cheese to the bowl.
3. Toss well to coat then place the asparagus in the air fryer basket.
4. Seal the fryer and Cooking Time: them for 8 minutes at 350 degrees F on Air fryer mode.
5. Garnish with parsley and lemon juice.
6. Enjoy warm.

Nutritional Values:
Calories 201
Total Fat 8.9 g
Saturated Fat 4.5 g
Cholesterol 57 mg
Sodium 340 mg
Total Carbs 24.7 g
Fiber 1.2 g
Sugar 1.3 g
Protein 15.3 g

852. Balsamic Artichokes

Preparation time: 10 minutes
Cooking time: 7 minutes

Total time: 17 minutes
Servings: 04
Ingredients:
- 4 big artichokes, trimmed
- ¼ cup olive oil
- 2 garlic cloves, minced
- 2 tablespoons lemon juice
- 2 teaspoons balsamic vinegar
- 1 teaspoon oregano, dried
- Salt and black pepper to the taste

How to Prepare:
1. Season artichokes liberally with salt and pepper then rub them with half of the lemon juice and oil.
2. Add the artichokes to a baking dish suitable to fit in the air fryer.
3. Place the artichoke dish in the air fryer basket and seal it.
4. Cooking Time: them for 7 minutes at 360 degrees F on air fryer mode.
5. Whisk remaining lemon juice, and oil, vinegar, oregano, garlic, salt and pepper in a bowl.
6. Pour this mixture over the artichokes and mix them well.
7. Enjoy.

Nutritional Values:
Calories 119
Total Fat 14 g
Saturated Fat 2 g
Cholesterol 65 mg
Sodium 269 mg
Total Carbs 19 g
Fiber 4 g
Sugar 6 g
Protein 5g

853. Tomato Kebabs

Preparation time: 10 minutes
Cooking time: 6 minutes
Total time: 16 minutes
Servings: 04
Ingredients:
- 3 tablespoons balsamic vinegar
- 24 cherry tomatoes
- 2 cups vegan feta cheese, sliced
- 2 tablespoons olive oil
- 3 garlic cloves, minced
- 1 tablespoon thyme, chopped
- Salt and black pepper to the taste

Dressing:
- 2 tablespoons balsamic vinegar
- 4 tablespoons olive oil
- Salt and black pepper to taste

How to Prepare:
1. In a medium bowl combine oil, garlic cloves, thyme, salt, vinegar, and black pepper.
2. Mix well then add the tomatoes and coat them liberally.
3. Thread 6 tomatoes and cheese slices on each skewer alternatively.
4. Place these skewers in the air fryer basket and seal it.
5. Cooking Time: them for 6 minutes on air fryer mode at 360 degrees F.
6. Meanwhile, whisk together the dressing ingredients.
7. Place the cooked skewers on the serving plates.
8. Pour the vinegar dressing over them.
9. Enjoy.

Nutritional Values:
Calories 231
Total Fat 20.1 g
Saturated Fat 2.4 g
Cholesterol 110 mg
Sodium 941 mg
Total Carbs 20.1 g
Fiber 0.9 g
Sugar 1.4 g
Protein 4.6 g

854. Eggplant And Zucchini Snack

Preparation time: 10 minutes
Cooking time: 8 minutes
Total time: 18 minutes
Servings: 04
Ingredients:
- 1 eggplant, cubed
- 3 zucchinis, cubed

- *2 tablespoons lemon juice*
- *1 teaspoon oregano, dried*
- *3 tablespoons olive oil*
- *1 teaspoon thyme, dried*
- *Salt and black pepper to taste*

How to Prepare:
1. *Take a baking dish suitable to fit in your air fryer.*
2. *Combine all ingredients in the baking dish.*
3. *Place the eggplant dish in the air fryer basket and seal it.*
4. *Cooking Time: them for 8 minutes at 360 degrees F on air fryer mode.*
5. *Enjoy warm.*

Nutritional Values:
Calories 361
Total Fat 16.3 g
Saturated Fat 4.9 g
Cholesterol 114 mg
Sodium 515 mg
Total Carbs 29.3 g
Fiber 0.1 g
Sugar 18.2 g
Protein 3.3 g

855. Artichokes With Mayo Sauce

Preparation time: 10 minutes
Cooking time: 6 minutes
Total time: 16 minutes
Servings: 4
Ingredients:
- *2 artichokes, trimmed*
- *1 tablespoon lemon juice*
- *2 garlic cloves, minced*
- *A drizzle olive oil*
- *Sauce:*
- *1 cup vegan mayonnaise*
- *¼ cup olive oil*
- *¼ cup coconut oil*
- *3 garlic cloves*

How to Prepare:
1. *Toss artichokes with lemon juice, oil and 2 garlic cloves in a large bowl.*
2. *Place the seasoned artichokes in the air fryer basket and seal it.*
3. *Cooking Time: the artichokes for 6 minutes at 350 degrees on air fryer mode.*
4. *Blend coconut oil with olive oil, mayonnaise and 3 garlic cloves in a food processor.*
5. *Place the artichokes on the serving plates.*
6. *Pour the mayonnaise mixture over the artichokes.*
7. *Enjoy fresh.*

Nutritional Values:
Calories 205
Total Fat 22.7 g
Saturated Fat 6.1 g
Cholesterol 4 mg
Sodium 227 mg
Total Carbs 26.1 g
Fiber 1.4 g
Sugar 0.9 g
Protein 5.2 g

856. Fried Mustard Greens

Preparation time: 10 minutes
Cooking time: 11 minutes
Total time: 21 minutes
Servings: 04
Ingredients:
- *2 garlic cloves, minced*
- *1 tablespoon olive oil*
- *½ cup yellow onion, sliced*
- *3 tablespoons vegetable stock*
- *¼ teaspoon dark sesame oil*
- *1-pound mustard greens, torn*
- *salt and black pepper to the taste*

How to Prepare:
1. *Take a baking dish suitable to fit in your air fryer.*
2. *Add oil and place it over the medium heat and sauté onions in it for 5 minutes.*
3. *Stir in garlic, greens, salt, pepper, and stock.*
4. *Mix well then place the dish in the*

air fryer basket.
5. *Seal it and Cooking Time: them for 6 minutes at 350 degrees F on air fryer mode.*
6. *Drizzle sesame oil over the greens.*
7. *Devour.*

Nutritional Values:
Calories 201
Total Fat 8.9 g
Saturated Fat 4.5 g
Cholesterol 57 mg
Sodium 340 mg
Total Carbs 24.7 g
Fiber 1.2 g
Sugar 1.3 g
Protein 15.3 g

857. Cheese Brussels Sprouts

Preparation time: 10 minutes
Cooking time: 8 minutes
Total time: 18 minutes
Servings: 04
Ingredients:
- *1-pound brussels sprouts, washed*
- *3 tablespoons vegan parmesan, grated*
- *Juice from 1 lemon*
- *2 tablespoons vegan butter*
- *Salt and black pepper to the taste*

How to Prepare:
1. *Spread the brussels sprouts in the air fryer basket.*
2. *Seal it and Cooking Time: them for 8 minutes at 350 degrees F on air fryer mode.*
3. *Place a nonstick pan over medium high heat and add butter to melt.*
4. *Stir in pepper, salt, lemon juice, and brussels sprouts.*
5. *Mix well then add parmesan.*
6. *Serve warm.*

Nutritional Values:
Calories 119
Total Fat 14 g
Saturated Fat 2 g
Cholesterol 65 mg

Sodium 269 mg
Total Carbs 19 g
Fiber 4 g
Sugar 6 g
Protein 5 g

858. Mushroom Stuffed Poblano

Preparation time: 10 minutes
Cooking time: 20 minutes
Total time: 30 minutes
Servings: 10
Ingredients:
- *10 poblano peppers, tops cut off and seeds removed*
- *2 teaspoons garlic, minced*
- *8 ounces mushrooms, chopped*
- *½ cup cilantro, chopped*
- *1 white onion, chopped*
- *1 tablespoon olive oil*
- *Salt and black pepper to taste*

How to Prepare:
1. *Place a nonstick pan over medium heat and add oil.*
2. *Stir in mushrooms and onion, sauté for 5 minutes.*
3. *Add salt, black pepper, cilantro and garlic.*
4. *Stir while cooking for 2 additional minutes then take it off the heat.*
5. *Divide this mixture in the poblano peppers and stuff them neatly.*
6. *Place the peppers in the air fryer basket and seal it.*
7. *Cooking Time: them for 15 minutes at 350 degrees F on air fryer mode.*
8. *Enjoy.*

Nutritional Values:
Calories 231
Total Fat 20.1 g
Saturated Fat 2.4 g
Cholesterol 110 mg
Sodium 941 mg
Total Carbs 20.1 g
Fiber 0.9 g
Sugar 1.4 g

Protein 4.6 g

859. Mushroom Stuffed Tomatoes

Preparation time: 10 minutes
Cooking time: 15 minutes
Total time: 25 minutes
Servings: 04
Ingredients:
- *4 tomatoes, tops removed and pulp removed (reserve for filling*
- *1 yellow onion, chopped*
- *½ cup mushrooms, chopped*
- *1 tablespoon bread crumbs*
- *1 tablespoon vegan butter*
- *¼ teaspoon caraway seeds*
- *1 tablespoon parsley, chopped*
- *2 tablespoons celery, chopped*
- *1 cup vegan cheese, shredded*
- *Salt and black pepper to the taste*

How to Prepare:
1. *Place a pan over medium heat, add butter.*
2. *When it melts, add onion and celery to sauté for 3 minutes.*
3. *Stir in mushrooms and tomato pulp.*
4. *Cooking Time: for 1 minute then add crumbled bread, pepper, salt, cheese, parsley, and caraway seeds.*
5. *Cooking Time: while stirring for 4 minutes then remove from the heat.*
6. *After cooling the mixture, stuff it equally in the tomatoes.*
7. *Place the tomatoes in the air fryer basket and seal it.*
8. *Cooking Time: them for 8 minutes at 350 degrees F on air fryer mode.*
9. *Enjoy.*

Nutritional Values:
Calories 361
Total Fat 16.3 g
Saturated Fat 4.9 g
Cholesterol 114 mg
Sodium 515 mg
Total Carbs 29.3 g
Fiber 0.1 g
Sugar 18.2 g
Protein 3.3 g

860. Spinach Stuffed Portobello

Preparation time: 10 minutes
Cooking time: 12 minutes
Total time: 22 minutes
Servings: 4
Ingredients:
- *4 portobello mushrooms, chopped*
- *10 basil leaves*
- *1 tablespoon parsley*
- *¼ cup olive oil*
- *8 cherry tomatoes, halved*
- *1 cup baby spinach*
- *3 garlic cloves, chopped*
- *1 cup almonds, chopped*
- *Salt and black pepper to the taste*

How to Prepare:
1. *Add all ingredients except mushrooms to a food processor.*
2. *Blend it all well until smooth then stuff each mushroom cap with the mixture.*
3. *Place the stuffed mushrooms in the air fryer basket and seal it.*
4. *Cooking Time: them for 12 minutes at 350 degrees F on air fryer mode.*
5. *Enjoy.*

Nutritional Values:
Calories 205
Total Fat 22.7 g
Saturated Fat 6.1 g
Cholesterol 4 mg
Sodium 227 mg
Total Carbs 26.1 g
Fiber 1.4 g
Sugar 0.9 g
Protein 5.2 g

861. Seasoned Potatoes

Preparation time: 10 minutes
Cooking time: 12 minutes
Total time: 22 minutes
Servings: 04

Ingredients:
- 1 tablespoon coriander seeds
- ½ teaspoon turmeric powder
- ½ teaspoon red chili powder
- 1 teaspoon pomegranate powder
- 1 tablespoon pickled mango, chopped
- 1 tablespoon cumin seeds
- 2 teaspoons fenugreeks, dried
- 5 potatoes, boiled, peeled and cubed
- Salt and black pepper to the taste
- 2 tablespoons olive oil

How to Prepare:
1. Take a baking dish suitable to fit in your air fryer.
2. Add oil, coriander, and cumin seeds to the dish.
3. Place it over medium heat and sauté for 2 minutes.
4. Stir in the rest of the ingredients.
5. Mix well then spread the potatoes in the air fryer basket.
6. Seal it and Cooking Time: them for 10 minutes at 360 degrees F on Air fryer mode.
7. Serve warm.

Nutritional Values:
Calories 201
Total Fat 8.9 g
Saturated Fat 4.5 g
Cholesterol 57 mg
Sodium 340 mg
Total Carbs 24.7 g
Fiber 1.2 g
Sugar 1.3 g
Protein 15.3 g

862. Black Bean Lime Dip

Preparation Time: 5 minutes
Cooking Time: 6 minutes
Servings: 4
Ingredients:
- 15.5 ounces cooked black beans
- 1 teaspoon minced garlic
- ½ of a lime, juiced
- 1 inch of ginger, grated
- 1/3 teaspoon salt
- 1/3 teaspoon ground black pepper
- 1 tablespoon olive oil

Directions:
1. Take a frying pan, add oil and when hot, add garlic and ginger and Cooking Time: for 1 minute until fragrant.
2. Then add beans, splash with some water and fry for 3 minutes until hot.
3. Season beans with salt and black pepper, drizzle with lime juice, then remove the pan from heat and mash the beans until smooth pasta comes together.
4. Serve the dip with whole-grain breadsticks or vegetables.

Nutrition:
Calories: 374 Cal
Fat: 14 g
Carbs: 46 g
Protein: 15 g
Fiber: 17 g

863. Beetroot Hummus

Preparation Time: 10 minutes
Cooking Time: 60 minutes
Servings: 4
Ingredients:
- 15 ounces cooked chickpeas
- 3 small beets
- 1 teaspoon minced garlic
- 1/2 teaspoon smoked paprika
- 1 teaspoon of sea salt
- 1/4 teaspoon red chili flakes
- 2 tablespoons olive oil
- 1 lemon, juiced
- 2 tablespoon tahini
- 1 tablespoon chopped almonds
- 1 tablespoon chopped cilantro

Directions:
1. Drizzle oil over beets, season with salt, then wrap beets in a foil and bake for 60 minutes at 425 degrees F

until tender.
2. When done, let beet cool for 10 minutes, then peel and dice them and place them in a food processor.
3. Add remaining ingredients and pulse for 2 minutes until smooth, tip the hummus in a bowl, drizzle with some more oil, and then serve straight away.

Nutrition:
Calories: 50.1 Cal
Fat: 2.5 g
Carbs: 5 g
Protein: 2 g
Fiber: 1 g

864. Zucchini Hummus

Preparation Time: 5 minutes
Cooking Time: 0 minute
Servings: 8
Ingredients:

- 1 cup diced zucchini
- 1/2 teaspoon sea salt
- 1 teaspoon minced garlic
- 2 teaspoons ground cumin
- 3 tablespoons lemon juice
- 1/3 cup tahini

Directions:
1. Place all the ingredients in a food processor and pulse for 2 minutes until smooth.
2. Tip the hummus in a bowl, drizzle with oil and serve.

Nutrition:
Calories: 65 Cal
Fat: 5 g
Carbs: 3 g
Protein: 2 g
Fiber: 1 g

865. Chipotle And Lime Tortilla Chips

Preparation Time: 10 minutes
Cooking Time: 15 minutes
Servings: 4
Ingredients:

- 12 ounces whole-wheat tortillas
- 4 tablespoons chipotle seasoning
- 1 tablespoon olive oil
- 4 limes, juiced

Directions:
1. Whisk together oil and lime juice, brush it well on tortillas, then sprinkle with chipotle seasoning and bake for 15 minutes at 350 degrees F until crispy, turning halfway.
2. When done, let the tortilla cool for 10 minutes, then break it into chips and serve.

Nutrition:
Calories: 150 Cal
Fat: 7 g
Carbs: 18 g
Protein: 2 g
Fiber: 2 g

866. Carrot And Sweet Potato Fritters

Preparation Time: 10 minutes
Cooking Time: 8 minutes
Servings: 10
Ingredients:

- 1/3 cup quinoa flour
- 1½ cups shredded sweet potato
- 1 cup grated carrot
- 1/3 teaspoon ground black pepper
- 2/3 teaspoon salt
- 2 teaspoons curry powder
- 2 flax eggs
- 2 tablespoons coconut oil

Directions:
1. Place all the ingredients in a bowl, except for oil, stir well until combined and then shape the mixture into ten small patties.
2. Take a large pan, place it over medium-high heat, add oil and when it melts, add patties in it and Cooking Time: for 3 minutes per side until browned.
3. Serve straight away

Nutrition:
Calories: 70 Cal

Fat: 3 g
Carbs: 8 g
Protein: 1 g
Fiber: 1 g

867. Tomato And Pesto Toast

Preparation Time: 5 minutes
Cooking Time: 0 minute
Servings: 4
Ingredients:

- *1 small tomato, sliced*
- *¼ teaspoon ground black pepper*
- *1 tablespoon vegan pesto*
- *2 tablespoons hummus*
- *1 slice of whole-grain bread, toasted*
- *Hemp seeds as needed for garnishing*

Directions:
1. *Spread hummus on one side of the toast, top with tomato slices and then drizzle with pesto.*
2. *Sprinkle black pepper on the toast along with hemp seeds and then serve straight away.*

Nutrition:
Calories: 214 Cal
Fat: 7.2 g
Carbs: 32 g
Protein: 6.5 g
Fiber: 3 g

868. Avocado And Sprout Toast

Preparation Time: 5 minutes
Cooking Time: 0 minute
Servings: 4
Ingredients:

- *1/2 of a medium avocado, sliced*
- *1 slice of whole-grain bread, toasted*
- *2 tablespoons sprouts*
- *2 tablespoons hummus*
- *¼ teaspoon lemon zest*
- *½ teaspoon hemp seeds*
- *¼ teaspoon red pepper flakes*

Directions:
1. *Spread hummus on one side of the toast and then top with avocado slices and sprouts.*
2. *Sprinkle with lemon zest, hemp seeds, and red pepper flakes and then serve straight away.*

Nutrition:
Calories: 200 Cal
Fat: 10.5 g
Carbs: 22 g
Protein: 7 g
Fiber: 7 g

869. Apple And Honey Toast

Preparation Time: 5 minutes
Cooking Time: 0 minute
Servings: 4
Ingredients:

- *½ of a small apple, cored, sliced*
- *1 slice of whole-grain bread, toasted*
- *1 tablespoon honey*
- *2 tablespoons hummus*
- *1/8 teaspoon cinnamon*

Directions:
1. *Spread hummus on one side of the toast, top with apple slices and then drizzle with honey.*
2. *Sprinkle cinnamon on it and then serve straight away.*

Nutrition:
Calories: 212 Cal
Fat: 7 g
Carbs: 35 g
Protein: 4 g
Fiber: 5.5 g

870. Thai Snack Mix

Preparation Time: 15 minutes
Cooking Time: 90 minutes
Servings: 4
Ingredients:

- *5 cups mixed nuts*
- *1 cup chopped dried pineapple*
- *1 cup pumpkin seed*
- *1 teaspoon garlic powder*
- *1 teaspoon onion powder*
- *2 teaspoons paprika*
- *1 teaspoon of sea salt*
- *1/4 cup coconut sugar*

- 1/2 teaspoon red chili powder
- 1/2 teaspoon ground black pepper
- 1 tablespoon red pepper flakes
- 1/2 tablespoon red curry powder
- 2 tablespoons soy sauce
- 2 tablespoons coconut oil

Directions:
1. Switch on the slow cooker, add all the ingredients in it except for dried pineapple and red pepper flakes, stir until combined and Cooking Time: for 90 minutes at high heat setting, stirring every 30 minutes.
2. When done, spread the nut mixture on a baking sheet lined with parchment paper and let it cool.
3. Then spread dried pineapple on top, sprinkle with red pepper flakes and serve.

Nutrition:
Calories: 230 Cal
Fat: 17.5 g
Carbs: 11.5 g
Protein: 6.5 g
Fiber: 2 g

871. Zucchini Fritters

Preparation Time: 10 minutes
Cooking Time: 6 minutes
Servings: 12
Ingredients:
- 1/2 cup quinoa flour
- 3 1/2 cups shredded zucchini
- 1/2 cup chopped scallions
- 1/3 teaspoon ground black pepper
- 1 teaspoon salt
- 2 tablespoons coconut oil
- 2 flax eggs

Directions:
1. Squeeze moisture from the zucchini by wrapping it in a cheesecloth and then transfer it to a bowl.
2. Add remaining ingredients, except for oil, stir until combined and then shape the mixture into twelve patties.
3. Take a skillet pan, place it over medium-high heat, add oil and when hot, add patties and Cooking Time: for 3 minutes per side until brown.
4. Serve the patties with favorite vegan sauce.

Nutrition:
Calories: 37 Cal
Fat: 1 g
Carbs: 4 g
Protein: 2 g
Fiber: 1 g

872. Zucchini Chips

Preparation Time: 10 minutes
Cooking Time: 120 minutes
Servings: 4
Ingredients:
- 1 large zucchini, thinly sliced
- 1 teaspoon salt
- 2 tablespoons olive oil

Directions:
1. Pat dry zucchini slices and then spread them in an even layer on a baking sheet lined with parchment sheet.
2. Whisk together salt and oil, brush this mixture over zucchini slices on both sides and then bake for 2 hours or more until brown and crispy.
3. When done, let the chips cool for 10 minutes and then serve straight away.

Nutrition:
Calories: 54 Cal
Fat: 5 g
Carbs: 1 g
Protein: 0 g

873. Rosemary Beet Chips

Preparation Time: 10 minutes
Cooking Time: 20 minutes
Servings: 3
Ingredients:
- 3 large beets, scrubbed, thinly sliced
- 1/8 teaspoon ground black pepper
- ¼ teaspoon of sea salt

- 3 sprigs of rosemary, leaves chopped
- 4 tablespoons olive oil

Directions:
1. Spread beet slices in a single layer between two large baking sheets, brush the slices with oil, then season with spices and rosemary, toss until well coated, and bake for 20 minutes at 375 degrees F until crispy, turning halfway.
2. When done, let the chips cool for 10 minutes and then serve.

Nutrition:
Calories: 79 Cal
Fat: 4.7 g
Carbs: 8.6 g
Protein: 1.5 g
Fiber: 2.5 g

874. Quinoa Broccoli Tots

Preparation Time: 10 minutes
Cooking Time: 20 minutes
Servings: 16
Ingredients:
- 2 tablespoons quinoa flour
- 2 cups steamed and chopped broccoli florets
- 1/2 cup nutritional yeast
- 1 teaspoon garlic powder
- 1 teaspoon miso paste
- 2 flax eggs
- 2 tablespoons hummus

Directions:
1. Place all the ingredients in a bowl, stir until well combined, and then shape the mixture into sixteen small balls.
2. Arrange the balls on a baking sheet lined with parchment paper, spray with oil and bake at 400 degrees F for 20 minutes until brown, turning halfway.
3. When done, let the tots cool for 10 minutes and then serve straight away.

Nutrition:
Calories: 19 Cal
Fat: 0 g
Carbs: 2 g
Protein: 1 g
Fiber: 0.5 g

875. Spicy Roasted Chickpeas

Preparation Time: 10 minutes
Cooking Time: 20 minutes
Servings: 6
Ingredients:
- 30 ounces cooked chickpeas
- ½ teaspoon salt
- 2 teaspoons mustard powder
- ½ teaspoon cayenne pepper
- 2 tablespoons olive oil

Directions:
1. Place all the ingredients in a bowl and stir until well coated and then spread the chickpeas in an even layer on a baking sheet greased with oil.
2. Bake the chickpeas for 20 minutes at 400 degrees F until golden brown and crispy and then serve straight away.

Nutrition:
Calories: 187.1 Cal
Fat: 7.4 g
Carbs: 24.2 g
Protein: 7.3 g
Fiber: 6.3 g

876. Nacho Kale Chips

Preparation Time: 10 minutes
Cooking Time: 14 hours
Servings: 10
Ingredients:
- 2 bunches of curly kale
- 2 cups cashews, soaked, drained
- 1/2 cup chopped red bell pepper
- 1 teaspoon garlic powder
- 1 teaspoon salt
- 2 tablespoons red chili powder
- 1/2 teaspoon smoked paprika
- 1/2 cup nutritional yeast
- 1 teaspoon cayenne
- 3 tablespoons lemon juice

- 3/4 cup water

Directions:
1. Place all the ingredients except for kale in a food processor and pulse for 2 minutes until smooth.
2. Place kale in a large bowl, pour in the blended mixture, mix until coated, and dehydrate for 14 hours at 120 degrees F until crispy.
3. If dehydrator is not available, spread kale between two baking sheets and bake for 90 minutes at 225 degrees F until crispy, flipping halfway.
4. When done, let chips cool for 15 minutes and then serve.

Nutrition:
Calories: 191 Cal
Fat: 12 g
Carbs: 16 g
Protein: 9 g
Fiber: 2 g

877. Red Salsa

Preparation Time: 10 minutes
Cooking Time: 0 minute
Servings: 8
Ingredients:

- 30 ounces diced fire-roasted tomatoes
- 4 tablespoons diced green chilies
- 1 medium jalapeño pepper, deseeded
- 1/2 cup chopped green onion
- 1 cup chopped cilantro
- 1 teaspoon minced garlic
- ½ teaspoon of sea salt
- 1 teaspoon ground cumin
- ¼ teaspoon stevia
- 3 tablespoons lime juice

Directions:
1. Place all the ingredients in a food processor and process for 2 minutes until smooth.
2. Tip the salsa in a bowl, taste to adjust seasoning and then serve.

Nutrition:
Calories: 71 Cal
Fat: 0.2 g
Carbs: 19 g
Protein: 2 g
Fiber: 4.1 g

878. Tomato Hummus

Preparation Time: 5 minutes
Cooking Time: 0 minute
Servings: 4
Ingredients:

- 1/4 cup sun-dried tomatoes, without oil
- 1 ½ cups cooked chickpeas
- 1 teaspoon minced garlic
- 1/2 teaspoon salt
- 2 tablespoons sesame oil
- 1 tablespoon lemon juice
- 1 tablespoon olive oil
- 1/4 cup of water

Directions:
1. Place all the ingredients in a food processor and process for 2 minutes until smooth.
2. Tip the hummus in a bowl, drizzle with more oil, and then serve straight away.

Nutrition:
Calories: 122.7 Cal
Fat: 4.1 g
Carbs: 17.8 g
Protein: 5.1 g
Fiber: 3.5 g

879. Marinated Mushrooms

Preparation Time: 10 minutes
Cooking Time: 7 minutes
Servings: 6
Ingredients:

- 12 ounces small button mushrooms
- 1 teaspoon minced garlic
- 1/4 teaspoon dried thyme
- 1/2 teaspoon sea salt
- 1/2 teaspoon dried basil
- 1/2 teaspoon red pepper flakes
- 1/4 teaspoon dried oregano
- 1/2 teaspoon maple syrup

- 1/4 cup apple cider vinegar
- 1/4 cup and 1 teaspoon olive oil
- 2 tablespoons chopped parsley

Directions:
1. Take a skillet pan, place it over medium-high heat, add 1 teaspoon oil and when hot, add mushrooms and Cooking Time: for 5 minutes until golden brown.
2. Meanwhile, prepare the marinade and for this, place remaining ingredients in a bowl and whisk until combined.
3. When mushrooms have cooked, transfer them into the bowl of marinade and toss until well coated.
4. Serve straight away

Nutrition:
Calories: 103 Cal
Fat: 9 g
Carbs: 2 g
Protein: 1 g

880. Hummus Quesadillas

Preparation Time: 5 minutes
Cooking Time: 15 minutes
Servings: 1
Ingredients:
- 1 tortilla, whole wheat
- 1/4 cup diced roasted red peppers
- 1 cup baby spinach
- 1/3 teaspoon minced garlic
- ¼ teaspoon salt
- ¼ teaspoon ground black pepper
- 1/4 teaspoon olive oil
- 1/4 cup hummus
- Oil as needed

Directions:
1. Place a large pan over medium heat, add oil and when hot, add red peppers and garlic, season with salt and black pepper and Cooking Time: for 3 minutes until sauté.
2. Then stir in spinach, Cooking Time: for 1 minute, remove the pan from heat and transfer the mixture in a bowl.
3. Prepare quesadilla and for this, spread hummus on one-half of the tortilla, then spread spinach mixture on it, cover the filling with the other half of the tortilla and Cooking Time: in a pan for 3 minutes per side until browned.
4. When done, cut the quesadilla into wedges and serve.

Nutrition:
Calories: 187 Cal
Fat: 9 g
Carbs: 16.3 g
Protein: 10.4 g
Fiber: 0 g

881. Nacho Cheese Sauce

Preparation Time: 5 minutes
Cooking Time: 10 minutes
Servings: 4
Ingredients:
- 3 tablespoons flour
- 1/4 teaspoon garlic salt
- 1/4 teaspoon salt
- 1/2 teaspoon cumin
- 1/4 teaspoon paprika
- 1 teaspoon red chili powder
- 1/8 teaspoon cayenne powder
- 1 cup vegan cashew yogurt
- 1 1/4 cups vegetable broth

Directions:
1. Take a small saucepan, place it over medium heat, pour in vegetable broth, and bring it to a boil.
2. Then whisk together flour and yogurt, add to the boiling broth, stir in all the spices, switch heat to medium-low level and Cooking Time: for 5 minutes until thickened.
3. Serve straight away.

Nutrition:
Calories: 282 Cal
Fat: 1 g
Carbs: 63 g
Protein: 3 g

Fiber: 12 g

882. Avocado Tomato Bruschetta

Preparation Time: 10 minutes
Cooking Time: 0 minute
Servings: 4
Ingredients:

- *3 slices of whole-grain bread*
- *6 chopped cherry tomatoes*
- *½ of sliced avocado*
- *½ teaspoon minced garlic*
- *½ teaspoon ground black pepper*
- *2 tablespoons chopped basil*
- *½ teaspoon of sea salt*
- *1 teaspoon balsamic vinegar*

Directions:

1. *Place tomatoes in a bowl, and then stir in vinegar until mixed. Top bread slices with avocado slices, then top evenly with tomato mixture, garlic and basil, and season with salt and black pepper.*
2. *Serve straight away*

Nutrition:
Calories: 131 Cal
Fat: 7.3 g
Carbs: 15 g
Protein: 2.8 g
Fiber: 3.2 g

883. Butter Carrots

Preparation time: 10 minutes
Cooking time: 10 minutes
Total time: 20 minutes
Servings: 04
Ingredients:

- *2 cups baby carrots*
- *1 tablespoon brown sugar*
- *½ tablespoon vegan butter, melted*
- *A pinch each salt and black pepper*

How to Prepare:

1. *Take a baking dish suitable to fit in your air fryer.*
2. *Toss carrots with sugar, butter, salt and black pepper in the baking dish.*
3. *Place the dish in the air fryer basket and seal the fryer.*
4. *Cooking Time: the carrots for 10 minutes at 350 degrees F on air fryer mode.*
5. *Enjoy.*

Nutritional Values:
Calories 119
Total Fat 14 g
Saturated Fat 2 g
Cholesterol 65 mg
Sodium 269 mg
Total Carbs 19 g
Fiber 4 g
Sugar 6 g
Protein 5g

884. Leeks With Butter

Preparation time: 10 minutes
Cooking time: 7 minutes
Total time: 17 minutes
Servings: 04
Ingredients:

- *1 tablespoon vegan butter, melted*
- *1 tablespoon lemon juice*
- *4 leeks, washed and halved*
- *Salt and black pepper to taste*

How to Prepare:

1. *Take a baking dish suitable to fit in your air fryer.*
2. *Toss the leeks with butter, salt, and black pepper in the dish.*
3. *Place the dish in the air fryer basket.*
4. *Seal the fryer and Cooking Time: the carrots for 7 minutes at 350 degrees F on air fryer mode.*
5. *Add a drizzle of lemon juice.*
6. *Mix well then serve.*

Nutritional Values:
Calories 231
Total Fat 20.1 g
Saturated Fat 2.4 g
Cholesterol 110 mg
Sodium 941 mg
Total Carbs 20.1 g
Fiber 0.9 g

Sugar 1.4 g
Protein 4.6 g

885. Juicy Brussel Sprouts

Preparation time: 10 minutes
Cooking time: 10 minutes
Total time: 20 minutes
Servings: 04
Ingredients:
- 1-pound brussels sprouts, trimmed
- ¼ cup green onions, chopped
- 6 cherry tomatoes, halved
- 1 tablespoon olive oil
- Salt and black pepper to taste

How to Prepare:
1. Take a baking dish suitable to fit in your air fryer.
2. Toss brussels sprouts with salt and black pepper in the dish.
3. Place this dish in the air fryer and seal the fryer.
4. Cooking Time: the sprouts for 10 minutes at 350 degrees F on air fryer mode.
5. Toss these sprouts with green onions, tomatoes, olive oil, salt, and pepper in a salad bowl.
6. Devour.

Nutritional Values:
Calories 361
Total Fat 16.3 g
Saturated Fat 4.9 g
Cholesterol 114 mg
Sodium 515 mg
Total Carbs 29.3 g
Fiber 0.1 g
Sugar 18.2 g
Protein 3.3 g

886. Parsley Potatoes

Preparation time: 10 minutes
Cooking time: 10 minutes
Total time: 20 minutes
Servings: 4
Ingredients:
- 1-pound gold potatoes, sliced
- 2 tablespoons olive oil
- ¼ cup parsley leaves, chopped
- Juice from ½ lemon
- Salt and black pepper to taste

How to Prepare:
1. Take a baking dish suitable to fit in your air fryer.
2. Place the potatoes in it and season them liberally with salt, pepper, olive oil, and lemon juice.
3. Place the baking dish in the air fryer basket and seal it.
4. Cooking Time: the potatoes for 10 minutes at 350 degrees F on air fryer mode.
5. Serve warm with parsley garnishing.
6. Devour.

Nutritional Values:
Calories 205
Total Fat 22.7 g
Saturated Fat 6.1 g
Cholesterol 4 mg
Sodium 227 mg
Total Carbs 26.1 g
Fiber 1.4 g
Sugar 0.9 g
Protein 5.2 g

887. Fried Asparagus

Preparation time: 10 minutes
Cooking time: 8 minutes
Total time: 18 minutes
Servings: 04
Ingredients:
- 2 pounds fresh asparagus, trimmed
- ½ teaspoon oregano, dried
- 4 ounces vegan feta cheese, crumbled
- 4 garlic cloves, minced
- 2 tablespoons parsley, chopped
- ¼ teaspoon red pepper flakes
- ¼ cup olive oil
- Salt and black pepper to the taste
- 1 teaspoon lemon zest
- 1 lemon, juiced

How to Prepare:

1. Combine lemon zest with oregano, pepper flakes, garlic and oil in a large bowl.
2. Add asparagus, salt, pepper, and cheese to the bowl.
3. Toss well to coat then place the asparagus in the air fryer basket.
4. Seal the fryer and Cooking Time: them for 8 minutes at 350 degrees F on Air fryer mode.
5. Garnish with parsley and lemon juice.
6. Enjoy warm.

Nutritional Values:
Calories 201
Total Fat 8.9 g
Saturated Fat 4.5 g
Cholesterol 57 mg
Sodium 340 mg
Total Carbs 24.7 g
Fiber 1.2 g
Sugar 1.3 g
Protein 15.3 g

888. Balsamic Artichokes

Preparation time: 10 minutes
Cooking time: 7 minutes
Total time: 17 minutes
Servings: 04
Ingredients:

- 4 big artichokes, trimmed
- ¼ cup olive oil
- 2 garlic cloves, minced
- 2 tablespoons lemon juice
- 2 teaspoons balsamic vinegar
- 1 teaspoon oregano, dried
- Salt and black pepper to the taste

How to Prepare:
1. Season artichokes liberally with salt and pepper then rub them with half of the lemon juice and oil.
2. Add the artichokes to a baking dish suitable to fit in the air fryer.
3. Place the artichoke dish in the air fryer basket and seal it.
4. Cooking Time: them for 7 minutes at 360 degrees F on air fryer mode.
5. Whisk remaining lemon juice, and oil, vinegar, oregano, garlic, salt and pepper in a bowl.
6. Pour this mixture over the artichokes and mix them well.
7. Enjoy.

Nutritional Values:
Calories 119
Total Fat 14 g
Saturated Fat 2 g
Cholesterol 65 mg
Sodium 269 mg
Total Carbs 19 g
Fiber 4 g
Sugar 6 g
Protein 5g

889. Tomato Kebabs

Preparation time: 10 minutes
Cooking time: 6 minutes
Total time: 16 minutes
Servings: 04
Ingredients:

- 3 tablespoons balsamic vinegar
- 24 cherry tomatoes
- 2 cups vegan feta cheese, sliced
- 2 tablespoons olive oil
- 3 garlic cloves, minced
- 1 tablespoon thyme, chopped
- Salt and black pepper to the taste

Dressing:

- 2 tablespoons balsamic vinegar
- 4 tablespoons olive oil
- Salt and black pepper to taste

How to Prepare:
1. In a medium bowl combine oil, garlic cloves, thyme, salt, vinegar, and black pepper.
2. Mix well then add the tomatoes and coat them liberally.
3. Thread 6 tomatoes and cheese slices on each skewer alternatively.
4. Place these skewers in the air fryer basket and seal it.
5. Cooking Time: them for 6 minutes

on air fryer mode at 360 degrees F.
6. Meanwhile, whisk together the dressing ingredients.
7. Place the cooked skewers on the serving plates.
8. Pour the vinegar dressing over them.
9. Enjoy.

Nutritional Values:
Calories 231
Total Fat 20.1 g
Saturated Fat 2.4 g
Cholesterol 110 mg
Sodium 941 mg
Total Carbs 20.1 g
Fiber 0.9 g
Sugar 1.4 g
Protein 4.6 g

890. Eggplant And Zucchini Snack

Preparation time: 10 minutes
Cooking time: 8 minutes
Total time: 18 minutes
Servings: 04
Ingredients:
- 1 eggplant, cubed
- 3 zucchinis, cubed
- 2 tablespoons lemon juice
- 1 teaspoon oregano, dried
- 3 tablespoons olive oil
- 1 teaspoon thyme, dried
- Salt and black pepper to taste

How to Prepare:
1. Take a baking dish suitable to fit in your air fryer.
2. Combine all ingredients in the baking dish.
3. Place the eggplant dish in the air fryer basket and seal it.
4. Cooking Time: them for 8 minutes at 360 degrees F on air fryer mode.
5. Enjoy warm.

Nutritional Values:
Calories 361
Total Fat 16.3 g
Saturated Fat 4.9 g
Cholesterol 114 mg
Sodium 515 mg
Total Carbs 29.3 g
Fiber 0.1 g
Sugar 18.2 g
Protein 3.3 g

891. Artichokes With Mayo Sauce

Preparation time: 10 minutes
Cooking time: 6 minutes
Total time: 16 minutes
Servings: 4
Ingredients:
- 2 artichokes, trimmed
- 1 tablespoon lemon juice
- 2 garlic cloves, minced
- A drizzle olive oil

Sauce:
- 1 cup vegan mayonnaise
- ¼ cup olive oil
- ¼ cup coconut oil
- 3 garlic cloves

How to Prepare:
1. Toss artichokes with lemon juice, oil and 2 garlic cloves in a large bowl.
2. Place the seasoned artichokes in the air fryer basket and seal it.
3. Cooking Time: the artichokes for 6 minutes at 350 degrees on air fryer mode.
4. Blend coconut oil with olive oil, mayonnaise and 3 garlic cloves in a food processor.
5. Place the artichokes on the serving plates.
6. Pour the mayonnaise mixture over the artichokes.
7. Enjoy fresh.

Nutritional Values:
Calories 205
Total Fat 22.7 g
Saturated Fat 6.1 g
Cholesterol 4 mg
Sodium 227 mg
Total Carbs 26.1 g

Fiber 1.4 g
Sugar 0.9 g
Protein 5.2 g

892. Fried Mustard Greens

Preparation time: 10 minutes
Cooking time: 11 minutes
Total time: 21 minutes
Servings: 04
Ingredients:

- 2 garlic cloves, minced
- 1 tablespoon olive oil
- ½ cup yellow onion, sliced
- 3 tablespoons vegetable stock
- ¼ teaspoon dark sesame oil
- 1-pound mustard greens, torn
- salt and black pepper to the taste

How to Prepare:

1. Take a baking dish suitable to fit in your air fryer.
2. Add oil and place it over the medium heat and sauté onions in it for 5 minutes.
3. Stir in garlic, greens, salt, pepper, and stock.
4. Mix well then place the dish in the air fryer basket.
5. Seal it and Cooking Time: them for 6 minutes at 350 degrees F on air fryer mode.
6. Drizzle sesame oil over the greens.
7. Devour.

Nutritional Values:
Calories 201
Total Fat 8.9 g
Saturated Fat 4.5 g
Cholesterol 57 mg
Sodium 340 mg
Total Carbs 24.7 g
Fiber 1.2 g
Sugar 1.3 g
Protein 15.3 g

893. Cheese Brussels Sprouts

Preparation time: 10 minutes
Cooking time: 8 minutes
Total time: 18 minutes
Servings: 04
Ingredients:

- 1-pound brussels sprouts, washed
- 3 tablespoons vegan parmesan, grated
- Juice from 1 lemon
- 2 tablespoons vegan butter
- Salt and black pepper to the taste

How to Prepare:

1. Spread the brussels sprouts in the air fryer basket.
2. Seal it and Cooking Time: them for 8 minutes at 350 degrees F on air fryer mode.
3. Place a nonstick pan over medium high heat and add butter to melt.
4. Stir in pepper, salt, lemon juice, and brussels sprouts.
5. Mix well then add parmesan.
6. Serve warm.

Nutritional Values:
Calories 119
Total Fat 14 g
Saturated Fat 2 g
Cholesterol 65 mg
Sodium 269 mg
Total Carbs 19 g
Fiber 4 g
Sugar 6 g
Protein 5g

894. Mushroom Stuffed Poblano

Preparation time: 10 minutes
Cooking time: 20 minutes
Total time: 30 minutes
Servings: 10
Ingredients:

- 10 poblano peppers, tops cut off and seeds removed
- 2 teaspoons garlic, minced
- 8 ounces mushrooms, chopped
- ½ cup cilantro, chopped
- 1 white onion, chopped
- 1 tablespoon olive oil

- Salt and black pepper to taste

How to Prepare:
1. Place a nonstick pan over medium heat and add oil.
2. Stir in mushrooms and onion, sauté for 5 minutes.
3. Add salt, black pepper, cilantro and garlic.
4. Stir while cooking for 2 additional minutes then take it off the heat.
5. Divide this mixture in the poblano peppers and stuff them neatly.
6. Place the peppers in the air fryer basket and seal it.
7. Cooking Time: them for 15 minutes at 350 degrees F on air fryer mode.
8. Enjoy.

Nutritional Values:
Calories 231
Total Fat 20.1 g
Saturated Fat 2.4 g
Cholesterol 110 mg
Sodium 941 mg
Total Carbs 20.1 g
Fiber 0.9 g
Sugar 1.4 g
Protein 4.6 g

895. Mushroom Stuffed Tomatoes

Preparation time: 10 minutes
Cooking time: 15 minutes
Total time: 25 minutes
Servings: 04
Ingredients:
- 4 tomatoes, tops removed and pulp removed (reserve for filling
- 1 yellow onion, chopped
- ½ cup mushrooms, chopped
- 1 tablespoon bread crumbs
- 1 tablespoon vegan butter
- ¼ teaspoon caraway seeds
- 1 tablespoon parsley, chopped
- 2 tablespoons celery, chopped
- 1 cup vegan cheese, shredded
- Salt and black pepper to the taste

How to Prepare:
1. Place a pan over medium heat, add butter.
2. When it melts, add onion and celery to sauté for 3 minutes.
3. Stir in mushrooms and tomato pulp.
4. Cooking Time: for 1 minute then add crumbled bread, pepper, salt, cheese, parsley, and caraway seeds.
5. Cooking Time: while stirring for 4 minutes then remove from the heat.
6. After cooling the mixture, stuff it equally in the tomatoes.
7. Place the tomatoes in the air fryer basket and seal it.
8. Cooking Time: them for 8 minutes at 350 degrees F on air fryer mode.
9. Enjoy.

Nutritional Values:
Calories 361
Total Fat 16.3 g
Saturated Fat 4.9 g
Cholesterol 114 mg
Sodium 515 mg
Total Carbs 29.3 g
Fiber 0.1 g
Sugar 18.2 g
Protein 3.3 g

896. Spinach Stuffed Portobello

Preparation time: 10 minutes
Cooking time: 12 minutes
Total time: 22 minutes
Servings: 4
Ingredients:
- 4 portobello mushrooms, chopped
- 10 basil leaves
- 1 tablespoon parsley
- ¼ cup olive oil
- 8 cherry tomatoes, halved
- 1 cup baby spinach
- 3 garlic cloves, chopped
- 1 cup almonds, chopped
- Salt and black pepper to the taste

How to Prepare:

1. Add all ingredients except mushrooms to a food processor.
2. Blend it all well until smooth then stuff each mushroom cap with the mixture.
3. Place the stuffed mushrooms in the air fryer basket and seal it.
4. Cooking Time: them for 12 minutes at 350 degrees F on air fryer mode.
5. Enjoy.

Nutritional Values:
Calories 205
Total Fat 22.7 g
Saturated Fat 6.1 g
Cholesterol 4 mg
Sodium 227 mg
Total Carbs 26.1 g
Fiber 1.4 g
Sugar 0.9 g
Protein 5.2 g

897. Seasoned Potatoes

Preparation time: 10 minutes
Cooking time: 12 minutes
Total time: 22 minutes
Servings: 04
Ingredients:
- 1 tablespoon coriander seeds
- ½ teaspoon turmeric powder
- ½ teaspoon red chili powder
- 1 teaspoon pomegranate powder
- 1 tablespoon pickled mango, chopped
- 1 tablespoon cumin seeds
- 2 teaspoons fenugreeks, dried
- 5 potatoes, boiled, peeled and cubed
- Salt and black pepper to the taste
- 2 tablespoons olive oil

How to Prepare:
1. Take a baking dish suitable to fit in your air fryer.
2. Add oil, coriander, and cumin seeds to the dish.
3. Place it over medium heat and sauté for 2 minutes.
4. Stir in the rest of the ingredients.
5. Mix well then spread the potatoes in the air fryer basket.
6. Seal it and Cooking Time: them for 10 minutes at 360 degrees F on Air fryer mode.
7. Serve warm.

Nutritional Values:
Calories 201
Total Fat 8.9 g
Saturated Fat 4.5 g
Cholesterol 57 mg
Sodium 340 mg
Total Carbs 24.7 g
Fiber 1.2 g
Sugar 1.3 g
Protein 15.3 g

898. White Chocolate Fudge

Preparation Time: 5 minutes
Cooking Time: 15 minutes, 4 hours refrigeration
Servings: 6
Ingredients:
- 2 cups coconut creaminutes
- 1 tsp vanilla extract
- 3 oz. butter
- 3 oz. unsweetened white chocolate
- Swerve sugar for sprinkling

Directions:
1. Pour the coconut cream and vanilla into a saucepan and bring to a boil over medium heat, then simmer until reduced by half, about 15 minutes.
2. Stir in the butter until the batter is smooth; turn the heat off.
3. Chop the white chocolate into small bits and stir into the cream until melted.
4. Pour the mixture into a 7 x 7 baking sheet and chill in the fridge for 3 to 4 hours.
5. After, cut into squares, sprinkle with a little swerve sugar, and serve.

Nutrition
Calories:297 , Total Fat:31.3g, Saturated Fat:25g, Total Carbs: 5g, Dietary Fiber:1g, Sugar:1 g, Protein:3g, Sodium:14 mg

899. Cheesecake With Blueberries

Preparation Time: 4minutes
Cooking Time: 1hour, 28minutes, overnight refrigeration
Servings: 6
Ingredients:

For the piecrust:
- *2 oz. butter*
- *1¼ cups* almond flour
- *2 tbsp* Swerve *sugar*
- *½ tsp vanilla extract*

For the filling:
- *3 tbsp flax seed powder + 9 tbsp water*
- *2 cups dairy-free cashew creaminutes*
- *½ cup coconut creaminutes*
- *1 tbsp Swerve sugar*
- *1 tsp lemon zest*
- *½ tsp vanilla extract*
- *2 oz. fresh blueberries*

Directions:
1. *Preheat the oven to 350 F and grease a 9-inch springform pan with cooking spray. Line with parchment paper.*
2. *To make the crust, melt the butter in a skillet over low heat until nutty in flavor. Turn the heat off and stir in the almond flour, swerve sugar, and vanilla until a dough forms.*
3. *Press the mixture into the springform pan and bake in the oven until the crust is lightly golden, about 8 minutes.*
4. *For the filling, mix the flax seed powder with water and allow sitting for 5 minutes to thicken.*
5. *In a bowl, evenly combine the cashew cream, coconut cream, swerve sugar, lemon zest, vanilla extract, and flax egg.*
6. *Remove the crust from the oven and pour the mixture on top. Use a spatula to layer evenly.*
7. *Bake the cake for 15 minutes at 400 F.*
8. *Then, reduce the heat 230 F and bake further for 45 to 60 minutes.*
9. *Remove to cool completely. Refrigerate overnight and scatter the blueberries on top.*
10. *Unlock, lift the pan and slice the cake into wedges. Serve immediately.*

Nutrition
Calories:598 , Total Fat:56g, Saturated Fat:18.8g, Total Carbs: 12g, Dietary Fiber:3g, Sugar:5 g, Protein:15 g, Sodium:762 mg

900. Lime Ice Creaminutes

Preparation Time: 10minutes
Servings 4
Ingredients:
- *2 large avocados, pitted*
- *Juice and zest of 3 limes*
- *1/3 cup erythritol*
- *1¾ cups coconut creaminutes*
- *¼ tsp vanilla extract*

Directions:
1. *In a blender, combine the avocado pulp, lime juice and zest, erythritol, coconut cream, and vanilla extract. Process until the mixture is smooth.*
2. *Pour the mixture into your ice cream maker and freeze based on the manufacturer's instructions.*
3. *When ready, remove and scoop the ice cream into bowls. Serve immediately.*

Nutrition
Calories:129 , Total Fat:8.2g, Saturated Fat:5.2g, Total Carbs: 7g, Dietary Fiber:1g, Sugar: 4g, Protein:7 g, Sodium: 52mg

901. Berry Coconut Yogurt Ice Pops

Preparation Time: 2 minutes, 8 hours refrigeration
Servings: 6
Ingredients:
- *2/3 cup avocado, halved and pitted*
- *2/3 cup frozen strawberries &*

blueberries, thawed
- 1 cup dairy-free sugar free coconut yogurt
- ½ cup coconut creaminutes
- 1 tsp vanilla extract

Directions:
1. Pour the avocado pulp, berries, dairy-free sugar free coconut yogurt, coconut cream, and vanilla extract. Process until smooth.
2. Pour into ice pop sleeves and freeze for 8 or more hours.
3. Enjoy the ice pops when ready.

Nutrition
Calories:240 , Total Fat:22.5g, Saturated Fat:13.8g, Total Carbs: 9g, Dietary Fiber:2g, Sugar: 6g, Protein:3 g, Sodium: 37mg

902. Berry Hazelnut Trifle

Preparation Time: 5minutes
Servings: 4
Ingredients:
- 1 ½ ripe avocado
- ¾ cup coconut creaminutes
- Zest and juice of ½ a lemon
- 1 tbsp vanilla extract
- 3 oz. fresh strawberries
- 2 oz. toasted hazelnuts

Directions:
1. In a bowl, add the avocado pulp, coconut cream, lemon zest and juice, and half of the vanilla extract. Mix the Ingredients with an immersion blender.
2. Put the strawberries and remaining vanilla in another bowl and use a fork to mash the fruits.
3. In a tall glass, alternate layering the cream and strawberry mixtures.
4. Drop a few hazelnuts on each and serve the dessert immediately.

Nutrition
Calories:321 , Total Fat:31.4g, Saturated Fat:19.2g, Total Carbs: 10g, Dietary Fiber:5g, Sugar:4 g, Protein: 2g, Sodium: 298mg

903. Avocado Truffles

Preparation Time: 4minutes
Cooking Time: 1minutes
Servings: 6
Ingredients:
- 1 ripe avocado, pitted
- ½ tsp vanilla extract
- ½ tsp lemon zest
- 1 pinch salt
- 5 oz. dairy-free dark chocolate, unsweetened
- 1 tbsp coconut oil
- 1 tbsp unsweetened cocoa powder

Directions:
1. Scoop the pulp of the avocado into a bowl and mix with the vanilla using an immersion blender. Stir in the lemon zest and a pinch of salt.
2. Pour the chocolate and coconut oil into a safe microwave bowl and melt in the microwave for 1 minute.
3. Add to the avocado mixture and stir. Allow cooling to firm up a bit.
4. Oil your hands with a little oil and form balls out of the mix.
5. Roll each ball in the cocoa powder and serve immediately.

Nutrition
Calories: 503, Total Fat:50g, Saturated Fat:30.9g, Total Carbs: 13g, Dietary Fiber:4g, Sugar: 7g, Protein:4 g, Sodium: 49mg

904. Mint Ice Creaminutes

Preparation Time: 10minutes, refrigeration time
Servings: 4
Ingredients:
- 2 avocados, pitted
- 1¼ cups coconut creaminutes
- ½ tsp vanilla extract
- 2 tbsp erythritol
- 2 tsp chopped mint leaves

Directions:
1. Into a blender, spoon the avocado pulps, pour in the coconut cream,

vanilla extract, erythritol, and mint leaves.
2. Process until smooth.
3. Pour the mixture into your ice cream maker and freeze according to the manufacturer's instructions.
4. When ready, remove and scoop the ice cream into bowls. Serve immediately.

Nutrition
Calories:373 , Total Fat:39.8 g, Saturated Fat: 24.7g, Total Carbs: 2 g, Dietary Fiber:0g, Sugar:2 g, Protein: 2g, Sodium:147 mg

905. Cardamom Coconut Fat Bombs

Preparation Time: 5minutes
Cooking Time: 2minutes
Servings: 6
Ingredients:
- ½ cup unsweetened grated coconut
- 3 oz. unsalted butter, room temperature
- ¼ tsp green cardamom powder
- ½ tsp vanilla extract
- ¼ tsp cinnamon powder

Directions:
1. Pour the grated coconut into a skillet and roast until lightly brown. Set aside to cool.
2. In a bowl, combine the butter, half of the coconut, cardamom, vanilla, and cinnamon.
3. Use your hands to form bite-size balls from the mixture and roll each in the remaining coconut.
4. Refrigerate the balls until ready to serve.

Nutrition
Calories:687 , Total Fat: 54.5g, Saturated Fat:27.4 g, Total Carbs: 9g, Dietary Fiber:2g, Sugar: 4g, Protein: 38g, Sodium:883 mg

906. Berries, Nuts, And Cream Bowl

Preparation Time: 10minutes
Cooking Time: 20minutes
Servings: 6
Ingredients:

For the dark chocolate cake:
- 5 tbsp flax seed powder + 2/3 cup water
- 1 cup dairy-free dark chocolate
- 1 cup butter
- 1 pinch salt
- 1 tsp vanilla extract

For the topping:
- 2 cups fresh blueberries
- 4 tbsp lemon juice
- 1 tsp vanilla extract
- 2 cups coconut creaminutes
- 4 oz. walnuts, chopped
- ½ cup roasted unsweetened coconut chips

Directions:
1. Preheat the oven to 320 F; grease a 9-inch springform pan with cooking spray and line with parchment paper.
2. In a bowl, mix the flax seed powder with water and allow thickening for 5 minutes.
3. Then, break the chocolate and butter into a bowl and melt in the microwave for 1 to 2 minutes.
4. Share the flax egg into two bowls; whisk the salt into one portion and then, 1 teaspoon of vanilla into the other.
5. Pour the chocolate mixture into the vanilla mixture and combine well. Then, fold into the other flax egg mixture.
6. Pour the batter into the springform pan and bake for 15 to 20 minutes or until a knife inserted into the cake comes out clean.
7. When ready, slice the cake into squares and share into serving bowls. Set aside.
8. Pour the blueberries, lemon juice,

and the remaining vanilla into a small bowl. Use a fork to break the blueberries and allow sitting for a few minutes.
9. Whip the coconut cream with a whisk until a soft peak forms.
10. To serve, spoon the cream on the cakes, top with the blueberry mixture, and sprinkle with the walnuts and coconut flakes.
11. Serve immediately.

Nutrition
Calories:49 , Total Fat: 45g, Saturated Fat: 29.9g, Total Carbs:12 g, Dietary Fiber:3g, Sugar: 6g, Protein: 3g, Sodium: 48mg

907. Chocolate Peppermint Mousse

Preparation Time: 10minutes, 30minutes refrigeration
Servings: 4
Ingredients:

- ¼ cup swerve sugar, divided
- 4 oz. dairy-free cashew cream, softened
- 3 tbsp unsweetened cocoa powder
- ¾ tsp peppermint extract
- ¼ cup warm water
- ½ tsp vanilla extract
- 1/3 cup coconut creaminutes

Directions:

1. Put 2 tablespoons of swerve sugar, the cashew cream, and cocoa powder in a blender. Add the peppermint extract, warm water, and process until smooth.
2. In a large bowl, whip the vanilla extract, coconut cream, and the remaining swerve sugar using a whisk. Fetch out 5 to 6 tablespoons for garnishing.
3. Next, fold in the cocoa mixture until thoroughly combined.
4. Spoon the mousse into serving cups and chill in the fridge for 30 minutes.
5. Garnish with the reserved whipped cream and serve immediately.

Nutrition
Calories:70 , Total Fat7.4: g, Saturated Fat: 4.6g, Total Carbs: 1g, Dietary Fiber:0g, Sugar:0 g, Protein: 0g, Sodium:8 mg

908. Keto Brownies

Preparation Time: 10minutes
Cooking Time: 20minutes, 2hour refrigeration
Servings: 4
Ingredients:

- 2 tbsp flax seed powder + 6 tbsp water
- 1/4 cup unsweetened cocoa powder
- 1/2 cup almond flour
- 1/2 tsp baking powder
- ½ cup erythritol
- 10 tablespoons butter 1/2 cup + 2 tbsp
- 2 oz dairy-free dark chocolate
- ½ teaspoon vanilla extract optional

Directions:

1. Preheat the oven to 375 F and line a baking sheet with parchment paper. Set aside.
2. Mix the flax seed powder with water in a bowl and allow thickening for 5 minutes.
3. In a separate bowl, mix the cocoa powder, almond flour, baking powder, and erythritol until no lumps from the erythritol remain.
4. In another bowl, add the butter and dark chocolate and melt both in the microwave for 30 seconds to 1 minute.
5. Whisk the flax egg and vanilla into the chocolate mixture, then pour the mixture into the dry Ingredients. Combine evenly.
6. Pour the batter onto the paper-lined baking sheet and bake in the oven for 20 minutes or until a toothpick inserted into the cake comes out clean.

7. Remove from the oven to cool completely and refrigerate for 30 minutes to 2 hours.
8. When ready, slice into squares, and serve.

Nutrition
Calories: 321, Total Fat: 40.3g, Saturated Fat:18 g, Total Carbs: 19 g, Dietary Fiber:5g, Sugar:4 g, Protein:2 g, Sodium:265 mg

909. Chia Bars

Preparation time: 10 minutes
Cooking time: 20 minutes
Servings: 6
Ingredients:

- 1 cup coconut oil, melted
- ½ teaspoon baking soda
- 3 tablespoons chia seeds
- 2 tablespoons stevia
- 1 cup coconut creaminutes
- 3 tablespoons flaxseed mixed with 4 tablespoons water

Directions:
1. In a bowl, combine the coconut oil with the cream, the chia seeds and the other ingredients, whisk well, pour everything into a square baking dish, introduce in the oven at 370 degrees F and bake for 20 minutes.
2. Cool down, slice into squares and serve.

Nutrition: calories 220, fat 2, fiber 0.5, carbs 2, protein 4

910. Fruits Stew

Preparation time: 10 minutes
Cooking time: 10 minutes
Servings: 4
Ingredients:

- 1 avocado, peeled, pitted and sliced
- 1 cup plums, stoned and halved
- 2 cups water
- 2 teaspoons vanilla extract
- 1 tablespoon lemon juice
- 2 tablespoons stevia

Directions:
1. In a pan, combine the avocado with the plums, water and the other ingredients, bring to a simmer and Cooking Time: over medium heat for 10 minutes.
2. Divide the mix into bowls and serve cold.

Nutrition: calories 178, fat 4.4, fiber 2, carbs 3, protein 5

911. Avocado And Rhubarb Salad

Preparation time: 10 minutes
Cooking time: 0 minutes
Servings: 4
Ingredients:

- 1 tablespoon stevia
- 1 cup rhubarb, sliced and boiled
- 2 avocados, peeled, pitted and sliced
- 1 teaspoon vanilla extract
- Juice of 1 lime

Directions:
In a bowl, combine the rhubarb with the avocado and the other ingredients, toss and serve.

Nutrition: calories 140, fat 2, fiber 2, carbs 4, protein 4

912. Plums And Nuts Bowls

Preparation time: 5 minutes
Cooking time: 0 minutes
Servings: 2
Ingredients:

- 2 tablespoons stevia
- 1 cup walnuts, chopped
- 1 cup plums, pitted and halved
- 1 teaspoon vanilla extract

Directions:
In a bowl, mix the plums with the walnuts and the other ingredients, toss, divide into 2 bowls and serve cold.

Nutrition: calories 400, fat 23, fiber 4, carbs 6, protein 7

913. Avocado And

Strawberries Salad

Preparation time: 5 minutes
Cooking time: 0 minutes
Servings: 4
Ingredients:

- *2 avocados, pitted, peeled and cubed*
- *1 cup strawberries, halved*
- *Juice of 1 lime*
- *1 teaspoon almond extract*
- *2 tablespoons almonds, chopped*
- *1 tablespoon stevia*

Directions:
In a bowl, combine the avocados with the strawberries, and the other ingredients, toss and serve.
Nutrition: *calories 150, fat 3, fiber 3, carbs 5, protein 6*

914. Chocolate Watermelon Cups

Preparation time: 2 hours
Cooking time: 0 minutes
Servings: 4
Ingredients:

- *2 cups watermelon, peeled and cubed*
- *1 tablespoon stevia*
- *1 cup coconut creaminutes*
- *1 tablespoon cocoa powder*
- *1 tablespoon mint, chopped*

Directions:
In a blender, combine the watermelon with the stevia and the other ingredients, pulse well, divide into cups and keep in the fridge for 2 hours before serving.
Nutrition: *calories 164, fat 14.6, fiber 2.1, carbs 9.9, protein 2.1*

915. Vanilla Raspberries Mix

Preparation time: 10 minutes
Cooking time: 10 minutes
Servings: 4
Ingredients:

- *1 cup water*
- *1 cup raspberries*
- *3 tablespoons stevia*
- *1 teaspoon nutmeg, ground*
- *½ teaspoon vanilla extract*

Directions:
In a pan, combine the raspberries with the water and the other ingredients, toss, Cooking Time: over medium heat for 10 minutes, divide into bowls and serve.
Nutrition: *calories 20, fat 0.4, fiber 2.1, carbs 4, protein 0.4*

916. Ginger Creaminutes

Preparation time: 10 minutes
Cooking time: 10 minutes
Servings: 4
Ingredients:

- *2 tablespoons stevia*
- *2 cups coconut creaminutes*
- *1 teaspoon vanilla extract*
- *1 tablespoon cinnamon powder*
- *¼ tablespoon ginger, grated*

Directions:
In a pan, combine the cream with the stevia and other ingredients, stir, Cooking Time: over medium heat for 10 minutes, divide into bowls and serve cold.
Nutrition: *calories 280, fat 28.6, fiber 2.7, carbs 7, protein 2.8*

917. Chocolate Ginger Cookies

Preparation time: 10 minutes
Cooking time: 20 minutes
Servings: 6
Ingredients:

- *2 cups almonds, chopped*
- *2 tablespoons flaxseed mixed with 3 tablespoons water*
- *¼ cup avocado oil*
- *2 tablespoons stevia*
- *¼ cup cocoa powder*
- *1 teaspoon baking soda*

Directions:
1. *In your food processor, combine the almonds with the flaxseed mix and the other ingredients, pulse well, scoop tablespoons out of this mix, arrange them on a lined baking*

sheet, flatten them a bit and Cooking Time: at 360 degrees F for 20 minutes.
2. Serve the cookies cold.

Nutrition: calories 252, fat 41.6, fiber 6.5, carbs 11.7, protein 3

918. Coconut Salad

Preparation time: 10 minutes
Cooking time: 0 minutes
Servings: 6
Ingredients:
- 2 cups coconut flesh, unsweetened and shredded
- ½ cup walnuts, chopped
- 1 cup blackberries
- 1 tablespoon stevia
- 1 tablespoon coconut oil, melted

Directions:
In a bowl, combine the coconut with the walnuts and the other ingredients, toss and serve.

Nutrition: calories 250, fat 23.8, fiber 5.8, carbs 8.9, protein 4.5

919. Mint Cookies

Preparation time: 10 minutes
Cooking time: 20 minutes
Servings: 6
Ingredients:
- 2 cups coconut flour
- 3 tablespoons flaxseed mixed with 4 tablespoons water
- ½ cup coconut creaminutes
- ½ cup coconut oil, melted
- 3 tablespoons stevia
- 2 teaspoons mint, dried
- 2 teaspoons baking soda

Directions:
1. In a bowl, mix the coconut flour with the flaxseed, coconut cream and the other ingredients, and whisk really well.
2. Shape balls out of this mix, place them on a lined baking sheet, flatten them, introduce in the oven at 370 degrees F and bake for 20 minutes.
3. Serve the cookies cold.

Nutrition: calories 190, fat 7.32, fiber 2.2, carbs 4, protein 3

920. Mint Avocado Bars

Preparation time: 10 minutes
Cooking time: 25 minutes
Servings: 6
Ingredients:
- 1 teaspoon almond extract
- ½ cup coconut oil, melted
- 2 tablespoons stevia
- 1 avocado, peeled, pitted and mashed
- 2 cups coconut flour
- 1 tablespoon cocoa powder

Directions:
1. In a bowl, combine the coconut oil with the almond extract, stevia and the other ingredients and whisk well.
2. Transfer this to baking pan, spread evenly, introduce in the oven and Cooking Time: at 370 degrees F and bake for 25 minutes.
3. Cool down, cut into bars and serve.

Nutrition: calories 230, fat 12.2, fiber 4.2, carbs 15.4, protein 5.8

921. Coconut Chocolate Cake

Preparation time: 10 minutes
Cooking time: 30 minutes
Servings: 12
Ingredients:
- 4 tablespoons flaxseed mixed with 5 tablespoons water
- 1 cup coconut flesh, unsweetened and shredded
- 1 teaspoon vanilla extract
- 2 tablespoons cocoa powder
- 1 teaspoon baking soda
- 2 cups almond flour
- 4 tablespoons stevia
- 2 tablespoons lime zest
- 2 cups coconut creaminutes

Directions:
1. In a bowl, combine the flaxmeal

with the coconut, the vanilla and the other ingredients, whisk well and transfer to a cake pan.
2. Cooking Time: the cake at 360 degree F for 30 minutes, cool down and serve.

Nutrition: calories 268, fat 23.9, fiber 5.1, carbs 9.4, protein 6.1

922. Mint Chocolate Creaminutes

Preparation time: 10 minutes
Cooking time: 0 minutes
Servings: 6
Ingredients:
- 1 cup coconut oil, melted
- 4 tablespoons cocoa powder
- 1 teaspoon vanilla extract
- 1 cup mint, chopped
- 2 cups coconut creaminutes
- 4 tablespoons stevia

Directions:
In your food processor, combine the coconut oil with the cocoa powder, the cream and the other ingredients, pulse well, divide into bowls and serve really cold.

Nutrition: calories 514, fat 56, fiber 3.9, carbs 7.8, protein 3

923. Cranberries Cake

Preparation time: 10 minutes
Cooking time: 30 minutes
Servings: 6
Ingredients:
- 2 cups coconut flour
- 2 tablespoon coconut oil, melted
- 3 tablespoons stevia
- 1 tablespoon cocoa powder, unsweetened
- 2 tablespoons flaxseed mixed with 3 tablespoons water
- 1 cup cranberries
- 1 cup coconut creaminutes
- ¼ teaspoon vanilla extract
- ½ teaspoon baking powder

Directions:

1. In a bowl, combine the coconut flour with the coconut oil, the stevia and the other ingredients, and whisk well.
2. Pour this into a cake pan lined with parchment paper, introduce in the oven and Cooking Time: at 360 degrees F for 30 minutes.
3. Cool down, slice and serve.

Nutrition: calories 244, fat 16.7, fiber 11.8, carbs 21.3, protein 4.4

924. Sweet Zucchini Buns

Preparation time: 10 minutes
Cooking time: 30 minutes
Servings: 8
Ingredients:
- 1 cup almond flour
- 1/3 cup coconut flesh, unsweetened and shredded
- 1 cup zucchinis, grated
- 2 tablespoons stevia
- 1 teaspoon baking soda
- ½ teaspoon cinnamon powder
- 3 tablespoons flaxseed mixed with 4 tablespoons water
- 1 cup coconut creaminutes

Directions:
1. In a bowl, mix the almond flour with the coconut flesh, the zucchinis and the other ingredients, stir well until you obtain a dough, shape 8 buns and arrange them on a baking sheet lined with parchment paper.
2. Introduce in the oven at 350 degrees and bake for 30 minutes.
3. Serve these sweet buns warm.

Nutrition: calories 169, fat 15.3, fiber 3.9, carbs 6.4, protein 3.2

925. Lime Custard

Preparation time: 10 minutes
Cooking time: 20 minutes
Servings: 6
Ingredients:
- 1 pint almond milk
- 4 tablespoons lime zest, grated

- *3 tablespoons lime juice*
- *3 tablespoons flaxseed mixed with 4 tablespoons water*
- *tablespoons stevia*
- *2 teaspoons vanilla extract*

Directions:
1. In a bowl, combine the almond milk with the lime zest, lime juice and the other ingredients, whisk well and divide into 4 ramekins.
2. Bake in the oven at 360 degrees F for 30 minutes.
3. Cool the custard down and serve.

Nutrition: calories 234, fat 21.6, fiber 4.3, carbs 9, protein 3.5

926. Brussels Sprouts Chips

Preparation time: 5 minutes
Cooking Time: time: 10 minutes
Servings: 2
Ingredients:
- *10 Brussels sprouts split leaves*
- *1 tablespoon olive oil*
- *¼ teaspoon sea salt*

Directions:
Preheat your oven to 350° Fahrenheit. Toss Brussels sprouts with olive oil. Season Brussels sprouts with salt. Spread Brussels sprouts in a baking dish and bake in preheated oven for 10 minutes. Serve and enjoy!

Nutrition:
Calories: 101
Fat: 7.3 g
Sugar: 2.1 g
Carbohydrates: 8.6 g
Cholesterol: 0 mg
Protein: 3.2 g

927. Baked Onion Rings

Preparation time: 5 minutes
Cooking Time: time: 25 minutes
Servings: 4
Ingredients:
- *2 eggs, organic*
- *½ teaspoon pepper*
- *½ teaspoon salt*
- *½ teaspoon garlic powder*
- *2 tablespoons thyme, sliced*
- *1 ½ cups almond flour*
- *2 large sweet onions, cut into rings*

Directions:
Preheat your oven to 400° Fahrenheit. In a mixing bowl, combine garlic powder, almond flour, thyme, garlic powder, and salt. Take another bowl, add eggs and whisk. Dip the onion ring in egg mixture then coat with flour mixture. Place the coated onion rings in a baking dish. Bake in preheated oven for 25 minutes. Serve immediately and enjoy!

Nutrition:
Calories: 130
Carbohydrates: 10.7 g
Fat: 7.4 g
Sugar: 3.5 g
Cholesterol: 82 mg
Protein: 6.1 g

928. Roasted Almonds

Preparation time: 5 minutes
Cooking Time: time: 5 minutes
Servings: 4
Ingredients:
- *2 cups almonds, blanched*
- *2 tablespoons rosemary*
- *1 teaspoon salt*
- *2 tablespoons olive oil*
- *1 teaspoon paprika*

Directions:
In a pan over medium-high heat add almonds and heat until toasted. Reduce heat to medium-low and add salt, paprika, and rosemary. Cooking Time: almonds for another 3 minutes. Serve immediately and enjoy!

Nutritional Values (Per Servings):
Calories: 342
Fat: 31.1g
Sugar: 2.1 g
Carbohydrates: 11.5 g
Cholesterol: 0 mg

Protein: 10.2 g

929. Cheese Fries

Preparation time: 5 minutes
Cooking Time: time: 4 minutes
Servings: 4
Ingredients:

- 8-ounces halloumi cheese, sliced into fries
- 2-ounces tallow
- 1 serving marinara sauce, low carb

Directions:
Heat the tallow in a pan over medium heat. Gently place halloumi pieces in the pan. Cooking Time: halloumi fries for 2 minutes on each side or until lightly golden brown. Serve with marinara sauce and enjoy!
Nutrition:
Calories: 200
Sugar: 0.3 g
Fat: 18 g
Carbohydrates: 1 g
Cholesterol: 42 mg
Protein: 12 g

930. Crunchy Parmesan Crisps

Preparation time: 5 minutes
Cooking Time: time: 3 minutes
Servings: 12
Ingredients:

- 12 tablespoons Parmesan cheese, shredded

Directions:
Preheat your oven to 400° Fahrenheit. Spray a baking tray with cooking spray. Place each tablespoon of cheese on a baking tray. Bake in preheated oven for 3 minutes or until lightly brown. Allow cooling time, serve and enjoy!
Nutrition:
Calories: 64
Carbohydrates: 0.7 g
Sugar: 0 g
Fat: 4.3 g
Cholesterol: 14 mg
Protein: 6.4 g

931. Cinnamon Coconut Chips

Preparation time: 5 minutes
Cooking Time: time: 2 minutes
Servings: 2
Ingredients:

- ¼ cup coconut chips, unsweetened
- ¼ teaspoon sea salt
- ¼ cup cinnamon

Directions:
Add cinnamon and salt in a mixing bowl and set aside. Heat a pan over medium heat for 2 minutes. Place the coconut chips in the hot pan and stir until coconut chips crisp and lightly brown. Toss toasted coconut chips with cinnamon and salt. Serve and enjoy!
Nutrition:
Calories: 228
Carbohydrates: 7.8 g
Fat: 21 g
Sugar: 0 g
Cholesterol: 0 mg
Protein: 1.9 g

932. Roasted Cashews

Preparation time: 5 minutes
Cooking Time: time: 3 hours
Servings: 4
Ingredients:

- 1 cup cashews
- 1 cup water
- 2 tablespoons cinnamon

Directions:
Add water and cashews to a bowl and soak overnight. Drain the cashews and place on a paper towel to dry. Preheat oven to 200° Fahrenheit. Place the soaked cashews on a baking tray. Sprinkle cashews with cinnamon. Roast in preheated oven for 3 hours. Allow cooling time and then serve and enjoy!
Nutrition:
Calories: 205
Sugar: 1.8 g
Fat: 15.9 g
Carbohydrates: 13.9 g
Cholesterol: 0 mg
Protein: 5.4 g

933. Crunchy Cauliflower Bites

Preparation time: 10 minutes
Cooking Time: time: 20 minutes
Servings: 8
Ingredients:

- *2 eggs, organic, beaten*
- *1 tablespoon Parmesan cheese, grated*
- *½ head cauliflower, cut into florets*
- *1 cup breadcrumbs*
- *Pepper and salt to taste*

Directions:
Preheat your oven to 395°Fahrenheit. Spray baking dish with cooking spray and set aside. In a shallow dish combine the cheese, breadcrumbs, pepper, and salt. Dip the cauliflower florets in beaten egg then roll in breadcrumb mixture. Place coated cauliflower florets onto prepared baking dish. Bake in preheated oven for 20 minutes. Serve hot and enjoy!
Nutrition:
Calories: 81
Sugar: 1.3 g
Fat: 2.4 g
Carbohydrates: 10.7 g
Cholesterol: 42 mg
Protein: 4.3 g

934. Crispy Zucchini Fries

Preparation time: 10 minutes
Cooking Time: time: 25 minutes
Servings: 4
Ingredients:

- *1 medium zucchini*
- *4 tablespoons almond meal*
- *4 tablespoons light ranch dressing*
- *3 tablespoons Franks hot sauce*
- *2 teaspoons Italian seasoning*
- *½ cup breadcrumbs*
- *2 tablespoons Parmesan cheese, grated*

Directions:
Preheat oven to 395°Fahrenheit. Spray a baking dish with cooking spray and set aside. Wash zucchini and cut into fries' size pieces. Place almond meal in a flat dish. Take another flat dish and mix the breadcrumbs, Italian seasoning, and cheese on it. In a bowl combine the hot sauce and ranch dressing. Roll zucchini pieces in the almond meal then dip in sauce mixture and finally coat with breadcrumb mixture. Place coated zucchini on prepared baking dish. Bake in preheated oven for 25 minutes. Flip zucchini fries once halfway through. Serve and enjoy!
Nutrition:
Calories: 149
Sugar: 2.6 g
Cholesterol: 11 mg
Fat: 8.1 g
Carbohydrates: 13.6 g
Proteins: 6 g

935. Crispy Kale Chips

Preparation time: 10 minutes
Cooking Time: time: 12 minutes
Servings: 2
Ingredients:

- *1 cup kale, fresh*
- *2 teaspoons garlic seasoning*
- *2 teaspoons sesame seeds, toasted*

Directions:
Preheat your oven to 325° Fahrenheit. Spray baking dish with cooking spray and set aside. Wash kale and pat dry with paper towel. Cut the kale and tear into pieces and place in a baking dish. Spray kale with cooking spray. Sprinkle sesame seeds and seasoning over the kale. Bake in preheated oven for 12 minutes. Serve and enjoy.
Nutrition:
Calories: 55
Carbohydrates: 5.2 g
Fat: 2.3 g
Sugar: 0 g
Cholesterol: 0 mg
Protein: 2 g

Dessert Recipes

936. Chocolate Brownies

Preparation time: 5 minutes
Cooking Time: time: 20 minutes
Servings: 4
Ingredients:

- 2 tablespoons cocoa powder
- 1 scoop protein powder
- 1 cup bananas, over-ripe
- ½ cup almond butter, melted

Directions:
Preheat the oven to 350° Fahrenheit. Spray the brownie pan with cooking spray. Add all ingredients in your blender and blend until smooth. Pour the batter into the prepared pan and bake in preheated oven for 20 minutes. Serve and enjoy!

Nutrition:
Calories: 82
Sugars: 5 g
Fat: 2.1 g
Carbohydrates: 11.4 g
Cholesterol: 16 mg
Protein: 6.9 g

937. Almond Butter Fudge

Preparation time: 15 minutes
Cooking Time: time: 2 minutes
Servings: 8
Ingredients:

- 2 ½ tablespoons coconut oil
- 2 ½ tablespoons honey
- ½ cup almond butter

Directions:
Combine coconut oil and almond butter in a saucepan and warm for 2 minutes or until melted. Add honey and stir. Pour the mixture into candy container and store in the fridge until set. Serve and enjoy!

Nutrition:
Calories: 63
Carbohydrates: 5.6 g
Fat: 4.8 g
Sugars: 5.4 g
Cholesterol: 0 mg
Protein: 0.2 g

938. White Chocolate Fat Bomb

Preparation time: 5 minutes
Cooking Time: time: 2 minutes
Servings: 8
Ingredients:

- 4 tablespoons butter
- 4 tablespoons coconut oil
- 4 tablespoons erythritol, powdered
- 4-ounces cocoa butter
- ¼ teaspoon salt
- ¼ teaspoon Stevia
- ½ teaspoon vanilla extract
- ½ cup walnuts, chopped

Directions:
Add your cocoa butter and coconut oil into a pan over medium heat for 2 minutes or until melted, then remove from heat. Add Stevia, vanilla extract, erythritol, salt, and walnuts. Mix well to combine. Pour mixture into silicone mold and place in the fridge for an hour. Serve and enjoy!

Nutrition:
Calories: 265
Fat: 20.2 g
Carbohydrates: 0.8 g
Protein: 0.9 g
Fiber: 0.5
Cholesterol: 15 mg

939. Brownie Balls

Preparation time: 20 minutes
Servings: 12
Ingredients:

- 6 dates, pitted
- ¼ cup chocolate chips
- ½ cup almond meal
- 2 tablespoons coconut butter
- 2 teaspoons vanilla extract

Directions:

Add your dates to your food processor and pulse for 3 minutes. Add all remaining ingredients except chocolate chips. Pulse until well combined. Add chocolate chips and pulse for 2 times. Form dough into 12 balls and place into the fridge for 1 hour. Serve and enjoy!

Nutrition:
Calories: 86
Fat: 6 g
Cholesterol: 1 mg
Carbohydrates: 7.3 g
Protein: 1.5 g

940. Peanut Butter Fudge

Preparation time: 15 minutes
Cooking Time: time: 2 minutes
Servings: 20
Ingredients:

- *12-ounces peanut butter, smooth*
- *4 tablespoons maple syrup*
- *4 tablespoons coconut cream*
- *3 tablespoons coconut oil*
- *Pinch of salt*

Directions:
Line baking tray with parchment paper. Melt the coconut and maple syrup in a pan over low heat for about 2 minutes or until melted. Add peanut butter, coconut cream, and salt into the pan, stir well. Pour fudge mixture into the prepared baking dish and place in the fridge for an hour. Cut into pieces serve and enjoy!

Nutrition:
Calories: 135
Carbohydrates: 6.2 g
Sugar: 4.1 g
Cholesterol: 0 mg
Fat: 11.3 g
Protein: 4.3 g

941. Instant Blueberry Ice Cream

Preparation time: 15 minutes
Servings: 2
Ingredients:

- *1 cup blueberries*
- *1 teaspoon lemon juice, fresh*
- *1 tablespoon Splenda*
- *½ cup heavy cream*

Directions:
Add all ingredients into a blender and blend until smooth. Serve immediately and enjoy!

Nutrition:
Calories: 176
Carbohydrates: 17.4 g
Sugar: 13.3 g
Cholesterol: 41 mg
Fat: 11.4 g
Protein: 1.2 g

942. Chia Raspberry Pudding

Preparation time: 3 hours and 10 minutes
Servings: 2
Ingredients:

- *4 tablespoons chia seeds*
- *½ cup raspberries*
- *1 cup coconut milk*

Directions:
Add the raspberry and coconut milk into your blender and blend until smooth. Pour the mixture into a mason jar. Add chia seeds and stir. Cap jar and shake. Place in the fridge for 3 hours then serve and enjoy!

Nutrition:
Calories: 408
Fat: 38.8 g
Sugar: 5.4 g
Carbohydrates: 22.3 g
Cholesterol: 0 mg
Protein: 9.1 g

943. Choco Mug Brownie

Preparation time: 5 minutes
Cooking Time: time: 30 seconds
Servings: 1
Ingredients:

- *½ teaspoon baking powder*
- *¼ cup almond milk*
- *1 scoop chocolate protein powder*
- *1 tablespoon cocoa powder*

Directions:
In a safe microwave, mug blend the protein

powder, cocoa, and baking powder. Add milk in mug and stir. Place the mug in the microwave for 30 seconds. Enjoy!
Nutrition:
Calories: 207
Carbohydrates: 9.5 g
Fat: 15.8 g
Sugar: 3.1 g
Cholesterol: 20 mg
Protein: 12.4 g

944. Pistachio Ice Cream

Preparation time: 20 minutes
Cooking Time: time: 3 minutes
Servings: 3
Ingredients:

- *2 egg yolks, organic*
- *1 ¾ cups coconut milk*
- *1 tablespoon oil*
- *1 tablespoon honey*
- *5 tablespoons pistachio nuts, chopped*
- *1 teaspoon vanilla*

Directions:
In a bowl, add honey, egg yolks, oil, coconut milk, salt, and whisk. Place the mixture into the fridge for an hour. In a pan over medium heat roast chopped pistachio nuts. Run ice cream mixture in ice cream maker and add in the roasted pistachios halfway through. Serve chilled and enjoy!
Nutrition:
Calories: 457
Carbohydrates: 15.8 g
Fat: 43.8 g
Sugar: 11.1 g
Cholesterol: 140 mg
Protein: 6.3 g

945. Strawberry Ricotta

Preparation time: 10 minutes
Servings: 2
Ingredients:

- *2 teaspoon Splenda*
- *1 cup strawberries, washed, sliced*
- *½ cup ricotta cheese*

Directions:
Add ricotta cheese to a shallow serving dish. Sprinkle with Splenda. Mash strawberries and pour over ricotta. Serve and enjoy!
Nutrition:
Calories: 129
Carbohydrates: 12.7 g
Fat: 5.1 g
Sugar: 7.7 g
Cholesterol: 19 mg
Protein: 7.5 g

946. No-Bake Raspberry Cheesecake Truffles

Preparation time: 3 hours
Servings: 48 (truffles
Ingredients:

- *½ cup erythritol, powdered*
- *8-ounces cream cheese softened*
- *1 teaspoon vanilla Stevia*
- *Pinch of salt*
- *1 ½ cups sugar-free chocolate chips, melted*
- *¼ cup coconut oil, melted*
- *Few drops of natural red food coloring*
- *3 teaspoons raspberry extract*
- *2 tablespoons heavy cream*

Directions:
In a stand mixer blend erythritol and cream cheese until smooth. Add the Stevia, cream, raspberry extract, salt, natural red food coloring and mix well. Slowly add in the coconut oil and continue to blend on high until it is incorporated. Scrape down the sides of the bowl to make sure it is all mixed well. Place in fridge for 1 hour. On a parchment-lined baking sheet scoop out the batter using a 1 ¼ inch mini cookie scoop. Should make 48 balls. Freeze for 1 hour before coating with melted chocolate. Drop one cheesecake truffle into chocolate at a time and place back on the lined baking pan. Place in fridge for 1 hour. Serve and enjoy!

DESSERTS AND DRINKS

947. Oatmeal Raisin Muffins

Preparation time: 10 minutes
Cooking time: 35 minutes
Total time: 45 minutes
Servings: 12
Ingredients:
- 2½ cups rolled oats
- ½ cup oat flour
- 1 teaspoon baking powder
- ½ teaspoon baking soda
- ½ teaspoon salt
- 1 tablespoon cinnamon
- ½ teaspoon ground nutmeg
- 4 ripe bananas, mashed
- 1 apple, grated
- ½ cup almond milk
- 2 teaspoons vanilla extract
- ½ cup raisins
- ½ cup chopped walnuts

How to Prepare:
1. Preheat your oven to 350 degrees F.
2. Whisk the dry ingredients in a mixing bowl, and wet ingredients in a separate bowl.
3. Beat the two mixtures together until smooth.
4. Fold in apples, walnuts and raisins, give it a gentle stir.
5. Line a muffin tray with muffin cups and evenly divide the muffin batter among the cups.
6. Bake for nearly 35 minutes and serve.

Nutritional Values:
Calories 398
Total Fat 6 g
Saturated Fat 7 g
Cholesterol 632 mg
Sodium 497 mg
Total Carbs 91 g
Fiber 3 g
Sugar 83 g
Protein 2 g

948. Applesauce Muffins

Preparation time: 10 minutes
Cooking time: 25 minutes
Total time: 35 minutes
Servings: 12
Ingredients:
- 2 cups whole wheat flour
- 1 teaspoon baking powder
- 1 teaspoon baking soda
- ½ teaspoon salt
- 1 teaspoon cinnamon
- ½ teaspoon ground allspice
- ½ cup brown sugar
- 15 ounces apple sauce
- ½ cup almond milk
- 1 teaspoon vanilla
- 1 teaspoon apple cider vinegar
- ½ cup raisins
- ½ cup apple, diced

How to Prepare:
1. Preheat your oven to 350 degrees F.
2. Separately, whisk together the dry ingredients in one bowl and wet ingredients in another bowl.
3. Beat the two mixture together until smooth.
4. Fold in apples and raisins, give it a gentle stir.
5. Line a muffin tray with muffin cups and evenly divide the muffin batter among the cups.
6. Bake for nearly 25 minutes and serve.

Nutritional Values:
Calories 232
Total Fat 8.9 g
Saturated Fat 4.5 g
Cholesterol 57 mg
Sodium 340 mg

Total Carbs 24.7 g
Fiber 1.2 g
Sugar 12.3 g
Protein 5.3 g

949. Banana Cinnamon Muffins

Preparation time: 10 minutes
Cooking time: 22 minutes
Total time: 32 minutes
Servings: 12
Ingredients:

- 3 very ripe bananas, mashed
- ½ cup vanilla almond milk
- 1 cup sugar
- 2 cups flour
- 1 teaspoon baking soda
- ½ teaspoon cinnamon
- ¼ teaspoon salt

How to Prepare:

1. Preheat your oven to 350 degrees F.
2. Separately, whisk together the dry ingredients in one bowl and the wet ingredients in another bowl.
3. Beat the two mixtures together until smooth.
4. Line a muffin tray with muffin cups and evenly divide the muffin batter among the cups.
5. Bake for 22 minutes and serve.

Nutritional Values:
Calories 427
Total Fat 31.1 g
Saturated Fat 4.2 g
Cholesterol 123 mg
Sodium 86 mg
Total Carbs 29 g
Sugar 12.4 g
Fiber 19.8 g
Protein 3.5 g

950. Cashew Oat Muffins

Preparation time: 10 minutes
Cooking time: 22 minutes
Total time: 32 minutes
Servings: 12
Ingredients:

- 3 cups rolled oats
- ¾ cup raw cashews
- ¼ cup maple syrup
- ¼ cup sugar
- 1 teaspoon vanilla extract
- ½ teaspoon salt
- 1½ teaspoon baking soda
- 2 cups water

How to Prepare:

1. Preheat your oven to 375 degrees F.
2. Separately, whisk together the dry ingredients in one bowl and the wet ingredients in another bowl.
3. Beat the two mixtures together until smooth.
4. Fold in cashews and give it a gentle stir.
5. Line a muffin tray with muffin cups and evenly divide the muffin batter among the cups.
6. Bake for 22 minutes and serve.

Nutritional Values:
Calories 398
Total Fat 13.8 g
Saturated Fat 5.1 g
Cholesterol 200 mg
Sodium 272 mg
Total Carbs 53.6 g
Fiber 1 g
Sugar 12.3 g
Protein 1.8 g

951. Banana Walnut Muffins

Preparation time: 10 minutes
Cooking time: 18 minutes
Total time: 28 minutes
Servings: 12
Ingredients:

- 4 large pitted dates, boiled
- 1 cup almond milk
- 2 tablespoons lemon juice
- 2½ cups rolled oats
- 1 teaspoon baking powder
- 1 teaspoon baking soda
- 1 teaspoon cinnamon

- ¼ teaspoon nutmeg
- ⅛ teaspoon salt
- 1½ cups mashed banana
- ¼ cup maple syrup
- 1 tablespoon vanilla extract
- 1 cup walnuts, chopped

How to Prepare:
1. Preheat your oven to 350 degrees F.
2. Separately, whisk together the dry ingredients in one bowl and the wet ingredients in another bowl.
3. Beat the two mixtures together until smooth.
4. Fold in walnuts and give it a gentle stir.
5. Line a muffin tray with muffin cups and evenly divide the muffin batter among the cups.
6. Bake for 18 minutes and serve.

Nutritional Values:
Calories 265
Total Fat 14 g
Saturated Fat 7 g
Cholesterol 632 mg
Sodium 497 mg
Total Carbs 36 g
Fiber 3 g
Sugar 10 g
Protein 5 g

952. Carrot Flaxseed Muffins

Preparation time: 10 minutes
Cooking time: 20 minutes
Total time: 30 minutes
Servings: 12
Ingredients:

- 2 tablespoons ground flax
- 5 tablespoons water
- ¾ cup almond milk
- ¾ cup applesauce
- ½ cup maple syrup
- 1 teaspoon vanilla extract
- 1½ cups whole wheat flour
- ½ cup rolled oats
- 1 teaspoon baking soda
- 1½ teaspoons baking powder
- ½ teaspoon salt
- 1 teaspoon ground cinnamon
- ¼ teaspoon ground ginger
- 1 cup grated carrot

How to Prepare:
1. Whisk flaxseed with water in a bowl and leave it for 10 minutes
2. Preheat your oven to 350 degrees F.
3. Separately, whisk together the dry ingredients in one bowl and the wet ingredients in another bowl.
4. Beat the two mixtures together until smooth.
5. Fold in flaxseed and carrots, give it a gentle stir.
6. Line a muffin tray with muffin cups and evenly divide the muffin batter among the cups.
7. Bake for 20 minutes and serve.

Nutritional Values:
Calories 172
Total Fat 11.8 g
Saturated Fat 4.4 g
Cholesterol 62 mg
Sodium 871 mg
Total Carbs 45.8 g
Fiber 0.6 g
Sugar 2.3 g
Protein 4 g

953. Chocolate Peanut Fat Bombs

Preparation time: 10 minutes
Cooking time: 1 hour 1 minute
Total time: 1 hour and 11 minutes
Servings: 12
Ingredients:

- ½ cup coconut butter
- 1 cup plus 2 tablespoons peanut butter
- 5 tablespoons cocoa powder
- 2 teaspoons maple syrup

How to Prepare:
1. In a bowl, combine all the ingredients.

2. Melt them in the microwave for 1 minute.
3. Mix well then divide the mixture into silicone molds.
4. Freeze them for 1 hour to set.
5. Serve.

Nutritional Values:
Calories 246
Total Fat 7.4 g
Saturated Fat 4.6 g
Cholesterol 105 mg
Sodium 353 mg
Total Carbs 29.4 g
Sugar 6.5 g
Fiber 2.7 g
Protein 7.2 g

954. Protein Fat Bombs

Preparation time: 10 minutes
Cooking time: 1 hour
Total time: 1 hour and 10 minutes
Servings: 12
Ingredients:

- 1 cup coconut oil
- 1 cup peanut butter, melted
- ½ cup cocoa powder
- ¼ cup plant-based protein powder
- 1 pinch of salt
- 2 cups unsweetened shredded coconut

How to Prepare:
1. In a bowl, add all the ingredients except coconut shreds.
2. Mix well then make small balls out of this mixture and place them into silicone molds.
3. Freeze for 1 hour to set.
4. Roll the balls in the coconut shreds.
5. Serve.

Nutritional Values:
Calories 293
Total Fat 16 g
Saturated Fat 2.3 g
Cholesterol 75 mg
Sodium 386 mg
Total Carbs 25.2 g
Sugar 2.6 g
Fiber 1.9 g
Protein 4.2 g

955. Mojito Fat Bombs

Preparation time: 10 minutes
Cooking time: 1 hour and 1 minute
Total time: 1 hour and 11 minutes
Servings: 12
Ingredients:

- ¾ cup hulled hemp seeds
- ½ cup coconut oil
- 1 cup fresh mint
- ½ teaspoon mint extract
- Juice & zest of two limes
- ¼ teaspoon stevia

How to Prepare:
1. In a bowl, combine all the ingredients.
2. Melt in the microwave for 1 minute.
3. Mix well then divide the mixture into silicone molds.
4. Freeze them for 1 hour to set.
5. Serve.

Nutritional Values:
Calories 319
Total Fat 10.6 g
Saturated Fat 3.1 g
Cholesterol 131 mg
Sodium 834 mg
Total Carbs 31.4 g
Fiber 0.2 g
Sugar 0.3 g
Protein 4.6 g

956. Apple Pie Bites

Preparation time: 10 minutes
Cooking time: 1 hour
Total time: 1 hour and 10 minutes
Servings: 12
Ingredients:

- 1 cup walnuts, chopped
- ½ cup coconut oil
- ¼ cup ground flax seeds
- ½ ounce freeze dried apples
- 1 teaspoon vanilla extract

- 1 teaspoon cinnamon
- Liquid stevia, to taste

How to Prepare:
1. In a bowl add all the ingredients.
2. Mix well then roll the mixture into small balls.
3. Freeze them for 1 hour to set.
4. Serve.

Nutritional Values:
Calories 211
Total Fat 25.5 g
Saturated Fat 12.4 g
Cholesterol 69 mg
Sodium 58 mg
Total Carbs 32.4 g
Fiber 0.7 g
Sugar 0.3 g
Protein 1.4 g

957. Coconut Fat Bombs

Preparation time: 10 minutes
Cooking time: 1 hour and 1 minute
Total time: 1 hour and 11 minutes
Servings: 12
Ingredients:

- 1 can coconut milk
- ¼ cup coconut oil
- 1 cup coconut flakes
- 20 drops liquid stevia

How to Prepare:
1. In a bowl combine all the ingredients.
2. Melt in a microwave for 1 minute.
3. Mix well then divide the mixture into silicone molds.
4. Freeze them for 1 hour to set.
5. Serve.

Nutritional Values:
Calories 119
Total Fat 14 g
Saturated Fat 2 g
Cholesterol 65 mg
Sodium 269 mg
Total Carbs 19 g
Fiber 4 g
Sugar 6 g

Protein 5g

958. Peach Popsicles

Preparation time: 10 minutes
Cooking time: 2 hours
Total time: 2 hours and 10 minutes
Servings: 2
Ingredients:

- 2½ cups peaches, peeled and pitted
- 2 tablespoons agave
- ¾ cup coconut cream

How to Prepare:
1. In a blender, blend all the ingredients for popsicles until smooth.
2. Divide the popsicle blend into the popsicle molds.
3. Insert the popsicles sticks and close the molds.
4. Place the molds in the freezer for 2 hours to set.
5. Serve.

Nutritional Values:
Calories 231
Total Fat 20.1 g
Saturated Fat 2.4 g
Cholesterol 110 mg
Sodium 941 mg
Total Carbs 20.1 g
Fiber 0.9 g
Sugar 1.4 g
Protein 4.6 g

959. Green Popsicle

Preparation time: 10 minutes
Cooking time: 2 hours
Total time: 2 hours and 10 minutes
Servings: 4
Ingredients:

- 1 ripe avocado, peeled and pitted
- 1 cup fresh spinach
- 1 can (13.5 ounce) full fat coconut milk
- ¼ cup lime juice
- 2 tablespoons maple syrup
- 1 teaspoon vanilla extract

Desserts

How to Prepare:
1. In a blender, blend all the ingredients for popsicles until smooth.
2. Divide the popsicle blend into the popsicle molds.
3. Insert the popsicles sticks and close the molds.
4. Place the molds in the freezer for 2 hours to set.
5. Serve.

Nutritional Values:
Calories 361
Total Fat 16.3 g
Saturated Fat 4.9 g
Cholesterol 114 mg
Sodium 515 mg
Total Carbs 29.3 g
Fiber 0.1 g
Sugar 18.2 g
Protein 3.3 g

960. Strawberry Coconut Popsicles

Preparation time: 10 minutes
Cooking time: 2 hours
Total time: 2 hours and 10 minutes
Servings: 2
Ingredients:
- 2 medium bananas, sliced
- 1 can coconut milk
- 1 cup strawberries
- 3 tablespoons maple syrup

How to Prepare:
1. In a blender, blend all the ingredients for popsicles until smooth.
2. Divide the popsicle blend into the popsicle molds.
3. Insert the popsicles sticks and close the molds.
4. Place the molds in the freezer for 2 hours to set.
5. Serve.

Nutritional Values:
Calories 205
Total Fat 22.7 g
Saturated Fat 6.1 g
Cholesterol 4 mg
Sodium 227 mg
Total Carbs 26.1 g
Fiber 1.4 g
Sugar 0.9 g
Protein 5.2 g

961. Fudge Popsicles

Preparation time: 10 minutes
Cooking time: 2 hours
Total time: 2 hours and 10 minutes
Servings: 2
Ingredients:
- 1 cup almond milk
- 3 ripe bananas
- 3 tablespoon cocoa powder
- 1 tablespoon almond butter

How to Prepare:
1. In a blender, blend all the ingredients for popsicles until smooth.
2. Divide the popsicle blend into the popsicle molds.
3. Insert the popsicles sticks and close the molds.
4. Place the molds in the freezer for 2 hours to set.
5. Serve.

Nutritional Values:
Calories 201
Total Fat 8.9 g
Saturated Fat 4.5 g
Cholesterol 57 mg
Sodium 340 mg
Total Carbs 24.7 g
Fiber 1.2 g
Sugar 1.3 g
Protein 15.3 g

962. Tangerine Cake

Preparation time: 10 minutes
Cooking time: 20 minutes
Servings: 8
Ingredients:
- ¾ cup coconut sugar
- 2 cups whole wheat flour

- ¼ cup olive oil
- ½ cup almond milk
- 1 teaspoon cider vinegar
- ½ teaspoon vanilla extract
- Juice and zest of 2 lemons
- Juice and zest of 1 tangerine

Directions:
1. In a bowl, mix flour with sugar and stir.
2. In another bowl, mix oil with milk, vinegar, vanilla extract, lemon juice and zest, tangerine zest and flour, whisk very well, pour this into a cake pan that fits your air fryer, introduce in the fryer and Cooking Time: at 360 degrees F for 20 minutes.
3. Serve right away.
4. Enjoy!

Nutrition: calories 210, fat 1, fiber 1, carbs 6, protein 4

963. Sweet Tomato Bread

Preparation time: 10 minutes
Cooking time: 30 minutes
Servings: 4
Ingredients:
- 1 and ½ cups whole wheat flour
- 1 teaspoon cinnamon powder
- 1 teaspoon baking powder
- 1 teaspoon baking soda
- ¾ cup maple syrup
- 1 cup tomatoes, chopped
- ½ cup olive oil
- 2 tablespoon apple cider vinegar

Directions:
1. In a bowl, mix flour with baking powder, baking soda, cinnamon and maple syrup and stir well.
2. In another bowl, mix tomatoes with olive oil and vinegar and stir well.
3. Combine the 2 mixtures, stir well, pour into a greased loaf pan that fits your air fryer, introduce in the fryer and Cooking Time: at 360 degrees F for 30 minutes.
4. Leave the cake to cool down, slice and serve.
5. Enjoy!

Nutrition: calories 203, fat 2, fiber 1, carbs 12, protein 4

964. Lemon Squares

Preparation time: 10 minutes
Cooking time: 30 minutes
Servings: 6
Ingredients:
- 1 cup whole wheat flour
- ½ cup vegetable oil
- 1 and ¼ cups coconut sugar
- 1 medium banana
- 2 teaspoons lemon peel, grated
- 2 tablespoons lemon juice
- 2 tablespoons flax meal combined with 2 tablespoons water
- ½ teaspoon baking powder

Directions:
1. In a bowl, mix flour with ¼ cup sugar and oil, stir well, press on the bottom of a pan that fits your air fryer, introduce in the fryer and bake at 350 degrees F for 14 minutes.
2. In another bowl, mix the rest of the sugar with lemon juice, lemon peel, banana, and baking powder, stir using your mixer and spread over baked crust.
3. Bake for 15 minutes more, leave aside to cool down, cut into medium squares and serve cold.
4. Enjoy!

Nutrition: calories 140, fat 4, fiber 1, carbs 12, protein 1

965. Sweet Cashew Sticks

Preparation time: 10 minutes
Cooking time: 15 minutes
Servings: 6
Ingredients:
- 1/3 cup stevia
- ¼ cup almond meal
- 1 tablespoon almond butter

- 1 and ½ cups cashews, chopped
- 4 dates, chopped
- ¾ cup coconut, shredded
- 1 tablespoon chia seeds

Directions:
1. In a bowl, mix stevia with almond meal, almond butter, cashews, coconut, dates and chia seeds and stir well again.
2. Spread this on a lined baking sheet that fits your air fryer, press well, introduce in the fryer and Cooking Time: at 300 degrees F for 15 minutes.
3. Leave mix to cool down, cut into medium sticks and serve.
4. Enjoy!

Nutrition: calories 162, fat 4, fiber 7, carbs 5, protein 6

966. Grape Pudding

Preparation time: 10 minutes
Cooking time: 40 minutes
Servings: 6
Ingredients:

- 1 cup grapes curd
- 3 cups grapes
- 3 and ½ ounces maple syrup
- 3 tablespoons flax meal combined with 3 tablespoons water
- 2 ounces coconut butter, melted
- 3 and ½ ounces almond milk
- ½ cup almond flour
- ½ teaspoon baking powder

Directions:
1. In a bowl, mix the half of the fruit curd with the grapes stir and divide into 6 heatproof ramekins.
2. In a bowl, mix flax meal with maple syrup, melted coconut butter, the rest of the curd, baking powder, milk and flour and stir well.
3. Divide this into the ramekins as well, introduce in the fryer and Cooking Time: at 200 degrees F for 40 minutes.
4. Leave puddings to cool down and serve!
5. Enjoy!

Nutrition: calories 230, fat 22, fiber 3, carbs 17, protein 8

967. Coconut And Seeds Bars

Preparation time: 10 minutes
Cooking time: 35 minutes
Servings: 4
Ingredients:

- 1 cup coconut, shredded
- ½ cup almonds
- ½ cup pecans, chopped
- 2 tablespoons coconut sugar
- ½ cup pumpkin seeds
- ½ cup sunflower seeds
- 2 tablespoons sunflower oil
- 1 teaspoon nutmeg, ground
- 1 teaspoon pumpkin pie spice

Directions:
1. In a bowl, mix almonds and pecans with pumpkin seeds, sunflower seeds, coconut, nutmeg and pie spice and stir well.
2. Heat up a pan with the oil over medium heat, add sugar, stir well, pour this over nuts and coconut mix and stir well.
3. Spread this on a lined baking sheet that fits your air fryer, introduce in your air fryer and Cooking Time: at 300 degrees F and bake for 25 minutes.
4. Leave the mix aside to cool down, cut and serve.
5. Enjoy!

Nutrition: calories 252, fat 7, fiber 8, carbs 12, protein 7

968. Chocolate Cookies

Preparation time: 10 minutes
Cooking time: 25 minutes
Servings: 12
Ingredients:

- 1 teaspoon vanilla extract
- ½ cup coconut butter, melted

- 1 tablespoon flax meal combined with 2 tablespoons water
- 4 tablespoons coconut sugar
- 2 cups flour
- ½ cup unsweetened vegan chocolate chips

Directions:
1. In a bowl, mix flax meal with vanilla extract and sugar and stir well.
2. Add melted butter, flour and half of the chocolate chips and stir everything.
3. Transfer this to a pan that fits your air fryer, spread the rest of the chocolate chips on top, introduce in the fryer at 330 degrees F and bake for 25 minutes.
4. Slice when it's cold and serve.
5. Enjoy!

Nutrition: calories 230, fat 12, fiber 2, carbs 13, protein 5

969. Simple And Sweet Bananas

Preparation time: 10 minutes
Cooking time: 15 minutes
Servings: 4
Ingredients:

- 3 tablespoons coconut butter
- 2 tablespoons flax meal combined with 2 tablespoons water
- 8 bananas, peeled and halved
- ½ cup corn flour
- 3 tablespoons cinnamon powder
- 1 cup vegan breadcrumbs

Directions:
1. Heat up a pan with the butter over medium-high heat, add breadcrumbs, stir and Cooking Time: for 4 minutes and then transfer to a bowl.
2. Roll each banana in flour, flax meal and breadcrumbs mix.
3. Arrange bananas in your air fryer's basket, dust with cinnamon sugar and Cooking Time: at 280 degrees F for 10 minutes.
4. Transfer to plates and serve.
5. Enjoy!

Nutrition: calories 214, fat 1, fiber 4, carbs 12, protein 4

970. Coffee Pudding

Preparation time: 10 minutes
Cooking time: 10 minutes
Servings: 4
Ingredients:

- 4 ounces coconut butter
- 4 ounces dark vegan chocolate, chopped
- Juice of ½ orange
- 1 teaspoon baking powder
- 2 ounces whole wheat flour
- ½ teaspoon instant coffee
- 2 tablespoons flax meal combined with 2 tablespoons water
- 2 ounces coconut sugar

Directions:
1. Heat up a pan with the coconut butter over medium heat, add chocolate and orange juice, stir well and take off heat.
2. In a bowl, mix sugar with instant coffee and flax meal, beat using your mixer, add chocolate mix, flour, salt and baking powder and stir well.
3. Pour this into a greased pan, introduce in your air fryer, Cooking Time: at 360 degrees F for 10 minutes, divide between plates and serve.
4. Enjoy!

Nutrition: calories 189, fat 6, fiber 4, carbs 14, protein 3

971. Almond And Vanilla Cake

Preparation time: 10 minutes
Cooking time: 30 minutes
Servings: 8
Ingredients:

- 1 and ½ cup stevia
- 1 cup flour
- ¼ cup cocoa powder+ 2 tablespoons

- ½ cup chocolate almond milk
- 2 teaspoons baking powder
- 2 tablespoons canola oil
- 1 teaspoon vanilla extract
- 1 and ½ cups hot water
- Cooking spray

Directions:

1. In a bowl, mix flour with 2 tablespoons cocoa, baking powder, almond milk, oil and vanilla extract, whisk well and spread on the bottom of a cake pan greased with cooking spray.
2. In a separate bowl, mix stevia with the rest of the cocoa and the water, whisk well and spread over the batter in the pan.
3. Introduce in the fryer and Cooking Time: at 350 degrees F for 30 minutes.
4. Leave the cake to cool down, slice and serve.
5. Enjoy!

Nutrition: calories 250, fat 4, fiber 3, carbs 10, protein 2

972. Blueberry Cake

Preparation time: 10 minutes
Cooking time: 30 minutes
Servings: 6
Ingredients:

- ½ cup whole wheat flour
- ¼ teaspoon baking powder
- ¼ teaspoon stevia
- ¼ cup blueberries
- 1/3 cup almond milk
- 1 teaspoon olive oil
- 1 teaspoon flaxseed, ground
- ½ teaspoon lemon zest, grated
- ¼ teaspoon vanilla extract
- ¼ teaspoon lemon extract
- Cooking spray

Directions:

1. In a bowl, mix flour with baking powder, stevia, blueberries, milk, oil, flaxseeds, lemon zest, vanilla extract and lemon extract and whisk well.
2. Spray a cake pan with cooking spray, line it with parchment paper, pour cake batter, introduce in the fryer and Cooking Time: at 350 degrees F for 30 minutes.
3. Leave the cake to cool down, slice and serve.
4. Enjoy!

Nutrition: calories 210, fat 4, fiber 4, carbs 10, protein 4

973. Peach Cobbler

Preparation time: 10 minutes
Cooking time: 30 minutes
Servings: 4
Ingredients:

- 4 cups peaches, peeled and sliced
- ¼ cup coconut sugar
- ½ teaspoon cinnamon powder
- 1 and ½ cups vegan crackers, crushed
- ¼ cup stevia
- ¼ teaspoon nutmeg, ground
- ½ cup almond milk
- 1 teaspoon vanilla extract
- Cooking spray

Directions:

1. In a bowl, mix peaches with coconut sugar and cinnamon and stir.
2. In a separate bowl, mix crackers with stevia, nutmeg, almond milk and vanilla extract and stir.
3. Spray a pie pan that fits your air fryer with cooking spray and spread peaches on the bottom.
4. Add crackers mix, spread, introduce into the fryer and Cooking Time: at 350 degrees F for 30 minutes
5. Divide the cobbler between plates and serve.
6. Enjoy!

Nutrition: calories 201, fat 4, fiber 4, carbs 7, protein 3

974. Easy Pears Dessert

Preparation time: 10 minutes
Cooking time: 25 minutes

Servings: 12
Ingredients:
- 6 big pears, cored and chopped
- ½ cup raisins
- 1 teaspoon ginger powder
- ¼ cup coconut sugar
- 1 teaspoon lemon zest, grated

Directions:
1. In a pan that fits your air fryer, mix pears with raisins, ginger, sugar and lemon zest, stir, introduce in the fryer and Cooking Time: at 350 degrees F for 25 minutes.
2. Divide into bowls and serve cold.
3. Enjoy!

Nutrition: calories 200, fat 3, fiber 4, carbs 6, protein 6

975. Sweet Strawberry Mix

Preparation time: 10 minutes
Cooking time: 20 minutes
Servings: 10
Ingredients:
- 2 tablespoons lemon juice
- 2 pounds strawberries
- 4 cups coconut sugar
- 1 teaspoon cinnamon powder
- 1 teaspoon vanilla extract

Directions:
1. In a pan that fits your air fryer, mix strawberries with coconut sugar, lemon juice, cinnamon and vanilla, stir gently, introduce in the fryer and Cooking Time: at 350 degrees F for 20 minutes
2. Divide into bowls and serve cold.
3. Enjoy!

Nutrition: calories 140, fat 0, fiber 1, carbs 5, protein 2

976. Sweet Bananas And Sauce

Preparation time: 10 minutes
Cooking time: 20 minutes
Servings: 4
Ingredients:
- Juice of ½ lemon
- 3 tablespoons agave nectar
- 1 tablespoon coconut oil
- 4 bananas, peeled and sliced diagonally
- ½ teaspoon cardamom seeds

Directions:
1. Arrange bananas in a pan that fits your air fryer, add agave nectar, lemon juice, oil and cardamom, introduce in the fryer and Cooking Time: at 360 degrees F for 20 minutes
2. Divide bananas and sauce between plates and serve.
3. Enjoy!

Nutrition: calories 210, fat 1, fiber 2, carbs 8, protein 3

977. Orange Cake

Preparation time: 10 minutes
Cooking time: 30 minutes
Servings: 4
Ingredients:
- Cooking spray
- 1 teaspoon baking powder
- 1 cup almond flour
- 1 cup coconut sugar
- ½ teaspoon cinnamon powder
- 3 tablespoons coconut oil, melted
- ½ cup almond milk
- ½ cup pecans, chopped
- ¾ cup water
- ½ cup raisins
- ½ cup orange peel, grated
- ¾ cup orange juice

Directions:
1. In a bowl, mix flour with half of the sugar, baking powder, cinnamon, 2 tablespoons oil, milk, pecans and raisins, stir and pour this in a greased cake pan that fits your air fryer.
2. Heat up a small pan over medium heat, add water, orange juice, orange peel, the rest of the oil and the rest of the sugar, stir, bring to a boil, pour

over the mix from the pan, introduce in the fryer and Cooking Time: at 330 degrees F for 30 minutes.
3. Serve cold.
4. Enjoy!

Nutrition: calories 282, fat 3, fiber 1, carbs 4, protein 3

978. Stuffed Apples

Preparation time: 10 minutes
Cooking time: 25 minutes
Servings: 5
Ingredients:

- 5 apples, tops cut off and cored
- 5 figs
- 1/3 cup coconut sugar
- ¼ cup pecans, chopped
- 2 teaspoons lemon zest, grated
- ½ teaspoon cinnamon powder
- 1 tablespoon lemon juice
- 1 tablespoon coconut oil

Directions:
1. In a bowl mix figs, coconut sugar, pecans, lemon zest, cinnamon, lemon juice and coconut oil and stir.
2. Stuff the apples with this mix, introduce them in your air fryer and Cooking Time: at 365 degrees F for 25 minutes.
3. Enjoy!

Nutrition: calories 200, fat 1, fiber 2, carbs 6, protein 3

979. Apples And Mandarin Sauce

Preparation time: 10 minutes
Cooking time: 20 minutes
Servings: 4
Ingredients:

- 4 apples, cored, peeled and cored
- 2 cups mandarin juice
- ¼ cup maple syrup
- 2 teaspoons cinnamon powder
- 1 tablespoon ginger, grated

Directions:
1. In a pan that fits your air fryer, mix apples with mandarin juice, maple syrup, cinnamon and ginger, introduce in the fryer and Cooking Time: at 365 degrees F for 20 minutes
2. Divide apples mix between plates and serve warm.
3. Enjoy!

Nutrition: calories 170, fat 1, fiber 2, carbs 6, protein 4

980. Almond Cookies

Preparation time: 10 minutes
Cooking time: 30 minutes
Servings: 12
Ingredients:

- 1 tablespoon flaxseed mixed with 2 tablespoons water
- ¼ cup coconut oil, melted
- 1 cup coconut sugar
- ½ teaspoon vanilla extract
- 1 teaspoon baking powder
- 1 and ½ cups almond meal
- ½ cup almonds, chopped

Directions:
1. In a bowl, mix oil with sugar, vanilla extract and flax meal and whisk.
2. Add baking powder, almond meal and almonds and stir well.
3. Spread cookie mix on a lined baking sheet, introduce in your air fryer and Cooking Time: at 340 degrees F for 30 minutes.
4. Leave cookie sheet to cool down, cut into medium pieces and serve.
5. Enjoy!

Nutrition: calories 210, fat 2, fiber 1, carbs 7, protein 6

981. Easy Pumpkin Cake

Preparation time: 10 minutes
Cooking time: 40 minutes
Servings: 10
Ingredients:

- 1 and ½ teaspoons baking powder
- Cooking spray

- 1 cup pumpkin puree
- 2 cups almond flour
- ½ teaspoon baking soda
- 1 and ½ teaspoons cinnamon, ground
- ¼ teaspoon ginger, ground
- 1 tablespoon coconut oil, melted
- 1 tablespoon flaxseed mixed with 2 tablespoons water
- 1 tablespoon vanilla extract
- 1/3 cup maple syrup
- 1 teaspoon lemon juice

Directions:
1. In a bowl, flour with baking powder, baking soda, cinnamon and ginger and stir.
2. Add flaxseed, coconut oil, vanilla, pumpkin puree, maple syrup and lemon juice, stir and pour into a greased cake pan.
3. Introduce in your air fryer, Cooking Time: at 330 degrees F for 40 minutes, leave aside to cool down, slice and serve.
4. Enjoy!

Nutrition: calories 202, fat 3, fiber 2, carbs 6, protein 1

982. Sweet Potato Mix

Preparation time: 10 minutes
Cooking time: 30 minutes
Servings: 8
Ingredients:
- 1 cup water
- 1 tablespoon lemon peel, grated
- ½ cup coconut sugar
- 3 sweet potatoes peeled and sliced
- ¼ cup cashew butter
- ¼ cup maple syrup
- 1 cup pecans, chopped

Directions:
1. In a pan that fits your air fryer, mix water with lemon peel, coconut sugar, potatoes, cashew butter, maple syrup and pecans, stir, introduce in the fryer and Cooking Time: at 350 degrees F for 30 minutes
2. Divide sweet potato pudding into bowls and serve cold.
3. Enjoy!

Nutrition: calories 210, fat 4, fiber 3, carbs 10, protein 4

983. Summer Day Brownies

Preparation Time: 30 Minutes
Servings: 12
Ingredients:
- 1 cup unsweetened cocoa powder
- 1 cup whole wheat pastry flour
- 1/2 cup packed brown sugar
- 1 cup nondairy milk
- 1 teaspoon vanilla extract
- 1/4 teaspoon salt
- 1/2 cup nondairy butter
- 1/2 teaspoon baking powder
- 2 tablespoons ground flaxseed
- 2 tablespoons warm water
- Powdered sugar, for serving

Directions:
1. Mix the flaxseed with the warm water and set aside.
2. Mix together all the dry ingredients in a separate bowl.
3. In a third bowl, beat together the butter and brown sugar. Stir in the flaxseed, vanilla, and milk before stirring in the dry ingredients a little bit at a time.
4. Place a cup of water in the bottom of the instant pot, and then place a rack on top.
5. Spray a baking dish or springform pan small enough to fit in your instant pot with nonstick spray.
6. Pour the brownie batter into the greased pan and lightly cover it with foil before lowering it onto the rack.
7. Seal the lid and Cooking Time: on high for 20 minutes, quick releasing the pressure when it is finished. Dust with powdered sugar.

984. Cranberry Cheesecake

Preparation Time: 35 Minutes
Servings: 8
Ingredients:

- 2 lbs soy yogurt
- 2 cups of sugar
- 4 tbsp flaxseed mixed with ¾ cup hot water
- 2 tsp lemon zest
- 1 tsp lemon extract
- ½ tsp salt
- 1 pie crust, dairy-free

For Topping:

- 7 oz dried cranberries
- 2 tbsp cranberry jam
- 2 tsp lemon zest
- 1 tsp vanilla sugar
- 1 tsp cranberry extract
- ¾ cup lukewarm water

Directions:

1. Preheat the oven to 350 degrees. In a large bowl, combine soy yogurt, sugar, flaxseed mixture, lemon zest, lemon extract, and salt. Using an electric mixer, beat well on low until combined.
2. Grease a medium-sized springform pan with some oil. Place crust in it and pour in the filling. Flatten the surface with a spatula. Leave in the refrigerator for about 30 minutes.
3. Meanwhile, prepare the topping. Combine cranberries with cranberry jam, lemon zest, vanilla sugar, cranberry extract, and water in a small pan. Bring it to a boil and simmer for 15 minutes over medium-low heat. You can add one teaspoon of cornstarch, but this is optional.
4. Fill your instant pot with ½ inch of water and position the trivet in the bottom. Set the cheesecake on the trivet and top with cranberries. Cover the stainless steel insert with a triple layer of paper towels and close the lid. Plug in your instant pot and set the steam release handle. Press "Manual" button and set the timer for 20 minutes.
5. Turn off the heat and let stand until the instant pot has cooled, 1 hour.
6. Run a sharp knife around the edge of your cheesecake. Refrigerate overnight.

985. Fig Spread Dessert

Preparation Time: 35 Minutes
Servings: 16
Ingredients:

- 1 cup of vegetable oil
- 1 cup of almond milk
- 1 cup of lukewarm water
- ½ cup of fig spread
- 1 ½ cup of all-purpose flour
- ½ cup of wheat groats
- ½ cup of corn flour
- 2 tsp of baking powder

Topping:

- 2 cups of brown sugar
- 2 cups of water
- ½ cup of fig spread

Directions:

1. First, you will have to prepare the topping because it has to chill well before using it. Place sugar, fig spread, and water in a heavy-bottomed pot. Bring it to a boil over a medium-high heat and Cooking Time: for 5 minutes, stirring constantly. Remove from the heat and cool well.
2. In another pot, combine oil with lukewarm water, almond milk, and fig spread. Bring it to a boil and then add flour, wheat groats, corn flour, and baking powder. Give it a good stir and mix well. Continue to Cooking Time: for 3-4 minutes. Chill well and form the dough.
3. Using your hands, shape 2-inches thick balls. This mixture should give you about 16 balls, depending on the size you want. Gently flatten the surface and transfer to a lightly greased stainless steel insert of your

instant pot. Press "Manual" button and set the steam release handle. Set the timer for 10 minutes.
4. When done, press "Cancel" button and turn off your pot. Perform a quick release and open the pot. Gently remove the fig spread and pour the cold topping over them. Set aside to cool completely.
5. Refrigerate for one hour and serve.

986. Crème Brulée

Preparation Time: 11 Minutes
Servings: 4
Ingredients:
- *3 cups of coconut cream*
- *3 tbsp flaxseed mixed with ½ cup hot water*
- *1 cup of sugar plus 4 tbsp for topping*
- *1 vanilla bean, split lengthwise*
- *¼ tsp of salt*

Directions:
1. In a large bowl, combine coconut cream with flaxseed mixture. Beat well with an electric mixer on high.
2. Using a sharp knife, scrape the seed out of your vanilla bean and add them to your cream mixture. I like to use the remaining of my vanilla bean. Finely chop it and add to the mixture. This, however, is optional. You can also add one teaspoon of pure vanilla extract for some extra flavor.
3. Now, whisk in the salt and beat well again. Pour the mixture into four standard-sized ramekins. Set aside.
4. Take 4 x 12" long pieces of aluminum foil and roll them up. You want to get snake-shaped pieces of the aluminum foil. Curl each piece into a circle, pinching the ends together. Place in the bottom of the stainless steel insert of your instant pot.
5. Place each ramekin on aluminum circle and pour enough boiling water to reach up to about 1/3 of the way.

Close the cooker's lid and set the steam release handle. Press "Manual" button and set the timer to 6 minutes. Cooking Time: on high pressure.
6. When done, release the steam pressure naturally for about 10 minutes, and then perform a quick release for any remaining steam.
7. Carefully remove the ramekins from the instant pot and add one tablespoon of sugar in each ramekin. Burn evenly with a culinary torch until brown.
8. Chill well and serve.

987. Chocolate Cake

Preparation Time: 45 Minutes
Servings: 12
Ingredients:
- *3 cups of soy yogurt*
- *3 cups of all-purpose flour*
- *2 cups of granulated sugar*
- *1 cup of oil*
- *2 tsp of baking soda*
- *3 tbsp of cocoa, unsweetened*

For the glaze:
- *7 oz dark chocolate*
- *10 tbsp of sugar*
- *10 tbsp of almond milk*
- *5 oz almond butter, unsalted*

Directions:
1. In a large bowl, combine soy yogurt, flour, sugar, oil, baking soda, and cocoa. Beat well with an electric mixer on high.
2. Transfer the mixture to a large springform pan. Wrap the pan in foil and place in your instant pot. Seal the lid and set the steam release handle. Press the "Manual" button and set the timer to 30 minutes.
3. When you hear the cooker's end signal, perform the quick release and open it. Gently remove the springform pan and unwrap. Chill well.

4. Meanwhile, melt the chocolate in a microwave. Transfer to a medium-sized bowl and whisk in almond butter, almond milk, and sugar. Beat well with an electric mixer and pour the mixture over your cake.
5. Refrigerate for at least two hours before serving.

988. Crème Caramel

Preparation Time: 30 Minutes
Servings: 4
Ingredients:

- ½ cup of granulated sugar, divided in half
- ½ cup of water
- 3 tbsp flaxseed, mixed with ½ cup hot water
- ½ tsp of vanilla extract
- ½ cup of almond milk
- 5 oz coconut cream, whipped

Directions:

1. Plug in your instant pot and press "Sautee" button.
2. In a stainless steel insert, combine ¼ cup of granulated sugar with water. Gently simmer, stirring constantly, until sugar dissolves evenly and turns into nice golden caramel. Press "Cancel" button and remove the steel insert. Set aside for 2-3 minutes, until bubbles disappear. Pour into ramekins and set aside.
3. Clean your steel insert and put it back in your instant pot.
4. Now, combine almond milk with whipped coconut cream and vanilla extract. Press "Sautee" button again and Cooking Time: for about 5 minutes, or until small bubbles form. Press the "Cancel" button and remove from the cooker.
5. Using an electric mixer, whisk the flaxseed mixture and remaining sugar. Gradually add the cream mixture and whisk until well combined. Now, pour the mixture into small ovenproof bowls and set aside.
6. Take a fitting springform pan and place ramekins in it. Fit the pan into your instant pot and pour enough water in the springform pan to reach half of the bowls. Cover the pan with a piece of foil and close the lid.
7. Press the "Manual" button and set the timer for 15 minutes. When you hear the cooker's end signal, perform a quick release and remove the lid. Crème caramel should be nice and set. If you're not sure, insert a toothpick in the middle. It will come out clean.
8. Remove the ramekins from your cooker and cool completely at a room temperature. Be careful not to refrigerate until completely chilled. Otherwise, the crème will have cracks and it will change its structure.

989. Lemon Dessert

Preparation Time: 45 Minutes
Servings: 10
Ingredients:

- 2 cups sugar
- 2 cups vegetable oil
- ½ cup all-purpose flour
- 1 tbsp dairy-free egg replacer
- 1 tsp baking powder

Lemon topping:

- 4 cups sugar
- 5 cups water
- 1 cup freshly squeezed lemon juice
- 1 tbsp lemon zest
- 1 whole lemon, sliced

Directions:

1. In a large bowl, combine egg replacer with sugar, oil, and baking powder. Gradually add flour until the mixture is thick and slightly sticky. Using your hands, shape the balls and flatten them to half-inch thick.
2. Place in a fitting springform pan and plug in your instant pot. Pour two

cups of water in a stainless steel insert and gently place the springform pan. Cover the springform with foil and seal the lid. Set the steam release handle and press the "Manual" button. Set the timer for 20 minutes.
3. After you hear the cooker's end signal, perform a quick release and open. Gently remove the springform and foil. Cool to a room temperature.
4. Now, add the remaining sugar, water, lemon juice, lemon zest, and lemon slices in your instant pot. Press the "Sautee" button and gently simmer until the sugar dissolves. Press "Cancel" button and remove the lemon mixture.
5. Pour the hot topping over chilled dessert and set aside, allowing it to soak the lemon dressing.

990. Simple Fig Dessert

Preparation Time: 30 Minutes
Servings: 4
Ingredients:
- 2 lbs fresh figs
- 1 lb sugar
- 2 tbsp lemon zest
- 1 tsp ground nutmeg
- 10 cups water

Directions:
1. Rinse well figs and drain in a large colander.
2. Plug in your instant pot and press the "Sautee" button. Add figs, sugar, water, nutmeg, and lemon zest. Give it a good stir and cook, stirring occasionally, until half of the water evaporates.
3. Optionally, you can add ½ cup of freshly squeezed lemon or lime juice to reduce the sweet taste.
4. Press the "Cancel" button and transfer figs with the remaining liquid into glass jars, without lids. Cool to a room temperature and close the lids. Refrigerate overnight before use.

991. Sweet Pumpkin Pudding

Preparation Time: 30 Minutes
Servings: 10
Ingredients:
- 2 lbs fresh pumpkin, chopped
- 1 cup brown sugar
- 2 tbsp pumpkin juice
- 4 tbsp cornstarch
- 2 tbsp lemon zest
- 1 tsp ground nutmeg
- 10 cups water

Directions:
1. Peel and prepare the pumpkin. Scrape out seeds and chop into bite-sized pieces.
2. Plug in your instant pot and place pumpkin in the stainless steel insert. In another bowl, combine sugar with pumpkin juice. Mix well until sugar dissolves completely. Now, pour the mixture into the cooker and stir in one cup of cornstarch. Add cinnamon, cloves, and water. Give it a good stir.
3. Close the lid and press "Manual" button. Set the timer for 10 minutes.
4. When you hear the cooker's signal, perform a quick release of the pressure. Open the cooker and pour the pudding into 4 serving bowls. Cool to a room temperature and then transfer to refrigerator.

992. Chill overnight.

Wild Berries Pancakes
Preparation Time: 20 Minutes
Servings: 3
Ingredients:
- 1 cup buckwheat flour
- 2 tsp baking powder
- 1 ¼ cup almond milk
- 1 tbsp flaxseed mixed with 3 tbsp of hot water
- ½ tsp salt

- *1 tsp vanilla sugar*
- *1 tsp strawberry extract*
- *1 cup coconut cream*
- *1 cup fresh wild berries*

Directions:
1. In a medium-sized mixing bowl, combine almond milk and flaxseed mixture. Beat well with a whisking attachment on high – until foamy. Gradually, add flour and continue to beat until combined.
2. Now, add baking powder, salt, and vanilla sugar. Continue to beat on high for 3 more minutes.
3. Plug in your instant pot and grease the stainless steel insert with some oil. Spoon 2-3 tablespoons of batter into the pot. Close the lid and set to low pressure. Press "Manual" button and set the timer for 5 minutes. Perform a quick release and repeat the process with the remaining batter.
4. Top each pancake with one tablespoon of coconut cream and wild berries. Sprinkle with strawberry extract and serve immediately.

993. Marble Bread

Preparation Time: 35 Minutes
Servings: 6
Ingredients:
- *1 cup all-purpose flour*
- *1 ½ tsp baking powder*
- *1 tbsp powdered stevia*
- *½ tsp salt*
- *1 tsp cherry extract, sugar-free*
- *3 tbsp almond butter, softened*
- *3 tbsp flaxseed, mixed with ½ cup hot water*
- *¼ cup cocoa powder, sugar-free*
- *¼ cup vegan sour cream*

Directions:
1. Combine all dry ingredients except cocoa in a large mixing bowl. Mix well to combine and then add the flaxseed mixture. Beat well with a dough hook attachment for one minute. Now, add vegan sour cream, almond butter, and cherry extract. Continue to beat for 3 more minutes.
2. Divide the mixture in half and add cocoa powder in one-half of the mixture. Pour the light batter into the stainless steel insert of your instant pot. Drizzle with cocoa dough to create a nice marble pattern.
3. Close the lid and adjust the steam release handle. Press "Manual" button and set the timer for 20 minutes. Cooking Time: on low pressure.
4. When done, press "Cancel" button and release the steam pressure naturally. Let it cool for a while before transfer to the serving plate.
5. Carefully remove using a large spatula and chill completely before serving.
6. Enjoy!

994. Blueberry Strudel

Preparation Time: 50 Minutes
Servings: 8
Ingredients:
- *1 cup fresh blueberries*
- *1 cup fresh raspberries*
- *1 tsp blueberry extract, sugar-free*
- *2 cups soy yogurt*
- *2 tbsp powdered stevia*
- *2 tbsp almond butter, softened*
- *¼ cup cornstarch*
- *2 puff pastry sheets, dairy-free*
- *¼ tsp salt*

Directions:
1. Place the blueberries along with stevia, cornstarch and salt in a food processor. Pulse until smooth and transfer to a heavy-bottomed pot. Add one cup of water and bring it to a boil. Briefly Cooking Time: for 3 minutes, stirring constantly. Remove

from the heat and set aside to cool completely.
2. In a medium-sized bowl, combine soy yogurt with blueberry extract- mix until completely smooth and set aside.
3. Unfold the pastry and cut each sheet into –inch x 7-inch pieces. Place approximately two tablespoons of blueberry mixture at the middle of each pastry. Fold the sheets and cut the surface with a sharp knife. Gently place each strudel into the stainless steel insert of your instant pot.
4. Plug in the instant pot and press "Manual" button. Set the timer for 25 minutes and Cooking Time: on low pressure.
5. When done, press "Cancel" button and release the steam naturally.
6. Let it chill for 10 minutes. Carefully transfer the strudels to a serving plate using a large spatula.

995. Vanilla Pancakes

Preparation Time: 37 Minutes
Servings: 6
Ingredients:
- 2 medium-sized bananas, mashed
- 1 ¼ cup almond milk
- 1 tbsp vegan egg replacer
- 1 ½ cup rolled oats
- 1 ½ tsp baking powder
- 1 tsp vanilla extract
- 2 tsp coconut oil
- 1 tbsp agave nectar
- ¼ tsp salt
- Non-fat cooking spray

Directions:
1. Combine all ingredients in a blender and pulse until completely smooth batter. Set aside.
2. Plug in your instant pot and grease the stainless steel insert with some cooking spray. Add about ¼ cup of the batter and close the lid. Press "Manual" button and Cooking Time: for 5 minutes on low pressure.
3. Repeat the process with the remaining batter.
4. Serve immediately.

996. Apple Pie Cups With Cranberries

Preparation Time: 120 Minutes
Servings: 6
Ingredients:
For the crust:
- 2 cups all-purpose flour
- ¼ tsp salt
- ¾ cup almond butter, softened
- 1 tbsp sugar
- ½ cup ice water

For the filling:
- 1 medium-sized Alkmene apple
- ½ fresh peach
- ½ cup blackberries
- ¼ cup cranberries
- 2 tbsp all-purpose flour
- 1 tbsp sugar
- ½ tsp cinnamon

Directions:
1. Place all the crust ingredients in a food processor and pulse until dough is crumbly, but holds together when squeezed. Remove from the food processor and place on a lightly floured work surface. Divide in 4 equal pieces and wrap in plastic foil. Refrigerate for one hour.
2. Meanwhile, place all filling ingredients in a medium-sized bowl. Toss to combine and set aside.
3. Roll each piece into 6-inch round discs. Add two tablespoons of the apple mixture at the center of each disc and wrap to form small bowls. Gently transfer to the stainless steel insert of your instant pot and sprinkle with cooking spray.
4. Plug in your instant pot and press "Manual" button. Set the timer for 25 minutes and adjust the steam release handle. Cooking Time: on low pressure.

5. When done, press "Cancel" button and release the steam naturally. Carefully transfer cups to the serving plate and enjoy!

997. Blueberry Peach Pie

Preparation Time: 75 Minutes
Servings: 6
Ingredients:
- 1 cup fresh blueberries
- 1 medium-sized peach, sliced
- 1 cup all-purpose flour
- 2 tbsp flaxseed, mixed with ¼ cup of hot water
- 1 tsp baking powder
- ½ tsp salt
- ¼ cup almond butter, softened
- ¼ cup powdered stevia
- ¼ tsp vanilla extract
- 2 tsp freshly squeezed lemon juice

Directions:
1. In a medium-sized bowl, combine flour, baking powder, and salt. Mix well and set aside.
2. In a separate bowl, combine flaxseed mixture and stevia powder. Using a hand mixer with a whisking attachment, beat well on high for 2 minutes, or until light and fluffy.
3. Place the flour mixture in a large mixing bowl. Add almond butter, vanilla extract, and lemon juice. Gradually add the flaxseed mixture, beating constantly. Continue to beat for 3-5 minutes.
4. Place the flour mixture into the stainless steel insert of your instant pot. Spread the batter evenly with a kitchen spatula. Arrange the fruit on top and close the lid. Adjust the steam release handle and press "Manual" button. Set the timer for 30 minutes. Cooking Time: on low pressure.
5. When done, press "Cancel" button and release the steam naturally. Remove from the pot and chill completely before serving.

998. Almond Cake

Preparation Time: 35 Minutes
Servings: 12
Ingredients:
- 1 cup rice flour
- 1 cup almond flour
- 2 tsp xanthan gum
- 1 tbsp baking powder
- 1 tsp baking soda
- ½ cup cocoa powder
- 2 cups sweetener, granulated
- 1 tbsp egg replacer
- 2 tsp vanilla extract
- 2 cups zucchini, shredded
- ½ cup almonds, roughly chopped
- 1 cup water
- ¼ cup applesauce, unsweetened
- ½ cup vegan butter, softened
- ½ tsp salt

Directions:
1. Combine rice flour, almond flour, xanthan gum, cocoa powder, baking powder, baking soda, and salt in a large mixing bowl. Mix with spatula until fully combined. In a separate bowl, combine egg replacer with ½ cup of water and add it to dry ingredients.
2. Gradually add applesauce, butter, and sweetener. Mix until all well combined and fluffy. Now, add zucchini, vanilla extract, and the remaining water.
3. Pour the mixture into a springform pan and flatten the surface with a spatula.
4. Fill your instant pot with ½ inch of water and position the trivet on the bottom. Set the pan on the trivet and top with almonds. Cover the stainless steel insert with a double layer of paper towels and close the lid. Plug in your instant pot and set the steam release handle. Press "Manual" button and set the timer for 20 minutes.
5. When done, press "Cancel" button and turn off the pot. Release the steam naturally.

6. Let it chill for a while before serving.

999. Agave Brownies
Preparation Time: 35 Minutes
Servings: 12
Ingredients:
- 1 cup all-purpose flour
- 1 tsp baking powder
- ½ tsp baking soda
- ½ cup brown sugar
- ½ cup agave nectar
- ¾ cup almond milk
- ½ cup vegan butter
- 4 tbsp flaxseeds, mixed with ½ cup hot water
- ½ cup water
- 1 tbsp vanilla extract

Directions:
1. In a large mixing bowl, combine flour, baking powder, and baking soda. Mix until combined and set aside.
2. In a separate bowl, combine maple syrup, almond milk, and vegan butter. Using an electric mixer, beat until well combined.
3. Now, combine prepared mixtures and the remaining ingredients. Mix until you get a nice batter. Grease a springform pan with some cooking spray and pour in the batter.
4. Plug in your instant pot and fill the stainless steel insert with ½ inch of water. Position the trivet on the bottom and set the springform pan.
5. Close the lid of your pot and set the steam release handle. Press "Manual" button and set the timer for 20 minutes.
6. When done, press "Cancel" button and turn off the pot. Release the steam naturally. Remove the pan from the pot and let it chill completely. Cut the brownies into desired shapes and serve immediately.

1000. Mango Cake
Preparation Time: 30 Minutes
Servings: 10
Ingredients:
- 2 cups mango juice, unsweetened
- ½ cup soft vegan butter
- 1 tsp vanilla extract
- ½ cup maple syrup
- ½ cup coconut whipped cream
- 4 cups all-purpose flour
- 1 tbsp baking powder
- 1 tsp salt

Directions:
1. Combine vegan butter and coconut cream in a large bowl. Gradually add maple syrup and vanilla and beat until smooth and creamy.
2. In a separate bowl, combine flour, baking powder, and salt. Mix until combined and add it to the butter mixture. Pour in the mango juice and stir until all well combined.
3. Pour the mixture into a lightly greased springform pan and flatten the surface with a spatula.
4. Plug in your instant pot and fill the stainless steel insert with ½ inch of water. Position the trivet on the bottom and set the springform pan.
5. Close the lid of your pot and set the steam release handle. Press "Manual" button and set the timer for 15 minutes.
6. When done, press "Cancel" button and turn off the pot. Release the steam naturally. Remove the pan from the pot and let it chill completely before serving.

1001. Caramel Sauce
Preparation Time: 17 MINUTES
Servings: 1 jar
Ingredients:
- 1/2 Teaspoon Baking Soda + 3 Tablespoons Warm Water (optional
- 1 14 Ounce Can Sweetened Condensed Coconut Milk
- 1 Cup Cold Water

Directions:
1. In a small bowl combine baking soda and water until dissolved.
2. In a stainless steel bowl that fits

inside instant pot add condensed coconut milk and baking soda mixture. Mix well.
3. Add cold water into the instant pot.
4. Place the bowl in the water and Cooking Time: on high pressure for 17 minutes. Allow to naturally release. Press cancel and let sit for 8 hours.
5. Serve with drinks, drizzled on desserts, oatmeal, warm or cold.
6. Enjoy!

1002. Chocolate Pudding

Preparation Time: 11 Minutes
Servings: 4-6

Ingredients:
- 1/4 Cup Organic Cornstarch
- 1/2 Cup Organic Cane Sugar
- 1/3 Cup Cacao Powder
- 1/8 Teaspoon Sea Salt
- 1 Teaspoon Vanilla
- 2 Cups Plain Unsweetened Almond Milk

Directions:
1. In a stainless steel bowl that fits into instant pot, whisk cornstarch, sugar, cacao, and sea salt.
2. Add vanilla, and almond milk.
3. Cover with foil.
4. Add 2 cups of water to instant pot and add trivet. Place bowl on top of trivet.
5. Close lid and seal. Cooking Time: on 9 minutes at high pressure.
6. Quick release.
7. Remove and place on counter top to cool. Remove foil and refrigerate for 4-6 hours.
8. Serve chilled and enjoy!

1003. Chocolate Tapioca Pudding

Preparation Time: 25 Minutes
Servings: 2

Ingredients:
- 1 Cup Water
- 3/4 Cup Full Fat Coconut Milk
- 1/3 Cup Agave or Maple Syrup
- 1 1/2 Teaspoon Vanilla Extract
- 1 Tablespoon Vegan Butter, melted
- 4 Tablespoons Cacao Powder
- 1/3 Cup Small Tapioca Pearls

Directions:
1. Pour 1 cup of water into the basin and insert steaming rack.
2. Combine all ingredients in an oven-safe bowl.
3. Place bowl on top of steaming rack, cover and seal lid.
4. On the manual setting, set to high pressure for 20 minutes.
5. When done, quick release and uncover.
6. Stir and transfer to refrigerator to cool and thicken.
7. Serve chilled and enjoy!

1004. Brownies

Preparation Time: 37 Minutes
Servings: 6

Ingredients:
- 2 Tablespoons flax meal + 5 Tablespoons Water
- 1/4 Cup Organic Cacao
- 1 Cup Organic Cane Sugar
- 3/4 Teaspoon Baking Powder
- 3/4 Cup All-Purpose Flour
- 5 Tablespoons Vegan Butter, melted
- 1/4 Tablespoon Vanilla
- 1 1/2 Cup Water

Directions:
1. In a small bowl combine flax meal and water. Set aside.
2. In a bowl add cacao, sugar, baking powder, and flour.
3. Add vegan butter, vanilla, and flax meal mixture.
4. Combine all ingredients together until wet.
5. Spray a cake pan with non-stick spray and pour in batter. Cover with foil.
6. Place the trivet into the instant pot and add 1 1/2 cups of water.
7. Place the cake pan on top of trivet.
8. Close lid and seal.

9. Set to 35 minutes on manual setting, high pressure.
10. Slow release by opening the valve slightly.
11. Let cool and remove.
12. Enjoy!

1005. Chocolate-Orange Espresso Pudding

Preparation Time: 30 Minutes
Servings: 5

Ingredients:

- 1 Cup Aquafaba (liquid from 1 can of chickpeas)
- 1/3 Cup Non-Dairy Dark Chocolate, chopped
- 1 Teaspoon Instant Espresso Granules
- 1/4 Teaspoon Orange Peel, grated
- 2 Tablespoons Agave or Maple Syrup

Directions:

1. Place trivet in instant pot with 1 1/2 cup of water.
2. In a bowl, whisk aquafaba or use an electric mixer until white and fluffy.
3. On stove top, melt chocolate over a pan of simmering water.
4. Mix in espresso, orange peel and agave or maple syrup.
5. Slowly whisk in the chocolate into the whipped aquafaba until well incorporated.
6. Pour mixture into heat-safe jars or ramekins.
7. Place the jars or ramekins on the trivet.
8. Close the lid and seal.
9. Press manual and Cooking Time: for 6 minutes.
10. When done, quick release and remove jars with oven mitts.
11. Allow to cool and refrigerate for 4-6 hours.
12. Serve chilled and enjoy!

1006. Pumpkin Cinnamon Mini Cakes

Preparation Time: 35 Minutes
Servings: 16

Ingredients:

- ½ cup of pumpkin puree, unsweetened
- 1 cup of almond milk
- 1 cup of vegetable oil
- 1 cup of lukewarm water
- 1 ½ cup of all-purpose flour
- ½ cup of corn flour
- 2 tsp of baking powder

For the topping:

- 2 cups of brown sugar
- 2 cups of water
- ½ cup of agave nectar
- 1 tsp cinnamon, ground

Directions:

1. Combine brown sugar, water, agave nectar, and cinnamon in a heavy-bottomed pot. Bring it to a boil over a medium-high heat and Cooking Time: for about 4-5 minutes. Remove from the heat and let it cool completely.
2. In a separate pot, combine almond milk, water, and oil. Bring it to a boil and then add flour, corn flour, pumpkin puree, and baking powder. Stir well and Cooking Time: for 5 more minutes. Let it chill for a while and then form the dough.
3. Using your hands, shape 2-inches thick balls. Flatten the surface of each ball and transfer to a lightly greased springform pan. Pour in ½ inch of water in the stainless steel insert and place the pan onto a positioned trivet on the bottom. Close the lid.
4. Plug in your instant pot and press "Manual" button. Set the steam release handle and set the timer for 10 minutes. When done, press "Cancel" and release the steam naturally. Pour the cold topping over and serve immediately.

1007. Oatmeal Cookies

Preparation Time: 20 Minutes

Servings: 18

Ingredients:
- *4 cups rolled oats, gluten-free*
- *½ cup flaxseed oil*
- *1 cup soy milk*
- *1 tsp vanilla extract*
- *½ cup agave nectar*
- *1 cup rice flour*
- *1 tsp xanthan gum*
- *½ tsp baking soda*
- *¼ cup stevia*

Directions:
1. *In a large mixing bowl, combine soy milk. Flaxseed oil, vanilla extract and agave nectar. Stir until combined and set aside.*
2. *In a separate bowl, combine the remaining ingredients and stir well.*
3. *Now, combine wet and dry ingredients and stir again until you get a nice batter.*
4. *Fill the stainless steel insert of your instant pot with ½ inch of water. Position a trivet and place the springform pan on top. Drop the tablespoon-sized portions of the batter onto the pan.*
5. *Close the lid and plug in your instant pot. Cover with a lid and set the steam release handle. Press "Manual" button and set the timer for 5 minutes. Cooking Time: on high pressure.*
6. *When done, press "Cancel" button and release the steam naturally. Let it cool before serving.*
7. *Enjoy!*

1008. Cherry Spread

Preparation Time: 20 Minutes
Servings: 10

Ingredients:
- *1 cup fresh cherries, pitted and chopped*
- *1 lb silken tofu*
- *½ cup powdered sugar*
- *3 tbsp all-purpose flour*
- *1 tsp xanthan gum*

Directions:
1. *Combine tofu, sugar, flour, and xanthan gum in a food processor. Blend until combined and transfer to the stainless steel insert of your instant pot.*
2. *Plug in your instant pot and press "Sautee" button and stir in the flour. Cooking Time: for 5 minutes and then add 1 cup water.*
3. *Close the lid and press "Manual" button. Set the steam release handle and set the timer for 5 minutes. Cooking Time: on high pressure.*
4. *When done, press "Cancel" button and turn off the pot. Perform a quick release and open the pot. Let it chill for a while before serving.*
5. *Store the cherry spread in the air-tight containers and refrigerate up to 2 weeks.*
6. *Enjoy!*

1009. Creamy Coconut Eggs

Preparation Time: 20 Minutes
Servings: 10

Ingredients:
- *4 oz vegan cheese cream cheese*
- *1 cup powdered sugar*
- *¾ cup mashed potatoes*
- *6 oz silken tofu*
- *1 tsp coconut extract*
- *2 cups vegan chocolate chips*
- *1 ½ cup shredded coconut, unsweetened*

Directions:
1. *Combine tofu and vegan cream cheese in a food processor and pulse until smooth and creamy. Add sugar, mashed potatoes, and coconut extract. Pulse again for one minute to combine. Transfer all to a large mixing bowl and stir in the shredded coconut. Mix with your hands until fully combined. Refrigerate the mixture for 15 minutes.*
2. *Line a springform pan with some*

cooking paper. Spoon the mixture into egg-shaped pieces. Freeze for about 10-15 minutes.
3. Melt the chocolate chips and drizzle over the egg-shaped pieces.
4. Fill the ½ inch water in the stainless steel insert of your instant pot. Place the trivet on the bottom and place the springform on top. Close the lid and plug in your instant pot. Set the steam release handle and press "Manual" button and set the timer for 5 minutes.
5. When done, press "Cancel" and turn off the pot. Release the pressure naturally.
6. Chill well before serving.

1010. Pumpkin Pancakes

Preparation Time: 20 Minutes
Servings: 6
Ingredients:
- 1 cup buckwheat flour
- 2 tsp baking powder
- 2 cups pumpkin, chopped
- ½ cup rice milk
- 1 tbsp egg replacer
- ½ tsp salt
- 1 tsp cinnamon, ground
- 1 tsp stevia
- ½ cup agave nectar

Directions:
1. In a medium-sized mixing bowl, combine rice milk and egg replacer. Beat well with a whisking attachment on high speed. Gradually, add buckwheat flour, pumpkin puree, baking powder, salt, cinnamon, and stevia powder. Continue to beat until combined.
2. Plug in your instant pot and grease the stainless steel insert with some oil. Spoon 2-3 tablespoons of batter into the pot. Close the lid and set to low pressure. Press "Manual" button and set the timer for 5 minutes.
3. When done, press "Cancel" and perform a quick release. Repeat the process with the remaining batter.
4. Top each pancake with some agave nectar and enjoy immediately.

1011. Orange Dessert

Preparation Time: 45 Minutes
Servings: 10
Ingredients:
- ½ cup all-purpose flour
- 2 cups brown sugar
- 2 cups olive oil
- 1 tbsp egg replacer
- 1 tsp baking powder

Orange topping:
- 3 cups powdered sugar
- 5 cups water
- 1 cup freshly squeezed orange juice
- 1 tbsp orange zest
- 1 large orange, sliced

Directions:
1. In a large bowl, combine egg replacer with brown sugar, oil, and baking powder. Gradually add flour until the mixture is thick and slightly sticky. Using your hands, shape the balls and flatten them to half-inch thick.
2. Place in a fitting springform pan and plug in your instant pot. Pour two cups of water in a stainless steel insert and position a trivet on the bottom. Gently place the springform pan onto the trivet. Cover the springform pan with foil and seal the lid. Set the steam release handle and press the "Manual" button. Set the timer for 20 minutes.
3. When done, press "Cancel" button and perform a quick release. Open and gently remove the springform and foil. Cool to a room temperature.
4. Now, add the remaining sugar, water, orange juice, orange zest, and orange slices in your instant pot. Press the "Sautee" button and gently simmer until the sugar dissolves. Press "Cancel" button and remove the orange mixture.
5. Pour the hot topping over chilled

dessert and set aside, allowing it to soak the orange dressing.

1012. Chocolate Bundt Cake

Preparation Time: 45Minutes
Servings: 8
Ingredients:

- 2 cups all-purpose flour
- ¾ cup cocoa powder
- 2 cups natural cane sugar
- 1 tsp baking soda
- ½ tsp salt
- 1 cup coconut oil, melted
- ½ cup coconut cream
- ¾ cup coconut milk
- 1 cup silken tofu

Directions:

1. In a large bowl, combine together all dry ingredients.
2. Place coconut oil, coconut cream, coconut milk, and tofu in a large mixing bowl. With a paddle attachment on, beat well on high speed until light and fluffy.
2. Slowly add the flour mixture and continue to beat until fully combined.
3. Spray a 6 cup bundt pan with some cooking spray and pour the mixture in it. Wrap the pan tightly with aluminum foil and set aside.
4. Add 2 cups of water in the stainless steel insert of your pot and place the trivet inside.
5. Place the wrapped bundt pan on top and seal the lid.
6. Press the 'Manual' button and set the timer to 35 minutes.
7. When you hear the cooker's end signal, release the pressure naturally and open the lid.
8. Cool to a room temperature before removing the cake from the pan.

1013. Chocolate Berry Cake

Preparation Time: 35Minutes
Servings: 6
Ingredients:

- 2 cups oat flour
- 2 tbsp shredded coconut
- 1 ½ tsp baking soda
- 1/3 cup cocoa powder
- ¼ tsp salt
- 3 cups silken tofu
- 1 tsp vanilla extract
- 1 cup coconut milk
- 3 cups soy yogurt
- 1 cup almond cream
- 5 oz vegan dark chocolate, melted
- 2 tsp agave nectar
- 1 tsp vanilla extract

Directions:

1. Brush a 7-inch pan with some oil and line with parchment paper. Set aside.
2. In a large mixing bowl, combine together oat flour, shredded coconut, baking soda, cocoa powder, and salt. Mix well and add tofu, vanilla extract, and soy milk. With a dough hook attachment, beat well for 3 minutes.
3. Transfer the batter into the prepared baking pan and set aside.
4. Add one cup of water to your instant pot and place the trivet. Gently place the pan onto the trivet and close the lid.
5. Set the steam release handle and press the 'Manual' button. Set the timer to 25 minutes.
6. When you hear the cooker's end signal, perform a quick release and open the lid. Remove the pan from the cooker and cool to a room temperature.
7. Meanwhile, in a bowl of a stand mixer, combine soy yogurt, almond cream, melted chocolate, agave nectar, and vanilla extract. Using a whisking attachment, beat well on high speed for 3 minutes.
8. Pour the mixture over chilled crust and refrigerate for 1 hour before serving.

1014. Mocha Brownies

Preparation Time: 30Minutes

Servings: 8

Ingredients:
- *2 cups oat flour*
- *¼ cup shredded coconut*
- *1 ½ tsp baking soda*
- *1/3 cup cocoa powder*
- *¼ tsp salt*
- *1 tsp vanilla extract*
- *1 tsp stevia powder*
- *¾ cup coconut milk*
- *¼ cup instant coffee*
- *3 tbsp ground flaxseed*
- *¼ cup water*
- *1 cup soy yogurt*
- *1 cup almond yogurt, vanilla flavored*
- *1/3 cup shredded coconut*
- *1 tsp vanilla extract*

Directions:
1. *Spray a 7-inch springform pan with some cooking spray and line with parchment paper. Set aside*
2. *In a large mixing bowl, mix together flour, shredded coconut, baking soda, cocoa powder, salt, and stevia powder. Add vanilla extract, coconut milk, and coffee. Using a paddle attachment beat well on high speed until fully incorporated.*
3. *Meanwhile, whisk together flaxseed and water. Pour the mixture into the bowl and continue to mix for 2 minutes.*
4. *Pour the mixture into the prepared springform pan and set aside.*
5. *Pour two cups of water into your instant pot and set the trivet. Place the springform pan onto trivet and seal the cooker's lid.*
6. *Press the 'Manual' button and set the timer to 20 minutes. When done, release the pressure naturally and open the lid.*
7. *Gently remove the springform pan from your instant pot and place on a wire rack to cool.*
8. *Meanwhile, combine the remaining ingredients in a mixing bowl and whisk together until fully combined. Optionally add 1 teaspoon of instant coffee for some more flavor.*
9. *Pour the mixture over chilled crust and refrigerate for one hour before serving.*

1015. Caramel Shortbread

Preparation Time: *50 Minutes*
Servings: 6

Ingredients:

For the crust
- *1 ½ cup all-purpose flour*
- *2 tsp stevia powder*
- *1 cup coconut oil*

For the caramel layer:
- *1 cup natural cane sugar*
- *½ cup almond butter*
- *2 tbsp agave nectar*
- *1 cup almond milk, unsweetened*

For the chocolate topping:
- *1 cup vegan chocolate, melted*
- *½ cup coconut cream*

Directions:
1. *In a large bowl, combine flour, stevia, and coconut oil. Beat well with an electric mixer on low. Using your hands, combine the dough evenly until crumbly. Press into 7-inch pan and wrap tightly with aluminum foil.*
2. *Pour 1 cup of water in your instant pot and set the trivet. Place wrapped pan onto trivet and seal the lid. Set the timer for 20 minutes.*
3. *When you hear the cooker's end signal, release the pressure naturally and open the lid. Gently remove the springform pan and remove the foil.*
4. *Meanwhile, combine sugar, butter, agave, and milk in a large bowl. Gently bring it to a boil over medium heat and simmer for 7-10 minutes, or until it begins to firm. Pour the warm mixture over crust and cool completely.*
5. *Finally, prepare the chocolate layer. Melt the chocolate in a double broiler or in a microwave. Stir in coconut*

cream and pour the mixture over chilled shortbread.

1016. Easy Hazelnut Cake

Preparation Time: 90 Minutes
Servings: 8
Ingredients:

For the crust:
- ½ almond flour
- ¼ cup cocoa powder, unsweetened
- 1 tsp baking powder
- 1 tsp stevia powder
- ½ cup almond milk
- ½ cup almond butter
- 4 tbsp chia seeds

For the topping:
- 2 cups almond yogurt
- ¼ cup cocoa powder
- ½ cup vegan dark chocolate, melted
- ¼ cup grated hazelnuts

Directions:
1. Line 3 8-inches round pans with parchment paper. Dust with some flour and set aside.
2. In a medium-sized bowl, combine almond flour, cocoa powder, baking powder, and stevia. Whisk together and gradually add milk. With a paddle attachment on, beat well for 2-3 minutes. Finally, add almond butter and continue to beat for 3 minutes. Pour the batter into prepared pans.
3. Add 2 cups of water in your pressure cooker and set the trivet. Place one pan in your pressure cooker and seal the lid. Set the 'Manual' mode for 20 minutes.
4. When you hear the cooker's end signal, perform a quick release and open the lid. Repeat the process with the remaining 2 pans. Cool each crust to a room temperature.
5. Meanwhile, combine almond yogurt, cocoa powder, melted chocolate, and hazelnuts. Spread the mixture over each crust, creating layers.
6. Refrigerate for one hour before serving.

1017. Pumpkin Parfait

Preparation Time: 45 Minutes
Servings: 6
Ingredients:
- 2 cups pumpkin, chopped
- ¾ cup brown sugar
- 2 tbsp egg replacer
- 1 tsp rum extract
- ½ tsp ground cinnamon
- ¼ tsp nutmeg
- 1 tbsp orange zest
- 2 cups pureed tofu
- 2 tsp vanilla extract
- ¼ cup agar powder

Directions:
1. Place chopped pumpkin in your instant pot and add enough water to cover. Seal the lid and press the 'Stew' button.
2. When done, release the pressure naturally and open the lid. The pumpkin should be fork-tender. Remove from the pot and transfer to a medium-sized bowl. Mash well to get a nice puree.
3. Now add sugar, egg replacer, rum extract, cinnamon, nutmeg, and orange zest. Stir well and place in the stainless steel insert. Press the 'Sauté' button and gently simper for 5-7 minutes, stirring constantly. Remove from the pot and set aside.
4. In another bowl, combine pureed tofu and vanilla extract.
5. In a large mixing bowl, combine the pumpkin mixture with the cream mixture and add agar powder. Pour the mixture in your instant pot and press the 'Sauté' button. Cooking Time: for 5 minutes.
6. Remove from the heat and divide between 6 parfait glasses. Optionally top with some whipped cream and refrigerate for 1 hour before serving.

1018. Banana Cheesecake

Preparation Time: 35 Minutes
Servings: 10

Ingredients:
- 6 large bananas
- ½ cup brown sugar
- 2 tbsp egg replacer
- 8 oz pureed tofu
- 1 tsp cinnamon, ground
- 1 tsp vanilla extract
- 10 oz original graham crackers (or any other vegan crackers
- ¼ cup almond butter

Directions:
1. Place crackers in a food processor and process to get an almost flour-like texture. Add almond butter and continue to process until smooth. Remove from the food processor and set aside.
2. Line a 7-inch springform pan with some parchment paper and add the cracker mixture. Press with your hands to create a crust.
3. Now prepare the topping. Combine the remaining ingredients in a food processor and process until smooth. Pour the mixture over the crust and flatten the surface using a kitchen spatula. Tightly wrap the pan with aluminum foil.
4. Set the trivet in your instant pot and pour in 2 cups of water. Gently place the springform pan and seal the lid.
5. Press the 'Manual' button and set the timer for 25 minutes.
6. When you hear the cooker's end signal, perform a quick release and open the lid. Remove the aluminum foil and cool to a room temperature.
7. Refrigerate overnight.

1019. Strawberry Pudding

Preparation Time: 25 Minutes
Servings: 4

Ingredients:
- 2 cups all-purpose flour
- 3 tsp baking powder
- 1 tsp salt
- 1 cup coconut oil
- ¼ cup breadcrumbs
- 1 cup brown sugar
- 2 tbsp egg replacement
- 1 ½ cup coconut milk
- 1 lb fresh strawberries, chopped
- ½ cup coconut cream, for serving

Directions:
1. Grease a 6 cup pudding basin with some coconut oil and set aside.
2. In a large mixing bowl, combine all dry ingredients and mix well. Add coconut oil, coconut milk, and chopped strawberries. Mix well again and transfer the mixture into the prepared pudding basin.
3. Pour 3 cups of water in your instant pot and set the steamer rack. Gently place the basin into the steamer and seal the lid.
4. Press the 'Steam' button and set the timer for 15 minutes.
5. When done, release the pressure naturally and open the lid. Remove the basin and cool to a room temperature. Transfer to the fridge and chill for 2-3 hours.

1020. Cookies 'N' Cream Cupcakes

Ingredients:
- 1½ cups flour
- 1 cup sugar
- ⅓ cup unsweetened cocoa powder
- 1 teaspoon baking soda
- ½ teaspoon salt
- cup water
- ½ cup olive oil
- tablespoons white vinegar
- 1 tablespoon pure vanilla extract
- 1 cup crushed vegan chocolate sandwich cookies

Frosting:
- 1 cup non-hydrogenated vegetable shortening
- cups powdered sugar
- 1 teaspoon pure peppermint extract
- non-dairy milk
- 2 cups crushed vegan chocolate

sandwich cookies

Directions:

1. To make the cupcakes: Preheat the oven to 350 degrees. Line two 12-cup cupcake pans with 16 cupcake liners.
2. In a large bowl, whisk together flour, sugar, cocoa, baking soda, and salt. In a separate bowl, whisk together coffee, oil, vinegar, and vanilla. Pour the wet mixture into the dry mixture and whisk until just combined. Fold in crushed cookie pieces.
3. Fill the cupcake liners about two-thirds full with batter. Bake for 16 to 20 minutes, or until a toothpick inserted in the center of the cupcake comes out dry, with a few crumbs clinging to it. Let the cupcakes cool completely before frosting.
4. To make the frosting: Using a stand or hand mixer, beat shortening until smooth. With the mixer running on low, add powdered sugar, peppermint extract, and 1 tablespoon nondairy milk at a time, as needed, until frosting reaches a spreadable consistency. Increase the speed to high and beat for 2 more minutes until light and fluffy. Add crushed cookie pieces and beat until incorporated. Add more nondairy milk, if needed.
5. To assemble the cupcakes: Spread a layer of vegan mint cookie frosting on the cupcakes.

1021. Carrot Cupcakes

Ingredients

Cupcake:

- 2 cups flour
- 1 cup sugar
- 1 teaspoon baking powder
- ½ teaspoon baking soda
- 1 teaspoon salt
- 1 teaspoon ground cinnamon
- ½ teaspoon ground nutmeg
- 1 cup carrot juice
- ½ cup olive oil
- 1 tablespoon vinegar
- 1 tablespoon pure vanilla extract
- 2 cups peeled, grated carrots
- 1 cup raisins

Glaze:

- 1½ cups powdered sugar
- 3 tablespoons maple syrup
- 3 tablespoons water

Directions:

1. To make the cupcakes: Preheat the oven to 350 degrees. Line two 12-cup cupcake pans with 16 cupcake liners.
2. In a large bowl, whisk together flour, sugar, baking powder, baking soda, salt, cinnamon, and nutmeg. In a separate bowl, whisk together carrot or orange juice, oil, vinegar, and vanilla. Pour the wet mixture into the dry mixture and whisk until just combined. Gently fold in carrots and raisins.
3. Fill the cupcake liners about two-thirds full with batter. Bake for about 20 minutes, or until a toothpick inserted in the center of the cupcake comes out dry, with a few crumbs clinging to it. Let the cupcakes cool completely before frosting.
4. To make the glaze: In a medium bowl, whisk together powdered sugar, maple syrup, and 1 tablespoon water at a time, until smooth.
5. To assemble the cupcakes: Drizzle the glaze over the cupcakes. Let set and serve.

1022. Coffee Cupcakes

Ingredients

- 1½ cups flour
- 1 cup sugar
- ⅓ cup unsweetened cocoa powder
- 1 teaspoon baking soda
- ½ teaspoon salt
- 1 cup canned coconut milk
- ½ cup olive oil
- 2 tablespoons apple-cider vinegar
- 1 tablespoon pure vanilla extract
- 2 teaspoons instant espresso powder

Frosting:

- 1 cup non-hydrogenated vegetable shortening
- 3 cups powdered sugar
- 1 teaspoon pure vanilla extract
- 3 tablespoons instant espresso powder dissolved in ¼ cup water

Ganache:
- cup vegan semisweet chocolate chips
- ¼ cup canned coconut milk, mixed well before measuring
- tablespoons olive oil
- 1 cup chopped toasted almonds

Directions:
1. To make the cupcakes: Preheat the oven to 350 degrees. Line two 12-cup cupcake pans with 14 cupcake liners.
2. In a large bowl, whisk together flour, sugar, cocoa, baking soda, and salt. In a separate bowl, whisk together coconut milk, oil, vinegar, vanilla, and espresso powder. Pour the wet mixture into the dry mixture and whisk until just combined.
3. Fill the cupcake liners about two-thirds full with batter. Bake for 16 to 20 minutes, or until a toothpick inserted in the center of the cupcake comes out dry with a few crumbs clinging to it. Cool the cupcakes completely before frosting.
4. To make the frosting: Using a stand or hand mixer, beat shortening until smooth. With the mixer running on low, add powdered sugar and vanilla, and beat to incorporate. Add 1 tablespoon of espresso liquid at a time, as needed, until it reaches desired frosting consistency and espresso flavor. Increase speed to high and beat for 2 more minutes until light and fluffy.
5. To make the ganache: Melt chocolate chips and coconut milk in a double boiler or microwave. Whisk in oil until smooth.
6. To assemble the cupcakes: Once the cupcakes are completely cooled, slice the dome off the top of each cupcake and pipe with a layer of frosting.

Place the top of the cupcake back on top of the frosting. Spread a thin layer of ganache over the cupcake and sprinkle with almonds.

1023. Pumpkin Gobs

Ingredients
Gobs:
- cups flour
- 1 cup sugar
- 1 teaspoon baking powder
- ½ teaspoon baking soda
- 1 teaspoon salt
- 1 teaspoon ground ginger
- 1 teaspoon ground nutmeg
- ½ teaspoon ground cloves
- ½ teaspoon ground cinnamon
- 1 cup pumpkin puree, canned or cooked fresh
- 1 cup canned coconut milk, mixed well before measuring
- ½ cup olive oil
- 1 tablespoon white or apple-cider vinegar
- 1 tablespoon pure vanilla extract

Buttercream:
- 1 cup non-hydrogenated vegetable shortening
- 2 cups powdered sugar
- 1 tablespoon pure maple syrup
- 1 teaspoon pure maple extract
- tablespoons non-dairy milk
- Powdered sugar, for serving

Directions:
1. To make the pies: Preheat the oven to 350 degrees. Lightly grease a whoopie pie pan or line a large baking sheet with parchment paper.
2. In a large bowl, whisk together flour, sugar, baking powder, baking soda, salt, ginger, nutmeg, cloves, and cinnamon. In a separate bowl, whisk together pumpkin puree, coconut milk, oil, vinegar, and vanilla. Pour the wet mixture into the dry mixture and whisk until just combined.
3. Scoop about 2 to 3 tablespoons of

batter into each cup of the whoopie pie pan or onto the prepared baking sheet, leaving about 4 inches between each whoopie. Bake for 10 to 12 minutes, or until a toothpick inserted in the center of the whoopie comes out clean. Let the whoopies cool completely in the pan before unmolding.
4. To make the buttercream: Using a stand or hand mixer, beat the shortening until smooth. With the mixer running on low, add powdered sugar, maple syrup, maple extract, and 1 tablespoon nondairy at a time, as needed, until frosting reaches a spreadable consistency. Increase speed to high and beat for 2 more minutes until light and fluffy.
5. To assemble the pies: Spread a layer of the buttercream on the flat bottom side of 16 pies and sandwich with the remaining pies. Dust with powdered sugar before serving.

1024. Saffron Cupcakes

Ingredients

Cupcakes:
- ¾ cups non-dairy milk
- ½ teaspoon saffron threads
- 1½ cups flour
- 1 cup sugar
- 1 teaspoon baking soda
- ½ teaspoon salt
- ½ cup olive oil
- 2 tablespoons white or apple-cider vinegar
- 1 tablespoon pure vanilla extract

Buttercream:
- 1 cup non-hydrogenated vegetable shortening
- 3 cups powdered sugar
- 1 teaspoon pure vanilla extract
- 3 to 5 tablespoons non-dairy milk

Directions:
1. To make the cupcakes: Preheat the oven to 350 degrees. Line a 12-cup cupcake pan with cup-cake liners and spray with nonstick cooking oil.
2. In a small saucepan, add nondairy milk. Bring to a boil, then remove from heat and let cool.
3. In a large bowl, whisk together flour, sugar, baking soda, and salt. In a separate bowl, whisk together cooled saffron mixture, oil, vinegar, and vanilla. Pour the wet mixture into the dry mixture and whisk until just combined.
4. Fill the cupcake liners about two-thirds full with batter. Bake for about 20 minutes, or until a toothpick inserted in the center of the cupcake comes out clean, with a few crumbs clinging to it. Let the cupcakes cool completely before frosting.
5. To make the buttercream: Using a stand or hand mixer, beat the shortening until smooth. With the mixer running on low, add powdered sugar, vanilla and 1 tablespoon nondairy milk at a time, as needed, until frosting reaches a spreadable consistency. Increase speed to high and beat for 2 more minutes until light and fluffy.
6. To assemble the cupcakes: Pipe or spread a thin layer of buttercream on the cupcakes. If desired, garnish with gold pearls or dust.

1025. Mocha Cupcakes

Ingredients

Cupcakes:
- 1½ cups flour
- 1 cup sugar
- ⅓ cup unsweetened cocoa powder 1 teaspoon baking soda
- 1 teaspoon ground cinnamon
- ½ teaspoon salt
- 1 cup canned coconut
- ½ cup olive oil
- 2 tablespoons apple cider vinegar
- 1 tablespoon pure vanilla extract
- 2 teaspoons instant espresso powder

Frosting:

- 1 cup non-hydrogenated vegetable shortening
- 3 cups powdered sugar
- 1 teaspoon pure vanilla extract
- 1 teaspoon ground cinnamon, plus extra for dusting
- 2 tablespoons instant espresso powder dissolved in ¼ cup water

Directions:
1. To make the cupcakes: Preheat the oven to 350 degrees. Line two 12-cup cupcake pans with 14 cupcake liners.
2. In a large bowl, whisk together flour, sugar, cocoa, baking soda, cinnamon, and salt. In a separate bowl, whisk together coconut milk, oil, vinegar, vanilla, and espresso powder. Pour the wet mixture into the dry mixture and whisk until just combined.
3. Fill the cupcake liners about two-thirds full with batter. Bake for 16 to 20 minutes, or until a toothpick inserted in the center of the cupcake comes out dry with a few crumbs clinging to it. Let the cupcakes cool completely before frosting.
4. To make the frosting: Using a stand or hand mixer, beat shortening until smooth. With the mixer running on low, add powdered sugar, vanilla, and 1 teaspoon cinnamon, and beat to incorporate. Add 1 tablespoon of espresso liquid at a time, as needed, until it reaches desired frosting consistency and espresso flavor. Increase speed to high and beat for 2 more minutes until light and fluffy.
5. To assemble the cupcakes: Pipe or spread a layer of frosting on the cupcakes. Dust with cinnamon and garnish with shaved chocolate.

1026. Raspberry Chocolate Mousse Cupcakes

Ingredients

Mousse:
- ½ cup non-dairy milk
- 1 teaspoon instant espresso powder, optional
- 1 cup vegan semisweet chocolate chips
- ½ cup powdered sugar
- 1 (13.5-ounce can of coconut milk

Filling:
- 12-ounce raspberries
- 2 tablespoons water
- ¼ cup sugar
- ⅛ teaspoon salt
- 1 teaspoon lemon juice

Cupcakes:
- 1½ cups flour
- 1 cup sugar
- ⅓ cup unsweetened cocoa powder
- 1 teaspoon baking soda
- ½ teaspoon salt
- 1 cup cold coffee or water
- ½ cup olive oil
- 2 tablespoons apple- cider vinegar
- 1 tablespoon pure vanilla extract

Directions:
1. To make the mousse: Chill the bowl and whisk of stand mixer in the freezer for 15 minutes. In the meantime, whisk the nondairy milk and espresso powder in a medium saucepan over medium heat. Once the espresso powder is incorporated, add the chocolate chips and whisk over low heat until the chocolate is melted and smooth. Pour the mixture into a large bowl, let cool, and then chill in the refrigerator until cool to the touch, about 15 minutes.
2. Scrape the cream from the top of the chilled coconut milk can into the bowl of the chilled stand mixer. Add powdered sugar and beat for 1 to 2 minutes until fluffy. Add the cooled chocolate mixture to the stand mixer and beat until incorporated. Let chill, covered, in the refrigerator overnight.
3. To make the filling: In a medium saucepan, Cooking Time: raspberries, water, sugar, and salt over medium heat for about 15 minutes, or until thick and saucy. Remove from heat

and stir in lemon juice. Let cool, then store in refrigerator.
4. To make the cupcakes: Preheat the oven to 350 degrees. Line two 12-cup cupcake pans with 14 cupcake liners.
5. In a large bowl, whisk together flour, sugar, cocoa, baking soda, and salt. In a separate bowl, whisk together coffee, oil, vinegar, and vanilla. Pour the wet mixture into the dry mixture and whisk until just combined.
6. Fill the cupcake liners about two-thirds full with batter. Bake for 16 to 20 minutes, or until a toothpick inserted in the center of the cupcake comes out dry with a few crumbs clinging to it. Let the cupcakes cool completely before frosting.
7. To assemble the cupcakes: Using a knife or spoon, gently cut out a couple teaspoons of cake from the top of the cupcake and discard (or eat!), to create a small hole. Fill the hole with a couple teaspoons of filling and top with mousse.

1027. Chocolate Cake

Ingredients
- 1½ cups flour
- ⅓ cup unsweetened cocoa powder
- 1 teaspoon baking soda
- ½ teaspoon salt
- 1 cup agave
- ¾ cup non-dairy milk
- ½ cup olive oil
- tablespoons white vinegar
- teaspoons pure vanilla extract

Directions:
1. Preheat the oven to 350 degrees. Lightly grease a 9-inch round cake pan and line the bot- tom with parchment paper.
2. In a large bowl, whisk together flour, cocoa, baking soda, and salt. In a separate bowl, whisk together agave, nondairy milk, oil, vinegar, and vanilla. Pour the wet mixture into the dry mixture and whisk until just combined.
3. Fill the prepared cake pan evenly with batter. Bake for 30 minutes, or until a toothpick inserted in the center of the cake comes out dry with a few crumbs clinging to it. Rotate the cake halfway through baking time. Let the cake cool completely before unmolding.

1028. Simple Vanilla Cake

Ingredients:
- 1¾ cups flour
- 1 teaspoon baking soda
- 1 teaspoon baking powder
- ½ teaspoon salt
- 1 cup non-dairy milk
- ¾ cup agave
- ½ cup olive oil
- 1 tablespoon white vinegar
- teaspoons pure vanilla extract

Directions:
1. Preheat the oven to 350 degrees. Lightly grease a 9-inch cake pan and line the bot tom with parchment paper.
2. In a large bowl, whisk together flour, baking soda, baking powder, and salt. In a separate bowl, whisk together nondairy milk, agave, oil, vinegar, and vanilla. Pour the wet mixture into the dry mixture and whisk until just combined. Batter will be thin.
3. Fill the prepared cake pan evenly with batter. Bake for about 30 minutes, or until a toothpick inserted in the center of the cake comes out dry with a few crumbs clinging to it. Rotate the cake halfway through baking time. Let the cake cool completely before unmolding.

1029. Almond Ice Cream

Ingredients
- 1 quart vegan vanilla ice cream
- 1 cup brown sugar
- ¼ cup vegan margarine
- 2 tablespoons non-dairy milk

- 1½ cups almond, toasted and chopped

Directions:
1. Soften ice cream in the refrigerator for about 15 to 30 minutes, unless using freshly made ice cream.
2. In a small saucepan over medium heat, heat brown sugar, margarine, and nondairy milk, stirring frequently. Once the mixture comes together, increase heat to medium-high for 1 minute. Remove from heat, stir in almonds, and let sit 15 to 20 minutes, stirring occasionally.
3. Transfer ice cream to a large bowl and fold in as much of the almond mixture as you'd like. Reserve any remaining almond mixture for another use. Cover bowl tightly with plastic wrap, making sure that the plastic wrap is pressed onto the top of the ice cream.

1030. Raspberry Ice Cream

Ingredients
- 1 (13.5-ouncecan coconut milk
- 2 cups raspberry
- ¾ cup agave
- tablespoons olive oil
- ½ teaspoon pure vanilla extract
- ⅛ teaspoon salt
- ¾ teaspoon xanthan gum
- 2 tablespoons water
- ¼ cup sugar
- 1 teaspoon lemon juice
- ⅛ teaspoon salt

Directions:
1. Add raspberry to a blender, process until smooth. In a small saucepan, combine coconut milk and almond or soy milk. Bring to a simmer and add rosemary. Reduce heat to low, and let cook, covered, for 20 minutes, stirring occasionally. Let cool completely.
2. Blend rosemary-infused milk, agave, oil, vanilla, salt, and xanthan gum in a blender until thoroughly combined. Chill in the refrigerator for 2 to 3 hours. Once the ice-cream base is chilled, pour it into an ice-cream maker and process per manufacturer's instructions.

1031. Gelato

Ingredients:
- 1 (13.5-ouncecan coconut milk
- 2 cups almond or soy milk
- ¾ cup agave
- ⅛ teaspoon salt
- ¾ teaspoon xanthan gum
- ½ cup unsweetened cocoa powder 3 tablespoons hazelnut butter
- 1 tablespoon hazelnut liqueur

Directions:
1. Blend coconut milk, almond milk, agave, salt, xanthan gum, cocoa, hazelnut butter, and liqueur in a blender. Chill in the refrigerator for 2 to 3 hours. Once the ice-cream base is chilled, pour it into an ice-cream maker and process following manufacturer's instructions.

1032. Coconut Sorbet

Ingredients
- 1 cup sugar
- ¼ water
- 1 cup cashews
- 1 pint coconut sorbet

Directions:
1. Line a large baking sheet with parchment paper. In a medium saucepan, combine sugar and water. Bring to a gentle boil, occasionally swirling the pan to mix, and let Cooking Time: for about 7 minutes until golden. Add cashews and remove from heat. Using two forks, lift out 1-inch clusters (about 3 to 4 cashewsand place them on the prepared baking sheet. Let cool completely.
2. Once cooled and hardened, transfer cashew clusters to a cutting board and roughly chop with a sharp knife. Store in freezer.

3. To serve, top a scoop of coconut sorbet with a spoonful of cashew brittle.

1033. Chocolate Mousse

Ingredients
- 1 cup vegan semisweet chocolate chips

Mousse:
- ½ cup non-dairy milk
- 1 teaspoon instant espresso powder, optional
- 1 cup vegan chocolate chips
- ⅓ cup powdered sugar
- 1 (13.5-ouncecan of coconut milk

Directions:
1. To make the cups: Melt chocolate chips over a double boiler until smooth. Line a 12-cup cup-cake tray with 10 paper liners and pour approximately 1 tablespoon melted chocolate into each cup. Use a pastry brush to evenly coat each cupcake liner and spread the chocolate up the sides of each liner, stopping about ½ inch from the top. Freeze tray for several hours or overnight. Peel off the cupcake wrappers. Store in freezer.

To make the mousse:
2. Chill the bowl and whisk of a stand mixer in the freezer for about 30 minutes. If they are not very cold, the mousse will not whip properly.
3. In the meantime, whisk nondairy milk and espresso powder in a medium saucepan over medium heat. Once espresso is incorporated, add chocolate chips and whisk over low heat until the chocolate is melted and smooth. Pour the mixture into a large bowl, let cool, and then chill in the refrigerator until cool to the touch, about 15 minutes.
4. Skim the solidified coconut cream from the chilled coconut milk and transfer the solids to the bowl of the stand mixer.
5. Add powdered sugar and beat for 1 to 2 minutes, until fluffy. Add the cooled chocolate mixture and beat until incorporated. Let chill, covered, in the refrigerator for 8 hours or over-night. Distribute evenly among 10 chocolate cups. Each serving will be a little about ¼ cup of mousse. Drizzle with Raspberry Sauce, if using.

1034. Crème Brûlée

Ingredients
- ¼ cup non-dairy milk
- ¼ cup cornstarch or arrowroot
- 1 (13.5-ouncecan coconut milk
- ½ cup sugar, plus extra for brulée
- ⅛ teaspoon salt
- 1 teaspoon pure vanilla extract

Directions:
1. In a small bowl, thoroughly mix nondairy milk and cornstarch with a whisk or fork and set aside.
2. In a medium saucepan, whisk together coconut milk, ½ cup sugar, and salt, and heat over medium-high heat just until boiling. Reduce the heat to medium and slowly drizzle the cornstarch mixture into the saucepan, whisking continuously. Let Cooking Time: until the mixture becomes very thick in texture, like pudding, about 5 minutes, whisking frequently. Remove from heat and whisk in vanilla and food coloring, if using.
3. Pour the custard evenly into 4 crème brulée dishes or ramekins. Smooth tops. Let cool for 10 minutes; then chill in the refrigerator for 8 hours or overnight.
4. Remove the custards from the refrigerator 1 hour before torching, so that they come to room temperature. Sprinkle about 2 teaspoons sugar onto each custard, then give it a little shake so that the sugar spreads evenly.
5. Hold a torch about 2 to 3 inches from the sugar and melt the sugar until it bubbles and turns slightly golden. Be

sure to move your torch back and forth continuously so that it does not burn in one spot. Once there is no more visible dry sugar, let the crème brulée sit for 3 to 5 minutes, then serve immediately.

1035. Toffee Pudding

Ingredients

Glaze:
- 1 cup canned coconut milk, mixed well before measuring
- 1 cup dark brown sugar
- tablespoons vegan margarine
- ¼ teaspoon salt

Pudding Cakes:
- 8 ounces dates, pitted
- 1 cup canned coconut milk, mixed well before measuring
- 2 cups flour
- ½ teaspoon baking soda
- teaspoon baking powder
- ½ teaspoon salt
- ½ teaspoon ground cinnamon 1 cup brown sugar
- ½ cup olive oil
- teaspoons white vinegar
- 1 tablespoon pure vanilla extract

Directions:

To make the glaze: In a medium saucepan, combine coconut milk, brown sugar, margarine, and salt. Bring to a boil over medium-high heat, stirring occasionally. Let Cooking Time: for about 5 minutes and remove from heat.

To make the cakes:

1. Preheat the oven to 350 degrees. Lightly grease two 12-cup cupcake pans. Prepare a grid cooling rack by fitting it on top of a large baking sheet.
2. Place dates in a small saucepan with water to cover, and bring to a slow boil. Let the dates boil gently for 10 minutes. Drain and place in a food processor or blender with coconut milk. Process until combined and set aside.
3. In a large bowl, whisk flour, baking soda, baking powder, salt, and cinnamon. In the bowl of a stand mixer, beat the date mixture, brown sugar, oil, vinegar, and vanilla. Slowly add the flour mixture and beat until just combined.
4. Fill the cupcake cups about two-thirds full with batter. Bake for 18 to 20 minutes, or until a toothpick inserted in the center of the cake comes out clean with a few crumbs clinging to it. Remove from oven and, using a toothpick, immediately tilt the cakes so that they sit in the cupcake pans at an angle. Pour 2 tablespoons of glaze into each cupcake cup, then nudge the cakes so that they sit back into the cups. Let soak for about 10 minutes, then flip onto the prepared cooling rack. Top each cake with an extra tablespoon of glaze and serve immediately.

1036. Rice Pudding With Raisins

Ingredients

- ¾ cup raisins
- tablespoons dark rum
- 1 cup uncooked white rice
- cups non-dairy milk
- ½ cup sugar
- ½ teaspoon salt
- ¼ teaspoon ground cinnamon
- 1 teaspoon pure vanilla extract

Directions:

1. In a small bowl, soak raisins in rum and set aside.
2. In a large pot, combine rice, nondairy milk, sugar, salt, and cinnamon. Bring to a boil over medium-high heat, then reduce heat to low. Simmer, uncovered, stirring occasionally, for 45 to 50 minutes until thickened. Transfer to a large bowl and stir in vanilla, raisins, and rum. Let cool completely, cover with plastic wrap, and chill in the refrigerator for 8

hours or overnight.

1037. French Custard

Ingredients:

- *1¼ cups water, divided*
- *¼ cup cornstarch*
- *½ cup shelled unsalted pistachios*
- *½ cup sugar*
- *⅛ teaspoon salt*
- *¼ cup vegan, semisweet chocolate chips*
- *Coconut Whipped Cream, optional, for serving*

Directions:

1. *In a small bowl, thoroughly mix ¼ cup water and cornstarch with a whisk or fork and set aside.*
2. *In a blender, make pistachio milk by combining remaining 1 cup water and pistachios. Blend on high for 2 minutes until completely smooth. In a medium saucepan, whisk together pistachio milk, sugar, and salt, and heat on medium-high just until boiling. Reduce the heat to low, and stir in chocolate chips. Let cook, whisking frequently, until completely smooth. Increase the heat to medium and slowly drizzle the cornstarch mixture into the saucepan, whisking continuously. Let Cooking Time: until the mixture becomes very thick in texture, like pudding, about 5 minutes, whisking frequently.*
3. *Pour the custard evenly into 4 ramekins or small cups. Smooth the tops. Let cool for 10 minutes, then chill in the refrigerator for 8 hours or overnight. If desired, top with Coconut Whipped Cream before serving.*

1038. Panna Cotta

Ingredients:

- *¼ cup non-dairy milk*
- *¼ cup cornstarch*
- *1 (13.5-ouncecan coconut milk*
- *1 cup sugar*
- *⅛ teaspoon salt*
- *1 teaspoon pure vanilla extract*
- *Raspberry Sauce, optional*

Directions:

1. *In a small bowl, thoroughly mix non-dairy milk and cornstarch with a whisk or fork and set aside.*
2. *In a medium saucepan, whisk coconut milk, sugar, and salt, and heat over medium-high just until boiling. Reduce heat to medium and slowly drizzle the cornstarch mixture into the saucepan, whisking continuously. Let Cooking Time: until the mixture becomes very thick in texture, like pudding, about 5 minutes, whisking frequently. Remove from heat and whisk in vanilla.*
3. *Pour the custard evenly into 4 ramekins. Smooth the tops. Let cool for 10 minutes; then chill in the refrigerator for 8 hours or overnight.*
4. *Remove the custards from the refrigerator 1 hour before torching, so that they come to room temperature. Sprinkle about 2 teaspoons sugar onto each custard, then give it a little shake so that the sugar spreads evenly.*
5. *Gently shake each ramekin to loosen edges. Place a plate on top of each ramekin and flip with force to unmold. Garnish with Raspberry Sauce, if desired.*

1039. Trifle

Ingredients:

- *1/2 ounces cranberries, fresh or frozen*
- *½ cup maple syrup*
- *¼ cup orange juice*
- *½ teaspoon ground cinnamon*
- *¼ teaspoon ground ginger*
- *Pinch salt*
- *1 teaspoon pure vanilla extract*
- *2 cups vegan vanilla wafers*
- *Vanilla Pastry Cream*

Directions:
1. To make the filling: In a medium saucepan, stir together cranberries, maple syrup, orange juice, cinnamon, ginger, and salt. Bring to a boil over medium-high heat. Reduce heat and let simmer, stirring frequently, for about 15 minutes, or until cranberries begin to pop and turn saucy. Remove from heat, mix in vanilla, and add more maple syrup to taste.
2. To assemble the parfaits: Pulse cookies in a food processor until they are coarse crumbs. Layer the cranberry filling, pastry cream, and cookie crumbs in cocktail or parfait glasses.

1040. Hot Cocoa

Ingredients
- 2 cups non-dairy milk
- ½ cup semisweet chocolate chips (dairy-free
- 1 tablespoon peanut butter
- 1 tablespoon sugar

Directions:
In a medium saucepan, combine all ingredients. Heat over medium, stirring frequently, until the chocolate has melted and the mixture is smooth. Remove from heat and serve.

1041. Pina Colada

Ingredients
- 1 pint coconut sorbet
- 1 cup pineapple juice
- 1 cup ice

Directions:
Blend coconut sorbet and pineapple juice until smooth. Add ice, and blend again until smooth. Add more pineapple juice, if needed. Pour into glasses and serve immediately.

1042. Pumpkin Spice Latte

Ingredients
- 1 cup non-dairy milk
- ¾ cup water
- ¾ cup pumpkin puree, canned or cooked fresh
- ¼ cup sugar
- 2 teaspoons instant espresso powder
- 1 teaspoon pumpkin pie spice
- ¼ teaspoon salt

Directions:
In a medium saucepan, whisk together all ingredients. Heat over medium heat, whisking frequently, until the mixture comes to a simmer. Remove from heat and serve.

1043. Simple Vanilla Milkshake

Ingredients:
- ¼ cup non-dairy milk
- 1 pint vegan vanilla ice cream
- 1 cup ice
- dates, pitted

Directions:
Blend non-dairy milk and ice cream until smooth. Add more nondairy milk, if needed. Add ice and blend again until smooth. Add dates and blend until dates are incorporated, leaving some chunky pieces remaining. Pour into glasses and serve immediately.

1044. Vanilla Raspberry Milkshake

Ingredients
- ¾ cup non-dairy milk
- 1 cup frozen raspberries
- 1 pint vegan vanilla ice cream

Directions:
Blend all ingredients until smooth. Add more vegan, vanilla milk, if needed. Pour into glasses and serve immediately.

1045. Frozen Mocha Latte

Ingredients
- 1 cup non-dairy milk
- 1 tablespoon instant espresso powder
- 1 teaspoon unsweetened cocoa powder
- 2 tablespoons agave
- 2 cups ice

Directions:

Blend non-dairy milk, espresso powder, cocoa, agave. Add ice, and blend again until smooth. Taste, and add more espresso powder if a stronger coffee flavor desired. For more sweetness, add more agave. Pour into glasses and serve immediately.

1046. Blueberry Margarita

Ingredients:

- 2 cups frozen blueberries
- ½ cup tequila
- ½ cup agave
- ¼ cup orange juice
- ¼ cup lime juice
- 3 cups ice

Directions:

Blend blueberries, tequila, agave, orange juice, and lime juice until smooth. Add ice, and blend again until smooth. Pour into glasses and serve immediately.

1047. Peanut Butter Chocolate Chip Milkshake

Ingredients

- ½ cup non-dairy milk
- ½ cup peanut butter
- 1 pint vegan vanilla ice cream
- 1 cup ice
- ½ cup semisweet chocolate chips (dairy-free

Directions:

Blend non-dairy milk, peanut butter, and ice cream until smooth. Add more nondairy milk, if needed. Add ice, and blend again until smooth. Add chocolate chips and blend until chips are finely chopped. Pour into glasses and serve immediately.

1048. Lemonade And Rum Cocktail

Ingredients:

- 2 cups sugar
- cups water, divided
- 2 cups lemon juice
- 1 cup rum

Directions:

In a medium saucepan, combine or sugar, and 1 cup water. Bring to a boil, and then reduce heat and let simmer for 5 minutes, stirring frequently. Remove from heat, strain liquid into a pitcher. Let cool completely. Stir in lemon juice and remaining 6 cups water. Taste, and add more water if needed. If using, add rum to taste. Chill and serve

1049. Peach Bellini

Ingredients:

- 1 bottle sparkling wine
- 1 cup peach nectar

Directions:

Pour 3 tablespoons peach nectar into each glass. Fill the rest of each glass with approximately ⅓ cup sparkling wine.

1050. Vanilla Ice Cream

Ingredients

- 1 (13.5-ouncecan coconut milk
- 1½ cups almond or soy milk
- ¾ cup agave
- 3 tablespoons olive oil
- 1 teaspoon pure vanilla extract
- ⅛ teaspoon salt
- ¾ teaspoon xanthan gum

Directions:

Process coconut milk, almond milk, agave, oil, vanilla extract, salt, and xanthan gum in a blender. Chill in the refrigerator for 3 hours. Once the ice cream base is chilled, prepare in an ice-cream maker per manufacturer's instructions.

CONCLUSION

Thanks for making to the end! I hope you enjoy all the recipes herein. If dieting seems very important to you and you need to do it right, then it is recommended that you visit a professional such as a nutritionist or dietitian to discuss your dieting plan and optimizing it for the better.

No matter how much you want to lose weight, it is not advised that you decrease your calorie intake to an unhealthy level. Losing weight does not mean that you stop eating. It is done by carefully planning meals.

A plant-based diet is very easy once you get into it. At first, you will start to face a lot of difficulties, but if you start slowly, then you can face all the barriers and achieve your goal.

CPSIA information can be obtained
at www.ICGtesting.com
Printed in the USA
LVHW061334251020
669765LV00034B/1457